The Birds of Gwent

Published with the assistance of

Llywodraeth Cynulliad Cymru
Welsh Assembly Government

Cyngor Cefn Gwlad Cymru
Countryside Council for Wales

The Birds of
GWENT

W. A. VENABLES
A. D. BAKER, R. M. CLARKE, C. JONES
J. M. S. LEWIS, S. J. TYLER, I. R. WALKER & R. A. WILLIAMS

On behalf of the
GWENT ORNITHOLOGICAL SOCIETY

With additional material by
J. R. BENNETT, C. M. HATCH, S. HOWE, H. P. JONES,
R. MOELLER, M. PLUNKETT, S. J. SMITH

CHRISTOPHER HELM
LONDON

Published 2008 by Christopher Helm, an imprint of A&C Black Publishers Ltd.,
38 Soho Square, London W1D 3HB

www.acblack.com

ISBN 978–0–7136–7633–4

A CIP catalogue record for this book is available from the British Library

This book is produced using paper that is made from wood grown in managed sustainable forests. It is natural,
renewable and recyclable. The logging and manufacturing processes conform to the environmental regulations
of the country of origin.

Commissioning Editor: Nigel Redman
Project Editor: Jim Martin

Design by J&L Composition, Filey, Yorkshire

Printed in China
Lion Productions Ltd

10 9 8 7 6 5 4 3 2 1

CONTENTS

FOREWORD
by Iolo Williams

Living in Montgomeryshire, I have always been jealous of Gwent's ornithologists. In the last 70 years, you have produced five books on the birds of the county. Over the same period, the good people of Montgomeryshire have produced nothing! We remain the only county in Wales not to have its own avifauna.

I didn't really feel that I knew Gwent until my umpteenth visit in the late 1980s. By then, I had helped to survey woodland birds in the Black Mountains, upland birds on the Blorenge, breeding waders on the Gwent Levels and goosanders on the rivers Wye and Usk. It was not until 1989, however, that I could claim familiarity with the county. In that spring and summer, I was able to accompany Jerry Lewis and Steve Roberts as they monitored breeding Goshawks, Hobbies, Barn Owls, Dippers and Grey Wagtails on what appeared to be every square inch of south-east Wales. It was an excellent introduction to a beautiful and varied county. Since that time, I have had the pleasure of returning time and again to revisit old sites and discover new areas.

This latest account of the Birds of Gwent is a valuable addition to our knowledge of the birds of this corner of Wales. It makes for both an encouraging and a depressing read. Encouraging because of the colonisation of the county by Little Egrets, Avocets and Dartford Warblers, and increases in species such as Goosander and Goshawk. Depressing because of the decline in birds such as the Lapwing, Lesser Spotted Woodpecker and Tree Sparrow, a trend reflected throughout Wales.

Heartiest congratulations to everyone who has been involved in the production of this excellent avifauna.

ACKNOWLEDGEMENTS

The production of this book would have been impossible without a number of unsung heroes who have given their time and expertise willingly and enthusiastically. We wish to express our gratitude to all these people, and they are acknowledged below in no particular order.

We are indebted to the staff of the BTO who have provided invaluable support, particularly Stuart Newson who produced the breeding population estimates from BBS data, provided tailor-made CBC/BBS trends data for the period between the two Gwent atlases, and on occasions when we have questioned particular trends, has explained patiently and informatively why they are as they are. We are also grateful to Mark Collier who provided WeBS analyses specific to Gwent, and has given other valuable advice on the use of WeBS data, and also to Jacqui Clarke and Sue Adams for providing ringing recovery data relevant to Gwent and responding to subsequent queries.

The species accounts owe much to the merciless and, therefore immensely valuable criticism of the first drafts by Julian Branscombe and Sam Bosanquet. Thanks go to Peter Randerson and Stuart Davies, both of Cardiff University, for their advice and help on statistical analysis of atlas data, and Helen Jones is thanked for assembling the bibliography.

The visual attractiveness of the book owes much to the beautiful cover paintings by John Gale and the charming vignettes drawn by Steve Roberts, Chris Hodgson and Helen Scourse. Steve is particularly thanked for the production of an extra six vignettes in three days when deadlines became very tight! We have also been fortunate in being able to call upon some very talented local photographers, and are grateful to Ray Armstrong, Andrew Baker, Dave Brassey, Richard Clarke, Colin Elliot, Kevin Dupe, Chris Hatch, Garry Howells, Jerry Lewis, Dave Lock, Mike Love, John Marsh, Steve Roberts, R. Smith and Darryl Spittle for the use of their excellent pictures. Thanks also to Mary Field for her excellent maps which are an essential feature of the 'Where to watch birds in Gwent' chapter, and also to Chris Field for much time spent on electronic formatting of maps and figures.

The Countryside Council for Wales and the Welsh Assembly Government are thanked for their generous financial support.

The fieldwork for the 2nd Gwent Atlas was an enormous undertaking. Those who organised it are listed in the separate chapter entitled the Gwent Breeding Atlases, but it is appropriate at this point to thank all those observers who gave so much of their time over a five-year period to produce some 25,000 data items. The names of all contributors are listed in Appendices 3 and 6. Previously unpublished data for tetrads on the Glamorgan/Gwent border (Appendix 4) is published with permission of the Glamorgan Bird Club, and we are grateful to Peter Howlett of the National Museum of Wales for making these data available.

The editors themselves also performed many essential tasks that are not apparent, and which should be acknowledged. In particular we should recognise the role of Alan Williams who, in 1997, proposed the carrying out of a second county breeding atlas to be followed immediately by the production of a new *Birds of Gwent*. Alan set up and chaired the early meetings of the organising committee, and subsequently laboured long in the production of the atlas distribution maps using D-Map. Together with Chris Field, Alan also spent much time on the revisions of map formats required for publication. Alan also assembled the final texts and artwork for dispatch to the publisher. Chris Jones is to be applauded for taking on the mammoth task of organising a review of all past rarity records for which there was any element of doubt, and cajoling the other members of the local records committee (John Bennett, Richard Clarke, Brian Gregory, Chris Hatch, Jerry Lewis, Al Venables) to play their part. Richard Clarke and Andrew Baker organised the procurement and selection of photographs, and Richard played a part in the final review of the species accounts; Richard also unearthed a good deal interesting historical data and wishes to acknowledge the assistance of the staff of Gwent Records Office in this exercise. Andrew Baker negotiated and liaised with our publishers, helped in the review of the first drafts, and assembled and edited the Habitats and Where to watch birds in Gwent chapters. Jerry Lewis devised two of our methods for collection of population size data and analysed the results obtained.

Finally we thank Jim Martin of Christopher Helm for his encouragement to press on with the book, without which we might still have been writing it today, copy editor Ernest Garcia for his many astute and helpful comments on the final manuscript, and Lindsay Tyler for proof-reading the entire book.

Al Venables
Editorial Chairman
October 2007

A BRIEF HISTORY OF
GWENT ORNITHOLOGY

The founding of the Gwent Ornithological Society was the result of a meeting of two birdwatchers who at that time did not know each other. Bert Hamar and Betty Morgan met while out birdwatching somewhere between their respective homes, perhaps along the canal between The Jockey Pitch and Goetre. This was in 1961 and they began discussing their new found hobby and how they should promote it. It was decided to form Pontypool Bird Club, not because they were experts who wanted to impart their knowledge but because they were beginners who wanted to find out more. Experts and other enthusiasts were found, amongst them Patrick Humphreys and W G Lewis and this emerging group was the foundation of what was to later become the Gwent Ornithological Society, the compilers of this volume. Patrick Humphreys went on to be the Society's President for 25 years. Other early members included the likes of H J Vernall, Mrs Queenie Saunders, Capt. W K Marshall, Barbara Thorne, Mrs S H Robbins, E T Sarson and Percy Playford. It was Percy who did so much pioneering work on Pied Flycatchers with his nestbox and ringing projects. The eminent ornithologists Dr Bruce Campbell and H. Morrey Salmon were Honorary Members who visited the Society from time to time.

The Pontypool Bird Club grew from the early days of meetings in the front room of Bert Hamar's house to become the Monmouthshire Ornithological Society in 1964 and, following the local government reorganisation of 1974, the Gwent Ornithological Society. With over 400 members, a well-established series of indoor meetings each year, and an active outdoor programme, the Society flourishes. The previously published county avifaunas (Ingram & Salmon, 1937; Humphreys, 1963) were complemented by the publication of *The Birds of Gwent* in 1977 and the *Gwent Atlas of Breeding Birds* in 1985. This volume builds on these two earlier publications and the series of annual reports to set out a current (2007) status of the birds of Gwent.

Sadly Bert Hamar died in 1993 and Betty Morgan passed away in 1999. Patrick Humphreys summed up Bert's contribution to the Society thus: 'More than anyone, Bert was the guiding light in local ornithology over the last thirty years, and without his quiet work and gently persuasive manner I doubt very much if the ornithological and conservation achievements that have come to fruition in that time would have been more than good intentions.' Bert left us a flourishing Society and Betty Morgan left a generous legacy: enabling us to purchase Goytre House Wood, a 12-acre site of mainly semi-natural woodland that is being managed in the interest of birds.

INTRODUCTION

Systematic bird recording did not start in Gwent until the mid-1960s, and it became steadily more extensive as the newly formed Gwent Ornithological Society increased its influence, and formed a focus for recording activities. Thus, in 1977, when the first *Birds of Gwent* was published, there was still a relatively small body of available information for inclusion in the book, limited mainly to thirteen *Gwent Bird Reports* (1964–76). Indeed, one of the reviewers remarked at the time that seventy pages of A5 size was somewhat small for the species section of a county bird book, and expressed some regret that bird-watching didn't seem to have occurred in Gwent before 1960! For the current publication, the authors have been in a much more fortunate position.

In the years since 1977, there has been a great increase in the systematic study of British birds, on both local and national scales. On a local scale our knowledge of the distribution of breeding birds in the county has been informed by two detailed atlas projects carried out during 1981–85 and 1998–03, which have yielded a wealth of data on the distribution of breeding species, and also on the changes in distribution that have occurred in the intervening period.

Data has also been collected in the county for the British Trust for Ornithology (BTO) 1988–91 National Atlas and Winter Atlas (1981/82–1983/84), while ringing records from the county have contributed to the *Migration Atlas*, which was published in 2002.

Gwent has also participated fully in the Breeding Birds Survey (BBS), which has taken over from the Common Birds Census (CBC) as the primary means for monitoring population changes, while data is also collected systematically from Gwent for the Wetlands Birds Survey (WeBS) and the Waterways Birds Survey (WBS). Local observers have also contributed to many special BTO surveys.

Apart from nationally organised surveys, since 1976 we have accumulated a wealth of records contributed by bird-watchers to a further 29 editions of the annually published *Gwent Bird Report*.

This book begins with a short introduction to the county, defining its boundaries and outlining its geography. This is followed by a description of the county's geology, including its geological history. The major bird habitats in the county are then described in some detail together with ways in which they are changing and the threats that posed to some of them.

In the Where to Watch Birds in Gwent chapter a selection of ten of the best sites in the county has been selected, with a view to maximising the range of species covered and also achieving a geographical spread over the county. A separate chapter is devoted the Gwent breeding atlases, describing how they were carried out and discussing the broad conclusions from them. Gwent is one of very few counties to have completed two tetrad breeding atlases, and the availabilty of results from these has enabled us to demonstrate with great clarity the changes in distribution that have occurred locally over the last two decades. This, we feel, is one of the main strengths of the book.

The main body of the book comprises accounts of the birds themselves, summarising their history in the county, recent trends and current status.

Thirty years after the publication of the 1977 *Birds of Gwent*, and twenty-two years after the completion of the first *Gwent Atlas of Breeding Birds*, the time is now ripe for an update on the ornithology of Gwent. In this book we have attempted to pull together all current knowledge of the county's birds, and produce a book that will not only be a useful source of reference for the serious bird-watcher, but also make an informative and, hopefully, stimulating read for those with a more light-hearted interest in the birds of the county. We hope that it will also help beginners and birdwatchers who are new to the county to develop an interest in our local avifauna.

THE COUNTY OF GWENT

Although this book is about the birds of Gwent, and this section is headed The County of Gwent, such a place no longer exists as a local government entity. County avifaunas usually refer to the relevant Watsonian vice-county as most biological recording systems use these boundaries. Unfortunately the latest Welsh local government reorganisation used the title Monmouthshire County Council to refer to only a part of the original Monmouthshire vice-county. To avoid confusion, therefore, the title Gwent has been retained, and the recording area is the County of Gwent as it was in the 1974 Local Government reorganisation with one exception. As current maps have lost the old Gwent county boundary following the merger of Islwyn Borough Council into Caerphilly County Council, the western boundary of the recording area is now the River Rhymney, a physical feature no bureaucrat can alter with the stroke of a pen.

Gwent is a county of great contrasts. Unfortunately most non-residents usually drive through the county *en route* to Gower or Pembrokeshire or other tourist spots in Wales. They do not linger to explore the wealth of habitats and scenery that the county has to offer. It stretches from the mudflats and saltmarsh of the Severn Estuary in the south to the heather moorlands of the Black Mountains in the Brecon Beacons National Park in the northwest. In the east is the River Wye, the wonderful Wye Valley woodlands and mixed forests on the plateau, and in the west the series of former industrial valleys, now greening over with new woodland and pastures, with the moorland ridges between the valleys. It is this diversity of habitats that accounts for the high total of bird species for a relatively small county, an area of about 138,000 hectares.

Good heather moorland with Red Grouse clothes the tops of the Black Mountains and The Blorenge near Abergavenny. Other heather moorland, peat bogs, cotton grass *Eriophorum* and Purple Moor Grass *Molinia caerulea* moor cover Coity Mountain, Mynydd Maen and other hills in the west. There Skylarks and Meadow Pipits abound.

Much of the centre of Gwent comprises low-lying farmland with a mosaic of pastures and arable land in the Rivers Usk and Trothy valleys as well as in the Monnow Valley in the northeast and on the Gwent Levels. Hedgerows and woodland divide up the generally small to medium-sized fields. Although much of the farmland is intensively managed there are pockets of species-rich grassland and wetland. The mixed farmland maintains good populations of Yellowhammers and some Yellow Wagtails although Tree Sparrows are struggling. As elsewhere in England and Wales silage and early cutting of this fodder crop has largely ousted ground-nesting waders.

Bird populations on the low-lying Gwent Levels with their network of drainage ditches or reens have also suffered from agricultural intensification. The development of the Newport Wetland Reserve, partly on former Uskmouth Power Station pulverised ash dumps, but also on farmland, has boosted the populations of waders, notably Lapwings and Redshanks. The brackish lagoons at Goldcliff have attracted breeding Avocets, while other waders have bred on the island, and a large number of passage and wintering waders and wildfowl make use of the site. The lagoons have become very popular with home-grown bird-watchers, and increasingly with those from outside the county also, and have relegated the Peterstone area into second place as a destination for wader enthusiasts.

There are important and diverse rivers and streams. In the east the River Wye forms the boundary between Wales and England, running from near Symonds Yat down to Chepstow. Below Bigsweir the Wye is tidal. The northeast boundary is largely formed by the River Monnow, a tributary of the Wye joining that river at Monmouth. The meandering Monnow with its sandbanks and shoals between Pandy and Monmouth is second only to the River Usk for its important but small breeding populations of Goosanders, Common Sandpipers, Kingfishers and Sand Martins. Dippers and Grey Wagtails on the upper fast-flowing rocky reaches of the Monnow and its tributaries, notably the Afon Honddu running down the Llanthony Valley, and on the Grwyne Fawr, an Usk tributary in the Black Mountains, have been well-studied for the last 30 years. The Usk enters the county northwest of Abergavenny and meanders down to Newport through farmland and thence into the Severn Estuary. Further west, the valleys' rivers, the Rhymney and Ebbw and their tributaries, support increasingly important bird populations as their quality improves.

Add to the estuarine and river habitats, the Monmouth & Brecon Canal and a wide range of lakes, reservoirs and ponds. Llandegfedd Reservoir is the largest water body and hosts important concentrations of wintering waterfowl. Other reservoirs range from Garnlydan and Carno in the northwest to Penyfan Pond near Blackwood,

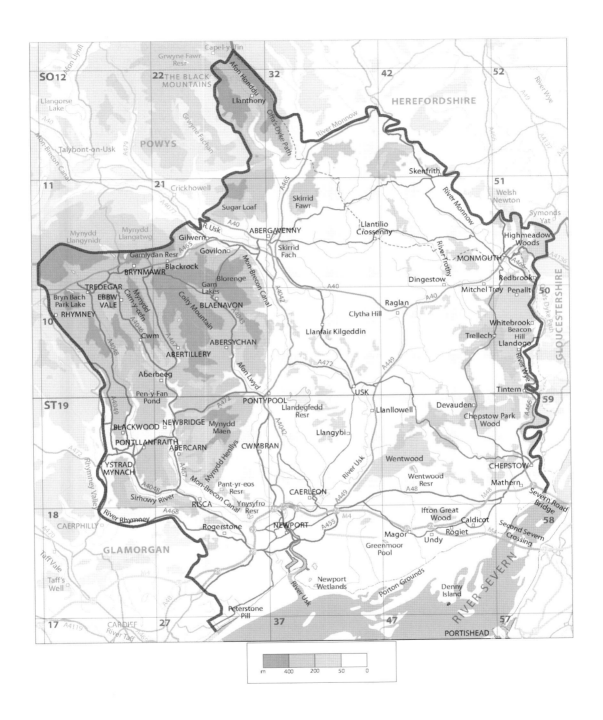

and Wentwood and Ynysyfro near Newport. There are old former industrial pools as at Llanwern steelworks, Alpha Steel, Uskmouth and Dunlop Semtex pond; these are all important waterbird habitats. There is also an increasing number of new ponds on farms, golf courses and on reclaimed opencast sites, such as the Bryn Bach lake near Ebbw Vale.

The spectacular Wye Valley woodlands, stretching from Chepstow to beyond Monmouth, are of international repute. These woodlands on the steep sides of the Wye Valley are predominantly mixed broadleaves with Ash, Wild Cherry, Small-leaved Lime and Oak all present. Conifers planted during the 1950s and 1960s are gradually being cleared from the valley sides so that ancient semi-natural woodland with native broadleaves predominates. These woodlands support healthy populations of woodland birds from tits and woodpeckers to Buzzards and Goshawks, as well as the elusive Hawfinches and scattered Wood Warblers. Small broadleaved woodlands are scattered throughout the county and those more open Oak, Ash, Alder and Birch woodlands in the north and west that are grazed by sheep, host good numbers of Pied Flycatchers and Redstarts.

Wentwood, a large mixed forest block in southern Gwent, and conifer forests on the Trellech Plateau, on the watershed between the Wye and Usk catchments, and in the former industrial valleys, are important habitats too. Clearfell areas and young restocked plantations support Nightjars and Woodcock whilst mature plantations encourage Redpolls, Siskins and Crossbills. Two areas of conifers on the Trellech Plateau are now being restored to heathland and already support Stonechats.

Gwent has a population of just over 450,000 with the majority of people concentrated in the south and west. Newport is the largest urban conurbation and now has city status. The main towns are Cwmbran, Pontypool, Ebbw Vale, Tredegar and Abertillery. The smaller market towns are Abergavenny, Chepstow, Monmouth and Usk. In Newport, and in towns and villages throughout Gwent, parks, churchyards and gardens provide more 'woodland' habitat for birds whilst factory roofs in Newport and the north-west of the county are favoured by nesting gulls.

THE GEOLOGY OF GWENT

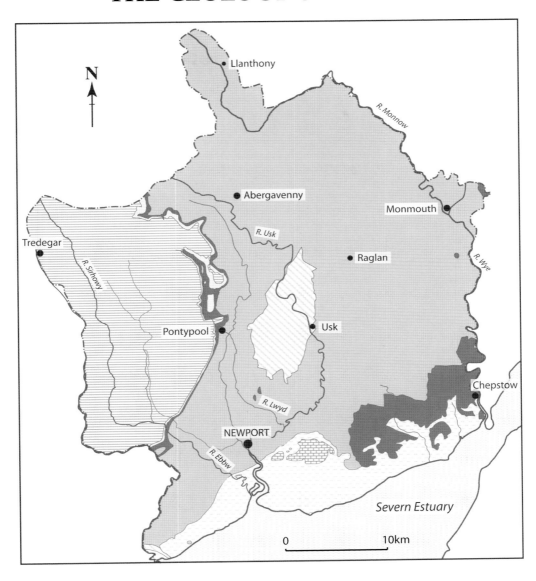

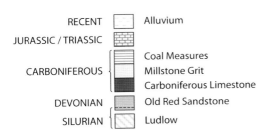

RECENT · Alluvium

JURASSIC / TRIASSIC

CARBONIFEROUS · Coal Measures · Millstone Grit · Carboniferous Limestone

DEVONIAN · Old Red Sandstone

SILURIAN · Ludlow

Apart from a tiny outcrop of igneous rock at the northern end of Wentwood, all of the rocks that underlie Gwent are of sedimentary origin and range in age from 425 million years old to the present day. A variety of rock types were deposited under a diverse range of environmental conditions as Wales drifted northwards across the face of the globe from a location south of the equator to its current latitude. Subsequent to their deposition these rocks were folded and faulted during periods of Earth movements and have suffered extensive periods of erosion. Geologically the county can be split into five areas: the eastern part of the South Wales coalfield, the Black Mountains, the Usk Anticline, the rolling country on the west bank of the Wye valley and the lowlands bordering the Severn Estuary.

The oldest rocks crop out in the core of the Usk Anticline, an elliptical up-folded dome that extends from Llanfrechfa in the south to Llanvihangel Gobion in the north. Of marine origin, they consist of richly fossiliferous limestones, shales and mudstones of Silurian age (425–418 million years ago) that were deposited in a subtropical, shallow sea at a time when Wales lay about 20° south of the equator.

Late in the Silurian Period plate movements resulted in the uplift of the seabed to form a mountain range over north and central Wales; its erosion produced the sediments that form the succeeding rocks of the Old Red Sandstone, which range in age from 418–360 million years ago. They consist of conglomerates, sandstones, siltstones, mudstones and thin limestones that were laid down on a large alluvial plain to the south of the mountains. Their outcrop covers about 50% of the county and produces distinctive red soils. The older beds contain a high proportion of soft siltstones and mudstones, and form a landscape of generally low relief, while the younger, harder and mainly coarser beds rim the coalfield, and form the prominent highlands of the Black Mountains.

The overlying Carboniferous rocks are divisible into three units: the Carboniferous Limestone, Millstone Grit and Coal Measures. The Carboniferous Limestone crops out in a narrow band around the edge of the coalfield, and in a broader one from Magor eastwards to the Wye Valley. It was deposited in a shallow sea that flooded the Old Red Sandstone landscape. The basal beds are made up of shales and thin limestones but most of the sequence comprises generally grey, sometimes massive limestones and dolomite. In the Magor-Wye Valley outcrop sandstones occur at some levels. The Carboniferous limestones are of high economic importance and have been extensively quarried. Many of these quarries form distinctive features within the landscape, and provide inland sites for cliff-nesting bird species. Where they outcrop at the surface they form calcareous soils which support a distinctive lime-loving flora.

During mid-Carboniferous times the land was uplifted and eroded and the shallow seas retreated, to be replaced by coastal swamps and river deltas in which the rocks of the Millstone Grit were deposited. These crop out in a narrow band around the edge of the coalfield. In the southern half of the county the rocks consist predominantly of shales with a few thin sandstones, while along the north crop of the coalfield hard, coarse conglomerates, grits and sandstones dominate, especially in the thick Basal Grits. Above these, freshwater shales with thin marine intercalations and a few thin coals occur. Along their outcrop the Basal Grits give rise to extensive areas of rough, acidic, heathery grasslands and bare rocky slopes. The Millstone Grit outcrop is commonly pockmarked with circular depressions, sometimes water-filled. These mark locations where layers of grit have collapsed into swallow holes, sink holes and dolines eroded into the surface of the underlying Carboniferous limestones.

The rocks of the succeeding Coal Measures were laid down in low-lying coastal swamps and river plains that lay close to the equator. Three units are recognised in the South Wales Coalfield. Of these, the upper or Pennant Measures are the most resistant to erosion and form the high ground between the valleys, with prominent rocky scarps. They comprise brown-grey sandstones and grits of deltaic origin which have been quarried extensively for building stone. The Lower and Middle Coal Measures are thinner and have a greater proportion of shale with some ironstones; they generally crop out in the valley bottoms. During the deposition of the Coal Measures minor tectonic movements led to rapid fluctuations in sea level, which produced a pattern of cyclic sedimentation. Periodically, at times of raised sea level, the low-lying land was flooded and the vegetation killed and buried under layers of mud and sand, where it was compacted and eventually turned into coal. The economically productive coal seams occur mainly in the lower two divisions.

Major earth movements at the end of the Carboniferous, during the succeeding Permian and Triassic periods, led to a lengthy period of uplift, folding and erosion, which lasted for about 80 million years. During this period the Carboniferous and older rocks were folded into the basin-like structure of the South Wales Coalfield. Due to this long period of folding and erosion the succeeding late Triassic age rocks (about 220 million years old) rest uncomformably upon the older sediments. The Triassic rocks were deposited in an arid, desert-like climate at a time when the area of the present day Severn Estuary was a low, undulating desert plain bounded to the northwest by rugged uplands.

The Triassic rocks occupy a narrow belt bordering the banks of the River Severn, where much of their outcrop is covered by recent alluvial deposits, although they are well-seen at Sudbrook. They comprise a variety of sediments deposited in and around a freshwater lagoon that was gradually inundated by the sea. Two major divisions are recognised. The older Mercia Mudstone Group comprises generally red siltstones and mudstones, capped by slightly harder pale green or beige mudstones, while the younger Penarth Group is made up of black shales, thin limestones and yellow calcareous mudstones. The latter were deposited in shallow, brackish water as the sea began to inundate the desert floor. Patches of fossil screes occur on the slopes and around the bases of former high ground. Known as 'Dolomitic Conglomerate', this consists of a coarse deposit of sub-angular pebbles (usually of Carboniferous Limestone) set in a pale-coloured matrix.

Minor earth movements led to uplift and some erosion at the very end of the Triassic Period, before the desert landscape was completely drowned under a shallow sea. At this time, and at the beginning of the succeeding Jurassic Period 200 million years ago, the marine grey, muddy limestones with shale partings belonging to the succeeding Blue Lias were deposited. These have a very limited outcrop around Newport.

These early Jurassic rocks are the youngest bedrock to be found in the county, leaving a gap of about 198 million years in the geological record before the sediments of the Pleistocene were deposited. During this interval the rocks were gently folded and faulted, probably during the Miocene between 23 and five million years ago. The whole area was uplifted, eroded and tilted gently to the southeast, and it was on this surface that the present day drainage pattern was initiated. It is thought three major platforms were developed during the Pliocene epoch (5 million to 1.8 million years ago): the High Plateau at 510–570m, the Middle Peneplain at 360–480m and the Low Peneplain at 210–330m. These represent former planation surfaces that became isolated as the river systems cut down into the landscape during regional uplift. Within Gwent the High Plateau is well seen in the Black Mountains and on the northern edge of the coalfield while the Middle Peneplain forms the high ground between the coalfield valleys.

Coastal erosion was probably responsible for the development of four other platform surfaces at heights of 60, 90, 120 and 180m. Although well seen farther to the west in South Wales, these are not particularly distinct within Gwent, although remnants of some of them can be detected. Their dating is problematic, and some may be products of the Pleistocene glaciations rather than being of earlier origin.

During the Pleistocene epoch (1.8 million to 10,000 years ago) there were periods of intense cold (glacials), when ice sheets developed on the higher ground and spread across much of the county. These alternated with much warmer conditions (interglacials) when the ice melted and sea level rose, sometimes to levels higher than today. There were a number of glacial advances, but it is mainly the effects of the last two that are visible in the landforms seen today. During the older of these, ice sheets derived from the Brecon Beacons and Black Mountains covered almost the whole county. Glacial deposits resulting from these are known as the 'Older Drift'. During the following Ipswichian Interglacial (275,000–120,000 years ago) the climate warmed sufficiently for animals such as hippopotamus to thrive, and sea level rose to a level 6–9m higher than it is today.

The final (Devensian) glacial period (120,000–10,000 years ago) reached its peak 18,000 years ago. At this time ice sheets and valley glaciers that originated in the Brecon Beacons, Black Mountains and Coalfield, extended as far as the southern edge of the coalfield, and eastwards to Usk and Raglan. The ice rounded the landscape and valley glaciers straightened and over-deepened the river valleys. Glaciers deposited moraines at their farthest extent, while meltwaters flowing from beneath the ice deposited patches of glacial sand and gravel. As the ice retreated a thick layer of glacial drift was left behind, covering the bedrock and forming generally hummocky, poorly-drained ground. Because the ice retreat occurred in pulses, it led to the formation of a series of moraines across the valley floors. Some of these blocked river courses and diverted the rivers along new channels, such as at Llanfihangel Crucorney, where a large moraine prevented the Honddu and Monnow rivers from flowing along their original pre-glacial route into the Usk.

Towards the end of the Devensian period periglacial conditions prevailed and heavy snowfall on the uplands eroded steep-sided cwms on the north and north-east facing sides of the coalfield valleys, the Blorenge escarpment and the Vale of Ewyas. Gravelly, sandy clay with coarse, angular rock fragments (head), which occurs along the steep valley sides, also originates from this time. Over-steepening of the valley sides caused instability and land sliding is common, such as is seen at Cwm Yoy and along the sides of the Skirrid. This probably started under the late Pleistocene periglacial climate but continues today.

The major rivers of the area, especially the Wye and Severn, show evidence of having flowed at much higher levels than today during the Pliocene epoch (5 million to 1.8 million years ago). The spectacular incised gorge of the river Wye between Monmouth and Chepstow shows that at one point the river was flowing across a flood plain some 200m higher than it is at the present day. Likewise, the Severn has also been subjected to a fall in level as evidence indicates that by the beginning of the Pleiostocene (1.8 million years ago) its drainage system probably lay about 60m higher than it does today. During the Pleistocene both rivers have responded to an overall fall in sea level as a result of the advance and retreat of ice sheets. However, the fall was not continuous. During glacial periods, sea level fell as water became trapped in the vast ice sheets whilst, in the warm interglacial periods, the ice sheets melted and water was released back to the sea, so leading to a rise in sea level. There were also periods of stability when the rivers flowed at the same level for long periods of time. After such periods, as sea level fell again and the river level dropped, remnants of the sediments deposited at the higher levels were left as flat-topped terraces along the sides of the valley. The terraces are typically composed of gravels, sand and sandy loam. Within the Severn valley five terraces have been identified, the highest being about 60m above current sea level.

During the Ipswichian Interglacial (130,000–115,000 years ago), sea level rose to more than 6m above present levels, which submerged many of the low-lying areas, such as the Caldicot Levels, which border the Severn Estuary. At this time the coast line would have lain at the foot of the rising ground to the north and some of the isolated low hills that now rise from the flat levels would have been small islands then.

At the height of the last, Devensian, glaciation (about 18,000 years ago), sea level fell to almost 100m below its current level, which led to rivers such as the Wye and Severn cutting down into their valley floors to a level well below those seen today. Today these over-deepened valleys appear as buried channels, now filled with more recent gravels and alluvium associated with the post-glacial Flandrian sea level rise.

Following the end of the Devensian Glaciation 10,000 years ago, the warming climate led to the development of widespread deciduous forests across the landscape. However, as the sea level rose it gradually inundated the lowlands around the Severn, killing the coastal forests and burying them under layers of fresh sediment. Their remains can be seen today as layers of peat within the clays that can be found along the shores of the estuary. Sea levels have continued to rise through historic times as evidenced by the abandoned Roman and later field systems that can be picked out in the muddy banks and mudflats of the estuary at low tide. Sea walls built to prevent flooding of the lowlands have had to be abandoned and moved further inland as sea levels continued to rise. At the present day sea level is still rising and, with global temperatures predicted to increase even further, the current sea protection barriers will either have to be raised even higher or abandoned altogether, and new ones built farther inland if the levels are to be protected. There has been much climatic variation over the last 10,000 years: for example, during periods of increased storminess coastal erosion was more rapid, and drifting sand was blown inland, covering some of the coastal areas. At the present day the estuary is suffering another episode of active erosion which is leading to the destruction of many of the coastal saltmarshes. As well as being an extremely valuable habitat for birds, saltmarshes also protect the shore from excessive wave action. In some places they have already been totally removed, so exposing the sea defences to the full force of the sea.

The climate and landscape of Gwent have changed considerably through the millennia and continue to do so today. What the future holds is hard to predict, but the landscape and environment will change through continuing geological processes, and thus so will the avifauna.

BIRD HABITATS IN GWENT

WOODLAND

Gwent has always been relatively well wooded and at one time had a higher percentage of its area covered by trees than any other county in Wales. The extent of woodland area has grown from around 9% in 1895, to 11% in 1947 and to 13.8% by 1997. However, the rate of afforestation has been even greater in some other counties in south and mid Wales, with the effect that Gwent has now fallen behind Glamorgan and Powys in extent of forest cover. The more modest afforestation seen in Gwent has been limited to the former heathland areas of the Trelleck ridge and in the western valleys on industrial reclamation sites.

There have been two recent national surveys of woodland area, which coincidentally (and fortuitously) correspond broadly with the two Gwent Breeding Bird Atlas periods. These are the Forestry Commission Census of Woodlands 1979–82, and the National Inventory of Woodland and Trees – Wales 2002, also published by the Forestry Commission.

Wales had some 11.6% woodland cover in 1980, which had increased to 14% by 1997. Most of this woodland (56%) is in private ownership and, coincidentally, the same proportion is also coniferous. The main increase between the two censuses has been in the larger woodlands (over 2ha) where the increase has been 19%, and the smaller copses (between 0.25–2ha) where the increase has been 15%. Small groups and lines of trees in contrast have declined extensively (down by 32%). The greatest loss between the censuses has been in the density of individual trees, from 100/km^2 in 1980 to just 33/km^2 in 1997.

The changes in Gwent have broadly followed those seen in Wales as a whole, although at the county level, direct comparisons are hampered by the use of slightly different methodologies in the two censuses. In 1980, there were 16,900ha of woodland over 2ha in Gwent and a further 3,800ha of smaller woods. Approximately half of this total was broadleaved, and this was well above the Welsh average. In 1997, there were 18,054ha of woodland over 2ha and a further 968ha of small woods (0.1–2ha). These totals indicate a slight reduction over the 1980 amount, which may be a reflection of areas smaller than 0.1ha being excluded from the later census. However, there may actually have been a small reduction in total woodland area due to the loss of small copses and groups of trees: these would not have been subject to felling control under the various Forestry Acts, and would not have had replanting conditions. Any changes, however, are too small at the tetrad scale to be picked up as differences in the woodland maps between the two Atlases. The current Gwent figure is some 13.8% woodland cover (19,000ha). Of this, 9,552ha (50%) is broadleaved, 5,425ha (29%) is coniferous and 2,926ha (15%) is mixed, with lesser amounts of coppice (229ha), felled (184ha) and open ground (704ha) (FC 2002). The current heathland restoration programmes on the Trellech plateau would have occurred mainly after the census.

Although a high proportion of Gwent woodlands are broadleaved, and some 2,249ha are classed as ancient semi-natural woodland, the county has suffered one of the greatest losses of such ancient woodland in the UK. Some 67% has been lost in Gwent in the last 40–50 years, mainly as a result of replacement by conifers, mostly in parts of the Wye Valley and in Wentwood. Despite these losses, there are still substantial areas of ancient semi-natural woodland left, a reflection of the considerable amount that was once present in some parts of the county.

In the east of the county, the Wye Valley woodlands extend in an almost unbroken chain for some 30km on both the Gwent and Gloucestershire sides of the River Wye, and then north-eastwards from Monmouth into Herefordshire. They are internationally important and contain some of the best areas in the UK for three different woodland types: Yew dominated woods with ash and whitebeam on limestone; lime/maple woods on base rich soils associated with rocky slopes, and beech woods on neutral/rich soils of lowland limestone. Although conversion to conifers has taken place in some parts in the past, the main broadleaved woodlands are designated as the Wye Valley Woodlands Special Area of Conservation (SAC). In Gwent, from Monmouth to Chepstow, these comprise nine individual woodland blocks: the Upper Wye Gorge, Fiddler's Elbow, Livox Wood, Harper's Grove/Lord's Grove, Graig Wood, Lower Hael Wood, Cleddon Shoots, Blackcliff-Wyndcliff and Pierce and Alcove & Piercefield Woods.

The Forestry Commission policy is now to encourage the replacement of conifers by broadleaves on the remaining ancient woodland sites, both here in the Wye Valley and elsewhere in the UK. One of the main features of the Wye Valley woodlands, and of the majority of the county's other broadleaved and mixed woodlands, is the variety of tree species. As well as those mentioned above, oak, birch, cherry, wych elm and holly are all relatively common, and small pockets of hornbeam can also be found. There is now a move to reintroduce coppicing into some of the Wye Valley woodlands, which is the method by which they would have been managed over a century ago.

There are two other SAC woodlands in Gwent, both in the north near Abergavenny. On the southern slopes of the Sugar Loaf, is the Abergavenny Woodlands SAC, one of the best areas in the UK for western acidic (sessile) oak wood and with a significant component of beech on neutral/rich soils of lowland limestone. A little to the west is the Cwm Clydach SAC, one of the best areas in the UK for beech on neutral/rich soils. An uncommon type of beech woodland (Atlantic beech with holly on acid soils) is also found in Cwm Clydach.

In addition to these internationally important woodlands there are a further 17 woodland Sites of Special Scientific Interest (SSSIs). They are mainly in the east and north of the county and, because of the county's rich geology, comprise varied woodland types. There are only two woodland SSSIs in the western valleys (Silent Valley and Plas Machen), a reflection of the degraded nature of the natural sessile oak woods there by past industrial activities and recent overgrazing, and the extent of replacement by conifer forests.

Sessile oak woods are found at Park House Wood (on the Trellech plateau), Strawberry Cottage Wood (north of Abergavenny) and Parc Seymour, which represents the last remnant of the former extensive Wentwood oak-woods. Pedunculate oak woods are at Bushy Close (south-west of Chepstow) and Gaer Lan (south-west of Monmouth), while Penhow Woodlands have a mixture of pedunculate oak and ash woodland types. One of the most extensive areas of coppice beech is found at Coed y Person, southwest of Abergavenny. Atlantic beech woodland is found at Silent Valley, near Ebbw Vale. Alder-dominated woods are at Coed y Cerrig and Gaer House Woods, north and northeast of Abergavenny, whilst mixed alder/oak woodland is at Plas Machen near Risca.

The Coombe Valley Woods between Chepstow and Wentwood are on rich calcareous soils. Mixed woods on flushed acid soils are found at Gaer Wood east of Raglan, at Maes yr Uchaf, Penarth Brook Woodland and Croes Robert: all on the Trellech plateau. Priory Wood, near Usk, is noted for having a wide variety of woodland types in a relatively small area.

The conifer plantations of the Wye Valley and Wentwood have extensive areas of larch and Douglas fir on the richer soils, with Scots pine on the poorer soils, especially on the millstone grit areas of the Trellech plateau, while Norway spruce is found on the wetter ground. Mynydd ddu forest in the north of the county, and Ebbw Forest: including the woodlands around Tredegar, Ebbw Vale, Abertillery and Abercarn in the western valleys, also have some larch and Douglas fir, but there are extensive areas of both Norway and sitka spruce, reflecting both the poorer nature of the soils and the higher altitude of these forests. A wide variety of other conifers have also been planted in small pockets, presumably to assess their growth potential. The main ones are western hemlock, Corsican pine, redwood and various species of fir and cypress.

The broad valley of the River Usk and the rolling countryside of central and northeastern Gwent are the main farmland areas of the county. There are few large woodland areas here other than where they are associated with the larger estates, such as near Llangibby, Llanover, Llanarth, Talycoed and the Hendre. These farmed areas are however rich in small, mainly broadleaved, woodlands, although there have been a few losses in the last 20 years since the earlier Gwent Atlas. Larger woodlands, mainly mixed, are also associated with the smaller hills of the north and north-east, such as on the Graig and Ysgyryd Fawr.

There are few parts of the county with no woodland; the lack of trees on the coastal belt and on the upland plateau in the northwest is understandable. Not so explicable is the broad treeless swathe of countryside running north-westwards from near Raglan. The absence of large estates in this area, whose owners generally emphasise landscape and shooting, is presumably the reason. These areas can be easily picked out on the woodland map and on some of the species maps.

The diversity of Gwent's woodlands has an important influence on the variety of birds present. There are however two recent national management policies that are likely to have a more fundamental effect on future bird populations. Firstly the reversion (over the long term) of conifer plantations on ancient woodland sites (PAWS) to native broadleaved high forest, and secondly the adoption of continuous cover forestry, which involves a reduction in the amount of clear felling.

PAWS is likely to benefit a whole range of typical woodland birds such as Woodcocks, Lesser Spotted Woodpeckers, Song Thrushes, Blackcaps, Garden Warblers, Spotted and Pied Flycatchers, Marsh and Willow Tits,

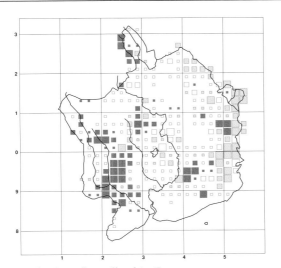

Woodlands

>60% conifer
- ■ >30% of tetrad wooded
- ■ 15%–30% of tetrad wooded
- ▪ <15% of tetrad wooded

Mixed woodland
- ▨ >30% of tetrad wooded
- ▨ 15%–30% of tetrad wooded
- ▫ <15% of tetrad wooded

>60% broadleaved
- □ >30% of tetrad wooded
- □ 15%–30% of tetrad wooded
- ▫ <15% of tetrad wooded

Figure 1. Distribution of woodland in Gwent

Nuthatches, Treecreepers and Hawfinches. Some others appear to do better in coniferous (or mixed) woodlands however, and benefits from this policy for Goshawks, Sparrowhawks, Great Spotted Woodpeckers, Goldcrests and Firecrests may not materialise.

With respect to those coniferous woodlands destined to remain as such, there are proposals for continuous cover and reductions in clear felling. The majority of woodland birds, especially the conifer specialists such as Goldcrests, Crossbills and Siskins, are likely to benefit from the more varied and natural age structure and a more consistent/predictable seed source. The Wood Warbler is not usually thought of as a species of coniferous woodland but it is found in high densities in larch plantations in Wentwood and other areas, where this decid-uous conifer allows some ground vegetation to develop but where plantation management and summer shade suppress the heavy growth of shrubs and ground flora. Continuous cover management and the development of a denser understorey is unlikely to benefit this declining species. A number of species have also become special-ists of the early growth stages following clear felling, the Nightjar being an obvious example where the county population is now at its highest level and virtually dependent on forest clearfells. These young scrubby planta-tions, in their first ten years of growth, also provide an important habitat for a range of other species, such as Tree Pipit, Stonechat, Lesser Redpoll, Linnets and perhaps Turtle Dove (whose last Welsh refuge is in the forest re-stocks of the Trelleck plateau), which are unlikely to benefit from continuous cover forestry. It is hoped that the two broad policies (PAWS and continuous cover), which in general terms are to be welcomed, do not have detrimental effects on a few bird species that are already in decline.

Most woodland birds appear to be influenced as much by the woodland structure as by the canopy species, and this is easily illustrated by the warblers: Willow Warblers, Chiffchaffs, Blackcaps and Garden Warblers all require dense ground cover, whereas Wood Warblers do not. Changes in woodland structure have been associ-ated with the current declines of many woodland birds. In some cases these changes result from over- browsing by Fallow Deer. The deer have become a problem in the Wye Valley and Wentwood in recent years by prevent-ing tree and herb regeneration, and there are proposals to reduce their numbers. Another factor not generally considered as affecting woodland birds is the increased mechanisation of forest operations. Long gone are the days of the woodman with his hook or chainsaw, now replaced by a machine which harvests the whole tree. Forest operations are now year-round activities with no respite during the breeding season and, at the local level, considerable numbers of bird nests must be destroyed. This mechanisation is akin to the agricultural intensification of the last century,which is now recognised as having such an adverse effect on farmland birds, and it can only be a matter of time before it becomes implicated in the decline of woodland birds.

MOORLAND

The moorlands of Gwent have variations in floral composition which influence the range of bird species present. The main plant species present are rush, moss and grass species typical of higher altitudes in Gwent. These ubiquitous species are however enriched in many areas by Bracken, Bilberry, Heather, Cowberry, Cross-leaved Heath and Gorse. It is those moorlands with a higher percentage of these latter species, which usually support a wider range of birds. Rough grassland present on all of the county's uplands support Skylarks and Meadow Pipits, but more specific habitat is required for other species. For example tall heather supports Red Grouse; heather, bracken and gorse provide habitat for Stonechats and Whinchats, whilst stony outcrops are necessary for Wheatears.

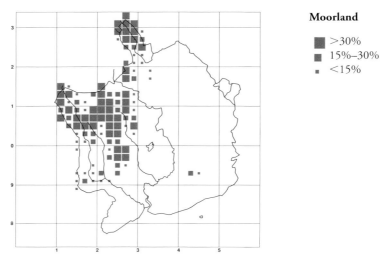

Figure 2. Distribution of moorland in Gwent

The main blocks of moorland are to be found in the north-west of the county on a series of parallel ridges and the occasional plateau running in a roughly north/south direction. The most easterly of the ridges starts just north of Pontypool with Mynydd Garn-wen which, moving in a northerly direction, merges into Mynydd Garnclochdy, Mynydd y Garn-fawr and The Blorenge. The moorland block becomes more diverse in flora and fauna as we move northwards. Mynydd Garnclochdy does have some patchy heather in addition to the rough grassland which predominates on Mynydd Garn-wen. Mynydd y Garn-fawr, which had previously been managed by controlled fires, was extensively burned in 2004 but has made a good recovery with a widespread growth of good quality dwarf shrub heath. The flanks of the Blorenge are covered in Bracken, and this has infiltrated onto some parts of the plateau with a resultant reduction in heather quality. The Blorenge has approximately 32ha of good quality dwarf shrub heath, with a further 150ha of poorer patchy growth. The three more northerly mountains support a great profusion of Skylarks and Meadow Pipits, and good densities of breeding Stonechats , Whinchats, Red Grouse and Wheatears . The northern flank of the Blorenge has a growth of small hawthorn trees and has a good population of Tree Pipits: at least three male Cuckoos are usually present in this area. Grouse shooting still takes place on the Blorenge and Mynydd y Garn-fawr during late summer.

The second ridge arises to the north of Risca at Twmbarlwm and Mynydd Henllys, before merging in a northerly direction with the Mynydd Maen/ Mynydd Llwyd/Mynydd Twyn-glas complex, which is covered by approximately 7km^2 of moorland. Bracken and rough grass are the main habitat, but there is a 15ha patch of good quality dwarf shrub heath on Mynydd Maen which can support Red Grouse. There is a further patch of this habitat on the northern edge of Mynydd Llwyd but this is of poor quality as it has been degraded by trail-bikers.

This ridge is bisected by a deep east/west valley before continuing as Mynydd Llanhilleth which then adjoins the largest moorland plateau in Gwent, consisting of Mynydd Farteg Fawr/Coety Mountain/Mynydd James, (and the more minor peaks of Brygwm, Waun Wen, Gwastad, Twyn Du, Mynydd Farteg Fach, Cefn Coch, Twyn Carncanddo and Mulfran) extending over at least 20 km². The dwarf shrub heath on the Coety Mountain/Mynydd Farteg Fawr area has been managed by mowing and until recently was of a very high quality (waist-deep in parts), very extensive (c.172ha), and had good densities of Red Grouse and a few pairs of Whinchats. Unfortunately the laying of a gas pipeline across the mountain created a track which has given access to large numbers of four-wheel drive vehicles and motorcycles. Consequently this excellent habitat has been illegally damaged and is likely to have a lowered bird population. Mynydd James also has about 14ha of good quality heather and has breeding Red Grouse. Where the bracken in the hill pasture or 'ffridd' areas on the slope meets the plateau, there are Whinchats and Stonechats and also Reed Buntings in the wetter areas. Wheatears breed in the rocky areas on the plateau fringes and Redstarts nest in some of the old stone walls on the top. Many birds of prey use this plateau to forage. They include Merlins (summer), Short-eared Owls (mainly winter), Long-eared Owls, Sparrowhawks, Peregrines, Hen Harriers (March–April and September), Hobbies (late summer) and occasional Red Kites.

To the north of the plateau but at a lower level is Waun Afon, a boggy area covered with rushes, which attracts Snipe, and in the winter Short-eared Owls and Hen Harriers. The ground rises again to the north of Blaenavon, with Tir Abraham-Harry and Cefn Garn-yr-erw: areas still covered by large mounds of mining waste, before the two ridges merge at Llanelly Hill and Gilwern Hill. There is a strong growth of about 2ha of gorse on the north side of Gilwern Hill which supports breeding Stonechats.

The remaining three ridges have smaller areas of moorland as they are narrower and isolated from each other by deep valleys. The third ridge begins to the north of Abertillery with Cefn yr Arail which runs into Mynydd Carn-y-Cefn, and largely consists of unvarying rough grassland. There are however two patches of dwarf shrub heath: 10ha of medium quality at the southern end of Mynydd Carn-y-cefn and 35ha of poor quality on Cefn yr Arail.

The fourth ridge arises at Mynydd Pen-y-fan near Aberbeeg and extends north through Cruglwyn and onto Cefn Manmoel. There are 15ha of medium quality dwarf shrub heath on Cefn Manmoel but this area is subject to a good deal of disturbance from four-wheel drive vehicles and motorcycles.

The final ridge begins with Mynydd Bedwellte running north to Tredegar and its habitat is rough grassland. These three ridges are generally less florally diverse and this comparative homogeneity of plant species supports fewer birds with Stonechats and Whinchats, for example, only found locally and Red Grouse not at all.

To the north of Tredegar in the far northwest of Gwent are Trefil Ddu, Trefil Las and Twyn Bryn-march, a broad area of moorland covering over 10km². Trefil Ddu has around 100ha of patchy dwarf shrub heath, and has breeding populations of Red Grouse, Stonechats, Whinchats and Wheatears. The latter species is particularly prevalent in the quarry area, as are Ravens. There is a damp rushy area just to the north of the quarry which often contains Snipe. Trefil Ddu also contains the last remaining haunt of the Ring Ouzel in Gwent.

The moorland continues eastwards, although it is somewhat fragmented to the north of Ebbw Vale by the reservoirs of Carno and Garnlydan, and the associated forest plantation. This upland block forms the southern edge of the more extensive Mynydd Llangynidr/Mynydd Llangatwg complex in the adjoining county of Powys. The more easterly part of this block consists of short rough grassland and dwarf shrub heath. The dwarf shrub heath is kept very short by overgrazing of sheep, and could improve if this was reduced.

To the north of Abergavenny, moorland is found on Skirrid Fawr, Sugar Loaf and Bryn Arw. Skirrid Fawr has some bracken on its flanks, with short grassland on its ridge. The small trees on its flanks are a good place to observe Yellowhammers. The south side of the Sugar Loaf is covered by dense bracken which gives way to rough grassland towards the summit. In contrast the north side of the Sugar Loaf has a particularly dense growth of dwarf shrub heath, covering about 60ha, and hosts Red Grouse, about five pairs each of Stonechats and Whinchats, and a couple of pairs of Linnets. Bryn Arw has a thick growth of gorse of approximately 4ha, which is excellent habitat for breeding Stonechats.

The Black Mountains range begins to the north of the Sugar Loaf, with a ridge to each side of the Vale of Ewyas. The more westerly ridge consists, from south to north, of Garn-wen, Bal-mawr, Bwlch bach and Chwarel y Fan and has an area of about 9km² of moorland. These mountains are covered by a vast area of heather, totalling around 350ha, although much of it is patchy. The easterly ridge, which has the county boundary running along it, begins as Hatterrall Hill to the north of Cwmyoy and runs north for about 8km before reaching the county border. There are also two small areas of moorland in the south-east of the county on Gray Hill and the neighbouring Mynydd Altir-fach.

WETLANDS

The county has abundant and varied watercourses ranging from large rivers, as the Wye and Usk, to a plethora of small streams in both the uplands and the lowlands. The Monmouth & Brecon Canal runs south to Newport from Abergavenny and the Brecon border whilst many kilometres of standing or slow-flowing water occur in the network of drainage channels, locally known as reens, on the Gwent Levels. In addition there are reservoirs, lakes and numerous ponds.

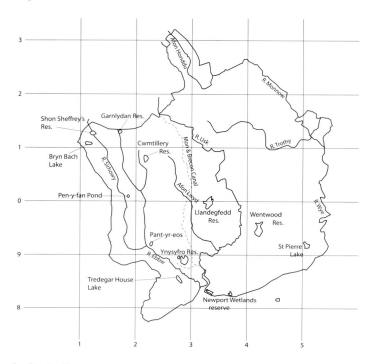

Figure 3. Water bodies in Gwent

In the west the Rhymney, the Ebbw and Sirhowy Rivers flow down to the Severn Estuary. The River Usk flows through the centre of Gwent from the Brecon border down to the Severn Estuary near Newport. The Afon Llwyd is a major tributary of the River Usk and there are a host of minor tributaries including the Gwernesney and Olway Brooks near Usk and the Grwyne Fawr in the Black Mountains. In the east the River Wye forms the Wales/England border from north of Monmouth down to Chepstow. A main tributary of the Wye, the River Monnow and its important tributary the Afon Honddu, arises in the Black Mountains. The River Monnow forms the country border with Herefordshire from near Pandy down to Skenfrith. Other Wye tributaries include the Mally Brook above Monmouth, the Trothy Brook which runs from near Abergavenny through Llantilio Crossenny and Dingestow to the Wye below Monmouth and a series of short tributaries such as the Black Brook, White Brook, Cat Brook and Angidy Brook that arise on the Trellech Plateau and drop steeply down to the Wye.

These watercourses provide diverse habitats for birds. There are excellent clean fast-flowing and rocky reaches on the Black Mountain's upland Grwyne Fawr, the Afon Honddu and River Monnow as well as on the short Lower Wye tributaries such as the Angiddy Brook. As so much of Gwent lies on Old Red Sandstone, some of which is lime-rich, and on limestone, the rivers do not suffer from acidification. They have good tree cover along much of their lengths and a diverse invertebrate fauna of mayflies, stone-flies and caddis flies and support good populations of Dippers and Grey Wagtails. The rivers of the Western Valleys, now that they are no longer grossly polluted, support Dippers and Kingfishers too. The River Monnow below Pandy and the River Usk meander across floodplains and there are many vertical sand cliffs and extensive areas of shoals. These stretches of river are favoured by Goosanders, Common Sandpipers, a small population of Little Ringed Plovers, Kingfishers and numerous Sand Martins as well as more Dippers and both Grey and Pied Wagtails. On the lower reaches of the Rivers Usk, Monnow and Wye, Mute Swans and Mallard prevail, and bankside vegetation may support Reed Buntings. In the winter months Goosanders and sometimes Teal occur on these lower stretches along with Cormorants. The division is not exact and many species such as Kingfisher and Grey Wagtail occur throughout the county on all rivers, even on tiny tributaries.

Sad to say the area of flood meadows is now much reduced because of flood prevention schemes along so many of the streams and rivers. However, fields along parts of the lower Usk and the fields alongside the Olway Brook still become inundated when rivers overtop their banks. In the south the Nedern Brook below Caerwent also has extensive flood meadows which support breeding Coots and Moorhens, feeding Little Egrets and wintering wildfowl.

The slow-flowing canal and numerous reens in the south of the county are favoured by Coots, Moorhens and Kingfishers with Grey and Pied Wagtails breeding at some of the canal locks and Reed Buntings frequent along the reens. In the autumn and winter months Stonechats are among the birds using the bushes and willows along the reens. Areas of reedbed occur mainly on the Levels although small areas exist at Llanover and on the lower estuarine reaches of the Rivers Usk and Wye. New large reedbeds have been created at the Newport Wetland Reserve augmenting the existing old reedbed in the old ash lagoon. Smaller reedbeds, sedgebeds and willow thickets occur at the Gwent Wildlife Trust Reserve at Magor Marsh, at Llanwern Steelworks and scattered through the reen network. These wetland habitats are busy in the summer months with Reed and Sedge Warblers and Reed Buntings whilst Cetti's Warblers have a healthy resident population. Less common visitors such as Bitterns, Marsh Harriers, Short-eared Owls and Bearded Tits have been recorded in recent years, mainly at the Newport Wetlands Reserve.

The largest open waterbody in the county is Llandegfedd Reservoir. This has been well watched over the years. It supports breeding Coots as well as Great Crested Grebes, large numbers of wintering wildfowl and a host of migrants on passage. Other important reservoirs for breeding birds or wintering wildfowl include Wentwood, Ynsyfro, Pant-yr-eos, Pen-y-fan Pond, Garnlydan and Carno. At the larger upland reservoirs Common Sandpipers sometimes breed. There are a host of small reservoirs and man-made ponds, many of those in the western valleys, such as the Dunlop-Semtex Pond, created during the industrial past. The series of ponds in the Whitebrook and Angiddy Valleys in the east of the county also owe their origins to the wireworks and paper mills which began to flourish in these valleys as long ago as the 16th and 17th centuries, respectively. These ponds support a few Little Grebes, Moorhens and Coots and their outflows are often used by Dippers and wagtails. Newer lakes created for recreation, fishing or conservation interests, include Brynbach near Ebbw Vale, Dingestow Court Lake renovated in the 1980s and The Hoop ponds near Penallt. Brynbach has become a regular site for flocks of Goosanders in the winter whilst Dingestow Lake and The Hoop ponds support a few wintering Tufted Ducks and Pochards and breeding Little Grebes, Canada Geese, Coots, Moorhens and Tufted Ducks. There are also new ponds on recently constructed golf courses. For example, ponds at Raglan Golf Course support breeding Coots and Moorhens and Canada Geese are regular. These ponds did not exist during the 1981–85 Gwent Atlas. Likewise wetland creation – scrapes and pools – on the Newport Wetland Reserve has provided more wildfowl and wader habitat.

Data from Blaenau Gwent and Newport Borough show that in these relatively small areas there are 225 and 200 ponds respectively. Numbers in Torfaen and Monmouthshire are unknown but must number well in excess of 500. The marked increase in Canada Geese and Coots since the 1st Gwent Atlas may be partly due to the creation of many new wetlands.

URBAN AND INDUSTRIAL

The extent of the built-up and industrial areas, as indicated on the map, differs surprisingly little from that shown in the 1st Gwent Atlas. Of the 393 tetrads common to both Atlas surveys, more than half (211) remain in the 'less than 3 %' category, and only 49 show a change of category. New industrial estates and housing developments account in almost equal numbers for the 36 tetrads showing a change to a higher category. This probably under-states the growth of these areas, since in several instances a new development crossed tetrad boundaries, and failed to show a significant increase in either tetrad. Thirteen tetrads show a decrease sufficient to show as a change of

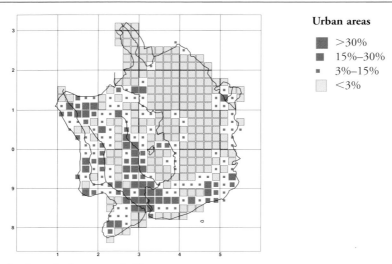

Urban areas

■ >30%
■ 15%–30%
■ 3%–15%
☐ <3%

Figure 4. Distribution of urban areas in Gwent

category: most of these are in the western valleys and relate to the reclamation and landscaping of the sites of coal mines and their associated spoil tips. As yet the grass and scrub on these sites remain young but could grow into habitat suitable for pipits, chats and warblers.

FARMLAND

Gwent is a predominantly pastoral county. Grazing by stock, mainly sheep and cattle, of pastures, rough hillsides and moorland is the main land use. Arable farming is largely confined to the Usk, Monnow and Trothy Valleys where cereals, oilseed rape and maize are the commonest crops.

In 1984, at the time of the 1st Gwent Atlas, there were about 82,000ha of farmland and 9,500ha of rough grazing on common land in the west and north-west. This comprised about 67% of the county's land area, the rest being woodland, urban, moorland and water. Much of the farmland was grade 3 or 4. The same situation prevails today but there have been marked changes in agriculture, as in the rest of Britain. Much old permanent pasture has been ploughed, sown with rye-grass and treated with artificial fertilisers, so that a thick growth of grass develops early in the season. The grass is now mostly cut for silage with two to three cuts in the season and little is left for a hay crop. The early cutting of rye grass leys has had detrimental effects on ground-nesting birds such as Curlews. The tall dense growth early in the season also adversely impacts on nesting Lapwings and on birds, such as Starlings, that prefer to feed in short swards. By contrast, corvids such as Jackdaws have fared well and their numbers have increased. Very little unimproved species-rich pasture remains, but in the Wye Valley and on the Trellech Plateau especially, there are a series of small steep pastures and hay meadows which have retained a diverse flora and a good insect fauna. A feature is the numerous Meadow Ant mounds that attract Green Woodpeckers. Since the first Atlas the numbers of dairy and beef cattle in Gwent have declined and those of sheep have correspondingly increased. Goats, red deer, llamas and alpacas occur in small numbers.

Although no statistics were available from the Welsh Office Agriculture Department for the amount of arable land in Gwent during the 2nd Gwent Atlas period, the area is probably rather similar to that in the 1980s (less than 10,000ha). It is the type of crop that has changed. Autumn-sown cereal crops (barley and wheat) have replaced spring-sown crops, to the detriment of finches and buntings that formerly fed on spilt grain and weed seeds in stubble fields during the winter months. On arable land there is also now much more oilseed rape as well as maize and other fodder crops such as mangolds and turnips. A range of additional arable crops occupy only small areas: these include flax, peas, beans, onions, potatoes and lupins as well as soft fruit. Lapwings favour nesting in maize, which is sown late in the spring, whilst Yellow Wagtails may nest in any arable crop.

Generally arable land is usually treated with a cocktail of pesticides and this in turn has led to a reduction in weed seed and in invertebrates, both of which are needed for food by many farmland birds. However, an increasing number of farms are going 'organic' and are not using pesticides and/or are entering into agricultural schemes, notably the Tir Gofal scheme, to safeguard and enhance wildlife habitats. In some cases this means leaving buffer strips around arable fields to provide cover for nesting birds or food in the form of weed seeds and invertebrates.

In the uplands of the north and west, the valley sides or ffridd habitats have in the past been enclosed by walls and fences and are now sheep-grazed but often dominated by bracken. Scattered hawthorns, rowans and birches occur in the fridd, especially in the steep-sided tributary valleys. Good examples are to be found in the Llanthony valley. There, Willow Warblers, Tree Pipits and Redstarts abound in the scrub and in the bracken on the ffridd, birds such as Whinchats occur. In the west, some former upland opencast sites, as along the Heads of the Valleys road, have been converted to rye-grass pasture that now supports sheep.

WHERE TO WATCH BIRDS IN GWENT

For a small county, Gwent is blessed with a wide variety of habitats. In this guide we have selected nine of the best birding sites in the county. In doing so we have attempted to detail areas which encompass the maximum diversity both of habitat and bird species, whilst ensuring a wide geographic spread that covers most areas of the county. We recommend that the relevant Ordinance Survey Explorer Map is used, with a compass and the site map included in this guide, at all sites other than the Newport Wetlands Reserve, Llandegfedd Reservoir, Castle Meadows and Llanfihangel Gobion.

1 NEWPORT WETLANDS RESERVE (NWR)

O.S Map Explorer 152 Newport and Pontypool
Grid reference: ST 334834

Please note that this new reserve is evolving. The information given was current in July 2006 and is subject to change.

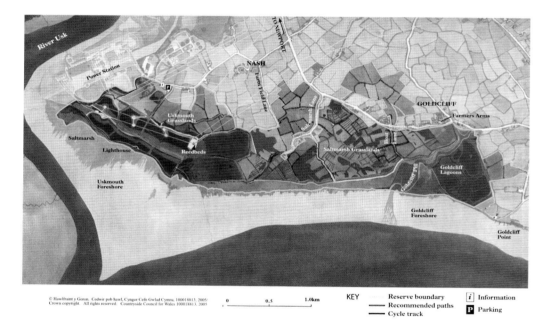

KEY

Reserve boundary   i Information
— Recommended paths   P Parking
— Cycle track

Habitat

Opened in 2000, the reserve is a narrow strip approximately 5km long lying along the north shore of the Severn Estuary, from the mouth of the River Usk eastwards to the village of Goldcliff. The reserve has three distinct habitat areas interspersed with trees and hedgerows. At the western end (Uskmouth) there is a large area of new reedbeds with open water pools. At the eastern end (Goldcliff), three saline lagoons have been created to encourage winter, breeding and passage waders. The central section is lowland wet grassland, managed to encourage breeding waders and over-wintering wildfowl.

The wetlands are maintained by pumping water from nearby sewage works through a special treatment reedbed from which clean water can be circulated through the reserve via the network of reens. Water levels are controlled throughout the reserve to provide suitable habitats. Volunteer wardens patrol the site.

Timing

At the Goldcliff lagoons the best time to visit is when the tide is in, particularly if it is high. Other than this, early morning is best as usual for birding.

Access

Facilities include a car park and single toilet, with disabled access, on West Nash Road between Nash Village and Uskmouth Power Station. From the east at M4 Junction 24 take the A48 to Newport Retail Park, then turn off towards the western entrance to Llanwern Steelworks and follow the 'brown duck' signs to the reserve car park which is open from 09.00–17.00 hrs (or dusk if earlier). From the west, at junction 28, take the A48 towards the docks. Then follow signs for Nash Village and you will pick up the 'brown duck' signs.

Several public footpaths pass through the reserve, as does a spur of the Sustrans Celtic Trail cycle route. At the time of writing, it is not possible to walk through the reserve from the car park at Uskmouth to the lagoons at Goldcliff using footpaths. Care must be taken if the stretch of road which runs through Nash village is used instead as there are no pavements.

At Uskmouth, several paths run between the reedbeds, including four way-marked routes. The Orchid Walk is suitable for pushchairs and wheelchair users. Other paths have rough surfaces. Dogs are allowed on clearly identified paths and must be kept on leads. Stout footwear and suitable clothing are recommended, bearing in mind that it is often windier and cooler on the reserve than further inland, with no shelter available. An interpretation board at the car park shows the routes, and leaflets are generally available. Leaflets can also be obtained by contacting the Countryside Council for Wales (CCW) at www.ccw.gov.uk.

Viewing platforms have been built overlooking the lagoons at Goldcliff. Handrails are provided for limited mobility visitors, but paths are unsurfaced and access was not suitable for wheelchair users in 2006.

A Visitor/Environmental Education Centre at Uskmouth was completed in 2007 and includes information, refreshment and toilet facilities. It is operated by the Royal Society for the Protection of Birds (RSPB). Other refreshments are available at The Waterloo Inn at Nash Village, The Farmers Arms at Goldcliff, and at Newport Retail Park. Details of walks and activities taking place at the Reserve can be found at www.ccw.gov.uk, www.gwentbirds.org.uk or www.rspb.org.uk/wales.

At the time of writing, bus 5B from Newport goes near to the Reserve. Contact Traveline Cymru at 0870 608 2608 for up-to-date information.

Species

The reserve was created as an amelioration measure to compensate for the habitat loss which resulted from the Cardiff Bay barrage. It has proved to be an exciting development for birdwatching in Gwent with over 170 bird species recorded. This includes new breeding species for the county such as Avocet and Bearded Tit. It provides interest all year around, though sometimes a visit can produce nothing of note. In winter there are wildfowl, waders, a spectacular starling roost just before dusk, the hope of hearing a Bittern (and better still of seeing one), and the possibility of watching Short-eared Owl hunting over the reedbeds accompanied by the explosive song of a Cetti's Warbler. In spring there is the anticipation of passage waders and the arrival of summer visitors. The summer brings the buzz of breeding Reed and Sedge Warblers, the diminutive song of the Reed Bunting, perhaps the distinctive sound of Bearded Tits, possibly the sight of a Hobby after dragonflies or, the confirmation of another new breeding species for Gwent. Then, what might turn up in the autumn?

Calendar

Resident Typical water/reedbed species may be seen in most months including: Little Egret, Grey Heron, Little Grebe, Shelduck, Gadwall, Tufted Duck, Oystercatcher, Lapwing, Dunlin, Curlew, Redshank, Water Rail (normally heard), Cetti's Warbler (normally heard), Reed Bunting along with Buzzard, Kestrel, Peregrine and many hedgerow species.

Winter Numbers of waders increase, particularly Dunlin, Curlew and Redshank, and large numbers of ducks such as Shelduck, Mallard, Wigeon, Teal, Pintail and Shoveler can be seen. Other possible species include Bittern, Hen Harrier, Merlin, Black-tailed Godwit, Short-eared Owl, Golden Plover, Grey Plover, Knot,

Stonechat, Fieldfare and Redwing. There is also an impressive Starling roost at Uskmouth reedbeds. Black Redstart is also a possibility.

Spring This is the time of regular spring wader passage, arrival of passage and breeding migrants, establishment of territories by resident and migrant breeding birds, and the arrival of some more unusual species. More regular species to look out for, although not always common, include: Oystercatcher, Avocet, Little Ringed Plover, Ringed Plover, Sanderling, Curlew Sandpiper, Ruff, Bar-tailed Godwit, Whimbrel. The scarcer waders recorded include Kentish Plover, Temminck's Stint and Purple Sandpiper as well as a series of rarities (see below). Passerines include Water Pipit, Yellow Wagtail, White Wagtail, Redstart, Whinchat and Wheatear. Regular/diligent observation at this time may produce many other species/rarities.

Summer The reserve holds many breeding/probable breeding species such as Little Grebe, Mute Swan, Canada Goose, Shelduck, Moorhen, Coot, Tufted Duck, Ruddy Duck, Oystercatcher, Avocet, Little Ringed Plover, Ringed Plover, Lapwing, Redshank, Cuckoo, Skylark, Cetti's Warbler (not often seen but characterised by its explosive song), Sedge Warbler, Reed Warbler, Lesser Whitethroat, Whitethroat, Chiffchaff, Willow Warbler, Bearded Tit, Linnet and Reed Bunting. Other birds that might be seen or heard between April and September include Spoonbill, Garganey, Marsh Harrier, Hobby and Grasshopper Warbler. Orchids, dragonflies, damselflies, butterflies and moths add additional interest to visits during summer.

Autumn This is the time of departure of migrant breeders, movement of passage waders, and the arrival of the more unusual. Species include some of those recorded as spring passage waders along with the possibility of: Red-necked Phalarope, Wood Sandpiper, Green Sandpiper, and flocks of Redwing and Fieldfare. Regular/ diligent observation at this time may produce many other species, including rarities.

Rarities Notable species which have been recorded on the reserve are Squacco Heron, White-rumped Sandpiper, Baird's Sandpiper, Pectoral Sandpiper, Hudsonian Whimbrel, Richard's Pipit, Dartford Warbler, Aquatic Warbler (by ringers), Yellow-browed Warbler, Woodchat Shrike and Lapland Bunting.

2 LLANDEGFEDD RESERVOIR

O.S Map Explorer 152 Newport & Pontypool
Grid references: Dam ST 325985, North End SO 333008 (Car park on map)

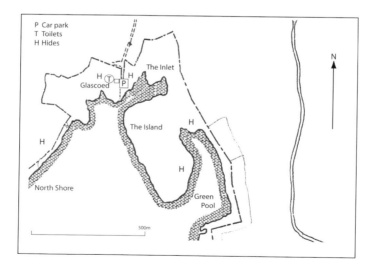

Habitat

A 174ha reservoir mainly consisting of open water but with some reedbeds and willow carr. Adjacent habitat includes marsh, small ponds, broadleaved woodland, hedgerows and hay meadows.

Conservation work has included the planting of reedbeds, construction of ponds and ditches, creation of wild flower meadows, tree planting, woodland management, planting of crops to encourage finches and buntings, provision of nest boxes and nesting islands, construction of Osprey nesting platforms, construction of a Sand Martin nesting bank, creation of breeding habitat for Lapwings and operation of a bird feeding station.

Species

The site is designated as an SSSI for wintering wildfowl. Large numbers of Wigeon, Mallard and Teal over-winter, together with smaller numbers of Pochard and Tufted Duck. Other winter visitors include Bewick's Swans, Goldeneye, Shoveler and Pintail.

Passage migrants regularly include Ospreys in spring and autumn, together with tern and wader species. Winter visitors regularly include diver species and rarer grebes. Breeding birds include Water Rails, Great Crested and Little Grebes, Tree Sparrows in small numbers and both Reed and Sedge Warblers.

The northerly (shallower) end is the best area for wintering wildfowl but species preferring deeper water are best observed from the dam. The western bank is good for observing gulls coming in to roost.

Timing

Early morning is best for birding, as usual. Winter is good for wildfowl, grebes and divers, spring and autumn for passage waders, terns and Osprey, and summer for breeding birds.

Access

The site is owned by Dwr Cymru-Welsh Water and managed by United Utilities Operational Services. Access is by permit only, obtainable either by joining the Gwent Ornithological Society or by purchase on site. Access to the northern end is for key holders only during the period 1 November–28 February: keys available from G.O.S. Some access restrictions apply during the winter months to protect grazing wildfowl.

There are six hides on site: five at the northern end, including one overlooking the bird feeding station, and one on the western bank. Other useful observation points are from the dam wall and from the education lodge at the north end.

Car parking is available at the north end, on the west bank, just below the treatment works and in the eastern picnic area. It is also possible to park near the dam. Permit holders are entitled to walk around the reservoir but access to the eastern bank is prohibited in winter. Disabled access is available at the northern end to the feeding station and inlet hides. No dogs or bicycles are allowed. The nearest points served by public transport, the railway station at Pontypool/New Inn and the village of New Inn, which is served by frequent buses, are both two miles distant.

Calendar

Resident Great Crested Grebe, Little Grebe, Coot, Moorhen, Water Rail, Mallard, Grey Heron, Lapwing; Green, Great Spotted and Lesser Spotted Woodpeckers, Buzzard, Sparrowhawk, Kestrel, Tree Sparrow, Yellowhammer, Reed Bunting, Willow Tit, Marsh Tit and many common species.

December to February Wigeon, Teal, Tufted Duck, Pochard, Pintail, Shoveler, Goosander, Bewick's Swan, occasional Black-throated and Great Northern Divers; Slavonian, Black-necked and Red-necked Grebes, Golden Plover, Snipe, Green Sandpiper, and large numbers of gulls, including occasional rarities.

March to May Osprey, Hobby, passage terns including Black Tern, passage waders, Little Ringed Plover, Common Sandpiper, Yellow Wagtail, Wheatear, Redstart, Tree Pipit, Reed Warbler, Sedge Warbler, Garden Warbler, occasional Cetti's Warbler.

June to July The breeding species are present plus a small flock of Common Scoter (in some years), Little Egret, terns, waders, Hobby.

August to November Osprey, waders, terns, returning wildfowl, migrant passerines.

3 THE WENTLOOGE COAST

O.S Map Explorer 152 Newport and Pontypool: all sites accessible from the B4239 coast road
Grid references: St Brides coast ST 300816, Peterstone Pill ST 278807, Sluice Farm ST 255790

Habitat

The Wentlooge Level is a large low-lying coastal area between Cardiff and Newport, protected from the sea by an earth sea wall. It was traditionally pastureland drained by ditches (known locally as reens) but some areas are now pipe-drained and arable, and there is also some land-fill, a golf course and a golf driving range. A path (not designated on the Explorer map) runs along the entire length of the sea wall, and gives excellent views of the tidal mudflats and saltmarshes that characterise this stretch of the Severn coast.

Timing

The waders and wildfowl of the Severn are the major interest and best views are obtained either on the rising or high tide, depending on the site.

General access

All sites are accessible from the B4239, the Cardiff to Newport coast road, but see under individual sites for details. St Brides and Peterstone are served by bus services 31A and 31C from Newport Bus Station (6–8 buses daily, but no Sunday service). Wheelchair access to the sea wall is really possible only at Peterstone Pill, and progress from there is soon blocked in both directions by stiles.

Species

A wide selection of winter wildfowl includes good numbers of Shelduck, Mallard, Teal, Pintail, Shoveler and Wigeon, and smaller numbers of less regular species. The most abundant winter wader species are Dunlin, Knot, Curlew, Black-tailed Godwit, Redshank and Oystercatcher, but many other species are regularly recorded. Passage periods produce species such as Garganey, Whimbrel, Curlew Sandpiper, Sanderling, Ringed Plover, Little Stint, Greenshank and Bar-tailed Godwit. Shelduck breed, as do several summer visitors including Reed and Sedge Warblers, and Yellow Wagtails (now very scarce).

ST BRIDES COAST

Grid reference: ST 300816

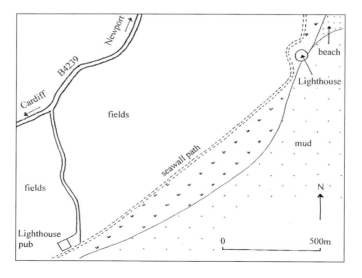

Access

Visit at high tide. Park in the large car park adjacent to the Lighthouse Inn at the above grid reference. Go through gate and walk east, either along seawall or along the seaward edge of the saltmarsh, which remains dry on all but the highest spring tides. According to season, the saltmarsh and inland meadows may have breeding Lapwings and Redshanks, feeding Curlews and Whimbrels, or (only on the saltmarsh) high tide roosts of Dunlin and Ringed Plover. Continue to just beyond the West Usk Lighthouse where a small beach has a regular high tide wader roost with a good range of species.

Calendar

Autumn-Winter Oystercatcher, Grey Plover, Ringed Plover, Knot, Dunlin, Curlew, Black-tailed Godwit, and occasionally Bar-tailed Godwit. Up to about 600 Shelduck offshore. Stonechats are regular on fences and reeds. Little Stint, Curlew Sandpiper during autumn passage.

Spring All the above wader species at the beach roost, but also including passage Whimbrel and Sanderling, though the latter has been only occasional in recent years. Breeding Oystercatcher, Lapwing, Ringed Plover, and Redshank. Cetti's, Reed and Sedge Warblers plus Reed Bunting in vegetated reens. Passage Wheatears and sometimes Whinchats on saltmarsh. Ravens breed in the large pylon.

Summer Breeding waders and passerines as listed for spring.

PETERSTONE PILL AND GOUT
Grid reference: ST278807

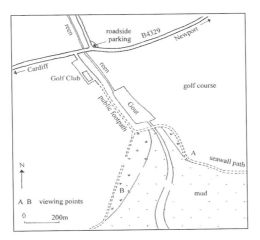

Broadway reen, which runs across the levels from Marshfield, drains into a large basin known as Peterstone Gout. This in turn drains, via sluices in the sea wall, into the estuary where it meanders over the mudflats as Peterstone Pill. The mud surrounding the Pill is a favoured feeding area for wildfowl and waders and, as it the last area to be covered by the rising tide, there is often a large concentration of birds just prior to full mud cover. The winter Shoveler flock is a particular attraction of the site. The Gout is also of interest, as some wildfowl and waders, particularly Redshanks, use it as a high tide roost, and when water levels are high it is used by Little Grebes and duck species for feeding.

Access

Arrive 2–3 hours before high tide. There is very limited parking on the roadside verge at the junction (see map). In the past, birdwatchers were permitted to park in the golf course overflow car park, but permission was withdrawn some years ago (it might just be worth asking?). Follow the public footpath through the golf club car park to the corner of the Gout: resist the temptation to cross the stile to look into the Gout (the light and the view are better from the far end) and proceed on the track down the west side of the gout to the sea wall. From here, look back into the Gout. You now need to find a vantage point from which you can observe birds feeding on the rising tide. The position of the sun is a major consideration: in the morning it is best to turn left along the seawall, cross the sluices and settle at viewing point A; in the afternoon, turn right along the seawall, cross the narrow saltmarsh and settle at viewing point B.

An alternative approach involves roadside parking 1km to the west at Peterstone village (ST268802). Take the public footpath alongside the church to the sea wall, and walk east to reach viewing point B.

Calendar

Winter Large numbers of wildfowl, including Shelduck, Mallard, Teal, Pintail, Wigeon and an impressive Shoveler flock; waders including Oystercatcher, Grey Plover, Ringed Plover, Knot, Dunlin, Curlew, Redshank. Also look out for Merlin and Short-eared Owl.

Spring All the above species, but in smaller numbers; additional passage species include Garganey (in some years), Whimbrel, Spotted Redshank, Greenshank, Common Sandpiper; breeding Cetti's, Reed and Sedge Warblers and Reed Buntings in vegetated reens; Yellow Wagtail in meadows; Common and Lesser Whitethroat in hedgerows; breeding Great Crested Grebe, Little Grebe and Tufted Duck in the gout.

Summer Shelduck broods feeding on mud-flats; a sprinkling of waders; occasional movements of Manx Shearwater offshore.

Autumn The same wildfowl and waders as in winter, but in smaller numbers, plus passage Curlew Sandpiper, both godwits, Whimbrel, Common Sandpiper, Wood Sandpiper, Ruff.

SLUICE FARM
Grid reference: ST255790

Saltmarsh with high tide wader roost. The turfed areas are favourite spots for Water Pipits, especially in early spring (March/April), when birds have often acquired their breeding plumage. The area is best covered on the hour either side of the higher tides when the wader roost: principally of Curlew, Oystercatcher and Redshank, has been pushed onto the higher areas of the saltmarsh by the rising tide and is more likely to be visible. The roost can be on either side of the large concrete building on the seaward side of the sea wall.

Access

Visit at high tide. There is roadside parking for several cars on the south side of the road opposite the farm: from there take the track to the sea wall. Alternatively, park at Peterstone village (ST268802), take the public footpath alongside the church to seawall, and walk west along the seawall towards Cardiff for about 1km.

Calendar

Summer/Autumn/Winter Similar selection of species to Peterstone Pill.

Spring Water Pipit. Otherwise again similar to Peterstone Pill.

4 THE RIVER USK

The River Usk is already a mature river when it enters the county at a point near Glangrwyney, on Gwent's north-west boundary. It runs in an easterly direction to Abergavenny, where it turns south-east until it reaches Llanfihangel Gobion, then due south to Newbridge-on-Usk (the tidal limit) and south-west to Newport, where it enters the Severn Estuary. In total it flows some 55km from the county boundary to the Severn. The river is designated as a Special Area of Conservation because of its high diversity of habitats and species of European importance.

Llandegfedd Reservoir (*Welsh Water plc*). The largest inland water body in Gwent, this reservoir attracts notable numbers of wildfowl, especially during the winter months.

Red-necked Grebe (*John Marsh*). Mostly a rare winter visitor to Gwent, but this summer- plumaged bird was at Llandegfedd Reservoir in May 1995.

Bewick's Swan (*John Marsh*). Small groups are found most winters at traditional sites in the Usk valley, but they have become scarcer in recent years.

Goldeneye (*R. Colin Elliott*). An uncommon winter visitor to the reservoirs of Gwent, its numbers having decreased in recent years.

Goldcliff Point and Newport Wetlands Reserve (*Kevin Dupé, Countryside Council for Wales*).

Goldcliff Lagoons, Newport Wetlands Reserve (*Kevin Dupé, CCW*)

Tufted Duck (*Dave Brassey*). A common winter visitor; first bred in the county in 1984.

Avocet (*R. Colin Elliott*). An uncommon passage migrant as well as a rare breeder.

Juvenile Avocets (*Steve Roberts*). The first recent successful breeding in Wales took place at Goldcliff in 2003.

Wigeon (*John Marsh*). Newport Wetlands Reserve has become this duck's major wintering site in the county.

Uskmouth Lagoons, Newport Wetlands Reserve (*Kevin Dupé, CCW*).

The Gout, Peterstone (*Mike Love*). Import-ant for wildfowl and waders.

Long-tailed Duck (*John Marsh*). This sea duck is a rare visitor to Gwent.

Ring-necked Duck (*Dave Brassey*). A very rare visitor to Gwent, first recorded in 2000.

Little Egret (*R. Colin Elliott*). Since this species was first recorded in Gwent in 1989, it has become a regular sight, especially on the coast.

Shelduck (*R. Colin Elliott*). A locally common breeding resident, but also a common passage migrant and winter visitor to Gwent.

Little Egret chicks (*Richard Clarke*). This species has bred in the county annually since 2001.

Goldcliff Saltmarsh, Newport Wetlands Reserve (*Kevin Dupé, Countryside Council for Wales*).

Redshank (*John Marsh*). A common winter visitor and passage migrant, and breeding resident in small numbers.

Greenshank (*John Marsh*). An uncommon passage migrant, mostly recorded in the autumn.

Spotted Redshank (*R. Colin Elliott*). A scarce passage migrant and rare winter visitor to Gwent. This individual was at the Red Pools, Nash in 1996.

Purple Sandpiper (*Al Venables*). A rare winter visitor and passage migrant to Gwent, this bird wintered at St Brides during January–March 1990.

Cormorant chicks on the nest, Denny Island (*Richard Clarke*). Cormorants have been breeding regularly on Denny Island since at least 1999.

Whimbrel (*John Marsh*). A fairly common passage migrant with higher numbers being noted during the spring.

(a) **White-rumped Sandpiper** (*Chris Hatch*). A rare vagrant recorded on just three occasions in Gwent. This bird was at Goldcliff in September 1999; (b) **Pectoral Sandpiper** (*R. Colin Elliott*). A rare vagrant. This individual was at Goldcliff in September 1999; (c) **Baird's Sandpiper** (*John Marsh*). A rare vagrant recorded on two occasions in Gwent. This immature bird was at Llandegfedd Reservoir in September 1997; (d) **Dunlin** (*John Marsh*). A common winter visitor and fairly common on passage, seen mostly on the coast.

Black-tailed Godwits (*John Marsh*). In addition to being an uncommon passage migrant, the species can be seen in both summer and winter.

Lapwing (*Ray Armstrong*). A common winter visitor and passage bird; the number of resident breeding pairs has declined substantially.

Yellow Wagtail (*Ray Armstrong*). An uncommon summer visitor and passage migrant that has declined considerably.

Blue-headed Wagtail (*John Marsh*). A scarce passage migrant in Gwent with the majority of records being in April or May.

Lesser Spotted Woodpecker (*R. Colin Elliott*). An uncommon breeding resident found in mature deciduous woodland, parks, orchards and alders alongside streams and canals. This bird was at St. Pierre Wood, Shirenewton.

Marsh Tit (*John Marsh*). A scarce breeding resident in Gwent that has shown a marked decline in range between breeding atlas periods.

Willow Tit (*Ray Armstrong*). A scarce breeding resident in Gwent that is in decline.

Hawfinch (*R. Colin Elliott*). Uncommon breeding resident and rare passage migrant.

Great Spotted Woodpecker (*John Marsh*). A common breeding resident that has increased its range in the county.

Green Woodpecker (*R. Colin Elliott*). Gwent has always been a stronghold for this species in Wales.

Woodcock (*Steve Roberts*). An uncommon winter visitor and scarce breeder that has shown a marked reduction in its breeding range.

Goshawk (*Jerry Lewis*). Gwent has a significant proportion of the Welsh breeding population, with an estimated population of some 50 pairs.

Pied Flycatcher (*R. Colin Elliott*). A fairly common breeding summer visitor and passage migrant. They breed mainly in the north and west of the county but some are found in the woodlands of the Wye and Usk Valleys.

Crosskeys in the Ebbw Valley (*Richard Clarke*).

Monmouthshire and Brecon Canal at Goytre (*Alan Williams*).

Siskin (*John Marsh*). An increasing breeding species, numerous winter visitor and passage migrant, which has benefited from maturing conifer plantations.

Crossbill (*John Marsh*). An uncommon breeder and occasional irruptive visitor.

Buzzard (*John Marsh*). A fairly common breeding resident throughout the county and absent only from a few urban areas in the west.

Redstart (*Ray Armstrong*). A breeding summer visitor that is locally common, mostly in the sessile oak woods of the northern uplands and the slopes of the western valleys.

Wye Valley (*Wye Valley AONB Office*). Looking upriver from Hadnock.

Turtle Dove (*John Marsh*). Until recently, Gwent was the only Welsh county where breeding regularly occurred, but the tenuous foothold the species had now looks to have been lost.

Wye Valley (*Wye Valley AONB Office*). Looking north from Redbrook.

Cuckoo (*R. Colin Elliott*). This species has declined significantly between atlases, particularly in lowland agricultural areas.

Usk Valley (*Andrew Baker*).

Kingfisher (*Dave Lock*). Occurs throughout the county at freshwater sites, but also found along the Gwent levels, especially during the autumn.

Sand Martin (*R. Colin Elliott*). A common breeding summer visitor, which is found mostly in colonies along the Usk, Wye and Monnow river valleys.

Dipper (*Ray Armstrong*). Fairly common breeding resident on suitable watercourses throughout the county.

Goosander (*Dave Brassey*). An uncommon winter visitor to the county and rare breeder since 1975.

Little Grebe (*R. Colin Elliott*). The number of breeding pairs of Little Grebe in Gwent has increased significantly between breeding atlas surveys.

Hobby (*Steve Roberts*). An uncommon summer visitor and breeder with an expanding population in Gwent.

Grey Partridge (*R. Colin Elliott*). This species has shown a dramatic 83% reduction in range in Gwent.

Quail (*Steve Roberts*). This rain-soaked bird was caught at Llanarth in September 1994 and was subsequently released successfully.

Trefil Quarries (*Andrew Baker*). These limestone quarries on the border with Powys are the only remaining breeding site for Ring Ouzel in the county.

Raven (*Ray Armstrong*). A bird found historically in the mountains of Gwent, but that can now be encountered in a range of habitats, including the coastal levels and urban areas.

Long-eared Owl (*Steve Roberts*). A scarce breeder and winter visitor in increasing numbers, especially in the north of the county.

Long-eared Owl chicks (*Steve Roberts*). Breeding records have increased in Gwent in recent years, but this is linked to a few enthusiastic individuals concentrating on the species.

Barn Owl (*R. Colin Elliott*). Breeding success and survival rates have increased since the mid-1970s, with Gwent now having an estimated population of 25–50 pairs.

Little Owl (*R. Colin Elliott*). A fairly common breeding resident, though this species has shown a noticeable decline in its range over recent years.

Redwing (*Ray Armstrong*). A regular winter visitor

Fieldfare (*John Marsh*). A common winter visitor, typically arriving in mid-October.

Black Redstart (*Darryl Spittle*). An uncommon passage migrant and winter visitor. This individual was trapped and ringed at Uskmouth power station in February 2003.

Dartford Warbler (*R. Colin Elliott*). A very scarce winter visitor that has bred in the county. This bird was at the Newport Wetlands Reserve, Uskmouth at the end of 2003.

Sabine's Gull (*John Marsh*). A rare passage migrant. This 1st-year bird was at Goldcliff Pill during April 1994.

Woodchat Shrike (*John Marsh*). A rare passage migrant in Gwent; this individual summered on the Caldicot Levels in 1993.

Desert Wheatear (*Richard Smith*). This confiding male bird was at Peterstone in December 1996.

American Bittern (*Tim Loseby*). This very rare vagrant to Britain was present at the Gwent Wildlife Trust's Magor Reserve between October 1981 and January 1982.

Aquatic Warbler (*Darryl Spittle*). A rare passage migrant that has been recorded on nine separate occasions on the Gwent levels, mostly at Uskmouth.

Night Heron (*Richard Smith*). One of two birds during April and May 1994 at Woodstock/ Morgans Pool, Newport.

Golden Oriole (*Dave Brassey*). This rare passage migrant was at Castle Meadows, Abergavenny during October 2004.

Waxwing (*John Marsh*). This individual was one of many birds recorded during the winter of 2005, when the UK was besieged by this irruptive species from northern Europe.

For most of its length it is a slow moving river with extensive meanders and a wide flood plain. Flooding is now less extensive and shorter lived than in historical times. It is most likely to occur above the town of Usk, where the flood plain is interrupted by rising ground that restricts the river's flow, and around the Llangybi bottoms, when high tides coincide with high river flows.

The river Usk provides an excellent riverine habitat along much of its length, but there are hotspots with a greater range of bird species, particularly if additional habitats such as shingle banks, cut-off meanders or river-ine woodland are in evidence. The sections that provide the best birding are at Llanwenarth, Castle Meadows (Abergavenny), Llanfihangel Gobion, Llanllowell and Llangybi. The latter two sites are privately owned and not accessible to the public, but large parts of the river can be explored via the various footpaths making up the long distance Usk Valley Walk. The river bank at Llanwenarth has been eroded and the footpath that followed it has unfortunately been lost in the course of the river. Until recently the route was still passable because the landowner allowed a stile to be moved inland as the river width expanded, but now the route has been blocked and so is not recommended.

CASTLE MEADOWS, ABERGAVENNY
O.S Map Explorer OL13 Brecon Beacons National Park (Eastern Area)
Grid references: Llanfoist River Bridge SO 292139: recommended start of the walk. Abergavenny sewage works bridge SO 302133: end of walk, return to the starting point following alternative footpath.

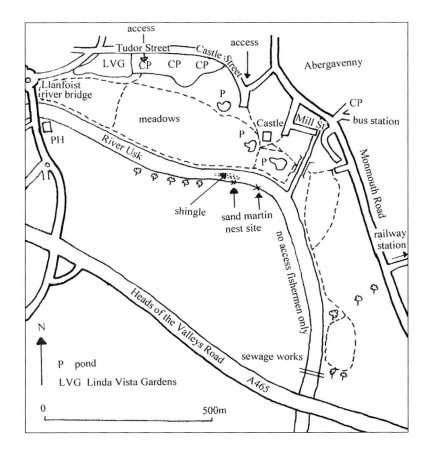

Habitat

Hay meadow, river, shingle bank, hedgerow, man-made ponds and small areas of woodland.

Species

An excellent range of birds characteristic of riverine habitat including Dippers, Grey Wagtails, Common Sandpipers, Kingfishers, Moorhens, Coots, Mute Swans, Pied Wagtails, Sand Martins, Reed Buntings, Grey Herons, Goosanders and the secretive Water Rails in winter.

The hedgerows provide excellent views of Greenfinches, Goldfinches, Blackcaps and Bullfinches, while the woodland areas provide the perfect habitat for Spotted Flycatchers, Nuthatches, Treecreepers, Willow Warblers, Chiffchaffs and Long-tailed Tits. All three British woodpeckers have been seen, though the Lesser Spotted is becoming more elusive. Swifts and hirundines are abundant in spring and summer.

Timing

Early morning is the best time for bird activity whatever the season, and will avoid disturbance from dog walkers. You can find something of interest at any time of year, although the summer months have to be a favourite, watching the Sand Martins darting with precision into the nest to feed their young.

Access

By car take the A40 into Abergavenny and make your way to Castle Street or Tudor Street car parks, signposted when entering Abergavenny in either direction. These car parks are ideal for the walk as both border the meadows. By public transport, the bus and railway station will take you onto the Monmouth road: take a first left into Mill Street just before you enter the town; you can enter the meadows near Abergavenny castle.

Most of the walk can be covered by disabled or wheelchair users as the paths are of good foundation and well maintained.

On entering the meadows turn right to head west towards Llanfoist River Bridge. This is a good starting point for the walk and also gives you an opportunity to check the hedgerow of Linda Vista Gardens for finch and thrush species.

Follow the path downriver until you come to a shingle bank, which is worth scanning during the breeding season for Common Sandpipers with young. The river bank opposite contains one of the largest Sand Martin colonies in Gwent, where the main colony can range from 150 to 300 nests. Continue to follow the path until you meet the River Gavenny where it is worth taking a break to view the river from the bridge for Dippers, Kingfishers and Pied and Grey Wagtails. The walk continues for another 500m to a small woodland area (unsuitable for wheelchair users) where you can see Nuthatches, Treecreepers and woodpeckers.

Return to the Llanfoist Bridge using the circular footpath ensuring you cover the whole of the meadows. At a leisurely stroll the walk should take 90 minutes.

LLANFIHANGEL GOBION (GOBION) NR ABERGAVENNY

O.S Map Explorer OL13 Brecon Beacons National Park (Eastern Area)
Grid references: Bryn village SO 331097; limited parking near church.Pant-y-Goitre Bridge SO 347089; very limited parking on road verges and farm gateway.

Habitats

Riverine habitats including shingle, earth banks, oxbows (recent and old), river meadows, woodland and scrub, bordered by farmed pasture and arable areas

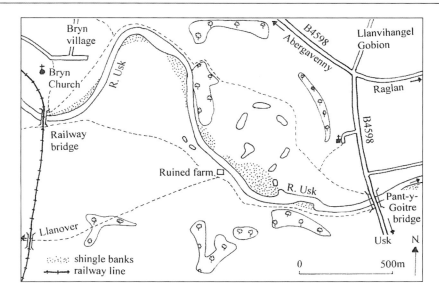

Species

Similar to Castle Meadows but because the area has less public use, disturbance is not such a problem. Breeding species along the river and ox-bows include Mute Swans, Goosanders, Moorhens, Coots, Common Sandpipers, Kingfishers, Sand Martins, Yellow Wagtails, Dippers and Reed Buntings, while one of the counties largest heronries is nearby. The woodlands contain the usual range of common birds and Hobbies nest in the area, frequently hunting the river area for martins and dragonflies.

There is a regular passage of wading birds (in small numbers but good variety) with Little Egrets, Greenshanks, Redshanks, Green Sandpipers and Little Ringed Plovers all regularly recorded, as well as Garganey, Mandarin and Blue-headed Wagtails in some springs.

During the winter, mixed flocks of Redpolls and Siskins can be found in the riverside alders and Fieldfares and Redwings are on the fields. These flocks sometimes attract hunting Merlins or Peregrines. Small numbers of ducks, mainly Teal and Tufted Ducks, can be found on the ox-bows. Rarer species such as the Long-eared Owl and Water Pipit are found occasionally. A wintering flock of approx 80 Lapwings sometimes ventures this far down the Usk valley.

Timing

Any time of year can be productive, although the spring and autumn passage periods are likely to produce the greatest variety of species.

Access

There are way-marked public footpaths on both the north and south sides of the river, but unfortunately it is not possible to do a circular route as the railway bridge at the upstream (Bryn) end has no footway. From the Bryn village there is a public footpath running all the way to Pant-y-Goitre bridge, some 2km away. The south ride of the river can only be accessed from a different public footpath from Pant-y-Goitre bridge. If crossing this bridge great care needs to be taken as there is no dedicated footway. Both of these footpaths deviate from the river bank in places so please respect the rights of the farmers and do not trespass off route. To do so during the breeding season could cause you to disturb nesting birds inadvertently. These walks are unsuitable for wheelchair users.

Calendar for both sites

Resident Mallard, Sparrowhawk, Buzzard, Moorhen, Coot, Kingfisher, woodpeckers, Meadow Pipit, Grey and Pied Wagtails, Dipper, Goldcrest, Long-tailed Tit, Coal Tit, Nuthatch, Treecreeper, Greenfinch, Goldfinch, Bullfinch, and Reed Bunting. Also Lesser Spotted Woodpecker at Gobion.

Spring-Summer Goosander, Hobby, Common Sandpiper, Swift, Sand Martin, Swallow, House Martin, Willow Warbler, Chiffchaff, Blackcap, Spotted Flycatcher,.

Spring and Autumn Mandarin, Little Egret, Little Ringed Plover, Green Sandpiper. Also Garganey, Greenshank, Redshank and Blue-headed Wagtail at Gobion.

Winter Water Rail, Fieldfare, Redwing, Siskin, Redpoll.

5 WENTWOOD FOREST

O.S Map Explorer OL 14 Wye Valley & Forest of Dean
Grid references: Cadira Beeches ST 424947, Foresters Oaks ST 428940

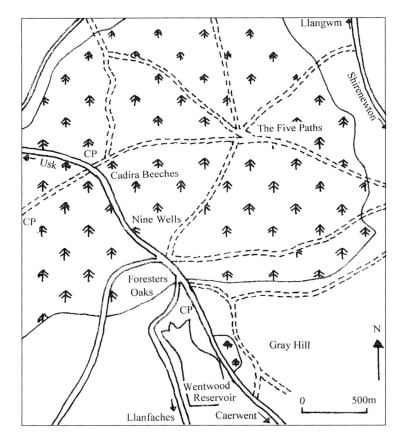

Habitat

The forest of Wentwood was originally a huge area mainly of beech and oak but is now much reduced in size. There are large areas that have been planted with conifers, mainly larch and Douglas Fir, which are periodically harvested forming different habitats. These range from bare clear-felled areas, through young plantations surrounded by scrub, to mature forest. Gray Hill, which requires a short but strenuous climb, has a small area of grassland at the summit with birch scrub, Gorse and Heather on its southern flank.

Species

Wentwood provides habitat for a wide variety of woodland species and a majority of those found in the county list have been recorded here. The forest is however especially noted for certain species. Firecrests were formerly present as a breeding species with upwards of ten pairs in some years, and can still be observed occasionally. Goldcrests are common. As a result of the periodic cropping of the conifer plantations, large clearings result which become colonised with a number of species during the new period of growth. The most significant is the Nightjar and several pairs are present in the larger clearings. These can be observed at dawn and dusk from mid-May to July together with roding Woodcock. Cuckoos are present in reasonable numbers from late April. Whitethroats, Garden Warblers and Tree Pipits are widespread and Stonechats breed occasionally. Willow and Marsh Tits both breed, as do the more common Coal, Blue and Great Tits.

Great Grey Shrikes regularly stop off on autumnal migration or even overwinter at this site, usually in the clearings. Crossbills are almost always present in winter, sometimes in large numbers, and often stay to breed. Bramblings may join the Chaffinch flocks and the numbers of Siskins and Redpolls increase especially in late winter. Gray Hill is a good vantage point to see raptors such as Goshawks, Sparrowhawks, Kestrels and Buzzards.

The reservoir holds a few Mallard and grebes throughout the year with a small number of Pochard and Tufted Ducks in winter. It has attracted a few rarities over the years such as Smew, Ring-necked Duck and Leach's Petrel. The road above the reservoir is a good vantage point but beware of the traffic.

Hawfinches and Pied Flycatchers can be observed but only infrequently because of the relative scarcity of native broadleaved trees.

The Common Spotted and Bee Orchids and the Broad-leaved Helleborine are among several types of orchid seen in spring and summer. The small meadow adjacent to the Foresters' Oaks car park contains some notable butterfly species, including Grizzled Skipper and Marbled White.

Timing

A good range of birds can be observed at any time of the year and early morning is generally the best for bird-watching. However, to see or hear Nightjars and Woodcock the site must be visited in the late evening, perhaps as late as 22.00 hrs in June or at around 04.00 hrs for the dawn.

Access

A good map is recommended if venturing far into the Forest which is criss-crossed with many wide tracks (for forestry vehicles) and smaller paths.

Cadira Beeches car park and picnic area are as good a place as any to start for observing woodland birds, and there are a number of wide tracks leading into the Forest here. A recommended option is to head towards The Five Paths. Part of the route is accessible to wheelchairs as it is broad and flat, but it does tend to deteriorate further into the forest, particularly in winter. Foresters' Oaks car park also gives access to this area but you need to cross the road. Gray Hill can be also be reached from here via a narrow steep track, and the road south from here overlooks Wentwood Reservoir.

Calendar

Resident Tawny Owl, Green and Great Spotted Woodpecker, Goldcrest, Willow and Marsh Tit, Nuthatch.

December to March Brambling, Siskin, Redpoll, Crossbill and winter thrushes.

April to July Woodcock, Cuckoo, Nightjar, Tree Pipit, Whitethroat, Garden Warbler, Wood Warbler, Firecrest.

August to November Passage migrants and Great Grey Shrike if you are lucky.

6 YNYSYFRO RESERVOIRS

O.S Map Explorer 152 Newport and Pontypool
Grid reference: ST 283890, about 1km. north of M4 junction 27, off the B4591 Newport/Risca road.

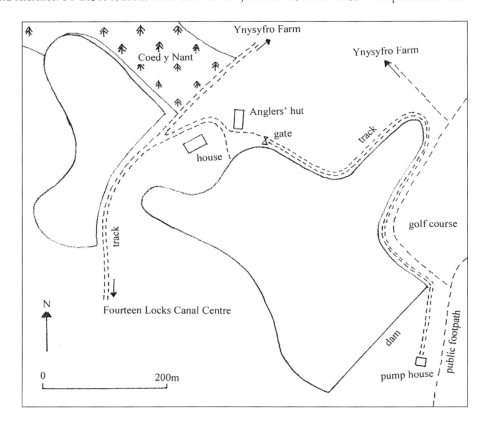

Habitat

Two reservoirs owned by Welsh Water, separated by a causeway, bounded by hedgerows and surrounded by fields, part of a golf course and a small conifer plantation. There is only one short stretch of riparian vegetation on the far side of the upper reservoir. Extensively used by fishermen from late March to autumn.

Species

Winter wildfowl are regular in small to moderate numbers. They are mainly Coot, Mallard, Tufted Ducks, Pochard, Little and Great Crested Grebes and Mute Swans. Canada Geese, in parties varying from ones and twos to 50 or more, visit intermittently. Other wildfowl visit occasionally during the winter months, especially when low water levels expose mud and weed along the water's edge. Kingfishers, Grey Wagtails and some of the smaller waders also visit occasionally. Records in recent years have included Black-necked Grebe, Ruddy and Ring-necked Ducks, and Scaup; also Water Pipits in some winters.

Access

By car leave the M4 Motorway at junction 27 and head north on the B4591. After approximately 800m turn right off the B4591 into Cefn Walk, signposted '14 Locks Canal Centre'. After about 400m, cross a narrow canal bridge (care needed here!) and turn right into the Canal Centre car park, which is open daily from 09.00 hrs to dusk. The track to the reservoirs, signposted 'Ynysyfro Reservoir', leaves the road immediately beyond the car park. It is a ten-minute walk walk to the causeway between the reservoirs.

By public transport, there are regular bus services along the B4591 to and from Newport, except on Sundays when services are minimal. Services R1/R3/R6 to/from Risca every 15 minutes and service 56 to/from Blackwood or Tredegar every 30 minutes, pass the end of Cefn Walk.

The track along the causeway is a public right of way and affords ample views of the upper reservoir and part of the lower. A public footpath runs along the edge of the golf course, close to the eastern bank of the lower reservoir. To reach this, continue along the track, past the houses, turn right towards the clubhouse, and right again, downhill along the hedgerow past the No. 1 tee. Access to the reservoir banks, and use of the parking at the reservoir, is by permit (GOS membership card).

Calendar

Resident Mute Swan (these usually breed), Mallard, Buzzard, Moorhen, Coot, Little Owl, Skylark.

Winter Tufted Duck, Pochard, Little and Great Crested Grebe regularly; other wildfowl occasionally. Also Canada Goose, Kingfisher, Grey Wagtail.

7 GRAIG GOCH WOODS

O.S Map Explorer 166 Rhondda & Merthyr Tydfil
Grid reference ST190908 alongside A4048, three miles west of Risca.

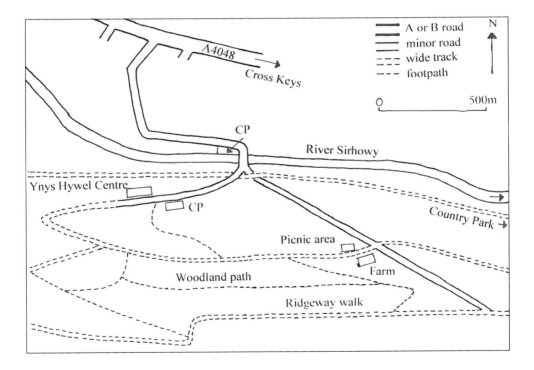

Habitat

Steep hillside with broadleaved woodland, mainly of sessile oak and birch with some ancient beeches, and also conifer plantations, mainly of western hemlock and Scots pine, leading up to high pasture with beech copses. On parts of the lower slopes there is a traditionally managed farm with cattle grazing and pig enclosures. A large number of tracks and footpaths enable the planning of short, medium and longer walks, on steep or flat terrain. The woodland path gives the best views of the more interesting species. Oddly there is no vehicle access to the picnic site. The lowest track (the former railway line) is fine for wheelchairs.

Species

The site offers an excellent selection of birds characteristic of upland woods in Wales, including Tree Pipits, Redstarts, Wood Warblers and Pied Flycatchers, together with Siskins and Crossbills in the conifer plantations, and a wide variety of the more general woodland/woodland edge species. At the foot of the hillside, the river Sirhowy holds Kingfishers, Grey Wagtails and Dippers, all of which can be seen from the bridge near the car park (though not necessarily all three on every visit!). The higher-level tracks either east or west from Graig Goch lead to more open habitats where Stonechats, Whinchats and Wheatears can be found. Ravens and Buzzards breed locally, and Peregrines and Merlins are sometimes sighted.

Access

By car, take the A4048 to the small town of Cwmfelinfach. Toward the east side of town turn south down Islwyn Street, signposted Ynys Hywel Centre. Follow this road to the bridge over the river and park just before the bridge in the Pont Lawrence car park. Alternatively, drive across the bridge, follow the road to the right and park at the Ynys Hywel Activity Centre. By public transport, take the No. 56 bus that runs a frequent service between Newport and Blackwood/Tredegar via Cwmfelinfach (alternate buses go through to Tredegar and display this route sign).

Calendar

Resident Buzzard, woodpeckers, Kingfisher, Coot, Grey Wagtail, Meadow Pipit, Dipper, Treecreeper, Nuthatch, Raven, Siskin.

Spring-Summer Tree Pipit, Meadow Pipit, Redstart, Garden Warbler, Blackcap, Chiffchaff, Willow Warbler, Wood Warbler, Pied Flycatcher, Crossbill. Also Stonechat, Whinchat and Wheatear at adjacent sites along the Ridgeway path.

8 THE BLORENGE

O.S Map OL13 Brecon Beacons National Park (Eastern Area)
Grid reference: Highest Point SO 270118

Habitat

This is a plateau of upland heath, with the main flora being Heather, Bilberry and Bracken, with steep sides covered mostly with Bracken, small trees and some rocky screes, and covers an area of about 5km².

Species

The mountain is inhabited by many bird species that are characteristic of upland Wales. The predominant species, Meadow Pipits and Skylarks, are present throughout the year, as are Red Grouse, Ravens and Buzzards. They are joined during the breeding season by Stonechats, Whinchats, Wheatears, Cuckoos, Tree Pipits, Willow Warblers, Redstarts and Linnets.

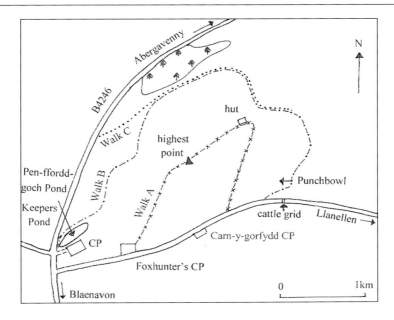

Access

Travelling from the north of the site: exit the A465 and turn on to the B4246 at either Gilwern or Llanfoist. Then take the B4246 for Blaenavon, which proceeds directly to the Blorenge. Travelling from the south of the site, from Blaenavon, join the B4246 for Abergavenny, which proceeds directly to the Blorenge. There is no access to the site via public transport. The nearest bus stops are at Blaenavon and Llanfoist. The site can be accessed from several starting points, with walks of varying length and gradient:

WALK A

Starting point: Foxhunter's car park, which is directly opposite the TV Masts.
Grid reference SO 264107.

Circular walk. Distance: 5km. Time: 2 hours. Difficulty: contains several slopes with a medium gradient. Access by wheelchair is not possible.

Scan from the car park for Wheatears, then take the path to the highest point. This is the best route to see or hear Red Grouse, particularly in spring or summer, and ideally in the early morning. Walk to the right of the brick hut, and carefully approach the edge of the plateau (there is a plunging drop) at SO 277123, before following the edge to the right, checking the stony banks immediately below you for Wheatears. Follow the track through the bracken and take the right track where it forks. This is a very good section to observe Whinchats and Tree Pipits. Turn right at the road and return to the starting point, pausing at Carn-y-gorfydd car park, to scan over the wall for Stonechats and Whinchats.

WALK B

Starting point: Park on the grassy verge just above the cattle grid.
Grid reference SO 278113

Circular walk. Distance 9km, or 6km if two cars are used and one is left at the Pen-fford-goch (Keepers) Pond SO 255107. Time: 4–5 hours. Difficulty: one climb of medium gradient and c.1km in length. Access by wheelchair is not possible.

Take the footpath to the left (north) of the cattle grid. Check the conifers close to the road for Siskins. Descend to the punchbowl listening for Blackcaps, Chiffchaffs and Garden Warblers. The path turns west above Pen-y-graig Farm, and this can be a pleasant place to rest on the grassy verge, whilst looking out for Redstarts in the dry stone wall area. The 1km stretch between here and the conifer woodland is excellent for Tree Pipits, Redstarts and Cuckoos, particularly to the right of the path. When the conifer wood approaches the path listen for Goldcrests and Coal Tits. At the point where the conifer wood butts against the path, take the bridleway which is signposted, up and to the left of the path. This walk through bracken is very good for Stonechats, Whinchats and Wheatears: this track can however become rather overgrown with bracken in late summer. When you reach the main path, turn right and continue to the paths end at Pen-fford-goch (Keepers) Pond car park. From here turn left on to the road, and then left again onto the next road, and back to the starting point.

WALK C

Starting point: Park on roadside verge at footpath sign marked 'Llanfoist 3.5 km' Grid reference SO 260122. There is only sufficient space for two to three cars.

Non-Circular walk. Distance: 4km. Time: 2–3 hours. Difficulty: level track with only slight gradients. The majority of this track (until it begins to descend) could be negotiated by wheelchair as it is flat, but with small undulations.

Begin along the footpath and immediately check the Gorse to the right for Whinchats, Stonechats, Linnets and Willow Warblers. The trees adjacent to the path are often used by Cuckoos as a vantage point. A few hundred metres along the track is a further patch of Gorse which should be checked for similar species. Scan and listen for Whinchats, Stonechats and Wheatears to either side of the path as you progress. Listen at the conifer forest for Goldcrests and Coal Tits. The next 1km stretch is very good for Tree Pipits, Redstarts and Cuckoos particularly to the left of the path. The path descends more steeply alongside a drystone wall, and looking over it, close to its end, can give excellent views of Redstarts. Finish the walk at the wall's end, above Pen-y-graig Farm, and return to the starting point. An alternative route back can be taken via the bridleway which begins at the conifer wood in Walk B. If this route is taken, turn right at Pen-fford-goch (Keepers) pond car park, and walk down the road to the starting point.

Calendar

Autumn-Winter Skylark, Meadow Pipit. Red Grouse on Walk A. .

Spring-Summer The above species plus Cuckoo, Tree Pipit, Redstart, Whinchat, Stonechat, Wheatear, Goldcrest, Coal Tit, Linnet. Also Blackcap, Garden Warbler, Chiffchaff, Siskin on Walk B.

9 WYE VALLEY WOODLANDS

The Wye Valley woodlands comprise the largest block of woodland in the county. These woods lie alongside the River Wye from the border with Herefordshire north of Monmouth, down to Chepstow. The steep sides of the Wye Valley are clothed mainly with broadleaved woodland, much of it classed as ancient and semi-natural. Although many conifers were planted on clear-felled areas on the valley sides in the 1960s and 1970s, the policy is fortunately now to remove the alien conifers and restore with native broadleaves. Gradually this is coming about. There are still some areas of conifers in the valley and more extensive blocks of conifers on the Trellech Plateau on former heathland, on the watershed between the Wye and Usk catchments. These are usually interspersed with broadleaved trees and there are two schemes to restore small areas of heathland.

Typically the Wye Valley woodlands include much Small-leaved Lime as well as the rarer Large-leaved Lime, Wild Cherry or Gean and Ash. On the plateau on drier soils there are woods of oak and birch. Tributaries of the Wye: the Black Brook, White Brook, Cat Brook and Angidy, drop down steeply through the woodlands on the Welsh side. The valley sides and plateau characteristically also have small fields edged with stone walls or well-developed hedges. Many have escaped modern intensive agriculture and still support a wealth of wildflowers and insects.

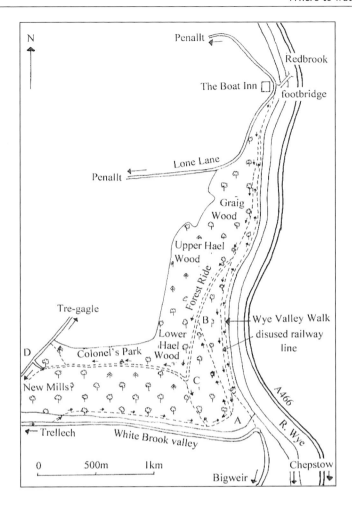

GRAIG WOOD, LOWER HAEL WOOD, UPPER HAEL WOOD, COLONEL'S PARK AND PWLLPLYTHIN WOOD AND THE RIVER WYE

This walk runs from Redbrook to Whitebrook with detours into Colonel's Park.

O.S Map Explorer OL14 Wye Valley & Forest of Dean

Grid reference: Redbrook car park SO 536098. Recommended start of walk.

Habitat

Broadleaved and coniferous woodland and the River Wye.

Species

Typical broadleaved woodland birds such as Great Spotted Woodpeckers, Nuthatches and Treecreepers abound in the woodlands. Green Woodpeckers favour the small steep-sided pastures adjacent to the woodland. Of particular note is the population of Hawfinches breeding in the Wye Valley. Whilst Song Thrushes and Bullfinches may have declined in England they are still numerous in these woodlands, especially in conifer thickets. Willow and Marsh Tits are not uncommon, the former favouring mixed conifer and broadleaves.

Access

Park at Redbrook just west of the A466. Walk over the railway bridge crossing the River Wye to the Boat Inn and turn left. After a few metres turn left again onto the disused railway line. You can follow this all the way to Whitebrook and then walk back along the River Wye footpath. Look out for Goosanders on the river during the winter and at other times there will be a range of waterbirds including Mute Swans, Little Grebes, Grey Wagtails and Kingfishers. This walk is flat and the railtrack is suitable for wheelchairs but the River Wye footpath is undulating and boggy in winter.

For the more energetic there are various tracks that take you into the woods. Just before Whitebrook you can take a small track up through lime, beech and ash woods and this eventually comes out on another forest track (A). You can go left to Whitebrook and walk back down the minor road in the valley to rejoin the railway line or you can turn sharp right here and walk up to a broad forest ride (B). If you turn right, downhill, you will soon rejoin the railway line. Alternatively you can walk uphill. There are several options if you do this. One is to walk up to a right-hand bend and there turn left (C) and drop down a sunken track to Whitebrook, where you turn left into the wood rather than walking out onto the minor road. The woodland track will bring you back where you started (A). If you continue on the broad track up to the New Mills to Tre-gagle road (D) you can either bear right at the road and then follow a track at the edge of the wood that loops back to the main track, or turn left along the road to New Mills and then follow the Whitebrook valley down, along the road and along a track following the stream. This is a recommended route, but it is fairly strenuous and up to 12km in length, and therefore can require six hours or more and a good level of fitness.

OTHER LARGE BLOCKS OF PREDOMINANTLY BROADLEAVED WOODLAND IN THE VICINITY INCLUDE:

1. Cuckoo Wood and Cleddon Shoots: access from parking area by bus shelter on Whitebrook road south of Bigsweir Bridge at Grid reference SO 537052
2. Lower Hale, Buckle and Glyn Woods and further west Ravensnest and Great Wenallt Wood. Access from Tintern. Take the minor road just south of Abbey Mill and after the hotel on the right (west side) towards The Cot. There is a parking area after a few hundred metres at SO 524002. Footpaths go up the Angidy Valley and into the woodlands. Alternatively follow the minor road towards The Cot past Ravensnest fishing ponds and park on the left above the ponds at the wide entrance to the forest at ST 503997.
3. Blackcliff and Wyndcliff Woods. Parking areas along main road at ST 526973 and ST 524974
4. Chepstow Park Wood. Accessible from several points along the road between Devauden and Chepstow (B4293), or between Devauden and Itton.

Calendar

Resident Sparrowhawk, Goshawk, Buzzard, Woodcock, all three woodpecker species, Goldcrest, tits, Nuthatch, Treecreeper, Raven, Bullfinch, Hawfinch.

Spring and Summer Hobby, Redstart, Wood Warbler, Pied Flycatcher.

Winter Mixed flocks of tits, woodpeckers, and finches such as Crossbill, Redpoll or Siskin. The latter two species are especially found in Alder trees along the river or in conifers.

TRELLECH PLATEAU

On the Trellech plateau to the west of the Wye Valley there are large areas of conifer plantations. These range from mature plantations to thickets, and there are scattered restocked and clear-felled areas which provide more interest. Cleddon and Beacon Hill, two areas recently cleared of conifers near Trellech, are being encouraged to revert to heathland and these are now fenced and grazed by Exmoor ponies.

For CLEDDON take the B4293 from Trellech and turn left as you drive south through the village of Cleddon. There is parking at Grid reference SO515038. From here walk around Cleddon Bog, Ninewells Wood and Broad Meend.

For BEACON HILL take the Cleddon road from Trellech but turn left at Cotland along below Beacon Hill. There is a parking area at SO511053. Explore Beacon Hill and Trellech Common.

Calendar

Resident As above for broadleaved woodlands; additionally Stonechat in restocks and clearfell areas, Coal Tit, Goldcrest, Crossbill in some years and Yellowhammer.

Spring and summer Nightjar, Turtle Dove (very small population), Tree Pipit, Whitethroat and occasionally Whinchat in clear-felled and restocked areas.

Winter Siskin and Redpoll.

THE GWENT BREEDING BIRD ATLASES

Two breeding atlas surveys, based on tetrads (2-km × 2-km squares), have been carried out in Gwent, in the periods 1981–85 and 1998–2003, and they are referred to throughout this book as the 1st and 2nd Gwent Atlases. The data derived from the two atlases are based on two identical sets of tetrads, and form the basis of our current knowledge of breeding bird distributions within the county, and also of the changes in distribution that have occurred in recent years. The data from the 2nd Gwent Atlas has also informed our estimates of breeding populations in Gwent. The ways in which atlas data have been used in estimation of population sizes is explained in the separate section on populations (Appendix 1).

From its outset, the aim of the second atlas was to produce data that were directly comparable with those produced by the first atlas, thus permitting strong conclusions to be drawn with regard to the changes in distribution that had occurred in the intervening period. In order to maximise the comparability, the methodology of the 2nd Gwent Atlas was, from the outset, designed to be as similar as possible to that used in the 1st Gwent Atlas.

Tetrad coverage

Tetrads comprise squares of dimensions 2-km × 2-km based on the National Grid. The tetrads analysed for each of the Gwent Atlases are identical, and are shown in Figure 1. For various reasons, the two atlases originally included slightly different sets of tetrads, but the comparative analysis of the atlas data has followed adjustments that have produced identical sets, each of 394 tetrads. The circumstances that gave rise to the need for adjustments, and the rationale involved in the selection of comparative sets is as follows.

Most biological recording at the county level is based on the Watsonian vice-county system. Southeast Wales comprises the adjacent vice-counties of Glamorgan (v.c.41) and Monmouthshire (v.c.35), the border between which is the River Rhymney. The 1st Gwent Atlas (1981–85) was based on the administrative county of Gwent, which corresponds broadly to v.c.35 but has some significant differences. Most relevant to the current discussion is the position of the western boundary of Gwent, which lies a few kilometres to the east of the River Rhymney for most of its length. The adjacent county of Glamorgan carried out a tetrad atlas survey during the period 1984–89, but although field recording was carried out up to the then-existing administrative boundary between Glamorgan and Gwent, only those tetrads that were at least 50% within the boundary of v.c.41 were included in the published *Birds of Glamorgan* (1995). This left a total of five tetrads between the River Rhymney and the western border of Gwent in 'no man's land' and data from them was not published in either the Gwent or Glamorgan atlases. Following discussions between the Gwent Ornithological Society and the Glamorgan

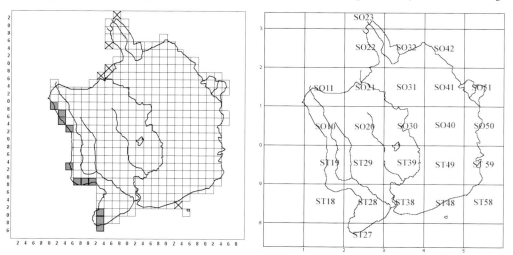

Figure 1a. Tetrads surveyed in the Gwent Atlases. ■ = tetrads incorporated from Glamorgan; × = tetrads deleted from current Atlas. **Figure 1b. 10-km square designations in the Gwent Atlases**

Bird Club, it was agreed that the 2nd Gwent Atlas would follow the western boundary of v.c.35 (the River Rhymney), and thus incorporate 11 border tetrads previously censused by Glamorgan, including the five that had been omitted from the published Glamorgan atlas. These 11 tetrads are shown in Figure 1 and listed in Table 1. Furthermore, in order to make the data from the 1st and 2nd Gwent Atlases comparable, the data collected by Glamorgan Bird Club from these eleven tetrads during 1984–89 (some of it previously unpublished) would be added to the data from the 1st Gwent Atlas. As the recording periods for the Glamorgan Atlas and the 1st Gwent Atlas overlapped (and much of the recording in the border tetrads was done in the overlap years by the same observers), this was considered to be a scientifically valid solution. In addition to the above, a different five tetrads (each with less than 1% of their area in Gwent, or with greater than 95% of their area offshore), which had been covered by the 1st Gwent Atlas, were omitted in the second atlas: these have been deleted from the comparative analysis (see Figure 1 and Table 1). In agreement with the Glamorgan Bird Club, the previously unpublished data from border tetrads are detailed in Appendix 4.

Tetrads covered by the Glamorgan Atlas, but added to the 1st Gwent Atlas	SO10E, 10H, 10I, 10L ST18U, 18Z,19L, 27I, 27J, 28E, 28F
Tetrads covered by the 1st Gwent Atlas that have been deleted from the comparative analysis	SO21I, 21P, 22M, 23R ST48G
Total tetrads analysed for each Gwent atlas	394

Table 1. Adjustments made to the 1st Gwent Atlas data

Duration of the two Gwent Atlases

In the 1st Gwent Atlas (1981–85), the main body of recording was accomplished in the first four years, and the fifth 'mopping-up' year was used to obtain data for a limited selection of tetrads that had, up till then, received no coverage or obviously incomplete coverage. In the 2nd Gwent Atlas (1998–2003), an identical approach had been planned but, in 2001, which would have been the final year of full recording, virtually no recording took place owing to the national outbreak of foot-and-mouth disease. The final year of recording was therefore postponed till 2002, while 2003 became the mopping-up year. Both Gwent Atlases thus comprised four full recording years and a mopping-up year, but spread over six years in the case of the 2nd Gwent Atlas.

Organisation of the 2nd Gwent Atlas

The county was divided into 10-km squares based on the National Grid, and each of these were further divided into 25 tetrads (2 × 2 km squares) labelled as shown in Figure 2. For example, if the 10-km square below is ST49 the tetrads shown are 49A to 49Z.

E	J	P	U	Z
D	I	N	T	Y
C	H	M	S	X
B	G	L	R	W
A	F	K	Q	V

Figure 2. Tetrad labelling within a 10-km square

The 10-km squares were split into four groups and a single organiser was appointed for each group. Sadly one of the original organisers, Dave Wood, became seriously ill and died in 1999. His place was taken by Ian Walker. The job of the organisers was to ensure that the tetrads within their area were covered, to distribute recording cards and other information to observers involved, and to collect completed cards at the end of each season. Data was then supplied on an annual basis to the overall atlas organiser, who entered and stored it on a spreadsheet. The overall organiser also entered records from casual record sheets into the spreadsheet. At the end of the atlas period, the spreadsheet was checked against the original recording cards and casual record sheets.

Organiser	10-km squares
Jerry Lewis	SO21, SO22, SO23, SO31, SO32, SO41, SO42, SO51
Mary Plunkett	SO40, SO50, ST49, ST59
Al Venables	SO10, SO11, SO20, ST18, ST19, ST27, ST28, ST29
Ian Walker (2000–03) } Dave Wood (1998–99) }	SO30, ST38, ST39, ST48, ST58
Al Venables	overall coordination
Alan Williams	map production

Table 2. The Atlas organisers

Data collection for the 2nd Gwent Atlas

The 1st Gwent Atlas adopted the recording system used by the 1968–72 National Atlas, and as one of our main objectives for the 2nd Gwent Atlas was to maximise comparability between the two Gwent Atlases, the methods to be used in the second survey were largely predetermined, having to be the same as those used on the first occasion. Observers were asked to record every species breeding within each tetrad that they covered, and to obtain the best possible evidence for breeding, on the basis of the criteria laid down by the European Ornithological Atlas Committee (as published in the 1968–72 National Atlas). These criteria are divided into three categories that provide of evidence of breeding at three levels, termed *possible*, *probable* and *confirmed*, and are listed below.

POSSIBLE BREEDING

H	Species observed in breeding season in suitable nesting HABITAT
S	SINGING male(s) present, or breeding calls heard in breeding season

PROBABLE BREEDING

P	PAIR observed in suitable nesting habitat in breeding season
T	Permanent TERRITORY presumed through registration of territorial behaviour (song etc.) on at least two different days (at least a week apart) in the same place
D	DISPLAY and courtship
N	Visiting probable NEST site
A	Agitated behaviour or ANXIETY calls from adults
I	Brood patch on adult examined in hand indicating probable INCUBATION
B	BUILDING nest, carrying nest material, or excavating nest hole

CONFIRMED BREEDING

DD	DISTRACTION display or injury feigning
UN	USED nest or egg shells found (occupied or laid within period of survey)
FL	Recently FLEDGED YOUNG (nidicolous species) or downy young (nidifugous species)
ON	Adults entering or leaving nest site in circumstances indicating OCCUPIED NEST (including high nests, contents of which cannot be seen), or adults seen on nest
FY	Adults carrying FOOD for YOUNG or faecal sac
NE	NEST containing EGGS
NY	NEST with YOUNG seen or heard

Table 3. Categories of breeding evidence, recording codes and nature of evidence

Observers were issued with recording cards similar to those used in the 1968–72 National Atlas and also in the 1st Gwent Atlas. As the layout of such recording cards has been previously published elsewhere (including in the above mentioned books), it is not repeated here. Observers were requested to cover all habitats present within each tetrad, to make at least four visits per year, and to spread visits throughout the breeding season. No upper limit was placed on the amount of recording time, and those observers who lived within their tetrad could make observations on a daily basis if they wished. Observers could take on as many or as few tetrads as they wished: at the extremes, some covered only the tetrad in which they lived, while a few (the most experienced observers) covered up to 20 tetrads (in some cases over 30) at different times during the main atlas period and the mopping-up year. In many cases, experienced observers who had recorded particular tetrads in years 1 and 2, took on different tetrads for years 3 and 4. There were a few cases where two or more observers wished to cover the same tetrad independently: this was permitted, as also was recording by groups of individuals. Analysis of the data produces no significant correlation between number of species recorded in a tetrad, and the number of observers who covered it, either independently or as a team.

Observers were also given casual recording sheets on which to record relevant observations from outside their own tetrads. These sheets were also made available to all members of the Gwent Ornithological Society. In year 4, an appeal made in the local press for the public to send in any confirmed breeding records from their gardens, resulted in a few useful records (particularly from urban areas) but was not very productive overall. An appeal in year 5 to members of the Gwent Wildlife Trust also produced a number of useful records.

In the mopping-up year, recording was limited to a selection of tetrads for which the total number of species recorded was at least 15% lower than in the 1st Gwent Atlas. At the end of the survey, *Gwent Bird Reports* (1998–2003) were searched for any records of the more uncommon breeding species.

Distribution maps

Data from the spreadsheet were converted to distribution maps by use of DMap software. The three breeding categories, *confirmed*, *probable* and *possible,* are shown on maps as three different sizes of dots. To enable distribution comparisons, data from the maps published in the 1st Gwent Atlas plus the additional data from border tetrads (as explained above) were also entered into electronic spreadsheets and again mapped via DMap.

To save space it was decided that for species present in over 95% of tetrads, where changes in distribution were only marginal, only the map for the most recent atlas would be published. For certain rare breeding species, no map has been published in order to protect them from possible disturbance.

Possible biases in data within and between atlas surveys

Absolute comparability between the 1st and 2nd Gwent Atlases was, of course, impossible to achieve. An obvious potential source of bias is the use of different sets of observers between the two atlases, and the consequent likelihood that there would have been a different distribution of observer expertise/experience across the county. However, although there was a substantial change in the identity of observers between atlases, it should be noted that in the second atlas 53% of tetrads were covered by just nine observers, all of whom were 'veterans' of the first atlas.

Concerns about possible observer bias are most relevant in areas of the county where large differences have been recorded between the two atlases. As discussed below, very significant increases in species diversity were noted for 10-km squares in the north-west of the county. Fortunately, in square SO10, where the greatest increase in diversity was recorded, there are seven tetrads (representing almost 40% of the SO10 tetrads within Gwent) that were covered by the same two (very experienced) observers in both atlas surveys. The mean increase in diversity recorded in these seven tetrads was in fact considerably higher than the mean for the 10-km square as a whole, which leads us to conclude that the increases recorded in this area are undoubtedly real. This conclusion is supported by comments of the relevant observers who attribute the changes mainly to major environmental improvement resulting from the greening of extensive former industrial sites.

In breeding atlas surveys that span several years, with different tetrads being surveyed in different years, biasses in results may arise from changes in species distribution that occur during the course of the survey. Owing to the interruption caused by the foot-and-mouth disease outbreak of 2001, the 2nd Gwent Atlas spanned a total of six years, and some significant population changes definitely occurred during this period. For example, the national indices for Garden Warbler, Willow Warbler and Wood Warbler all declined steeply during the atlas period, so the maps for these species may show a wider distribution than actually existed at the end of the survey in 2003. Conversely, the national index for Stonechat increased sharply during the years of the survey, and the map probably underestimates its disribution in 2003. However, although the presence of such biasses needs to be taken into consideration, they detract relatively little from the basic value of the maps as indicators of change since the 1st Gwent Atlas.

Summary of results from the 2nd Gwent Atlas, and changes since the 1st Gwent Atlas

The current distributions and observed trends for individual species are discussed elsewhere, in the Systematic List and the chapter entitled Conclusions and Comparisons. Nevertheless, it is appropriate at this point to discuss some of the broader conclusions from the 2nd Gwent Atlas and changes that have occurred since since the 1st Gwent Atlas.

Table 4 shows that the total numbers of breeding species recorded in the 2nd Gwent Atlas was 137, an increase of seventeen over the earlier survey. As Short-eared Owl bred successfully only in a border tetrad at a site just outside the county boundary, the number of species recorded breeding actually within the county was 136 (121 being *confirmed*).

	Number of species				
Atlas period	Confirmed breeding	Probable breeding	Possible breeding	Total	Change in total
1981–85	112	6	2	120	–
1998–2003	122	10	5	137	+14%

Table 4. Numbers of species recorded in the two Gwent breeding atlases

The mean number of species recorded per tetrad has fallen from 54.7 in the first atlas to 52.5 in the second atlas (–2.2 species), while the number of *probable* plus *confirmed* species per tetrad has risen from 42.8 to 44.5 (+1.7 species).

The range of diversity in tetrads is shown in Table 5. Only 5% of tetrads have 70 or more species, 9% have fewer than 40, and those with 50–59 species form the largest block. The distribution of tetrads with 50 or more breeding species in shown on the map in Figure 3. Concentrations of high-scoring tetrads occur in a broad sector in the northwest, and also along the Usk Valley, and in parts of the Wye Valley. They are also scattered elsewhere at locations with high habitat diversity, such as the Newport Wetlands Reserve and Llandegfedd Reservoir. Much of the farmland in the east and north of the county is relatively impoverished, with fewer than 50 species, as also are the southern areas of the western valleys, parts of the coastal levels and and moorlands of the extreme northwest.

Number of species	70 or more	60–69	50–59	40–49	Fewer than 40
% tetrads	5	18	40	28	9

Table 5. Range of species diversity in tetrads

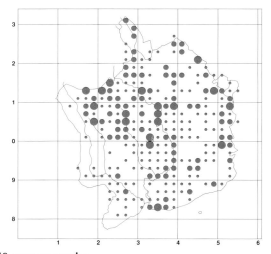

Figure 3. Tetrads with 50 or more species
Large dot = 70–85 species; medium dot = 60–69 species; small dot = 50–59 species

A list of all tetrads with precise numbers of species recorded in each of the breeding categories (*confirmed*, *probable* and *possible*) can be found in Appendix 3.

The two tetrads with the highest numbers of species are those that encompass Llandegfedd Reservoir (SO30F and ST39J), which have 85 and 82 species respectively. However, because the reservoir is a heavily-watched site where spring passage is well recorded, an unusually high proportion of the atlas records are of *possible* breeding, and many are likely to refer only to passage migrants. For this reason, the tetrads that really have the highest diversity of breeding species are better indicated by ranking on the basis of the *probable* plus *confirmed* breeding categories. When this is done, the Llandegfedd Reservoir tetrads lose their exalted status.

The five tetrads with the highest numbers of *probable* plus *confirmed* breeders are shown in Table 6. As would be expected, they all contain a variety of habitats and the presence of a river is a feature common to all. When considering the other end of the scale – the tetrads with the lowest numbers of breeding birds – it is necessary to exclude those coastal tetrads that comprise only a small fragment of land. Having done that, it is found that the species-poor tetrads tend to be those that are dominated by a single, species-poor habitat type, such as bare treeless moorland. Tetrads with extensive urban habitats, such as occur in the city of Newport, usually have at least a small area of parkland and, compared with open moorland, are relatively rich in species, having no representatives that rank in the bottom thirty.

Tetrad	Identifying place name	Number of species	Major habitat types
SO30N	Llanfair Kilgeddin	75	River Usk,, broadleaved woodland, mixed farmland
SO20T	Gallowsgreen	70	Afon Lwyd, mixed woodland, meadows, moorland
SO10X	Cwm	69	River Ebbw, mixed woodland, moorland, urban
SO30P	Pant-y-Goitre	69	River Usk, parkland, pastoral farmland, broadleaved woodland
SO21B	Cwm Clydach	69	River Clydach, moorland, broadleaved woodland, urban

Table 6. Tetrads with highest numbers of probable plus confirmed breeding species

Table 7 compares the species diversity in each of the 10-km squares in the county. Square ST38, with 107 species, has the greatest diversity, and this is largely due to the presence of the Newport Wetlands Reserve, which provides habitats that are absent or scarce in other parts of Gwent. The three other squares with over 100 species contain long stretches of the River Usk together with a share of Llandegfedd Reservoir (ST39 and SO30) or a combination of the River Usk plus uplands with open moorland and both coniferous and broadleaved woodland (SO21). Large increases in diversity are seen in the squares in the north-west (SO10, SO11, SO20 and SO21), and probable reasons for this are discussed in Conclusions and Comparisons chapter. The Wye Valley squares (SO50, SO51 and ST59) show a surprising range of changes (+10, -6 and +2 species, respectively) for which there is no obvious explanation.

Changes in diversity at the 10-km square level are only a crude indicator of the general state of the county's breeding birds, as the presence of any particular species may depend entirely on a single patch of good habitat somewhere in the square. This is certainly the case for ST38, where several species are present only in the Newport Wetlands Reserve, and SO30, where the diversity is boosted by the presence of the north end of Llandegfedd Reservoir.

Changes in the average number of species per tetrad within the 10-km square are a much more sensitive indicator than overall change in the square. These are shown in Table 8. It can be seen that whereas ST38 had a large increase in overall diversity (+13 species), data in Table 8 shows that the average number of species recorded per tetrad has remained unchanged, thus demonstrating that the overall increase for the 10-km square depends on the colonisation of a very localised area (Newport Wetlands Reserve in this instance). Similarly, 10-km square SO30 has maintained high species diversity owing to the presence of the north end of Llandegfedd Reservoir, but the average tetrad occupancy has fallen by a remarkable eight species. By contrast, the big increases in species diversity in the north-west 10-km squares are reflected strongly in the average increases per tetrad, demonstrating a general colonisation of these squares and suggesting, among other possible factors, a general improvement in habitat.

10-km square (number of tetrads)	1st Gwent Atlas 1981–1985 Number of species	2nd Gwent Atlas 1998–2003 Number of species	Change in number of species
SO10 (18)	74	94	+20
SO11 (11)	76	93	+17
SO20 (25)	83	97	+14
SO21 (19)	91	103	+12
SO22 (12)	79	81	+2
SO30 (25)	99	101	+2
SO31 (25)	92	99	+7
SO32 (16)	81	84	+3
SO40 (25)	90	98	+8
SO41 (24)	84	90	+6
SO42 (8)	83	82	−1
SO50 (12)	82	92	+10
SO51 (9)	86	80	−6
ST19 (11)	72	75	+3
ST28 (21)	98	95	−3
ST29 (25)	91	86	−5
ST38 (21)	94	107	+13
ST39 (25)	97	102	+5
ST48 (15)	91	93	+2
ST49 (25)	89	89	0
ST59 (10)	93	95	+2

Table 7. Species diversity in 10-km squares. 10-km squares SO23 (3), ST18 (2), ST27 (4) and ST58 (3) have been omitted from this analysis because they contain so few tetrads

It is a matter for concern that no fewer than 12 of the eighteen 10-km squares listed in Table 8 have shown a mean decrease in number of species per tetrad. As the coastal levels form a well-defined habitat that is easily mapped on a tetrad level, the changes in species diversity are shown separately for these areas. Both the Wentlooge and Caldicot Levels can be seen to have suffered statistically significant losses of 5.9–7.5 species per tetrad.

10-km Square	Mean change in number of species per tetrad	10-km square or other area	Mean change in number of species per tetrad
SO10	+9.4 (± 3.5)	ST19	+2 (± 3.0)
SO11	+3.5 (± 4.0)	ST28	−5.1 (± 1.7)
SO20	+10.7 (± 3.1)	ST29	−3.8 (± 0.8)
SO21	+1.2 (± 3.3)	ST38	+0.1 (± 0.96)
SO30	−8.2 (± 2.4)	ST39	−4.8 (± 1.5)
SO31	−4.4 (± 1.7)	ST48	−4.7 (± 2.2)*
SO32	−3.1 (± 2.1)	ST49	−4.5 (± 2.0)
SO40	−2.6 (±2.6)	ST59	−5.5 (± 3.8)
SO41	−5.2 (± 2.2)	Wentlooge Level	−7.5 (± 2.4)
SO50	−2.3 (± 2.4)	Caldicot Level	−5.9 (± 2.0)

Table 8. Mean change in numbers of species per tetrad for each 10-km square and for the Wentlooge and Caldicot Levels. Figures in parentheses are standard errors of the mean. Figures in bold are statistically significant changes at the 95% level. *The figure for ST48 figure is on the borderline of significance. Data for SO22 was not appropriate for analysis in this way

Correlation between distribution change and population change.

In the discussion of individual species in the Systematic List, we have made the logical assumption that expansions or contractions in range between the two atlas periods, reflect increases or reductions, respectively, in population size. The validity of this assumption is supported by statistical analysis, which shows a highly significant correlation between percentage distribution change in Gwent and the change in the CBC/BBS population index for the UK between the two Gwent atlases (n = 50; r = 0.69; P<0.001). This analysis used data for 50 widespread and common breeding species, omitting only:

(a)   those with specialised habitats of limited occurrence (e.g. medium-large open water bodies), and

(b)   very common species for which the UK index has increased but, being already present in at least 90% of Gwent tetrads during the 1st Gwent Atlas, there was little scope for increase in distribution.

The percentage change in tetrads with *confirmed* breeding shows an even higher correlation with the change in UK index (r = 0.74; P <0.001), as also does the percentage with *confirmed* plus *probable* breeding (r = 0.73; P<0.001). These correlations support our assumption that increases in the number of *confirmed*, or *confirmed* plus *probable,* breeding records reflect increases in population density, probably because higher population densities increase the chance that recorders will observe evidence of breeding.

It is interesting that significant correlation was not found between distribution changes in Gwent and the comparable Wales population indices. This suggests that in terms of trends in breeding bird populations, Gwent is more typical of the UK as whole, than of Wales, but inspection of data for individual species shows exceptions to this generalisation.

BIRDS IN GWENT
A SYSTEMATIC LIST

INTRODUCTION

This section inludes accounts of all species that have been reliably identified in the county of Gwent up to 31 December 2005. Analyses of records of common breeding species include data up to 31 December 2004, and of common winter visitors up to winter 2003/04. Records of scarce or unusual species during 2005 are included. At the time of going to press, records for 2006 had not been published, but authors have included a sprinkling of the more interesting records from that year where they have been available.

Authentication of records

Up to 1974 all records of birds in Gwent were accepted at the discretion of the editors of the Gwent Bird Report, sometimes in consultation with members the the General Committee of the Gwent Ornithological Society. From 1975 onwards, all records of species that are unusual or rare for the county have been assessed by a local records committee prior to acceptance. Also, since 1975 records of all national rarities have been approved by either the Welsh Records Panel or the British Birds Rarities Committee (as appropriate) prior to their acceptance. For the purposes of the current publication, all past records for the county that were unusual, and had not been scrutinised by either of the above national bodies, were reviewed by the Gwent Records Committee, with the result that a number of previously published records have been re-classified and placed in a separate list (Appendix 2).

The order of species follows the seventh edition of the British Ornithologists' Union's *British List* (Dudley *et al.*, 2006). The English species names used are the traditional names in common usage, though with the latest BOU names (Dudley *et al.,* 2006) indicated in parentheses where appropriate. Welsh names are those used by the 1994 *Birds in Wales.*

CONTENT OF SPECIES ACCOUNTS

Status in Gwent

Each species account begins with a short statement that summarises the species' current status in Gwent; definitions of status are as follows:

Very rare	Five or fewer county records
Rare	Less than annual, many years may pass between records
Very scarce	Less than annual, but typically recorded every 2 or 3 years
Scarce	Recorded in very small numbers in most years
Uncommon	Recorded in low numbers in each year
Fairly common	Occurs in reasonable numbers in suitable habitat
Common	Occurs in good numbers in suitable habitat
Abundant	Occurs in large numbers in suitable habitat

Conservation status in Wales and the UK

For breeding birds and the commoner winter visitors the conservation status in both Wales and the UK is shown. Information for Wales was taken from the *The Status of Birds in Wales 2003*; information for the UK was taken from the BTO website (see reference section for details). The conservation listings are defined as follows:

Red-listed: Those species that are globally threatened according to International Union for Conservation of Nature and Natural Resources criteria; those with a population or range that has declined rapidly in recent years; and those that have declined historically and not shown a substantial recent recovery.

Amber-listed: Those species with an unfavourable conservation status in the UK and Europe; those with a population range that has declined moderately in recent years; those with a population that has declined historically but made a substantial recovery; rare breeding birds; and those with internationally important or localised populations.

Green-listed: Any species not meeting any of the above criteria.

Breeding atlas data

Maps generated by the 2nd Gwent Atlas (1998–2003) have been included for all current breeding species, with the exceptions of a few sensitive species where observers had asked for sites to be kept confidential, and a few others where breeding occurred at only one or two locations that could be conveniently described in the text. Except for the very common species that were recorded in over 95% of tetrads, the maps from the 1st Gwent Atlas (1980–85) have also been included. This permits direct visual comparison to be made between the distributions found in the two periods. The same symbols are used for both maps: large dot = *confirmed* breeding; medium dot = *probable* breeding; small dot = *possible* breeding. In cases where the text refers directly to atlas data, the three categories of breeding are italicised (as above) to indicate that they are used in the defined sense of the atlas definitions for each category, and not in a more general sense.

For all breeding species there is a standardised table that summarises data from the two Gwent Atlases and includes an estimate of the size of the county breeding population.

Other standard tables

Accounts for the commoner species include one or more standardised tables at the end. For breeding species there is a table that gives the estimated population for Wales (taken from the 2002 *Birds in Wales*), population trends for Wales and the UK, and the current national conservation status (Red, Amber or Green-listed). Where possible the trends for Wales and the UK represent combined CBC/BBS trends for the period between the two Gwent Atlases (1985–2003), which were prepared specially for this book by Stuart Newson of the BTO. In cases where sample sizes were too small (<20) for such trends to be reliable (usually affecting only Welsh data) the 1994–2004 BBS trend has been used.

Each of the common winter wildfowl and wader species have a table that includes the mean annual peak WeBS counts for the 5-year period 1999/00–2003/04 for both Gwent and Great Britain. The figure for Gwent is replaced by a mean peak count from *Gwent Bird Report*s if this is significantly higher. This table also includes the threshold population figures at which sites are classed as nationally or internationally important for the species, and also the winter conservation status of the species (the use of Great Britain, rather than UK, data for for WeBS peak counts and importance thresholds reflects the form in which this information is published in WeBS reports). Wildfowl and wader accounts also have tables showing long- and medium-term trends (where available) for winter numbers in Wales and the UK.

In all standard tables other than the Gwent Atlas table, alternative sources of trends and population data have occasionally been used if available, and if no source of relevant data data has been available, sections have been left blank, or the entire table omitted.

General approach to species accounts

Each account has generally attempted to summarise the known history of species in the county by making reference to accounts from the 1937 and 1963 editions of the *Birds of Monmouthshire*, but strong emphasis has been placed on the the most recent 40–50 years, for which much more information is available, and which are of most relevance to the current ornithology of the county.

As a total of eleven authors has contributed to the species accounts, variations in style have been inevitable, but the editors have not been overly concerned by this, seeing such variety as a strength rather than a weakness. Similarly, the choice of whether to use of tables or figures to illustrate analyses has generally been left to the discretion of the authors.

Sources of data

The annually published *Gwent Bird Report* has provided the vast bulk of the information on Gwent's birds. This source has generally not been referenced in the text, so it should be assumed to be the source of data unless otherwise stated. Trends for the UK arising from BTO long-term studies such as BBS, WBS and CES have been sourced directly from the BTO website, and Welsh trends from *The State of Birds in Wales 2003*. Much information on national trends and populations of wildfowl and waders has been taken from the annual Wetlands Birds Survey reports, and these are referenced simply as WeBS (see reference section for full citation); dates have not generally been given as the data has usually been summarised from issues spanning several years. Data on trends in wintering wildfowl and waders were sourced from the WeBS Alerts site via the BTO website.

List of abbreviations used

BTO	British Trust for Ornithology
CBC	Common Birds Census
CCW	Countryside Council for Wales
BBS	Breeding Birds Survey
WBS	Waterways Birds Survey
WeBS	Wetlands Birds Survey
WOS	Welsh Ornithological Society
WWT	Wildfowl and Wetlands Trust

Abbreviated place names

Peterstone	Peterstone Wentlooge
St Brides	St Brides Wentlooge

Mute Swan
Alarch Dôf

Cygnus olor

An uncommon resident, widespread but usually in small numbers

The Mute Swan is a widespread breeding resident in the lowlands of Britain. Apart from the lowland border counties and the lower reaches of river valleys, most of Wales is unsuitable for the species.

The 1963 *Birds of Monmouthshire* recorded it as a common resident, breeding throughout the county. It also mentioned censuses that were conducted in the county in 1955 and 1956, which produced totals of 17 and 13 nests respectively, and a total of about 150 non-breeding birds. The *1970 Gwent Bird Report* records a count, also from 1955, of 84 birds around the River Usk at Llanllowel, south of the town of Usk, thus suggesting that about half the county population was located at this site.

During the 1960s and early 1970s, the number of nests reported each year was in the range 5–9, and gatherings of non-breeding birds were very small, with no flocks of greater than ten reported. The 1970s and most of the 1980s were bad times for Mute Swans in Britain: the great increase in coarse angling resulted in large amounts of lead shot being lost or discarded into fresh waters, and its ingestion by Mute Swans caused a high incidence of death by lead-poisoning. Despite this problem, the number of nests reported annually in the county continued to vary mostly between five and 11 (though there was only one in 1977), and the county total of nine nests recorded in each of the national censuses of 1978 and 1983 (Table 1) was therefore typical of the period. Following a change in the law in 1987, lead fishing weights were replaced by a non-toxic alternative. This resulted in a fairly rapid and gratifying improvement in the health of Mute Swans over the succeeding years, and the census of 1990 produced a total of 15 nests in Gwent, the highest since 1956.

Year	Territorial pairs	Nests	Broods	Non-breeders
1978	18	9	8	14*
1983	15	9	5	28*
1990	25	15	11	89

*Both these figures are underestimates, as the peak counts in the Usk Valley alone were higher in both years.

Table 1. Mute Swan census data for Gwent

The breeding population has continued to expand, assisted in more recent years by the construction of golf courses and associated pools. In the 1st Gwent Atlas breeding Mute Swans were shown to be concentrated mostly in the Usk Valley with a scattering in other parts of the county. The 2nd Gwent Atlas shows that while the Usk Valley remains an important breeding area, a big expansion has occurred on the rivers Wye and Monnow, while the reens and pools of the levels have been extensively colonised, most recently extending to the newly created Newport Wetlands Reserve. Breeding was confirmed in 46 tetrads over the period of the 2nd Gwent Atlas, and in some tetrads there was more than one nest. The highest number of nests reported in a single year was 23 in 2002, but this figure does not represent full coverage of the county. Combining these figures, and taking into account that not all 46 tetrads would have been occupied in every year of the atlas period, it seems likely that the breeding population is currently in the range of 50–60 territorial pairs and 30–50 nests.

The numbers of non-breeding Mute Swans reported in Gwent increased during the mid 1970s and early 1980s, but probably mainly as a result of better observation rather than an increase in population. This was particularly true of the Usk Valley, where regular observation from 1974 onward, showed sizeable flocks to be present during winter months at Llangybi, with peaks of 20–35 birds in most winters. The immature birds from these flocks often lingered on local farmland into May, causing some crop damage, and resulting in attempts by farmers to drive them away. This area of the Usk Valley has continued to support significant numbers: the national census of 1990 produced a total of 46 between Chain Bridge and Llanllowel, and a flock of 44 was reported at Llangybi in March 2003. Since the mid 1980s non-breeding flocks, usually of 20–35 birds, have also been regularly reported from other locations on the River Usk, notably at Gobion and The Bryn. The River Wye also holds a sizeable population, and there have been two recent counts of over 50 on the stretch from Tintern to the county border in the north. Ynysyfro Reservoir has held up to 12 birds, the golf course lakes and meadows at Peterstone up to 48 and, in years of high winter rainfall, the Nedern Wetlands have held up to 21.

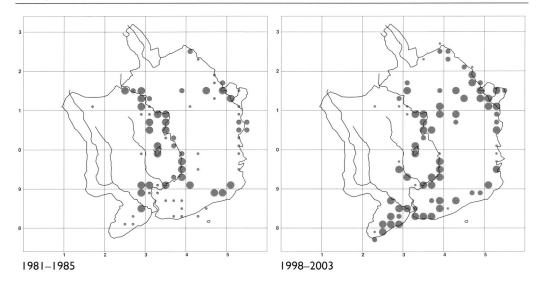

1981–1985   1998–2003

Most significantly, the Newport Wetlands Reserve has recently become the major site for non-breeding Mute Swans in Gwent, with maximum counts of 96, 86, 76 and 56 in the years 2000–03, and 60 in 2004 and 2005.

Although generally thought of a sedentary species, birds from the north and east of Britain often move south and west for the winter, and some indulge in moult migrations of moderate distances (*Migration Atlas*). Among birds ringed in Gwent, most have been recovered within 10km of the ringing site but there have been three instances of movements exceeding 100km, while among recoveries in the county, six have travelled over 100km from their site of ringing. These nine long-distance recoveries demonstrate movements between Gwent and the following counties: Berkshire (3), Warwickshire (2), Yorkshire, Shropshire, Hampshire and Dyfed. They show no obvious pattern in relation to season or age but one proves survival of a nestling to its eighth year of life.

Gwent Breeding Atlas data and population size

Gwent Atlas	Confirmed tetrads	Probable tetrads	Possible tetrads	Total tetrads	Change in total	Gwent population
1981–1985	26	13	31	70		–
1998–2003	46	19	15	80	14%	30–50 nests

National breeding data and conservation status

Estimated Welsh population	Welsh trend	UK CBC/BBS trend 1985–2003 trend	Welsh & UK conservation status
100–200	Not available	+83%	Not listed

Bewick's Swan (Tundra Swan)   *Cygnus columbianus*
Alarch Bewick

An uncommon winter visitor to a few traditional sites, which has declined severely in recent years

This small and attractive swan breeds on the arctic tundra of northern Russia and Siberia, and is a winter visitor to Britain. Its occurrence in Gwent appears to be a fairly recent development, as the 1963 *Birds of Monmouthshire* lists only one known record prior to 1960 – that of a bird found dead near Newport in November 1909. Since 1960, however, it has been recorded annually. During the 1960s, almost all records were from Caldicot Moor, beginning with two birds in winter 1959/60, three the following winter, and up to 22 in 1961/62. Numbers continued on an upward trend during the remainder of the decade, peaking with 36 birds in winter 1968/69. However, following a complete absence during the following winter, a count of 28 in

December 1971 proved to be the last significant record at this site. Extensive drainage of the site was doubtless the major factor in this decline.

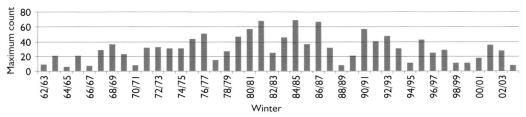

The disappearance of Bewick's Swans from Caldicot Moor coincided with the build up of a wintering flock in the Usk Valley. There had previously been three records there during the 1960s, including a flock of 20 at Llandegfedd Reservoir in December 1963, but winter 1969/70 began an unbroken sequence of records that has persisted into the present century. Although fluctuating from winter to winter, numbers showed an increasing trend during the 1970s and 1980s, and in three of the six winters 1981/82 to 1986/87 the peak winter count was between 66 and 68 (see Figure 1). The birds frequented the meadows adjacent to the River Usk, generally near to Llangybi, but also ranged northwards to Llanllowel and Llanbadoc. In many years there have also been reports from the meadows alongside the nearby Olway Brook, which probably refer to the same birds. The flock has usually roosted on Llandegfedd Reservoir, which has resulted in the submission of similar counts from both sites.

Figure 1. Annual maxima of Bewick's Swans in Gwent

In many years a moderate sized flock has also wintered in the south of the county on the Nedern Wetlands. Records from the Nedern began in 1981/82 and have since occurred in all but four winters up to the present time. A flock of 70 in January 1983 is the largest single flock recorded in the county, and other large numbers have included 63 in January 1996 and 46 in December 1985, although 10–35 birds has been the usual range. The average annual peak count in both of the last two decades is 25. The Usk Valley/Llandegfedd Reservoir and the Nedern are the only significant regular wintering sites for this species in southern Wales. [A reference in the 2002 *Birds in Wales* to 168 Bewick's Swans at Llandegfedd Reservoir during winter 2000/01 is erroneous.]

In winter 1983/84 there were two coordinated counts of the Usk Valley and the Nedern Wetlands. These were carried out in January and February and gave totals of 62 and 71 birds respectively. A coordinated count of flocks at both the Olway meadows and Llangybi in January 1985 produced 81 birds, which is the highest total ever recorded in the county.

The increase of Bewick's Swans in Gwent during the 1970s coincided with large increases in the numbers wintering in Britain as a result of a relocation of their wintering grounds from the Netherlands. In winter 1991/92 many fewer wintered in Britain, beginning a decade of slow decline which seems to have halted in the most recent years (WeBS). The wintering population has also redistributed – many fewer have come to western Britain, with the result that no birds have been recorded on WeBS counts in Wales since winter 1998/99.

Reflecting the situation in Wales, the numbers wintering in Gwent have declined severely, and records have become sporadic. In particular, the wintering flock has failed to appear in the Usk Valley and records at the site have become occasional. In the most recent decade the peak count for the county has varied between 47 and seven, with an average of only 23. A bird with a numbered neck-collar, observed at Collister Pill in December 1992, was seen at Slimbridge, Gloucestershire the following month; however, there is no other evidence to indicate any interchange between Gwent and Slimbridge, and peak numbers at the two sites have shown little correlation.

The first birds of the winter generally arrive in Gwent during the early weeks of November, though on three occasions there have been sightings in the last week of October, and, most exceptionally, four birds settled in at Llandegfedd Reservoir as early as 8th September in 1980. The maximum number for winter has usually been recorded during December–February, most often in January. Departure begins in late February, and last records are generally during mid-March, though stragglers have sometimes lingered as late as 7th April. In the Usk Valley they have often fed on winter wheat, which has not endeared them to local farmers but, as their departure has been early enough to allow recovery of the crop, they have generally been tolerated.

Occurrences at other minor sites are as follows. Flocks of 2–25 have been recorded sporadically at coastal sites, including Peterstone, Rogiet, Caldicot Pill and Mathern. Inland, there have been two records from Ynysyfro Reservoir, including 15 in November 1989, two on the River Wye at Redbook in February 1980, and one at Beaufort Pools in March 1996. Very unusually, an apparently healthy immature bird fed with domestic geese at Gobion during 11th March–1st May 1985.

WeBS data 1999/2000–2003/04 and conservation status

Average annual peak count for Gwent	19*
Threshold number for importance in GB	81
Threshold number for international importance	290
GB average peak count	6,200
Wales and UK winter conservation status	Amber-listed

*Data from Gwent bird reports, not WeBS.

National winter population trends (WeBS)

Wales long term	Wales medium term	UK long term	UK medium term
−100%	−100%	−50%	−75%

Long-term = the 25-year period 1977/78–2002/03; medium-term = the 10-year period 1993/94–2002/03.

Whooper Swan
Alarch y Gogledd

Cygnus cygnus

A very scarce winter visitor

Almost the entire Icelandic breeding population of around 20,000 birds winters in the British Isles. However, apart from a concentration in eastern England on the Ouse Washes, they have a northerly distribution in the UK and there are no concentrations of national or international importance in the Principality, although several sites in north and mid-Wales regularly hold small to moderate numbers.

The first record of Whooper Swans in Gwent was of a flock of 14 birds seen on Caldicot Moor on 9th February 1960, with almost certainly the same group of birds seen several miles to the east at Llanmartin on the 11th. Following a flock of five birds, again at Caldicot Moor, during 25th February–11th March 1961, flocks of up to ten birds were recorded annually during the years 1963–71, mostly from the Caldicot Moor/Magor area, although with several records from Llandegfedd Reservoir and the Olway Meadows.

Following a short break in records, a flock of five birds was present in fields adjacent to the regular Bewick's Swan flock in the Usk valley at Llangybi on 28th December 1974, with three birds again present on 19th January 1975. Subsequently there have been records in 14 of the 29 years to 2004, when the last genuinely wild birds, a single immature at Llandegfedd Reservoir during 18th November–2nd December, and three adults at Newport Wetlands Reserve on 11th December 2004 were recorded. During this period there has been a total of 23 records from at least 12 widely spread sites, typically of up to four individuals, although a flock of eight flew over Llandevaud on 5th January 1981, and five were present at Llandegfedd Reservoir on 1st January 1977.

There are two records thought to refer to birds of captive origin; one from Ynysyfro Reservoir where two birds were present during 26th–28th June 1990, and the other at Newport Wetlands Reserve where there was a single bird from April 2001 to August 2003.

All county records of Whooper Swan were reviewed by the Gwent Records Panel prior to the production of this book. The Panel was of the opinion that among the records included in the above analysis, some of those dating from the 1960s and 1970s may have been based on mis-identification. However, in the absence of conclusive evidence it was decided to leave these records in the analysis.

Bean Goose
Gŵydd y Llafur

Anser fabalis

A very rare winter visitor

The Bean Goose is an extremely local winter visitor to the UK, with regular flocks at only two locations, one in Scotland and the other in eastern England.

The only record in Gwent concerns a single bird of the nominate race *fabalis*, that was initially seen on the Nedern Wetlands on 31st January and then on the nearby Mathern foreshore during 10th–18th February 1996. This was presumably the same individual that had also been seen along the River Ogmore at the Watermill, Mid Glamorgan during 22nd–27th January.

Pink-footed Goose
Gŵydd droed-binc

Anser brachyrhynchus

A rare winter visitor

Most of the world's Pink-footed Geese, numbering around 275,000 birds, spend the winter in the UK (WeBS). They are found mainly in Scotland and northern England, and are scarce and irregular visitors to Wales.

Although it is now a rare visitor to Gwent, records in the 1963 *Birds of Monmouthshire* of 'many' at Llanwern during October–December 1899, and of three large flocks at Peterstone on 24th December 1935 suggest this species may have been a more frequent visitor to the county in the past. In more recent times there has been a total of just 11 records.

1970	25 December	Undy foreshore	1	
1975	9 November	Peterstone	12	flying NE
1977	15 April	Peterstone	2	flying NE
1982	30 January–12 April	Llangybi Bottom	1	
1987	24–30 January	Llanbadoc	1	
1987	24 November	Collister Pill	1	
1987	7 December	Uskmouth	4	
1992	October–November	Sluice Farm	1	also seen on Rumney Great Wharf, Glamorgan
1993	7 November	Black Rock	6	
1997	5 January	Llandegfedd Reservoir	1	also seen on the River Usk at Llanbadoc 10–11 January
1998	7–15 November	Coedkernew	1	

Table 2. Pink-footed Goose records in Gwent

European White-Fronted Goose Gŵydd Dalcen-wen

Anser albifrons albifrons

A very scarce and irregular winter visitor

Two races of the White-fronted Goose winter in Britain; the European race, which breeds in northern Russia and winters in southern and eastern England, and the Greenland race that winters mainly in Scotland and Ireland, but with very small numbers in parts of West Wales. It is the European race that normally occurs in Gwent.

The White-fronted Goose is described in the 1963 *Birds of Monmouthshire* as a fairly regular winter visitor, but only two detailed records are listed, of 60 at Marshfield and 30 at nearby Peterstone on 1st February 1952. Detailed records began only in the winter of 1962/63 and since then there have been about 100 records of White-fronted Geese and 46 records of 'grey geese'. The latter comprise sightings of geese (almost always in flight) that were definitely of the genus

Anser but could not be confidently identified to species level. It is likely that most, if not all, of these records refer to White-fronted Geese, partly because this is the *Anser* species that is by far the most common around the Severn Estuary, with a traditional wintering site at Slimbridge, Gloucestershire, but also because in many cases the observer was of the opinion (though not conviction) that this was the identity of the birds concerned. In this account, records should be assumed to refer to authentic White-fronted Geese unless the term 'grey geese' is specifically used.

In the very severe winter of 1962/63 Titcombe (1998) noted about 15 sightings of grey geese in the south of the county between 30th December and 16th February, in flocks ranging from eight to about 100 birds. Most were considered to have been White-fronts, but an emaciated individual, found dead, was the only certain identification. There were also four records of White-fronts elsewhere that winter, including a flock of 80 at Newbridge-on-Usk in early February, and 200 at Peterstone on 3rd March, which is the largest flock ever recorded feeding in the county. Figure 2 shows that over the next 30 years White-fronts and grey geese were regular visitors to the county with 2–6 records in most winters, and notable peaks in 1967/68 and 1978/79. The latter peak was associated with severe weather that also brought increased numbers of the species to neighbouring Glamorgan (Hurford & Lansdown, 1995).

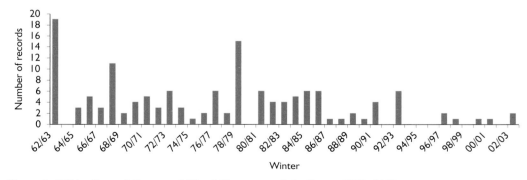

Figure 2. White-fronted Goose and 'Grey' Goose records in Gwent 1962–2003

Around 65% of the 100 White-fronted Goose records have been on or near the coast and most of the remainder have been in the Usk Valley, particularly on the wet meadows around Llangybi. By contrast, less than 20% of grey geese records have been on the coast, reflecting the fact that such records generally concern high-flying birds over inland locations. Numbers of White-fronts have often been small, with a little over half of all records involving ten or fewer birds, and a further third comprising flocks of 11–50. However there have been eleven records in excess of 50, the four largest flocks (all dating from the 1960s) comprise 1,000 birds that flew over Abergavenny on 7th March 1969, 200 over Caldicot on 30th April of the same year, 150 over Llanfoist in December 1967 and the 200 at Peterstone in 1963 (referred to above).

Figure 3 shows that records of White-fronts and grey geese are most numerous in the mid-winter months from December to February, but a few birds have occurred as early as 19th October, while at the end of the season there have been several large flocks in March, and a few as late as 30th April. Most county records have been transitory: over a third have involved birds flying over, and most of the rest have been one-day stops. Only four stays have lasted longer than two days, and these have involved six birds at Caldicot for 21 days in February 1968, up to 11 birds on flooded meadows at Llanfrechfa for 11 days in January 1968, 11 at Llangybi for eight days in December 1982, and up to ten at Peterstone from 24th December 1978 to 6th January 1979.

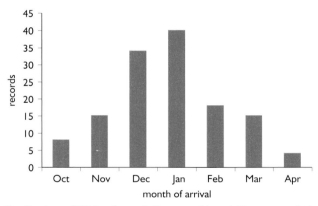

Figure 3. Monthly distribution of White-fronted Goose and 'grey' Goose records in Gwent 1962–2003

Since 1993, records of White-fronted and grey geese have been very scarce and irregular in Gwent. This relates directly to the great reduction in numbers of European White-fronts wintering in the UK, which has occurred over the last decade and seems to result from a shift of wintering grounds to continental Europe (WeBS).

WeBS data 1999/2000–2003/04 and conservation status

Average annual peak count for Gwent	6*
Threshold number for importance in GB	58
Threshold number for international importance	10,000
GB average peak count	2,704
Wales and UK winter conservation status	Amber-listed

*Data from Gwent Bird Reports, not WeBS.

National winter population trends (WeBS)

Wales long term	Wales medium term	UK long term*	UK medium term*
–33%	+288%**	–57%	–44%

**Of little significance, as based on such small numbers. *Long-term = the 25-year period 1977/78–2002/03; medium-term = the 10-year period 1993/94–2002/03.

Greenland White-fronted Goose   *A. a. flavirostris*

This race of White-fronted Goose winters mainly in Scotland and Ireland, but Wales also has a small number (usually 100–200) based mainly on the Dyfi Estuary. The only Gwent record concerns a single bird at Llandegfedd Reservoir in March 1974, though it is possible that other birds have been overlooked.

Greylag Goose   *Anser anser*
Gŵydd Wyllt

A scarce passage migrant. Feral birds are now resident and have bred in recent years

The Greylag Goose has a complex status in Britain. Historically it was a widespread native breeding bird, and a significant remnant of this wild population remains in northern Scotland and the Western Isles (Amber-listed owing to their very limited distribution). From the middle of the 20th century, offspring from the wild population were reintroduced successfully into many localities in Britain, mostly in England but also to Anglesey in Wales (1988–92 National Atlas). The reintroduced population has established well, has recently been increasing at rate of greater than 5% per year (Mead, 2000), and currently stands at around 25,000–30,000 birds in the UK (Rowell *et al.*, 2004). In addition, the Icelandic breeding population winters in Scotland (also Amber-listed), and the *Migration Atlas* cites ringing recoveries that indicate a few Scandinavian breeders may wander to England in winter.

Greylags have occurred in Gwent in 23 of the 30 years since 1974. It is often difficult to assess the origins of these birds. However, Britain's reintroduced populations are known generally to be very sedentary, so short-stay records (defined here as birds flying over or recorded on only one day) may often represent birds from wild populations. This assumption is supported by analysis (Figure 4), which shows that short-stay records occur mainly in the passage periods, particularly in April and May, the period when wintering birds from migratory populations are known to return to their breeding grounds. These passage records have usually involved very small numbers, most often ones or twos, but occasionally up to 8. Another record that almost certainly concerned wild birds was a party of nine, thought to be birds of the Eastern European race (*A. a. rubrirostris*), in the company of Bewick's Swans at Olway Meadows on 13th February 1993. Some longer-staying birds have also behaved as wild, including a pair at Llandegfedd Reservoir for eight weeks in winter 1986, and a single bird at Gobion from 9th–13th April 1988.

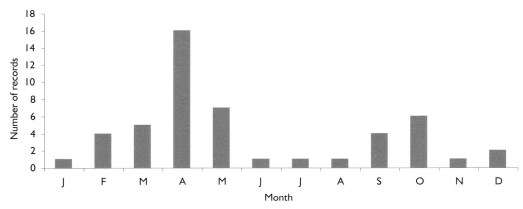

Figure 4. Monthly distribution of short-stay Greylag records in Gwent

Apart from the above, all long-stay records in Gwent have been assumed to comprise reintroduced birds. The first of these involved a moulting bird at Llandegfedd Reservoir during September 1967, and there were no others until 1985 when a very tame bird stayed at Pant-y-Goitre from February to April. 1993 saw the start of a period in which occurrence of reintroduced birds became more frequent; a bird at Dunlop Semtex Pond stayed from May to December, and in the following year a pair nested near Raglan, and 4–8 birds were recorded at Dingestow Court from July to December. 1995 saw records at the Hendre, Dingestow Court and a lake at The Warrage, while a flock of 19 at Llandegfedd Reservoir in August was the largest group ever recorded in the county.

Records became a little scarcer in the next four years, but in summer 2000 a pair bred successfully at a pond in the grounds of the steelworks at Llanwern. A single pair continued to breed at this site annually between 2001 and 2003, and then three pairs bred in 2004 and 2005 and possibly four pairs in 2006. Seven birds from Llanwern were fitted with colour Darvic rings in the summer of 2004, and subsequent sightings of these have been made in the Cardiff area, in particular at the Llanishen and Lisvane Reservoirs and at Roath Park Lake. The majority of these birds later returned to Llanwern. During autumn 2004 there were up to 27 birds present at Llanwern, which is an unprecedented number for the county.

One of the Llanwern birds has also been seen locally at the Newport Wetlands Reserve, paired with an unringed bird. Up to five Greylags have been present for long periods at Newport Wetland Reserve since 2000, and ones and twos have spent long periods at other sites, including the River Usk at Newport, Ynysyfro Reservoir and Bassaleg. It appears that the colonisation of Gwent is under way, so we can expect increases in future years.

(Greater) **Canada Goose**   *Branta canadensis*
Gŵydd Canada

A locally common resident, a regular breeder since 1989

The Canada Goose is a native of North America but was introduced into Britain in the 17th century. The 1968–72 National Atlas showed that it had become a widespread feral breeding species in Britain, with a total of 681 occupied 10-km squares, mainly in England. By the time of the 1988–91 National Atlas the number of occupied squares had increased to almost 1,200, but these were still mostly in England and only around 4% were in Wales.

There are no recorded occurrences of Canada Geese in Gwent prior to 1960, the year in which a wildfowling club attempted to introduce the species to the county by releasing moderate numbers into the wild. A further release was made in 1962, but despite successful breeding at Newbridge on Usk during 1964–69 and at Undy Pool in 1968, the introduction failed to get established, and during the next fourteen years (1970–83) the Canada Goose reverted to its former rare status. During this period there were two years in which there were no records at all, and eight years with only single records, while 1973 was somewhat exceptional with a total of five records that included a flock of about 20.

The year 1984 began a sequence of five years in which records became more numerous; there were 5–8 sightings annually, usually of six or fewer birds, and generally in the first half of the year, particularly in spring. Following this period, records in the county increased again, with an unprecedented 11 records in 1989, again mostly in spring, while a pair that reared young at Kentchurch constituted the first breeding record since 1969. In 1990 and 1991, successful breeding at Dingestow Court Lake was accompanied by widespread spring records at other sites, while in 1992, breeding spread to Peterstone and the Hendre, and other records included six flocks of ten or more birds.

During and since the 1990s the population of Canada Geese in Gwent has increased steadily and dramatically, and many birds are now present throughout the year. A flock of 55 at Dingestow in September 1995 was remarkable as the biggest ever recorded in the county, but autumn and winter flock sizes have continued to increase since then, and numbers of well over 100 are now of annual and widespread occurrence. In 2003 the largest flocks recorded were 192 at the Celtic Manor Lakes in January, 205 at Peterstone in August, 121 at Llandegfedd Reservoir in September and 252 at the Newport Wetland Reserve in December. Numbers continue to grow, and in 2005 peak counts comprised 400 at Newport Wetlands Reserve in September and 290 at Llandegfedd reservoir in December.

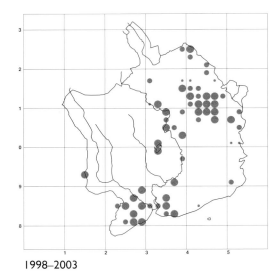

1998–2003

The 2nd Gwent Atlas map shows that successful breeding occurred in 32 tetrads during this period, mostly in the south-west, centre and north-east of the county. The sites occupied included reservoirs, ornamental ponds, wetlands and slow-flowing rivers. Probable breeding was recorded in a further 23 tetrads and the species was present during the breeding season in another seven. Some tetrads contained more than one breeding pair, but some others were not occupied in every year of the Atlas, so the total breeding population must be about 50 pairs, and increasing.

As the Canada Goose is an introduced species, no threshold numbers for importance are set, and it is not given a conservation status listing. During 1999/00–2003/04 the mean annual peak counts were 264 for Gwent and 52,600 for Britain.

Gwent Breeding Atlas data and population size

Gwent Atlas	Confirmed tetrads	Probable tetrads	Possible tetrads	Total tetrads	Change in total	Gwent population
1981–1985	0	1	0	1	–	–
1998–2003	31	23	7	61	+600%	c.50 territories

National breeding data and conservation status

Estimated Welsh population	UK WBS waterways trend 1981–2003	UK BBS trend 1994–2004	Welsh & UK conservation status
Not available	+108%	+74%	Not listed

WeBS data 1999/2000–2003/04 and conservation status

Average annual peak count for Gwent	264*
Threshold number for importance in GB	None set
Threshold number for international importance	None set
GB average peak count	52,600
Wales and UK winter conservation status	Not listed

*Maxima from minor inland sites have been added to WeBS data.

Barnacle Goose
Gŵydd Wyran

Branta leucopsis

A rare winter visitor and passage migrant

Upwards of 80,000 Barnacle Geese from the Greenland and Svalbard populations spend the winter in the British Isles, but are found almost entirely in Ireland, Scotland and northern England (WeBS). In Gwent, as elsewhere in Wales, they are rare visitors, and the existence in the UK of a substantial and increasing feral population derived from captive collections, makes it difficult to assess the status of visitors to the county.

Ten records of unringed birds, showing wild behaviour, that are considered likely to comprise genuinely wild individuals are shown in Table 3.

1970	10 October	Llanbadoc	1	on the River Usk.
1979	24 February	Peterstone	3	flew overland from the estuary
1980	25 October–1 November	Peterstone	2	
1983	29 April–12 May	Collister Pill	2	grazing on the salt marsh.
1985	25 May	Goldcliff Pill	2	feeding on the saltmarsh before flying off NW at a considerable height
1986	31 March	St Brides	1	seen with Shelducks
1987	25 January–1 February	Chepstow Wharf	1	
1989	23 December	Black Rock	1	near the lighthouse
1997	13 January	St Brides	1	
1998	6 December	St Brides	16	seen also at Sluice Farm on 13 December.

Table 3. Barnacle Goose records in Gwent

Brent Goose
Gŵydd Ddu

Branta bernicla

An uncommon but regular winter visitor and an occasional passage migrant

Brent Geese breed on tundra in the high arctic and winter on muddy coasts in temperate latitudes. Two distinct races of the Brent Goose, the Dark-bellied (*B. b. bernicla*), and the pale-bellied (*B. b. hrota*) spend their winter in the British Isles. The dark-bellied birds come from the Russian arctic and they winter along the east and south coasts of England where numbers have been in the range 90,000–100,000 in recent years. Their nearest wintering area to Gwent is the Burry Inlet (80km to the west), which regularly holds over 1,000 birds. Among the pale-bellied birds, 2,000–3,000 from the Svalbard and eastern Greenland population winter mainly in north-east England around Lindisfarne, while up to 20,000 from the Canadian breeding population winter in Ireland. As the closest winter concentrations to Gwent all comprise dark-bellied birds, it is not surprising that most of the county's visitors also belong to this race. However, because identification of race is not always possible in the field, and observers do not always specify it in their reports, the following account does not make any distinction between races, apart from a concluding summary of definite pale-bellied (*B. b. hrota*) records.

Formerly it was regarded as a very rare visitor to Gwent, with only two records, dating from 1928 and 1929 (1963 *Birds of Monmouthshire*), and a further two occurrences in 1972. However, from 1976 onwards Brent Geese have been recorded almost annually and the total number of records is now over 140. They may occur anywhere along the coast from Sluice Farm in the west to Chepstow Wharf in the east and they feed on both inter-tidal mud and saltmarsh. Figure 5 shows that most records fall in the winter months from November to January, with fewer than 25% outside this period. Numbers in Gwent are tiny in comparison with the national populations, and 70% of sightings have involved only one or two birds. However there have been 12 records of ten or more birds. The largest of these is a historical record of 70 on the coast in February 1929 (1963 *Birds of Monmouthshire*), and the three largest modern records in the winter period comprise 60 at Goldcliff Pill in November 1986, 18 at Collister Pill in December 1978, and 13 at Goldcliff Pill in late October 1990.

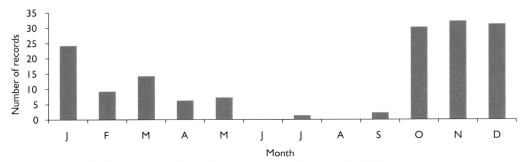

Figure 5. Monthly distribution of Brent Goose records in Gwent 1973–2003

There have been about 30 records in the passage periods, mostly between March and May, and usually of single birds (occasionally up to six), but including two sizeable flocks: 36 at Chepstow Wharf on 9th March 1988 and 16 at Peterstone on 11th April 1983. The solitary July record was of a single bird, as also were the two September records.

Single birds have occasionally occurred inland, particularly at Llandegfedd Reservoir where there have been six records between 1981 and 2001, spread between October and February, and one passage record on 24th–26th May 2001. Other inland sightings have been in the Usk Valley at Gobion, Llanbadoc and Llangybi.

WeBS data 1999/2000–2003/04 and conservation status

Average annual peak count for Gwent	2*
Threshold number for importance in GB	981
Threshold number for international importance	2,200
GB average peak count	78,100
Wales and UK winter conservation status	Amber-listed

*Data from Gwent bird reports, not WeBS.

National winter population trends (WeBS)

Wales long term	Wales medium term	UK long term	UK medium term
+420%	+24%	+46%	−33%

Pale-bellied Brent Goose   *Branta bernicla hrota*

The pale-bellied race of Brent Goose (*B. b. hrota*) is known to have occurred in Gwent on only nine occasions but, owing to the factors mentioned above, it is possible that a few birds have been missed. A party of seven, reported by many observers, between Peterstone and Goldcliff during 17th November–6th December 1987, five at Black Rock on 24th March 1986, three at Redwick on 4th May 2003, and two at Peterstone on 27th December 2003 are the only records referring to more than one bird. Of the single birds, one is a historical record from

January 1928, one was seen at Llangybi in December 1985, and the remaining three occurred at coastal locations in November 1986, January 1989 and January 1997.

Egyptian Goose
Gŵydd yr Aifft

Alopochen aegyptiaca

A rare winter visitor

The five county records of this African species have undoubtedly involved birds from the feral breeding population, centred on eastern England. Following the first at Abergavenny Sewage Works on 3rd April 1971, two birds were present on an ornamental pond in the grounds of the former Llanwern Steelworks complex during 3rd–6th April 1983 and a further single at the same location during 10th–12th March 1993. Single birds were also recorded at Llandegfedd Reservoir on 18th April 2003, and on the River Wye at Monmouth on 18th July 2004.

(Common) Shelduck
Hwyaden yr Eithen

Tadorna tadorna

A locally common resident, mostly on the coast, and an abundant passage migrant and winter visitor

The Shelduck breeds widely around the estuarine coasts of Britain, and winter numbers are swollen by the arrival of immigrants from the northern Europe, particularly from the Baltic breeding populations (*Migration Atlas*). The species has a long-established presence along the coast of Gwent, as both a breeding and a wintering bird (1937 and 1963 *Birds of Monmouthshire*).

The Shelduck's usual breeding requirements are large areas of estuarine mud adjacent to terrain that contains nesting sites with concealment and overhead cover. The coastal habitats of Gwent amply fulfil these conditions, and Shelducks breed commonly. Nesting sites known to have been used in the county include rabbit burrows, the bases of dense hedgerows, small quarries, barns, a cave, and a tree hole some 6m above ground that had previously been used by a pair of Tawny Owls. Such sites may be as much as 3–4km, occasionally further, from the coast. After hatching, the young are led overland, by both parents, to a 'nursery territory' on the estuarine mud. This will have been established early in the spring, and defended by the male during the incubation period. The young are tended there by their parents for two to three weeks, after which they often become part of larger crèches tended by a single pair of adults. Family parties are very conspicuous on the coast, so breeding is easily proved, but whether the nest was in the same tetrad is usually a matter of conjecture, so the distribution map may contain some inaccuracies. Shelducks also breed on the tidal reaches of Gwent's major rivers, with one or two pairs noted on the Usk near Caerleon in many years, and up to eight pairs on the Wye below Wyndcliff.

The 1988–91 National Atlas noted an increasing tendency for Shelducks to breed in association with inland waters in parts of England, possibly as a result of the increase in the population size and consequent saturation of coastal habitats. The first case of breeding at an inland water in Gwent was at Wentwood Reservoir in 1977 when a brood of eight was successfully raised. Single broods continued to be raised at this site until 1983 (with two broods in 1982), but in 1984 no young were seen and breeding has not occurred since. Breeding was also recorded at Llandegfedd Reservoir in most years from 1990 to 1998, usually just one pair, but two in 1992, and three in 1993. The Uskmouth/Goldciff area has long been an important breeding site, which now falls within the the Newport Wetland Reserve: in 2002 there were 17 pairs there, nine of which raised a total of 56 young.

The breeding distribution as shown in the 2nd Gwent Atlas is very similar to that found in the 1st Gwent Atlas, and no significant change seems to have occurred. The size of the coastal breeding population can be determined by counting territorial pairs early in the spring, and two such counts, in 1992 and 1999, yielded totals of 90 and 186 pairs respectively. However, counts of broods that appear on the shore later in the season have given much smaller numbers. During the 1980s up to 20 broods were commonly reported, with a combined total of up to 190 ducklings, while in the 1990s the number of broods seldom exceeded ten and the duckling total was in the range 28–63. It is apparent, therefore, that only a small proportion of territory holders breed successfully, probably because some are immature birds not old enough to breed, some may not find nest sites, and some may lose their broods to predators on the trek to the coast. The reason for the decline in success during the 1990s is not known. The estimated breeding population for the county is 100–200 pairs, of which probably only 10–30 are successful in any one year.

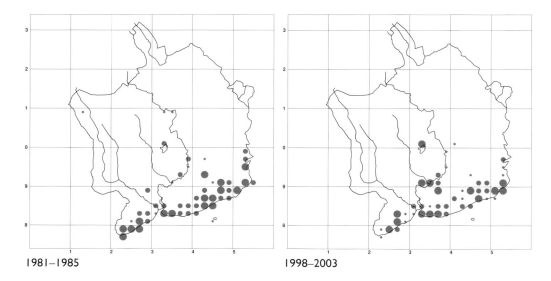

1981–1985   1998–2003

In late June and July, immature birds, failed breeders and those whose ducklings have gone into a crèche, gather into flocks preceding their migration to the Wadden See or the Helgoland Bight where they moult. In many years these pre-migration flocks have been quite large: in the 1970s June/July flocks on the Undy shore often contained 400–600 birds, though in subsequent decades 100–300 has been the norm at this site, and with similar numbers on the Uskmouth shore. At Peterstone pre-migration flocks have not been recorded in every summer but in many years have contained around 100–200 birds.

In August and September, following the departure of the moult migrants, very few Shelducks can be found on the Gwent coast apart from the young of the year, so a count of 160 at Undy in September 2001 was exceptional. Small numbers begin to appear again in October. A count of 375 at Peterstone in October 1997 was exceptionally high for this month and corresponded with unusually high numbers elsewhere in Britain (WeBS 1997/98).

The Severn Estuary is one of the top ten wintering sites for Shelducks in Britain, and its average peak count of over 3,000 birds makes it a site of international importance. The Gwent coast holds a high proportion of the estuary population and is in itself a site of national importance. Significant arrivals usually begin in November, though sometimes not till December, and the largest numbers are found along the Wentlooge (Sluice Farm-Peterstone-St Brides) stretch of the estuary, where the average maximum has increased steadily over the last 40 years to around 800 in the last decade (Table 4). The highest counts recorded on this stretch comprise 1,130 in January 1982, 1,350 in December 1993 and 1,370 in November 1999. Substantial, but smaller, numbers also occur regularly on the coast of the Caldicot Level at Uskmouth and Undy, with recent maxima of over 600 at Uskmouth in November 2004 and 2005, and 320 at Undy in January 2004. As on the estuary as a whole, the peak count in Gwent usually occurs in the period December–February, though occasionally in November, and there is often a secondary peak in March, or even April, suggestive of passage birds.

1963/64–1972/73	1973/74–1982/83	1983/84–1992/93	1993/94–2003/04	Maximum
184	391	654	805	1,350

Table 4. Average winter peak counts of Shelducks on the Wentlooge coast

During the passage periods, particularly in spring, small numbers (usually fewer than ten birds) may turn up at Llandegfedd Reservoir and occasionally other inland locations, which have included the Usk at Llangybi and Gobion, Woodstock Pool, Newport, and the Nedern Wetlands where, exceptionally, 46 were recorded in May 1986.

Gwent Breeding Atlas data and population size

Gwent Atlas	Confirmed tetrads	Probable tetrads	Possible tetrads	Total tetrads	Change in total	Gwent population
1981–1985	17	24	10	51	–	–
1998–2003	15	16	16	47	−4%	100–200 territories

National breeding data and conservation status

Estimated Welsh population	Welsh trend	UK CBC/BBS trend 1985–2003	Welsh & UK conservation status
500–800 pairs	Not available	−41%	Green-listed

WeBS data 1999/2000–2003/04 and conservation status

Average annual peak count for Gwent	1,114
Threshold number for importance in GB	782
Threshold number for international importance	3,000
GB average peak count	57,000
Wales and UK winter conservation status	Amber-listed

National winter population trends (WeBS)

Wales long term	Wales medium term	UK long term*	UK medium term*
+58%	−10%	+7%	−18%

*Long-term = the 25-year period 1977/78–2002/03; medium-term = the 10-year period 1993/94–2002/03.

Mandarin Duck
Hwyaden Gribog
Aix galericulata

A very scarce resident which has arrived recently

The Mandarin originates from Asia, and was introduced to Britain as a captive ornamental species as early as the mid-18th century. A feral population became established during the 20th century, initially in southeast England, but spreading north and west in recent decades.

The first record in Gwent was of a male at Llandegfedd Reservoir during 14th–15th November 1987, with possibly the same individual being seen again on 25th February and 2nd October 1988. Since then there have been a few reports (1–3 per year) of single birds or pairs in 11 out of 15 years, at widely scattered sites, including Llandegfedd and Ynysyfro Reservoirs, locations on the Rivers Usk, Wye and Honddu, Llanwern Steelworks, and Cwmbran boating lake. However, the Mandarin is notoriously shy and secretive, often remaining concealed by marginal vegetation, so the scattering of Gwent records may represent only an indication of a more substantial presence within the county.

With its breeding population increasing steadily in the nearby Forest of Dean, it was perhaps only a matter of time before this species was added to the county breeding list. This may have occurred as early as 1999, when a female with small ducklings was observed on the River Wye at Redbrook, but the possibility that the nest had been based on the Gloucestershire side of the river could not be ruled out. Breeding in the county was confirmed four years later when a nest with six eggs was found in a rotten tree stump alongside the canal at Pencroesoped on 7th May 2003.

(Eurasian) **Wigeon**   *Anas penelope*
Chwiwell

A common and increasing winter visitor and passage migrant; rare in summer

The Wigeon is mainly a winter visitor from Fennoscandia and northern Russia, and is widespread in Britain during the winter months. In its winter quarters it feeds predominantly by grazing and is found chiefly in association with estuaries. Considerable numbers also occur at appropriate inland localities, particularly flooded grassland, or lakes and reservoirs that have shallow margins or adjacent pasture.

The 1963 *Birds of Monmouthshire* described it as a winter visitor to the county, that occurred in flocks of up to 300 around the mouths of rivers and other outflows into the Severn, such as the Peterstone Pill and Goldcliff Pill. However, 1963 saw the completion of Llandegfedd Reservoir, which immediately began to attract wintering Wigeon, and by the winter of 1967/68 it had become the major site for this species in the county. Peak counts at the reservoir, always occurring in the months December to February, were 450 in 1967/68, rising to 600 in 1971/72, and 1,000 in 1973/74. Peak counts remained high for the next 13 years, usually between around 750 and 1,300, but with exceptionally high numbers of 1,850 in 1978/79, 2,000 in 1981/82, and 2,000 again 1986/87. The very high counts were all associated with severe winter weather.

Following 1986/87, numbers visiting Llandegfedd showed a sharp decline, and apart from 812 in 1991/92 and 750 in 1995/96, peak counts have since been well below 700. Table 5 illustrates the decline in Wigeon numbers over the last three decades.

	1973/74–1982/83	1983/84–1992/93	1993/94–2002/03	Highest
Llandegfedd Reservoir	136	881	455	2,000 (1986/87)
Caldicot Level coast	217	630	446	1,200 (1995/96)

Table 5. Average peak counts of Wigeon at Llandegfedd Reservoir and the Caldicot Level coast

Despite the emergence of Llandegfedd Reservoir as the main wintering site in the late 1960s, numbers of Wigeon remained high on the Severn Estuary, and flocks of 300–600 have occurred at various locations along the Caldicot Level coast, including Goldcliff, Undy, Black Rock and Mathern in most winters from 1972/73 to 2002/03 (Table 5). West of the River Usk, on the Peterstone and St Brides coasts, there have also been regular winter flocks, but with smaller numbers, usually in the range of around 15–100. In the three winters 1984/85 to 1986/87, all of which had spells of very cold weather, counts on the estuary were unusually high, with peaks of 1,000 birds east of Uskmouth and 90–350 to the west. The highest coastal number recorded is 1,200 at Undy in October 1995 (too early to have been caused by the severe weather later that winter)

The saltmarsh grasslands at Goldcliff on the recently completed Newport Wetland Reserve have provided another excellent habitat for Wigeon, and peak counts there have built-up rapidly from 1,100 in winter 2001/02 to 2,260 in December 2005. This reserve has now replaced Llandegfedd Reservoir as the major wintering site in the county for the species. Recent WeBS trends for Wigeon, both in Wales and the UK as a whole, are strongly positive, so numbers using the site may not yet have reached their peak.

In addition, Wigeon often occur in small to moderate numbers on flooded fields in river valleys, particularly in the Usk Valley around Llangybi and Llandenny. Flocks there usually contain no more than about 20 birds but can be much larger in severe weather; notably 600 at Llangybi in February 1979, and around 400 in December 1981 and December 1985. The Nedern Wetlands also hold small numbers in many years, but exceptionally there were about 1,000 birds there in January 1987, again in response to hard weather. Small flocks, usually of fewer than 20 birds but occasionally up to 100 or more, have also been recorded at some time on most sizeable water bodies in the county, including Ynysyfro and Wentwood Reservoirs.

In some years a few birds arrive at wintering sites in the county as early as August, but September is more usual, and numbers do not begin to build-up significantly till October. Departure begins in March, and usually only the stragglers remain in April. In some years, small peaks occur in autumn and spring that are suggestive of passage. Birds rarely remain over the summer months and those that do are usually injured individuals. A female with an injured wing remained at Llandegfedd Reservoir for 12 years beginning in the mid-1980s, and in several summers a single male, occasionally two, kept her company: there was, however, no suggestion of breeding. The 1977 *Birds of Gwent* records breeding as having apparently occurred in the south of the county from 1965 to 1968, but this was subsequently discounted for lack of hard evidence (Lovegrove *et al.*, 1980).

There are two ringing records relevant to Gwent, both involving birds ringed at Haarsteeg in the Netherlands in winter 1969: one was recovered later the same winter at Redwick, while the other was recovered seven winters later at Magor.

WeBS data 1999/2000–2003/04 and conservation status

Average annual peak count for Gwent coastal habitats	1,874
Threshold number for importance in GB	4,060
Threshold number for international importance	15,000
GB average peak count	377,960
Wales and UK winter conservation status	Amber-listed

National winter population trends (WeBS)

Wales long term	Wales medium term	UK long term*	UK medium term*
+45%	+13%	+100%	+29%

*Long-term = the 25-year period 1977/78–2002/03; medium-term = the 10-year period 1993/94–2002/03.

American Wigeon
Chwiwell America

Anas americana

A very rare vagrant

There are two records of this American counterpart of the Eurasian Wigeon. A female was present at Dingestow Court Lake during 25th August–10th September 1995 and an immature male was recorded at Peterstone during 31st October–27th November 1999, and subsequently at nearby Goldcliff Pill on 28th November 1999.

Gadwall
Hwyaden Lwyd

Anas strepera

A common resident at a few sites, but breeding proved at only one; also a scarce but widespread passage migrant and winter visitor

The Gadwall has a complex status in Britain: there is an expanding breeding population, the establishment of which was helped historically by some introductions; some of these birds migrate to south-west Europe for the winter. In addition, winter visitors that originate in Iceland and eastern Europe arrive in Britain during the autumn (*Migration Atlas*).

The species was formerly a very rare bird in the county, and prior to 1967 the only documented record is of a bird shot at Rumney (Monmouthshire) in October 1954 (1963 *Birds of Monmouthshire*). In the second half of

1967 there were four records and since then it has been recorded annually in small numbers, but with a very gradual increase culminating in its current status.

Since winter 1999/00 Gadwall has become a common resident at the newly created Newport Wetlands Reserve (Table 6). Moderate numbers have been present in all months and the peak winter count has reached 62. Breeding behaviour has been evident every year, and in 2001, as many as four pairs are thought to have nested, but failed to produce young. Gadwall have also become regular at ponds in Llanwern steelworks, where they are present in most months of the year, with a maximum of 21 birds in March 2005, and up to three pairs in recent springs. Breeding was proved at this site when a female with ducklings was observed in 2006 and again in 2007. Breeding has also been suspected periodically at Greenmoor Pool for over 15 years. This began with lone pairs, probably on passage, in the years 1986–89, but there were two pairs present during spring 1990, three pairs in 1991 and five in 1992. Paired birds were recorded again in spring 1993 and in several subsequent years, but though breeding has been strongly suspected, it has never been proved.

Winter	1999/00	2000/01	2001/02	2002/03	2003/04
Count	10 (Mar)	62 (Feb)	61 (Feb)	45 (Feb)	65 (Feb)

Table 6. Peak winter counts of Gadwall at Newport Wetlands Reserve

Magor Marsh has held moderate numbers in some recent years, notably in winter 1995–96, and 1996–97 when maxima were 13 and 17 respectively, the latter being a record count for the county at the time.

Apart from the above, the Gadwall is a scarce but widespread passage migrant and winter visitor, usually in ones and twos, but sometimes in flocks of up to eight or more, to a wide variety of sites, including (maxima in brackets) Llandegfedd Reservoir (6), St Pierre Lake (9), Ynysyfro Reservoir (6), Wentwood Reservoir (2), the Nedern Wetlands (5), Beaufort ponds (5), various locations on the River Usk (4), and on the coast at Peterstone (11), Goldcliff Pill (4) and Uskmouth (5). Spring passage records generally occur from mid March to mid May, and as pairing occurs in the winter range (in common with most other duck species), the spring migrants are often paired. Autumn passage is usually from August to mid-September.

The change in status seen in Gwent reflects the national situation. The Gadwall has undergone a spectacular expansion in Britain over the last 40 years. Between the two National Atlases (1968–72) and (1988–91) the number of 10-km squares in which it occurred tripled, while WeBS counts have shown a prolific and unremitting increase since the mid-1960s. The peak WeBS count for the UK in winter 1999/00 was over 15,000 and represented a doubling of numbers during the 1990s. An interesting observation made by WeBS reports is that in the 1960s the winter status of Gadwall was similar to that of the Smew or the Slavonian Grebe today.

WeBS data 1999/2000–2003/04 and conservation status

Average annual peak count for Gwent	50
Threshold number for importance in GB	171
Threshold number for international importance	600
GB average peak count	15,030
Wales and UK winter conservation status	Green-listed

(Eurasian) **Teal**   *Anas crecca*
Corhwyaden

A common winter visitor and passage migrant; a very rare breeder

The Teal is a widespread winter visitor to Britain, and is common on both inland and estuarine waters that provide extensive shallows for feeding. Since the beginning of WeBS counts in the mid-1960s, numbers of Teal wintering in Britain have shown an increasing trend. In Gwent, the major winter concentrations are at Llandegfedd Reservoir and on the Severn Estuary, particularly at Peterstone, St Brides and Uskmouth.

The 1963 *Birds of Monmouthshire* described the Teal as a common winter visitor, especially on the coast and in the Usk Valley. A more quantitative assessment of its status in the county was not possible until the start of systematic counts, and they began at Llandegfedd Reservoir, shortly after its completion in the early 1960s.

Numbers at Llandegfedd invariably reach a maximum during December–February and the average peak count in the last 30 years has been about 300 (Table 7). Occasionally numbers have been very much higher than average, notably during the four winters 1983/84 to 1986/87 when the peak count averaged 660, and included 940 in January 1986, the highest ever count for the site. Another high count of 600 was recorded in December 1995.

	1974/75–1983/84	1984/85–1993/94	1994/95–2003/04	**Highest**
Llandegfedd Reservoir	238	417	284	940 (1985/86)
Peterstone	266	576	536	1,500 (1985/86)

Table 7. Average peak counts of Teal at Llandegfedd Reservoir and Peterstone

On the estuary at Peterstone the winter maximum has averaged about 450 in the last 30 winters, showing an increasing trend during the first 10 years but remaining fairly stable since (Table 7), and the highest recorded number was 1,500 in February 1986 during a period of severe cold weather. The mouth of the River Usk is another site where large concentrations are noted in many, but not all, winters: flocks of 300–500 are not unusual, and the highest-ever number was 1,400 in January 1996. Since its completion in 1999/2000, the Newport Wetland Reserve has become a major wintering site for Teal, with peak counts exceeding 1,000 in December 2000 and February 2002, and up to 860 in subsequent winters.

The Severn Estuary as a whole is of international importance for wintering Teal. The peak winter count averages well over 4,000 and the estuary ranks between 8th and 11th (depending on the year) in the WeBS list of most important UK sites for this species. The Gwent coast has had a mean peak count of around 1,400 in recent years, and thus holds a substantial proportion of the total Severn population. The importance of the Gwent coast was confirmed by the WeBS low tide counts of winter 1998/99, which showed the Peterstone/St Brides stretch of shore to hold one of the highest feeding concentrations on the estuary.

Teal also occur on passage, and this is often indicated at Peterstone by the occurrence of a small peak in numbers during September or October, well before the main winter influx. Passage and winter records occur at many other sites in the county, notably on the River Usk at Llanfoist where numbers have reached 100, and at Gobion where up to 140 have been recorded. Other sites with large numbers have included (maxima in brackets) the Nedern Wetlands (300), ponds at Llanwern steelworks (100), Greenmoor Pool (55) and Magor Marsh (40). Spring passage occurs in March and April but it generally involves fewer birds than in autumn and is not always distinguishable as a peak in numbers.

The Teal is a widespread but scarce breeder in Wales, and in Gwent there have been only four *confirmed* breeding records, all associated with the River Usk. The first two records were at Llandowlais in 1943 where two pairs were described as 'nesting' (1963 *Birds of Monmouthshire*). The remaining two were at Gobion where single females accompanied by broods of ducklings were recorded in summers 1982 and 1985. During the 2nd Gwent Atlas pairs were observed in spring, in suitable habitat at Greenmoor Pool and in tetrad 40W but, as there was no further indication of breeding, it is likely these birds were late passage migrants. A dead juvenile bird found in the Uskmouth reedbeds in July 2006 is thought most likely to have originated locally.

There are three interesting ringing records: a bird ringed in May 1956 in Swedish Lapland was recovered in January 1958 near Newport; one ringed in winter at the Camargue in France was recovered the following autumn near Newport; and one ringed in the Netherlands in winter 1983/84 was recovered near Newport in winter 1986/87. These records are consistent with the known migration patterns of the species, which involve movements of Fennoscandian and other northern European birds to wintering grounds in western and southern Europe.

WeBS data 1999/2000–2003/04 and conservation status

Average annual peak count for Gwent coastal habitats	1,393
Threshold number for importance in GB	1,920
Threshold number for international importance	4,000
GB average peak count	160,630
Wales and UK winter conservation status	Amber-listed

National winter population trends (WeBS)

Wales long term	**Wales medium term**	**UK long term***	**UK medium term***
+114%	+41%	+102%	+28%

*Long-term = the 25-year period 1977/78–2002/03; medium-term = the 10-year period 1993/94–2002/03.

Mallard
Hwyaden Wyllt

Anas platyrhynchos

A common and widespread resident, abundant passage migrant and winter visitor

The Mallard is Britain's commonest duck species and is both a breeding resident and winter visitor. Its basic requirement is shallow water in the form of lakes, ponds, rivers, streams or estuarine coast. National breeding numbers have increased in recent years but wintering numbers have declined, probably owing to fewer continental birds coming so far west.

The 1st Gwent Atlas showed Mallard to have a widespread breeding distribution in the county, occurring in 66% of tetrads but with a few gaps in eastern areas, where open water is not common, and a surprising absence from most of the valleys in west. The 2nd Gwent Atlas shows that a significant colonisation of the western valleys has occurred in the intervening years, resulting in the current presence of the Mallard in 76% of Gwent's tetrads, with breeding recorded as *probable* or *confirmed* in 66%. This increase in breeding strength reflects the situation in

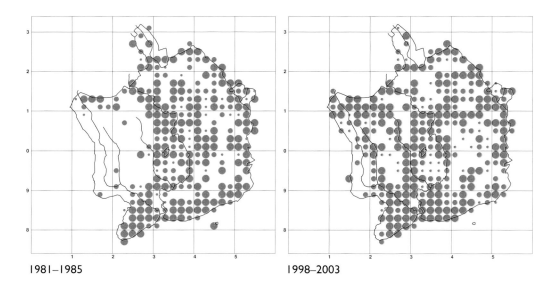

1981–1985   1998–2003

the UK as a whole where the trend shows an increase of 30% between the two Gwent Atlases, but contrasts with a decline in Wales of 37% in the last decade. Using the BBS-based method, the population for the county is estimated as 2,700–3,500 pairs. A figure of 5,500–7,500 was suggested by the 1st Gwent Atlas on the basis of data from two CBC plots, but these were unlikely to be representative and that figure was certainly too high.

The nest is usually placed in dense vegetation but cavities are also used. In Gwent there is a record of a nest in a hole in a tree, which was 4–5m above ground and had previously had Kestrels as its tenants, while on the Gwent Levels the brush that collects in the crowns of Pollarded willows has also been a common nesting site, again at heights of 4–5m. An unusual breeding record concerned two females incubating at a nest at Monmouth that contained 23 eggs, 22 of which hatched successfully. Predators of newly hatched ducklings in Gwent have been observed to include Carrion Crows, Magpies and Grey Herons.

Post-breeding flocks begin to gather during late May and June at locations that offer good feeding. Larger water bodies tend to be favoured as they also offer safety from predators during the period of the moult. In Gwent the largest post-breeding flocks occur on the estuarine coast and a June congregation of 400–600 has been usual at Peterstone during most of the last 30 years, though in 1984 it was as high as 760. As the males take no part in incubation of the eggs or care of the young, they usually predominate in the early post-breeding flocks, a fact that is well illustrated by the estimate of 90% males in a flock of 300 at Peterstone in late May 1984. Smaller numbers occur in May/June at other locations on the estuary and at inland waters, particularly Llandegfedd and Wentwood Reservoirs. Since its recent construction, the Newport Wetland Reserve has fast become a favoured haunt of post-breeding Mallard, with numbers in June 2003 exceeding 300.

Numbers at coastal locations usually decline in August but peak again in September, as autumn passage gets underway. September counts at Peterstone are normally in the range 500–800 but are higher in some years and the largest recorded is 1,150 in September 1983. Again the Newport Wetlands Reserve is becoming important for this species, and there were over 950 birds there in September 2005. Smaller autumn numbers, usually fewer than 200 but occasionally up 450, are also recorded less regularly at other locations on the estuary, particularly Goldcliff and Uskmouth. The autumn peak at Llandegfedd Reservoir exceeds 100 in some years and has on rare occasions reached this figure at Ynysyfro Reservoir also.

Many Mallard spend the winter in Gwent. Llandegfedd Reservoir was the main wintering site in the county during the late 1960s and throughout the 1970s. Peak counts were generally recorded in December or January and exceeded 1,000 birds in seven of the ten winters from 1969/70 to 1978/79, with a maximum of 1,700 in December 1976. During and after the 1980s, winter numbers at Llandegfedd declined steadily and in the last ten winters the peak counts have ranged from 105 to 300.

	1964/65– 1973/74	1974/75– 1983/84	1984/85– 1993/94	1994/95– 2003/04	**Highest**
Llandegfedd Reservoir	815	842	475	239	1,700 (1976/77)
Peterstone	–	394	444	443	890 (1981/82)

Table 8. Average winter peak counts of Mallard at Llandegfedd Reservoir and Peterstone

However, the decline of winter numbers at Llandegfedd coincided with some increase on the Severn Estuary at Peterstone, which thus became the most important wintering site in Gwent during the 1980s and 1990s. The peak count during these decades occurred generally in the period December–February and was usually in the range 400–600, but as high as 890 in January 1982 following very cold weather in December. The importance of this location was emphasised by the WeBS Low Tide Counts in 1998/99, which showed that the stretch of inter-tidal mud between Peterstone and St Brides held a greater concentration of feeding Mallard than any other in the Severn Estuary. In the four most recent winters (2001/02–04/05) winter maxima have been exceptionally low at Peterstone, averaging only around 270 in comparison with around 500 for the previous seven years. Factors influencing this decline may include a change in food availability stemming from the cessation during 2002 of local sewage discharge into the estuary, the development of the Newport Wetlands Reserve and the decline in national wintering numbers. Large winter flocks also occur in most years on the Severn Estuary to the east of Peterstone, and counts ranging from around 200 to 650 birds may be recorded irregularly from St Brides, Uskmouth, Goldcliff, Undy, Collister Pill or Mathern. Newport Wetland Reserve has begun to attract large numbers of wintering Mallard, with over 600 in winter 2002–03.

The average WeBS winter peak count, which approaches 1,400, can only be a conservative estimate of the county population, partly because it includes some incomplete counts, but perhaps more importantly because WeBS does not cover the great diversity of small inland sites used by this species.

Gwent Breeding Atlas data and population size

Gwent Atlas	Confirmed tetrads	Probable tetrads	Possible tetrads	Total tetrads	Change in total	Gwent population
1981–1985	153	73	29	255	–	–
1998–2003	174	86	38	298	+17%	2,700–3,500 pairs

National breeding data and conservation status

Estimated Welsh population	Welsh BBS trend 1994–2004	UK CBC/BBS trend 1985–2003	Welsh & UK conservation status
7,000–8,000 pairs*	−3%	+30%	Green-listed

*1994 Birds in Wales.

WeBS data 1999/2000–2003/04 and conservation status

Average annual peak count for Gwent coastal habitats	1,383*
Threshold number for importance in GB	3,520
Threshold number for international importance	20,000
GB average peak count	141,500
Wales and UK winter conservation status	Green-listed

*Probably too low as includes incomplete counts in one or more years.

National winter population trends (WeBS)

Wales long term	Wales medium term	UK long term	UK medium term
−13%	−27%	−19%	−19%

Long-term is the 25-year period 1977/78–2002/03; medium-term is the 10-year period 1993/94–2002/03.

(Northern) **Pintail**   *Anas acuta*
Hwyaden Lostfain

A fairly common winter visitor and passage migrant mostly to coastal sites. Winter numbers exceed the threshold for International Importance

The Pintail, perhaps our most elegant duck, winters widely in Britain. Although its numbers in Wales have fluctuated over the last 30 years, the overall trend for the period shows a very large increase (WeBS). It has long been an attractive member of Gwent's winter wildfowl population, and was described by the 1937 and 1963 *Birds of Monmouthshire* as a regular winter visitor to the county, occurring principally on the mudflats of the estuary and in numbers up to about 100.

In the years following 1963 there were regular winter records from the coastal sites of Caldicot Moor and Undy Pool, and also from the newly constructed Llandegfedd Reservoir, but numbers were never large and the highest count was 46 at Caldicot Moor in February 1966. Pintails ceased using the above coastal sites when they were drained during the late 1960s, and although they continued to use the adjacent estuarine shore at Undy, with counts of 40 and 30 in February 1971 and 1972, this site was also abandoned as a regular wintering site during the early 1970s. The pattern at Llandegfedd Reservoir was similar, with regular records during the 1960s being replaced by sporadic occurrence during the 1970s, though a count of 14 in January 1975 was the largest recorded for this water.

During the 1970s, the Peterstone shore became the only regular site for Pintail in the county, and this situation persisted through the 1980s. Records began with a flock of 100 in February 1972, which was the largest recorded in the county for many years, and it was followed by 60 in October of the same year. However, these counts proved atypical for the period, and over the subsequent 12 winters, peak counts were never higher than 18, and in some years as low as four. In the neighbouring county of South Glamorgan, a large wintering flock, usually exceeding 300 birds, became established at the Rhymney Estuary during the 1970s. In the early years this flock remained on the South Glamorgan stretch of the coast but in February 1988 some 195 birds, borne by the fast-flowing waters of a very high tide, came into Gwent waters off Sluice Farm. This visitation heralded a change in behaviour that has subsequently seen birds from the Rhymney flock make regular movements along the Gwent coast, reaching as far as St Brides, Goldcliff and Undy.

As a result of the mobility of the Rhymney flock, large numbers of Pintail are now recorded every winter at Peterstone, and in six of last ten winters the peak count has exceeded 200 with a maximum of 520 in January 2001. The growth of Pintail numbers at Peterstone is shown in Table 9.

Period	1974/75–1978/79	1979/80–1983/84	1984/85–1988/89	1989/90–1993/94	1994/95–1998/99	1999/00–2003/04	Highest
Peak count	10	14	60	122	254	347	520(2000/01)

Table 9. Five-year average winter peak counts of Pintail at Peterstone

Further east, at St Brides, the maximum count has been 200, and at Goldcliff Pill 300, while Nash Pools have often held large numbers in recent years, with as many as 122 in September 1997. The newly-constructed Newport Wetlands Reserve has also become a regular wintering site, with an average peak count of 258 during the five winters 1999/2000 to 2003/04. These latter birds appear to be additional to those previously wintering in the county, and have contributed to a raising of the mean WeBS peak count for Gwent to 682, compared with only 350 in the five preceding winters.

Owing to the mobility of the coastal flocks, it is difficult to ascertain whether increases/decreases at a particular site reflect migration or merely local movements. However, in the 1970s and 1980s, prior to the establishment of the big mobile flocks, the winter peak at Peterstone occurred in September–October in nine years, and in March in six years, indicating the passage of migrating birds. It is thought that birds arriving in Britain in early autumn may be Icelandic breeders, whereas the later arrivals comprise continental birds (WeBS, 1997/98). There is a single ringing recovery of relevance to Gwent: a bird ringed in Suffolk in October 1977 was recovered in January 1980 on the Gwent coast. This is consistent with the autumn arrival in eastern England of birds from the continent, followed by movement further west as the winter progresses.

Inland, Pintails have occurred at Llandegfedd Reservoir in twelve of the last twenty years, usually numbering fewer than ten but with a maximum of 15 in February 1996. They also occur sporadically at many other inland sites, including the Nedern Wetlands and various locations on the River Usk, and on reservoirs including Ynysyfro, Garnlydan and Wentwood.

Britain holds almost half of the north-west European winter population of Pintail, and the species is well represented in Wales, with the Dee Estuary and the Burry Inlet usually holding internationally important numbers of above 5,000 and 3,000 respectively. The Severn Estuary is also a site of international importance with an average peak count of around 850, most of which are found on the Gwent coast, which therefore qualifies in its own right as a site of international importance.

WeBS data 1999/2000–2003/04 and conservation status

Average annual peak count for Gwent	682
Threshold number for importance in GB	279
Threshold number for international importance	600
GB average peak count	24,050
Wales and UK winter conservation status	Amber-listed

Wales long term	Wales medium term	UK long term*	UK medium term*
+367%	+154%	+10%	+3%

*Long-term = the 25-year period 1977/78–2002/03; medium-term = the 10-year period 1993/94–2002/03.

Garganey
Hwyaden Addfain

Anas querquedula

A scarce passage migrant and very rare breeder

The Garganey is unique among British ducks in being a summer visitor that winters in Africa. Britain is at the north-west extremity of its summer range and numbers arriving have always been small and somewhat variable from year to year. However, they have shown an increasing trend during the last century, and in recent years the total pairs recorded by the Rare Breeding Birds Panel has averaged over 100.

Most of the breeding birds are found in southern and eastern England. Breeding in Wales is rare, and in Gwent there have been only two confirmed records, both at Magor Reserve, which is one of very few sites in the county that provides the Garganey's preferred habitat of extensive shallows with dense emergent vegetation for cover. In 1965 a female with young was observed on two occasions in June, and in 1969 a female with up to eight young was seen twice in mid May. It is possible that breeding occurred at Magor again in 1970 but, after that, thirty years were to elapse before breeding was again suspected in the county, this time in the newly constructed Newport Wetlands Reserve, where up to up to two birds were recorded throughout the spring and summer of 2000. Two years later, in 2002, breeding was again suspected. The Newport Wetlands Reserve provides extensive good habitat for Garganey, so we can expect further breeding records in future years.

The Garganey is a regular but scarce spring and autumn passage migrant to the county. Since 1964 it has been recorded in all except three years (1972, 1973 and 1977), with an average of 3–4 records per year, and 1–2 birds per record. The mean number of birds recorded per year is five. Figure 6 shows that spring passage occurs from late March through April and May, while autumn passage occurs during August and September. The earliest dates recorded are 7th and 14th March, but all other March records have been in the last week of the month. WeBS counts show that national numbers of passage Garganeys are very small, with an average peak count in recent years of around 65 birds and flock sizes rarely reaching double figures.

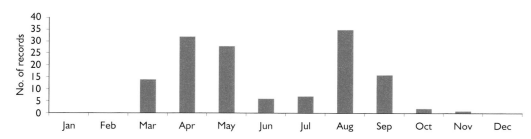

Figure 6. Monthly distribution of Garganey records 1964–2003

In Gwent, passage birds occur widely along the estuary shore but particularly at Peterstone, which accounts for over a third of all county records. The Peterstone birds are recorded most often on the shore, and to a lesser extent in the Gout and the nearby reens. Passage birds have also been regularly recorded at Newport Wetlands Reserve since 2000. The major inland passage location is Llandegfedd Reservoir, where there have been thirteen records over the last 40 years, while there have also been occasional records from the following sites: Magor Reserve (6), Nedern Wetlands (5), Greenmoor Pool (4), Garnlydan Reservoir (2), various locations along the River Usk (7), and single records from Ynysyfro Reservoir, Woodstock Pool, and Olway meadows.

(Northern) **Shoveler**
Hwyaden Lydanbig

Anas clypeata

A common winter visitor at two sites, where numbers exceed the threshold for National Importance. Also a scarce passage migrant and rare breeder

The Shoveler is mainly a winter visitor to Britain, with most birds originating in Scandinavia and northern Russia, and is an uncommon breeding bird mainly in the east of the country.

The 1963 *Birds of Monmouthshire* describes it as 'formerly uncommon but now seen regularly in numbers up to 200', but gives no clue as to where such flocks might have been seen. The Severn Estuary at Peterstone is a likely location, as this has been the county's most important site for Shoveler during most of the last 35 years, and the peak numbers recorded there regularly exceed the threshold for national importance. The WeBS low tide survey of winter 1998/99 concluded that feeding Shoveler on the lower Severn Estuary were largely confined to the Peterstone shore. Peterstone is one of only three nationally important sites for Shoveler in Wales, the others comprising the Burry Inlet and the RSPB Malltraeth Reserve.

Numbers begin to build-up at Peterstone in October and by December or January the winter flock usually comprises 100–150 birds: feeding in the shallows at the edge of the rising tide, this forms one of Gwent's more impressive ornithological sights. In most years the flock declines slowly during February and then more rapidly to only single figures by mid-March. The Peterstone flock has been counted regularly since the early 1970s and from around 1980 has shown a slow but steady increase. This is shown in Table 10, which indicates a 136% increase in winter maximum over three decades. This increase reflects the trend in Britain as a whole, which has seen winter numbers rise steadily since the mid 1960s, though some of the most recent increase at Peterstone may reflect local movements of birds from Newport Wetlands Reserve (see below). Maximum numbers of Shovelers in Britain are recorded in autumn (September–November) with many of these birds moving on to winter in France and Spain (WeBS Reports). The Peterstone flock, however, has almost always peaked in December or January, and is comprised, therefore, of true winter visitors rather than passage migrants. However, it is notable that in three very recent years it has peaked in November, and this may presage some change in status.

Period	1974/75– 1978/79	1979/80– 1983/84	1984/85– 1988/89	1989/90– 1993/94	1994/95– 1998/99	1999/00– 2003/04	Highest
Peak count	69	80	107	100	127	163	190 (1998/99)

Table 10. Five-year average winter peak counts of Shoveler at Peterstone

The only other traditional wintering site in Gwent has been the flood meadows of the Nedern Wetlands, but the suitability of this site varies from year to year according to whether significant water is present and for how long. Consequently, Shovelers have been recorded at the Nedern in only about half of the last 40 winters. The average peak winter count has been 18, but four counts have exceeded 30 and the highest record is of 65 in January 2001. The peak count at the Nedern has usually been in January or February. Small numbers have also been recorded in about 50% of winters at Llandegfedd Reservoir, but apart from an exceptional 20 birds in January 1997, numbers have generally been lower than six.

Since its completion, the Newport Wetlands Reserve has rapidly established itself as a second site of national importance for Shoveler in Gwent, with peak counts of 163 in January 2001, 215 in January 2002, 150 in February 2003, 122 in February 2004, and 184 in February 2005. Although this site is only about 6km from Peterstone, and some interchange between the two locations is known to occur, most of its birds seem to be new to the county, as they have contributed to a doubling of the average WeBS peak winter count for Gwent.

Small numbers, almost always fewer than ten birds, may be reported sporadically from a wide variety of locations, either in winter or during the passage periods of April–May and July–August. These have often included, in addition to the major sites mentioned above, flood meadows at Llangybi, various locations on the River Usk, Greenmoor Pool, Llanwern steelworks pools, Ynysyfro Reservoir, Magor Marsh and numerous coastal sites, and have occasionally included St Pierre Lake, Garnlydan Reservoir, Woodstock Pool, Dunlop Semtex Pond, Pen-y-Fan Pond and others.

The Shoveler is a very scarce breeder in Wales, with possibly up to 90 pairs in total (*2002 Birds in Wales*). The only definite record of breeding in Gwent was in 1966 when a duck with six young was seen at Undy Pool on 6th July. However the occurrence of adult pairs at suitable locations in late spring has often led to breeding being suspected. From 1989 to 1993 there were many records of pairs from Greenmoor Pool in late April and early May, and at the Nedern Wetlands in 1986, when a pair was present in early May, with only the male visible later in the month until the 26th. There were three pairs present throughout the summer in 2000 at the Newport Wetlands Reserve, and 3–4 pairs again in 2002. With several pairs summering regularly, it seems only a matter of time before breeding is proved at this site.

WeBS data 1999/2000–2003/04 and conservation status

Average annual peak count for Gwent coastal habitats	219
Threshold number for importance in GB	148
Threshold number for international importance	400
GB average peak count	11,190
Wales and UK winter conservation status	Amber-listed

National winter population trends (WeBS)

Wales long term	Wales medium term	UK long term*	UK medium term*
+50%	+147%	+46%	+9%

*Long-term = the 25-year period 1977/78–2002/03; medium-term = the 10-year period 1993/94–2002/03.

Red-crested Pochard
Hwyaden Gribgoch

Netta rufina

A scarce visitor of increasing occurrence

This attractive duck has a scattered feral breeding population in Britain, derived from birds that have escaped from captive collections. Recent expansion of the population in southern England has led to increasing occurrences in south-east Wales.

The first Gwent record, an adult male, was recorded at Ynysyfro Reservoir on 22nd December 1972. Since then there have been a further ten records, involving a total of 13 birds. These are listed in Table 11 and were female or immature birds except where indicated.

1986	5 September	Wentwood Reservoir	1	
1989	3 September	Goldcliff Pill	1	eclipse male
1990	19 August	Ynysyfro Reservoir	1	
1995	8 January	Llandegfedd Reservoir	1	
1995	8 July–3 August	Llandegfedd Reservoir	4	3 eclipse males and a female,
1995	7 August–14th October	Ynysyfro Reservoir	4	same birds as above
1997	21–23 July	Llandegfedd Reservoir	1	
1999	17 April	Sluice Farm	1	
2000	10 August–17 August	NWR	2	
2001	16 August–15 September	NWR	1	
2002	13 October–26 November	Ynysyfro Reservoir	1	

NWR = Newport Wetlands Reserve

Table 11. Red-crested Pochard records in Gwent from 1986

(Common) **Pochard** **Hwyaden Bengoch**

Aythya ferina

A fairly common winter visitor, but declining. A few remain in summer

The 1963 *Birds of Monmouthshire* describes the Pochard as the commonest diving duck in the county and cites a flock of 125 at Wentwood Reservoir in January 1961, presumably as the largest number recorded at that time. In more recent years Pochard numbers have declined and the Tufted Duck now has the distinction of being the most numerous diving duck in Gwent.

Undy Pool, a seasonally flooded area on the Caldicot Level, had traditionally been an important site for this species but recorded counts date only from the late 1960s when it was being drained. Significant counts are 200 in January 1966, 82 in March 1967 and 80 in December 1968.

Soon after its completion in 1963, Llandegfedd Reservoir became the most important wintering site for Pochards in Gwent, with an average winter peak count of 241 during the winters 1964/65 to 1973/74, and a maximum 400 in January 1968. In the early 1970s, numbers began to decline and Table 12 shows the average peak counts stabilising at around 150 during the late 1970s and 1980s, but sinking further to 57 during the most recent decade. A count of 205 in January 1996, occasioned by a hard-weather influx, is the only instance since winter 1990/91 in which the peak count has exceeded 100. This decline reflects a long-term decline across the UK, which has been more rapid in the last five years (WeBS 2003/4). The peak winter count at Llandegfedd Reservoir has typically occurred in the mid-winter months of December–February (in 33 out of 38 winters) and in November on only five occasions.

Period	1964/65– 1973/74	1974/75– 1983/84	1984/85– 1993/94	1994/95– 2003/04	Highest
Count	241	143	137	57	400 (1967/68 & 1985/86)

Table 12. Average winter peak counts of Pochard at Llandegfedd Reservoir

Pochards occur regularly at other inland waters, of which Ynysyfro Reservoir is probably the most important. The winter flock is very reliable at this water and the average winter maximum has exceeded 60 for each of last four decades. Flocks of 220 in 1972/73, 200 in 1973/74, 160 in 1995/96 and 100 in 1997/98 are the four largest peak counts. In contrast to Llandegfedd, the peak counts at Ynysyfro have almost all been during October–December (in 39 out of 43 years) suggesting that many of the birds that occur here are on passage.

Wentwood Reservoir regularly held a significant wintering Pochard flock in the years up to 1992/93, when winter peak counts were usually in range 30–60, with an average of 50 and a maximum of 100 in January 1968/69. Since 1992/93, however, the peak winter count has not exceeded 28, and has averaged a mere 13. Dunlop Semtex Pond had an average peak count of 45 during the winters 1982/83 to 1997/98, with a maximum of 100 in November 1991/92, but recent peak counts have not exceeded 18 and averaged only ten.

Small numbers, but occasionally up to around 50, are recorded irregularly from many other inland waters including Bryn Bach Lake, Dingestow Court Lake, St Pierre Lake, Pant yr Eos and Garnlydan Reservoirs, the Nedern Wetlands, Llanwern Steelworks and numerous locations on the River Usk. The reedbed pools at Uskmouth, now part of the Newport Wetlands Reserve, have held up 68 birds in winter 2001/02, 26 in 2002/03 and 31 in 2003/04.

During the 1960s and 1970s there had been sporadic records of small numbers on the coast, but in January 1979 an unprecedented flock of 260 appeared offshore at Peterstone. These birds appeared to have been displaced from inland waters by the prevailing freezing conditions, and Lisvane Reservoir, Cardiff, was a nearby and likely source. In the next four winters, numbers of Pochard at Peterstone were small, but in 1983/84 there was a flock of 130 and by 1985/86 this had increased to 375. For the next 14 years the peak count seldom fell below 300 and averaged about 350. Peak counts of 490 in 1988/89, 480 in 1991/92 and 720 during the cold winter of 1995/96 all exceeded the threshold for national importance at that time. The month of maximum flock size was almost always in the December–February period (in 19 years out of 22). The cessation of sewage discharge into the Severn in the year 2002 resulted in an immediate decline of this flock, with no significant records since.

Pochards are not known to have bred in Gwent (reports in the *2002 Birds in Wales* of breeding at Llandegfedd Reservoir are erroneous), but in many years a few spend all or part of the summer on Gwent waters, and this has become more frequent since the early 1980s. Largest numbers have been nine at Wentwood Reservoir in 1984, nine at Ynysyfro Reservoir in 1990 and ten at Llandegfedd Reservoir in 1996. Ones and twos have occurred frequently on other waters also. In summer 2000 a male Pochard mated with a Tufted Duck at Newport Wetland Reserve and five hybrid young were fledged. In subsequent years Pochards of both sexes have been recorded in summer at this site, with courtship display observed during 2003. It seems likely that breeding will occur at this site in the near future. In Wales as whole, the Pochard is a scarce breeder with totals of 28–52 pairs reported during 1997–99 (2002 *Birds in Wales*).

WeBS data 1999/2000–2003/04 and conservation status

Average annual peak count for Gwent	183*
Threshold number for importance in GB	595
Threshold number for international importance	3,500
GB average peak count	32,000
Wales and UK winter conservation status	Amber-listed

*Maxima from minor inland sites have been added to WeBS data. Inflated by inclusion of the last two large Peterstone counts of 1999/2000 and 2000/01; 70–80 would be a more realistic current mean.

National winter population trends (WeBS)

Wales long term	Wales medium term	UK long term	UK medium term
−39%	−43%	−19%	−15%

Long-term is the 25-year period 1977/78–2002/03; medium-term is the 10-year period 1993/94–2002/03.

Ring-necked Duck
Hwyaden Dorchog

Aythya collaris

A very rare vagrant. Frequent records in recent years are probably of the same individual

At least three individuals of the Ring-necked Duck, the American counterpart of the Tufted Duck, have occurred in the county. The first record was a male which was first observed at the Nedern Wetlands during 8th–10th and 20th–22nd May 2000. A bird that is presumed to be the same individual has since been recorded at various locations in the county as summarised in Table 13.

2001	21 January	Wentwood Reservoir
2001	29 January–25 February	Uskmouth reedbed pools
2001	17 March	Uskmouth reedbed pools
2001	14–22 May	Uskmouth reedbed pools
2001	16 October	Ynysyfro Reservoir
2001	18 October–1 May 2002	Uskmouth reedbed pools*
2002	17 March	Nedern Wetlands*
2002	5 April	Ynysyfro Reservoir*
2003	6 April	Uskmouth reedbed pools
2003	11 Oct–23 May 2004	Uskmouth reedbed pools
2004	25 March	Llanwern Steelworks
2005	3–18 February	Uskmouth reedbed pools
2005	31 May	Goldcliff lagoons
2006	30 April	Uskmouth reedbed pools

*During March–May 2002, sightings occurred at both the Uskmouth reedbed pools and the Goldcliff lagoons, and it is possible that two different birds were involved. The same bird (or birds) is thought to account for sightings at the Nedern Wetlands and Ynysyfro Reservoir during this period.

Table 13. Records of male Ring-necked Duck(s) in Gwent 2000–2006

The two remaining records both involve females that were present at the Goldcliff lagoons during 4th–17th October 2001 and on the sea at Sluice Farm on 1st May 2003; this latter bird having been seen the previous day at Lisvane Reservoir, South Glamorgan.

Ferruginous Duck
Hwyaden Lygadwen

Aythya nyroca

A very rare visitor

There are only three Gwent records of this mainly eastern European species. The first was of a juvenile present at Pant-yr-eos Reservoir during 28th October–3rd November 1973. Subsequently pairs have been seen on the River Usk at Llanfihangel Gobion on 27th December 1982 and at Wentwood Reservoir on 19th March 1987.

Tufted Duck
Hwyaden Gopog

Aythya fuligula

A widespread and fairly common winter visitor. Less common in summer and a scarce breeder

The Tufted Duck is a widespread breeding bird in most of Britain but is scarce in Wales, owing to the shortage of well vegetated lakes and sluggish reaches of rivers which constitute their preferred habitat (*1992 Birds in Wales*). It is also a well-distributed winter visitor from Iceland, Fennoscandia and north-eastern Europe.

Gwent possesses suitable breeding habitat for Tufted Ducks, and they have bred in the neighbouring county of Glamorgan since 1922, so it is somewhat surprising that the first record of successful breeding in the county was as recent as 1988. This occurred at Pen-y-fan Pond and followed a failed attempt at a reservoir near Brynmawr in 1984. In 1989, breeding occurred at the Hendre Lake, where two broods were raised and Pen-y-fan Pond again held a successful pair in 1990. Breeding has occurred in every year since 1990 and in 1998 at least nine pairs raised broods at a total of seven different sites. During the 2nd Gwent Atlas period, *confirmed* breeding was recorded at a total of seventeen sites, and *probable* breeding at eight others. Surprisingly, neither Hendre Lake nor Pen-y-fan Pond featured among the atlas breeding records. The expansion of the Tufted Duck as a breeding species in Gwent has been aided by the construction of new pools at golf courses and other sites, and also by the improvement and extension of the Uskmouth reedbed lagoons, and the construction of the Goldcliff saline lagoons at the Newport Wetland Reserve. This reserve and the golf course pools at Peterstone are now the most breeding important sites in the county, holding totals of 7–8 pairs in some recent years. Breeding did not occur in all occupied tetrads in every year of the Atlas, but some tetrads held several pairs; the total population for Gwent is estimated in the range of 20–30 pairs.

The 1963 *Birds of Monmouthshire* described the Tufted Duck as a regular but not very numerous winter visitor along the coast and to inland waters, and gave details of only one record: a flock of 50 seen offshore at Peterstone in February 1952. The completion of Llandegfedd Reservoir in 1963 stimulated the start of systematic wildfowl recording in the county, and the reservoir quickly developed into the most important site for the species in Gwent. The peak winter count during the ten winters 1968/69 to 1977/78 ranged from 100 to 180 (average c.130), occurring usually in November–January. However, the very next winter of 1978/79 saw the peak count drop to a mere 30 and, with the notable exception of 1985/86 when the peak count was 175, low

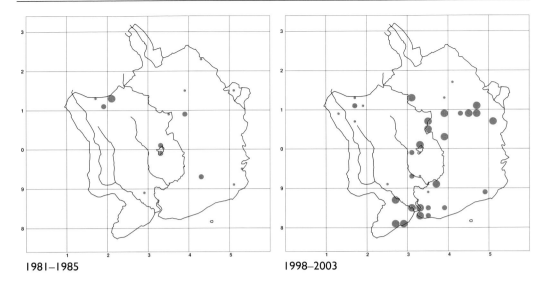

1981–1985   1998–2003

numbers became the norm, seldom reaching 50 and with an average maximum of only 33 during the most recent decade (1994/95 to 2003/04).

Published Tufted Duck records for Ynysyfro Reservoir began in winter 1969/70 when a maximum of 200 was reported in November. This number was described at the time as being much higher than previous years, so it is certain Ynysyfro had been a wintering site for this species prior to 1969, possibly for many years. During the first decade of recording, the average winter maximum at Ynysyfro was 96, but in contrast to Llandegfedd there was no subsequent decline and Ynysyfro is now the most important inland wintering site in the county, with maximum counts ranging between 46 and 118 (average 88) over the most recent decade. It is interesting that the month of maximum winter count at Ynysyfro has only twice been later than December and has generally (in 27 out of 33 winters) been in the September–November period, suggesting that significant numbers of autumn arrivals are passage birds that move on to other sites in mid-winter.

As with Pochards, the hard weather of 1978/79 coincided with the appearance in January of a very large flock on the estuary at Peterstone, which was estimated at 500 birds. This flock remained a regular feature over the subsequent 21 years, with winter maxima ranging from 280 in 1992/93 to 1,100 in 1985/86, and with an over-all mean maximum of 490. The month of maximum flock size was almost always (in 19 years out of 22) in the December-February period. As with Pochards, the cessation of sewage discharge into the Severn in 2002 resulted in an immediate decline of this flock, and maximum winter counts at Peterstone have been lower than ten in each of the four years 2001/02 to 2004/05. At its peak, the Peterstone flock represented about 2% of the peak winter population of Britain and was above the threshold for national importance.

There are a number of other sites in Gwent that regularly attract wintering Tufted Ducks, most notably Wentwood Reservoir, Dunlop-Semtex Pond, Pant-yr-eos Reservoir and Llanwern steelworks ponds, all of which can hold maxima of up to around 30 birds. In very recent years the Newport Wetlands Reserve has become an important wintering site with respective maxima of 84 (January); and 121, 83, 86 and 51 (all in March) in the five winters to 2004/05.

Jan	Feb	Mar	Apr	May	Jun	Jul	Aug	Sep	Oct	Nov	Dec
30	26	24	10	6	4	19	47	23	53	57	38

Table 14. Monthly maxima of Tufted Ducks at Ynysyfro Reservoir during 2003

In addition to providing winter habitat, Gwent's waters are used by Tufted Ducks as safe moulting sites in July and August. Dunlop Semtex Pond, and the Pant-yr-eos and Ynysfro Reservoirs are most notable in this respect, each typically holding between 20 and 30 birds during the late summer months. In some years

Llandegfedd and Wentwood Reservoirs, and the coast at Peterstone also hold moulting flocks, giving a total of between 100–150 moulting birds in recent years. In most years these birds show up statistically as a distinct peak in summer followed by a dip in numbers before wintering birds begin to arrive in October. This pattern is well illustrated by the monthly maxima at Ynysyfro Reservoir for 2003 (Table 14).

Gwent Breeding Atlas data and population size

Gwent Atlas	Confirmed tetrads	Probable tetrads	Possible tetrads	Total tetrads	Change in total	Gwent population
1981–1985	1	5	8	14	–	–
1998–2003	17	8	11	36	+157%	20–30 pairs

National breeding data and conservation status

Estimated Welsh population	Welsh BBS trend 1994–2003	UK CBC/BBS trend 1985–2003	Welsh & UK conservation status
c.100 pairs	Not available	+86%	Green-listed

WeBS data 1999/2000–2003/04 and conservation status

Average annual peak count for Gwent	486*
Threshold number for importance in GB	900
Threshold number for international importance	12,000
GB average peak count	57,150
Wales and UK winter conservation status	Amber-listed

*Maxima from minor inland sites have been added to WeBS data. Inflated by inclusion of the last large counts at Peterstone of 1999/2000 and 2000/01; c400 would be a more realistic current total.

National winter population trends (WeBS)

Wales long term	Wales medium term	UK long term	UK medium term
+15%	+21%	+24%	+18%

Long-term = the 25-year period 1977/78–2002/03; medium-term = the 10-year period 1993/94–2002/03.

(Greater) **Scaup**   *Aythya marila*
Hwyaden Benddu

A winter visitor in small to moderate numbers. An uncommon passage migrant in spring

The Scaup is a marine duck that is a winter visitor to British coastal waters, mainly in Scotland. On the coast of Wales it is widespread but nowhere very numerous and its numbers fluctuate greatly from year to year (2002 *Birds in Wales*).

In Gwent, detailed records date only from 1966 but Ingram and Salmon (1937 *Birds of Monmouthshire*) described it as a regular visitor to the Monmouthshire coast, sometimes in considerable numbers. Since 1966 it has been recorded almost annually and, although it is mostly a winter visitor, it has occurred in every month of the year. The majority of records are from the Severn Estuary, with largest numbers at Peterstone, and much smaller numbers at various locations higher up the estuary. Numbers recorded at Peterstone show very large annual fluctuations, which are illustrated in Figure 7.

Thus, between winters 1984/85 and 1996/97 maximum flock sizes in the range 30–76 were recorded on eight occasions, whereas before, during and after this period there have been many years when the winter total has not exceeded three birds. Considering all coastal records, most have involved fewer than five birds but flocks of ten or more have been recorded on 39 occasions. Winter 1996/97 was the last time a big flock of Scaup occurred at Peterstone and in the succeeding winters they have been very scarce. It is worth noting that the onset of this decline preceded the cessation of sewage discharge at the site in 2002 by five years and the two developments are not, there-fore, directly connected. Although Wales has very few wintering birds, WeBS trends show a strong increase over the last 25 years, in contrast to a decline in Britain as a whole.

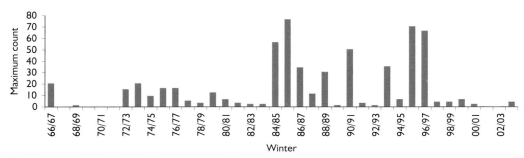

Figure 7. Maximum Greater Scaup counts at Peterstone

The graph of monthly totals over 30 years (Figure 8) shows that small numbers in the county increase during the autumn months, building to a peak in February and March that falls away rapidly during April. This pattern resembles that seen Northern Ireland rather than the typical pattern in Scotland, which shows a January peak (WeBS).

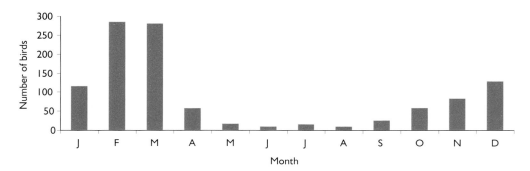

Figure 8. Monthly distribution of Greater Scaup in Gwent 1973–2004

Records for the May–August period are infrequent and always of very small numbers, seldom exceeding two birds, but have included extended stays: such as the male that was present at Peterstone during May–July 1973. The progress of this bird from breeding plumage to eclipse plumage was noted with interest by several regular observers.

Visits to inland waters are regular, having occurred in all months except August, but are usually of very small numbers. Of a total of about 60 inland records, two thirds have involved single birds and a further thirteen have involved two birds, while 12 birds at Wentwood Reservoir in November 1971 is the only inland record that reaches double figures. Half of the inland records have been at Llandegfedd Reservoir, with most of the remainder at Ynysyfro Reservoir and four at Wentwood Reservoir. Other inland records have included single birds on the Nedern Wetlands during winter 2000/01, at Pant-yr-Eos Reservoir in December 1975, on Pen-y-fan Pond in March–April 1992, and in winter on the Rivers Usk (at Llantrisant) and Wye (at Whitebrook).

WeBS data 1999/2000–2003/04 and conservation status

Average annual peak count for Gwent coastal habitats	1
Threshold number for importance in GB	76
Threshold number for international importance	3,100
GB average peak count	3,950*
Wales and UK winter conservation status	Amber-listed

*In common with other sea ducks, many are not detected by shore-based WeBS counts so the peak count greatly underestimates the actual population.

National winter population trends (WeBS)

Wales long term	Wales medium term	UK long term	UK medium term
+146%	+36%	−30%	0

Long-term = the 25-year period 1977/78–2002/03; medium-term = the 10-year period 1993/94–2002/03.

(Common) **Eider**   *Somateria mollissima*
Hwyaden Fwythblu

A scarce and irregular visitor, most often in spring

The Eider is a widespread resident around the UK coast, particularly from Cumbria and Northumberland northwards, and the British population in 2003 was estimated as 73,000 birds (WeBS). In Wales there are regular (but non-breeding) flocks at only two locations: the nearest of these to Gwent is the Burry Inlet (Glamorgan) where numbers have ranged from around 30 to over 200 in the last twenty years.

Historically the Eider was unknown in Gwent and the 1977 *Birds of Gwent* listed just one record, the first for the county, of a female seen offshore at Peterstone on 27th September 1972. There were no further records for the next 11 years but in 1984 there was a dramatic change in its status and records became almost annual, occurring widely along the coast in ten of the 14 years to 1997. Over two thirds of records have been in the spring passage period of March–May, but there have been occurrences in all months of the year. About half of all records have been of single birds but there have also been flocks of ten or more birds, the largest being 16 birds at Black Rock on 25th May 1985 and up to 10 birds remaining in the Peterstone-Sluice Farm area from mid-February to mid-September in 1989.

Following 1997 there was a gap of six years until a record of a flock of 13 seen at Peterstone and subsequently at Collister on 30th–31st May 2003.

Long-tailed Duck   *Clangula hyemalis*
Hwyaden Gynffon-hir

A scarce winter visitor and a passage migrant in very small numbers

The Long-tailed Duck is one species guaranteed to add excitement when it occurs on a Gwent wildfowl count, particularly if it is a male in its spectacular breeding plumage, but such occurrences are not at all common. Although an estimated 16,000 Long-tailed Ducks winter in British coastal waters, the great majority of them are found off northern Scotland and they are comparatively scarce elsewhere, including Wales, though concentrations of 10–30 can occur off the Meirionedd and Caernarfon coasts (WeBS; the 2002 *Birds in Wales*).

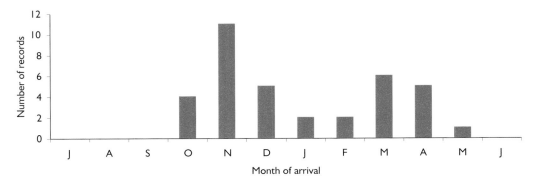

Figure 9. Long-tailed Duck records in Gwent

There have been approximately 34 records in Gwent, generally of three or fewer birds, but, exceptionally, five were seen at Collister Pill on 28th November 1988 and four at Llandegfedd Reservoir during 12th April–7th May 1989. Apart from a single bird at Pen-y-fan Pond on 30th November 1991, all records have been from reservoirs: usually Llandegfedd, and the coast: particularly at Peterstone.

Including the first county record, when two males were present at Wentwood Reservoir during 3rd–4th April 1965, Long-tailed Ducks have been recorded in 26 of the 40 years up to 2004, occurring at any time during the lengthy period of October (earliest date 12th) to May (latest date 23rd). Records divide fairly distinctly into short stays of between one day and 2–3 weeks, and long stays that have spanned all the winter months.

There have been several of the latter, principally at Llandegfedd Reservoir, where a female was present during 18th December–1st March 1966/67, up to four birds during 5th December–10th May 1988/89 and up to two during 16th November–2nd May 1991/92. Another long stay involved a female on the newly created Uskmouth reedbed lagoons at Newport Wetlands Reserve during 7th November–26th April 1999/00. The short-stay records are much more numerous and are concentrated in the passage months of November, March and April (Figure 9).

Common Scoter   *Melanitta nigra*
Môr-hwyaden Ddu

A regular non-breeding summer visitor in small to moderate numbers. Also a passage migrant and winter visitor, generally in small numbers

The Common Scoter is a marine duck that occurs widely around British coasts throughout the year. It is most numerous as a winter visitor but substantial numbers of non-breeders are present during spring and summer and these are joined by moulting birds from mid-summer onwards. Largest numbers occur in bays that provide shallow waters. Wales has three flocks of national importance in Colwyn Bay, Conwy Bay and Cardigan Bay, and one of international importance in Carmarthen Bay, which in many years holds over 20,000 birds (WeBS).

The muddy, estuarine waters of the Gwent coast would not be considered ideal habitat for this species but, despite that, the 1937 *Birds of Monmouthshire* described it as a regular visitor to the coast, sometimes in large flocks, adding that it was occasionally also recorded on inland waters. The first modern record dates from October 1963 when four were observed at Ynysyfro Reservoir, and the next was of two at Collister Pill in October 1966. Following this, Common Scoters have been recorded every year, but until regular and systematic coastal observation began in the early 1970s, records remained scarce, and the maximum number of birds recorded was only five. Figure 10 shows that 1974 began a period of 23 years during which flocks of ten or more birds, sometimes 20 or more, were recorded in most years. Since 1996 numbers have declined and the maximum flock size has exceeded eight on only one occasion. The relatively large flocks of 1974–96 occurred mostly on the coast and this is also true of records outside this period: of a county total of around 320 records since 1963, over three quarters have been coastal, occurring on almost any stretch but particularly at Peterstone, which accounts for 60% of them.

During 1974–1996, offshore records were likely to occur in any month of the year, and the seasonal pattern is effectively shown in Figure 11. There were numerous records of long stays, examples including up to 26 present during November–January 1974/75, up to 22 during April–May 1978 and up to 24 during June–July 1985.

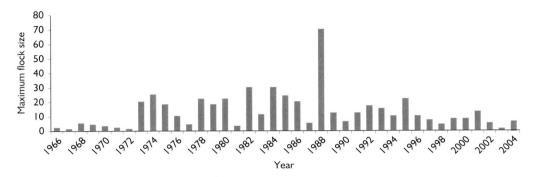

Figure 10. Annual maxima of Common Scoter in Gwent

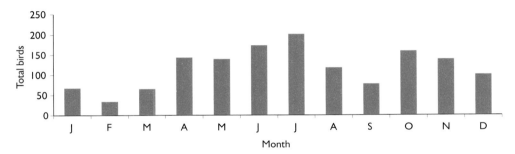

Figure 11. Monthly distribution of Common Scoters in Gwent 1973–2002

It was therefore possible in most years to talk of a passage peak during April–May, followed by a summer population of non-breeders that built-up from May to July and then declined during August and September. This was followed in turn by a second passage peak in October–November that gave way to a wintering population during December to March.

Numbers were often smaller than the examples given above. Half of all coastal records have involved no more than one or two birds but there have been thirty-seven records of ten or more and thirteen of 20 or more, and flocks of about 30 were seen off Collister Pill in October 1982 and June 1984. Exceptionally, a flock of 70 was displaced temporarily into Gwent waters following stormy weather on 5th January 1988.

Occurrences on inland waters have been many fewer than on the coast but still fairly regular: the two major locations have been Llandegfedd Reservoir and Ynysyfro Reservoir, which have had 62 and 11 records respectively. Flock sizes on inland waters have generally been much smaller than on the coast, with only five records of ten or more birds. Maxima at Llandegfedd have been 17 in July 1992 and 13 in July 2001, while the maximum at Ynysyfro was four in October 1963. Although inland records have occurred in all months, there has been a strong bias towards the summer, with over half during June–August. It is noteworthy that since the decline in coastal records, occurrences at Llandegfedd Reservoir have become more prominent and in four recent years (1992, 1997, 1999, 2001) the July flock has been the largest Gwent count for the year. Other inland records over the years have involved five birds at Wentwood Reservoir in June 1979, and single birds on Pant-yr-eos Reservoir, the River Wye at Redbrook and the River Usk at Llanllowel.

The decline in Gwent records since 1996 may be connected to the Sea Empress disaster, which occurred in that year and resulted in a dramatic drop in the Common Scoter population of Carmarthen Bay. However, although the Carmarthen Bay population had recovered to its former strength by the winter of 1998/99 (Pollitt *et al.*, 2003), this recovery had not yet been reflected in the numbers of birds visiting Gwent by 2006.

Velvet Scoter
Môr-hwyaden y Gogledd

Melanitta fusca

A rare passage migrant and winter visitor

The Velvet Scoter is a winter visitor to Britain from arctic and sub-arctic breeding grounds, occurring mostly on the east coast of Scotland where numbers can reach several thousand. It is a scarce visitor to Wales, though small numbers (usually up to about 15) occur regularly off the coasts of Caernarfon and Meirionedd. There are just twelve records for Gwent, mostly offshore (Table 15).

1938	29 December	Peterstone	1	immature female. Shot.
1969*	26 October	Goldcliff Point	1	flying down-channel
1969*	7 December	Peterstone	1	
1980	3 November	Peterstone	1	probably a male
1980	12 December	Peterstone	1	
1984	11 April	Uskmouth	4	
1984	11 November	St Brides	1	flew up the river Usk
1985	30 October	Peterstone	4	
1991	22 November	Llandegfedd Reservoir	1	
1992	17–18 April	Peterstone	1	probably a male, flew down-channel on both days
2000	28 October	Peterstone	1	flying down-channel
2004	11 October	Llandegfedd Reservoir	1	female

* Erroneously dated as 1970 in the 1977 *Birds of Gwent*.

Table 15. Records of Velvet Scoters in Gwent

(Common) **Goldeneye**
Hwyaden Lygadaur

Bucephala clangula

An uncommon winter visitor which has decreased in recent years

Goldeneyes are mainly winter visitors to the UK and are distributed widely on both salt and fresh water. In Wales the largest concentrations are found at locations on the northern coast but there are no sites where numbers reach the threshold for national importance (WeBS).

Gwent records begin with the 1963 *Birds of Monmouthshire*, which cites a number of winter records of up to three birds at a variety of locations, including the River Usk, the Severn Estuary and Ynysyfro Reservoir. The advent, in the mid-1960s, of regular recording on the River Usk and at the newly completed Llandegfedd Reservoir revealed the Goldeneye to be a regular winter visitor in moderate numbers.

Arrival is generally in November but peak numbers are not normally recorded until January or February and, in common with the national situation, there is sometimes a second peak in March, which may represent the passage of a different population. First arrivals are sometimes in October, with occasional earlier records such as two flying past Goldcliff on 27th August 1968, four at Llandegfedd Reservoir on 28th August 1991, and, most exceptionally, one at Pen-y-fan Pond on 29th June 2002. Last records often stretch into April: the latest recorded was on April 14th.

During the 1970s and 1980s the major wintering site in Gwent was the River Usk, from where it enters the county near Gilwern downstream to Caerleon. Over such a long stretch of river (over 60km) observation was understandably fragmented, with regular counts coming mostly from Caerleon to Llanhennock, Pwll-y-Llwnch to Llanbadoc, Pant-y-Goitre to The Bryn, and Abergavenny to Llanwenarth. Totals from these stretches were commonly in excess of 30, and sometimes over 50 during January and February so, allowing for uncounted stretches, the total wintering population on the Gwent Usk was probably over 70 birds in many years. During these years the mid-winter population on Llandegfedd Reservoir was commonly in the range 4–10, but counts were sometimes increased to around 20–30 birds, usually by arrivals at dusk, which almost certainly represented birds from the River Usk coming in to roost.

Beginning in 1988, a decline was apparent, and apart from a count of 22 at Llanllowel in January 1990, numbers on the River Usk have seldom reached double figures since then, and have never exceeded 16 birds. The decline on the Usk was reflected in lower counts at Llandegfedd Reservoir, and although there were maxima of 30 in 1991 and 25 in 1997, numbers have otherwise not exceeded 12 in the last decade. A count of ten at Llandegfedd Reservoir in January 2004 was the first count to exceed two since 1998. WeBS counts show that the winter Goldeneye population has been declining in Britain since 1996/97, but the decline in Gwent preceded this by about ten years, and shows a similarity to the trend observed in Northern Ireland. Goldeneye numbers at other sites in Wales have not shown any obvious recent decline (2002 *Birds in Wales*), and the ten-year trend is only slightly negative.

Since 1999, Goldeneyes have occurred at the Newport Wetlands Reserve and the peak counts here of 12 in winter 2002/03, nine in winter 2003/04 and ten in 2004/05 suggest this site may become Gwent's main wintering site in the future. Thirteen birds at nearby Nash Pools in January 2003 are likely to have included the same birds.

Apart from the sites discussed above, Goldeneyes occur regularly at Ynysyfro Reservoir, usually in numbers fewer than five but there were nine in winter 1985/86 and seven in 1970/71. They also turn up sporadically at most other inland waters including (maxima in brackets) Dunlop Semtex Pond (4), Pant-yr-eos Reservoir (3), Dingestow Court Lake (3), Beaufort Ponds (2) and Wentwood Reservoir (2). Small numbers (up to 4) also occur offshore at Peterstone, St Brides, Goldcliff and other coastal locations in many years.

WeBS data 1999/2000–2003/04 and conservation status

Average annual peak count for Gwent	17*
Threshold number for importance in GB	249
Threshold number for international importance	4,000
GB average peak count	14,000
Wales and UK winter conservation status	Amber-listed

*Includes non-WeBS counts.

National winter population trends (WeBS)

Wales long term	Wales medium term	UK long term*	UK medium term*
+47%	−4%	+36%	−12%

*Long-term = the 25-year period 1977/78–2002/03; medium-term = the 10-year period 1993/94–2002/03.

Smew
Lleian Wen

Mergus albellus

A very scarce winter visitor

The Smew comes to Britain from breeding grounds northern Scandinavia and is found mostly in East Anglia and south-east England. Total numbers are small and peak counts have been around 250 in recent winters (WeBS). It is a scarce visitor to Wales, and most likely to occur when driven west by severe weather.

From an analysis of records in Gwent, it is considered that there have been approximately 26 records of 38 individuals, although it is possible that there may have been some duplication of birds recorded during the winters of 1978/79 and 1986/87, following influxes into Britain during particularly severe weather.

The first records for the county were at Llandegfedd Reservoir in 1970, a female on 5th January, a male on 8th February, and a pair on 15th February. Since then it has been recorded in 14 out of 34 winters, but sometimes with gaps of several years: the record in November 2004 follows a gap of five winters when there were none. The monthly distribution of all records is summarised in Table 16. Records are limited to November–March period and earliest and latest dates are 15th November and 22nd March respectively.

Jul	Aug	Sep	Oct	Nov	Dec	Jan	Feb	Mar	Apr	May	Jun
0	0	0	0	3 (3)	6 (7)	9 (16)	6 (9)	2 (3)	0	0	0

Number of records based on month of arrival; number of birds involved in brackets.

Table 16. Monthly distribution of Smew records in Gwent

Llandegfedd Reservoir has been the main location, with ten records involving a total of at least 15 birds, while stretches of the River Usk between Llanvihangel Gobion and Llanllowel have hosted four records involving ten birds. Other locations (number of records in brackets) are Peterstone (4), Dunlop Semtex Pond, Brynmawr (3), Wentwood Reservoir (2), Garnlydan Reservoir (1) and Ynysyfro Reservoir (1). The peak winter for records was 1978/79 when severe weather brought a minimum of six (two males and four females) and possibly as many as 16 birds into the county. There are only two March records, of two at Llandegfedd Reservoir on 21st March 1979 and one on a reen at Sluice Farm during 1st–22nd March 1987. The three records at Dunlop Semtex Pond involved a female, almost certainly the same returning individual, during most of November–December 1980, 8th December 1982 and 15th November 1983.

Red-breasted Merganser *Mergus serrator*
Hwyaden Frongoch

A very scarce winter visitor and passage migrant

Red-breasted Mergansers breed in both freshwater and marine habitats in northern and western parts of the UK. In winter, the resident population is joined by birds from Iceland and central Europe and the species is then much more widely distributed around British coasts, with an estimated population of around 10,000 birds (Winter Atlas; *Migration Atlas*). The Burry Inlet (Glamorgan) is the nearest regular wintering site to Gwent and typically hosts around 20–30 birds.

The earliest documented record for Gwent is of two birds in the mouth of the River Usk in 1920, one of which was shot (1937 *Birds of Monmouthshire*). There were no further records until 1968, when a female was recorded at Llandegfedd Reservoir on 17th November, and a male was seen on both 1st and 15th December. Subsequent to this, records became much more frequent, and in the 1970s there were approximately 29 records involving a total of some 57 birds. Llandegfedd Reservoir was the major location during this period and hosted a total of 15 records during 1968–78. Most records have involved fewer than four birds, although five were seen at Llandegfedd Reservoir on 21st January 1974 and six at Collister Pill on 16th April 1976. Since 1977, sightings of Red-breasted Mergansers have become much scarcer in Gwent and the main location has changed from Llandegfedd Reservoir to sites along the Severn Estuary where there has been a total of 20 records in this period.

All modern Gwent records are summarised in Table 17, which shows that records occur more frequently in the passage periods of spring and autumn than in the mid-winter months.

	Jan	Feb	Mar	Apr	May	Jun	Jul	Aug	Sep	Oct	Nov	Dec	Totals
1965–69	–	–	–	–	1	–	–	–	–	–	2	2	5
1970–74	2	2	2	4	1	–	–	–	–	3	1	1	16
1975–79	1	–	2	3	3	–	–	–	2	1	1	–	13
1980–84	2	–	–	2	–	–	–	–	–	1	1	–	6
1985–89	–	–	–	1	–	–	–	–	–	–	–	1	2
1990–94	–	–	2	1	–	–	–	–	–	4	–	1	8
1995–99	–	2	2	–	–	–	–	–	–	–	2	–	6
2000–04	1	–	–	1	–	–	–	–	–	–	–	–	2
2005	–	–	–	1	–	–	–	–	–	–	–	1	2
Totals	6	4	8	13	5	–	–	–	2	9	7	6	59

Table 17. Temporal distribution of Red-breasted Merganser records in Gwent

Goosander
Hwyaden Ddanheddog

Mergus merganser

An uncommon winter visitor and rare breeder

This striking sawbill duck has colonised Britain since 1871, spreading down from the north. Its numbers are swollen in winter by the arrival of birds from Fennoscandia and northern Russia. It was unknown in Gwent as a breeding bird until 1975 when a family party was seen on the River Usk near Chain Bridge. This was then the second breeding record for Wales (the first being in 1970) and the most southerly in Britain: since then they have bred in Devon. Breeding took place again in 1976 and 1977 at the same location but was not proven again until 1985 and 1986, when females with small young were seen above Abergavenny and at Gobion on the River Usk.

There has been a marked increase in breeding numbers between the 1st and 2nd Gwent Atlases with the number of ocupied tetrads almost tripling. During the 2nd Atlas there were five *confirmed* breeding records on the River Usk, most being between Abergavenny and Usk. However, Goosanders now occur also on the River Monnow where there was a breeding record in June 2002. Other birds were seen lower down the Monnow but as yet there has been no other breeding record. Birds were seen too, in 2002, on the Rhymney River. Although breeding occurs on the River Wye in Herefordshire there has been no proven breeding on this river in Gwent. The *possible* and *probable* records may refer to late wintering birds from further north.

In Wales an estimated 100 pairs bred on 14 rivers by 1985, and by 1991 this had risen to 150 pairs. The current figure is unknown but is likely to be in excess of 200 pairs. The Gwent figure is likely to be about ten pairs, assuming that some breeding attempts failed or that some families were overlooked during the atlas fieldwork.

It is interesting to reflect that prior to about 1965 the Goosander was an irregular visitor to Gwent with only eight records between 1896 and 1945. Wintering birds began to be recorded regularly in the late 1960s and numbers built during the 1970s, with most records from the River Usk and Llandegfedd Reservoir in the November–March period. Passage or wintering birds were, however, seen at the reservoir as late as 18th May in 1983. The River Usk may support up to 50 birds during the day, while Llandegfedd Reservoir has been an important roost site perhaps largely made up of birds that feed on the Usk (Table 18).

The River Wye has only become of importance in recent years. In February 1986 the first wintering birds (four) were noted on the river but in the last decade up to 28 have been regularly recorded in winter between The Biblins and Tintern. Birds also occur on tributaries such as the Afon Llwyd (three in December 1988) and River Monnow (one at Maypole in February 1996).

	1980/81–1984/85	1985/86–1989/90	1990/91–1994/95	1995/96–1999/00	2000/01–2004/05	Maximum
Llandegfedd Reservoir	26	45	43	22	12	97 (1986/87)
Bryn Bach	–	–	24	15	20	41 (2001/02)
Garnlydan Reservoir	–	–	27	24	7	30 (1992/93)

Most maxima occurred during December–February.

Table 18. Five-year means of maximum count of Goosanders at three sites in Gwent in the winter months since the winter of 1980/81

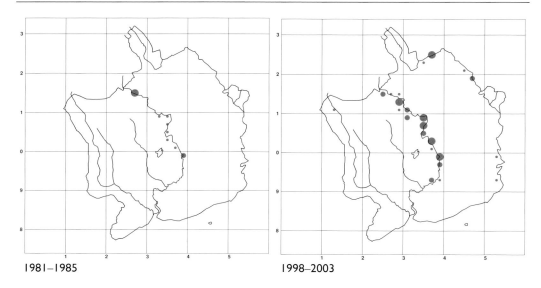

1981–1985   1998–2003

Starting in winter 1980/81, small flocks began to occur sporadically at Garnlydan Reservoir, but from 1991/92, records became more regular and numbers increased greatly (maximum flock size 41 in winter 2001/02). Similar numbers began to visit the lake at Bryn Bach Park at this time, and both waters have now become important wintering locations in the county Table 18). The numbers of birds recorded at Garnlydan and Brynbach are usually similar, and as they are no more than 5km apart, it is very likely that the Goosanders at these two waters are the same birds.

Small numbers also occur on smaller waters: for example, Ynysyfro Reservoir has held between one and four Goosanders at various times in most winters since 1969/70. Birds have turned up more occasionally on other lakes or reservoirs, which include (maximum count in brackets): Dunlop Semtex Pond (16), Cwmtillery Lakes (8), Machine Ponds (18), Beaufort Ponds (20), Cwmbran boating lake (18) and many others. There are also regular records of small numbers passing along the coast.

Numbers of Goosanders wintering in Britain have declined steeply since the mid-1990s, possibly as a result of the milder winters during this period. The short-term WeBS trend for Wales is strongly negative, and this has been reflected in declining numbers at the main Gwent sites.

Gwent Breeding Atlas data and population size

Gwent Atlas	Confirmed tetrads	Probable tetrads	Possible tetrads	Total tetrads	Change in total	Gwent population
1981–1985	1	1	6	8	–	–
1998–2003	6	7	10	23	+188%	c.10 pairs

National winter population trends (WeBS)

Wales long term	Wales short term	UK long term	UK short term
+67%	−36%	+61%	−33%

Long-term = the 25-year period 1977/78–2002/03; medium-term = the 5-year period 1998/99–2002/03.

Ruddy Duck
Hwyaden Goch

Oxyura jamaicensis

A rare visitor, mainly in winter. Breeds at one location

The Ruddy Duck is an American species that has colonised Britain following its escape from captive collections. It first bred in Wales in 1976, and in 1990 the breeding population was estimated at about 70 pairs, mostly in the north and with over half in Anglesey (2002 *Birds in Wales*).

The first record for Gwent was a single female at Wentwood Reservoir in December 1977. The next was in January 1979 when severe weather brought a flock of four to Llandegfedd Reservoir; this had grown to six by the time of the last sighting on 4th March. There were further records at Llandegfedd Reservoir of two in January 1980, seven in December 1981 and up to two during January and February 1982. The first records for Ynysyfro Reservoir occurred in this period and comprised single birds in January–February 1980 and December 1981. There followed a period of two winters (1982/83 and 1983/84) when there were no records in the county.

Records began again with two at Llandegfedd Reservoir in October 1984, and since then the species has been recorded almost annually at this site, occasionally during October–December, but mostly during January–March, with usually only one or two birds present, but there were up to 13 in 1986, six in 1996 and 12 in January 1997: probably a cold-weather influx. There have also been two records in each of the months of April, June, July and August, always of one or two birds apart from seven on 28th April 1997.

The only other regular site has been Ynysyfro Reservoir, where there have been records in twelve winters since 1980, almost all of single birds, but there were five in November 1995 and three in December 1996. A single bird during July–August 1994 is the only summer occurrence at this site.

Apart from the above sites, there have been four records of up to three birds at Peterstone (in the Gout or on the trout lake), and single birds at Dunlop Semtex Pond, Dingestow Court Lake, Nash Pools, the Nedern Wetlands, Pant-yr-eos Reservoir and Bryn Bach Park Lake.

Since 2000, Ruddy Ducks have been recorded regularly in the reedbed lagoons at Newport Wetlands Reserve and are currently present in all months of the year, with a maximum count of 15 in July 2003. Successful breeding has occurred in each of the years 2001–2005, with single broods produced in the first two years, two broods in 2003 and probably three in 2004.

The Ruddy Duck, though an attractive addition to our avifauna, is a potential conservation disaster, as it has spread to continental Europe and threatens the extinction of its Old World equivalent, the White-headed Duck *Oxyura leucocephala*. A national programme for its extermination in Britain was trialled in winters 1999/00 and 2000/01, and has been followed by an ongoing cull (WeBS Reports 1997/98 to 2003/04).

Red Grouse (Willow Ptarmigan)
Grugiar

Lagopus lagopus scotia

An uncommon and declining resident on heather uplands

The Red Grouse, a subspecies of the Willow Ptarmigan, is a bird of open moorland, feeding almost exclusively on a diet of heather. Its distribution is therefore restricted to moorland that is heather dominated. Gwent has the distinction of possessing the most southerly indigenous grouse moor in the British Isles – the grouse on Dartmoor and Exmoor originate from introductions in the early 20th century. The species is confined to the hills of the north and west of the county where dwarf shrub heath (i.e. *Calluna/Erica*) is present.

Earliest records are of shoots noted in estate game books. Pontypool Park Estate: 1882, 25 brace taken over four days at Mynydd Maen; and 1898, one brace taken on 21st September at Maesderwen. Llanover Estate: 1905, 22 brace taken at Abercarn on 14th August; 1906, 26 brace taken at Abercarn between 13th August and 1st October; 1905, ten brace taken at Manmoel on 21st August; 1907, 26 brace taken at Abercarn on 26/27th August. Subsequent shoots at the estate accounted for 14 brace in 1908, 18 brace in 1909 and 25 brace in 1910. In the late 19th century the grouse on the Blaenavon moors were preserved as game, the population then being probably well over 1,000 birds.

In 1937 Ingram and Salmon noted in the *Birds of Monmouthshire* that the species was resident and that it bred on moors that were preserved on the hills, and that it did so in fair numbers on the Black Mountains. They also noted that it appeared to have deserted the Sugar Loaf grouse moor since the area was opened to the public: this moor had accounted for 14–20 brace on 12th August during the first quarter of the 20th century. Blaenavon Grouse Moors extended over 9,000 acres at that time and had been preserved as such for over 100 years by the then Marquis of Abergavenny. Seasonal bag averages were 205 brace, the record being 417 brace in 1905, and the best day, 12th August, 1903, when 11 guns accounted for 821/2 brace. Pairs were noted to wander off to the surrounding hills to breed and had occasionally been seen as far south as Twm Barlwm.

The 1963 *Birds of Monmouthshire* reported that since the war and subsequent nationalisation of the coal industry and open cast mining, Blaenavon Grouse Moor was reduced to a very low level of population: '*probably not more than a dozen pairs are resident and these are in constant peril from predators and un-controlled trigger-happy urban youth from neighbouring towns*'. The opinion was expressed that even if keepering and vermin control could be achieved, it was doubtful if the moor could be repopulated without birds being introduced from elsewhere.

Birds of Gwent (1977) reported the species as being widespread and regularly seen on the high ground in the north-west, though usually only in small numbers. Records at that time suggested that Coity Mountain was one of the main strongholds of the species (35 birds were recorded there in 1970) with other regular sightings, usually only in twos and threes and only occasionally over ten, reported from most of the other highland areas.

Breeding areas included surrounding areas around Garnlydan Reservoir, Trefil Quarries and in the Black Mountains. Records from the 1st Gwent Atlas referred to pairs in suitable habitat, with seven of the 14 tetrads with *confirmed* records involving sightings of chicks. Although the population size was estimated at this time, it was subsequently revised downwards. Some 67–74 pairs were estimated by assessing the extent of suitable habitat, and field surveys over selected upland areas to record bird density. This arrived at an overall figure of 1.5 pairs/km^2 – 6 pairs per tetrad (Lewis, 1990).

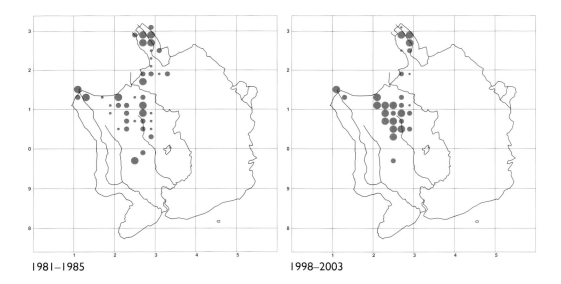

1981–1985   1998–2003

The distribution of the species in Gwent has shown a decline of 29% between Gwent Atlases from being present in 41 tetrads during 1981–85 to 29 tetrads during 1998–2003.

Numbers are currently declining throughout the British Isles. Although the BBS shows no overall trend since 1994, shooting bags have revealed long-term declines, apparently driven by loss of habitat caused by lack of management, and a loss of moorland owing to agricultural improvements and afforestation, increased predation, and an increasing incidence of viral disease (Hudson, 1992; Newton, 2004). Red Grouse abundance varies in cycles, with periods that vary regionally, that are linked to the dynamics of infection by a nematode parasite (Dobson & Hudson, 1992; 1988–91 National Atlas). All population data should therefore be interpreted in this context. The species is Red-listed in Wales as it has declined severely between 1800 and 1994. Its decline has coincided with a decline in sporting interests in Wales, with subsequent heavy stocking of moors by sheep resulting in loss of grouse habitat. No information is available on status or trends of the Welsh population outside nature reserves. However, the range of the Red Grouse has declined from 99 to 73 10-km squares between 1968–72 and 1988–91 (National Atlases).

Further evidence of a decline in recent years comes from casual records reported in Gwent Bird Reports. In the early 1980s good numbers were found in the autumn on Coity Mountain/Waen Wen: 19 on 25th September; 14 brace were shot during the season. However, recent autumn visits there have revealed a maximum of only two pairs and no coveys. In arriving at a current population estimate for Gwent, the area of suitable habitat (dwarf shrub heath) found in the county was first assessed. Lewis (1990) calculated this as being some 47km^2 in 1990, but since then there has been further erosion of heather quality on the moors. By applying local knowledge of the current state of the moors to the 1990 position, a new estimate of some 40km^2 is arrived at. This is comparable to information derived from the BTO's Land Habitat Map (2000). Lewis considered bird density in Gwent to be some 1.5 pairs/km^2 and by applying this to the habitat area we arrive at a possible current Gwent population of Red Grouse of some 60 pairs.

Gwent Breeding Atlas data and population size

Gwent Atlas	Confirmed tetrads	Probable tetrads	Possible tetrads	Total tetrads	Change in total	Gwent population
1981–1985	11	18	12	41	–	–
1998–2003	15	10	4	29	−29%	60 pairs

National breeding data and conservation status

Estimated Welsh population	Welsh trend	UK BBS trend 1994–2005	Welsh & (UK) conservation status
5,000	Not available	−15%	Red (Amber)-listed

Black Grouse
Grugiar Ddu

Tetrao tetrix

A former resident species, not recorded since 1977

Black Grouse undoubtedly bred in Gwent in former times but documented records are scarce and fragmentary. The 1963 *Birds of Monmouthshire* records that they were formerly described as 'common on the hills in the 19th century' and they were reported to have bred on the Monmouthshire side of the Sugar Loaf in 1926. The only record for the Blaenavon moors was of a 'greyhen' shot on the Blorenge in the 1870s but birds were also reported as far south as Twmbarlwm, although there are no documented records to support this. In the middle of the 20th century it was reported as 'still occasionally seen in the Black Mountains and the Llanthony Valley, and 6 blackcocks seen at the latter location on 6th February 1952'.

In more recent times, single blackcocks were noted as follows: on the Blorenge during the winter of 1971/72 and again on 15th September 1972, displaying at Trefil quarries on 7th April 1974, along the ridge south of Llanthony Abbey on 2nd May 1974; and on the Gaer mountain, Fforest Coalpit during September 1977.

The loss of the Black Grouse from Gwent reflects the great contraction of its range in Britain that has been occurring for many years and still continues today.

Red-legged Partridge
Petrisen Goesgoch

Alectoris rufa

An uncommon resident. The population is augmented by releases

This attractively marked game bird was first introduced into Britain in the 18th century, and after repeated introductions, not all of them successful, it became established as a self-sustaining breeding population that probably reached its maximum during the 1930s. It has a preference for arable over pastureland and an aversion to high rainfall, so its strongholds have always been in south and east England, with the Welsh population limited mainly to Anglesey and the border counties (1988–91 National Atlas).

The species was first recorded in Gwent in 1921 when five were seen (one of which was shot) at Walnut Tree Farm, Llandegfedd. In the 1937 *Birds of Monmouthshire*, the Red-legged Partridge was described as an introduced species that was uncommon but 'occasionally observed'. It had been recorded at Penrose, Llandewi, Rhyd-derech, Malpas Court, Ponthir and Abergavenny. The 1963 *Birds of Monmouthshire* considered it to be very uncommon and listed only two further records for the county, at Llandegfedd in 1946 and at Llanarth in 1962, while the 1977 *Birds of Gwent* described it as irregularly recorded with one definite breeding record at Ponthir in 1973 and two other instances of possible breeding: near Bassaleg and near Magor in 1971. In addition, there were fourteen other records up until 1975.

It is possible that at this time its abundance was underestimated, as only a few years later it was recorded in 82 tetrads of the 1st Gwent Atlas, with *probable* or *confirmed* breeding in 54 of these. The occupied tetrads were almost all in the eastern two-thirds of the county, with just a few outliers in the western valleys and the Wentlooge Level. There were numerous records in 1986, the year after atlas recording work had finished, including three in new tetrads in the south of the county, and it thus appeared that the species was continuing to increase its range. However, in 1989 very few records were received and this scarcity has remained the case in most subsequent years to the present time. Unsurprisingly, therefore, the 2nd Gwent Atlas has shown a picture of severe decline in which the number of occupied tetrads has decreased by 46% and the number with *confirmed*

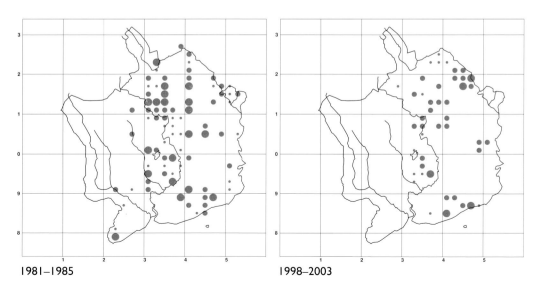

1981–1985

1998–2003

breeding by 74%. This appears to reflect a national decline in which the UK population has dropped by 37% over the same period. The estimate for the Gwent population during the 2nd Gwent Atlas period, based on sample tetrads, is only 40–65 pairs.

Assessment of the status of Red-legged Partridge in Gwent, as elsewhere in the country, is complicated by the continued release of birds for sporting purposes. The most recent that the authors are aware of concerns the release of over 100 at Dingestow in 2003. Thus, although the number of records in any year is small, the sizes of the groups seen are often disproportionately large, and probably refer to flocks of recently released birds. With that proviso in mind, the largest groups recorded in county comprise 29 at Llanarth in 1984, 22 at Llanhennock in autumn 1989, 30 at Ysgyryd Fawr in December 1992, and 34 at West Pill in October 2003.

Gwent Breeding Atlas data and population size

Gwent Atlas	Confirmed tetrads	Probable tetrads	Possible tetrads	Total tetrads	Change in total	Gwent population
1981–1985	19	35	28	82	–	–
1998–2003	5	26	13	44	−46%	40–65 pairs

Grey Partridge
Petrisen

Perdix perdix

An uncommon resident that has shown a dramatic decline over recent years

The Grey Partridge occurs in family coveys during the greater part of the year where historically it was found predominantly in hedgerows, path sides and other 'edge' areas of cultivated land where weed seeds form its staple diet. The earliest records in the county are found in estate game books going back to the last quarter of the 19th century. Some significant bags were shot from this time through to the start of the 20th century (Table 19). It is not clear to what extent wild birds were supplemented with releases during this period but from the size of some of the bags it is likely that some of the birds were releases.

The 1937 *Birds of Monmouthshire* recorded that the Grey Partridge was resident and breeding in fair numbers in suitable localities, but noted that the county was 'not good Partridge country' and that the species was decreasing in some districts. The 1963 *Birds of Monmouthshire* made the point that the species was 'not preserved to any extent'. Presumably the estate releases that must have accounted for the good game bags in the late 19th and early 20th centuries were no longer being undertaken, although an autumn population of 100+ birds was reported from the Llanover Estate in 1967, which suggests that a release was still being undertaken in at least this area. At the time of the 1977 *Birds of Gwent* the species was recorded regularly throughout most of the county with coveys of up to 20 seen, especially in the autumn months. Strongholds were the coastal areas and the Usk Valley, although regular reports also came from other areas including Monmouth and Cwmavon. Records from the north of the county were, however, comparatively sparse. At a national level, the species started to decline dramatically from the late 1970s, probably because of the effects of agricultural intensification (specifically herbicides) on the food plants of young chicks' insect prey (Potts, 1986). Extensive research and the introduction of a government Biodiversity Action Plan (Aebischer & Ewald, 2004) have not as yet born fruit, as the CBC/BBS data continues to show a decline. In Wales, there has been a major fragmentation and contraction of range with pairs being found in just fifty-five 10-km squares compared to 161 squares in 1968–72 (*State of Birds in Wales 2002*).

Furthermore, the 2002 *Birds in Wales* states that by 2000 it was highly likely that the species had become extinct as a breeding species in most Welsh counties, with populations only being maintained by releases for shooting.

Estate	Summary of game bags
Llanover Estate (Ochran)	In 1876, six were shot on 4th October. Bags subsequently increased to some 50 birds a season by the late 19th century and then declined to just ten birds by 1911.
Itton Court, Chepstow	The estate accounted for 304 birds in 1896 and 291 in 1898
Hendre	30–40 per day was the usual bag during 1856–1870 (*Shooting in Monmouthshire, 1923*) and subsequently 252 birds in 1890/91, 443 in 1900/01 (with 64 birds being shot there on 9th September) and 112 during 1909/10.
Talycoed	Three were shot in 1882 and 31 in 1915: the largest bags being during the 1898/99 and 1899/00 seasons, with 137 and 169 respectively.
Llantillio	A total of 316 were shot during the 1901 season and 371 in 1902.

Table 19. Grey Partridge shoots at estates in Gwent

In common with the national picture, a dramatic reduction in range is seen in Gwent. The 2nd Gwent Atlas data shows a dramatic 83% reduction in range compared to the 1st Gwent Atlas. Sadly, the optimism of the 1st Gwent Atlas, which considered the species not to have been affected by agricultural changes as it was present over much of the farmland regions of the county, has not been realised. The former strongholds of the Usk Valley and Gwent Levels have all but disappeared. A resident population is found in the north-west of the county on the moorland edge but its hold must surely be tenuous. Although difficult to calculate, the estimated population has declined considerably from some 600–700 pairs in the 1st Gwent Atlas period to some 50–100 pairs currently. The fate of the species on the Wentlooge Level has already been described succinctly by one county observer – 'the Grey Partridge has gone from being fairly common in the 1970s to rare in the 1980s and absent in the 1990s'. It remains to be seen if the fate of the species as a breeding resident in the county as a whole will be described in such a stark way in the not too distant future.

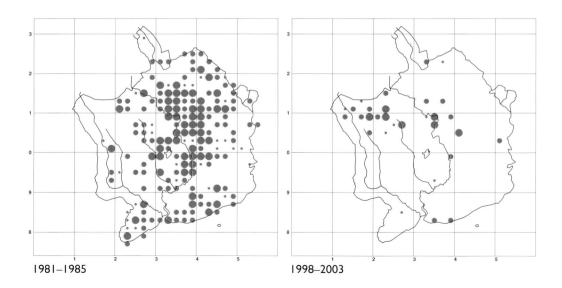

1981–1985   1998–2003

Gwent Breeding Atlas data and population size

Gwent Atlas	Confirmed tetrads	Probable tetrads	Possible tetrads	Total tetrads	Change in total	Gwent population
1981–1985	59	91	30	180	–	–
1998–2003	7	15	8	30	−83%	50–100 pairs

National breeding data and conservation status

Estimated Welsh population	Welsh trend	UK CBC/BBS trend 1985–2003	Welsh & UK conservation status
Almost extinct	Severe decline	−76%	Red-listed

(Common) **Quail**
Sofliar

Coturnix coturnix

A very scarce summer visitor

The Quail is a widespread but scarce summer visitor to Britain, seldom seen but readily identified by its distinctive 'wet my lips' call. In some years it is much more common owing to large invasions from the continent. In the last 50 years, such invasions have occurred in 1964, 1970, 1983 and 1989 (1988–91 National Atlas).

It is an irregular visitor to the Gwent and has been recorded in only 14 of the 40 years since 1965. Table 20 summarises the temporal distribution of all county records in ten-year intervals, and shows that the mid-summer months of June to August are the time when the species is most likely to be encountered. The irregularity of records is not apparent from the table, and it should be noted that of the 5 records in the 1970s, 3 were in the invasion year of 1970, while of the 14 records during the 1980s, 9 were recorded in the invasion year of 1989. The invasion of 1964 produced no county records, and that of 1983 only one.

	Jan	Feb	Mar	Apr	May	Jun	Jul	Aug	Sep	Oct	Nov	Dec	Date unknown	Total
Pre 1949	–	–	–	–	–	–	–	–	–	–	–	–	2	2
1950–59	–	–	–	–	–	–	–	1	–	–	–	–	–	1
1960–69	–	–	–	–	–	–	–	1	–	–	–	–	1	2
1970–79	–	–	–	–	–	1	2	1	–	–	–	–	1	5
1980–89	–	–	–	1	2	6	3	1	–	1	–	–	–	14
1990–99	–	–	–	–	–	4	1	1	1	–	–	–	–	7
2000–05	–	–	–	–	–	–	3	1	–	–	–	–	–	4
Total	0	0	0	1	2	14	7	5	1	1	0	0	4	35

Table 20. Temporal distribution of Quail records in Gwent

Nearly all records refer to single birds, although five were noted at Llantrisant in 1970, and during the 1989 influx there were up to five calling at Llandewi Skirrid during 17 July–13th Aug and four at Llanllowell during 16th–23rd June. Up to three calling birds were recorded at same site in Llandewi Skirrid in subsequent years until 1994.

Breeding is difficult to prove in such a secretive species and there are only two such records for Gwent: an incubating female killed at Llanvapley in 1965 and eight birds (presumed to be a family party) flushed at Trostrey in August 1967. There were two *possible* breeding records during the 1st Gwent Atlas (in tetrads SO30Z and SO40N), and one in the 2nd Gwent Atlas on the southern slopes of the Sugarloaf (SO21T).

The earliest date recorded is of a single bird heard at dusk at Lydart Hill, Monmouth on 21st April 1988, while the latest comprise a rain-soaked bird found at Llanarth on 15th September 1994 and one flushed on several occasions from a field at Michaelstone-y-Fedw during 13th–15th October 1988.

(Common) **Pheasant**
Ffesant

Phasianus colchicus

A common resident

This large and strikingly-plumaged game bird was introduced into Britain by the Normans in the 11th century and has since become very much a part of the British scene, its far-carrying call one of the characteristic sounds of lowland countryside. Its basic requirements are open areas for feeding, coupled with cover for breeding and roosting. Wooded farmland, preferably arable, is its favoured habitat.

The Pheasant is easily the most numerous game bird in Gwent but the annual autumn release of thousands of captive-bred birds for shooting is a major factor in the maintenance of its numbers. Indeed, as Gwent is on the edge of the Pheasant's main range in Britain, it is possible it might not be self-sustaining in the county and would die out in the absence of continued releases.

Estate game books give an insight into the scale of releases and shoots in the county at the end of the 19th and start of the 20th centuries. The earliest record relates to 1875 when 105 birds were shot at Llantilio, followed by similar numbers there in 1881 and 1901, and then 350 in 1902. The largest releases and shoots relate to the Hendre, where 6,000–7,000 birds were being reared during the 1890s and into the early 20th century, with shoots of over 4,000 birds in the 1896/97 season and some 5,000 in 1900/01, 1905/06 and 1909/10. Elsewhere, shoots were almost annual at Talycoed between 1882 and 1915 with the bag varying considerably in size over the years from tens to several hundred, the largest bag being in the winter of 1904/05 when over 600 were shot. Smaller numbers were shot at other estates in the county, including Itton Court, Tredegar Park and Blackbrook & Glen Monnow.

The 1st Gwent Atlas showed a distribution that corresponded fairly well to areas where releases occur and an absence from the western valleys and the southwest corner of the county. This was consistent with the status briefly outlined in earlier years by both the 1937 and 1963 *Birds of Monmouthshire*.

The 2nd Gwent Atlas paints a similar picture but records increases of 8% in total tetrads occupied, and of 16% in tetrads with *probable* or *confirmed* breeding. Most of this increase results from greater penetration into the western valleys and coastal areas east of Newport. The expansion of the Pheasant's range in Gwent has taken place against the backdrop of a UK population increase of 42% over the corresponding period, which may be driven by rising numbers of captive-bred birds released.

Estimation of a total county population is not feasible when so many birds continue to be released. However there is evidence that the number of territory holding birds is determined more by the amount of habitat than

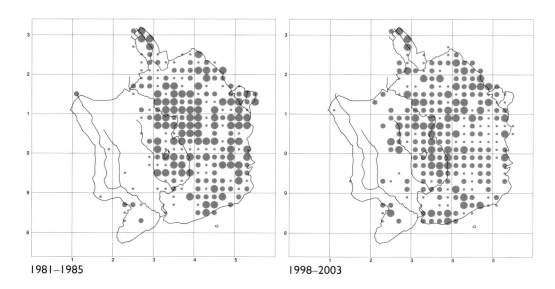

1981–1985   1998–2003

the number of males in the population (1988–91 National Atlas), so determination of the number of territory holders is probably an achievable objective. The 1988–91 National Atlas quotes an average density of 3.9 territories/km² for Britain (excluding mountains and moorlands) and if this figure is applied to the total number of Gwent tetrads with *probable* or *confirmed* breeding, a county population of about 3,000 territories is obtained. At the time of the 1st Gwent Atlas, data from CBC plots in the county suggested a population of 900–1,200 territories.

The creation of small copses for Pheasants and the provision of winter feeders have influenced the habitat of large areas of central Gwent, and this has been to the benefit other species as well as the Pheasant. However there may also be negative effects of high Pheasant densities on native birds, possibly including changes in the structure of the field layer, the spread of disease and parasites, and competition for food (Fuller *et al.*, 2005).

Gwent Breeding Atlas data and population size

Gwent Atlas	Confirmed tetrads	Probable tetrads	Possible tetrads	Total tetrads	Change in total	Gwent population
1981–1985	87	70	76	233	–	–
1998–2003	58	124	69	251	+8%	c.3,000 territories

Red-throated Diver   *Gavia stellata*
Trochydd Gyddfgoch

A rare winter visitor and passage migrant

The Red-throated Diver is a scarce breeder in Scotland but in most parts of the UK it is known only as a winter visitor, often to inland waters but most numerous offshore, particularly on the east coast. Recent aerial and boat-based surveys have shown the UK winter population to be considerably in excess of 10,000 birds. It is thinly spread around the coast of Wales, apart from north Cardigan Bay which is a site of national importance and held 732 birds in winter 2001/02 (WeBS).

With a total of just 12 records involving 16 birds, this is the rarest of the three diver species to be recorded in the Gwent. Records have occurred at a wide variety of sites, although predominantly from locations along the estuary, and are scattered throughout the year (Table 21).

1964	16 April	Newport Docks	1	adult in winter plumage found dead
1976	4–6 April	Pen-y-fan Pond	1	
1980	21 December	Collister Pill	1	oiled; found dead on the shoreline
1984	15–21 January	Tredegar House	1	an oiled bird on the lake; despite being caught and cleaned, it was eventually found dead.
1985	14 September	Goldcliff Point	1	flying down-channel.
1990	4 March	Peterstone	1	appeared to be in distress, with oiling on its belly
1991	8–10 February	Monmouth	1	on the river Wye; possibly present from the 2nd.
1991	6 May	Black Rock	5	winter-plumaged birds with two summer-plumaged Black-throated Divers
1992	23–28 April	Llandegfedd Reservoir	1	moulting into summer plumage
1992	28 Nov–03 Dec	Peterstone	1	on the Trout Lake; apparently present for 2–3 weeks
2003	27 April	Goldcliff Point	1	winter-plumaged; flying down-channel
2004	5 April	Goldcliff Point	1	winter-plumaged; flying down-channel

Table 21. Records of Red-throated Divers in Gwent

Black-throated Diver
Trochydd Gwddfddu

Gavia arctica

A very scarce winter visitor and passage migrant

The Black-throated Diver breeds in Scotland but, like the Red-throated Diver, is better known in other parts of the UK as a winter visitor. It is the rarest of the divers in winter and occurs mostly in coastal waters.

There have been 15 Gwent records involving 18 individuals. It has been recorded from only three sites and, in contrast to Red-throated Diver, has occurred principally at Llandegfedd Reservoir. The distribution of all county records is shown in Table 22, and details of records in Table 23.

	Jan	Feb	Mar	Apr	May	Jun	Jul	Aug	Sep	Oct	Nov	Dec	Total
Black Rock	–	–	–	–	1	–	–	–	–	–	–	–	1
Llandegfedd Reservoir	4	3	1	–	1	–	–	–	–	1	2	1	13
Newport	–	1	–	–	–	–	–	–	–	–	–	–	1
Total	4	4	1	–	2	–	–	–	–	1	2	1	15

Table 22. Distribution of Black-throated Diver records in Gwent

1915	5 February	Newport	1	found dead in a garden
1975	14–28 December	Llandegfedd Reservoir	1	
1976	10 October	Llandegfedd Reservoir	1	
1978	28 February	Llandegfedd Reservoir	1	late Feb [exact dates not recorded]
1985	7 January	Llandegfedd Reservoir	3	
1987	9–22 May	Llandegfedd Reservoir	1	in winter plumage, despite the late date
1991	10–24 February	Llandegfedd Reservoir	1	
1991	6 May	Black Rock	2	in summer plumage; with five Red-throated Divers
1996	6 January–21 February	Llandegfedd Reservoir	1	
1996	21 November–15 December	Llandegfedd Reservoir	1	in full summer plumage
1997	25 January	Llandegfedd Reservoir	1	
1998	7–16 November	Llandegfedd Reservoir	1	often with a Great Northern Diver
2001	14 January	Llandegfedd Reservoir	1	
2002	3–10 February	Llandegfedd Reservoir	1	
2002	8–9 March	Llandegfedd Reservoir	1	

Table 23. Records of Black-throated Divers in Gwent

Great Northern Diver
Trochydd Mawr

Gavia immer

A rare winter visitor

The coasts of the British Isles are the major wintering ground for the Greenland and Icelandic breeding populations of Great Northern Divers. Sites with nationally or internationally important numbers (50 birds) are all found on the coasts of Scotland and north and west Ireland. The Cleddau Estuary, which has held an average of five birds in recent winters, appears to be the most important site in Wales (WeBS 2003/04).

The 1963 *Birds of Monmouthshire* lists four records for the county, but only three of them, in 1929, 1931, and 1938 are dated. Since the early 1960s, when systematic bird recording began in the county, Great Northern Divers have occurred in 12 out of 41 winters, involving a total of 19 further records, all except one of which refer to single birds. The only record of a multiple occurrence was of two at Llandegfedd Reservoir in February 1974.

Of the 19 more recent records, 16 have been at Llandegfedd Reservoir and one each at Goldcliff, Wentwood Reservoir and Pen-y-fan Pond. Apart from two occurrences in October, which can be a passage month for this species, records have been confined to the winter period of November–March. A summary of all records is shown in Table 24.

	Jan	Feb	Mar	Apr	May	Jun	Jul	Aug	Sep	Oct	Nov	Dec	?	Total
Blackwood	–	–	1	–	–	–	–	–	–	–	–	–	–	1
Caerleon	–	–	1	–	–	–	–	–	–	–	–	–	–	1
Goldcliff Point	–	–	–	–	–	–	–	–	–	–	1	–	–	1
Llanbadoc	–	–	–	–	–	–	–	–	–	–	–	–	1	1
Llandegfedd Reservoir	3	2	1	–	–	–	–	–	–	–	6	4	–	16
Pen-y-fan Pond	–	–	–	–	–	–	–	–	–	–	1	–	–	1
Wentwood Reservoir	1	–	–	–	–	–	–	–	–	–	–	–	–	1
Ynysyfro Reservoir	–	–	–	–	–	–	–	–	–	1	–	–	–	1
Total	**4**	**2**	**3**	**–**	**–**	**–**	**–**	**–**	**–**	**1**	**8**	**4**	**1**	**23**

? = date unknown

Table 24. Summary of Great Northern Diver records in Gwent

Diver sp.

There have been 13 records of divers in Gwent that have not been identified to species level. Table 24a shows their monthly distribution, which is concentrated in the passage periods of spring and late autumn. Eight of the records are from the coast and five from inland waters.

Jan	Feb	Mar	Apr	May	Jun	Jul	Aug	Sep	Oct	Nov	Dec
2	–	1	4	–	1	–	–	–	2	3	–

Table 24a. Monthly distribution of unidentified diver records in Gwent

Little Grebe   *Tachybaptus ruficollis*
Gwyach Fach

An uncommon resident

The Little Grebe is the smallest of the resident British grebes. It has a dumpy appearance and sits high on the water. It readily dives when disturbed, surfacing unseen some distance away. Its distinctive whinnying trill often betrays its presence.

The 1937 and 1963 editions of *Birds of Monmouthshire* both described the species as a resident, breeding regularly on suitable inland waters throughout the county. The 1977 *Birds of Gwent*, however, described the species as a winter visitor and passage migrant in moderate numbers, rarely breeding and with just three confirmed nesting records since 1965. Subsequently the 1st Gwent Atlas described breeding records as being few and sporadic in the previous twenty years. The period of the 1st Gwent Atlas did however coincide with a genuine increase in breeding numbers.

The three confirmed breeding records referred to above were at Undy Pool in 1966, Skenfrith in 1969 and Miers Bog, Llanfoist in 1970. Although breeding was suspected on the River Monnow in 1972, it was not until 1981 that breeding was confirmed again, this time at a small pool at Tredegar Park House, Newport where a pair successfully reared two broods. In 1984, breeding was reported from an unprecedented total of three sites: at Tredegar Park House, Greenmoor Pool and at a small pond at Uskmouth. Since then breeding has been reported annually, with the number of sites and pairs increasing gradually, although the number of pairs remained in single figures until the new Millennium: thereafter there was an unprecedented increase. Most sites generally hold just single pairs, and include those already mentioned plus Magor Reserve, the Hendre, Dingestow Court, Pant-yr-eos Reservoir, Pen-y-fan Pond and Ynysfro Reservoir, although this last site has in some years held more than one pair. Since 2000, two significant breeding sites have become apparent: various pools at the Llanwern Steelworks site which have held six pairs regularly, and the shallow lagoons developed as part of the Newport Wetlands Reserve, where the number of pairs has increased dramatically from three or four in 2000, to eight in 2001, 12 in 2002 and then eight again in 2003. Table 25 summarises confirmed breeding data as reflected in Gwent Bird Reports, and is therefore not a complete survey of the county in any one year.

1993	1994	1995	1996	1997	1998	1999	2000	2001	2002	2003
8–9	5	9	8	7	7	8	13–14	18	25	23

Table 25. Number of breeding pairs of Little Grebes reported in Gwent during 1993–2003

The increase in breeding strength shown in Table 25 is reflected in the results from the 2nd Gwent Atlas which show that the number of occupied tetrads has increased by 142%, and the number with confirmed breeding has risen from five to 26.

A population estimate was not given at the time of the 1st Gwent Atlas, although based upon the numbers of *confirmed* and *probable* tetrad records a range of 5–10 breeding pairs seems likely. For the 2nd Gwent Atlas, 30–45 breeding pairs is suggested, based on extrapolation from sample tetrads.

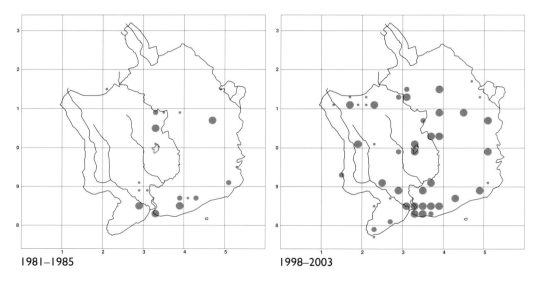

1981–1985   1998–2003

Little Grebes are present in the county throughout the winter and the 1977 *Birds of Gwent* noted that most records in the years 1965–1974 were between November and March, with few from August and into May and none (apart from breeding birds) in June or July. The *Gwent Bird Report* for 1981 estimated the total birds present in the county at particular times; the following conservative totals for the winter months were suggested: January, 16; February, 20; March, 16; October, 11; November, 21; December, 14.

Larger counts relate mostly to the winter months, with ten at Llanwenarth in January 1972, and 13 at Ynysfro Reservoir in November 1981. At the time these were the largest concentrations ever recorded in the county. Subsequently, high counts have also come from Ynysfro Reservoir with 16 in August and October 1990 and again in September 1991; 23 there in August 1993 and 1995, and then 20 in November 1996 and 22 in September 1997. More recent high counts come from the Newport Wetlands Reserve where the largest concentration of breeding pairs has become established. Counts at this site include 42 in September 2002, 34 in August 2003 and 29 in August 2004.

		Gwent Breeding Atlas data and population size				
Gwent Atlas	**Confirmed tetrads**	**Probable tetrads**	**Possible tetrads**	**Total tetrads**	**Change in total**	**Gwent population**
1981–1985	5	4	10	19	–	–
1998–2003	26	8	12	46	+142%	30–45 pairs

National breeding data and conservation status			
Estimated Welsh population	**Welsh trend**	**UK CBC/BBS trend 1985–2003**	**Welsh & UK conservation status**
120–150 pairs	Not available	+33%	Green-listed

Great Crested Grebe
Gwyach Fawr Gopog

Podiceps cristatus

An uncommon winter visitor and scarce resident

The Great Crested Grebe is our best known grebe, its colourful breeding plumage and display making it a distinctive and popular species. It breeds predominantly on large, shallow waters, such as lakes and reservoirs with vegetated fringes where nests are usually concealed. In winter the species may also be found in a variety of other aquatic habitats including deep lakes, slow-moving rivers, estuaries, coastal pools and inshore waters.

The first Monmouthshire avifaunas of 1937 and 1963 described the status of the species only as a migrant in spring and autumn, and an occasional winter visitor. Today, it is present in mostly small numbers all year; there is a noticeable passage movement especially during March and April; and the species has become a regular, yet scarce breeder. The increase in its presence is consistent with an increase noted nationally.

Llandegfedd Reservoir is the stronghold for the species where the largest number of breeding pairs is to be found and where the greatest numbers of birds congregate. Peak counts of 110, 113 and 99 were recorded there in July–August 2002 and August 2004. Such counts are exceptional, enhanced significantly by successful breeding at the site. Great Crested Grebes are also recorded in reasonable numbers at Llandegfedd outside the breeding season, especially during the winter months. Peak annual counts during these times include: 57 birds between March and May 1976, 52 between October and December 1998, 53 in November 2001 and 67 in April 2002.

Elsewhere, birds are occasionally recorded at other water bodies, including the reservoirs in the north-west of the county and the Wentwood and Ynysfro reservoirs in the south. During the past 25 years it has also been recorded in most years on the Severn Estuary. Half of such records are from the period April to June and possibly relate to migratory and non-breeding birds. Generally no more that one or two birds are recorded at these other locations at any one time and the number of birds seen across all of them averages 16 birds a year.

Great Crested Grebes have only fairly recently been recorded as a regular breeding species in Gwent. The first records were in 1971 at St Pierre Lake and, again at this site and also at Llandegfedd Reservoir, in 1972. The absence of breeding before this time is attributed to the lack of suitable breeding habitat and disturbance at sites where habitat was suitable. After the first definite breeding records almost a decade passed before breeding was suspected again, at St Pierre in 1981 and then confirmed at Llandegfedd Reservoir in 1985, both recorded during survey work for the 1st Gwent Atlas.

Breeding attempts have been recorded annually in Gwent since 1987, with up to nine pairs being noted in any one year. Llandegfedd Reservoir supports the largest breeding population with seven pairs attempting to

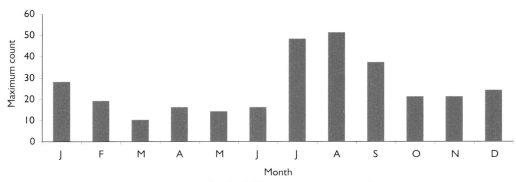

Figure 12. Average monthly maxima at Llandegfedd Reservoir 1995–2004

breed there in 1993, but more usually up to five pairs are present. Breeding success is, however, very dependent upon water levels being maintained during the season. Where they are not, nests are generally destroyed by predators as happened in 1989 when at least five pairs failed due to falling water levels that resulted in predation of nests by foxes.

Other sites where breeding has been attempted include: Ynysfro Reservoir (1991, 1992, 1997); Wentwood Reservoir (1989, 1998, 1999); north-western water bodies including Bryn Bach Park (1995, 1998, 1999, 2000, 2003), Garnlydan (1993) and Beaufort Ponds (2001); the Warrage at Raglan (1996, 1997); the Nedern Wetlands (2000); and on the Usk at Llanllowell: where in 1993 and 1994 a pair nested in tree branches overhanging the river. With the exception of Llandegfed Reservoir, and Wentwood Reservoir in 1999 when two pairs nested, all other sites had single pairs.

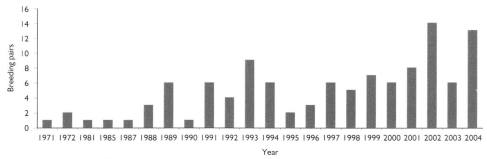

Figure 13. Number of breeding pairs of Great Crested Grebe in Gwent 1971–2004

The Great Crested Grebe will colonise new sites quickly after they become available and this has been the case in Gwent: noticeably at the Newport Wetlands Reserve, pools on the Wentlooge Level and at the Celtic Manor golf course. An increase in suitable habitat in the county is reflected in the Gwent Atlases with a marked increase in the number of tetrads supporting *confirmed* breeding from just one in the 1st Gwent Atlas to 13 in the 2nd Gwent Atlas. The overall number of tetrads where the species was recorded also shows a marked increase between atlases, having doubled from nine to 18.

Gwent Breeding Atlas data and population size

Gwent Atlas	Confirmed tetrads	Probable tetrads	Possible tetrads	Total tetrads	Change in total	Gwent population
1981–1985	1	5	3	9	–	–
1998–2003	13	3	2	18	+100%	6–14 pairs

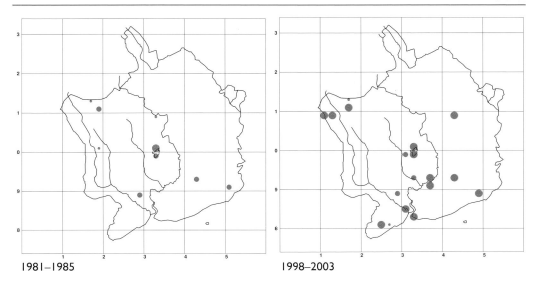

1981–1985   1998–2003

National breeding data and conservation status

Estimated Welsh population	**Welsh trend**	**UK BBS trend 1994–2004**	**Welsh & UK conservation status**
100–120 pairs	Not available	+38%	Green

Red-necked Grebe
Gwyach Yddfgoch

Podiceps grisegena

A rare visitor, in winter or on passage

The Red-necked Grebe is a scarce winter visitor to the UK from eastern and northern Europe. It is found mainly on the east coast and is rare in the west, including in Wales.

It is the rarest species of grebe to be seen in Gwent and there are just nine records, all of single birds (Table 26).

Year	Date	Site	Notes
1978	3 December	Llandegfedd Reservoir	
1979	11 March	Llandegfedd Reservoir	
1980	1 November	Peterstone	On the estuary
1984	8–9 September	Peterstone Gout	
1994	27 November	Pant-yr-eos Reservoir	
1995	14 May	Llandegfedd Reservoir	In full breeding plumage
1996	14 February	Llandegfedd Reservoir	
2004	11–12 October	Llandegfedd Reservoir	
2004	2 December	Llandegfedd Reservoir	

Table 26. Red-necked Grebe records in Gwent

Slavonian Grebe
Gwynach Gorniog

Podiceps auritus

A rare winter visitor and passage migrant

Small numbers of Slavonian Grebes breed in Scotland but the species is a widespread winter visitor to the remainder of the UK, mainly occurring on the coast but also less commonly on inland waters. In Wales there are about six sites where it occurs regularly in small to moderate numbers, the nearest to Gwent being Whiteford Point, Glamorgan, where 5–11 birds (14 in 1998/99) have been usual in recent winters (2002 *Birds in Wales*).

There is a historical record of a Slavonian Grebe shot at Marshfield in the late 19th (1937 *Birds of Monmouthshire*), but the first modern record for Gwent was in the winter of 1969/70, and subsequently it has been recorded in exactly half of the 36 winters to 2005/06 (the term winter is used here in its broadest sense to include passage periods). The number of records totals 34, involving 40 different birds, most of which have been at Llandegfedd Reservoir where there have been 20 records, involving a total of 26 birds. Omitting the undated historical record, the remainder are summarized in Table 27.

The species is principally recorded during the winter months, November to March, although five individuals have been recorded during passage periods, at Llandegfedd Reservoir on 24th October 1971 and 17th–20th April 1986; at Peterstone on 1st October 1984, 30th October 1995, and 25th October 2005; and at Goldcliff Lagoons (Newport Wetlands Reserve) during 19th–24th September 2000.

All records involving more than one bird have been from Llandegfedd Reservoir where there were three present on one occasion and two on four occasions.

	Jan	Feb	Mar	Apr	May	Jun	Jul	Aug	Sep	Oct	Nov	Dec	Total
Goldcliff Lagoons	–	–	–	–	–	–	–	–	1	–	–	–	1
Llandegfedd Reservoir	5	1	2	1	–	–	–	–	–	1	4	6	20
Newbridge-on-Usk	–	–	–	–	–	–	–	–	–	–	–	1	1
Wentwood Reservoir	–	–	–	–	–	–	–	–	–	–	–	3	3
Ynysyfro Reservoir	1	3	–	–	–	–	–	–	–	–	–	1	5
Peterstone	–	–	–	–	–	–	–	–	–	3	–	–	3
Total	6	4	2	1	0	0	0	0	1	4	4	11	33

Table 27. Summary of Slavonian Grebe records in Gwent

Black-necked Grebe
Gwyach Yddfddu

Podiceps nigricollis

A very scarce winter visitor and passage migrant

The Black-necked Grebe has a very small but widely scattered breeding population in the UK, comprising perhaps as many as 40 pairs (1988–91 National Atlas). It is also a winter visitor, chiefly to sheltered coastal waters in the south and southwest, with a total population of around 120 birds (Winter Atlas). There are no regular wintering sites in South Wales.

The 1963 *Birds of Monmouthshire* lists two records of Black-necked Grebes: at Ynysyfro Reservoir in 1923 and on the Usk at Llanbadoc in 1948, but modern records began in 1965, since when the species has been recorded in about half of the 41 years to 2005. There is a total of 39 records for the county, involving 51 birds, and, as with the Slavonian Grebe, Llandegfedd Reservoir has been the principal site: with 29 records comprising a total of 39 birds. Groups of three birds have been recorded at Llandegfedd Reservoir on 26th August 1968 and during 26th–27th April 2001, and at Ynysyfro Reservoir during 7th December 2005–29th March 2006.

In contrast to the Slavonian Grebe, there are records in the county for every month of the year, with a bias towards April–May and July-October, when birds are recorded on passage. It is notable in this context, that in some years passage birds produce the peak WeBS count for the UK, for example 73 in April 2002 (however there were no Gwent records in that year).

	Jan	Feb	Mar	Apr	May	Jun	Jul	Aug	Sep	Oct	Nov	Dec	Total
Llanbadoc	–	–	1–	–	–	–	–	–	–	–	–	–	1
Llandegfedd Reservoir	5	1	–	3	2	–	–	8	3	2	–	5	29
Ynysyfro Reservoir	–	1	–	1	–	–	–	–	2	1	–	1	6
St Brides	1	–	–	–	–	–	–	–	–	–	–	–	1
Uskmouth	–	–	–	–	–	–	1	1	–	–	–	–	2
Total	6	2	1	4	2	0	1	9	5	3	0	6	39

Month of arrival for each record is shown.

Table 28. Summary of Black–necked Grebe records in Gwent

(Northern) **Fulmar**
Aderyn–Drycin y Graig

Fulmarus glacialis

A scarce but regular wind–driven visitor, usually occurring from spring to autumn

The Fulmar extended its breeding range southward in the UK for most of the 20th century and it is now widespread around our coasts, occurring wherever there are suitable cliffs for nesting (1988–91 National Atlas). Its eastward expansion along the South Wales coast brought it to the Vale of Glamorgan coast in the 1980s, and this remains its closest breeding site to Gwent (1994 *Birds in Wales*; 2002 *Birds in Wales*).

With just three records of single birds detailed in the 1977 *Birds of Gwent*: one wrecked inland at Llanfihangel Ystern Llewern on 7th September 1967, another flying around the mouth of the river Wye on 19th August 1969 and one found dead on the Undy foreshore on 6th November 1976, this species was then considered to be a very rare visitor to the county.

Following further records of two birds off the Redwick coast on 24th October 1979, at least five off Sluice Farm on 3rd May 1981, single birds past Peterstone on 12th and 25th August 1981 and one past Peterstone on

13th June 1983, this species was then recorded in every year, except 1999, up to 2005. This increase may be related to the species' continued expansion in the southern half of Britain but could also be due in part to increased observer awareness of the weather conditions that are usually required to bring seabird species into the Severn Estuary. Similar increases have also been recorded for other seabird species during this period, including Manx Shearwater, Gannet, petrels and skuas.

Fulmars are generally recorded during April–October and are usually seen over the estuary following periods of south–westerly gales, although there have been occasions when birds have been seen during calmer conditions. Some of the more significant movements, all observed from Goldcliff Point, have included 15 on 9th June 1991, 22 on 31st May 1993, 29 on 3rd June 1994, 14 on 9th June 1998 and 28 on 27th April 2003.

Records are less frequent during the winter months November–March, with just three sightings of single birds: at Black Rock in February 1987 and December 1989 and the Caldicot shore in January 1998, and a record five at Goldcliff Point in December 1994.

An exceptional record concerns an individual, initially seen flying north, and then returning and disappearing in a southward direction over Llangybi Village in the Usk Valley on 19th August 1994.

Cory's Shearwater
Aderyn-Drycin Cory

Calonectris diomedea

A very rare storm-blown visitor

The only record is of a single bird sitting just offshore at Peterstone on 7th September 1983, which subsequently swam out into the estuary. This record followed a period of exceptionally strong south-westerly winds, which also resulted in a number of other seabirds being recorded in the Severn Estuary. It is quite possible that a Cory's Shearwater seen a few days later in the Parrett Estuary, Somerset on 11th and 19th September was the same individual.

Manx Shearwater
Aderyn-Drycin Manaw

Puffinus puffinus

A regular visitor to the estuary in summer, usually wind-driven

The Manx Shearwater is a summer visitor to the British Isles, breeding in large colonies, mostly on islands off the western coasts. The nearest colonies to Gwent are Lundy Island, Devon, and the Pembrokeshire islands of Skokholm and Skomer.

The majority of Gwent records, 15 of 19 prior to 1977, were of birds that were found wrecked following September gales. The remaining four records: 17 at Peterstone on 5th July 1973, 130 at Undy on 23rd June 1974, 140 flying past Peterstone on 27th June 1975 and, exceptionally, c.1,000 seen flying around the estuary between Sudbrook and New Passage, Gloucestershire on 6th June 1977 were all considered to be associated with movements of non-breeding birds that arrive in the south-western approaches of Britain in June (1977 *Birds of Gwent*). There are a number of similar records from other locations in neighbouring counties along the Bristol Channel and Severn Estuary.

The above pattern of occurrences continued to 1985, with a further six records of wrecked birds, and six records of up to 20 birds seen offshore at Peterstone between June and August. In addition, there was a series of seven September records, all following south-westerly gales, involving up to three birds at several locations along the estuary, and also an early spring record of two offshore at Black Rock on 13th April 1985.

From 1986, beginning with 39 birds seen from Goldcliff on 27th May, records became more closely associated with periods of westerly or south-westerly gales, probably due to an increasing observer awareness that such conditions are the most productive for sea watching on the Gwent coast. Goldcliff Point is generally the favoured viewing location for these movements, although birds can be seen from any location along the estuary. Late May through July is the most likely period to record large numbers of Manx Shearwaters, with significantly smaller numbers being noted into late September. Exceptionally, there are three records of birds recorded in October, the latest being of two off Goldcliff Point on 9th October 1987 and one off Black Rock on 9th October 1997.

Most weather-related movements are of fewer than 50 birds, although counts of up to 300 and more have occasionally been recorded. The most impressive numbers recorded from Goldcliff Point are: 170 on 7th August 1986, 1,283 on 9th July 1990, 600 on 21st June 1997, 1,180 on 9th June 1998 and 860 on 25th May 2002. Further down the estuary at Sluice Farm, notable movements have included 204 on 24th June 1994 and 506 on 29th May 1995.

Other than the individuals found 'wrecked', there are two inland records of single birds at Llandegfedd Reservoir on 15th July 1986 and 22nd June 1997.

(European) **Storm-petrel**   *Hydrobates pelagicus*
Pedryn Drycin

A very scarce wind-driven visitor from spring through to autumn

The Storm Petrel, like its larger relative, the Manx Shearwater, is a summer visitor that breeds in colonies on offshore islands in the far north and on the western coasts of the British Isles. The nearest colonies to Gwent are on the Pembrokeshire Islands of Skokholm and Skomer.

At the time of the 1977 *Birds of Gwent* it was considered a very rare species in the county, with only two records, both of storm-wrecked birds: one found alive near Pontypool on 13th October 1963 and the other found dead at Chepstow on 14th November 1964. The next records followed the severe gales in south-western Britain during the first week of September 1983, when daily totals of up to 14 birds were seen off-shore at Peterstone during 4th–6th September. Subsequently, with increased awareness of the weather conditions required to bring seabirds into the Severn Estuary, records became more frequent, and Storm Petrels were recorded in 14 of the 22 years between 1983 and 2004, seen mainly from either Goldcliff or Peterstone.

Table 29 summarises the temporal distribution of all records in five-year periods, excluding sightings over consecutive days as these may possibly involve the same birds moving up and down the estuary with the rise and fall of the tide.

	Jan	Feb	Mar	Apr	May	Jun	Jul	Aug	Sep	Oct	Nov	Dec	Total
Prior to 1965	–	–	–	–	–	–	–	–	–	1	1	–	2
1980–84	–	–	–	–	–	–	1	–	2	1	–	–	4
1985–89	–	–	–	–	–	3	1	1	–	2	–	–	7
1990–94	–	–	–	–	2	2	1	1	–	–	–	–	6
1995–99	–	–	–	–	–	2	1	–	–	–	–	–	3
2000–04	–	–	–	–	2	1	1	–	–	–	–	–	4
Total	–	–	–	–	4	8	5	2	2	4	1	–	26

Table 29. Temporal distribution of Storm Petrel records in Gwent

Late May to early July is the period when records are most likely and sightings generally involve fewer than five birds. Counts of 12 on 15th June 1991 and 12 again on 25th May 2005, both seen from Goldcliff Point, were unusual. These were eclipsed by an exceptional 40 birds flying south-west past Goldcliff Point during a five-hour sea watch on 13th June 1991. In recent times, there is only a one record of a wrecked bird, which was found at Trelleck, following a period of gales on 15th September 1983. There is also a remarkable record of one seen flying around offshore at Peterstone during mid-afternoon on 14th July 1984 during hot, calm weather conditions.

Leach's Storm-petrel   *Oceanodroma leucorhoa*
Pedryn Gynffon-fforchog

A rare storm-blown visitor, mostly in autumn and early winter

Leach's Petrel breeds only on remote islands, in Britain mostly off the Scottish coast, and records in Wales are almost all of wind-driven birds in autumn.

The 1977 *Birds of Gwent* detailed just five records. These comprised single birds shot at Llantarnam pre-1937 and at Rhymney on 28th December 1948, and, as a result of a widespread 'wreck' during the autumn of 1952, dead birds found at Newport in October, Peterstone in November and at Chepstow early the following year. It is surprising that only three Gwent records resulted from the 1952 wreck as 250+ were recorded at Severn Beach, Gloucestershire, and several thousand along the Somerset coast.

There were no further records until 23rd November 1984 when a single bird was seen offshore at Black Rock, and then in 1988, when a wrecked bird was picked up at Abergavenny in January. Following a period of storms during mid-December 1989 there was an influx of birds into the Severn Estuary and eight were noted at Black Rock on 17th December and up to ten during 23rd–24th December, with other birds noted elsewhere in the estuary at Peterstone (6), Uskmouth (1) and Goldcliff Point (2). Wrecked birds were also picked up inland during this period, at Monmouth on 23rd and Raglan on 24th, when a live bird was also seen briefly at Wentwood Reservoir.

There are four other records, all of single birds, two of which were from Llandegfedd Reservoir on 7th September 1990, and Sluice Farm on 5th January 1998. The other two were in the surprisingly early month of June, both during periods of south-westerly gales: one past Goldcliff Point on the 13th June 1991, during an exceptionally large movement of Storm Petrels, and the other past Sluice Farm on 5th June 1999.

(Northern) **Gannet**   *Morus bassanus*
Hugan

An uncommon, but annual visitor, usually wind-driven

The Gannet breeds in large colonies, usually on offshore islands but also on some mainland cliffs. Wales has a colony of over 30,000 pairs on the island of Grassholm, Pembrokeshire, and it is likely that this is the origin of most birds that stray into Gwent waters.

The 1963 *Birds of Monmouthshire* lists six records. The earliest is of a party of four birds at Denny Island in September 1893, while others are of single wrecked birds that were (respectively) shot at Llanwern in 1926, picked up dead at Llantarnum on 25th May 1942, at Chepstow on 2nd February 1945 and 3rd November 1951 and picked up alive near Pontypool in November 1960.

By the time of the 1977 *Birds of Gwent*, the number of county records had increased to 14 and, with just two further records to 1982, it was considered at this time a very scarce visitor to the county. However, following four records in 1983, including one of 11 birds at Collister Pill on 3rd September, Gannets have been recorded annually (except in 1995 and 2005), and the total number of records for the county is now approaching one hundred. Most records are of fewer than ten birds, although there have been nine records of 10–20 birds. These were however, eclipsed by a movement off Goldcliff Point on 27th April 2003 in which at least 51 birds were seen flying down-channel following a period of south-westerly gales. The temporal distribution of all dated records in five-year periods is shown in Table 30.

	Jan	Feb	Mar	Apr	May	Jun	Jul	Aug	Sep	Oct	Nov	Dec	Total
Prior to 1960	–	1	–	–	1	–	–	–	1	–	1	–	4
1960–1964	–	–	–	–	–	–	–	–	–	–	1	–	1
1965–1969	–	–	–	1	–	–	1	–	–	–	–	–	2
1970–1974	–	–	–	–	1	1	1	–	1	–	–	–	4
1975–1979	–	–	–	–	–	–	–	–	1	–	–	–	1
1980–1984	–	–	–	–	1	1	3		2	–	–	–	7
1985–1989	1	–	–	–	5	4	5	3	3	–	–	–	21
1990–1994	–	–	1	–	5	8	2	2	–	–	–	1	19
1995–1999	–	–	–	–	7	3	4	–	–	–	–	1	15
2000–2004	–	–	–	3	9	5	2	–	2	–	–	–	21
Total	**1**	**1**	**1**	**4**	**29**	**22**	**18**	**5**	**10**	**0**	**2**	**2**	**95**

Two undated records are excluded.

Table 30. Temporal distribution of Gannet records in Gwent

May–July is the period when Gannets are most likely to be encountered in the county, although there are records from all months of the year except October. Most records have been from Goldcliff Point, which offers the best vantage point for seabird observation in the county.

Occurrences inland are rare with just seven records and usually comprise storm driven/wrecked individuals, although there is a very unusual record of an adult bird seen flying down the River Wye about half a mile upstream of Monmouth in 1972.

(Great) **Cormorant**   *Phalacrocrax carbo*
Mulfran

A fairly common resident and winter visitor. Breeding since at least 1999

The Cormorant is a very conspicuous species: its size and distinctive posture when drying its wings after feeding are familiar to most observers.

The 1937 *Birds of Monmouthshire* reported the species as regularly observed along the coast and on inland waters during autumn and spring, and penetrating far inland up the rivers. Forty years on, the 1977 *Birds of Gwent* stated that the species was a resident and winter visitor, birds being found throughout the year, with peak numbers of approximately 50 recorded in most winters. Today it can be encountered at any time of the year on suitable feeding grounds and, furthermore, it has become a breeding resident since at least 1999.

The first record of possible breeding came on 17th June 1963 when a nest, believed to be that of a Cormorant, was found on Denny Island (Boyd, 1963). Some 30 years elapsed before breeding was suspected again, when 62 birds including 12 juveniles were noted in August 1993 at the island. The following year, a possible nest was noted in May on the parapet of Black Rock lighthouse, in the Severn Estuary. Conclusive proof of breeding came in 1999, when members of the Portishead Yacht Club observed nesting birds on Denny Island and breeding has been confirmed there annually since then.

Surveys of Denny Island by the Goldcliff Ringing Group since 2000 have shown that over a seven-year period the mean number of nests has been 67.5. The number of nests has shown considerable variation between years (Table 31).

Year	Occupied nests	Used nests*	Total nests (used & occupied)
2000	21	68	89
2001	12	41	53
2002	12	28	40
2003	31	45	76
2004	24	70	94
2005	9	40	49
2006	17	55	72

*Used nests: those used in the season but not occupied during visit.

Table 31. Number of Cormorant nests found at Denny Island 2000–2006

Ringing recoveries have shown that most Cormorants recovered in the Severn Estuary area have historically originated primarily from breeding colonies in west Wales, but some originate from north-west Wales and a few from Scotland and Ireland. Since 2001, nestlings from Denny Island have been colour ringed and sightings/recoveries of these birds have provided an insight into dispersal patterns and winter feeding grounds. The majority of sightings come from inland waters during the winter months: Llandegfedd Reservoir, Chew Valley Lake in Somerset, Cotswold Water Park in Wiltshire and the gravel pits near Newbury in Berkshire. Elsewhere, birds have been reported at water bodies in a number of Welsh counties, as well as in Leicestershire, Staffordshire, Buckinghamshire, Oxfordshire, Herefordshire, Sussex, Surrey, the Isle of Wight and, perhaps more surprisingly, Stellendam in the Netherlands.

The wintering population in Gwent has shown an increase over the past 30 years. During the 1960s numbers recorded were small with peak counts only reaching double figures on one occasion. In excess of 100 birds are now thought to winter in the area. The numbers visiting Llandegfedd Reservoir vary between months, with noticeable peaks in March and August and the lowest counts during May, when breeding birds are presumably at nesting colonies. Average monthly maxima for March and August in the period 1991–1997 was 37 birds and for May, two birds. During the 1975–1990 numbers feeding at the reservoir remained fairly constant between years, but between 1991 and 1997 they doubled in almost all months from those recorded in the earlier period (Clarke, 2002).

Several night roosts are found in Gwent: at Piercefield (Chepstow), Denny Island, Pill-mawr (Caerleon) and Uskmouth. During the mid to late 1980s the Piercefield roost in trees on the cliff face above the river Wye was possibly the most significant, with over 100 birds being present during the winter months of 1986 to 1988. More recent counts during 2001–2003 have shown a two-thirds reduction in the number of birds there. A reduction in numbers of birds feeding in the Wye Valley was also noted around this time, and a link to a national cull of birds undertaken during the 1990s has been suggested as the cause (*Gwent Bird Reports 1988–1999*). Since the mid 1990s, birds have been noted roosting on Denny Island during the winter period October to February. An exceptional count of up to 200 birds was seen flying to the island from Avon at dusk in December 1994. The only recent count of this roost was made in January 2003, when 27 birds were seeing flying to the island from Avon. At Pill-mawr, the roost is located in trees along the bank of the river Usk. First noted in 1999, it is occupied mostly during the winter months. Peak counts here are 58 in January 2002, 64 in January 2003, 75 in February 2004 and 79 in November 2004. The Uskmouth roost on an electricity pylon and wires was first noted in 1996, and is occupied mostly during late summer, August being the peak month. Some 34 to 52 birds were using this roost between 1996 and 2000, though it is largely unoccupied during winter months.

Day roosts or loafing sites are plentiful throughout Gwent, with birds recorded regularly along the county coastline and at reservoirs, rivers and other suitable water bodies close to feeding sites. The most prominent of these are the Garth, Abergavenny, Monmouth and on pylons over the river Usk at Bulmore, Caerleon.

Birds showing characteristics of the continental race *P. c. sinensis* were recorded in 1976, 1978, 1980, 1982, 1983, 1984, 1986, 1997 and 2005. The majority of these involve records of one or two birds at Llandegfedd Reservoir, Gobion and Peterstone with sightings occurring between mid February and early April. The highest counts were in 1986, when three were at the Piercefield roost in February and six at Llandegfedd Reservoir in March.

National breeding data and conservation status

Estimated Welsh population	Welsh trend 1985–88/1998–2002*	Britain/Ireland trend 1985–88/1998–2002*	Welsh & UK conservation status
1,700	−2%	+15%	Amber-listed

* The Seabird 2000 census of Britain and Ireland (Mitchell et al., 2004).

(European) **Shag**
Mulfran Werdd

Phalacrocorax aristotelis

A very scarce visitor, usually in autumn

The Shag breeds widely on rocky coasts around the UK, apart from those of east and south-east England. The coast of the Gower peninsula is the nearest breeding site to Gwent.

Although a species of the open coast, it is rarely affected by severe winds, which reflects the total of just 13 occurrences totalling 14 birds recorded in Gwent to date. The 1963 *Birds of Monmouthshire* lists just three records, which comprise a bird shot at Uskmouth in February 1907, another found at Newport on 11th October 1938: which had been ringed in Anglesey on 2nd July 1938, and two immatures found in Llantarnam on 13th March 1962: which were part of a country-wide wreck of the species at that time. In more recent times there have been a further ten records, all of single birds (Table 32). Eight of these have occurred in September–November, and six of seven whose age was specified were immature.

1977	16 November	Sluice Farm	1	adult
1979	9 November	Peterstone	1	immature; on rocks and in the sea
1980	26 October	Peterstone	1	flying up-channel
1983	7 September	Peterstone	1	flying up-channel
1988	7 March	Usk	1	1st winter female picked up 'wrecked'; released on following day at Beachley Head Glos. Found dead nearby at Piercefield on 13th March.
1988	4 September	Caldicot	1	immature found wrecked; died later
1994	11 December	Black Rock	1	immature
2004	19 September	St Brides	1	immature on rocks; flew off up-channel
2004	19–20 September	Llandegfedd Reservoir	1	
2005	4–10 September	Llandegfedd Reservoir	1	first-year immature

Table 32. Records of Shag in Gwent since 1977

(Great) **Bittern**
Aderyn y Bwn

Botaurus stellaris

A very scarce winter visitor; regular at one site since 2002

The Bittern is a rare breeding resident and winter visitor in Britain, confined to regions where there are large areas of undisturbed wet reedbeds, and it is Red-listed in the UK owing to its scarcity. In recent years, most records in Wales have been of winter visitors, and breeding is not known to have occurred since the 1980s (1994 *Birds in Wales*; 2002 *Birds in Wales*).

Eight records are detailed in the 1963 *Birds of Monmouthshire,* all of birds shot between 1889 and 1926 from a variety of locations, generally in the south of the county. Subsequent records are listed in Table 33.

Prior to the construction of the Uskmouth reedbed pools in the Newport Wetlands Reserve, the county lacked large areas of wet reedbed suitable for Bitterns, and this was reflected in the scarcity and irregularity of records. Since the completion of Newport Wetlands Reserve, the Uskmouth reedbed pools have provided ideal habitat and up two birds have been regularly recorded in the January to March period since 2002.

1967	24 October	1	Goldcliff	in a reen
1968	3 May	1	Newport	on canal bank
1969	8 November	1	Uskmouth	found dead
1975		1	Llanfoist	
1975	12 September	1	Whitson	found dead
1976	1 April	1	Llanover	near canal
1985	January	1	Undy	
1985	23 January	1	Peterstone	flushed from reen
1995	9 December	1	Llanwern steelworks	
1997	24 March	1	Peterstone	flushed from reen
2002	3 February	1	Magor Marsh	
2002	January–March	1	Uskmouth	reedbed pools
2003	January–March	1–2	Uskmouth	reedbed pools
2004	2 March	1	Magor Marsh	
2004	January–March	1	Uskmouth	reedbed pools
2005	January	1	Magor Marsh	

Table 33. Bittern records in Gwent 1967–2005

American Bittern
Aderyn-bwn America
Botaurus lentiginosus

A very rare vagrant

There is one county record of this transatlantic vagrant. A single bird, which became a local celebrity owing to the large number of visiting birdwatchers, was present at Magor Marsh from 29th October 1981 until 7th January 1982.

Little Bittern
Aderyn-bwn Leiaf
Ixobrychus minutus

A very rare vagrant

This diminutive heron is a widespread summer visitor to many parts of continental Europe but a rare visitor to Britain. The only Gwent record concerns an adult male, seen briefly in flight after it was flushed from the margins of a small reed-fringed pool at Nash Pools, Newport on 15th May 1994.

(Black-crowned) Night Heron
Crëyr y Nos
Nycticorax nycticorax

A very rare vagrant

The Night Heron is a widespread summer visitor to southern Europe but a rare visitor to Britain. In Gwent there have been three records to date, involving four birds. Following an adult at Magor Marsh during 22nd–25th May 1983, two (an adult and a first-year bird) were present at Woodstock/Morgans Pools, Newport during 6th–25th May 1994, and a juvenile was present at Llandegfedd Reservoir during 7th–30th July 1997. This last record is of particular interest as it was the earliest date that a juvenile bird had been recorded in Britain.

Cattle Egret
Crëyr y Gwartheg

Bubulcus ibis

A very rare vagrant

The Cattle Egret occurs in Britain as a vagrant from southwest Europe. The only Gwent record is of an immature bird found dead at Llandenny on 1st March 1981.

Little Egret
Crëyr Bach

Egretta garzetta

An uncommon throughout the year. Breeds at one location

The Little Egret is a recent colonist of the UK from continental Europe. Numbers of non-breeding birds increased steadily through the 1980s and early 1990s, and breeding first occurred in Dorset in 1996. By 2002 the UK population had expanded to 146 confirmed pairs at 22 localities (Ogilvie, 2004).

As the Little Egret became a more frequent visitor to Britain during the early-mid 1980s, it was only a matter of time before it was recorded in Gwent. This came to pass when a single bird was seen along the shore at Sluice Farm during 5th–6th May 1989, and was quickly followed by a record of another at Llandegfedd Reservoir on 11th June 1989.

Following a further occurrence on the river Usk at Llanvihangel Gobion during 12th–18th July 1992, records then became annual in the county and increasingly more frequent, with up to four birds recorded from Llandegfedd Reservoir, the river Usk at Llanvihangel Gobion and various locations along the coast during both passage periods: April–May and July–September. The first record outside the passage months came from the Nedern Wetlands where a single bird was present during 22nd–23rd January 1995, and the first overwintering individual was recorded at Peterstone from 28th November 1998 until 4th April 1999.

Following the construction of the Newport Wetlands Reserve in 1999, the areas of shallow water and the saline lagoons proved an attractive habitat for Little Egrets and appeared to provide the catalyst for further expansion of the Gwent population. Numbers at Newport Wetlands Reserve increased rapidly during 2000–02, and from 2001 onwards the species has been ever-present there (Table 34).

	Jan	Feb	Mar	Apr	May	Jun	Jul	Aug	Sep	Oct	Nov	Dec
2000	–	–	1	2	1	–	11	30	10	4	3	3
2001	3	3	3	5	4	7	10	27	23	24	6	5
2002	5	26	15	19	9	5	14	23	36	25	7	8
2003	19	10	19	16	10	15	13	15	22	26	5	13
2004	17	8	30	15	20	17	22	24	26	20	20	31
2005	10	5	16	18	13	20	16	39	63	38	16	12

Table 34. Monthly maxima of Little Egrets at Newport Wetland Reserve 2000–05

With increasing numbers of birds present in the county during the summer months, and a rapid expansion of the species' breeding range in the UK, commencement of breeding in Gwent was widely anticipated. It duly happened in 2001 when a pair reared four young at a location in the south of the county, providing not only the first breeding record for Gwent but for Wales also. Breeding was subsequently recorded annually at this same site, with ten juveniles seen on nests in 2002, nine in 2003, and 11 in 2004. It is difficult to determine the exact number of breeding pairs at the colony. However it is possible to say that a minimum of five pairs has bred successfully each year. During the 2nd Gwent Atlas, there were records from possible breeding habitat in three other tetrads, suggesting that birds might, in future, start nesting outside their existing known colony: in the absence of any other evidence of breeding, these have been omitted from the atlas data table.

Between 2002 and 2006, some 31 juvenile birds were ringed at the Gwent colony. Subsequent sightings of colour-ringed birds indicate only a limited movement, with most birds remaining close to their natal colony, though several have been seen at the Goldcliff lagoons and one at Llandegfedd Reservoir. Further afield, individual birds have also been sighted in Cornwall and north-east England (Goldcliff Ringing Group, unpublished data).

Continued immigration into Gwent is indicated by the sighting of a colour-ringed juvenile at Llandegfedd Reservoir during July and August 2004 that had been ringed at Gosport, Hampshire in May of the same year.

Gwent Breeding Atlas data and population size

Gwent Atlas	Confirmed tetrads	Probable tetrads	Possible tetrads	Total tetrads	Change in total	Gwent population
1981–1985	0	0	0	0	–	–
1998–2003	1	0	0	1	–	5 pairs

Great White Egret   *Ardea alba*
Crëyr Mawr Gwyn

A very rare vagrant

The only record of this vagrant from the European mainland is of a single bird seen briefly in the Gout at Peterstone and then on the nearby shore on 28th June 1995. It is presumed that this was the same individual that had been seen flying north-east from the Wildfowl and Wetlands Trust reserve at Penclacwydd, Carmarthenshire late the previous evening.

Grey Heron   *Ardea cinerea*
Crëyr Glas

A fairly common resident

The Grey Heron is frequently seen in the county at all seasons almost anywhere there is water but especially on the coastal levels, reservoirs and rivers.

The 1937 *Birds of Monmouthshire* noted three heronries in the county, the largest being near Llanwern, which had some 30 nests. The others were at Tredegar Park and near Llanover where pairs rarely numbered more than 6–10. The 1963 *Birds of Monmouthshire* noted that the Tredegar Park heronry was no longer in use: however, there was a heronry at nearby Cefn Llogell at this time. The 1963 avifauna gave no mention of the Llanwern heronry but it was still occupied up to at least 1943. Heronries surveyed in 1961 included: Piercefield near Chepstow (5 nests); Llantarnam Hall near Cwmbran (1 nest); New Wood near Caerleon (6 nests, but deserted in 1962); Rookery Wood at Pant-y-Goitre (10 nests) and Llanmartin (16 nests).

The Birds of Gwent (1977) records three well-established heronries: Pant-y-Goitre, Piercefield Woods and Whitson, which at that time held some 70 pairs between them, and a fourth heronry at Part-y-seal which was declining but where there had been 20 nests in 1975. The Whitson heronry was first recorded in 1968 at Pill Farm, but this site went into decline in the early 1980s and a new site was established at nearby Whitson Court.

Six heronries were noted at the time of the 1st Gwent Atlas: at Pant-y-Goitre, Piercefield, Whitson, Llanhennock, Peterstone and at Part-y-Seal, which had just two nests by 1984, but birds established a new heronry nearby on the border with Herefordshire at Kentchurch. Between Gwent Atlas periods heronries were established at Llandegfedd Reservoir, Llangybi, Crucorney and Crosskeys/Pontywaun, while the Kentchurch heronry declined and was last reported in 1994.

During the 2nd Gwent Atlas, 13 tetrads recorded heronries where breeding was *confirmed* at some point during the survey. There were also a number of other developments: nest counts of 15, 13 and 12 were made during the first three survey years at the Crosskeys/ Pontywaun heronry but it declined shortly afterwards, possibly as a consequence of hillside fires that had raged out of control around the site in 2000. Birds from Crosskeys most probably relocated, as a new heronry emerged at Risca just south of Crosskeys around this time. A second new heronry was discovered at Pill-mawr, Newport, beside the river Usk, which increased from one nest in 1998 and 1999 to six, 15, 11 and six nests during the remainder of the atlas period. Single nests were also found at Tredegar House Park in 2003 and at the southern end of Llandegfedd Reservoir in 1999. *Probable* breeding was also recorded in three other tetrads, at Machen and in two tetrads in the NW of the county. Since the 2nd Gwent Atlas work, two pairs nested at a new site at Aberbeeg in 2006.

Site	Founded/first recorded	Most recent count	Peak count
Piercefield, Chepstow	1954	26 in 2005	36 in 1995
Pant-y-Goitre (Rookery Wood)	1963	24 in 2005	49 in 1991
Whitson Court	1981	27 in 2005	51 in 1998
Llanhennock	1981	8 in 2003	18 in 1991
Crucorney (Bryn Arrw)	1986	8 in 2005	8 in 1996, 2003, 2005
Llandegfedd Reservoir	1989	17 in 2005	25 in 1999
Llangybi	1993	10 in 2005	10 in 2005
Pill-mawr, Glebelands	1998	10 in 2005	15 in 2001
Pontywaun, Crosskeys	1990	3 in 2005	15 in 1998
Risca	2001	15 in 2005	18 in 2001
Aberbeeg	2006	2 in 2006	2 in 2006

Table 34. Details of heronries currently occupied in Gwent

The long-term BTO Heronries Census shows the species to be more abundant now than ever before. The general increase that underlies these fluctuations may stem from reduced persecution, improvements in water quality, the provision of new habitat and increased feeding opportunities at freshwater fisheries (1988–91 National Atlas, Marchant *et al.*, 2004). This increase is very apparent in Gwent records with the total number of known nests in the county generally being below 50 during the 1960s up until 1972. In 1973, however, total nests exceeded 50 for the first time and by 1977 there were over 100 nests. The number of nests then remained within a range of 80–100 up until 1989, when 133 nests were recorded, and since then the total number of nests has remained over 100 in any one year. Peak counts occurred in 1995 and 2002 when there were 168 and 166 nests respectively. Outside the breeding season and away from the breeding sites, the highest numbers of birds occur mostly on the coast, although parties of up to ten birds are not uncommon at many locations. More significant counts come from Black Rock: 25 in January 1988, 25 in November 1995, 53 seen flying up channel from Black Rock in December 1997 and 22 in January 2000. Unusual records include 14 birds seen flying across the Severn Estuary into Gwent from Avon in January 1998, and a striking melanistic bird seen at Broadway Reen, Peterstone on 31st October 1996.

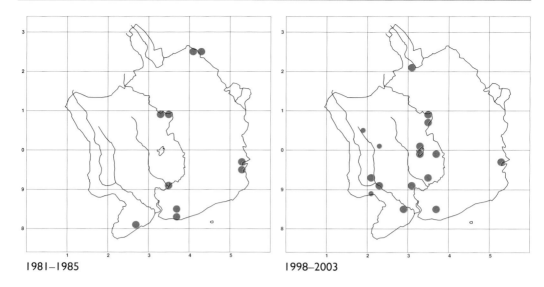

| 1981–1985 | 1998–2003 |

There are just two records of movements of birds ringed in Gwent: one ringed at Llanmartin April 1944 was found at Mountain Ash, Glamorgan in March 1945; and a bird ringed at Llanwern in April 1943 was found at Chepstow in June the same year. There are three records of birds recovered in Gwent having been ringed elsewhere in the UK: one found on the river Monnow near Pandy in October 1993 had been ringed as a juvenile at Tyne & Wear in April 1993; a bird found at Bute Town, Rhymney in May 1980 had been ringed at Llansantffraed, Powys in June 1977; and a bird found at Llantarnam, Newport in May 1959 had been ringed originally at Buscot, Oxfordshire in May 1955. Overseas-ringed birds recovered in Gwent include one from Raudoy, Norway and two from the Netherlands: one found at Chepstow in 1976 having been ringed at Callantsoog in 1975 and one found at the Nedern in 1991 having been ringed at Haren in 1987.

Gwent Breeding Atlas data and population size

Gwent Atlas	Confirmed tetrads	Probable tetrads	Possible tetrads	Total tetrads	Change in total	Gwent population
1981–1985	10	–	–	10	–	–
1998–2003	13	3	–	16	+60%	140–160 pairs

National breeding data and conservation status

Estimated Welsh population	Welsh Breeding population trend BTO Heronries Census	UK Breeding population trend BTO Heronries Census	Welsh & UK conservation status
600–700 pairs	Stable	Moderate increase	Green-listed

Purple Heron
Crëyr Porffor

Ardea purpurea

A very rare vagrant

The Purple Heron is a summer visitor to continental Europe and a rare visitor to Britain. There are only three records for Gwent. Following the first record for the county of an immature bird, flushed from a reen on several occasions just west of Goldcliff Pill on 26th September 1993, there were single birds seen in the Usk Valley, just south of Caerleon on 3rd May 1994 and, possibly the same individual, at St Brides on 24th May 1994.

White Stork
Ciconia Gwyn

Ciconia ciconia

A very rare summer visitor

The White Stork is a widespread and increasing species in western Europe, northern populations especially being migratory, but a rare visitor to the UK. There are only two Gwent records: a single bird was seen at two locations around the outskirts of Usk on 22nd June 1986, and presumably the same individual was flying over Cwmbran on 24th June 1986; a single bird was observed soaring over Caerleon on 15th May 2005 before it flew off in a westerly direction.

Glossy Ibis
Crymanbig Ddu

Plegadis falcinellus

A very rare vagrant

Glossy Ibis is a vagrant to the UK from southern Europe. The only Gwent record is of an adult male which was shot at Caerleon on 11th October 1902 and which was presented to Newport Museum.

(Eurasian) **Spoonbill**
Llwybig

Platalea leucorodia

A very scarce summer visitor, but almost annual in recent years

Substantial numbers of Spoonbills breed as near as the Netherlands and, with summering birds now regular in eastern England, colonisation of Britain appears imminent. There have been 15 records in Gwent, involving at least 21 individuals. All records up to 1996 were from the Peterstone-St Brides stretch of the coast, where they frequented the muddy shore, whereas more recent records have all been from Newport Wetlands Reserve, particularly the Goldcliff lagoons.

1973	7–21 June	Peterstone	4	on the shore
1989	16–17 April	Peterstone	1	Sluice Farm
1992	29 July	St Brides	1	on the shore between St Brides and Sluice Farm
1994	12–15 June	Peterstone	1	in the Gout
1996	15–18 May	Peterstone	1	in the Gout
2000	3–6 May	Goldcliff lagoons	1	
2000	11 June–2 July	Newport Wetland Reserve	2	one at Saltmarsh Grasslands on 11th June, joined by a 2nd from 26th, both remaining until 2nd July
2002	14 April	Goldcliff lagoons	1	
2002	8 August	Goldcliff lagoons	1	
2003	18 June–2 July	Goldcliff lagoons	3	up to 3 present during the period.
2003	11–19 July	Goldcliff lagoons	1	
2004	20 May–19 August	Goldcliff lagoons	1	immature
2005	2 April–11 September	Goldcliff lagoons	3	up to 3 immature birds present during the period

Table 35. Spoonbill records in Gwent

One of the birds present at Goldcliff lagoons during 18th June–2nd July 2003 had been colour-ringed at Middelplaten in the Netherlands on 7th July 2002. It undertook an amazing jaunt during its stay in Gwent, flying out from the lagoons on 22nd June, to be found at Poole Harbour, Dorset later the same day, and returning to Goldcliff on the 28th. The bird at Goldcliff during 11th–19th July had been colour-ringed at Schiermonnikoog, Netherlands on 22nd May 1999.

Honey Buzzard (European Honey-buzzard)   *Pernis apivorus*
Bod y Mêl

A rare summer visitor and passage migrant, which has probably bred in recent years

The Honey Buzzard is generally only ever seen in flight, occasionally circling over woodland or on migration. Its plumage varies considerably across all ages; typical adults have greyish-brown upperparts and whitish under-parts. It feeds mainly on wasp larvae, which it digs out, although on first arriving on our shores in the summer it is also known to feed on amphibians, mostly frogs. Nesting British birds have previously seen the unwelcome attention of egg collectors, and for this reason breeding sites have often been kept secret to protect them. Numbers are increasing, possibly as a result of upland conifer forests coming into maturity. Owing to the small size of the breeding population, it is Amber-listed in the UK.

There is just one historical record of the Honey Buzzard in Gwent, of a bird in the possession of Mr John Morris, Solicitor, Cardiff, which had been obtained in 1876 from Machen Wood (1990 *Birds of Glamorgan*). Another was shot in the same year close by at Ruperra, and then one at nearby Cefn Mably in 1880, but both birds were just over the county border in Glamorgan. There were no further records until June 1975 when one was seen near Abergavenny. The *Migration Atlas* indicates that birds arrive from their African winter quarters in mid May and depart from mid August, adults leaving about two weeks before the juveniles. Between 1991 and 1998 there were five records in Gwent during the May arrival period, at Sudbrook in 1991, Ebbw Forest in 1992, Caerleon in 1993, Trelleck in 1995 (a very early bird on 3rd May) and near Chepstow in 1998.

The 1994 *Birds in Wales* predicted colonisation and, after an increasing number of records since 1980, the first Welsh breeding record was in 1992. Breeding has now been proved in several locations in both north and south Wales and the Welsh population is probably about eight pairs.

A bird was seen in the south of the county in the summer of 1998 and, in 1999, intensive watching over many days located three different birds in August, including a very distinctive white male. The birds were seen throughout the month, and the male performed an extended display flight on 7th before flying off to another woodland some 5km away. Because of the very wide-ranging nature of the birds, views were often over consid-erable distances, and individuals were not often recognised. In 2000, the first sighting was on 20th May, and in

June the white male was seen carrying nest material. Two birds were seen throughout July and another was seen on 10th August at St Arvans (incorrectly recorded in the *Gwent Bird Report* as Cwmyoy). In 2001, two birds were found on 31st May, but were only noted occasionally until last seen on 30th July. In 2002, two birds were seen displaying on 23rd May. They were both thought to be males but a female was identified on 1st June and an empty nest was found later in the month. The last bird seen that year was on 14th July, and in 2003 there was only a single sighting on 18th May. Although breeding was not confirmed, with hindsight, and a much greater understanding of the species' behaviour, the observers consider it probably occurred (in 2000 and 2002), but that it was not successful.

In 2000, a major displacement of Scandinavian birds took place in September into eastern Britain. Five of these birds reached Gwent and were seen passing Goldcliff; with three on 23rd and single birds on 29th and 30th. A dark-phase individual on passage flew over High Cross, Newport on 27th September 2002.

Black Kite   *Milvus migrans*
Barcud Du

A very rare visitor

There are two records of this migratory European raptor. One flew into Gwent air space over Lady Park Wood, from Symonds Yat, Gloucestershire on 15th May 1985, and another, quite remarkably, was recorded independently by two observers as it flew over Tredegar Park and then High Cross, Newport on 5th June 2002.

Red Kite   *Milvus milvus*
Barcud Coch

A formerly rare visitor, now frequent. Bred in 2006

The 1963 *Birds of Monmouthshire* states that the Red Kite was recorded as having bred in the Railway Wood at Nantyderry during the 1870s and that two specimens in Newport Museum, from the Tredegar collection, were said to have been shot locally. More recently, the first documented record is of an individual seen flying along the Undy foreshore on 22nd September 1968.

The summary data in Table 36 shows that Red Kite records in the county remained scarce and sporadic until the mid-1980s after which there was a steep increase that has since been maintained. Records are generally of single birds, but records of two birds have occurred as follows: over Lasgarn Wood on 9th July 1976, at Tredunnock on Usk during 17th February–2nd Mar 2002, at Blaenavon on 5th May 2002, at Garn-yr-erw on 28th March 2003 and in the Trefil area during 9th–17th April 2004. The species continues to increase in the county and in 2005 there was an unprecedented total of 27 records.

Red Kites bred successfully at one location in Gwent in 2006 and thus have been restored to the list of breeding species for the county after an absence of over a century.

	Jan	Feb	Mar	Apr	May	Jun	Jul	Aug	Sep	Oct	Nov	Dec	Total
1965–69	–	–	–	1	–	–	–	–	1	–	–	–	2
1970–74	–	–	1	2	–	1	1	1	1	–	–	–	7
1975–79	–	–	3	1	–	–	1	–	–	–	1	–	6
1980–84	–	–	–	1	–	–	–	–	1	–	–	–	2
1985–89	–	–	1	1	3	–	–	2	–	–	–	–	7
1990–94	1	–	1	1	1	1	2	1	–	1	–	–	9
1995–99	1	2	2	2	2	2	1	3	–	1	–	1	17
2000–04	–	1	3	3	9	3	3	2	1	–	–	2	27
Total	2	3	11	12	15	7	8	9	4	2	1	3	77

Table 36. Temporal distribution of all documented Red Kite records in Gwent to 2004

The increase in Gwent records reflects the fortunes of the population in central Wales which has been increasing and expanding for many years, but much more rapidly since the mid-1980s. Reintroduction schemes in several areas of England and Scotland that began during the 1990s have also been very successful and will also have contributed to the increases recorded in Gwent. The total British breeding population was approaching 450 pairs in 2002, with over half of these in Wales (Ogilvie, 2004).

(Western) **Marsh Harrier**   *Circus aeruginosus*
Bod y Gwerni

A scarce passage migrant

Marsh Harriers almost became extinct in the UK during the 1960s but have since made a remarkable recovery concentrated mostly in eastern England, with the total number of breeding females exceeding 250 in recent years (Ogilvie, 2004). The reasons for recovery are complex but are thought to include the banning of insecticides such as DDT, increased immigration from the continent, increased protection in the UK, and expansion of breeding habitat from traditional reedbeds to include cereal fields.

The 1977 *Birds of Gwent* detailed just four records, the first of which was a female at Peterstone on 31st August 1959. Between 1976 and 1999 there were another 17 records, and the most recent period, 2000–05, has seen an enormous increase, with 26 further records. All records are summarised in Table 37. The recent remarkable increase in records is considered to be partly a result of the continued expansion of the breeding population in England but, probably more significantly, may be due to the attraction of the wet grassland and reedbed habitat created at the Newport Wetland Reserve in 1999. This site accounted for 23 of the 26 records during 2000–05.

	Jan	Feb	Mar	Apr	May	Jun	Jul	Aug	Sep	Oct	Nov	Dec	Total
Prior to 1965	–	–	–	–	–	–	–	1	–	–	–	–	1
1965–69	–	–	–	1	–	–	–	–	1	–	–	–	2
1970–74	–	–	–	–	1	–	–	–	–	–	–	–	1
1975–79	–	–	–	–	1	–	–	–	–	–	–	–	1
1980–84	–	–	–	1	1	–	–	–	–	–	–	–	2
1985–89	1	–	–	2	1	1	–	–	–	–	–	–	5
1990–94	–	–	–	1	2	1	–	–	–	1	–	–	5
1995–99	–	–	–	1	2	–	–	1	–	–	–	–	4
2000–04	–	–	1	5	7	1	–	8	–	1	–	–	23
2005	–	–	–	1	1	–	–	–	–	1	–	–	3
Total	1	–	1	12	16	3	–	10	1	3	–	–	47

Table 37. Temporal distribution of Marsh Harrier records in Gwent

Spring passage records have occurred chiefly during the period 19th April–14th June, and autumn passage records from 5th August–13th September. There is an unusually early record of an immature male at the

Newport Wetlands Reserve on 15th March, and late records on 10th October at Peterstone in both 1993 and 2000 and of up to two at the Newport Wetlands Reserve during 13th October–1st November 2005. There is also a mid-winter record of an individual seen over the Severn Estuary at Black Rock on 9th January 1988. There are few records away from the coastal levels, these comprising two over Penhow on 9th May 1976 and single birds at Bulmore, Caerleon on 20th May 1989, at Trelleck: hunting over hay and barley fields on 11th June 1992, and at Dingestow on 4th May 2002.

Hen Harrier *Circus cyaneus*
Bod Tinwen

A scarce passage migrant and winter visitor

The Hen Harrier is a scarce breeding bird in the uplands of northern and western Britain, and around 20 pairs nest in north and mid-Wales (2002 *Birds in Wales*). It is also an uncommon but widespread winter visitor to Britain (Winter Atlas).

The 1963 *Birds of Monmouthshire* lists four documented records, the earliest of a bird that was shot at the mouth of the River Wye on 10th October 1925, and the remainder of single birds in the winters of 1939/40, 1943/44 and 1955/56.

Since the mid-1960s it has been recorded almost annually in the county, with a total of 103 further records (Table 38). It has occurred in all months except July but is most commonly encountered from September to May, with just four records in August and two in June. Visitors to the county thus include passage migrants in both spring and autumn, and also winter visitors. Records are widespread throughout the county, but have been most frequent from the Uskmouth area (12), Mynydd Garn-clochdy (6) and the coast at Peterstone (6).

The only breeding record was in 1975, when a pair nested on the Gwent/Powys border, but owing to lack of detail it was not possible to determine whether it had been on the Gwent side of the border. There are two other records suggestive of breeding: of males on Mynydd Garnclochdy on 4th June 1997 and again on 2nd June 1998.

	Jan	Feb	Mar	Apr	May	Jun	Jul	Aug	Sep	Oct	Nov	Dec	Total
1925–64	–	1	–	–	–	–	–	–	–	1	–	2	4
1965–69	–	4	–	–	–	–	–	2	–	1	3	3	13
1970–74	1	–	–	1	2	–	–	–	1	1	1	1	8
1975–79	–	–	1	–	–	–	–	–	2	3	1	–	7
1980–84	–	1	–	4	–	–	–	1	1	3	–	2	12
1985–89	–	3	–	–	2	–	–	1	2	–	1	–	9
1990–94	1	–	1	–	–	–	–	–	1	–	2	–	5
1995–99	3	1	4	4	2	2	–	–	1	2	–	3	22
2000–04	3	4	1	2	1	–	–	–	2	–	6	1	20
2005	–	–	2	–	–	–	–	–	1	3	1	–	7
Total	**8**	**14**	**9**	**11**	**7**	**2**	**–**	**4**	**11**	**14**	**15**	**12**	**107**

Table 38. Temporal distribution of Hen Harrier records in Gwent

Montagu's Harrier *Circus pygargus*
Bod Montagu

A rare summer visitor and passage migrant

Montagu's Harrier is a scarce summer visitor to Britain, with just a handful of breeding pairs in southern and eastern England. It has bred in Wales in the past. In Gwent it is by far the rarest of the harrier species, with only ten records to date. The 1937 *Birds of Monmouthshire* gives only one record: a single bird seen at Peterstone on

21st September 1935. All more recent records are listed in Table 39. The records at Peterstone in 1964 and 1967 are notable for being relatively late and early dates, respectively, while the May–July records, particularly those at Wentwood in 1969, are suggestive of breeding.

1964	12 October	Peterstone	1	
1967	3 April	Peterstone	1	
1968	25 August	Bulmore, Caerleon	2	'a pair' along the ridge at Bertholey, Bulmore.
1969	19–31 May	Wentwood Forest	2	a pair present
1969	21 June	Wentwood Forest	1	
1972	27 July	Pant-yr-eos Reservoir	1	
1973	May-June	Pontllanfraith	1	a single bird during late May and early June
1973	9 June	Sugar Loaf	1	on heather slopes north of the Sugar Loaf.
1993	12 May	Llandewi Skirrid	1	

Table 39. Records of Montagu's Harrier in Gwent since 1964

(Northern) **Goshawk**   *Accipiter gentilis*
Gwalch Marth

An uncommon resident but in increasing numbers

The Goshawk is elusive for such a large raptor, best observed during late winter/early spring when aerial displays are common in fine weather. The British population has become established from escaped (or released) falconers' birds. The 1977 *Birds of Gwent* gives the first record for the county as 11th June 1966 at Llanellen. There were no further records until March and May 1971, when a bird frequented Wentwood, and this forest produced several more sightings in August 1974 and summer 1975. The latter year also produced sightings from near Usk. Throughout the mid 1970s, individuals were noted at several other areas: Peterstone (1973 and 1974), Parc Seymour/Penhow (1973 and 1976), Abergavenny (1974) and Goldcliff (1976). In 1977, there was only a single record: at Peterstone in November.

During the 1st Gwent Atlas there were breeding season records in all years but, because of the risks from persecution, it was only listed as having 'bred in the county during the Atlas period'. The 1988–91 National Atlas indicates that the its establishment was hampered by egg/chick thefts in many areas and the Gwent decision for secrecy has subsequently proved to have benefited the species, which has bred successfully and rapidly colonised the county. The number of records submitted has continued to grow, but with only the occasional breeding record listed.

The species has been closely monitored since 1979 when the first nesting pair was found. This pair subsequently moved into an adjacent county, and it was not until 1984 that breeding was again proved (old nests from 1983 were found at two different sites), and four sites were known in 1985. This increased to 11 pairs by 1990, 27 by 1995, 30 by 2000 and 36 by 2003. From 1995, breeding numbers are likely to be underestimated, because most time has been taken up monitoring known sites, with little time left to survey new areas (J. Lewis and S. Roberts, pers. comm.).

Collection and measurement of moulted feathers has confirmed that the original colonists were the large, pale, north European birds. Monitoring work has revealed that there have been several years of low productivity, and although this is generally related to adverse weather, there were several years when human-related failures were influential. In 1990 and 1991 there were some egg robberies (the culprit was subsequently caught) but in other years (1996 and 1999 especially) it was attributable to disturbances from forestry operations. Breeding birds are found in both state and private forests, and forestry operations are now the main cause of nest failure and hence of low productivity. Although generally associated with extensive areas of woodland, pairs are also found breeding in fragmented woodland in farmland areas. Territorial pairs generally nest approximately 1.5km apart but nests have been found as close as 700m in prime woodland habitat.

The Winter Atlas states that the species is mainly sedentary, although adult females may move further than males outside the breeding season, with only an occasional vagrant arriving in Britain from the continent. Goshawks take a wide variety of birds and mammals of an appropriate size, and in Britain there is generally an abundant food supply within the breeding territories, no matter how severe the winter. Nationally, the main centres of population are Wales/Welsh border, the southern Pennines, the English/Scottish border and north-east Scotland. As dispersal is generally short-distance (*Migration Atlas*) there is little interbreeding between these, essentially isolated, populations. It is not a bird of conservation concern and is Green-listed.

When dispersing, young birds tend to settle at their first opportunity and areas become fully occupied before birds venture further. Recoveries of ringed birds show 42% of deaths (where the cause is given) are human-related but this figure is certainly under-represented. There are 42 recoveries on the BTO database for Gwent. The majority (29) were ringed and recovered in Gwent, and involved movements of less than 9km. The remainder were mainly movements to/from adjacent counties, of which only two involved distances greater than 20km: a female from the Wye Valley that was found near Bromyard, Herefordshire (48km) in its third autumn and a male from Crychan Forest, Carmarthanshire killed near Raglan (65km) in its first autumn.

Illegal persecution of first-year birds is considerable in July and August, when Goshawks can cause considerable damage at pheasant release pens and thus come into conflict with game-keeping interests. Between 1991 and 2001, 13 ringed (plus a few unringed) birds were reported killed at just one pheasant release pen, reflecting both the level of persecution and the potential damage to commercial shooting interests. Any young birds dispersing out of the forest area will almost certainly encounter one of the many pheasant shoots that are found throughout Gwent and the adjoining counties. A handful of breeding attempts in private woodlands are also known to have failed through persecution of the adults, and three former breeding sites are no longer occupied. A more fortunate, long-lived individual was trapped in 2004, having been ringed as a chick, 20km away, ten years earlier.

Wales is undoubtedly a UK stronghold for this species and the Welsh population was estimated at 200–250 pairs (2002 *Birds in Wales*). Gwent makes a significant contribution to this total, with an estimated population of 50 pairs.

Gwent Breeding Atlas data and population size

Gwent Atlas	Confirmed tetrads	Probable tetrads	Possible tetrads	Total tetrads	Change in total	Gwent population
1981–1985	4			Not specified	–	–
1998–2003	39	10	28	77	–	c.50 pairs

(Eurasian) **Sparrowhawk**   *Accipiter nisus*
Gwalch Glas

A fairly common resident, with recent declines noted in some areas

The Sparrowhawk is found in a variety of habitats, including coniferous and mixed woodlands, parks and gardens. It is a common and widespread breeding species found throughout Wales and is second only to the Buzzard as the most common diurnal raptor.

The first mention of the Sparrowhawk in Gwent came in 1923, when *Shooting in Monmouthshire* described the species as vermin and reported that a number had been killed at the Llangibby Estate. Subsequently, a male was taken at Chepstow in 1925 and a female at Llantilio Crossenny in 1928, the skins of which are now housed in the National Museum of Wales, Cardiff. Further evidence of the persecution of the species was noted in the 1937 *Birds of Monmouthshire*, which stated that the species was a fairly common resident breeding species throughout the county in areas where there was no game preserving. At the time of the 1963 *Birds of Monmouthshire*, the Sparrowhawk was 'reduced almost to rarity' status, following continued persecution and a drastic decline in the 1950s (as nationally) due to poisoning from

organochlorine pesticides. It increased from the mid 1960s to about 12 pairs in 1969–1973, with a stronghold in the central parts of the county. The position continued to improve so that by the time of the 1977 *Birds of Gwent* it was resident and breeding in moderate numbers: this increase and spread continued until it had become one of the most common raptors by the time of the 1st Gwent Atlas, with an estimated population of 500–1,000 pairs (2–4 pairs per tetrad).

During the late 1980s and 1990s, the number of submitted records continued to increase, with 10–20 confirmed breeding records in most years. Where estimates of numbers were given, these were 3–4 pairs in 2km^2 of the Skirrid Fach, 8–10 pairs in 4km^2 of the Hendre woods and seven pairs in the Nantyglo area. Most recent records have been from the south and central parts of the county, with fewer records being received from the western valleys and the Trelleck Ridge/Wye Valley area.

In the 1st Gwent Atlas, Sparrowhawks were recorded in 71% of tetrads, while in the 2nd Gwent Atlas they were recorded in 75% of tetrads. Despite the slight overall increase, a closer inspection of the two distribution maps shows differences that have been alluded to in *Gwent Bird Reports*. The current distribution shows a major consolidation of *confirmed* records in central Gwent and areas to the west of this, but little change in the southern half of the county, and some reductions in the north and the Wye Valley/Trelleck Ridge areas. In areas of the county where Goshawks have become well established, it is possible that predation by that species may be implicated in the observed decline. The increase in numbers since the 1960s has now probably stabilised, or it may even have decreased to the lower end of the 1981–85 range. The population is now estimated to be near the upper end of the a range of 430–610 pairs. The UK National index during the same period, derived from CBC/BBS data, shows an increase of 36% but this figure would have included data from parts of the country where the species was still recovering.

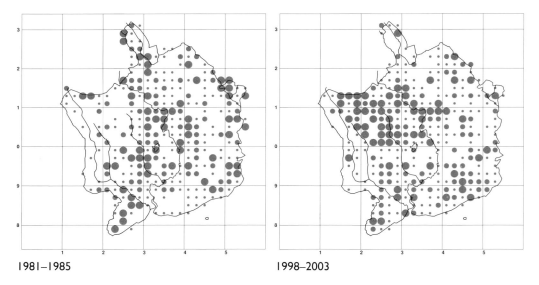

1981–1985   1998–2003

The *Migration Atlas* indicates that this species is non-migratory and relatively sedentary, in fact more sedentary than other British raptors. Most disperse less than 20km (median distance only 8km), with females moving further than males. Following post-fledging dispersal, most juveniles settle and remain in the same general area throughout their lives. There is some movement of north European birds (mainly from Norway and Denmark) into Britain for the winter but there is no evidence that any reach Gwent.

There have been 28 ringing recoveries affecting Gwent, the majority (20) being ringed and recovered in the county. Of these, 13 had moved less than 9km, 12 from 10–99km (most nearer the lower end of the range) and four over 100km. The four longer-distance movements involved two ringed as chicks: a male from the Skirrid Fach to Devon (13 months later and 132km) and a female from the New Forest to Chepstow (five months and 116km), and two ringed in their first autumn: a male from Uskmouth to Shropshire (32 months and 152km) and a female from Llanfoist to Shropshire (one month and 115km), having also been found at Llanvihangel Crucorney on the way.

Gwent Breeding Atlas data and population size

Gwent Atlas	Confirmed tetrads	Probable tetrads	Possible tetrads	Total tetrads	Change in total	Gwent population
1981–1985	61	70	148	279	–	–
1998–2003	65	77	153	295	+ 5%	430–610 pairs

National breeding data and conservation status

Estimated Welsh population	Welsh trend	UK CBC/BBS trend 1985–2003	Welsh & UK conservation status
3,100 pairs	Not available	+36%	Green-listed

(Common) Buzzard
Bwncath

Buteo buteo

A fairly common resident throughout the county

The Buzzard is synonymous with Wales, being found throughout the principality due to its affinity for woodland and farmland habitat. It is however less plentiful in north-west Wales and is rare on Anglesey. Having been persecuted by gamekeepers between the 18th and early 20th centuries, the Welsh population has now fully recovered in most areas and densities here are possibly higher than anywhere else in Britain (1994 *Birds in Wales*).

The earliest record of breeding in Gwent is referred to in *Shooting in Monmouthshire*, which mentions a Buzzard's nest containing one juvenile being found at Llangibby Park in 1922. This nest was probably one of the two nests in the Usk Valley referred to in the 1937 *Birds of Monmouthshire,* the second nest being found in 1926. By 1937, however, the species' residence was thought to be doubtful, although it was still seen frequently in the county during autumn and winter.

Its numbers increased during and after the second world war but it subsequently suffered setbacks in the 1950s due to myxomatosis reducing its preferred prey, and again in the 1960s due to poisoning from organochlorine pesticides. By the time of the 1977 *Birds of Gwent,* the Buzzard was described as being widespread in moderate numbers with probably c.25 pairs being present. It was however absent, or rare as a breeder, in the low-lying coastal areas and in the south-east of the county.

The 1st Gwent Atlas found the Buzzard in all parts of the county but noted that it was still patchily distributed in the urban areas, the bare high ground of the north-west and the coastal levels. The population was thought to be 200–250 pairs: higher than the 7–9 pairs per 10-km square suggested in the 1968–72 National Atlas.

During the late 1980s, the Buzzard continued its spread into coastal areas and, by the early 1990s, it was by far the most commonly seen raptor anywhere in the county, being well established on both the Caldicot and Wentlooge Levels. During the period 1986–98, there was an average of 27 breeding records reported per year, with densities of up to 3–5 pairs per tetrad at Sor Brook, Cleppa Park and Ysgyryd Fach: at the latter site two successful nests were only 80m apart in 1995. The number of records submitted decreased during the late 1990s but this was almost certainly a reflection of familiarity with the species by observers, rather than a decrease in the population.

The largest concentrations are usually seen in the spring, when birds are riding thermals, or during the winter when they are found feeding on worms, often in the company of gulls on fields. During the late 1980s, the maximum numbers reported were generally about ten birds (maximum 13 at Llanddewi Skirrid in 1988, and at Llanwenarth in 1989). By the late 1990s, this had increased up to threefold, with 25 or more reported regularly. For example, there were 26 in a field at Kemeys Commander in September 2004 and a maximum of 30 over Wentwood in February 1998.

The 2nd Gwent Atlas found Buzzards in 97% of tetrads, with an increase of 18% in occupied tetrads since the 1st Gwent Atlas. This increase, however, does not reflect the whole picture, as density had also increased from an estimated 1 pair/tetrad in 1981–85, to an average of 2.3 pairs/tetrad in 1998–2003. This higher density has also enabled a much higher proportion of records to be of *confirmed* breeding. The estimated population is now thought to be around 500–800 pairs, almost four times the estimate of the 1st Gwent Atlas. This increase

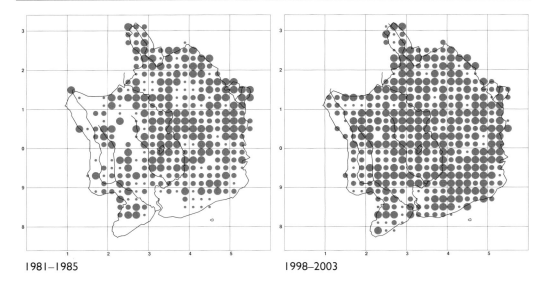

1981–1985   1998–2003

is well above both the Wales CBC/BBS trend of +70% and the UK CBC/BBS increase of +223% for the same period.

The Winter Atlas indicates that the distribution is markedly similar to that during the breeding season, with adults remaining on territory all year. The species is largely sedentary and birds have a tendency to move back to their natal area following initial post-fledging dispersal (*Migration Atlas*). There have been 17 recoveries of ringed birds relevant to Gwent; all were ringed as nestlings in the county and 14 of these were also recovered here, only three having crossed the border into England. The majority (ten) had moved less than 9km, with more significant movements being from Ebbw Vale to Monmouth 18 months later (12km), and from Trelleck to Newport six months later (19km). Where the cause of recovery was known, two were road casualties, one was killed on a railway line and, unfortunately, two were shot.

Gwent Breeding Atlas data and population size

Gwent Atlas	Confirmed tetrads	Probable tetrads	Possible tetrads	Total tetrads	Change in total	Gwent population
1981–1985	136	123	64	323	–	–
1998–2003	215	130	36	381	+18%	500–800 pairs

National breeding data and conservation status

Estimated Welsh population	Welsh CBC/BBS trend 1985–2003	UK CBC/BBS trend 1985–2003	Welsh & UK conservation status
3,800 pairs	+70%	+223%	Green-listed

Rough-legged Buzzard   *Buteo lagopus*
Bod Bacsiog

A very rare winter visitor

The Rough-legged Buzzard is an uncommon winter visitor to eastern England and, apart from the occasional years when large influxes occur, it is rarely seen in the west. There are only three records for Gwent, which probably involve just two individuals. Following the first at Crick on 21st January 1973, one was seen briefly at Garnlydan Reservoir on 9th October 1998, and possibly the same individual at Peterstone on 15th November of the same year.

Golden Eagle
Eryr Euraid

Aquila chrysaetos

Vagrant

Although it is considered to have bred regularly in Wales some 300 years ago (1994 *Birds in Wales*), the Golden Eagle is nowadays restricted to mountainous areas of northern Britain, chiefly in Scotland. The occurrence of a bird in Gwent in 1985 is therefore most remarkable. The bird in question was an immature, and was watched for about 15 minutes as it was mobbed by Buzzards, over Coed-y-prior Common on 24th March. What was almost certainly the same individual had also been seen in central Wales several weeks earlier.

Osprey
Gwalch y Pysgod

Pandion haliaetus

A scarce passage migrant, regular in recent years

Formerly extinct in Britain, the Osprey recolonised Scotland during the latter half of the 20th century. As its population has expanded, it has spread into England and has recently bred in North Wales.

The first documented record for Gwent was of a single bird flying over the river Usk at Abergavenny on 11th September 1965. Since then there has been a total of approximately 85 birds noted in the county. Temporal distribution of all records is summarised in Table 40.

The striking increase in records from 1990 is assumed to be associated with the increasing breeding population in the north of Britain.

Most birds are noted on passage, either as they fly north during April–May, or on their return migration during August–October, although there have also been four records of individuals during June and July. The earliest recorded date is of one flying over Newport on 25th March 2005, while the latest concerns one at Llandegfedd Reservoir on 29th November 1976. The majority of records are of single birds although there are two records of two birds: flying along the River Wye at Monmouth in early May 1973 and at Tredunnock-on-Usk on 24th August 1995.

	Jan	Feb	Mar	Apr	May	Jun	Jul	Aug	Sep	Oct	Nov	Dec	Total
1965–1969	–	–	–	1	–	–	–	1	3	–	–	–	5
1970–1974	–	–	–	–	1	–	–	3	–	–	–	–	4
1975–1979	–	–	–	–	1	–	–	–	1	–	1	–	3
1980–1984	–	–	1	1	–	–	–	1	–	1	–	–	4
1985–1989	–	–	–	–	–	–	–	–	–	1	–	–	1
1990–1994	–	–	–	2	4	–	2	2	5	1	–	–	16
1995–1999	–	–	–	2	5	–	1	5	3	–	–	–	16
2000–2004	–	–	–	8	4	–	1	2	10	2	–	–	27
2005	–	–	2	1	2	1	–	–	2	–	–	–	8
Total	–	–	3	15	17	1	4	14	24	5	1	–	85

Table 40. Temporal distribution of Osprey records in Gwent

(Common) Kestrel
Cudyll Coch

Falco tinnunculus

A fairly common resident; declining since the early 1990s

The Kestrel is found breeding in a wide variety of habitats and is Britain's most common and widespread small falcon. It is Amber-listed nationally in England and Wales because of a moderate decline in the UK breeding population over the last 25 years and an unfavourable conservation status in Europe.

The earliest records of Kestrels in Gwent both relate to 1934 with a male taken at Monmouth and a female at Peterstone, the skins of which are now housed in the National Museum of Wales in Cardiff. The 1937 *Birds of Monmouthshire* recorded it as being a common resident breeding species that was well distributed and probably increasing slightly in numbers. The Kestrel was not as badly affected in Wales by the organochlorine pesticides as were other raptors, and by the time of the 1963 *Birds of Monmouthshire*, it was still being recorded as a well distributed common resident, that was showing no signs of decreasing. This account was presumably written before the harsh winter of 1962–63 when many birds died. By the time of the 1977 *Birds of Gwent*, its former status had been regained and submitted breeding records were averaging 11 per year. An exceptional gathering of 20 was noted at Twmbarlwm in July 1971.

In the early 1980s, the 1st Gwent Atlas recorded the Kestrel in 86% of tetrads and estimated a county population of 600–1,000 pairs (2–3 pairs per occupied tetrad). *Gwent Bird Reports* up to the early 1990s confirmed this common status with an average of ten confirmed breeding records per year and five reports of 10+ birds together. The largest of these were 17–20 at Peterstone in September 1989 and 15 at Caerwent in March 1990. The habit of hunting alongside trunk roads became well established from the 1970s and the frequency with which birds were seen by motorists may have masked a decline caused by agricultural intensification. However, during the early 1990s, a change in status was being reported with decreases in the Trelleck area and on the trunk roads. Although quick to take advantage of new road verges, the species was being replaced by Buzzards on older verges, presumably as the verge habitat succeeded to scrub and became less suitable for hunting Kestrels. By the mid 1990s, declines were still being reported, and the species was thought to be more unusual than the Hobby in the farmed areas of central Gwent, although still regular on the ffridd and upland areas of the west. The areas of decline were those that contained the greatest percentage of agricultural land or where agricultural intensification had been most severe: a process linked nationally to reductions in the numbers of small mammals (1988–91 National Atlas). Nevertheless, pockets of set-aside rough grassland often continued to hold pairs in otherwise unsuitable intensively farmed areas.

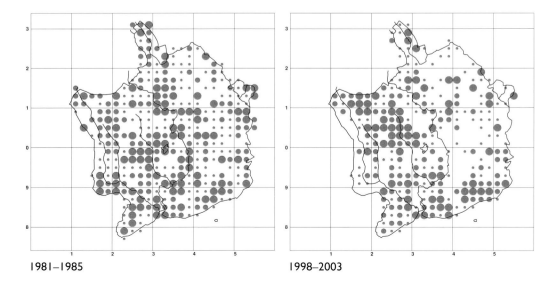

1981–1985

1998–2003

The 2nd Gwent Atlas recorded the Kestrel in 68% of tetrads, a 21% decrease in range since 1981–85. The estimated population falls in the range of 90–200 pairs (assuming 1.32 pairs per tetrad), well below the lower end of the range of the earlier atlas, and represents a substantial decline. A patchy distribution is now apparent in the north-eastern half of the county, approximately north-east of a line from Chepstow to Abergavenny. Numbers of records on the coastal levels and in the hills north-west of Pontypool appear to have remained stable or even increased. The 1988–91 National Atlas abundance map shows the species as scarce in parts of Wales, and not particularly common in Gwent. Although the most abundant UK raptor, it may have been over-taken by the Buzzard and the Sparrowhawk in Gwent (as elsewhere in Wales) by the early 1990s (1994 *Birds in Wales*). The 2002 *Birds in Wales* considers the species surprisingly scarce considering the extent of upland rough grazing, with the main declines in the improved farmland (pasture) areas. The Wales CBC/BBS trend of a 47% decline during the period between the two Gwent Atlases has been counter to the UK trend of a 16% increase, calculated over the same timescale.

Kestrels are largely sedentary in Britain but with some migratory tendencies. Birds in western Britain have a greater tendency to migrate, with lower numbers remaining in the winter than is the case further east. Young birds disperse randomly from July onwards, but long distance movements at this time are rare. Longer distance migratory movements occur from September onwards but in Britain most birds are recovered locally. Females are more likely to move than males, the latter being more inclined to remain on territory.

There have been 55 Gwent ringing recoveries, 20 were ringed and recovered in Gwent and six involved exchanges with other Welsh counties, including Denbighshire and Pembrokeshire. The other recoveries show a migratory movement with 23 being recovered in south-western and southern English counties, three in north-ern England (Yorkshire and Northumberland), one in Ireland (Co. Wicklow) and two in France (La Garnache and Plougonven). Twelve of the birds had moved less than 9km, 24 from 10–99km and 19 had travelled further than 100km. The majority of birds were ringed as nestlings and recovered mainly in their first autumn (peaks in August and October) or winter (peaks in November and February). There was a mainly southerly orientation to the movements. Details of ringing recoveries are listed in Appendix 9.

Gwent Breeding Atlas data and population size

Gwent Atlas	Confirmed tetrads	Probable tetrads	Possible tetrads	Total tetrads	Change in total	Gwent population
1981–1985	91	108	143	342	–	–
1998–2003	67	83	119	269	−21%	90–200 pairs

National breeding data and conservation status

Estimated Welsh population	Welsh CBC/BBS trend 1985–2003	UK CBC/BBS trend 1985–2003	Welsh & UK conservation status
800–1000	−47%	16%	Amber-listed

Merlin
Cudyll Bach

Falco columbarius

An uncommon winter visitor and scarce breeder

The Merlin requires extensive areas of open country in which to hunt, at higher altitude during the breeding season and at lower altitude during the winter. With the variety of Gwent's landscape, it is therefore not surprising that it both breeds and winters in the county. The Merlin hunts small birds, such as the Meadow Pipit, which form its staple prey.

The 1963 *Birds of Monmouthshire* records the Merlin as a scarce winter visitor on the coast and a former resi-dent of the hills. Breeding was reported in 1900 at Blaenavon and nestlings were taken for falconry. Two skins are in the National Museum of Wales: a male from Peterstone in 1916 and a female from Aberbeeg in 1928. The 2002 *Birds in Wales* reported a long, steady decline since 1900, with only three pairs remaining in the uplands of Monmouthshire by 1939. However, there was an indication of a slight recovery from the 1980s, when breeding was first discovered in the edges of conifer plantations. The 1988–91 National Atlas also indicated a Welsh recovery in this period.

The 1977 *Birds of Gwent* recorded small numbers at all seasons, but confirmed breeding was rarely reported, with only one record since 1965. However, there were regular sightings, averaging nine per year, with records split between the hills of the north-west, coastal areas and the rest of the county. There was a seasonal bias towards the November–February period for the coastal records.

The 1st Gwent Atlas suggested the Black Mountains were one of the South Wales strongholds but the species was never common. Breeding was still irregular in the hills of the north and west, and only two confirmed records were received during the atlas years (1981–85). This period corresponded with a special study of the species but fieldwork was targeted at the traditional (ffridd) nesting areas. The switch to nesting in conifer plantations, which also occurred at this time, may have gone undetected and has made the interpretation of population trends difficult

Most of the Gwent breeding records have been in abandoned crows' nests in trees on the ffridd, as occurs in most of South Wales, where ground nesting is rarely recorded: although there have been single instances in a Raven's nest on a cliff (1977) and on the ground in heather (1978). The first plantation nest was discovered in 1986, with the birds using an artificial site (a refurbished crow's nest) in the following year. Breeding season records from 1986 suggest a maximum of five or six locations in any year (1989, 1999, 2000), but in general there were only two or three locations reported and in some years there were none.

The species still retains a tentative foothold as a breeder in Gwent and there are still several potential nesting sites,in the western valleys and in the Black Mountains. During the 2nd Gwent Atlas (1998–2003) the total number of tetrads with *probable* or *confirmed* records over the survey period declined by 67% and the population is now generally unlikely to be above three pairs. The majority of the *possible* records (as with the 1st Gwent Atlas) are presumed to refer to wandering or passage birds. In addition to these, there were two further sightings during the breeding season in tetrads that did not contain suitable breeding habitat.

Merlins are recorded on passage from all Welsh counties and offshore islands, with peak movements noted from the latter during March–April and September–November (1994 *Birds in Wales*). In Gwent, some of the birds encountered in spring and autumn are undoubtedly on passage, especially individuals seen on the coast. Merlins are generally thought to winter near the coast but they rarely desert the high ground in the county. In Gwent, the ratio of coastal to inland winter records has changed from equality in 1986–90 to 2–3 times the number on the coast thereafter. This could of course represent observer bias to coastal areas in the winter period. There has been a general stability in winter records during 1986–2003 (averaging 15 records per year and with slightly higher numbers in the mid-1990s).

The *Migration Atlas* indicates most birds remain in Britain (although a few reach the Continent) but move to lower elevations, with a median recovery distance of 68km. There are four Gwent ringing recoveries, all ringed as nestlings. Two have come from the Black Mountains breeding population and were found in their first autumn at Monmouth (1978) and at Ebbw Vale (1982). Two others had moved from more northerly breeding grounds: a female at Abergavenny in October 1996 had been ringed in Tayside (a movement of 554km south), and a male found at Gwehelog, Usk in November 2001 had been ringed in North Yorkshire in 1997 (a movement of 257km SSW). This could suggest that Gwent's wintering birds are not of local origin, which would explain why there is a stable wintering population and a declining breeding population.

Gwent Breeding Atlas data and population size

Gwent Atlas	Confirmed tetrads	Probable tetrads	Possible tetrads	Total tetrads	Change in total	Gwent population
1981–1985	2	7	12	21	–	–
1998–2003	1	2	22	25	+ 19%	3 pairs

National breeding data

Estimated Welsh population	Welsh trend	UK trend	Welsh & UK conservation status
90–100 pairs	Not available	Not available	Amber-listed

(Eurasian) **Hobby**
Hebog yr Ehedydd

Falco subbuteo

An uncommon summer visitor and breeder with an expanding population

The Hobby is a short-staying summer visitor, being on our shores for just five months before undertaking its trans-Saharan migration. Traditionally it has been found over central and southern England, but birds have been known to bred in south-east Wales since the early 20th century. It is a superb aerial acrobat, hunting large insects and small birds, particularly hirundines and Swifts. Its current conservation status is Green-listed in the UK but it is Amber-listed in Wales.

At the time of the 1937 and 1963 *Birds of Monmouthshire*, the Hobby was a scarce summer visitor with just three breeding records: Wentwood 1910, near Usk 1934 and near Chepstow 1938. At the latter two sites, birds were unfortunately shot: victims to game preserving interests, and a skin of a juvenile female from Usk is in the National Museum of Wales. There were only two other sightings: at Ponthir in September 1942 and in the north of the county in April 1953.

The 1977 *Birds of Gwent* recognised the Hobby's former rare breeding status, but recorded it at that time as an occasional summer visitor and passage migrant, although breeding was thought to have been probable in one area in 1966. Otherwise, between 1963 and 1977 there had been just 17 records all of single birds, mainly in the Usk Valley. A record from Llanover in December 1975 is now thought to be unproven.

The 1988–91 National Atlas detailed a westward and northward extension of the Hobby as the traditional heathland population expanded into mixed farmland areas. The first Gwent nest of recent times was found in 1985, although records of fledglings had come to light from 1966, 1980, 1982 and 1984 (Roberts & Lewis 1985). An artificial nest platform was used at the 1985 site in the following year (Roberts & Lewis 1986). A reassessment of records since 1980 suggested regular breeding had occurred during the 1st Gwent Atlas years (1981–85) at up to nine different sites with a maximum of four pairs in any year (Roberts & Lewis, 1990). The increase in sightings and breeding records has continued since that time (see Table 41).

Period	1986–90	1991–95	1996–00	2001–03
Probable/confirmed breeding	5.5	6	9	9
Sightings	8	13	17	33

Table 41. Mean annual number of Hobby records submitted to the Gwent Ornithological Society

A total of 83 tetrads were occupied in the 2nd Gwent Atlas, which represents a four-fold increase over the 1st Gwent Atlas. *Confirmed* or *probable* breeding was recorded in 28 tetrads. When newly arrived, birds can spend some time over water bodies or on the hills hawking insects, and this could account for some of the *possible* breeding records where birds have been located away from their eventual breeding area. Nesting birds are elusive and difficult to locate, and the actual number of breeding pairs is probably under-represented by the 18 *confirmed* tetrads in the 2nd Gwent Atlas. In one area of the county, nests have been found 6.5km apart (Roberts & Lewis, 1988), whereas in another area, three nests were found only 2–3km apart, with a mean distance of 2.4km for this grouping and 3.1km overall (Roberts & Lewis, 1990). These distances are clearly comparable with figures given for farmland-nesting Hobbies in the Midlands (Fuller *et al.*, 1985). The concentration of records in central parts of Gwent is likely to reflect the extensive fieldwork carried out there, rather than a preference over other farmed areas.

The Gwent population is estimated to be in excess of 20–28 pairs: occasional tetrads are known to hold more than one pair, and some *possible* records undoubtedly relate to additional breeding pairs rather than wandering individuals. Even though Gwent is known to be the Welsh stronghold, the latest Welsh population estimate of '20–25 pairs, possibly in excess of 30' (2002 *Birds in Wales*) must be well short of the true figure.

The entire Hobby population migrates to Africa for the winter. The average arrival date in Gwent is 25th April (earliest 23rd March 1989), and last date is 26th September (latest 13th October 1991). Birds generally return to near their natal area to breed and a median displacement of 25km is recorded in the *Migration Atlas*. There have been two local ringing recoveries that conform to this pattern, with chicks ringed in Gwent nests and found subsequently in the breeding season. One from 1992 was found injured near Hereford three years later while the other was

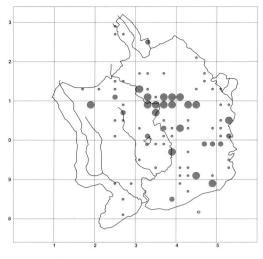

1998–2003

ringed in 2000 and was caught and released at Llangorse Lake, near Brecon the following summer. A third recovery was of a bird ringed in Derbyshire in July 1999 and found at Llanthony the following July, a distance of 163km south-west.

Gwent Breeding Atlas data and population size

Gwent Atlas	Confirmed tetrads	Probable tetrads	Possible tetrads	Total tetrads	Change in total	Gwent population
1981–1985	4	9	8	21	–	–
1998–2003	18	10	55	83	+ 295%	20–28 pairs

Peregrine Falcon
Hebog Tramor

Falco peregrinus

A scarce or uncommon resident; more numerous now than ever recorded previously in the county

The Peregrine is a large and powerful falcon that is swift and agile in flight as it hunts its prey. It feeds predominantly on medium-sized birds, especially pigeons, but also on wading birds and small ducks. Prey is taken in the air, either by outflying or by striking it with stooping dives from height.

The 1963 *Birds of Monmouthshire* listed the Peregrine Falcon as uncommon, a doubtful breeder and only occasionally seen. It documented only one breeding record: a clutch of four eggs collected from Denny Island in 1927. Ratcliffe established a baseline population estimate for Monmouthshire of an average of three pairs during the period 1930–39 and four territories within the county, which were either regularly or irregularly occupied in the period 1900–1960 (Ratcliffe, 1980). These included the Denny Island pair and a pair in the lower Wye Valley as well as one or two pairs that had previously been reported as breeding in the hills of the north (1937 *Birds of Monmouthshire*). These northern pairs presumably refer to the Cwmyoy area, where a site was occupied from as long as anyone could remember to 1956 (Dr Walker pers comm.), and to another nearby site just outside the county boundary. Research work at known nest sites, using metal detectors to find old pigeon rings, suggests that six Peregrine Falcon territories in Gwent were occupied in at least one year during the pre-pesticide era between 1900–60 (Dixon & Lawrence, 1999).

The species was extinct as a breeding bird in Gwent by 1960 and the situation had changed little by the time of the 1977 *Birds of Gwent*. Sightings were, however, more common with 38 birds seen in the period 1966–1975, mainly during the non-breeding periods, 11 of which were in 1974. This low point in the Gwent population reflected the national situation, when the species had been severely affected in the late 1950s – early 1960s by organochlorine pesticides causing eggshell thinning. At the time of the 1st Gwent Atlas (1981–85) there had been a recovery, with a pair returning to Cwmyoy in 1979 and rearing three young in both 1980 and 1981 (Roberts & Lewis, 1989). Numbers increased rapidly during the Gwent Atlas survey years with six known pairs and a predicted future population of 10–12 pairs, if all potential sites were occupied. Most birds were breeding in old quarry workings and were well distributed in the western valleys.

The 1988–91 National Atlas indicated that the species was numerically at its highest known level and had recovered from the pesticide era crash. In some parts of Wales it was twice as abundant as ever known before, with tiny crags and working quarries occupied. This dramatic increase was attributed to good food supplies and greater protection, although persecution from pigeon fanciers was a problem in the South Wales valleys. The benchmark era for assessing population levels was 1930–39, and three sites were attributed to the old vice-county of Monmouthshire.

During the 1991 national Peregrine survey, ten sites were located in the county, and breeding was proved at seven, although success was poor (Lewis, 1992). By 1995, 11 sites were located, three of which were in the south of the county and away from the traditional upland areas. During that year, three breeding attempts failed and two of them could be attributed to human persecution. Protection of the early breeding attempts no doubt helped numbers to increase and, although it was now no longer possible to provide that level of protection to all sites, a few were still guarded.

By 1996 it had become the most commonly reported raptor in the county, with many recorders reporting every sighting: 90 winter records were received in that year. Regular sightings around Newport suggested that some breeding sites were still remaining undetected in the urban areas. Another year of high persecution was 1997, and at one site, five different adult birds were found dead during the breeding season: perhaps indicating the numbers of non-breeding birds available to occupy any vacant territories. In 1998, there were ten confirmed breeding records and the first breeding site on a pylon was discovered near Newport. The maximum number of confirmed breeding records in any year was 13: in 1999, when only one site was away from the western valleys; and in 2001, when two were in the south. Both years are likely to be underestimates however, as in 2003, of nine sites monitored, two were on pylons and two on buildings, all in the Newport area. Although there is now a stable breeding population in the county, productivity is well below the national average of 1.28 young per occupied nest (1988–91 National Atlas).

The 2nd Gwent Atlas shows a 35% increase in the total number of tetrads since 1981–85. The species was also recorded in an additional 39 tetrads which apparently held no suitable breeding site, but with the discovery of pylon nesting this number should perhaps also be added to the possible figure. The distribution is clearly concentrated in the western valleys and the Black Mountains but with an increasing number of records in the

south and south-east of the county. As illegal persecution is still a problem in the South Wales valleys, the distribution map shows all records in the centre of each 10-km square. One site is known to be outside the county boundary, although within a border tetrad, and three confirmed breeding records are known to represent birds moving between adjacent tetrads in different years. The county population is known to be at least 15 pairs.

The Winter Atlas indicated a similar distribution to the 1988–91 National Atlas. The species is however named after its habit of wandering and appearing outside the breeding season in areas where it does not nest. There are more records in this season from lowland and coastal areas and birds can turn up anywhere, especially if there is prey available. In Gwent, all breeding areas are within relatively easy access to winter hunting areas and sightings suggest birds only move to our coast in the late winter if feeding conditions warrant it.

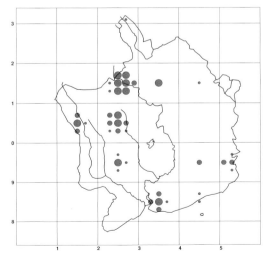

1998–2003

The *Migration Atlas* suggests that movements largely follow the prey availability, but young birds disperse to find a territory of their own. The median distance travelled is 45km (a minority moved over 200km) with females moving slightly further than males. The longest movements are undertaken during the first year, and thereafter birds are mainly faithful to the breeding territory. There have been 14 recoveries of ringed birds in Gwent. Of these, four had moved less than 9km, six from 10–99km and four over 100km. Recoveries were spread throughout the year with a slight bias to the breeding season, and at least five of these were killed (shot or poisoned) at breeding sites in the South Wales valleys. Long-distance movements of Gwent-ringed birds include recoveries from Kingsbridge, Devon, 170km SSW; Didcot Power Station, Oxfordshire, 120km E; Salisbury, Wiltshire, 102km SE; and, Lincolnshire, 277km NE. The first-listed bird also had the longest interval between ringing and finding (14 years).

Gwent Breeding Atlas data and population size

Gwent Atlas	Confirmed tetrads	Probable tetrads	Possible tetrads	Total tetrads	Change in total	Gwent population
1981–1985	9	8	20	37	–	–
1998–2003	19	15	16	50	+ 35%	15 pairs

National breeding data and conservation status

Estimated Welsh population	Welsh trend	UK trend	Welsh & UK conservation status
350 pairs	Not available	Not available	Amber-listed

Water Rail
Rhegen y Dŵr

Rallus aquaticus

An uncommon winter visitor and resident

The Water Rail is an elusive species, its favoured habitat of dense marshy vegetation and skulking nature make it very difficult to see. Its presence is usually recorded as a result of it calling, but even then it may not be recognised as its calls are very often not bird-like. It is widely but sparsely distributed in Britain (1988–91 National Atlas), and has been Amber-listed owing to contraction of its breeding range. The estimated population for Wales is only 100–200 pairs.

The earliest record of the Water Rail in Gwent, and for that matter Wales, comes from Roman times. Remains of the species were discovered in Roman drains at Caerleon dating back to the 1st and early 3rd centuries (1994 *Birds in Wales*).

In more recent years, the 1937 *Birds of Monmouthshire* described it as a resident in small numbers, breeding in suitable localities in central and southern districts and frequent on the coastal levels in winter. *Gwent Bird Reports* record birds mostly on the Gwent Levels in the winter months; with Peterstone, Magor Marsh and the Uskmouth reedbeds producing birds annually.

Conclusive records of breeding are infrequent. The earliest was near Abergavenny in 1971 and then at Peterstone in 1973, but subsequent records are few. The 1st Gwent Atlas recorded the species in 13 tetrads but breeding was not *confirmed* in any of these, and was *probable* in just two: at sites near Pontypool and Llanwern. A stronghold for the species noted around Abergavenny in the 1977 *Birds of Gwent* had apparently disappeared by the time of the 1st Gwent Atlas. Breeding possibly occurred at a site near Raglan in 1988 and two years on, in August 1990, it was confirmed when adult and juvenile birds were seen at Magor Reserve. In the 2nd Gwent Atlas, birds were found in 11 tetrads, two fewer than in the previous atlas period. With such a small range, the -15% change between atlas periods is probably not very meaningful. Neither atlas produced *confirmed* breeding records but there was a noticeable increase in the number of *probable* breeding birds between the two atlas periods.

The breeding distribution for the Water Rail is almost entirely restricted to the Gwent Levels and its stronghold is undoubtedly the reedbeds at the Newport Wetlands Reserve. Between 1996 and 2005 the site was

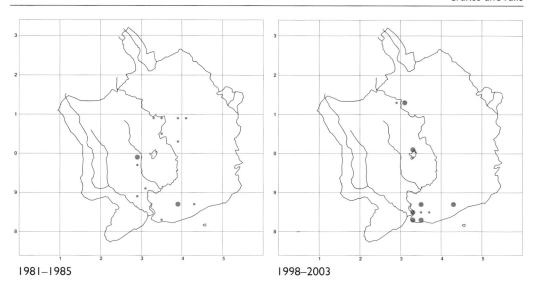

1981–1985   1998–2003

surveyed for breeding birds using tape lures to induce calls, and the survey period covered the years pre- and post establishment of the Reserve. The creation of substantial new reedbeds at the site is reflected in the number of pairs recorded, with 2–3 in 1996 increasing significantly to 20–24 by 2005. The highest single count of birds recorded in Gwent was made during this survey when on 2nd April 2005, 56 birds were noted (Clarke, 2006).

Assessing the size of a breeding population is difficult owing to the secretive nature of the species and because wintering birds can still be present until early spring. However, by combining the latest atlas findings and the survey work at Uskmouth a Gwent population of around 30 breeding pairs is produced.

The majority of winter records in Gwent are of small numbers of birds, the exception being at the Uskmouth where counts of over 10 birds have been recorded since the establishment of the new reedbeds. Elsewhere, 14 were at Llanarth in the winters of 1966 and 1968. Records are more widespread during this time of year with birds noted at breeding sites and a variety of other water bodies, including small ponds and along the Monmouthshire to Brecon canal. Typically, around 20 birds are recorded annually, of which half are at Uskmouth.

The Winter Atlas suggested that the British and Irish summer population remains during the winter, and that numbers are considerably augmented by incoming migrants. Possible evidence of winter immigration to Gwent comes from three ringing records. A bird ringed at Dungeness, Kent in late March 1964 and recovered at Llanwenarth in November 1964 possibly relates to a continental migrant. The second record, a bird ringed at Mellum, Germany in August 1953 and recovered at Blackwood in January 1955, is consistent with the suggestion that the majority of continental migrants that winter in Britain originate from Germany (*Migration Atlas*). The third record concerns a bird ringed at Pandy, Abergavenny in January 1976, and recovered near Glasgow, Strathclyde some ten years later in June 1986. A similar long-distance movement between Wales and Scotland is noted in the *Migration Atlas* with a bird moving between Gwynedd and Tayside.

Gwent Breeding Atlas data and population size

Gwent Atlas	Confirmed tetrads	Probable tetrads	Possible tetrads	Total tetrads	Change in total	Gwent population
1981–1985	0	2	11	13	–	–
1998–2003	0	7	4	11	−15%	c.30 pairs

Spotted Crake
Rhegen Fraith

Porzana porzana

An uncommon passage migrant and rare winter visitor

This very secretive species is a summer visitor to Britain, with a very small breeding population of fewer than 50 pairs in most recent years (Ogilvie, 2004). It has bred sporadically in Wales but not proved to do so since the mid-1980s (2002 *Birds in Wales*). The Winter Atlas lists a small number of winter records.

The 1937 *Birds on Monmouthshire* records an opinion that 'a few pairs may have bred some years ago' in the county, but states there are no definite records of this. In total, there are twelve documented records of Spotted Crakes, all of which are from localities in the south of the county. Four date from the early half of the 20th century: birds shot at Newport in 1903 and 1917, a one seen at Peterstone in August 1940 and one found dead at Llanwern on 15th November 1946. The remaining eight records, all of single birds, and dating from 1975 are detailed in Table 42.

Apart from a sighting in December at Magor Marsh, all recent records have been in the passage periods, with three in spring and four in autumn. Peterstone Gout has been a favoured autumn location, hosting three stays of 16–25 days duration. The May record from Greenmoor Pool was suggestive of breeding, and owing to this, the location was not published at the time.

1975	5–20 September	Peterstone	1	present in the Gout
1977	15 October	Chepstow	1	a single found dead near Chepstow.
1981	16 December	Magor Marsh	1	seen with 4 Water Rails.
1984	25 March	Uskmouth	1	
1988	28 May	Greenmoor Pool	1	heard calling
1989	29 August–21 September	Peterstone	1	in the Gout
1993	24–25 April	Uskmouth	1	heard calling from reedbeds
1994	2–26 September	Peterstone	1	in the Gout

Table 42. Modern records of Spotted Crakes in Gwent

Corn Crake
Rhegen yr Ŷd

Crex crex

A rare passage migrant, formerly bred

The 1963 *Birds of Monmouthshire* describes the Corn Crake as very rare summer visitor that was previously considered to be a well distributed breeding species, especially in the hay meadows of the coastal levels, which were still thought to hold a few pairs up to 1938.

There are 14 documented records (Table 43), the first being from Llanbadoc in 1948, and the most recent being of an individual heard at Lower Coed Morgan during the late evening/early morning of the 6th and 7th June 1984. Of the remaining records, there has been only one instance of confirmed breeding, from Llanarth in 1965. There have also been three records where pairs are thought likely to have bred, and these have involved birds seen/heard at Llanellen during 1st May–12th June 1967; at Abernant, near Caerleon during 9th May–17th June 1968, and at Ponthir during the spring of 1982.

1948		Llanbadoc	1	
1958	13 August	Usk	1	killed by collision with wires
1965	summer	Llanarth	1	bred; fledged young seen
1966	14 September	Grosmont	1	found in an exhausted condition after a storm; later released.
1967	1 May–12 June	Llanellen	1	probably bred
1967	September	Clytha	1	

1967	16 September	Coed-y-bwnydd	1	seen on the road at dusk
1968	9 May–17 June	Abernant, Caerleon	1	probably bred
1969	7 October	Rodge Wood, Caerwent	1	
1971	14 August	Central Gwent	1	listed only as 'alongside the Mon-Brecon canal'
1973	19 September	Caldicot	1	Brockwells farm
1976	16 July	Abergavenny	1	Hardwick Farm
1982	spring	Ponthir	1	probably bred
1984	6–7 June	Lower Coed Morgan	1	singing

Table 43. Documented records of Corn Crakes in Gwent

(Common) **Moorhen** Iâr Ddŵr

Gallinula chloropus

A common and widespread resident

The Moorhen is common and widely distributed in the lowlands of Britain. The 1994 *Birds in Wales* notes that a decline in the coalfield valleys of South Wales during the industrial era was reversed when the coal mines closed and the river quality improved. The 1963 *Birds of Monmouthshire* described it as common, especially in the reens of the coastal flats and on canals.

Moorhens remain common and widespread in Gwent, though quite scarce on high ground in the north and west. In the 1977 *Birds of Gwent* they were noted as being also scarce in the western valleys. They occur at any pond, lake or reservoir where there is good emergent vegetation or overhanging branches for nest sites. Even garden pools may be utilised. They also occur on the less disturbed sections of the Monmouth & Brecon Canal and on the network of reens on the Gwent Levels, where the species is numerous, as well as on slower-moving sections of rivers. For example, a few records come from the River Wye near Monmouth and the lower Monnow up to Monmouth Cap.

In the 1st Gwent Atlas Moorhens were found in 47% of tetrads and confirmed breeding in 33%. In the 2nd Gwent Atlas they were found in a similar number (47.5%) of tetrads, with confirmed breeding in 35%, showing, therefore, very little change in overall numbers of occupied tetrads between the two surveys. Distribution

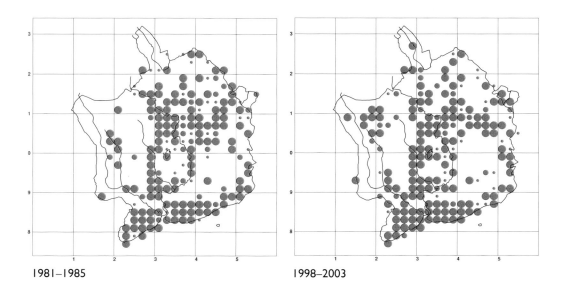

1981–1985   1998–2003

was also similar although there were more records in the northwest than previously, probably reflecting the improvement of water quality in both the rivers and many former industrial ponds.

The Gwent Levels, Usk Valley and farmland in the Raglan area remained strongholds. The many new ponds on farmland and on golf courses, as well as wetlands at the Newport Wetlands Reserve have provided much new habitat for the species over the last two decades, and although distribution has changed little, there may now be more birds per tetrad. In 1985 the 1st Gwent Atlas suggested that up to 15 pairs per tetrad might occur on the reens on the levels, with two to three pairs per occupied tetrad elsewhere, giving a county population of around 1,000 pairs. This may still be true although the plethora of ponds would suggest an even higher figure. However, current estimates derived from BBS data and sample tetrads give a population of no more than 325–380 pairs, which is considered too low.

There have been concerns nationally that feral mink have caused heavy losses of eggs or chicks, but the mink population has now stabilised or even declined. Recent data shows a marked short-term increase in Moorhens in the U.K. during 1994–02 (Eaton *et al.*, 2003), while the WBS waterways survey shows no change during 1994–2003. In Gwent, Moorhens still remain common at most sites.

British Moorhens are very sedentary, so during the autumn and winter they occur at the same sites as in the breeding season but numbers may be augmented by winter visitors from France, The Netherlands and Denmark (*Migration Atlas*). There is only one ringing record of interest: a juvenile ringed at Raglan in August was recovered 38km SSE in Bristol in the following February.

Gwent Breeding Atlas data and population size

Gwent Atlas	Confirmed tetrads	Probable tetrads	Possible tetrads	Total tetrads	Change in total	Gwent population
1981–1985	129	24	31	184	–	–
1998–2003	137	24	26	187	0%	330–380 pairs

National breeding data and conservation status

Estimated Welsh population	Welsh trend	UK CBC/BBS trend 1985–2003	Welsh & UK conservation status
16,000 pairs	Not available	+29%	Green-listed

(Common) **Coot**   *Fulica atra*
Cwtiar

A common and increasing breeding species at suitable wetlands; also a winter visitor

The Coot is a well-distributed breeding bird in the UK, absent only from northern Scotland and the far south-west of England (1988–91 National Atlas). In the breeding season it requires open water with areas of emergent vegetation in which to build the nest. Although tending to avoid the smallest farm or garden ponds, pairs now breed on relatively small ponds on golf courses as well as on larger lakes and reservoirs.

In Gwent there has been a marked increase in breeding Coots since the publication of the 1977 *Birds of Gwent* and the 1st Gwent Atlas. In the 1970s and early 1980s there were few regular breeding sites, amongst which were St Pierre Lake, the steelworks wetlands at Llanwern and the canal near Llanellen. In the mid 1980s, they started breeding at Llandegfedd Reservoir: where four pairs

bred in 1986, seven in 1990 and 11–15 in 1994, since when two to three pairs have bred most years. The other main breeding areas in the 1980s were in the Usk Valley between Abergavenny and the town of Usk, and in the coastal areas. The 1st Gwent Atlas showed birds to be present in 40 tetrads, representing a mere 10% of tetrads in the county, and with *confirmed* breeding in only 27.

Since then new breeding sites have included Ynysyfro Reservoir, Dunlop Semtex Pond at Brynmawr (six pairs by 1995), the Nedern Wetlands (3–4 pairs), Magor Marsh (two pairs), Dingestow Court Lake (2–3 pairs), Llantilio Crossenny and Woodstock Pond. Numbers at Peterstone rose to 8–10 pairs by 1996, with pairs noted at the Gout and the trout lake. Birds were also found breeding at Hendre Golf Course Lakes (2–3 pairs), Beaufort Ponds (three pairs), Brynmawr machine ponds, and The Hoop above Whitebrook for the first time in 1995. Other newly colonised sites were Pant-yr-eos Reservoir and Abergavenny Golf Course in 1997, and Bryn Bach Park (three pairs), Ysgyryd Fach and Peterstone Golf Course in 1998. In 1999, pairs bred at 14 sites including single pairs at Gobion, Chain Bridge and Coldbrook. In 2000, Caldicot Castle, Waun-y-Pound, Coedkernew, Penyfan Pond, Garn Lakes and Bulmore Golf Course were added to the list of sites. By then at least 30 pairs were also breeding at the Newport Wetlands Reserve. In 2001 yet another new site was the lake at Ebbw Vale Festival Park. In 2002 three more sites, comprising ponds on Raglan Golf Course (three pairs), Celtic Manor and Llanfoist Ponds were occupied, whilst in 2003 a pool at Bassaleg, Fedw Pond at Tintern and Wentwood Reservoir also held breeding pairs. The county population has doubled since 1981–85 with birds occurring in 21% of tetrads in the 2nd Gwent Atlas.

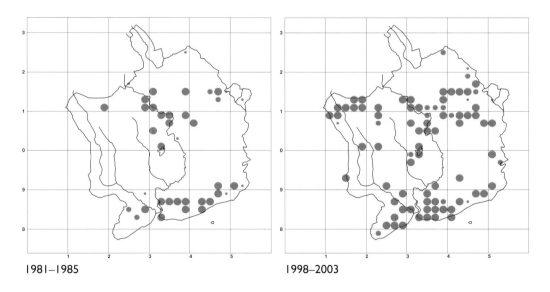

1981–1985   1998–2003

Up to 1977 the total population was about 20 pairs. By 1985 the estimated population was 50–100 pairs but this has now increased to over 100, possibly up to 200 pairs. Our estimated current population of 130 to 160 pairs may be too conservative, but we considered it likely that the BBS-based estimate of 420 pairs (see Appendix 1) was too high, being inflated by the inclusion of two BBS squares in the Newport Wetland Reserve, where there are atypically high numbers.

In autumn the British Coot population is increased by immigration from as far east as Russia (*Migration Atlas*), and although some of these birds doubtless come to Gwent, the the only ringing evidence for immigration from the east concerns a bird ringed at the rather less exotic location of Lincolnshire.

During the winter, birds gather in large numbers at favoured sites. In the 1970s the main wintering sites were Llandegfedd and Ynysyfro Reservoirs. At these sites numbers increased from September or October to peak counts in December or January, after which numbers decreased again, with few or none present from May to August. A record count at Llandegfedd Reservoir of more than 1,100 Coots was made in December 1974, but winter maxima more commonly reached only 500–600 birds during the 1970s. From the early 1980s winter numbers at Llandegfedd declined and the pattern of occurrence changed, with peak numbers sometimes occurring in the summer as the breeding population increased. At Ynysyfro, winter counts have, by contrast, increased from fewer than 50 in the early 1970s to over 100 in 1982, 1986 and 1988, and about 200–230 in most winters from 1989/90 to 1994/95. Then there were 290 in November 1995 and a maximum of 320 in January 1997. Numbers were low in 1998/99 and again in 1999/2000, but since then peak winter counts have ranged from 217–292.

Other regular wintering sites for up to 50 Coots include St Pierre Lake, Tredegar House Lake, Liswerry Pond, Coedkernew, British Steel Corporation wetlands at Llanwern, Woodstock Pool and Wentwood Reservoir. Small numbers occur too on the River Usk, on the Nedern Wetlands, and small numbers are occasinally recorded on the sea. Although Uskmouth ashponds always held a few Coots, the expanded Newport Wetlands Reserve held 243 in February 2001 and 149 in February 2002. The lake at Bryn Bach now regularly holds 50–60 Coots in mid winter with 131 recorded in November 2000. Dunlop Semtex Pond and Pant-yr-eos Reservoir are also now regular wintering sites for up to 100 birds. An increase in winter numbers is evident, and this is consistent with a rise in the WeBS index for Wales of around 40% during 1994–2003.

Gwent Breeding Atlas data and population size

Gwent Atlas	Confirmed tetrads	Probable tetrads	Possible tetrads	Total tetrads	Change in total	Gwent population
1981–1985	27	4	9	40	–	–
1998–2003	66	13	5	84	+110%	130–160 pairs

National breeding data and conservation status

Estimated Welsh population	Welsh trend	UK CBC/BBS trend 1985–2003	Welsh & UK conservation status
3,500 pairs	Not available	+74%	Green-listed

WeBS data 1999/2000–2003/04 and conservation status

Average annual peak count for Gwent	450–500*
Threshold number for importance in GB	1,730
Threshold number for international importance	17,500
GB average peak count	109,000
Wales and UK winter conservation status	Green-listed

*Data from Gwent Bird Reports, not WeBS.

Common Crane   *Grus grus*
Garan

A very rare visitor

This spectacular species is an annual visitor to Britain, usually in very small numbers during the migration period, but since 1981 there have been several breeding pairs in eastern England. It is a rare visitor to Wales but has occurred in all months except June, July and November (2002 *Birds in Wales*).

There are just four records of Common Crane in Gwent, three of them in mid-winter, and one in spring. Details of these are as follows: a single bird was seen following the course of the River Wye at Dixton, near Monmouth on the 25th January 1978; two birds, which had been present at several other South Wales locations at the end of 1999, were seen flying over St Brides on 2nd January 2000; four [two adults and two immature birds] were present along the Rhymney Valley at Michaelston-y-fedw during 13th–16th January 2001, and also seen briefly at Peterstone on 14th January; a single bird was present on the saltmarsh grasslands at the Newport Wetlands Reserve during 11th–12th April 2002.

(Eurasian) **Oystercatcher** **Pioden y Môr**

Haematopus ostralegus

A winter visitor and passage migrant in moderate to large numbers. A few pairs breed

The combination of smart black and white plumage with bright orange bill and legs ranks the Oystercatcher among our most attractive and most conspicuous shoreline birds. This, together with its far-carrying call, its conspicuous display behaviour and its almost entirely coastal distribution in Gwent, makes it unlikely that any breeding pairs were overlooked during either Gwent Atlas survey (1981–85 & 1998–2003).

The Severn Estuary's large tidal range, exposing considerable quantities of molluscs daily, readily explains the presence of breeding Oystercatchers on the Gwent coast. Suitable coastal breeding habitat; whether saltmarsh, sand or shingle, is very limited, and much of it suffers disturbance by various human activities. This equally readily explains the clear indication on the map of a small, irregularly distributed but numerically stable, breeding population. The 1977 *Birds of Gwent* refers only to breeding on Denny Island prior to 1899, and at an unspecified coastal location from 1971 to 1975. The 1st Gwent Atlas estimated the breeding population at about 15 pairs; more recent *Gwent Bird Reports* have referred to up to six pairs, but in a variety of locations, so a present estimate of about ten breeding pairs looks reasonable. The establishment of the lagoons at Goldcliff, where three pairs attempted to breed in 2003, may well lead to an increase in coastal breeding numbers.

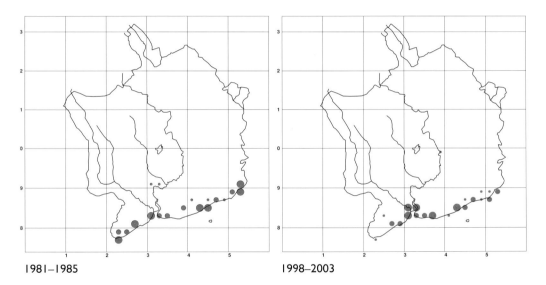

1981–1985   1998–2003

Two trends noted on a national scale in recent years may also lead to increased numbers breeding in Gwent. First, the 1988–91 National Atlas notes that the widespread distribution of breeding Oystercatchers in northern Britain is the result of colonisation of shingle banks along rivers and on lake shores; its maps indicate this change spreading into north and mid-Wales. Secondly, and in part a consequence of this spread, Oystercatchers have increasingly adopted arable fields as nest sites, a trend most strikingly noted in the intensely farmed areas from Norfolk northwards along the east coast. Neither trend has become marked in Gwent as yet, but there have been occasional nests in fields at St Brides and it is possible this behaviour may increase in the future. These developments are reflected in national population trends, where the overall recent UK trend from BBS sites has been –5%, whereas the WBS (Waterways Birds Survey) has shown a 10% increase over a similar ten year period and a 114% increase over a thirty-year period. The recent overall Welsh trend has been +23% and the contrast with the decline in the UK as a whole, probably reflects the remaining relatively larger scope for expansion into these new inland habitats in Wales.

The 1988–91 National Atlas estimated the British breeding population at 33,000–43,000 pairs in the mid-1980s, while the 2002 *Birds in Wales* gives a range of 600–800 pairs for the Welsh breeding population 'at present'. The Gwent breeders form only a minute fraction of both of these, so that any comparison of variation in their numbers with published population trends can have little if any significance.

The Winter Atlas indicates that Oystercatchers wintering on the west coasts of Britain originate from Scotland, the Faeroe Islands or Iceland. The 2002 *Birds in Wales* concurs with this, adding that some Welsh wintering birds also come from Norway. In recent years, WeBS counts indicate average winter totals of about 500–600 birds in the county, and most of these are on the coastal stretch west of Newport. This represents a considerable increase over the numbers in the 1980s and 1990s, when 100–200 were more typical winter totals, and an even greater increase over the estimates in the 1977 *Birds of Gwent*, which gave peak winter and passage numbers of 30–80. The Cardiff Bay barrage was closed in November 1999, displacing about 100 Oystercatchers (Burton, 2006), many of which relocated to the nearby Rhymney estuary. Thus, if any birds relocated to the Gwent coast, their numbers will have been far too small to have had a noticeable impact on the winter totals quoted above.

Even in summer, coastal totals of up to 200 are not uncommon; most of these are, presumably, non-breeding subadults from the northern populations. Ringing recoveries cited in the 2002 *Birds in Wales* indicate that first-year birds from Wales move south into south-west Britain, France and Portugal; thus the Gwent winterers are unlikely to be of local origin. On a national scale, the British winter population is of the order of 250,000 birds; about one-fifth of these are in Wales, and the Dee Estuary and the Burry Inlet are sites of international importance with populations of about 22,000 and 15,000 respectively. The Gwent winter population is very small by comparison.

Gwent Breeding Atlas data and population size

Gwent Atlas	Confirmed tetrads	Probable tetrads	Possible tetrads	Total tetrads	Change in total	Gwent population
1981–1985	7	7	5	19	–	–
1998–2003	5	8	8	21	+11%	c.10 pairs

National breeding data and conservation status

Estimated Welsh population	Welsh trend 1994–2003*	UK BBS trend 1994–2004 (WBS 1993–2003)	Welsh & UK conservation status
600–800 pairs	+23	−5% (+10)	Amber-listed

*From *The State of Birds in Wales 2003.*

WeBS data 1999/2000–2003/04 and conservation status

Average annual peak count for Gwent	530
Threshold number for importance in GB	3,200
Threshold number for international importance	20,000
GB average peak count	248,900
Wales and UK winter conservation status	Amber-listed

Black-winged Stilt
Hirgoes

Himantopus himantopus

A very rare vagrant

The only record of this spectacular and unmistakable species is of a pair of birds that was present on flooded pasture in the Undy area one spring in the early 1950s, probably in one of the years 1952–54. They can be identified unequivocally from photographs taken at the time and apparently attempted to breed but failed, possibly as a result of disturbance from the flow of local people that came to see them.

(Pied) **Avocet**
Cambig

Recurvirostra avosetta

An uncommon passage migrant and winter visitor. Has bred since 2003

The Avocet recolonised Britain in late 1940s, breeding initially in Suffolk. It has since expanded in both numbers and range and the current population stands at over 1,000 pairs, still centred mainly on eastern England (Ogilvie, 2004). It has also increased as a winter visitor, mostly on the south and east coasts of England, with peak counts of around 6,000 birds in recent years (WeBS).

The 1937 *Birds of Monmouthshire* gives only two records: of a 'flock' reported from the Severn Estuary in 1906 and a single bird shot at Ynysyfro Reservoir in 1907. The 1977 *Birds of Gwent* details a further four records: of a single bird at Peterstone during 4–6th April 1968, two seen on a reen at Bishton on 10th May 1969, one at Collister Pill on 20th June 1974 and two on the shore at Peterstone on 2nd August of the same year.

There were a further six records during the late 1970s and early 1980s but, following this, occurrences became progressively more frequent and have been annual since 1987. Almost all records have been at coastal locations, with a single bird at Llandegfedd Reservoir during 24–25th June 1995, as the only inland occurrence. All documented records for the county are summarised in Table 44, and show a strong peak in the spring passage period, with less frequent occurrences at other times of year. Records generally comprise one or two birds, but have included small flocks at Peterstone: of ten birds during 16–17th April 1989 and 13 during 30th November–14th December 1994, and at Goldcliff Pill where there were nine on 7th October 1998.

	Jan	Feb	Mar	Apr	May	Jun	Jul	Aug	Sep	Oct	Nov	Dec	Total
1965–69	–	–	–	1	1	–	–	–	–	–	–	–	2
1970–74	–	–	–	–	–	1	–	1	–	–	–	–	2
1975–79	–	–	–	–	1	–	–	1	1	–	–	–	3
1980–84	–	–	–	–	1	–	–	1	1	–	–	–	3
1985–89	–	–	–	3	1	–	–	–	–	–	–	1	5
1990–94	1	–	–	–	4	–	–	–	–	1	1	1	8
1995–99	3	–	–	–	1	1	–	–	–	1	1	–	7
2000–04	–	–	3	2	1	1	–	1	–	–	–	–	8
2005	–	–	1	–	–	–	–	–	–	1	–	–	2
Total	4	–	4	6	10	3	–	4	2	3	2	2	40

Table 44. Temporal distribution of Avocet records in Gwent (breeding records excluded)

Following the construction of the Goldcliff Lagoons at the Newport Wetlands Reserve in 1999, a pair of Avocets was seen displaying at the site in April 2002, and successful breeding occurred there in 2003. Subsequently two pairs raised five young in 2004, and three pairs raised nine young in 2005. These are the first breeding records for Wales.

Research undertaken into items found at the Roman archaeological sites in Caerleon (Parker, 1988) identified the remains of this species amongst late 1st century food refuse found at the Fortress Baths. It is presumed that birds would have been caught at the nearby estuary, an area where the Second Legion Augusta carried out extensive drainage and reclamation works in the 2nd and 3rd Centuries.

Stone Curlew
Rhedwr y Moelydd

Burhinus oedicnemus

A rare visitor during passage periods

The Stone Curlew is a scarce and local summer visitor to Britain, breeding very locally in places that provide extensive open habitat with sandy or stony soils, in southern and eastern England (1988–91 National Atlas).

There are eight Gwent records of this generally secretive species, all involving single birds, and mostly in either April or August. Following the first on the Undy shore on 10th April 1970, there were three other records in the next 12 years: from the Undy shore on the late date of 11th November 1972 and again on 15th June 1973, and from Peterstone on 5th August 1982.

The next occurrence was not till 1990, when a juvenile was seen at Sluice Farm on 22nd August: this bird had been in nearby Glamorgan during 20th–21st August, and had been ringed as a juvenile on Salisbury Plain, Wiltshire earlier in the year. Other records have been at Llanfihangel Gobion on 14th April 1995, on the Offa's Dyke footpath at Hatterall Hill on 9th April 1997 and at Redwick on 8th August 1998.

Black-winged Pratincole
Cwtiadwennol Aden-ddu

Glareola nordmanni

A very rare vagrant

The only record of this aerial wader species in Gwent, and the 2nd for Wales, was of a single bird seen on several occasions on 25th June 2001 at the Goldcliff lagoons, Newport Wetlands Reserve. Unfortunately, this bird occurred during the time when the public were excluded from the reserve, owing to the national foot-and-mouth disease epidemic, and it was therefore seen only by the staff of the reserve. A bird subsequently seen in Anglesey, during 4th–20th July 2001 is assumed to have been the same individual.

Little Ringed Plover
Cwtiad Torchod Bach

Charadrius dubius

An uncommon passage migrant and scarce summer visitor

The Little Ringed Plover is a summer visitor to Britain and a fairly recent colonist, beginning in 1938 with a single pair in eastern England. Since then it has spread north and west, reaching Wales in the early 1970s, and becoming established at many widespread localities. In 2000, the Welsh population was estimated as about 100 pairs (2002 *Birds in Wales*).

The earliest records in Gwent were all of single passage birds at Peterstone, the first in July 1964, and the next two in August 1967 and April 1968 respectively. From 1971, records became annual and for the next 12 years continued to involve only passage birds, fairly evenly distributed between spring and autumn seasons, and between Llandegfedd Reservoir and coastal sites such as Peterstone Gout and St Brides beach.

Breeding first occurred in 1984 when three pairs were discovered on a gravel shoal in the River Usk, one of which hatched two clutches of eggs, and another pair at a similar site was seen with chicks. The species has bred in the county in every subsequent year, with the number of locations fluctuating from year to year between one and about four. In the early years, the occupied sites continued to be mostly on gravel shoals in the River Usk, but industrial sites such as Newport Docks have also been used, as have gravelly areas on the coast. In 1999, four pairs bred at Newport Wetlands Reserve (three at the Goldcliff lagoons and one at the Uskmouth reedbed lagoons. Since then, the Goldcliff lagoons have become the major breeding site in the county with up to eight pairs recorded. In 1999 in addition to eight pairs at Newport Wetlands Reserve, there were two on the River Usk, and another at a site in the north of the county, making a total of 11 pairs in the county.

Data from the two Gwent Atlases are tabulated in the standard way but maps have not been published in order to minimise disturbance at breeding sites.

Since the advent of breeding in the county, there have continued to be passage records in both spring and autumn, reported mostly from Llandegfedd Reservoir, and more occasionally from coastal locations. Passage records doubtless occur at Newport Wetlands Reserve but are difficult to separate from the arrival of breeders. Earliest arrival dates used to be in the first week of April, but have been in March in ten of the last fifteen years, with the 18th as the earliest date. Few birds are recorded in September, and there have been only a handful in October, with the latest on the 14th.

Gwent Breeding Atlas data and population size

Gwent Atlas	Confirmed tetrads	Probable tetrads	Possible tetrads	Total tetrads	Change in total	Gwent population
1981–1985	3	0	0	3	–	–
1998–2003	5	2	2	9	+200%	8–12 pairs

Ringed Plover
Cwtiad Torchog

Charadrius hiaticula

Mainly a passage migrant but some birds stay through the year. Has bred sporadically, becoming regular in recent years

The Gwent coast is almost completely devoid of the sandy and shingle beaches which form the Ringed Plover's favoured breeding habitat, and such small patches that exist are often liable to disturbance by a variety of shoreline users. It is thus not surprising that, prior to the establishment of the Newport Wetlands Reserve in 1999, which has provided suitable undisturbed habitat at Goldcliff, breeding had been recorded in only seven years. The earliest were in 1971–73, at Newport Docks, where breeding was attempted 'on Llanwern shale', but no information was given about the outcome. Later attempts in 1984 (site undisclosed, one chick raised) and 1994 (Goldcliff, nest washed out by high tides) were followed in 1998–2000 at St. Brides by one or two pairs, with at least one chick being raised in two of these years. In subsequent years up to four pairs have attempted to breed at St Brides but with no confirmation of success.

Since 1999, *probable* or *confirmed* breeding has occurred annually on the new saline lagoons at Goldcliff; most recently in 2003, when three pairs fledged a total of at least four young, while in 2002, 2–4 pairs raised some young (number not stated). This gives grounds for hope that Ringed Plovers will establish a colony of at least moderate size on the shingle of the reserve pools.

The 1988–91 National Atlas shows that, in eastern Britain, the Ringed Plover has extended its breeding range inland to an increasing extent, colonising gravel pits and similar wetland sites. This had not then (1991) occurred in Wales or SW England, but the possibility remains that the margins of reservoirs like Llandegfedd may yet host the occasional breeding pair, although most are probably too muddy, and too subject to disturbance, to be suitable.

Apart from the breeders, and in spite of the absence of sandy or shingle beaches, Ringed Plovers are regularly seen in small to moderate numbers throughout the year and at many coastal sites. As in the UK as a whole, the largest numbers usually occur on autumn passage, with a smaller but still marked spring passage. As an indication of the numbers involved, Table 45 gives mean values of the maximum monthly count at any one coastal site:

Jan	Feb	Mar	Apr	May	Jun	Jul	Aug	Sep	Oct	Nov	Dec
24	15	9	26	89	26	10	109	91	28	37	23

The means are for 1992–2000 inclusive, for comparison with data in the 2002 *Birds in Wales*.

Table 45. Mean values of maximum counts of Ringed Plovers on the Gwent coast

The 2002 *Birds in Wales* estimates peak autumn passage numbers in the Principality of at least 1,000–2,000 birds over the same years, whilst the Severn Estuary has a mean August peak of around 600, which easily exceeds the national importance threshold (300) for autumn passage (WeBS). The Gwent proportion of this, though small, is larger than might be expected in view of the lack of ideal habitat. Wintering numbers in the UK have declined steadily to around two-thirds of what they were 15 years ago, and the recent mild winters have produced some redistribution from west coast to east coast, thus accentuating the decline in Wales (WeBS).

The 2002 *Birds in Wales* also indicates that 'very few Welsh breeders are ringed, so that there is very little information on their movements (outside the breeding season)'; its maps show only one recovery in South Wales, of a bird ringed on the Wash. Two other ringing records confirm assertions made in the Winter Atlas on the breeding areas of British passage and wintering birds: first, that most wintering birds breed elsewhere in Britain or on the near Continent: a nestling ringed near Amsterdam in May 1975 had its ring read in the field at Llandegfedd Reservoir the following August. Secondly, that birds from the larger Arctic breeding population occur only on passage in Britain: a bird ringed (presumably on the coast) at Magor in May 1973 was killed on Ellesmere Island, north-east Canada, in July 1979.

Inland records occur fairly regularly in autumn, from late July to early October, in most years most frequently at Llandegfedd Reservoir and usually in small numbers, although maxima of 10–18 birds occur occasionally between late August and mid-September. Spring records here are much less regular, as are passage records in either season at other inland sites, where ones and twos are the norm. Thus a sighting of 25 at Llandegfedd Reservoir in early May 2000 was most unusual.

Gwent Breeding Atlas data and population size

Gwent Atlas	Confirmed tetrads	Probable tetrads	Possible tetrads	Total tetrads	Change in total	Gwent population
1981–1985	1	1	6	8	–	–
1998–2003	2	0	0	2	−75%	4–8 pairs

National breeding data and conservation status

Estimated Welsh population	Welsh long-term trend*	UK trend	Welsh & UK conservation status
c.250 pairs	−6%	Not available	Green-listed

*From *The State of Birds in Wales 2003*.

WeBS data 1999/2000–2003/04 and conservation status

Average annual peak count for Gwent	c.100
Threshold number for importance in GB	330
Threshold number for international importance	730
GB average peak count (August)*	16,570*
Wales and (UK) winter conservation status	Red (Amber) listed

*Peak winter counts can be only 25% of this figure. WeBS is estimated to detect only about two-thirds of the winter population, the remaining third occurring on non-estuarine coasts.

Kentish Plover   *Charadrius alexandrinus*
Cwtiad Caint

A rare visitor in passage periods

There are just eight passage records of this scarce plover, all involving single birds (Table 46).

1978	21–22 April	St Brides
1981	22 August	Peterstone
1983	13 April	St Brides

1989	21 May	Sluice Farm
1983	15–20 September	Goldcliff Pill
1998	18 April	Coldharbour Pill
2000	9 April	Goldcliff lagoons, Newport Wetlands Reserve
2004	11 October	Llandegfedd Reservoir

Table 46. Records of Kentish Plovers in Gwent

Greater Sand Plover   *Charadrius leschenaultii*
Cwtiad y Tywod Mwyaf

A very rare vagrant

The Greater Sand Plover is an Asian species that is extremely rare in Britain. The only Gwent record, and the first for Wales, was of a single bird at St Brides on 16th May 1988. This individual was considered to be the same bird that had been present at Dawlish Warren, Devon during 27th April–4th May 1988.

(Eurasian) Dotterel   *Charadrius morinellus*
Hutan y Mynydd

A very rare passage migrant

There are just five Gwent records to date of this upland wader. Following a single immature at Hafod-yr-Ynys on 1st September 1972, four were seen on spring passage at Mynydd Llanwernarth on 8th May 1980, two at Collister Pill during 25–27th August 1984 and one along the Offa's Dyke footpath at Llanthony on 20th October 1984. Following a gap of twenty years two were seen, again by the Offa's Dyke footpath near Llanthony, on 30th April 2005.

    The Dotterel is a summer visitor that breeds in the highlands of Scotland, and the 1994 *Birds in Wales* describes it as a regular passage migrant through Wales, particularly in spring, occurring mostly at hilltop locations in Cardiganshire and Carmarthenshire. In view of this, the rarity of records on the high ground of Gwent is perhaps surprising.

(Eurasian) Golden Plover   *Pluvialis apricaria*
Cwtiad Aur

A winter visitor and passage migrant in small to moderate numbers. Bred formerly, probably only in small numbers

Although described in the 1977 *Birds of Gwent* as breeding 'in the hills around Abertillery, Tredegar and Abergavenny' about 120 years ago, the Golden Plover has now disappeared from Gwent as a breeding species. Both *Gwent Atlas* records of probable breeding (one in each *Atlas*) and a July record in 1985 of an adult thought to be accompanying four juveniles (*Gwent Bird Report*) refer to the moorland area north of the Heads of the Valleys, of which only a small part lies within Gwent. It is thus at least possible that these records refer to birds which actually bred beyond the county boundary. Otherwise, the only breeding season records since 1985 have been the single possible breeding

record in the 2nd Gwent Atlas (1998–2003), and two other isolated sightings in its favoured moorland habitat. This reflects locally the results of other recent surveys, which indicate the continuing contraction of its breeding range in Wales; the 2002 *Birds in Wales* indicates a population of only about 80 breeding pairs, with its stronghold in the Elenydd region which straddles the Ceredigion/Powys border in mid-Wales.

Winter records are annual but sparse, referring to either cold-weather movements of substantial numbers or, more usually, small numbers mainly at coastal localities. The assertion in the 1977 *Birds of Gwent* that flocks of more than 100 are uncommon remains true, these having occurred in only five winter seasons since 1985, although records of 20–60 have become more frequent. In recent years the largest numbers recorded were in January 1987, at the onset of a spell of freezing weather, when 800–1,200 were noted on the Wentlooge Level for just one day, and in the following March, when up to 280 were seen in the lower Usk Valley. These unusually high numbers still fall well below the exceptional numbers recorded at Undy in the winter of 1970/71, which peaked at 3,000 in January and 2,000 in March. Small numbers are also regularly recorded on both spring and autumn passage, again mainly at coastal sites.

The Winter Atlas estimates the British Isles winter population to have been of the order of 300,000 birds in the early 1980s. Its distribution map confirms the indication given in the 2002 *Birds in Wales*, that most Welsh wintering birds are in the south-west. This source also gives figures of 7,000–12,000 birds wintering at the most favoured sites in Carmarthenshire and, while giving no figure for the overall Welsh wintering population, suggests this is of the order of 20,000 birds. Thus the small numbers usually seen in Gwent are far from typical of the wider scene.

Gwent Breeding Atlas data and population size

Gwent Atlas	Confirmed tetrads	Probable tetrads	Possible tetrads	Total tetrads	Change in total	Gwent population
1981–1985	0	1	0	1	–	–
1998–2003	0	1	1	2	+100%	0–1 pairs

National breeding data and conservation status

Estimated Welsh population	Welsh population trend 1994–2004	UK BBS trend 1994–2004	Welsh & (UK) conservation status
c80 pairs	−27%	+2	Red (Green)-listed

WeBS data 1999/2000–2003/04 and conservation status

Average annual peak count for Gwent	2
Threshold number for importance in GB	2,500
Threshold number for international importance	9,300
GB average peak count	154,830
Wales and UK winter conservation status	Green-listed

Grey Plover
Cwtiad Llwyd

Pluvialis squatarola

A winter visitor to the coast in moderate numbers, with some indication of birds on passage

Grey Plovers are most frequently recorded in winter along the coast, from Peterstone to Undy, with occasional sightings further east. Table 47 gives mean monthly maxima over ten winter seasons for four of the most well-watched coastal sites. The winter seasons chosen as typical were 1989/90 – 1998/99.

Site	Oct	Nov	Dec	Jan	Feb	Mar
Peterstone	10	25	80	86	73	17
St Brides–Uskmouth	1	15	56	56	50	11
Goldcliff–Redwick	30	40	97	31	30	16
Undy	36	27	33	59	40	4

Table 47. Mean monthly maxima of Grey Plovers at four Gwent coastal sites

These figures give a fair indication of the typical seasonal pattern. There is, however, considerable variation in maximum numbers. In particular, unusually large maxima of 750, 400 and 500 were recorded at Goldcliff–Redwick in February and October 1992 and February 1996, respectively, which have been omitted in calculating the figures in Table 47.

The Winter Atlas describes a complex pattern of migration during the whole of the non-breeding season, so it would be unwise to infer total numbers on the Gwent coast from these data; but an average winter population of about 400 birds is suggested for the county. This appears to be about one-fifth of the Welsh wintering population, but only a small fraction of the British Isles wintering population of about 20,000 (Winter Atlas). The Gwent Grey Plovers are very significant in a local context, as the WeBS Low Tide Counts of 1998/99 found virtually the entire Severn Estuary population to be feeding on the Gwent coast. WeBS counts have given mean annual peak counts of 100–120 in the periods 1994/95–1998/99 and 1999/00–2003/04, which is lower than the total of 400 suggested above, but contains some incomplete counts.

Numbers of Grey Plovers wintering in Britain showed an increasing trend from the mid-1970s to the mid-1990s. However since then numbers have declined again, and this has particularly affected west coast sites such as the Burry Inlet and Morecambe Bay, possibly because the long run of mild winters has meant that a higher proportion of birds has stayed at east coast sites (in this context it is notable that numbers on the Wash have increased substantially). This is illustrated in the population trends table, and is reflected in Gwent numbers which were on average significantly higher during the mid-1970s than in 1995–2005.

Records for June in recent years suggest a small number of summering non-breeders, usually fewer than ten; only once in the ten summers 1990–99 were more than ten seen at any of the four sites listed in Table 47.

Inland records of Grey Plover are very scarce: in the ten winters 1989/90 to 1998/99 there were records on only four dates, all between late November and early January, all from Llandegfedd Reservoir, and all but one were of a single bird.

	National winter population trends		
Wales long term	**Wales short term**	**UK long term**	**UK short term**
−38%	−58%	+185%	−4%

WeBS data 1999/2000–2003/04 and conservation status	
Average annual peak count for Gwent	109
Threshold number for importance in GB	530
Threshold number for international importance	2,500
GB average peak count	41,390
Wales and UK winter conservation status	Green-listed

(Northern) **Lapwing**
Cornchwiglen

Vanellus vanellus

Breeds in moderate but decreasing numbers, over a sizeable but rapidly contracting range. A passage migrant and winter visitor in substantial numbers

Discovering the presence of breeding Lapwings is one of the surveyor's easier tasks; their acrobatic display flight, and their aggressive and noisy feints at potential predators, betray their presence very quickly. It is thus likely that few breeding pairs were overlooked, so that the substantial decrease shown by the maps of the Gwent Atlases is unquestionably a real one. The 'apparent recovery in numbers after a period of decline' mentioned in the 1963 *Birds of Monmouthshire* was, at best, only temporary.

Both the 1988–91 National Atlas and the 1994 *Birds in Wales* indicate that this decrease is the local manifestation of a widespread and lengthy decline, first in evidence in Wales from about the 1920s, but now affecting much of western Britain. The 1994 *Birds in Wales,* citing the results of the 1987 BTO Lapwing Survey in a sample of Welsh tetrads, indicates a density equivalent to three pairs per occupied tetrad in south-east Wales. This would suggest a Gwent population of 600–700 pairs in 1987, rather below the estimate of 1,000 pairs given in the 1st Gwent Atlas.

of 1,500 in November 2005 and 1,800 in January 2006, are the only recent counts over 1,000. However, data from WeBS also include a whole-coast count of 3,050 in February 1996. Data from *Gwent Bird Reports* prior to 1994 and in the 1977 *Birds of Gwent* suggest that maxima in thousands, rather than hundreds, were the norm in past years; the latter source cites over 10,000 at Peterstone in February 1969 and at Undy in December 1973, with most observations of 3,000–5,500 birds. The 1963 *Birds of Monmouthshire,* while confirming the general pattern, cites peak numbers over 1,000 only in 1951 and 1953. 'Considerable variation in numbers observed' may well have been as true then as nowadays.

The pattern shown is consistent with the movements of British wintering Knots as described in the Winter Atlas. Autumn arrivals in Britain coming directly from their breeding grounds in Greenland and eastern Canada are augmented by arrivals from (mainly) the Wadden See in the Netherlands (where they have moulted), which then move to estuaries around the Irish Sea before returning to their breeding grounds in spring. Only a small number stay in Britain through the summer; during 1994/95–2003/04 the single site maximum for May to July never exceeded 12 birds, thus giving only limited opportunities for Gwent observers to see the handsome breeding plumage from which its modern international name 'Red Knot' derives.

Inland records are scarce. Since 1990 there have been only nine inland records, scattered through the passage and winter seasons, all of single birds and mostly at Llandegfedd Reservoir. One unusual sighting was of a bird at Gobion in January 1996, presumably seen by or close to the river.

Substantial numbers also occur on other Welsh estuaries, the Dee hosting internationally important numbers. However, as with several other wader and wildfowl species, the much milder winters of the last decade have resulted in many more Knots staying on the east coast, and proportionately fewer coming as far west as Wales. Thus the Burry Inlet, which as recently as winter 2000/01 was an internationally important site with a five-year mean of over 5,000 birds, has now declined to to the lesser status of 'nationally important' with a mean of around 3,500 birds. However, as noted earlier in respect of Gwent, numbers wintering in Wales vary considerably from year to year.

National winter population trends

Wales long term	Wales short term	UK long term	UK short term
−81%*	−50%*	+11%	+3%

*Data from *The State of Birds in Wales 2003.*

WeBS data 1999/2000–2003/04 and conservation status

Average annual peak count for Gwent	50**
Threshold number for importance in GB	2,800
Threshold number for international importance	4,500
GB average peak count	258,800*
Wales and (UK) winter conservation status	Red (Amber) listed

**Down from 540 in previous 5-year period.

Sanderling
Pibydd y Tywod

Calidris alba

A passage migrant, in small numbers; has declined in recent years. A few summer records

Sanderlings come to Britain from the high Arctic tundra, some from across the Atlantic in Greenland and Northern Canada, and others from the east in Siberia. Many of them, mostly Siberian birds, spend the winter on our shores, while others pass through to winter as far south as South Africa (*Migration Atlas*).

The Gwent coastline has none of the long stretches of sandy shore which are the Sanderling's favoured passage and winter habitat, so records are confined almost entirely to the few small stretches of sandy beach that are available, of which St Brides is the best example.

The 1963 *Birds of Monmouthshire* described the Sanderling as 'a rather scarce passage migrant, as a rule in very small numbers', and listed only six known records between 1929 and 1952. However, it is almost certain that this understated its true status, as the advent of regular recording on the coast, which began in the mid-

1960s, quickly revealed the species to be a regular passage migrant chiefly in the spring. Records in the 1960s came mainly from the high-tide roost at Undy but during the 1970s it became apparent that the small sandy beach to the east of St Brides, just inside the mouth of the River Usk, was the main feeding and roosting location in the county.

The great majority of records occur on spring passage, generally in early May, but with peak numbers occasionally in late April. Table 49 gives the mean number of bird-days recorded for the whole of the Gwent coast, over a recent ten-year period, and illustrates the typical pattern of occurrence. Winter records are rare, and the only such occurrence during the period of Table 49 was a single bird at Goldcliff in late November. Autumn numbers are always small, so a flock of 50 at Undy in August 1969 was most exceptional.

	Mar	Apr	May	June	July	Aug	Sep
Mean number of bird-days	1	6	59	3	3	4	5

1990–99 chosen as a typical ten-year period for Sanderling records.

Table 49. Monthly mean numbers of Sanderling bird-days for the Gwent coast, 1990–99

Spring passage numbers vary considerably from year to year. In some years the largest recorded flock does not exceed 10, but in May 1979, when there was an exceptionally heavy passage through Britain, largest flocks were 125 at Peterstone, 124 at St Brides and 100 at Undy. During the 1980s there were four years when the St Brides flock exceeded 50 birds, but numbers then declined, and apart from May 1993, when 80 were seen there, such numbers have not been recorded since. Figure 14 shows the largest flock recorded in the county each year (mostly at St Brides until the 1990s), and illustrates the generally much lower numbers since the late 1980s together with a dramatic decline in the current millennium.

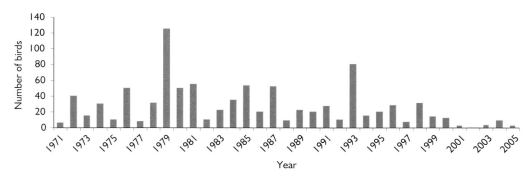

Figure 14. Single-site maxima for Sanderling in Gwent

The beach at St Brides was destroyed in 1991 when, together with the adjacent foreshore, it was used illegally as a landfill site. Much of the landfill was subsequently removed, but the beach took several years to reform at an adjacent site. These events show some coincidence with the onset of the decline of passage Sanderling numbers in the county, but whether there is any causal connection is uncertain. The winter population of Sanderlings has declined generally in the west of the UK and this is thought to be a consequence of the recent very mild winters, which have resulted in many birds remaining further north and east during the winter (WeBS). However, a decline in passage numbers along the west coast, though it would be more difficult to detect, has not been apparent.

Recent national counts show that about 7,000–8,000 Sanderlings winter in the British Isles, of which the 2002 *Birds in Wales* implies that Wales hosts about 1,000. Carmarthen Bay is a nationally important wintering site with a mean winter population of over 1,000 birds in recent years. Also, in many years, Carmarthen Bay and Swansea Bay exceed the national importance threshold for passage numbers (300). The 2002 *Birds in Wales* gives, for a comparable period, peak spring and autumn counts in the ranges 250–700 and 100–400 respectively. Numbers recorded in Gwent are very small in comparison.

Inland records are only occasional, and during 1990–99 there just four: in May (2), September and October. Three of these were from Llandegfedd Reservoir, the fourth (of a single bird in May) at the unusual upland site of Garnlydan Reservoir.

WeBS passage data 1999/2000–2003/04 and conservation status

Average annual peak count for Gwent (spring)	6*
Threshold number for importance in GB	300
GB average peak count (autumn)	15,110
Wales and UK winter conservation status	Green-listed

*Data from Gwent Bird reports instead of WeBS.

Little Stint
Pibydd Bach

Calidris minutus

A passage migrant, rarely in more than small numbers

Most Gwent records of Little Stints refer to birds on autumn passage from their breeding grounds in the Arctic tundra to their winter quarters, which for most are in West Africa south of the Sahara. There is, however, an increasing tendency for birds to overwinter around the Mediterranean and on the Atlantic coasts of Europe, the British Isles being at the extreme north of this range. Both the Winter Atlas and recent WeBS counts indicate an average winter population of about 20–25 birds, though with considerable annual variation. Since the 1977 *Birds of Gwent*, there has been only one winter record in Gwent, a single bird in November 1984, though there have been five elsewhere in the Severn Estuary in two very recent winters.

The typical pattern of autumn passage records in the county is of a steady increase from early August to a peak in late September and a rapid decrease during October. By contrast, spring passage records are scarce. Table 50 gives an indication of the numbers involved:

	May		June		Aug		Sep		Oct	
Half-month:	1	2	1	2	1	2	1	2	1	2
Gwent	3	2	3	1	10	21	61	122	31	3
All Wales	30		20		80		1,100		110	

The 'all Wales' figures were estimated from the histogram given in the 2002 *Birds in Wales;* this comparison determined the choice of years for analysis of Gwent data in the table.

Table 50. Total numbers of Little Stints recorded in Gwent and estimated for all Wales, for 1992–2000

These figures do, however, mask the considerable annual variability. For instance, in 1994 there were three spring records of single birds and none at all in autumn. By contrast, substantial numbers were seen over the whole of Wales in September 1996: of a Welsh total of at least 330 birds between 21st and 25th September, 48 were recorded in Gwent, of which there were 36 at Llandegfedd Reservoir on 23rd September. The latter is the only inland site where Little Stints occur regularly, accounting for about a quarter of all records. Most of the coastal records are from Goldcliff or Peterstone. The most recent WeBS data, for 1999/2000–2003/04, indicate average autumn peak numbers of four in September and seven in October, with no spring records at all. The recent establishment of the lagoons at Goldcliff, allowing both more extensive passage habitat and better opportunities for detecting these minute waders, may well lead to an increase in records in future years.

The 1963 *Birds of Monmouthshire* cites only five autumn passage records and one, very improbably early, spring passage record: four at St.Brides on 3rd March 1932. The regularity of sighting in more recent years very probably reflects an increase in both the amount of coastal observation time and the level of observational skills on the part of local birdwatchers, since small parties of Little Stints can easily pass undetected among large flocks of Dunlins.

Temminck's Stint   *Calidris temminckii*
Pibydd Temminck

A rare passage migrant, usually in autumn

Temminck's Stint is an extremely rare breeding bird in Scotland and in the remainder of the UK it is a scarce passage migrant, mostly in the east. There are seven Gwent records of this tiny, skulking wader, all of single birds (Table 51).

1987	18 May	Llanvihangel Gobion
1993	17–20 September	Nash Pools
1999	10–15 September	Goldcliff lagoons, Newport Wetlands Reserve
2002	3–6 September	Goldcliff lagoons, Newport Wetlands Reserve
2002	19–20 September	Goldcliff lagoons, Newport Wetlands Reserve
2004	16 May	Goldcliff lagoons, Newport Wetlands Reserve
2004	30 August	Goldcliff lagoons, Newport Wetlands Reserve

Table 51. Temminck's Stint records in Gwent

White-rumped Sandpiper   *Calidris fuscicollis*
Pibydd Tinwen

A very rare vagrant

White-rumped Sandpiper is a regular transatlantic vagrant to the British Isles. There are three Gwent records, surprisingly all of adult birds, and all from the Goldcliff area. Following the first, during 11th–17th August 1995 on Goldcliff Pill, further individuals have been seen on the Goldcliff Lagoons, Newport Wetlands Reserve during 14th–21st September 1999 and on 2nd July 2003.

Baird's Sandpiper   *Calidris bairdii*
Pibydd Baird

A very rare vagrant

There are just two Gwent records of this transatlantic vagrant, both of immature birds: at Llandegfedd Reservoir during 26th September–4th October 1997, and at the Goldcliff lagoons, Newport Wetlands Reserve, intermittently during 3rd–13th October 2000.

Pectoral Sandpiper   *Calidris melanotos*
Pibydd Cain

A rare vagrant

There are eleven Gwent records, eight since 1999, of this regular transatlantic vagrant to Britain (Table 52). As is typical for vagrants from America, most records are from the autumn period. The recently constructed

Goldcliff lagoons have proved a strong attractant for this species and may be responsible for the increase of records since 1999.

1963	17 September	Peterstone	1	
1976	3 April	Peterstone	1	
1979	10 August	Peterstone	2	
1999	9–21 September	Goldcliff lagoons	1	immature
2000	4 June	Goldcliff lagoons	1	adult
2000	23 September–4 October	Goldcliff lagoons	1	immature
2001	21–22 September	Collister Pill	1	immature
2002	31 August–5 September	Goldcliff lagoons	1	immature
2004	5–11 September	Goldcliff lagoons	1	immature
2005	4 August	Goldcliff lagoons	1	
2005	7–10 September	Goldcliff lagoons	1	

Table 52. Pectoral Sandpiper records in Gwent

Curlew Sandpiper
Pibydd Cambig

Calidris ferruginea

A passage migrant, usually in small numbers, mainly in autumn

Curlew Sandpipers occur in Britain mainly on autumn passage from their breeding range in eastern Arctic Asia, from where only a part of the population migrates westwards through Europe. Numbers vary greatly from year to year, depending on breeding success and weather patterns at the time of migration. Peak counts for Britain have ranged from 116 to over 1,000 in recent years (WeBS).

The same pattern occurs in Gwent, and Table 53 illustrates the numbers involved during the period 1992–2000. These figures are fairly typical of the period since the early 1970s when regular coastal recording began in the county.

	Apr		May		June		July		Aug		Sep		Oct		Nov
Half-month	2	1	2	1	2	1	2	1	2	1	2	1	2	1
Gwent	0	13	5	0	0	0	3	0	60	99	50	10	4	0
All Wales	<10		80		10		30		380		1100		180		20

The all Wales figures were estimated from the histogram given in the 2002 *Birds in Wales;* this comparison determined the choice of years for analysis of Gwent data in the table.

Table 53. Total numbers of Curlew Sandpipers recorded in Gwent, and estimated for all Wales, 1992–2000

While showing that the main passage occurs in late August and through September, these figures mask substantial annual variations in the Gwent numbers. For instance, at least 38 birds were seen during a concentrated movement between 5th and 10th September 1998, a year when record numbers passed through Britain, whereas the autumn passages of 1992 and 1995 produced only one and two birds respectively. During 1992–2000, no other single flock has approached the size of the largest seen in Gwent, which involved 30 at Goldcliff on 5th September 1985. It is possible that the figures given understate the numbers actually present, since Curlew Sandpipers may easily pass undetected among a large flock of Dunlins.

By contrast, the 1963 *Birds of Monmouthshire* cites only five records of Curlew Sandpipers, of which four were in late August or September. There can be little doubt that increased observation is a major factor in the increase in recorded numbers in recent years.

Almost all records are from the coast and birds can occur anywhere from Sluice Farm in the west to Collister Pill in the east. There have been only seven inland records in the past 35 years . These have included single birds at Garnlydan and Ynysyfro reservoirs, up to 5 on the River Usk near Caerleon in September 1988, 4–8 birds at Llandegfedd Reservoir in the years 1996, 1998 and 1999, and four at the newly constructed pools on the golf course at Bulmore in 1998. The only other inland record involves two birds at The Bryn in mid-November 1988. Since their completion in 1999, the saline lagoons at the Newport Wetlands Reserve have attracted Curlew Sandpipers in most years and may lead to increased numbers of this attractive wader in the county.

Winter quarters for most Curlew Sandpipers migrating through Europe are in sub-Saharan Africa, and very few birds winter north of the Mediterranean. Only two Gwent records, in 1983 and 1988, both for mid-November, could refer to overwintering birds, while the fifth record in the 1963 *Birds of Monmouthshire* refers to 'one picked up dead near Rumney, Christmas 1932'. The Winter Atlas noted only 12 records in the whole of the British Isles over the three winters 1981/82–1983/84, including one of the November records referred to above and one other in the Bristol Channel.

Purple Sandpiper   *Calidris maritima*
Pibydd Du

A very scarce visitor, mostly in passage periods

The Purple Sandpiper is the most maritime of the sandpipers. It is a widely distributed winter visitor around the British coast wherever there are stretches of open rocky shore, which provide its favoured habitat. The muddy, estuarine coastline of Gwent is little to its liking and records are correspondingly scarce.

The 1963 *Birds of Monmouthshire* lists only four records, all from Peterstone, and since then there have been a further eleven records on the coast and one unusual inland occurrence at Llandegfedd Reservoir. All records are listed in Table 54. Of fourteen dated records, three have occurred in spring (April–May), nine in autumn (August–November) and only two in winter. One of the winter records was a six-week stay along a sewage outfall pipe that is covered by imported rocks and gravel to protect it from tidal action and forms one of Gwent's best bits of rocky 'shore'.

1933	10 October	Peterstone	1	
1936	7 November	Peterstone	1	shot
1950	6 December	Peterstone	1	
1954	14 November	Peterstone	1	
1969	14 September	Undy shore	1	
1970	undated	Undy shore	1	seen in a mixed flock of waders.
1971	6–7 May	Collister Pill	2	2 birds on 6th and one on 7th.
1973	12 May	Magor Pill	1	
1977	21 April	Collister Pill	2	
1981	29 August	St Brides	1	
1983	22 October	Llandegfedd Reservoir	1	
1987	10–12 August	Peterstone	1	
1989	31 August	Goldcliff Pill	1	
1990	27 January–11 March	St Brides	1	present along the sewage outfall pipe
2000	19 November	Goldcliff Pill	1	

Table 54. Records of Purple Sandpipers in Gwent

Dunlin
Pibydd y Mawn

Calidris alpina

A winter visitor to the coast in large numbers, with some passage birds. Formerly an occasional breeder in very small numbers

The 1977 *Birds of Gwent* states that 'a few pairs of Dunlin breed irregularly', although evidence for this is scanty. The record it cites for breeding in 1973, at an undisclosed site on moorland in the north of Gwent, is the last county record of *confirmed* breeding. The three *probable* records in the 1st Gwent Atlas (1981–85): in the uplands at the Heads of the Valleys, and occasional records of display at Garnlydan Reservoir up to 1988, and again once near this site during the 2nd Gwent Atlas survey (1998–2003), may have involved birds which actually bred on the Powys side of the county boundary. The 1988–91 National Atlas shows breeding in square SO 11, which straddles the boundary, while the 2002 *Birds in Wales* cites breeding in the Black Mountains in 2000 as the site nearest to the Gwent border. There is no evidence to suggest that the Dunlin was ever more than a scarce breeder in Gwent, although the 1963 *Birds of Monmouthshire* asserts that it nested on the hills near Abergavenny in the past, with only the implied suggestion of regularity. Britain is at the southern extremity of the Dunlin's breeding range; only the few remaining pairs on Dartmoor breed further south than Gwent.

By contrast, the Dunlin is both numerous and conspicuous as a coastal winter visitor. The acrobatic gyrations of flocks of hundreds, and often thousands, over the foreshore at high tide are an unforgettable spectacle. Records indicate their presence all along the coast in thousands from November to February. Over the winter seasons 1992/93–2000/01, maximum numbers at any one site in Gwent often reached 8,000–10,000, the largest being an estimated 13,000 at Peterstone in February 1993. More recently, data both in *Gwent Bird Reports* and from WeBS indicate peak estimates of about 5,000. All these numbers, however, fall well below the largest single-site estimates for the Gwent coast, in January 1975 (15,000–20,000) and January and November 1983 (20,000–30,000 in both months). Total numbers involved are harder to assess, since there is almost certainly movement between sites, but figures given in *Gwent Bird Reports* suggest a peak winter population of about 20,000 in the early 1990s, and about 10,000–12,000 more recently. Comparison with data from the 2002 *Birds in Wales* suggests that Gwent shores host about a quarter of the Welsh winter population. This in turn is only a small fraction of the total British winter population, estimated in recent WeBS counts to reach a peak of about 400,000 birds. The Severn Estuary as a whole is a site of international importance for Dunlins, and is currently the fifth most important site in Britain, with a mean peak count of around 23,000 in recent years. WeBS Low Tide Counts in 1998/99 showed the density of Dunlins feeding on the Peterstone–St Brides stretch of the Gwent shore was the highest in the estuary.

The pattern of seasonal variation on the Gwent coast is shown in Tables 55 and 56.

July	Aug	Sep	Oct	Nov	Dec	Jan	Feb	Mar	Apr	May	Jun
120	240	300	720	1,500	7,200	6,700	6,000	2,300	170	360	24

The period chosen for tabulation corresponds as closely as possible to the period covered in the *2002 Birds in Wales* for comparison, even though this source gives no monthly breakdown of numbers.

Table 55. Mean monthly maximum numbers of Dunlins at any one Gwent coastal site, for April 1992–March 2001

July	Aug	Sep	Oct	Nov	Dec	Jan	Feb	Mar	Apr	May	Jun
51	355	312	1,100	1,100	3,600	5,000	4,800	121	132	1,250	73

Numbers over 1,000 have been rounded to the nearest 50. No counts were made during the spring of 2001 due to foot-and-mouth disease restrictions; thus the spring data set is necessarily incomplete.

Table 56. WeBS data: Peak monthly counts of Dunlins on the whole of the Gwent coast, for 1999/2000–2003/04

Both tables show a clear indication of spring passage, mostly in May, but the presence of autumn passage, spread through July to October, is masked to a great extent by the arrival of wintering birds.

The BTO conducted a long-term study of the effects on wintering waterbirds of the Cardiff Bay barrage, which was closed in November 1999. Describing the results, Burton (2006) gives a figure of the order of 3,300 for the mean peak annual count of Dunlins in Cardiff Bay during the preceding ten winters. He also notes that 'due to an ongoing decline in the Severn population, it was not possible to determine whether displaced [Dunlin] were able to relocate successfully'. The data in Tables 56 and 57 above, which correspond roughly to the 'pre-barrage' and 'post-barrage' periods respectively, certainly give no evidence of successful relocation of winter Dunlins to the Gwent coast.

Most autumn passage birds are of the race *C. a. schinzii*, which breeds mainly in Iceland, south-east Greenland and south from southern Norway (including the British breeders); nearly all of these winter on the coasts of north-west Africa. The bulk of the British winter visitors are of the northern race *C. a. alpina*, which breeds in the north of Scandinavia and Russia, and migrates via the Baltic Sea. The 2002 *Birds in Wales* maps the distribution of birds ringed on the Severn shore and recovered on migration, or vice versa; most of these show movement between the Severn and the shores of the Baltic. The third race, *C. a. arctica,* which breeds only in northern Greenland, probably occurs in Wales only on passage.

Inland records of passage and wintering Dunlin occur annually but only in small numbers and at scattered sites, of which Llandegfedd Reservoir is the most frequently noted; a flock of 40 at this site in September 2000 is exceptionally large for an inland sighting.

Gwent Breeding Atlas data and population size

Gwent Atlas	Confirmed tetrads	Probable tetrads	Possible tetrads	Total tetrads	Change in total	Gwent population
1981–1985	0	3	0	3	–	–
1998–2003	0	1	0	1	−67%	0–1 pairs

National breeding data and conservation status

Estimated Welsh population	Welsh CBC/BBS trends	UK BBS trend 1994–2004	Welsh & UK conservation status
50–70 pairs	Not available	Not available	Amber-listed

WeBS data 1999/2000–2003/04 and conservation status

Average annual peak count for Gwent	5,000
Threshold number for importance in GB	5,600*
Threshold number for international importance	13,300
GB average peak count	387,600
Wales and UK winter conservation status	Amber-listed

*Winter threshold; passage threshold = 2,000.

Broad-billed Sandpiper
Pibydd Llydanbig

Limicola falcinellus

A very rare vagrant

Broad-billed Sandpipers breed as near as Scandinavia but their passage route is south-easterly, as they winter in southern Asia and Australia, and occurrences in Britain are rare. There are two records for Gwent, both of single birds: the first at Peterstone Pill on 7th May 1979 and the second at Sluice Farm on 15th May 1988. The individual seen in 1988 was considered to have been the same bird that had been present at Dawlish Warren, Devon on 1st May 1988 and then at Severn Beach Gloucestershire on 16th May 1988.

Buff-breasted Sandpiper
Pibydd Bronllwyd

Tryngites subruficollis

A rare vagrant, usually in autumn

Buff-breasted Sandpipers are the second commonest transatlantic vagrants to the British Isles and there are six records for Gwent. They have a preference for grassland habitat, so Gwent records have usually been on the short turf of the saltmarsh between the seawall and the muddy shore.

The first was at St Brides during 13th–15th September 1978, a bird which moved to Sluice Farm during 16th–17th September, and which had also been present on the Rumney Great Wharf, South Glamorgan. There are two records from Collister Pill during 26th–30th September 1980 and, on exactly the same dates again, 26th–30th September 1984; and another from Goldcliff Pill on 17th September 1989.

Spring records in Britain are very rare, so a bird on Chepstow Wharf during 23rd–29th May 1990, which was also seen on the English side of the estuary at New Passage, Avon on 22nd–23rd May, was particularly surprising. The most recent record is from Goldcliff lagoons, Newport Wetlands Reserve during 12th–30th September 2000.

Ruff
Pibydd Torchog

Philomachus pugnax

A passage migrant in small numbers; a few winter records

The Ruff's main breeding range is from Scandinavia eastwards across northern Siberia, from which many birds migrate through Europe to their winter quarters in Africa from the Sahara southwards. Most British records are of birds seen on autumn passage. The return passage in spring is usually much smaller. Some birds winter in Britain, usually singly or in small parties; the peak winter count can exceed 1,000 but varies considerably from year to year (WeBS).

The 1963 *Birds of Monmouthshire* described the Ruff as a rare vagrant to the county, citing only one spring record and three autumn records, but this is almost certainly a reflection of limited observation before 1963. Records for Gwent in more recent years reflect the national pattern in miniature, although with a smaller proportion of winter visitors compared with passage birds. At present, most winter records are isolated sightings of single birds on or near the coast, though one notable exception is of up to nine birds in January and February 2002 at the Goldcliff lagoons at Newport Wetlands Reserve.

Since the completion of the Newport Wetlands Reserve in 1999 there has been a substantial increase in sightings of Ruffs through much of the year, and Figure 15 shows that almost all of this increase comes from records from the above reserve. The figure also illustrates the seasonal pattern of records, with passage peaks in March and August–September.

Spring passage records are usually isolated sightings of single birds, although occasionally small parties of up to 8–10 are noted, again mostly from coastal sites. An exceptionally heavy spring passage occurred in 1987, with the peak numbers of 26 at St. Brides and 20 at Peterstone within a day or two of records of similarly large numbers at several other sites across Wales (1994 *Birds in Wales*). The exotic sight of a male in full breeding

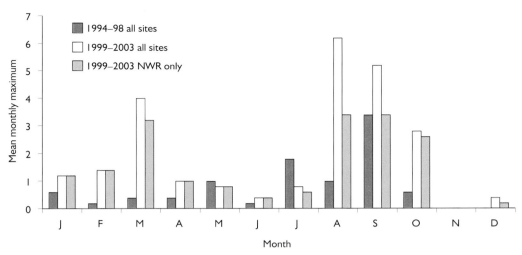

Figure 15. Ruff: comparison of records 1994–1998 and 1999–2003

plumage is very rare in Gwent: only four have been recorded and it seems unlikely that many more would have been overlooked.

Autumn passage, which may start at the end of June and continue well into October, also usually involves sightings of single birds or small parties, although they are more widely and more regularly seen. Not since 1977 has an autumn passed without any records, and totals of 6–10 birds during the passage period is typical. In recent years no autumn passage numbers have even approached those of spring 1987 cited above.

Inland records are thinly, and fairly widely, scattered across Gwent; not surprisingly, Llandegfedd Reservoir is the most favoured site.

Jack Snipe
Gïach Fach

Lymnocryptes minimus

A winter visitor in small numbers

The Jack Snipe is among our least known birds, both in Gwent and on a national scale. This is in large measure due to its secretive behaviour. Its small size (from which its vernacular name 'Half Snipe' derives), its superb camouflage, its crepuscular habits, its habit of sitting tight until almost trodden upon, its usually silent flight and its reluctance to gather even in small parties, all contribute to the secrecy. It is thus inevitable that, both locally and nationally, the extent to which any estimates of numbers reflect its true status must be open to question; it would be unwise to infer more than general indications from the analysis of Gwent records.

Of the 59 records for the ten recent winter seasons 1993/94–2002/03 about four-fifths refer to single birds, with five the largest party, at Goytre in December 1993. Less recent records suggest that parties of four or five were more frequently seen in earlier years, with two records, both from the Peterstone area, of eight together as the largest groups. Just over half the records in the above period are of birds at sites on the coast or the coastal levels, the rest referring to well-scattered inland sites, some at quite high altitudes in the uplands. Numbers recorded each season have varied from none at all in 2000/01 to 11 in 1996/97; in the latter winter, most records were during the spell of hard weather in late December and early January. Table 57 shows the distribution of records by months:

Sept	Oct	Nov	Dec	Jan	Feb	Mar
3	6	4	14	18	10	4

Table 57. Records of Jack Snipe in Gwent, 1993/94–2002/03

In these winters, the earliest and latest dates were 19th September and 10th March respectively. In earlier years, and again in 2006, there have been records up to mid-April. This distribution fits well with the migration pattern described in the Winter Atlas, of the main arrival from its breeding grounds,mainly in northern Scandinavia and Russia, during October–November, with the main return passage during April. The 1963 *Birds of Monmouthshire* similarly describes it as a winter immigrant in varying numbers, but 'not at all common'; this still indicates its status fairly well.

The Winter Atlas also gives two indications of the British wintering population in the early 1980s. Quoting results obtained from samples of numbers of both Common and Jack Snipe in sportsmen's bags, it suggests 'a wintering population of about 100,000; field work, however, indicates a total well below this, probably of the order of several thousand'. Similarly, data in the Concise BWP imply a British wintering population of only a few thousand. In view of the Jack Snipe's extreme reluctance to leave cover, the evidence from sportsmen's bags, arising as a result of targeting this and similar species, may well give a truer picture of numbers than is obtainable from birdwatchers' largely casual records, especially in the upland areas. Thus an average winter population of the order of 50, rather than the fewer than 10 the data from *Gwent Bird Reports* would indicate, may not be too exaggerated.

Common Snipe   *Gallinago gallinago*
Gïach Gyffredin

A winter visitor in moderate numbers; a small, and probably decreasing, breeding population

Although the 1963 *Birds of Monmouthshire* commented that 'the Common Snipe breeds regularly in suitable localities throughout the county', this is clearly no longer the case. The assessment in the *Concise BWP* that for British breeders 'there has been a marked decrease since the 1950s, especially in lowland areas' is a much fairer reflection of the recent trend in Gwent.

The ideal breeding habitat for Common Snipe contains damp ground that remains soft throughout the breeding season, enabling their long bills to probe beneath the surface for food: mainly worms and cranefly larvae, with tussocks of grass or similar cover, and lookout posts. In Gwent this combination occurs in two distinct types of terrain, the uplands of the north and west, and lowland marshy grasslands. The two Gwent Atlas maps reflect this situation, showing a distribution centred on the bare uplands in the north-west but with scattered pockets on the wetter parts of the coastal levels. Between the two atlases there has been a decline in distribution of 50%.

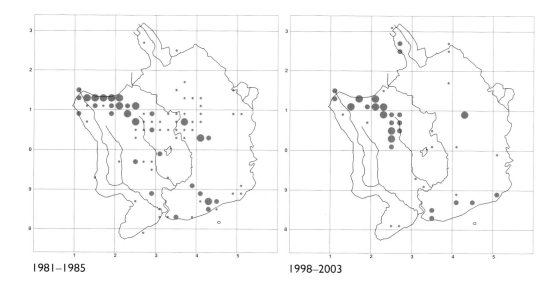

1981–1985   1998–2003

Table 58 analyses the distributions shown by the Gwent Atlases. In the upland tetrads, which in the 1st Gwent Atlas contained about three-quarters of the *probable* and *confirmed* records, the margins of pools and reservoirs, or patches of moorland bog, provide suitable habitat. The drumming and display flights of breeding Common Snipe are conspicuous, so it is improbable that many breeding birds were overlooked; thus the decline from 30 to 23 occupied tetrads is likely to be a fair indication of the true situation. It also seems likely that disturbance or destruction of suitable habitat could have contributed to this decrease; this is known to have happened at Waun-y-Pound, Ebbw Vale, where in 1996 industrial development started on a site that had previously hosted several pairs. Numbers involved are very hard to assess accurately, due to the difficulty of surveying upland areas comprehensively. Records in recent *Gwent Bird Reports* are of up to 8–12 pairs or displaying birds at favoured upland sites such as Waunafon or Trefil, suggesting an upland breeding population of the order of 20 pairs.

		Confirmed	Probable	Possible	Total
Upland	1981–1985	9	9	12	30
tetrads	1998–2003	8	11	4	23
Lowland	1981–1985	3	8	40	51
tetrads	1998–2003	1	5	12	18

Table 58. Breeding records of Common Snipe for both Gwent Atlases, from upland and lowland tetrads

In lowland areas, poorly drained pastures subject to winter flooding provide the best habitat, and it is in these areas that the decline is most marked; from 51 down to 18 occupied tetrads. The intensification of agriculture has led to the loss of much of this habitat through improved drainage, and this has probably been a major factor in the decline of lowland breeding Snipe through much of southern Britain. The Gwent Atlas maps give the impression of disappearance of most of the lowland breeders, especially in the Usk Valley in mid-Gwent. However, many of the now-deserted tetrads recorded only *possible* breeding in the 1st Gwent Atlas and, as was suggested at the time, many of these birds could actually have been late-departing winter visitors, so the true decrease in breeding numbers may be less drastic than the tabulated figures imply. Records from *Gwent Bird Reports* of breeding in lowland areas are regular only from Magor Marsh, where several pairs were frequently noted in the 1960s and 1970s; more recent records imply only one or two pairs there. Other breeding records are both well-scattered and intermittent.

During the autumn, substantial numbers of Snipe arrive in Britain from northern Europe, some of which may move on to Ireland or France, especially in hard weather. The winter population in the UK has been estimated as at least 100,000, and probably nearer 300,000 (WeBS reports 2001–03), but only a very small proportion of these are detected on WeBS counts. The Winter Atlas asserts that 'many of these (arrivals) will have bred in the countries around the Baltic Sea'; the 1994 *Birds in Wales* cites a small number of instances of birds ringed in northern Europe, from as far east as Poland, and recovered in Wales. One bird showing the dark rufous plumage characteristic of the Faeroes race *G. g. faeroeensis* was seen at Llandegfedd Reservoir in late August 1991; it is possible that a small number of birds of this race, which breeds in Iceland, winter in Gwent, although most are believed to winter in Ireland and north and west Scotland.

Winter gatherings of up to 50–70 birds, with occasional records of up to 300, are reported from a variety of lowland sites mainly on the coastal levels,. In recent years the Llanwern steelworks site has hosted the largest numbers, frequently up to 200 in December or January; presumably the suitable habitat here is less subject to disturbance than at other more public sites. Overall winter numbers are difficult to assess, since Snipe rely heavily on their superb camouflage, and become conspicuous only when flushed, which makes normal counting techniques virtually impossible. Thus the indications from numbers given in *Gwent Bird Reports,* of a winter population of several thousand, are little more than a judicious guess. The Severn Estuary is in the top four UK WeBS sites for Snipe, easily passing the national reporting threshold (200) with a five-year mean peak of around 550. The only other significant Welsh site is the Cleddau Estuary complex in Pembrokeshire.

Gwent Breeding Atlas data and population size

Gwent Atlas	Confirmed tetrads	Probable tetrads	Possible tetrads	Total tetrads	Change in total	Gwent population
1981–1985	12	18	52	82	–	–
1998–2003	9	16	16	41	−50%	20–30 pairs

National breeding data and conservation status

Estimated Welsh population	Welsh trend	UK BBS trend 1994–2004	Welsh & UK conservation status
300–450 pairs	Not available*	+54%**	Amber-listed

*Decline of 34% between National Atlases of 1968–72 and 1988–91. **Mostly due to large increases in Scotland.

WeBS data 1999/2000–2003/04 and conservation status

Average annual peak count for Gwent	23*
Threshold number for importance in GB	200**
Threshold number for international importance	20,000
GB average peak count	7,240
Wales and UK winter conservation status	Green-listed

*Many Snipe frequent non-WeBS habitats, so these figures greatly underestimate total populations. **No threshold has been set, but WeBS uses 200 as a 'reporting threshold'.

Long-billed Dowitcher
Gïach Gylfin-hir

Limnodromus scolopaceus

A very rare vagrant

There are just two just two Gwent records of this transatlantic vagrant, both of single birds: one heard calling and seen flying east at Peterstone on 14th September 1985, and another in breeding plumage at Sluice Farm on 9th April 1989. The latter bird had been present on the lower reaches of the River Rhymney, South Glamorgan during 10th March-18th April 1989.

There are three records of birds that were not identified to species level, which refer to either this species or the very similar Short-billed Dowitcher *L.griseus*. Two of these were from the Undy foreshore, where up to two birds were present during 16th September–30th October 1971, and a single bird was present on 29th August 1976. More recently another individual was present on several days at the Goldcliff lagoons in Newport Wetlands Reserve during 20th–27th March 2005.

(Eurasian) Woodcock
Cyffylog

Scolopax rusticola

An uncommon winter visitor and scarce breeder

The 1963 *Birds of Monmouthshire* recorded the Woodcock as a resident that had bred in small numbers, but acknowledged that a lack of recent records made its present breeding status uncertain. The 1977 *Birds of Gwent* listed it as a scarce breeding resident, more widely reported in small numbers in the winter.

The 1st Gwent Atlas showed Woodcock to be largely restricted to the Wye Valley woodlands, the Wentwood ridge and the north of the county. Some *possible* breeding records in central Gwent may have referred to migrant birds, as suitable breeding habitat is restricted there. The population was estimated at probably not in excess of 200 pairs. However, as this is a particularly difficult species to census, owing to the potential of roding males to mate with several females and its crepuscular habits, this is likely to have been an

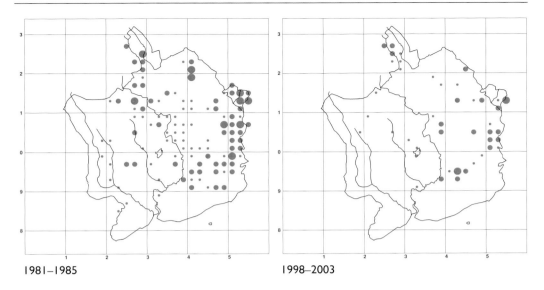

| 1981–1985 | 1998–2003 |

overestimate. There have been only occasional breeding records for subsequent years: one or two 2 records in 1988, 1990, 1992, 1993 and 2001, and three or four records in 1986 and 1989.

The 2nd Gwent Atlas shows a marked reduction in occupied tetrads since the earlier survey, although the same general areas are occupied. The reduced numbers of roding birds reported since the early 1990s also suggest there has been a decrease in numbers. There is an obvious scarcity during the breeding season in the western valleys, which is indicated in both Gwent Atlases and in records from the intervening years; with confirmed breeding only in 1986 from the lower Sirhowy Valley, and just three roding records. The Wye Valley/Wentwood areas are undoubtedly the breeding stronghold. During Nightjar surveys in 2004, five different roding flights were recorded in the Trelleck area and 17 were found in an incomplete survey of Wentwood. The county population is now estimated at about 100 pairs.

The Gwent reduction corresponds to the national situation where the CBC/BBS trend for the same period indicates a drop of 42%. The 1988–91 National Atlas suggests no change in range but a reduction in the number of squares occupied and this was attributed to a change in habitat characteristics. The favoured new plantations had progressed to the thicket stage by the time of the survey work, and these are generally avoided until the plantation matures and is once more suitable.

The Winter Atlas acknowledges underestimates of distribution and numbers. In winter a wider range of woodland types and age classes, as well as other habitats such as bracken and heather covered hillsides, marshes and hedgerows, are utilised. This is reflected locally with birds being flushed from Llanwern reedbeds in early 2000 and October 2002, from a Llangybi garden in November 2001, and from the Newport Wetlands Reserve in January 2002. Considerable numbers of continental winter migrants begin arriving at the October/November full moon period (which presumably helps with night migration), and some make landfall in unsuitable locations, e.g. one found injured amongst packing cases in Newport docks in December 1995. The return passage is in April. Cold weather in Europe may cause birds that would normally winter further to the north and east, to move to Britain and then to Ireland. Thus the severity of the continental winter has a marked influence on numbers that pass through or winter in Gwent. During the late 1980s, when there were some cold winters, there were 20–35 winter records, including a record of seven flushed in Wentwood on 9th March 1986, but there has been a reduction of records during the subsequent predominantly mild winters. This would ordinarily suggest declining numbers but casual records for such a secretive species cannot give an accurate impression of trends.

When trained dogs are used to find birds (generally for shooting purposes), many more birds are located, and records from shooting areas do not seem to support declining numbers. In general, only 1 bird may be shot for every two or three flushed (S.J.Roberts, pers. comm.), and these game bag records may be a more useful indication of winter status. Table 59 gives details of numbers recorded from three estates, which are supplemented by previously unpublished game records from one of the Estates (Llanarth) and S.J. Roberts. The figures show the annual variation in numbers present (a reflection of the severity of the winter), in just a few small woodland areas in the centre of Gwent. Prior to the 1986/7 winter an average of 16 had been shot per year for the previous decade on Clytha Estate. The large numbers recorded during the severe1988/9 and 1990/1 winters are reflected in individual records of '18 shot in one day' and '12 shot in one plantation' respectively.

Winter	Ysgyryd fach	Clytha Estate	Llanarth Estate	Roberts
1986/87	13	13		
1987/88				
1988/89	24	large numbers	large numbers	
1989/90		more in Nov/Dec	more in Nov/Dec	
1990/91		large numbers	large numbers	
1991/92	8 (Nov/Dec)		23	1
1992/93		low numbers	5	13
1993/94		19	14 (Oct–Dec)	14
1994/95			8	8
1995/96			4	10
1996/97		6 (8th Nov)	24	13
1997/98			10	15
1998/99			13	5
1999/00			3	14
2000/01			7	2
2001/02	15 (Jan–Mar)		10	10
2002/03			14	9

Table 59. Game bag records for Woodcock from four Gwent shoots in winters 1986/87–2002/03

There are also historical shooting records (Tyler, 1923) from several areas, covering a period of 28 years from 1884 –1911. These show generally much smaller bags than those indicated for recent years in Table 59, but comparisons cannot readily be drawn to indicate population trends. In the historical records, the shooting was very much geared to large Pheasant drives, with other game being of lesser interest. Currently the woodland management to encourage Pheasants is not so intensive, and the thicker understorey and ground cover of today's woods is more conducive to Woodcock (S.J. Roberts, pers. comm.).

The *Migration Atlas* shows the British population to be largely sedentary, with north European birds migrating here. Most British reared birds are found within 30km of their ringing location, with only a small proportion from northern Britain making significant movements of over 500km. Migrants may outnumber the residents by 13:1 during some winters and Wales/southern England appears to be the main wintering area for Finnish, Russian and Latvian birds. This is borne out by Gwent recoveries: one (ringed as a chick in Norway in June 1997) was found near Newport in November, a movement of 1,442km. Two others were shot near Raglan having been ringed a few months earlier near St Petersburg, Russia (September – December 1995 and November 2001 – January 2002), both movements in excess of 2,200km. Finally a bird caught on passage in the Netherlands in December 1968 was shot later in the month at Abergavenny (587km).

Gwent Breeding Atlas data and population size

Gwent Atlas	Confirmed tetrads	Probable tetrads	Possible tetrads	Total tetrads	Change in total	Gwent population
1981–1985	10	45	54	109	–	–
1998–2003	2	18	23	43	−61%	c.100 pairs

National breeding data and conservation status

Estimated Welsh population	Welsh CBC/BBS trend 1985–2003	UK CBC/BBS trend 1985–2003	Welsh & (UK) conservation status
<100 pairs	Not available	−42%	Green (Amber) listed

Black-tailed Godwit
Rhostog Gynfonddu

Limosa limosa

A regular passage migrant and winter visitor in increasing numbers. Some birds stay through the summer

Until very recently, the majority of Gwent records of Black-tailed Godwits were of birds on autumn passage from their breeding grounds in Iceland, or on return spring passage. The 1977 *Birds of Gwent*, and subsequent *Gwent Bird Reports*, indicate typical maximum numbers at any one coastal site of c.25 in autumn and c.15 in spring. The 1963 *Birds of Monmouthshire* cites only ten records, only one of these (in autumn) being of more than ten birds. Figures given in The 2002 *Birds in Wales* show that the Gwent birds formed only a tiny fraction of the Welsh passage birds; peak passage numbers for the whole of Wales were between 1,000 and 2,200 during the years 1992–2000. Larger numbers did occur occasionally in Gwent: prior to 1997, the largest gathering was of 52 at Peterstone in March 1986, with several other records of 30–40 together. However, from 1997, when a flock of 70 was at Peterstone from September to early November, numbers of birds on passage have increased significantly and single-site numbers of 40 or more have occurred annually.

Similarly, there has been a recent dramatic increase in wintering numbers. The Winter Atlas showed that, although some coastal areas of Britain and, more notably, Ireland, hosted hundreds of wintering birds with an overall total of about 14,000, the Severn Estuary numbers were very small. Most of the Welsh wintering population was concentrated on the Dee estuary and the Menai Straits. The 1977 *Birds of Gwent* gives no winter records before 1967/68. WeBS counts also show the Severn Estuary low on the list of nationally important wintering areas. Until 2000, single-site wintering numbers in Gwent have exceeded 20 only once, in 1992, with 27 in January and 23 in February, both at Peterstone. Before 1995, winter sightings of Black–tailed Godwits were the exception rather than the rule.

As an indication of the scale of recent increases, Table 60 compares the monthly figures of maximum numbers at any one site on the Gwent coast, for the nine years 1992 – 2000, for 2003, the year when numbers began to increase, and for the two years 2004–05.

Period	Jan	Feb	Mar	Apr	May	Jun	Jul	Aug	Sep	Oct	Nov	Dec
1992–00*	6	9	12	15	15	5	7	14	25	14	13	2
2003	1	3	14	40	35	13	42	300	220	150	250	340
2004–05**	310	242	244	220	81	74	122	193	205	184	227	171

* An average of the maximum numbers recorded at any one Gwent coastal site, over the years 1992 to 2000. Dates were chosen for comparison with data in the *2002 Birds in Wales*. ** Mean data for the two years.

Table 60. Single-site maximum numbers of Black-tailed Godwits on the Gwent coast

Many of the recent records were from the new lagoons at Goldcliff in Newport Wetlands Reserve, which provides a clue to one possible reason for increased numbers. Black-tailed Godwits feeding on exposed intertidal mud are driven off by the rising tide and need relatively undisturbed refuges on fields close to the estuary while the mudflats are covered; the new reserve provides such a refuge, with soft or waterlogged ground which enables them to continue feeding. The possibility of watching a flock of a hundred or more Black-tailed Godwits at close range, using rapid vertical probing with their long bills almost in synchrony, is an added bonus for bird-watchers. Apart from local factors, there has been a steady rise in numbers of passage and wintering birds in the UK since 1980, which is related to an expansion of the Icelandic breeding population (WeBS). It is likely that this has also contributed to the increase seen in Gwent.

There are only eight records from inland sites, all in May and July–October and all from reservoirs or riverside sites; none of these refers to more than three birds.

The *Concise BWP* notes that large numbers of non-breeders summer south of their breeding ranges; it seems fair to infer that birds seen on the Gwent coast in summer are in this category. More than ten are rarely seen during the summer, the largest June figure being 23 at Peterstone in 1989. As yet there is no evidence that the Black-tailed Godwit has ever attempted to breed in Gwent. Their nearest breeding site is on the Somerset Levels, 60km away, and their stronghold is on the Ouse and Nene Washes in East Anglia. In 2003, however, a spring record of a bird in display flight at Goldcliff indicates the possibility that this may yet occur. The Newport Wetlands Reserve would appear to provide a suitable disturbance-free habitat.

WeBS data 1999/2000–2003/04 and conservation status

Average annual peak count for Gwent	64
Threshold number for importance in GB	150
Threshold number for international importance	350
GB average peak count	24,520
Wales and (UK) winter conservation status	Amber (Red) listed

Bar-tailed Godwit
Rhostog Gynffonfrith

Limosa lapponica

A regular spring and autumn passage migrant. Small numbers remain throughout the year

Bar-tailed Godwits breed in the Arctic, and since at least the early 1970s have been regularly observed in Gwent on both spring and autumn passage, almost always in their favoured habitat on the shore of the Severn Estuary. By contrast, the 1963 *Birds of Monmouthshire* cites only seven records, from 1932–33 and in 1955, which must be partly attributable to limited observation. In most years, the largest numbers are recorded during spring passage, typically in late April or early May, with 20–40 birds at any one site. Autumn passage numbers are usually smaller, mainly in September and typically of about 20 birds. However, in some years, spectacularly large numbers are seen, in which upwards of 200 have been noted at one site. The heaviest recorded passage occurred in 1990, in the Chepstow Wharf/Black Rock coastal area, where the first seven days in May yielded counts of 90, 130, 87, 305, 159, 162 and 77 birds; the observers noted that many birds were seen to move on each day. Records from elsewhere in Britain indicate that exceptionally large numbers were observed nationwide at the time. Similar large numbers were recorded at Gwent coastal sites in May 1976 (200), April–May 1984 (300–450), August 1992 (150) and May 2000 (121). To set these figures in context, Table 61 gives mean values of single coastal site maxima for the years 1992–2000:

Jan	Feb	Mar	Apr	May	June	July	Aug	Sep	Oct	Nov	Dec
6	2	5	17	26**	4	2	2**	19	3	2	2

*The years 1992–2000 were chosen for comparison with data in the 2002 *Birds in Wales,* which covers the same period; figures given are the nine-year means of the maximum numbers observed at any one Gwent coastal site during that month. **The figures for August 1992 and May 2000 quoted in the text have been excluded from the calculation, to indicate the more typical level of numbers.

Table 61. Mean numbers of Bar-tailed Godwits in Gwent, 1992–2000*

Birds on spring passage often move through rapidly, so some may have been missed through absence of observers on the critical days, or even at the critical times of day. It is thus possible that the large numbers cited earlier may be less atypical than their infrequent occurrence suggests.

The 2002 *Birds in Wales* gives no details of passage numbers over Wales as a whole, but notes site counts of 100–300 on spring passage in three of the nine years 1992–2000, and on autumn passage also in three of these years. These suggest that Welsh passage numbers may regularly be of at least several hundred, to which the Gwent records contribute a relatively small fraction.

The Winter Atlas shows a fairly widespread coastal distribution of wintering Bar-tailed Godwits in Britain and Ireland, reflecting their use of both sandy and muddy shores. The UK wintering population is estimated to number about 60,000 in all, though with substantial variation between years. Wintering birds in Wales are concentrated on the Burry Inlet and on the north coast. The 2002 *Birds in Wales* indicates a population of between 500 and 1,300 birds but, as Table 61 indicates, very few of these are in Gwent. WeBS data for 1999/00–2003/04 give a mean of eight and a maximum of 22 for the winter population on the Gwent coast. Many birds winter further south, some going as far as the coasts of west Africa.

The Bar-tailed Godwits passing through and wintering in Britain breed in the high Arctic, from northern Scandinavia eastwards to central Siberia. The 1963 *Birds of Monmouthshire* cites one local ringing record consistent with this distribution, of a bird ringed in Norway in August 1949 and recovered at Peterstone in January

1955. No Bar-tailed Godwits breed in Britain, so the small number of birds, nearly always in single figures, remaining in Gwent during the summer are non-breeders, possibly juveniles from the previous year.

There have been only three inland records in Gwent, all from Llandegfedd Reservoir: in April 1976 (three birds), May 1985 (one) and August 1994 (two); this reflects the Bar-tailed Godwit's strong preference for coastal habitats.

WeBS data 1999/2000–2003/04 and conservation status

Average annual peak count for Gwent	15
Threshold number for importance in GB	620
Threshold number for international importance	1,200
GB average peak count	52,460
Wales and (UK) winter conservation status	Red (Amber) listed

Whimbrel
Coeglfinir

Numenius phaeopus

A regular passage migrant in moderate numbers. Small numbers stay through the summer

Large numbers of Whimbrel pass through the British Isles on migration between their breeding grounds in Iceland, Scandinavia and western Siberia, and their winter quarters in West Africa. On the west coast of Britain, largest numbers are recorded on spring passage, whilst on the east coast, largest numbers are recorded in autumn. Peak WeBS counts for spring passage in the UK have averaged around 1,700 since 1998 but the total number of birds passing through must be much greater than this.

Both the 1963 *Birds of Monmouthshire* and the 1977 *Birds of Gwent* describe the Whimbrel as a regular passage migrant. Although the first source adds 'not normally very numerous', citing only one large party, of 60 in late April, the second gives several records of much larger numbers.

More recent records show that passage through Gwent reflects its west coast location, with the largest numbers of Whimbrel occurring during a short period in late April or early May, although smaller numbers are regularly seen from mid-April until early June, and also on autumn passage from July to September.

Table 62 gives the mean values for maximum single-site counts in the county from a selection of recent years, and clearly indicates the relatively short spring passage period and the more protracted autumn passage. While indicating the relative numbers involved, it is likely that the actual numbers involved are considerably larger: for instance, coordinated counts on the Gwent coast in spring 1991 gave totals of 547 on 28th April and 559 on 5th May, the corresponding single site maxima being only 213 and 237 respectively.

	Mar	Apr		May		Jun		Jul		Aug		Sep		Oct
Half-month	2	1	2	1	2	1	2	1	2	1	2	1	2	1
No.	<1	8	113	102	19	4	6	9	35	26	17	3	1	<1

*From 1996 to 1999 inclusive, and before 1987, *Gwent Bird Reports* gave monthly, rather than half-monthly, figures; pre-1987 records were also less complete. The figures given are the combined means for these periods of the maximum counts at any single coastal site during that half-month.

Table 62. Combined half-monthly means of single-site counts of Whimbrel on the Gwent coast, 1987–95* and 2000–03*

The latter figures represent the highest single-site maxima in recent years, but the years previous to 1987 commonly saw larger numbers than these, for example, gatherings in April of 400–500 at Peterstone in 1983 and Undy in 1984. Figure 16 shows the mean maxima for single-site counts over a 30-year period, and demonstrates that the largest concentrations are now only about one-third the size of those from the mid-1970s to the mid-1980s.

In April 1976 there was a most exceptional record of c.1,000 birds at Undy. However, both the Winter Atlas and the 1977 *Birds of Gwent* refer to a roost on Steart Island, in Bridgwater Bay, in the mid-1970s of the

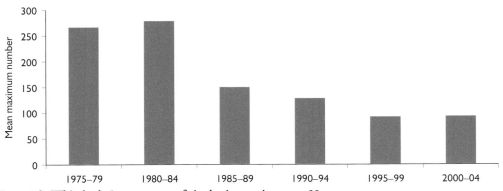

Figure 16. Whimbrel: 5-year means of single-site maxima over 30 years

order of 1,500–2,000 birds; the 1976 record, in an exceptionally dry spring, was thought to be a possible 'overspill' from this roost.

Records also occur inland, mostly during spring passage, though of smaller numbers than seen on the coast, and Llangybi is a particularly favoured site; other sites are widely scattered. Among inland records there are several of birds heard passing overhead at night, most regularly along the low-lying corridor north-eastwards from Newport.

The 1994 *Birds in Wales*, citing the results of counts made during 1972–75, indicated that nearly three-quarters of the British Whimbrel counted in May were on the Severn Estuary. It has been suggested (Ferns *et al.*, 1979) that this may well be because, at that time, the Gwent and Somerset levels constituted the last major feeding area for Icelandic breeders on their northward passage. Figures given in recent WeBS reports indicate that, while the Severn area remains important, other staging posts such as the Burry Inlet or Morecambe Bay, are used by similar or larger numbers of spring passage birds in recent years. The decline in numbers visiting Gwent may stem from changes in land use on the Levels, which have greatly reduced the amount of damp pasture favoured by Whimbrels.

Numbers of birds remaining through June are usually very small, typically in only single figures. It seems likely that these birds are non-breeding juveniles from the previous year, and some may be very late spring or very early autumn migrants. During the more prolonged autumn passage, site maxima of more than 50 birds are unusual, as are inland site records of more than ones and twos. Thus the flock of 55 seen over Ynysyfro Reservoir in late July 1988 must be rated as most exceptional.

Very few Whimbrel winter in Britain; the Winter Atlas estimated 20 as the upper limit of the British wintering population, while recent WeBS counts indicate even fewer than this. There has been one record of a wintering bird in Gwent, in early 1997, when a bird was seen at Goldcliff in January and (presumably the same bird) at Redwick in February.

Since 1974 the earliest spring arrival date has varied between 16th March and 23rd April, with a median date of 12th April. The latest autumn record has varied between 15th September and 27th October, with a median of 30th September. There has been no obvious trend in dates of first arrivals and last departures.

The probable breeding and wintering areas of the Gwent birds are indicated by two ringing records: an adult colour-ringed in Iceland in July 1999 was seen at Peterstone the following May, while an adult ringed at Collister Pill in April 1976 was caught in Senegal, West Africa, in December 1979.

Hudsonian Whimbrel   *Numenius phaeopus hudsonicus*

A single bird of the American race of Whimbrel, known as the Hudsonian Whimbrel, was present at the Goldcliff lagoons, Newport Wetlands Reserve, during 6th–7th May 2000. This was just the 3rd British record and the 7th for the Western Palearctic of Hudsonian Whimbrel, and it offered the first opportunity for British birdwatchers to see this subspecies side by side with its Eurasian counterpart. Remarkably, what seems likely to have been same bird was present again at the same site during 3rd–4th May 2002.

(Eurasian) **Curlew**
Gylfinir

Numenius arquata

Breeds in small numbers. Also a winter visitor and passage migrant in large numbers

The 1963 *Birds of Monmouthshire* describes the Curlew as 'resident, breeding locally, apparently more numerous than before', while the 1977 *Birds of Gwent* asserts 'breeding recorded widely in the north and west'. Over the last century, British breeders have spread from their traditional habitat on moorlands and damp upland grasslands and have increasingly colonised lowland regions, breeding in both pasture and arable areas.

Both Gwent Atlas maps show that breeders occupy both upland and lowland habitats, although there are very few on the coastal levels. The 1963 *Birds of Monmouthshire* indicates breeding on the Levels as occurring 'only recently', but gives no dates. Between the two atlases there has been a considerable reduction in range, with 30% fewer tetrads occupied. Data in Table 63, strongly suggest that most of this decline has occurred outside the upland areas.

	Upland*	Other
1st Gwent Atlas	28	87
2nd Gwent Atlas	27	60

Table 63. Breeding records of Curlews in upland and lowland areas in Gwent, in both Atlas surveys.
*Upland refers to the hills of the north and west; other refers to the remainder of the county.

Current population analyses indicate a Gwent breeding population within the range 20–130 pairs, indicating a substantial reduction of the 150–200 pairs estimated in the 1st Gwent Atlas. However, the upper end of the current estimate assumes that all tetrads with *confirmed* or *probable* breeding are occupied every year, which is unlikely to be the case.

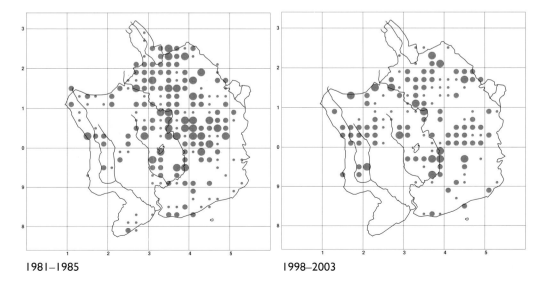

1981–1985   1998–2003

Records from recent *Gwent Bird Reports* regularly give much lower figures for the numbers of breeding pairs. This may well be because many Curlews breed in areas of agricultural land with little other ornithological interest, so that records received represent only a small proportion of the actual population. The *Gwent Bird Report* records show a fall in the numbers of occupied territories, including instances of confirmed breeding, from about 25–30 in the late 1980s to single figures since 2000. Figure 17 illustrates the trend, showing the five-year moving average for these records for the period 1989 to 2002:

For the years 1997 to 2003, records are sufficiently detailed to be separable into 'upland' and 'other': the mean number of occupied territories for these years is 4.6 for upland areas and 6.3 elsewhere. If Figure 17 accurately reflects the overall population trend, the 150–200 breeding pairs estimated in the 1st Gwent Atlas would have fallen to about 60–80 pairs at the time of the 2nd Gwent Atlas. Thus a figure of about 70 breeding pairs, close to the middle of the range given above, seems a fair estimate of the present breeding population.

Much larger numbers are regularly seen on the Gwent coast during the autumn passage (July–October) and in winter (November–February), with usually smaller numbers on spring passage and during the summer. Wintering Curlews tend to be site-faithful, moving only short distances during the whole winter season; thus the sum of monthly maximum numbers at different coastal sites can be expected to give reasonable estimates of total numbers during the winter months. Table 64 gives the estimated mean monthly totals over the ten years 1994–2003:

Jan	Feb	Mar	Apr	May	June	July	Aug	Sep	Oct	Nov	Dec
790	720	570	340	80	160	730	970	980	1030	730	680

These figures are based on the assumption of short term site-fidelity, and therefore that counts on different parts of the coast in the same month (though not necessarily on the same day) are additive. They give the means over the ten years, of the sum of the maximum numbers recorded at all Gwent coastal sites in each month. No records are available for March–May 2001, due to foot-and-mouth disease restrictions; the figures for these months have been adjusted to allow for this.

Table 64. Mean monthly totals of Curlews on the Gwent coast, 1994–2003

Not all sites yielded counts every year, so the figures in table 64 may be underestimates to a small but irregular degree. They are, however, reasonably consistent with the summary in the 1994 *Birds in Wales*, which gives an estimate of about 12,000 wintering Curlews in Wales, of which about 1,000 are on the coast of Gwent. Recent WeBS data also indicate 1,000–1,200 birds wintering on the Gwent coast, and these comprise about a third of the nationally important Severn Estuary population. The 2002 *Birds in Wales* indicates several other

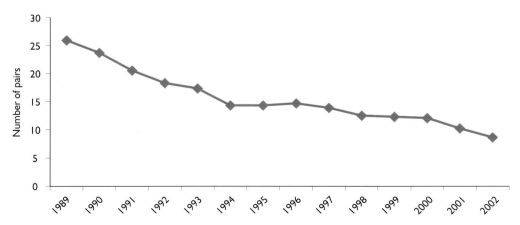

Figure 17. Breeding pairs of Curlew reported in Gwent
Data from *Gwent Bird Reports* expressed as five-year moving averages for the period 1987–2004. 'Breeding records' includes instances of *probable* and *confirmed* breeding according to Atlas criteria. The five-year moving average is used to smooth out irregularities resulting from varying weather conditions and variation in observer coverage.

Welsh coastal sites with peak winter counts of well over 1,000 birds: most notably the Burry Inlet, the Cleddau in Dyfed and Traeth Lafan in Gwynedd. The 2002 *Birds in Wales* also shows the recovery sites of 13 birds ringed in north-west Wales. Of these, three were recovered further north in Britain and seven in Scandinavia, suggesting that the Welsh wintering population is a mixture of British and north-east European breeders. Birds are also known to move to estuaries in western Britain in response to the onset of hard weather further east and this may account for some of the winter influx into Gwent.

Table 64 also shows the decrease in numbers in late autumn, indicating that many autumn passage birds move on before the onset of winter. The Winter Atlas suggests their destination may be the coasts of Ireland or further south in France or Iberia.

Gwent Breeding Atlas data and population size

Gwent Atlas	Confirmed tetrads	Probable tetrads	Possible tetrads	Total tetrads	Change in total	Gwent population
1981–1985	33	86	72	191	–	–
1998–2003	15	72	46	133	−30%	20–130 pairs

National breeding data and conservation status

Estimated Welsh population	Welsh trend 1994–2003	UK CBC/BBS trend 1985–2003	Welsh & (UK) breeding conservation status
c.2,000 pairs	−31%	−28%	Red (Amber)-listed

WeBS data 1999/2000–2003/04 and conservation status

Average annual peak count for Gwent	1,120
Threshold number for importance in GB	1,500
Threshold number for international importance	4,200
GB average peak count	87,300
Wales and UK winter conservation status	Amber-listed

Spotted Redshank   *Tringa erythropus*
Pibydd Coesgoch Mannog

Mainly a passage migrant in very small numbers, with sporadic summer and overwintering records

As in other parts of Britain, most records of Spotted Redshanks in Gwent refer to birds on autumn passage from their breeding grounds in northern Scandinavia or Russia. In recent autumns the mean peak count for Great Britain has been lower than 250 and most of these are recorded on the east coast (WeBS), so numbers passing through Gwent are predictably small.

While the 1963 *Birds of Monmouthshire* cites only four records, describing the Spotted Redshank as a rare vagrant, records have been regular since at least the late 1960s. Numbers have always been very small, most often single birds, but occasionally two or three together. The seven together at Undy on two dates in August–September 1969 was an exceptionally large party. The 1977 *Birds of Gwent* noted only six spring records up to 1975 but since then there has been at least one spring record in all but three years. Nearly all sightings are still of single birds; twos are scarce and there has been only one more record of three together, at Peterstone in April 1984. The latter birds, like many others seen in spring or summer, were in their handsome dark breeding plumage, from which the bird's alternative name Dusky Redshank derives.

As an indication of overall numbers and passage periods, Figure 18 shows the distribution by half-months of all the records outside the winter months for the 28 years following the period covered in the 1977 *Birds of Gwent*. The data show that in the two half-periods (1976–89 and 1990–2003) numbers of spring and late autumn records are roughly similar, but summer and early autumn records have decreased significantly. The regularity and intensity of observation in Gwent since the 1970s have varied little so these decreases are almost certainly real. However, the reality of the apparent shift in peak passage times must be less certain, since such small numbers are involved.

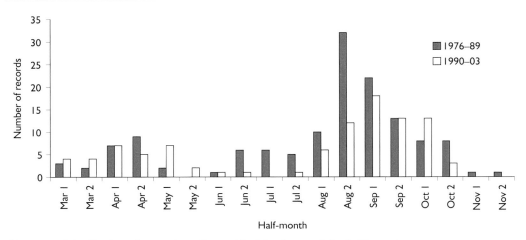

Figure 18. Distribution of non-winter Spotted Redshank records by half-month

Britain is at the northern extremity of the Spotted Redshank's wintering range, which extends down the Atlantic coasts of Europe and north Africa and into the Mediterranean. The Winter Atlas and recent WeBS reports have estimated a British wintering population in the range 80–200 birds, while in recent years Spotted Redshanks are known to have wintered regularly in small numbers in south-west Wales. It is thus surprising that, during the 28 years referred to above, overwintering birds have been recorded in Gwent in only eight winters, and with the exception of February 1998, when a long-term winter resident at Peterstone was briefly joined by a second bird, all records have involved only single birds.

Inland records, which account for about one tenth of the total number of records during the above 28 years, occur irregularly during autumn passage, most frequently at reservoirs or riverside sites; one at Llandegfedd Reservoir at the end of March 1969 is the only inland spring record. Most inland sightings are of single birds; the three together in August 1987, also at Llandegfedd Reservoir, is the largest inland party recorded.

Common Redshank   *Tringa totanus*
Pibydd Coesgoch

Breeds in small numbers, mainly on the coast. Also a passage migrant and winter visitor in moderate numbers

Although the 1937 *Birds of Monmouthshire* cites Redshanks breeding at a site near Abergavenny, the Gwent Atlas maps show that their breeding range in Gwent is now almost entirely restricted to the coastal levels, where the favoured habitats are saltmarshes and damp pastures. It is clear that breeding is now concentrated in just three areas: the Wentlooge Level, the Newport Wetlands Reserve at Goldcliff and the Nedern Wetlands near Caldicot. The Goldcliff site has held at least six territories each year since 2001, while at least this many have been noted on the Wentlooge Level for most of the years for which detailed records are available. The 1988–91 National Atlas shows the Cardiff end of the Wentlooge Level as one of only three areas in Wales supporting high breeding densities. It seems probable, however, that this reflects limited availability of suitable coastal habitat in Wales more than any other factor.

The maps also show that, since the 1st Gwent Atlas, the breeding population on the Caldicot Level which was first noted there in 1961 (1963 *Birds of Monmouthshire*) has all but disappeared, the occasional pair or pairs at the Nedern Wetlands being the last survivors. In this area, records have been sporadic since 1984, when the estimated population was 17 pairs, and have ceased altogether since the mid-1990s, apart from those at the Nedern Wetlands. The small breeding population in the Usk Valley near Usk, and at the nearby Olway meadows, has also disappeared. Breeding records from the former stronghold in the Llangybi area ceased to be regular in 1986 and even sightings have been only sporadic since then. The causes of the decline appear to be changes in agricultural

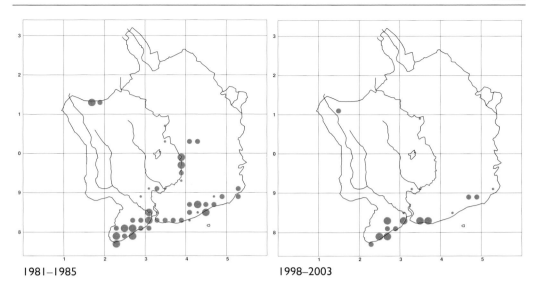

1981–1985   1998–2003

practice: higher stocking levels in pastures creating more disturbance, conversion of pastures to fast-growing ryegrass, so reducing their suitability for breeding Redshanks, improved drainage yielding unsuitably dry meadows, and a switch from pasture to arable on a sizeable scale, have probably all been contributory factors. The 1994 *Birds in Wales* indicates similar reasons for declines in numbers over much of Wales, and cites the results of a wider breeding season survey in 1991. This indicated about 180 breeding pairs in Wales, of which about 160 pairs were on or near the coast. Of these, 12–14 coastal pairs and six inland pairs were in Gwent. By comparison, current population estimates indicate 15–30 breeding pairs in Gwent, suggesting the population may have stabilised at this low level.

Upland breeding seems never to have been widespread in Gwent, being restricted to a very small number of pairs around the Heads of the Valleys. The loss of the site at Waun-y-Pound, Ebbw Vale to industrial development in 1996 was a major setback. The 1988–91 National Atlas shows that, unlike Scotland and northern England, upland areas in Wales supported only scattered patches of low densities of breeders.

As many field workers will know, breeding Redshanks will give loud and persistent alarm calls on the appearance of an intruder near nests or young, a habit that gives rise to its nickname 'warden of the marshes.' Thus it seems likely that, if suitable habitat is visited, few if any breeders will be overlooked, so that the decreases indicated are almost certainly real.

Although records clearly show that large numbers arrive on autumn passage and that many stay during the winter, it is difficult to give more than a rough indication of the numbers involved, since tabulated records in *Gwent Bird Reports* for many sites contain blanks which may mean either no birds or no counts made. Apart from the breeding site at Goldcliff, the coast near Peterstone has been the most consistently watched in recent years. As an indication of relative passage and wintering numbers, Table 65 gives figures for Peterstone only, over the most recent ten years for which complete records are available:

Jan	Feb	Mar	Apr	May	June	July	Aug	Sep	Oct	Nov	Dec
115	55	85	100	10	75	135	50	95	160	170	70

Numbers are rounded to the nearest five birds. No records are available for March–May 2001, due to foot-and-mouth disease restrictions: the figures for these months have been adjusted to allow for this.

Table 65. Mean monthly maxima of Redshanks at Peterstone, 1994–2003

These figures clearly show a relatively limited passage in July and the main passage in the autumn. The data in *Gwent Bird Reports,* although incomplete for other coastal sites, clearly indicate larger numbers at these times on the coast generally, and especially at some regularly-favoured sites. For instance, Hunger Pill at the mouth of the River Wye has frequently hosted flocks in hundreds, in many years peaking at 400–600 birds between September and November. Similar, but usually smaller, parties are also noted at the Nedern Wetlands, by the River Usk between Caerleon and Newport Docks, and at other coastal sites, although less regularly. The non-breeding Redshank population in Britain has remained stable for the last fifteen years, and numbers in Gwent appear to reflect the national situation.

The BTO's long-term study to monitor the effects of the Cardiff Bay barrage, which was completed in November 1999, concentrated in particular on the relocation and winter survival of the displaced Redshanks. Describing its results, Burton (2006) notes that most Redshanks moved to the Rhymney estuary, 3km south-west of the Gwent border, with only a few birds going further away. This is entirely consistent with the figures in Table 66, which compares the BTO results as given by Burton with figures for Peterstone, the Gwent coastal site nearest to Cardiff Bay.

	Cardiff Bay	Peterstone
Pre-barrage	404	241
Post-barrage	37	253

Pre-barrage winters were 1989/90–1998/99; Post-barrage winters were 1999/2000–2002/03.
The BTO counts for Cardiff Bay were done twice monthly from November to March inclusive. Peterstone figures are from *Gwent Bird Reports* for those winters.

Table 66. Mean peak winter counts of Common Redshanks at Cardiff Bay and Peterstone

Most years see a few records of Redshanks inland, nearly always during the passage seasons. These birds visit riverside sites or reservoirs, usually in ones and twos, although up to six birds together have been noted.

Although passage and winter numbers in Gwent are of only moderate size, the Severn Estuary as a whole is a site of international importance for Redshanks, with a mean peak count of 2,530 in recent years. There are also several other sites in Wales that hold larger numbers than the Gwent coast, the most notable of which is the Dee Estuary, which is currently the second most important wintering site in Britain with a mean peak count of over 6,000, and which was the top passage site in autumn 2003, with a count of over 11,000 birds.

The Winter Atlas asserts that 'it is likely that the majority of our wintering birds are of Icelandic origin'. The 1994 *Birds in Wales*, however, cites data on recoveries of birds ringed on the Severn Estuary which indicated that about one-third of these wintering birds breed in Iceland and the rest in northern Britain.

The 2002 *Birds in Wales* map of recoveries of Welsh-ringed Redshanks is consistent with this pattern. However, the same source indicates 'too few Redshank chicks ringed [in Wales] to give any information on their movements'. It is thus not known whether the small Gwent breeding population remains here during the winter, or moves further south or west. Four records of winter visitors shot at Peterstone between 1933 and 1940 are included in the 1963 *Birds of Monmouthshire* as 'Iceland Redshank', but no supporting evidence for this is cited.

Gwent Breeding Atlas data and population size

Gwent Atlas	Confirmed tetrads	Probable tetrads	Possible tetrads	Total tetrads	Change in total	Gwent population
1981–1985	12	22	10	44	–	–
1998–2003	6	6	6	18	−59%	15–30 pairs

National breeding data and conservation status

Estimated Welsh population	Welsh CBC/BBS trends	UK BBS trend 1994–2004	Welsh & UK conservation status
c180 pairs	Not available	+23%	Amber-listed

WeBS data 1999/2000–2003/04 and conservation status

Average annual peak count for Gwent	390
Threshold number for importance in GB	1,200
Threshold number for international importance	1,300
GB average peak count	92,640
Wales and UK winter conservation status	Amber-listed

(Common) **Greenshank**   *Tringa nebularia*
Pibydd Coeswerdd

A passage migrant in small numbers, mainly in autumn. There are a few winter records

Many coastal observers in autumn will be familiar with the sight of a slightly larger and more contrasted bird among a party of Redshanks, or with the sound of a clear triple-note call, both of which are typical of the Greenshank. Most records have been of birds on autumn passage from their breeding grounds, which extend from northern Scotland into Scandinavia and eastwards from the Baltic states across northern Russia. Most of these birds continue southwards to winter in west Africa south of the Sahara, although some may remain in the western Mediterranean or north-west Africa, and a small number remain in Britain, mostly in the south-west. Return passage through Gwent in spring usually involves much smaller numbers. The descriptions of the Greenshank's status in Gwent in both the 1963 *Birds of Monmouthshire* and the 1977 *Birds of Gwent* indicate that this has changed very little since at least the early 1960s.

Table 67 gives an indication of both the numbers involved and the timing of spring and autumn passage in recent years. The figures given are the sums of the half-monthly maxima at two well-watched sites, Llandegfedd Reservoir and the coast at Peterstone, for the two five-year periods before and after the establishment of the Newport Wetlands Reserve in 1999:

Site	Period /half-month	Apr 1	2	May 1	2	Jun 1	2	Jul 1	2	Aug 1	2	Sep 1	2	Oct 1	2
Llandegfedd	1994–1998	1	0	4	1	0	0	1	7	4+	4+	11+	7+	1	1
	1999–2003	0	1	0	0	0	0	0	3	8	10	14	6	1	0
Peterstone	1994–1998	0	3	8	5	2	0	4	7	5	13+	15	3+	2	0
	1999–2003	2	0	1	0	0	0	0	3	8	15	4	7	3	2
Newport Wetlands Reserve	1999–2003	5	7	25	8	2	0	5	13	20	47	36	29	6	6

+ indicates incomplete records

Table 67. Totals over two five-year periods of half-monthly maxima of Greenshanks at three sites

Figures in Table 67 exclude one untypical record, of a flock of 20 at Llandegfedd Reservoir on 27th August 1997. Other records for late August 1997 indicate an unusually heavy passage at that time through much of Gwent. Overall numbers have clearly increased since the establishment of the Newport Wetlands Reserve although it is not yet clear whether this is due to extension of suitable habitat or to increased intensity of observation.

Over the 20-year period 1981–2000, the median dates for first and last passage birds in spring have been 18th April and 17th May, and in autumn, 9th July and 21st October.

Apart from the above sites, records are mostly from other sites on the coast or the coastal levels, or from inland riverside and reservoir sites. Among the latter, birds are frequently noted by the River Usk at Gobion, and also at upland sites such as Garnlydan Reservoir.

Records from *Gwent Reports* prior to 1994 conform broadly to the pattern indicated in Table 67; single site maxima of 5–8 birds on autumn passage, in late August or early September, appear to have been normal for many years, while spring records of more than two or three birds at any one site have been exceptional. Even in autumn, records in double figures are uncommon; in recent years only the 1997 record of 20 cited above has even approached the exceptional record cited in the 1977 *Birds of Gwent*, of 36 at Uskmouth in September 1973.

It is likely that, in some years at least, overall numbers may be considerably larger than this. For instance, in late August and early September 1984, three coastal sites held maxima of between 12 and 20 birds, while a linear count along the River Usk from Caerleon to Gilwern on 20th–21st August revealed 26 birds in all.

Nearly all June records are for dates near the beginning or end of the month, so these may refer either to birds staying through the summer, or to late spring or early autumn passage birds. Very rarely do records occur at both ends of June in the same year, so the latter explanation seems the more probable.

Records in the Winter Atlas indicate that, of a British and Irish wintering population of the order of 1,000 birds, about 60–100 were found around Welsh estuaries; it is thus surprising that none were from the Gwent coast. The 1977 *Birds of Gwent* cited three instances of birds staying well into December: in 1966 at Peterstone and in 1971 and 1972 at Wentwood Reservoir. It is equally surprising that only three sightings since then have referred to probably wintering birds: one in mid-February 1976 at Collister Pill and two in late November; in 1994 at Peterstone and in 2000 at the Newport Wetlands Reserve. Other early- or mid-November records, in 1978 and 1979, and two early March records, in 1985 (two birds) and 1989, both at Gobion, may well refer to passage birds departing very late or arriving very early, respectively.

The 1994 *Birds in Wales* suggested that the timing of spring records indicated that Welsh overwinterers breed in Scotland, and that spring passage birds breed further north, possibly in Scandinavia. Direct evidence in the form of recoveries of ringed birds is still awaited. The Cleddau Estuary and Carmarthen Bay are the only sites currently of national importance in Wales for this species.

WeBS data 1999/2000–2003/04 and conservation status

Average annual peak count for Gwent (autumn)	13
WeBS passage qualifying level*	50*
GB average peak count (autumn)	2,060
Wales and UK winter conservation status	Green-listed

*No threshold is set for importance of a site to passage birds, but WeBS uses 50 as a qualifying level for reporting.

Lesser Yellowlegs   *Tringa flavipes*
Melyngoes Bach

A very rare vagrant

The only record of this vagrant from America is of an immature bird seen briefly on the shore at Peterstone on 25th September 1981.

Green Sandpiper   *Tringa ochropus*
Pibydd Gwyrddd

An uncommon passage migrant and scarce winter visitor

Green Sandpipers breed in northern latitudes across Europe, and winter in south-west Europe and Africa. They occur in Britain chiefly as passage migrants with peak WeBS counts of usually 400–600 birds occurring in August. There is also a small wintering population of perhaps 500–1,000 birds (*Winter Atlas*).

They have been recorded in Gwent in all months. In parallel with the national picture, numbers are highest from July to September, especially in August (Figure 19) with few birds recorded in May or June. Since 1990 there have been just two May records, one on 9th May 1991 at Peterstone and the other on 4th May 1995 at Gobion. Six birds seen in May 1987 at Gobion constitutes the largest spring flock recorded in the county. This status seems little changed from that described in the 1963 *Birds of Monmouthshire* for the first half of the 20th century.

Green Sandpipers occur at any wetland, being frequent on the coastal reens and pools as at Peterstone, as well as at reservoirs, such as Llandegfedd, Ynysyfro and less commonly Carno Reservoir; at lakes such as Woodstock Pond and on shoals by rivers, notably the Usk and Monnow. Birds on the River Usk are most regularly reported on the stretch from Gobion to The Bryn but can turn up anywhere. During 21st–22nd August 1984, 39 individuals were counted scattered along the River Usk from Caerleon up to the Gwent/Brecon border.

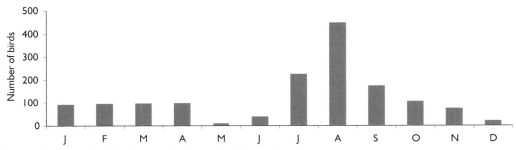

Figure 19. Monthly distribution of Green Sandpipers in Gwent

Birds are usually reported as singly or in twos or threes but occasionally larger numbers occur at a site: for example ten on 8th August 2003 at Nash Pools and 20 at Llandegfedd Reservoir in July 2003. Particularly high counts were 25 in August 1987 on the Gobion/The Bryn stretch of the River Usk, and a flock of 26 at Gobion on 28th July 1984.

Wood Sandpiper
Pibydd y Graean

Tringa glareola

A scarce passage migrant, mainly in the autumn but there are a few spring records

Small numbers of Wood Sandpipers breed in northern Britain but the majority of birds passing through Gwent are from breeding populations in Scandinavia and eastwards.

The 1963 *Birds of Monmouthshire* lists only one definite record for Gwent, a single bird at Peterstone on 20th August 1952. The 1977 *Birds of Gwent* described it as a rare autumn passage migrant with only 13 records, four of these being inland and the rest at freshwater pools or by reens on the coastal levels. Records were all of single birds seen between 23rd June and 12th October.

Since 1977, records have become almost annual, though usually with only one record per year, and all records up to 2003 have been of single birds except for three of two birds, two of three birds and one record of four birds. However, 2004 was a remarkable year for this species, with an exceptional passage at Goldcliff lagoons, where numbers built up from three during 4th–8th August to a peak of 12 on 10th August, and then down to three again on 24th August. The distribution of all records for the county is summarised in Table 68.

Only six Wood Sandpipers have been recorded during April–May, compared with 63 during June–October. The earliest autumn date was 23rd June in 1973 in the gout at Peterstone, and the latest on 12th October 1968 at Abergavenny Sewage Works. Peak passage occurs from the second week of August to the end of August.

	Jan	Feb	Mar	Apr	May	Jun	Jul	Aug	Sep	Oct	Nov	Dec	Total
Prior to 1960	–	–	–	–	–	–	–	1	–	–	–	–	1
1960–64	–	–	–	–	–	–	–	1	–	–	–	–	1
1965–69	–	–	–	–	–	–	–	2	2	1	–	–	5
1970–74	–	–	–	–	–	1	–	2	2	–	–	–	5
1975–79	–	–	–	–	–	–	–	1	3	–	–	–	4
1980–84	–	–	–	–	–	–	–	7	–	–	–	–	7
1985–89	–	–	–	1	2	–	–	5	3	–	–	–	11
1990–94	–	–	–	–	–	–	–	7	1	–	–	–	8
1995–99	–	–	–	–	1	–	–	4	1	–	–	–	6
2000–04	–	–	–	–	–	–	5	11	1	–	–	–	17
2005	–	–	–	–	–	1	–	1	1	–	–	–	3
Total	0	0	0	1	3	2	5	42	14	1	0	0	68

Table 68. Temporal distribution of Wood Sandpiper records in Gwent

Birds have been recorded mainly on the coast, traditionally at Peterstone (20 records), but since 2000, 18 out 20 records have been at the Newport Wetlands Reserve. Other locations have included Collister Pill, Nash Pools, St Brides and Undy. Away from the coast, single birds have turned up six times at Llandegfedd Reservoir and twice at Abergavenny sewage works. Single birds have occurred once each at Llanvihangel Gobion and Garnlydan Reservoir, with three birds once at Ynysyfro Reservoir and two on one occasion at Llangybi.

Common Sandpiper   *Actitis hypoleucos*
Pibydd y Dorlan

An uncommon passage migrant and scarce winter visitor. An uncommon breeder

Common Sandpipers breed in the vicinity of either standing or fast-flowing freshwater. Lakes, reservoirs, upper reaches of rivers and meandering middle stretches may all be used, provided that there are rocks, stones, gravel or shingle beds at the edge. Higher densities occur, however, on broader open rivers with abundant shoals. Good Common Sandpiper rivers may hold 4.7 pairs/km but typical densities are 0.7–2.4 pairs/km (1988–91 National Atlas).

The 1994 *Birds in Wales* indicated a slight contraction of range into upland areas and a general decline during the 20th century, with a decrease evident in central and west Wales since the 1950s.

The Common Sandpiper was described by the 1937 *Birds of Monmouthshire* as a summer visitor breeding locally along the River Usk, Honddu and other tributaries, and a passage migrant seen commonly on the coast. In the early 1980s, the 1st Gwent Atlas showed the Rivers Usk and Monnow to be the strongholds for the species in the county. It was found in 56 tetrads and probably no more than 30–40 pairs bred in any year.

In the 2nd Gwent Atlas Common Sandpipers were found in fewer than 46 tetrads, with *confirmed* breeding in 22 of these as compared with 20 in the 1st Gwent Atlas. Although found in fewer tetrads in the second atlas, no marked change in breeding numbers is apparent between the two atlas periods. The Rivers Usk and Monnow were shown still to be the strongholds for the species in the county, although birds were found breeding at more sites in eight tetrads in the north-west than previously. Breeding birds were for example, found at Garnlydan and Carno Reservoirs and Garn Lakes.

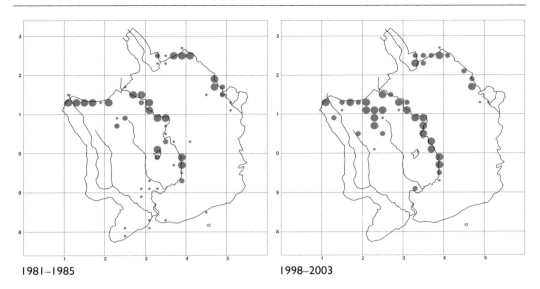

1981–1985   1998–2003

Despite the Rivers Usk and Monnow still being important, there were fewer confirmed breeding records on the River Monnow in the 2nd Gwent Atlas. Between the Honddu confluence at Altyrynys down to Grosmont there were up to 15 pairs during the 1980s, but only six territories were located in 2002 on the Monnow from Altyrynys all the way down to Monmouth. The population on the River Usk has apparently increased though, with more *confirmed* breeding records in the second than in the first atlas. On the River Usk they breed from above Newbridge-on-Usk up to the Breconshire border. The most important stretches are near Llanfoist, between Llanvihangel Gobion and The Bryn, with an estimated 15–20 pairs on this stretch, and between Llanlowell and Kemeys Commander. In 1991 there were at least 14 territories on the Usk between Kemeys Commander and Abergavenny, and in 1992 eight pairs were found on 5km stretch near Llanwenarth. Few of the River Usk's tributaries support any breeding Common Sandpipers, except close to their confluence with the Usk.

On the lower Wye, Common Sandpipers are scarce other than as late summer passage birds although a pair has held territory on the Wye at Monmouth in recent years and a survey in 1977 (RSPB, 1978) showed one territory between Goodrich and Redbrook.

Rather few Common Sandpipers are ringed each year in Gwent but a bird caught as a nestling at Gobion on the River Usk in June 1993 was controlled as a breeding bird the following June at Talybont-on-Usk in Breconshire.

Moderate numbers are recorded on passage through the county, especially in the autumn, with maximum numbers usually in July. Records from Llandegfedd Reservoir are frequent, with maxima of up 20 not unusual and a record number of 30 on 29th June 1971. Numbers at coastal locations are usually smaller, with maxima usually in the range 8–15 but with occasionally up to 20 at Peterstone, and 25 there in July 1987. At least 20 birds passed through Ynsyfro Reservoir during the late summer 1976, though the maximum number on any one day was eight on 9th July, which illustrates the fact that maximum counts of passage migrants greatly underestimate the true numbers of birds passing through. The mean date of first arrivals in spring is 8th April and the mean last date in autumn is 4th October.

The Winter Atlas recorded no Common Sandpipers in Britain but in recent years they have been wintering in increasing numbers and were recorded at 48 sites in 2003/04 (WeBS). Accordingly, very small numbers have begun to winter in Gwent and they occur in a wide variety of wetlands, including coastal habitats. Wintering records in recent years include single birds at Llandegfedd Reservoir from 20th–28th December 2000, at Llanwern and Abergavenny in November 2001, at Llanfair Kilgeddin in January 2002, at Gobion from January to March 2002, on the River Wye at Piercefield in January 2003 and at Abergavenny in November 2003. There was a very unusual concentration of 16 on the River Wye near Wyndcliff on 4th February 1996.

Gwent Breeding Atlas data and population size

Gwent Atlas	Confirmed tetrads	Probable tetrads	Possible tetrads	Total tetrads	Change in total	Gwent population
1981–1985	20	9	28	57	–	–
1998–2003	22	16	8	46	−2.3%	25–40 pairs

National breeding data and conservation status

Estimated Welsh population	Welsh trend	UK WBS trend 1985–2003	Welsh & UK conservation status
470 pairs	Not available	−37%	Green-listed

Spotted Sandpiper
Pibydd Brych

Actitis macularius

A very rare vagrant

There is just a single record of this American counterpart to the Common Sandpiper. A single bird over-wintered at Peterstone from 26th October 1980 to 25th April 1981, by which time it had developed its distinctive breeding plumage. This was first occasion that this species had been recorded wintering in Britain.

(Ruddy) **Turnstone**
Cwtiad y Traeth

Arenaria interpres

A passage migrant and winter visitor in moderate numbers. A few birds stay through the summer

The Turnstone is a common winter visitor and passage migrant to Britain, where rocky maritime shores are its preferred habitat. The Gwent coast is, therefore, far from ideal and this is reflected in the comparatively small numbers recorded in the county.

The 1937 and 1963 *Birds of Monmouthshire* both reported it as a frequent autumn passage bird to the county, though only in small numbers (up to 20), and an occasional winter visitor in larger numbers after stormy weather. This was almost certainly an underestimate of its status, as following the start of systematic recording in the county during the 1960s, it immediately began to be recorded in larger numbers and at other times of year; for example, there was a flock of c.100 at Caldicot in April 1966. Subsequently, during the late 1960s and early 1970s, it was recorded regularly in all months of the year, with maximum numbers occurring at Undy, where the peak spring passage counts were generally over 300, and as high as 600 in May 1971 and 500 in April 1973.

From the mid-1970s numbers have been much lower and the maximum annual counts have exceeded 100 in only ten of the thirty years from 1976. During this period the maximum single-site count has been in spring in 14 years, in winter in 12 years and in autumn in four years.

The pattern of recent records is shown in Table 69 which compares monthly WeBS totals for the whole Gwent coast with counts for Goldcliff published in *Gwent Bird Reports*. The latter indicate Goldcliff as the site at which Turnstones have been most consistently recorded, thus giving the best indication of the monthly pattern of numbers. The data indicate a presence throughout winter, with discernible passage peaks in both spring and autumn. Very few birds are present in June and July.

	Jul	Aug	Sep	Oct	Nov	Dec	Jan	Feb	Mar	Apr	May	Jun
WeBS:												
Mean:	1	5	1	20	11	6	11	26	22	8	2	1
Peak:	2	25	1	146	43	40	45	80	53	35	11	2
Goldcliff:												
Mean:	3	18	26	15	14	7	16	26	58	32	13	3
Peak:	4	50	54	55	21	11	33	38	110	56	50	7

Numbers given are the mean monthly maxima over the ten years April 1994–March 2004, the most recent ten years for which WeBS data were available. The Goldcliff figures for the same period are given for comparison.

Table 69. Numbers of Turnstones on the Gwent coast 1994/95–2003/04

Turnstones are usually counted at high-tide roosts, which are generally on offshore structures where they are available. The remains of the salmon putchers (traps) at Goldcliff are a long established roost that has been used for many years. In places where such structures are absent, birds tend to roost on the boulders of the sea-defences, where they can be very inconspicuous, and this may lead to some birds going unrecorded. Counting at low tide can result in different birds being counted. An example of this was seen in the late 1980s and early 1990s when large numbers, as high as 300 in May 1989, were recorded feeding on rocky substrates low on the shore at Mathern; these birds are known to roost on the other side of the Severn so would not have been picked up by WeBS counts in Gwent, which are carried out at high tide.

Beginning in the mid-1980s there has been a severe decline in the number of Turnstones wintering in Britain and this has been particularly pronounced in Wales. The WeBS index for Wales fell by around 80% between 1985 and 2003. As with other species, such as the Ringed Plover, this decline appears to be a consequence of the recent amelioration of the winter climate, which has resulted in many birds remaining further north or east than previously during the winter months. The extent to which passage numbers have been affected is unknown as WeBS counts, which are the main source of information on wader numbers, do not effectively assess numbers passing through the country.

In attempt to assess trends in Turnstone numbers in Gwent, Figure 20 shows five-year means of the maximum single-site count recorded in the county since 1970, excluding the Mathern birds. A decline is clearly shown until the 1990s, since when numbers appear to have stabilised.

The Winter Atlas indicates that nearly all Turnstones observed in Britain come from one of two distinct populations. Birds from the first, which breed in Greenland and northern Canada, winter on the coasts of Britain and Western Europe. Those from the second, which breed in northern Scandinavia and western Russia, pass through Britain on their way south to winter on the coasts of west Africa, but do not return via Britain in spring. As confirmation of this, the 1994 *Birds in Wales* cites instances of birds ringed in Iceland and Greenland and recovered in Wales, and of birds ringed in Wales and recovered in France and north-west Africa.

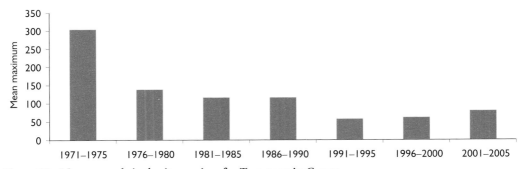

Figure 20. Mean annual single-site maxima for Turnstone in Gwent

WeBS data 1999/2000–2003/04 and conservation status

Average annual peak count for Gwent	45 (winter)*
Threshold number for importance in GB	500
Threshold number for international importance	1,000
GB average peak count	12,320**
Wales and UK winter conservation status	Amber-listed

*Average autumn peak is higher at 56. **Total population is much higher than this, as WeBS does not count on open rocky coasts, where many Turnstones are found.

Red-necked Phalarope   *Phalaropus lobatus*
Llydandroed Gyddfgoch

A very rare vagrant

Although a few Red-necked Phalaropes breed in the far north of Britain, they are mostly Arctic breeders with large populations in Scandinavia and Iceland. Small numbers occur on passage in Britain but mainly on the east coast (*Migration Atlas*).

There are just four Gwent records of this delightfully delicate wader. The first was present on a sludge pond at Lower House Farm, Coed Morgan on the very late dates of mid-November to late December 1972. It was initially identified as a Grey Phalarope, although subsequently re-identified following examination of photographs. Other records are of juveniles: at Goldcliff lagoons, Newport Wetlands Reserve during 9th–11th August 2002 and 15th August 2006, and at Llandegfedd Reservoir during 12th–16th September 2004.

Grey Phalarope   *Phalaropus fulicarius*
Llydandroed Llwyd

A rare autumn passage migrant, usually wind-driven

The Grey Phalarope breeds on arctic coasts and migrates over the North Atlantic to offshore wintering areas in the South Atlantic. In Britain it occurs as a scarce passage migrant on south-western coasts, chiefly after periods of strong westerly winds.

There are sixteen records in Gwent, the majority of which have occurred under the typical circumstance of south-westerly gales. Thirteen of the records have fallen during the short period 3rd September–9th October, with the three remaining records during late November to early December. All records are listed in Table 70. The records during September 1974 were of single birds seen variously in the areas of Chapel Farm and Magor Pill, and assumed to relate to the same individual. Most occurrences have been on the coast, but there are three records for Llandegfedd Reservoir and two for Ynysfro Reservoir.

1933	9 September	Peterstone	1	
1954	5 December	Rogerstone	1	
1968	7 October	Llandegfedd Reservoir	1	probably the same bird at Usk on 9th October
1969	29 November	Llandegfedd Reservoir	1	
1974	4–9 September	Undy foreshore	1	various sightings of a single bird
1974	9 September	Ynysfro Reservoir	1	
1983	4 September	Peterstone	1	
1983	22–23 September	Peterstone	1	
1984	30 September	Collister Pill	1	
1988	3 September	Black Rock	1	seen drifting up-channel on the rising tide
1989	20 September	St Brides	1	
1989	21 September	Peterstone	2	one on 23rd September

1996	2–3 October	St Brides	1	in the reen behind the sea wall
1998	24 September	West Pill	1	
2001	4–8 October	Llandegfedd Reservoir	1	
2003	8 October	Ynysyfro Reservoir	1	seen to depart high to the west

Table 70. Grey Phalarope records in Gwent

Pomarine Skua
Sgiwen Frech
Stercorarius pomarinus

A scarce passage migrant, chiefly in spring; formerly very rare

Pomarine Skuas breed in the Arctic and migrate to winter quarters in the southern reaches of the North Atlantic. They are recorded on both the east and west coasts of Britain during spring and autumn passage.

There are thirteen Gwent records, of which ten have been on spring passage during the period 29th April–7th June. These are listed in Table 71. There is only one autumn passage record, of a single bird flying past Peterstone on 8th October 1988.

The remaining two records are of immature birds. One of these was sighted on at least ten occasions during 23rd March–27th May 1986 at a variety of locations along the estuary between Sluice Farm in the west and Black Rock in the east, and the other was seen at Sluice Farm on at least nine dates during 27th March–1st May 1989.

1983	21 May	Peterstone	3	dark phase birds seen flying north-east
1985	6 May	Black Rock	3	light phase birds, initially seen drifting down-channel on the falling tide, before flying off north-east
1986	15 May	Black Rock	1	
1987	14 May	Goldcliff Pill	5	flying north-east
1990	7 June	Sluice Farm	1	harrying Lesser Black-backed Gulls
1997	9 May	Goldcliff Point	4	light phase birds moving south-west
1997	9 May	Peterstone	11	10 light phase and 1 dark phase seen moving south-west before returning north-eastwards
2002	25 May	Goldcliff Point	6	5 light phase and 1 dark phase flying south-west
2003	29 April	Sluice Farm	1	flying south-west
2004	5 May	Goldcliff point	10	flying north-east

Table 71. Spring passage records of Pomarine Skuas in Gwent

Arctic Skua
Sgiwen Gogledd
Stercorarius parasiticus

A scarce but regular passage migrant offshore; often wind-driven

This piratical seabird has a small breeding population in Scotland but most breed further north in arctic and sub-arctic latitudes. Winter quarters are in the South Atlantic and passage migrants occur commonly on both east and west coasts of Britain.

It is regularly recorded offshore in Gwent but, unlike the Great Skua, is restricted mainly to the period April–October (Table 72). Spring passage is more marked than autumn passage, and May has the greatest number of records. Single birds at Uskmouth on 7th January 1995, Goldcliff on 5th November 2005, and at Black Rock on 23rd December 1989 and 22nd December 1991, constitute the only records outside the usual period.

	Jan	Feb	Mar	Apr	May	Jun	Jul	Aug	Sep	Oct	Nov	Dec	Total
Prior to 1970	–	–	–	–	–	–	–	1	–	1	–	–	2
1970–74	–	–	–	–	1	–	–	2	–	–	–	–	3
1975–79	–	–	–	–	–	–	1	1	–	–	–	–	2
1980–84	–	–	–	2	1	1	2	–	2	–	–	–	8
1985–89	–	–	–	1	5	1	3	6	5	3	–	1	25
1990–94	–	–	–	1	5	9	2	2	3	1	–	1	24
1995–99	1	–	–	1	4	1	1	1	–	1	–	–	10
2000–04	–	–	–	2	3	1	–	–	–	–	–	–	6
2005	–	–	–	–	1	–	–	–	1	–	1	–	3
Total	1	–	–	7	20	13	9	13	11	6	1	2	83

* excludes an undated record from 1946

Table 72. Temporal distribution of Arctic Skua records in Gwent*

As with most seabird species recorded in the county, numbers of Arctic Skuas have seen a significant increase in records in the last twenty years, with just eight records up to 1979, but 76 in the period 1980–2005. Sightings were particularly numerous in the decade 1985–94, and have declined somewhat since then. The majority of records have involved 1–4 birds, and have generally followed a period of strong west/south-westerly winds, although there are instances when birds have occurred during calmer conditions. The largest numbers recorded on passage along the Estuary are nine past Goldcliff Point on 4th May 2004, eight past Sluice Farm on 25th August 1989, eight past Goldcliff Point on 31st May 1995, and records of five birds at each at Charston Sands on 14th April 1985, Goldcliff Pill on 4th September 1985 and Goldcliff Point on 13th June 1991.

There are six inland records. The 1963 *Birds of Monmouthshire* recorded a bird found at Abergavenny after gales in the autumn of 1946, which was also the first record for the county. Single birds occurred at Llandegfedd Reservoir on 10th June 1990, 13th September 1993, 31st August 1997 and 20th October 1998. The most remarkable record concerns a flock of 17 seen flying in a south-westerly direction over Ynysyfro Reservoir on 29th August 1992.

Long-tailed Skua   *Stercorarius longicaudus*
Sgiwen Lostfain

A very rare passage migrant

There are only two records of this, the rarest of the skuas, both of single birds flying south-west past Goldcliff Point. The first was an adult on 4th October 1970 and the second an immature on 14th September 2004.

Great Skua   *Stercorarius skua*
Sgiwen Fawr

A very scarce visitor at all seasons, usually wind-driven

The Great Skua breeds in Scotland and further north in Iceland and Norway. Passage migrants occur regularly on all British coasts as they move between their breeding grounds and wintering quarters off the coasts of south-west Europe.

The earliest documented record of this species in Gwent is of one harrying Arctic Terns at Peterstone on 21st September 1953 (1963 *Birds of Monmouthshire*). The 1977 *Birds of Gwent* records another found exhausted at Redwick in late March 1968, and the only other pre-1980 record is of the fresh remains of a bird found at Llandegfedd Reservoir on 16th October 1977.

As with several other seabird species, records in the county became more regular during the 1980s, at least partly as a consequence of increased levels of observation of offshore bird movements. This resulted in a further

36 records up to 2004, of which 18 were recorded during the five-year period 1985–89. From 1985 to 1998, birds were sighted almost annually, usually following periods of strong west to south-westerly winds, but since then the frequency has declined again and there have been only two records in the new millennium. All records are summarised in Table 73, and the distribution shows a fairly even spread across all months, including those of mid-winter.

	Jan	Feb	Mar	Apr	May	Jun	Jul	Aug	Sep	Oct	Nov	Dec	Total
Prior to 1980	–	–	1	–	–	–	–	–	1	1	–	–	3
1980–1984	–	–	–	–	–	1	–	–	2	–	1	–	4
1985–1989	1	–	–	2	1	2	1	3	2	3	–	3	18
1990–1994	–	1	–	–	2	–	–	–	–	–	2	1	6
1995–1999	1	–	1	–	–	2	1	–	–	–	–	1	6
2000–2005	–	1	–	1	–	–	–	–	–	–	–	–	2
Total	2	2	2	3	3	5	2	3	5	4	3	5	39

Table 73. Temporal distribution of Great Skua records in Gwent

Records are generally of single birds, although five were noted off Charston Sands on 13th April 1985 and the Caldicot shore on 4th January 1998, while four were seen at Black Rock on 11th April 1989.

The 1963 *Birds of Monmouthshire* mentions a specimen in Newport Museum which was apparently shot at the mouth of the river Usk, but no other details are given.

Mediterranean Gull
Gwylan Mor-y-Canoldir

Larus melanocephalus

A scarce passage migrant and winter visitor

Most of the world population of this small but strikingly attractive gull breeds in eastern Europe, in the vicinity of the Black Sea. However, owing to a range expansion during the last 60 years, there are now small breeding colonies in most west European countries, including Britain, which was first colonised during the 1960s (1988–91 National Atlas). It is also a scarce but widespread winter visitor to coasts of Wales and England.

The first Gwent record was on 3rd April 1975 when two adults in summer plumage were present at Peterstone. With an increasing number of birds being recorded in southern England and south-west Wales through the 1970s, further Gwent records were only to be expected and immature birds were subsequently noted, again at Peterstone, on 12th and 17th May 1979, on five dates during April–May 1981 and during 13th April–9th June 1983, when at least eight different individuals were seen. From 1983 onwards Mediterranean Gulls have been recorded annually in the county with, typically, the pattern of occurrence shown in Table 74:

Late March–mid June	Passage mainly of first-year birds through coastal localities
Late June–August	Post-breeding dispersal, mostly of adults, through coastal localities
July–September	Occasional records of juveniles
September–March	Immatures/adults at a variety of coastal and inland locations

Table 74. Occurrence pattern of Mediterranean Gulls

The species has been recorded from all coastal localities, but the presence of two offshore sewage outfalls on the St Brides/Sluice Farm stretch made this the most favoured location until their closure in 2001. Since closure of the outfalls, the frequency of Mediterranean Gull records from this section of the estuary has declined dramatically, along with numbers of other gull species. A similar reduction in records has also been noted along the Cardiff (South Glamorgan) shore following the closure of the sewage outfall at the Rhymney Estuary.

Away from the estuary, individuals have been recorded at the Nedern Wetlands, Ynysyfro and Llandegfedd Reservoirs, the Usk Valley, and Olway Meadows. They have also been recorded among flocks of commoner gull species that occur in areas around Raglan, Dingestow and Monmouth. The large gull roost that gathers on Llandegfedd Reservoir during evenings from September to March also frequently contains individual Mediterranean Gulls. There are no records in the west from the valleys or from northern areas of the county.

The majority of records are of single birds although up to six were present at Sluice Farm in May–June 1995, and also at Olway Meadows/Llandegfedd Reservoir during 8th–20th January 1998, while five first-year birds were present at Sluice Farm on 30th May 1992.

Sightings of colour-ringed birds indicate that most Mediterranean Gulls wintering in Britain originate from colonies in western Europe but all four marked birds sighted in Wales have been from a single colony in Hungary (2002 *Birds in Wales*).

Little Gull   *Larus minutus*
Gwylan Fechan

A scarce passage migrant and winter visitor

This diminutive gull breeds across northern Europe and winters around the coasts of western Europe and the Mediterranean. It occurs chiefly as a passage migrant in Britain but some winter here (*Migration Atlas*).

The first records of Little Gulls in Gwent were of immature birds at Llandegfedd Reservoir on 16th August 1972 and Peterstone during 29th–30th June 1973. Subsequently they have been recorded almost annually in the 31 years to 2005 with just three blank years: in 1975, 1977 and 1987. Figure 21 shows that they are recorded predominantly during the passage periods, March–May (74 records) and July–September (45 records), but have turned up in every month of the year. Most records have been from Llandegfedd Reservoir and locations along the coast, principally Peterstone. Frequency of records has varied from an average of one or two per year in the 1970s, to six per year in the 1970s and 1980s, and back down to three per year in the new millennium. The recent decline has also been noted in neighbouring counties, and may to some extent be connected with the general decrease of gulls in the Severn Estuary following the closure of sewage outfalls in 2001.

The majority of records refer to groups of fewer than five birds, although there are four records of over ten: 12 birds at Llandegfedd Reservoir on 12th May 1974, 11 at Peterstone on 30th June 1974, up to 17 at Black Rock during 30th April–2nd May 1984, and 13 at Black Rock on 4th May 1990.

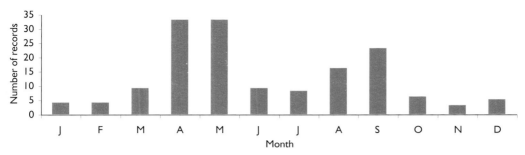

Figure 21. Monthly distribution of Little Gull records in Gwent

Sabine's Gull   *Larus sabini*
Gwylan Sabine

A very scarce passage migrant; usually wind-driven in autumn

Sabine's Gull breeds in arctic regions and winters pelagically south of the equator. Those breeding in eastern Canada and Greenland pass through the eastern North Atlantic and may be driven onto western coasts of Europe by westerly gales (*Migration Atlas*). Particularly large wind-driven influxes occurred in the autumns of 1983, 1987 and 1997, all years in which records occurred in Gwent.

In Gwent there are possibly as many as 12 records. Following the south-westerly gales of 3rd–4th September 1983, three adult birds were seen offshore at Sluice Farm on the evening of 5th September and possibly a further bird was then seen off Peterstone on the evening 6th September. Again following south-westerly gales, one was seen at Black Rock and a winter plumaged adult bird at Peterstone, both on 17th October 1987, with an immature bird seen at Llandegfedd Reservoir on 13th November of the same year. Single juvenile birds were recorded at Peterstone on 4th September 1988 and at Sluice Farm during 31st August–1st September 1993.

In 1994 a first-summer immature bird on a flooded field at Goldcliff Pill during the 9th–11th April was a particularly surprising find, as spring records are much rarer than autumn records, and there have been fewer than six in Wales (1994 *Birds in Wales;* 2002 *Birds in Wales*). There were further records in 1994, all at Sluice Farm, and again on unusually early dates: two on 7th July, two on 8th July, including a juvenile, and possibly the same juvenile bird on 14th July. Finally, immature birds were seen at Peterstone on 31st August 1997, 25th September 2004 and 29th September 2005.

Black-headed Gull   *Larus ridibundus*
Gwylan Penddu

A winter visitor and passage migrant in large numbers. Smaller numbers remain in summer; a few pairs may breed

The Black-headed Gull is both the most numerous and, for much of a typical year, the most widely observed of the gull species seen in Gwent. Paradoxically, of the four gull species known to breed in Gwent, it is both the least numerous breeder and also the least successful.

The 1977 *Birds of Gwent* notes that 'Gwent is the only Welsh county where this species has not been known to breed.' This remained true until 1982 when six pairs attempted to breed at Garnlydan Reservoir. Since then there have been definite breeding attempts in only six more years, at this and two similar upland sites, all of which offer its favoured breeding habitats: bogs, moorland pools and the islands and margins of inland fresh water bodies. None of these breeding attempts was known to be successful. This very limited distribution is shown in the two Gwent Atlas maps. Since the 2nd Gwent Atlas, the newly established Goldcliff lagoons at the Newport Wetlands Reserve have provided another suitable habitat and one pair nested there, unsuccessfully, in 2005.

The 1988–91 National Atlas clearly shows the Black-headed Gull as a widespread British breeder, but in only in small numbers in South Wales. The 2002 *Birds in Wales* gives breeding population estimates for Wales of about 8,700 pairs in 1973 and 2,100 pairs 'at present'. However, the latter source inexplicably quotes breeding figures for Gwent of c.1,700 pairs in 1973 and c.200 pairs at present, neither of which is correct. It seems likely that these are transcription errors in the table of estimates covering all Wales, and therefore that the correct estimates for Wales would be c.7,000 pairs in 1973 and 1,900 pairs 'at present'. As confirmation of the latter figure, *The State of Birds in Wales 2003* quoting the *JNCC Seabird 2000* project, gives just under 2,000 pairs as the present Welsh breeding population.

Recorded numbers of wintering birds regularly reach several thousands, the largest estimates being of roosting birds at Llandegfedd Reservoir, which reached peak numbers of 15,000–20,000 in the winters of 1993/94 and 1994/95. The absence of systematic roost counts in recent years makes it uncertain whether these numbers are typical or exceptional. Winter feeding flocks of up to 3,000 have been occasionally recorded in the low-lying areas around Usk and very probably these roost at the reservoir.

On the coast, autumn passage numbers are largest during August, with records of up to 6,000–8,000, although up to 1,000 have been noted as early as late June. Substantial numbers, typically 2,000–3,000, remain during the winter months. Most of the overwintering birds leave during March and, while occasional passage records from the coast may refer to up to 200 in April or early May, Black-headed Gulls can be quite scarce in Gwent until the return passage begins.

For comparison, the 2002 *Birds in Wales* cites the results of a survey in January 1993 which gave a Welsh wintering total of nearly 86,000 birds. The same source also indicates autumn passage numbers of the order of 15,000 birds at coastal sites in Glamorgan and Carmarthenshire.

The Winter Atlas suggests a British Isles wintering population of the order of 3,000,000 birds, of which about two-thirds are of Continental origin and also indicates the countries around the Baltic Sea as areas of origin. This is confirmed for Welsh wintering birds in the 2002 *Birds in Wales,* which notes that of 43 birds ringed overseas and recovered in Wales in 1992–2000, three originated from Lithuania, five from Finland and six from Denmark or north Germany. There are eleven instances of foreign-ringed birds recovered in Gwent, their countries of origin being Lithuania (four), Belgium, Denmark, Estonia (two each) and Finland (one). Two of these, both birds found dead at Llandegfedd Reservoir, had been ringed as nestlings in Lithuania eight months previously and in Denmark 18 years previously. The 1963 *Birds of Monmouthshire* also cites a Danish-ringed bird recovered in Newport five years later. If this sample is at all typical, it may be that Black-headed Gulls from a wide swathe of northern Europe use Gwent as winter quarters.

Gwent Breeding Atlas data and population size

Gwent Atlas	Confirmed tetrads	Probable tetrads	Possible tetrads	Total tetrads	Change in total	Gwent population
1981–1985	2	0	0	2	–	–
1998–2003	1	0	4	5	+150%	0–1 pairs

National breeding data and conservation status

Estimated Welsh population	Welsh trends; coastal (inland) 1985–88 – 1999–2002	UK trend 1985–88 – 1998–2002	Welsh & UK conservation status
c.2,000 pairs*	−15 (−43)%*	+2%**	Amber- listed

*From *The State of Birds in Wales 2003.* **From *Seabird 2000.*

Ring-billed Gull   *Larus delawarensis*
Gwilan Fodrwybig

A very rare vagrant

There are twelve Gwent records of this now-regular American visitor to British shores (Table 75) all of single birds, and all in the period 1981–1996.

1981	28 May	Peterstone	1	1st summer
1981	11 June	Sluice Farm	1	2nd summer
1981	24 June	Peterstone	1	1st summer
1983	15 May	Peterstone	1	Adult
1984	19 February	Llandegfedd Reservoir	1	Adult; also seen on 29th February
1984	16–18 April	Peterstone	1	Adult
1984	15–16 July	Sluice Farm	1	in transitional plumage from 1st summer to 2nd winter
1988	7–9 July	Peterstone	1	in transitional plumage from 1st summer to 2nd winter.
1990	22 July -	Sluice Farm	1	moulting from 1st summer to 2nd winter plumage.
1991	19 May -	St Brides	1	2nd summer
1996	23 March -	Ynysyfro Reservoir	1	Adult
1996	4–5 May	Sluice Farm	1	Adult

Table 75. Ring-billed Gull records in Gwent

Common Gull (Mew Gull)   *Larus canus*
Gwylan Gweunydd

A passage migrant and winter visitor in large numbers; there is a small non-breeding summer population

Of the five gull species regularly observed in Gwent, the Common Gull is the only one that does not breed in the county and has never done so, as far as is known. Also, although its numbers are often large in winter and at least moderate during autumn and spring passage, it is less widely distributed over the county than its smaller relative the Black-headed Gull. These factors indicate that its better-known name 'Common Gull' has been something of a misnomer in Gwent; only in the north of Britain, or during the winter months, is 'common' a fair indication of its status.

The 1977 *Birds of Gwent* noted a regular winter roost of Common Gulls at Llandegfedd Reservoir, with up to 200 birds, and substantial winter flocks, presumed to be pre-roost gatherings, on low-lying meadows, mainly in the Usk area. This is still essentially true, although numbers have increased dramatically. In recent years roosting numbers are usually in thousands, the largest estimate being 13,000 in the winter of 1997/98, with three other maxima of 9,000–10,000 birds. These counts equal or exceed the threshold for national importance of 9,000 birds. Not surprisingly, the 2002 *Birds in Wales* cites Llandegfedd Reservoir as one of the main Welsh roost sites. Similarly, winter flocks elsewhere have occasionally contained thousands of birds, although hundreds are more usual; these have also been noted more widely both in the lowland areas of Gwent and along the coastal levels. In recent years, however, systematic roost counts have been sporadic and other records submitted have been sparse. There must, therefore, be considerable uncertainty as to whether the numbers and trends cited are typical or exceptional.

The 1977 *Birds of Gwent* also noted smaller peaks in numbers in the spring and autumn periods, with a few remaining during the summer. Again, more recent records are consistent with this pattern, with passage numbers occasionally up to 250, and well spread over the low-lying coastal and Usk Valley areas, and with June the only month lacking records of more than small numbers.

In the wider context, the 2002 *Birds in Wales* cites winter counts of 1,000–2,000 at other Welsh coastal sites, although less than regularly, and names the Burry Inlet as the only Welsh site with consistently large summer or autumn numbers, of the order of 1,000–5,000 birds in the 1990s. The Winter Atlas gives an estimate for the early 1980s of 700,000 birds wintering in the British Isles. Thus both the Gwent and the Welsh wintering birds form only a small proportion of the British total.

Lesser Black-backed Gull
Gwylan Gefnddu Leiaf

Larus fuscus graellsii

Breeds in moderate and increasing numbers; also a common winter visitor and passage migrant

During the last 50 years, the Lesser Black-backed Gull has undergone a major change in both its seasonal behaviour and, in Gwent, its breeding status. From being a non-breeding, predominantly summer visitor to the county, it is now seen in considerable numbers throughout the year and has established itself as a regular breeder. Its natural breeding habitat, usually cliff-top areas with grass or low vegetation, not being available on the Gwent coast, it has emulated its close relative the Herring Gull by using large industrial rooftops for its nest sites. This was first recorded in 1969, with about ten pairs around the Newport Docks area, although earlier breeding may have escaped detection. This had not changed significantly at the time of the 1st Gwent Atlas. The atlas maps show a sizeable increase in range between the two atlas periods, both within Newport and to the Heads of the Valleys, where similar buildings are utilised.

Numbers involved are difficult to assess, since Lesser Black-backed and Herring Gulls tend to intermingle on the same roof spaces, which are often hard to see completely from available vantage points.

The breeding population was not censused during the 2nd Gwent Atlas period, but early findings from a survey carried out in 2007 (R M Clarke, A Survey of Breeding *Larus* Gulls in Gwent during 2007, unpublished), involving counts of apparently occupied nests at most known sites, recorded some 375+ nests, which is considered a good estimate of the recent county population.

Unlike the other large gulls, the Lesser Black-backed Gull seems not to have established itself as a breeder on Denny Island. The only confirmed records there are of 2–4 nests during 1982–85. The island does not appear to have been visited during any breeding season from 1987–1999, and visits during 2000–2003 found no breeders at all.

If, as seems probable, the Gwent populations of both Lesser Black-backed and Herring Gulls represent overspill from the large breeding colonies on Steepholm and Flatholm, there must be considerable scope for further expansion, since many apparently suitable industrial roofs still remain unoccupied. Combined with both species' skill as inveterate scavengers, this indicates the potential for continued growth in numbers, probably limited only by the effects of diseases such as botulism, which checked the local growth in numbers of both species in the 1970s (1st Gwent Atlas).

From being predominantly a summer visitor, this species has, in recent years, become a common winter visitor and passage migrant in the county. It is interesting that *The Popular Handbook* (1975), in noting the increas-

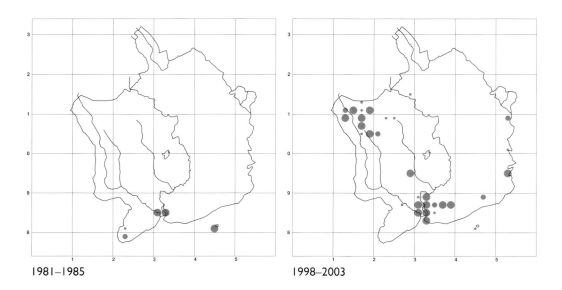

1981–1985   1998–2003

ing tendency of Lesser Black-backed Gulls to overwinter in the British Isles, cites the upper Bristol Channel as one region where this trend had been most evident. The 1977 *Birds of Gwent* indicated that winter flocks of more than 50 were scarce, the largest recorded by then being about 200, compared with larger summer numbers, sometimes up to about 500. Similarly, winter counts in 1975/76 found maxima of more than ten at only six of the nineteen Gwent rubbish tips surveyed. In recent years, however, winter gatherings, particularly at the Llandegfedd Reservoir roost, can number 2,000–5,000. Although such numbers do not occur every year, records of over 100 are frequent. By contrast, maximum summer numbers do not seem to have changed significantly.

Many Welsh-ringed Lesser Black-backed Gulls, mainly nestlings, are given Darvic rings, which can be read at a distance. The 2002 *Birds in Wales* refers to 410 such 'recoveries', most of which are presumably 'resightings'. Some of these are from sites scattered over the British Isles, the Channel coasts of France and the Low Countries. Most, however, are from the coasts of Iberia and Morocco and thus support the accepted view that first-year Lesser Black-backed Gulls still migrate as far as north-west Africa, despite the fact that many adults now remain near to their breeding quarters. No significant recoveries of Gwent-ringed birds are listed but it may be safe to assume that their migrations also follow this pattern.

Evidence for the movement of birds into Gwent is provided by seven recoveries (or sightings) in Gwent, of birds ringed as nestlings 250km or more outside the county. Five of these have been from colonies in northern England, and one each from Scotland and Suffolk. One bird was nine years old at the time of recovery.

Gwent Breeding Atlas data and population size

Gwent Atlas	Confirmed tetrads	Probable tetrads	Possible tetrads	Total tetrads	Change in total	Gwent population
1981–1985	3	1	1	5	–	–
1998–2003	16	5	11	32	+540%	c.375 apparently occupied nests

National breeding data and conservation status

Estimated Welsh population	Welsh trends; coastal (urban) 1985–87 – 1999–2002	UK trend 1985–88 – 1998–2002	Welsh & UK conservation status
c21,000 pairs*	+3 (+96)%*	+42%**	Amber-listed

*From *The State of Birds in Wales 2003*.
**From *Seabird 2000*.

Larus fuscus intermedius

Most Gwent records of this species are assumed to refer to the British race *L. f. graellsii*. Birds showing characteristics of the continental race *L. f. intermedius* have been recorded seven times in the last 30 years; the largest number in any single year was three at Llandegfedd Reservoir in 1999. In the 1977 *Birds of Gwent*, some of the early Gwent records were attributed to the Scandinavian race *L. f. fuscus*. Following the separation of the races *fuscus* and *intermedius*, this attribution is now considered extremely unlikely to be correct.

Yellow-legged Gull   *Larus michahellis*
Gwylan Goesmelyn

This species from the western Mediterranean was previously regarded as a subspecies of Herring Gull *Larus argentatus*, until given full species status in October 2005 by the BOU Records Committee. For this reason it is difficult to determine when it was first recorded within the county, as early records from the mid 1980s–90s often described it merely as 'showing characteristics of the yellow-legged subspecies'; full descriptions were not required and such records were not scrutinised by the local records committee. However, full details were documented and recorded of two adult birds that were seen in the gull roost at Llandegfedd Reservoir on 28th December 1984, and this therefore constitutes the first formal county record. Subsequently there was a third-year immature at Peterstone on 19th July 1986, and the species has since been recorded almost annually to 2004, with 1988 and 2002 as the only years without records.

Occurrences have developed a discernable pattern, with birds generally recorded from coastal areas during the July–October, and then from inland sites during the winter months December–February. Most records to date refer to individual birds, although at Peterstone up to six were present during 29 June–12 October 1997 and five on 23 August 1990.

Herring Gull
Gwylan y Penwaig

Larus argentatus argenteus

Breeds in moderate numbers; also a winter visitor in large numbers

The Herring Gull, familiar to many as the holiday-makers' 'seagull', breeds widely around British coasts, and has frequented Gwent in sizeable numbers for many years. Like its close relative the Lesser Black-backed Gull, it is a skilled and opportunist scavenger, frequently found foraging on rubbish tips. Herring Gulls have suffered moderate declines over the past 25 years and over half of their UK breeding population is confined to fewer than ten sites.

The Herring Gull's natural breeding habitat is on rocky islands or cliff ledges. In Gwent, such sites exist only on Denny Island, the lower reaches of the River Wye near Chepstow and in quarries.

Denny Island has hosted a colony since at least 1961, whose numbers have varied between eight and 120 nesting pairs, this peak being attained in the 1970s, and maintained at 70–120 nests/pairs until at least 1981 (Martin & Venables,1981), with 30–40 pairs up to 1985. More recent records, however, of only two nests with young in 2002 and ten chicks ringed in 2000, indicate a sharp decline in numbers. This may be due to overcrowding as a result of the success of the island's Cormorant colony. No nests were recorded on the island between 2002–2005 but a single pair raised three juveniles in 2006.

Herring Gulls were first recorded as breeding on the River Wye cliffs near Chepstow in 1947 but at this time they were confined to the English bank of the river and not until 1958 did they spread across to the Welsh side, near Chepstow Castle and further upstream near Lancaut, Pen Moel and Woodcroft. Five and eight nests respectively were present in a railway cutting below Bulwark in 1965 and 1975, as well as a few on various rooftops in Chepstow, from 1966, and occasionally on the river bridges (Ferns & Mudge, 1979). The 1977 *Birds of Gwent* notes that 'numbers breeding on the Gwent side of the river have always been very small', and recent records confirm that this is still the case; since 1990, up to five pairs have nested, or attempted to nest, on Chepstow Castle or the nearby cliffs. However, in 1994 a pair bred successfully on the simulated cliff formed by the ruins of Tintern Abbey, and up to three pairs have bred there regularly since then. At least four pairs nested at Livox quarry in the Wye Valley in 1973, with 12 pairs there in 1975 and up to eight pairs during the 1980s. This site, although on the Welsh side of the river, lies in a tetrad that is almost entirely on the English side and was thus omitted from both Gwent Atlas surveys.

Comparison of the two Gwent Atlas maps shows a big expansion in the distribution of breeding Herring Gulls in the county, in particular a colonisation of around ten tetrads in the Heads of the Valleys area. This spread has been made possible by the colonisation of roofs of factories and other industrial premises and the bulk of the county breeding population now occupies such habitats.

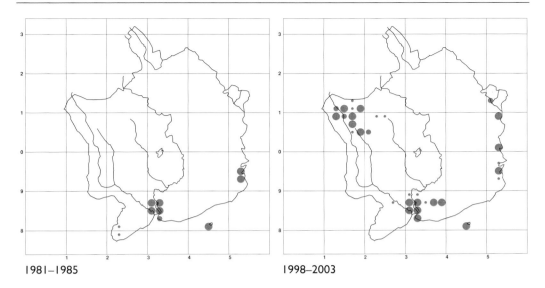

1981–1985   1998–2003

Roof-top nesting was first noted around Newport Docks in 1969, although in view of the size of the colony (about 100 pairs), it is very likely to have started some years previously. Subsequently, in 1975 a count of 61 nests was made in the Newport Docks area. Numbers involved are difficult to assess, in part because of the mix of species in these colonies, both Herring Gull and Lesser Black-backed Gulls being present, but also because access by observers is generally not possible and nests are often not visible from the ground.

The breeding population was not censused during the period of the 2nd Gwent Atlas. However, early findings from a survey carried out in 2007 (R M Clarke, A Survey of Breeding *Larus* Gulls in Gwent during 2007, unpublished), involving counts of apparently occupied nests at most known sites, recorded a total of some 170+ nests, which is considered a good estimate of the recent county population.

Numbers cited in non-breeding records have varied enormously from year to year and it seems likely that much of the variability arises from inconsistency of recording. Counts at rubbish tips have, not surprisingly, been conspicuous by their scarcity, the most recent systematic counts being in 1978 when nineteen Gwent tips were surveyed. At all of these the Herring Gull was by far the most numerous gull, with counts of over 100 at all but four of these tips. Most of the tips surveyed in 1978 have been closed in recent years and just two landfill sites now remain in use: at Silent Valley, Blaina Gwent and Maesglas, Newport. The loss of such feeding areas undoubtedly has had an impact on the species but, unfortunately, due to a lack of data it is not possible to draw any conclusions other than to draw attention to the fact that the breeding colonies at Newport and at the Heads of the Valleys are both near the two remaining landfill sites.

The largest numbers recorded have been of flocks along the coast and at the winter roost at Llandegfedd Reservoir, the annual maxima in both cases being in the range 500–5,000 birds. For comparison, the Winter Atlas indicated a British winter population in 1983 of at least 275,000 birds, based on roost counts, with an estimate of the order of 500,000 birds for the whole of the British Isles.

The 2002 *Birds in Wales* gives only one indication of the breeding areas of Welsh wintering birds: a bird ringed in northern Norway was recovered in South Wales. In view of the size of the winter immigration, it is surprising that this was the only Welsh recovery of an overseas-ringed bird during 1992–2000. Of around 40 ringed Herring Gulls that have been recovered in Gwent, most originate either from Gwent, elsewhere in Wales or the counties on the other side of the Severn Estuary. The exception concerns a breeding adult at Denny Island seen in 1984 that had been ringed and colour dyed on a Glasgow tip in the winter of 1982/3. No bird ringed in Gwent has been recovered further than 12km from the ringing site.

In both the Gwent Atlas surveys, records of Herring and Lesser Blacked-Gulls in urban areas were discarded unless there were appropriate nesting sites in the tetrad.

Gwent Breeding Atlas data and population size

Gwent Atlas	Confirmed tetrads	Probable tetrads	Possible tetrads	Total tetrads	Change in total	Gwent population
1981–1985	7	1	0	8	–	–
1998–2003	17	3	11	31	+287%	170+ apparently occupied nests

National breeding data and conservation status

Estimated Welsh population	Welsh trends; coastal (urban) 1985–87 – 1999–2002	UK trend 1985–88 – 1998–2002	Welsh & UK breeding conservation status
c.16,000 pairs*	+26 (+137)%*	−17%**	Amber-listed

*From *The State of Birds in Wales 2003*. **From *Seabird 2000*.

Larus argentatus argentatus

There are three records of birds showing the characteristics of this Scandinavian race. The first was at Peterstone on 11th September 1988. A bird in transitional 4th year/adult plumage was seen at Peterstone during July–September 1990. Finally, a 4th-winter bird was at Afon Ebbw on 26th December 1997.

Iceland Gull   *Larus glaucoides*
Gwylan yr Arctig

A very scarce winter visitor and spring passage migrant

The Iceland Gull is an uncommon winter visitor from Greenland that occurs on all coasts of Britain, but with a strong bias towards the west. The Winter Atlas puts the average winter population at no more than 70–80 birds, but this was quadrupled in 1983 and 1984 when there were exceptional influxes.

The first record for Gwent occurred during the 1984 influx, when a single immature bird was found in the large gull roost at Llandegfedd Reservoir on 20th January. Records continued at this site for some weeks, with up to five immature birds recorded in the evening roost until 21st March. It was thought likely that these birds then moved to feeding sites on the coast, as several birds similar in plumage to those seen at Llandegfedd Reservoir were located at coastal sites in the following weeks. These records were at Sluice Farm during 18–19th March and 13th and 28th April, and at Uskmouth on 17th April. In subsequent years there have been a further 14 records, all of immature birds, which are detailed in Table 76.

1986	27 January–9 February	Llandegfedd Reservoir	1	
1988	5 January	Black Rock	1	seen also on 9th January
1990	26–27 February	Llandegfedd Reservoir	1	
1991	16–17 February	Llandegfedd Reservoir	1	partly oiled; seen again on 23rd–24th February
1991	11 April	Sluice Farm	1	seen again on 14th April
1993	21–22 February	Sluice Farm	1	
1994	8 February	Ynysyfro Reservoir	1	
1994	11 April	Sluice Farm,	1	seen again on 24th April
1998	24 January	Peterstone Pill	1	
1998	4 May	St Brides	1	
1998	11–12 May	Sluice Farm	1	2nd year
2000	16 May	Uskmouth	1	1st year
2003	9 December	Llandegfedd Reservoir	1	
2004	27 March	Sluice Farm	1	

Table 76. Records of Iceland Gull in Gwent, since the 1984 influx

Glaucous Gull
Gwylan y Gogledd

Larus hyperboreus

A very scarce winter visitor and spring passage migrant

This species, the larger of the two 'white-winged' gulls, breeds in arctic and sub-arctic regions, and is a winter visitor to Britain, with a strong bias toward the north. The Winter Atlas gives a British population size of 200 to about 500 birds in most winters.

There are twelve documented Gwent records, the earliest of which is of a bird shot at Marshfield on 10th March 1893 (1963 *Birds of Monmouthshire*). The first record of a live bird was not until 1981, when an immature was seen at St Brides on 20th May; this may have been the same individual seen at Sluice Farm several months later on 4th July. All records are listed in Table 77.

1893	10 March	Marshfield	1	shot
1981	20 May	St Brides	1	possibly same bird at Sluice Farm, 4th July
1984	25 April–13 May	Sluice Farm	1	immature
1986	28 January–12 February	Llandegfedd Reservoir	1	1st year, seen on several dates in the gull roost
1987	17 January	Chepstow Wharf	1	adult
1987	19 January	Ynysyfro Reservoir	1	1st winter
1987	26 May	Sluice Farm	1	1st summer / 2nd winter
1992	11 January	Llandegfedd Reservoir	1	1st winter
1993	13 November	Black Rock	1	immature
1997	10 May	Nash Pools	1	1st summer imm.
1999	3 January	Llandegfedd Reservoir	1	1st winter imm.
2000	2 April	Peterstone	1	2nd winter

Table 77. Glaucous Gull records in Gwent

Great Black-backed Gull
Gwylan Gefnddu Fwyaf

Larus marinus

Resident; breeds in moderate numbers

Apart from the Kittiwake, the Great Black-backed Gull is the most maritime of the British breeding gulls. Its natural breeding sites are on rocky coasts, mainly on stacks and small islands. It is therefore not surprising that Denny Island is the only site in Gwent where this species is known to breed. Breeding on the island was first recorded in 1954. Table 78 gives all estimates of the breeding population in subsequent years; different criteria (nests found, young found, territorial pairs) were used in different years, so the figures are not always directly comparable.

Year	1954	1955	1961	1962	1969	1974	1975	1976	1980	1982	1984	1985	1993
Nests	1	>3	25	38	33	39	39	>30	40	60	36	52	>23

Table 78. Numbers of breeding Great Black-backed Gulls on Denny Island

A visit to the island in 1981 (Martin & Venables, 1981) showed that most of the nests were hidden among the stems of tree mallow *Lavatera arborea* which formed a thicket on the island top. In recent years the extent and density of the thicket has been variable, sometimes being almost completely absent. No recent nest counts have been made, but based on the number of adult birds and recently hatched juveniles seen on the island during annual visits between 2002 and 2006, a breeding population estimate of 20–30 pairs is thought likely (Goldcliff Ringing Group annual reports). The Denny island colony was the only breeding site during the 1st Gwent Atlas.

The Gwent population is very small compared to numbers elsewhere in Wales. The 2002 *Birds in Wales* gives c.320 pairs in Pembrokeshire in 1997 while the 1988–91 National Atlas suggests

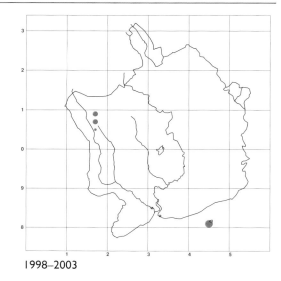

1998–2003

up to 150 pairs further north in Wales. Similarly, the Gwent population is only a tiny fraction of the British breeding population, for which the 1988–91 National Atlas gives an estimate of 23,000 pairs.

It is possible that Denny Island may lose its unique status in Gwent as a breeding site for this species, since up to seven pairs were observed on factory roofs in Ebbw Vale during the 2nd Gwent Atlas period. *Probable* or *possible* breeding was recorded in three tetrads in this area and *possible* breeding also in two tetrads in Newport.

The 2002 *Birds in Wales* cites one instance of roof-top breeding, on a chimney stack at the Old College, Aberystwyth, in 1998, as 'the first in Wales so far'. The *Seabird 2000* project gave totals of 21 and 61 apparently occupied nests on roof-tops in England and Scotland respectively, and also noted 136 apparently occupied nests at a major Scottish industrial site in the Cromarty Firth. It may well only be a matter of time before the Great Black-backed Gull follows the example of its close relatives and adopts industrial rooftops as a regular nesting habitat.

At least 43,100 Great Black-backs winter in Britain (Burton, 2003) but, owing to its relatively 'inland' position, Gwent holds only a very small fraction of these and does not see winter gatherings in hundreds, as elsewhere in Wales, still less in thousands as on the east coasts of the British Isles. Flocks, typically of 15–30 birds and occasionally up to 60 can be seen, often in autumn and winter, and mostly on the coast; these frequently include immature birds. Inland records, well scattered over the county, usually refer to small numbers, although since 1981 two instances of 20–30 together have been noted: at the Little Skirrid in October 1982 and at Goytre in March 1984.

Recoveries of young birds ringed on Denny Island have generally been in the local area except for one that was found dead in Lancashire almost nine years later, and individuals found in Gloucestershire and Dorset. A youngster ringed in spring on the Calf of Man and recovered the following January in Gwent is the only proved instance of winter immigration into the county.

Gwent Breeding Atlas data and population size

Gwent Atlas	Confirmed tetrads	Probable tetrads	Possible tetrads	Total tetrads	Change in total	Gwent population
1981–1985	1	0	0	1	–	–
1998–2003	1	2	3	6	+500%	20–30 pairs

National breeding data and conservation status

Estimated Welsh population	Welsh trend 1985–87 – 1999–2002	UK trend 1985–88 – 1998–2002	Welsh & (UK) breeding conservation status
c.430 pairs*	+47%*	–6%**	Amber (Green) -listed

*From *The State of Birds in Wales 2003*. **From *Seabird 2000*.

(Black-legged) **Kittiwake**   *Rissa tridactyla*
Gwylan Goesddu

An uncommon visitor, usually wind-driven; most frequent in winter

Around half a million pairs of Kittiwakes breed in Britain (1988–91 National Atlas). The largest colonies are in Scotland and north-east England, and the population in Wales has been estimated at over 9,000 pairs (1994 *Birds in Wales*). Most birds are pelagic in winter.

The Kittiwake is a sea-going gull and, though it breeds close to Gwent, it was formerly a very rare visitor to the county, with a total of just eight records to 1979. The earliest of these was of an individual at Newport Docks on 25th February 1928 (1963 *Birds of Monmouthshire*), and there were no further records until three were seen flying past Peterstone on 6th January 1968.

As with records of other seabird species in Gwent, there was a significant increase from the early 1980s. This, in part, is thought to result from increased observer awareness of the most productive weather conditions in which to look for the birds in the estuary: usually following periods of south-west/westerly gales. However, in the case of the Kittiwake it could also be partly attributable to an increased population in the Bristol Channel arising from the expansion of breeding colonies during the 1960s and 1970s along the Gower peninsula and the north Devon coast. Records have now been annual for the last 20 years or more, and they are summarised in Table 79.

In the early 1980s there were some spectacular flocks noted in the upper reaches of the Severn Estuary, principally in the Sudbrook/Black Rock area, where up to 600 were seen during January–April 1983, and where subsequent large counts have included 500 on 1st April 1991 and 320 on 12th November 1987. Movements of this scale have not been noted since and records of up to 50 birds have been the norm. Records in the estuary are most likely in winter and spring and less likely in summer and early autumn.

	Jan	Feb	Mar	Apr	May	Jun	Jul	Aug	Sep	Oct	Nov	Dec	Total
pre-1974	1	1	–	–	–	–	–	–	–	2	–	–	4
1975–79	–	–	1	–	1	1	–	1	–	–	–	–	4
1980–84	6	5	5	1	3	1	1	3	1	5	5	4	40
1985–89	7	3	13	5	9	6	6	5	3	8	3	8	76
1990–94	10	4	2	6	6	2	3	2	–	1	1	9	46
1995–99	11	4	3	2	4	2	1	2	–	1	–	2	32
2000–04	3	2	1	3	4	–	1	–	–	1	–	–	15
2005	–	–	–	–	–	–	–	1	–	–	–	–	1
Total	38	19	25	17	27	12	12	14	4	18	9	23	218

Table 79. Temporal distribution of Kittiwake records in Gwent

Since 2000, there has been a decline in the number of records of Kittiwakes and also of several other seabird species. It is possible this may result partly from a reduction of observer coverage of the estuary following the construction of the Newport Wetlands Reserve, which has become a major attractant for local birdwatchers and where most observation takes place on the inland side of the seawall and not over the shore.

The increase in offshore records during the 1980s was reflected in an increase in inland records. Following the first, an immature at Llanfihangel Gobion on 8th March 1979, there has been a total of 25 inland records, which are summarised in Table 80.

	Jan	Feb	Mar	Apr	May	Jun	Jul	Aug	Sep	Oct	Nov	Dec	Total
Llandegfedd Reservoir	3	2	2	–	–	–	1	1	–	–	–	1	10
Ynysyfro Reservoir	2	–	–	–	–	–	–	–	–	–	2	1	5
Other inland sites	4	3	2	1	–	–	–	–	–	–	–	–	10
Total	9	5	4	1	–	–	1	1	–	–	2	2	25

Table 80. Distribution of inland Kittiwake records in Gwent

Gull-billed Tern
Morwennol Ylfinbraff

Gelochelidon nilotica

A very rare vagrant

The only record of this mainly southern European species is of a bird that was found shot at Church Farm, St Brides on 5th July 1979 and subsequently handed to the National Museum of Wales. There have been only ten records of this species in Wales (2002 *Birds in Wales*).

Sandwich Tern
Morwennol Bigddu

Sterna sandvicensis

A scarce passage migrant

The Sandwich Tern is a summer visitor, with about 14,000 pairs breeding in Britain. The only Welsh colonies are on Anglesey where there are about 1,000 pairs (Mead, 2000).

The first documented Gwent record was of a single bird seen from the Undy shore on 26–27th August 1967, and it has since been recorded in 35 of the 39 years to 2005. Records usually comprise 1–2 birds, and the largest number recorded is 11 at Peterstone on 15th September 1974.

This species is generally one of the early migrants to arrive back in the UK, and individuals have been recorded on 26th March at Uskmouth in 1989, and twice on 1st April: in 1990 and 1994. Data in Table 81 show that records are fairly evenly spread across the months April–September, though there are discernible passage peaks in April and August. There are just four October records, of two birds at Peterstone on 2nd October 1997, two at Llandegfedd Reservoir on 2nd October 1998, two again at Peterstone on 11th October 1986, and a single bird at Collister Pill on 24th October 1985.

	Jan	Feb	Mar	Apr	May	Jun	Jul	Aug	Sep	Oct	Nov	Dec	Total
1965–69	–	–	–	3	–	–	–	1	–	–	–	–	4
1970–74	–	–	–	–	–	–	1	2	1	–	–	–	4
1975–79	–	–	–	–	1	1	1	1	2	1	–	–	7
1980–84	–	–	–	1	2	2	3	3	–	–	–	–	11
1985–89	–	–	1	–	–	3	3	4	4	2	–	–	17
1990–94	–	–	–	5	2	3	2	3	2	–	–	–	17
1995–99	–	–	–	1	1	2	–	3	–	1	–	–	8
2000–04	–	–	–	3	1	–	3	–	–	–	–	–	7
Total	–	–	1	13	7	12	13	17	9	4	–	–	75

Table 81. Temporal distribution of Sandwich Tern records in Gwent

Most records have been from the coast, but there are thirteen (under 20% of the total) from inland waters, principally Llandegfedd Reservoir; although single birds have also occurred at the Dunlop Semtex Pond on 15th September 1986 and Garnlydan Reservoir on 4th September 1993, whilst two were recorded at Usk on 25th September 1969 and a flock of 10 stayed briefly on flooded fields at the Moorings, Newport on 25th September 1988.

Roseate Tern
Morwennol Wridog

Sterna dougallii

A rare passage migrant

Small colonies of this graceful sea-tern are found in a few scattered locations around the coasts of the British Isles. Its numbers have greatly decreased in recent years, and hunting for food and sport in its winter home of West Africa has been identified as the major cause of winter mortality. Anglesey is the only breeding site in Wales.

In Gwent, as elsewhere, it is the rarest of the sea-terns, and there are just six records, all of single birds. Following, the first, an adult, at Peterstone on 7th July 1982, further individuals were noted flying north-east past Sluice Farm on 5th May 1984, at Peterstone Pill on 9th August 1985, at the mouth of the River Wye on 30th April 1988, and at Sluice Farm on 12th June 1995 and 29th April 2002.

Common Tern   *Sterna hirundo*
Morwennol Gyffredin

Arctic Tern   *Sterna paradisaea*
Morwennol Gogledd

Regular passage migrants, usually in larger numbers in spring; a small number may appear through the summer

The 1977 *Birds of Gwent* treated these species in a combined entry since, at that time, most of the records submitted were of 'Common/Arctic' terns (or, with the usual hybrid name 'Commic Terns'). Since then, the much larger number of records contains a larger proportion of sightings definitely identified as Common or Arctic. This reflects the increase in the number of observers competent in distinguishing the two species. However, the same treatment is used in the present account, for two reasons. First, the patterns of definite records reveal features common to both species, so a combined account avoids unnecessarily repetitive statements. Secondly, the largest numbers recorded involve hundreds of birds, frequently passing rapidly, and are submitted as 'Commic Terns'; it is highly probable that some parties of this size contain a mixture of the two species, as well as other tern species, and even the most experienced and skilled observer can rarely hope to identify more than a sample of the birds passing.

Both species breed in Wales, but only in Flintshire and Anglesey. Both the 2002 *Birds in Wales* and the *Seabird 2000* project indicate total Welsh populations of about 640 pairs of Common Terns and 1,700 pairs of Arctic Terns. Larger numbers breed elsewhere around British coasts, mainly in Scotland and north-eastern England. However, the 1988–91 National Atlas shows that, since 1972, Common Terns have increasingly colonised inland waters in eastern and central England, where lakesides and gravel pit margins offer relatively undisturbed alternatives to the species' preferred shingle beaches. As the nearest of these sites is in the Cotswolds, it seems at least possible that Common Terns will colonise Gwent before long. It is also possible that birds *en route* to these inland colonies account for some of the increase in Gwent records in recent years.

Table 82 indicates the number of bird-days for the two species and the indeterminate birds, for the most recent 20-year period, for both inland and coastal sites:

	Spring (April–June)		Autumn (July–November)	
	Coastal	Inland	Coastal	Inland
Common	157	26	168	312
Arctic	c.1,470	12	95	110
'Commic'	c.3,100	35	159	33

The 20 years 1985–2004 are the most recent for which complete data are available at the time of writing.

Table 82. Numbers of bird-days for Common, Arctic and 'Commic' Terns in Gwent, 1985–2004

It is clear that by far the largest numbers are recorded at coastal sites on spring passage, usually late in April or early in May. The 1990s saw some records of impressively large concentrations, all but one recorded as 'Commic': on 26th April 1995, c.1,800 were noted passing up-channel at Goldcliff in 30 minutes, and on 4th and 5th May 1991, 455 and 765 respectively were noted passing up-channel at Black Rock. Five other records in the 1990s, all on 1st, 2nd or 3rd May, refer to totals of over 100 birds, while several more refer to 50 or more birds; also, 125 were recorded passing Goldcliff on the later date of 26th May 1994. Totals of 370 recorded passing Black Rock on 1st to 3rd May 1998 and c.700 passing Goldcliff on 3rd May 2004 were specified as Arctic. The 1998 birds were the local part of a very large movement of Arctic Terns through Britain on these dates. Large movements like these are often associated with stormy weather, which delays their northward progress; in particular, the observers of the terns at Black Rock in 1991 noted that they were migrating steadily into a fresh to strong north-east wind. More typically, before 1990 and in many recent years, most coastal records have been of up to ten birds, although flocks of 20–30 are occasionally noted.

By contrast, the relatively few spring records from inland sites are almost always of small numbers, the largest numbers being recorded at Llandegfedd Reservoir, and involving 30 'Commic' on 5th May 1978 and 57 Arctic over the three days 4th–6th May 1974.

Records for June may refer to birds over-summering in the Bristol Channel area, rather than to passage migrants. Of the 45 records since 1976, five specify Arctic Terns and these are all of one or two birds noted at coastal sites. Another 25 specify Common Terns, again usually in small numbers, the largest numbers being 13 and nine in 1984 and 1991 respectively, both at Peterstone. A few of these records are from inland sites, including one, unexpectedly, at Garnlydan in June 1999. It is possible that some early July records, including one of 37 'Commic' at Peterstone in 1989, belong in the 'summer', rather than 'autumn passage', category.

Data in Table 82 also suggest that autumn passage records are more numerous at inland sites than on the coast. This is correct, although the table, showing 'bird-days', exaggerates the difference, since many autumn visitors tend to stay at inland waters for several days. Not surprisingly, Llandegfedd Reservoir produces most sightings: few years since 1966, and none since 1982, lack an autumn record there, and these are most numerous from early August to mid-September, with peaks of ten or more in nearly half of the sixteen autumn passage periods between 1988 and 2004. In most years both Common and Arctic are specifically identified, the respective maxima being: for Common, 34 in 1994 and 27 in 2002, both in early August; and for Arctic, eight in early September 1992. Other autumn records from inland sites are mainly of ones and twos, well scattered over the county.

Coastal autumn records usually are less frequent and involve smaller numbers: the largest numbers recorded are of 51 Arctic Terns at Peterstone in late August 1989, and 25 and 16 Common Terns at Goldcliff two days apart in mid-September 1985. Only three other records refer to more than ten birds.

Table 83 gives the earliest and latest sightings recorded. Common Terns winter in African waters and Arctic Terns spend our winters in Antarctic waters so it is rather surprising that there appears to be no significant difference in arrival and departure times between the two species.

	Spring		Autumn	
	Earliest	**Median**	**Median**	**Latest**
Common	11th April	24th April	22nd September	22nd October
Arctic	13th April	27th April	28th September	13th October
All records	1st April	27th April	28th September	5th November

Table 83. Dates of earliest and latest records of Common and Arctic Terns in Gwent

Very few birds of either species overwinter in the British Isles and no instance has been recorded in Gwent. The 2002 *Birds in Wales* cites only one record in nine years, an Arctic Tern at Carmarthen in January 1992, while the Winter Atlas cites one record of an Arctic Tern and five Common Terns in three years, only one of which was in the Bristol Channel.

There is only one ringing record relevant to Gwent: a juvenile Arctic Tern ringed on the Farne Islands, Northumberland in 1955 was recovered at Beaufort, Gwent in May 1958.

National breeding data and conservation status

Common Tern		Arctic Tern		Welsh
Welsh population	**Welsh trend 1985–87 – 1999–2002**	**Welsh population**	**Welsh trend 1985–87 – 1999–2002**	**conservation status (both species)**
674	+31%	1,705	+133%	Amber-listed

*From *The State of Birds in Wales 2003*. **From *Seabird 2000*.

Little Tern
Morwennol Fechan

Sternula albifrons

A scarce passage migrant

This diminutive tern breeds in small colonies on sand and shingle beaches scattered around most of the UK coastline but it is conspicuously absent from southwest England and South Wales (1988–91 National Atlas).

In Gwent, it occurs only on passage, and there are approximately 55 records. The 1963 *Birds of Monmouthshire* stated that it had occurred in the past on migration but the only documented record was of three seen at different locations along the River Wye on 7th June 1938. The next record, again at an inland site, was on 17th May 1970 at Llandegfedd Reservoir, when two birds were present. Since then there has been an average of one or two records per year and their distribution is shown in Table 84.

	Jan	Feb	Mar	Apr	May	Jun	Jul	Aug	Sep	Oct	Nov	Dec	Total
1970–1974	–	–	–	–	4	–	–	–	1	–	–	–	5
1975–1979	–	–	–	–	3	2	2	1	1	–	–	–	9
1980–1984	–	–	–	–	–	2	5	1	–	–	–	–	8
1985–1989	–	–	–	1	3	1	1	5	4	–	–	–	15
1990–1994	–	–	–	–	2	4	1	1	–	–	–	–	8
1995–1999	–	–	–	–	2	1	1	–	1	–	–	–	5
2000–2004	–	–	–	–	1	–	1	–	–	–	–	–	2
2005	–	–	–	1	–	–	1	1	–	–	–	–	3
Total	–	–	–	2	15	11	12	9	7	–	–	–	55

Table 84. Temporal distribution of Little Tern records in Gwent

Birds have been recorded throughout the period May–September, with the highest numbers in May. The earliest date recorded saw seven at the mouth of the River Wye on 30th April 1988, and the latest a single bird at Peterstone on 29th September 1995. Records are generally of up to three birds, although there were four at Peterstone on 29th August 1987, seven at the mouth of the River Wye on 30th April 1988, and up to 14 seen off Black Rock on 2nd May 1990 during an exceptionally heavy tern passage.

Whiskered Tern
Corswennol Farfog

Chlidonias hybrida

A very rare vagrant

The only record of this marsh tern from southern Europe is of an adult that was present at Llandegfedd Reservoir during 15th–18th July 1994.

Black Tern
Corswennol Ddu

Chlidonias niger

A fairly common passage migrant, mostly on the coast

The Black Tern is a common breeding species in eastern Europe but has a much more scattered distribution in the west. Apart a very few sporadic attempts, it has not bred in Britain for well over a century (Mead, 2000), and occurs only on passage.

The 1963 *Birds of Monmouthshire* described it as an irregular spring and autumn passage migrant, but since systematic recording began in the county it has been recorded almost every year and there is now a total of approximately 147 Gwent records, involving well over 600 birds. Of these, ten records were of irregular occurrences prior to 1969, the earliest being of single birds 'received', presumably shot, at Llanwern in 1898, Beaufort

Hill on 23rd August 1903, Beaufort on 30th April 1912 and Ynysyfro Reservoir on 9th May 1915. A summary of all records is shown in Table 85.

On spring passage, birds generally move through very quickly in the fairly short period of 22nd April–17th May, although there are two later records: from Black Rock of two on 23rd May 1984 and at Goldcliff Point where three flew past on 27th May 2000. Flock size in this period is generally smaller than ten, although up to 17 were present off Black Rock during 25th–30th Apr 1984 and 11 were at Newport Wetlands Reserve on 7th May 2000. During 2nd–4th May 1990, however, there was an exceptional passage off Black Rock when a flock of at least 286 was counted.

	Jan	Feb	Mar	Apr	May	Jun	Jul	Aug	Sep	Oct	Nov	Dec	Total
Prior to 1965	–	–	–	2	1	–	–	1	2	1	–	–	7
1965–1969	–	–	–	–	1	–	1	–	–	1	–	–	3
1970–1974	–	–	–	1	4	–	–	5	5	1	–	–	16
1975–1979	–	–	–	2	1	–	–	3	2	1	–	–	9
1980–1984	–	–	–	1	1	–	1	4	4	2	–	–	13
1985–1989	–	–	–	–	3	–	1	7	4	–	–	–	15
1990–1994	–	–	–	2	8	–	–	11	8	–	–	–	29
1995–1999	–	–	–	2	3	–	–	8	15	–	–	–	28
2000–2004	–	–	–	1	4	–	1	6	9	4	–	–	25
2005	–	–	–	–	1	–	–	–	1	–	–	–	2
Total	–	–	–	11	27	–	4	45	50	10	–	–	147

Table 85. Temporal distribution of Black Tern records in Gwent

The autumn passage is typically more protracted, with birds noted during the lengthy period of 22nd July–10th October, although there is an exceptionally early record from Peterstone of three on 4th July 1985. There are also four later records, all of single birds: at Llanfihangel Gobion on 22nd October 2001, St Brides on 24th October 1948, Uskmouth Ashponds during 24th–26th October 1976 and at St Brides on 29th October 1984. Records during the autumn period are typically of fewer than ten birds, although 18 were seen at St Brides on 21st September 1957, and 36 and 20 were present at Llandegfedd Reservoir on 21st August 1970 and 8th September 1970, respectively.

White-winged Black Tern
Corswennol Adeinwen

Chlidonias leucopterus

A very rare vagrant

There are two Gwent records of this eastern European species, both from Llandegfedd Reservoir: a 2nd-summer immature during 29th–31st May 1991 and an immature on 24th September 2000.

(Common) **Guillemot**
Gwylog

Uria aalge

A very scarce visitor, usually wind-driven

The Guillemot breeds commonly on offshore and mainland cliffs around the coast of Britain but is absent from most of the east coast of England and also the south-east. The nearest colony to Gwent is at Worms Head (Gower), which holds up to around 100 pairs, while a little further away the Pembrokeshire colonies hold around 25,000 pairs (2002 *Birds in Wales*).

There have been just twenty Gwent records, usually of wind-driven birds seen after periods of westerly or south-westerly gales. They have occurred on all stretches of the coast from Black Rock in the east to Sluice Farm in the west. The first was a winter plumaged bird, shot at Peterstone on 24th September 1935 (1963 *Birds of Monmouthshire*), and the next was not until 21st January 1973 when a bird was seen on the estuary at Undy, with presumably the same individual being found dead there six days later. The distribution of subsequent records is shown in Table 86. There have been records in all months except March, July and August, with a peak in May when six of the twenty records have occurred.

Year	1984	1985	1987	1988	1989	1991	1994	1998	2000	2002
No. of birds	3*	2*	2	1	2	4	1	1	8	1

* The 1984 birds and one in 1985 were found dead or dying

Table 86. Guillemot records in Gwent since 1984

Razorbill
Llurs

Alca torda

A very scarce visitor, usually wind-driven

The Razorbill breeds commonly around British coasts on offshore and mainland cliffs, but, like the Guillemot, it is absent from most of the east coast of England and also the south-east. The small colony at Worms Head (Gower), which holds up to around 80 pairs is the nearest to Gwent, and only slightly further are the Pembrokeshire colonies which hold around 7,000-8,000 pairs (2002 *Birds in Wales*).

The 1963 *Birds of Monmouthshire* mentions that Razorbills were recorded in the Birds of Glamorgan (1900) as having been seen as far up the Severn Estuary as Portskewett, but there are no other details. There are twelve documented records for the county, the first two of which occurred in 1970, at Goldcliff Point on 30th August, where one was watched swimming a few metres offshore, and the second at Peterstone on 20th September. Other than a bird found dead on a road at Llangua on 13th February 1981, all remaining records have been seen at various locations along the coast, usually after periods of south-westerly gales. All records are summarised in Table 87. Five records have occurred in May, two in October, and one each in January, February, June, August and September.

1970	1981	1984	1986	1987	1989	1991	1998	2001
2	1	1	1	2	2	1	1	1

Table 87. Razorbill records in Gwent

Little Auk
Carfil Bach

Alle alle

A very rare vagrant, usually wind-driven

This diminutive auk breeds in the Arctic and winters far out to sea, with British waters at the southern end of its range. It tends to be seen inshore only after onshore gales, when large 'wrecks' may occur.

There are five Gwent records. A bird was shot at Magor during the winter of 1912 (1937 *Birds of Monmouthshire*). One found on a factory roof in Risca on 18th December 1968 flew off strongly when released at Goldcliff the following day. Single birds were also found wrecked in the Llanthony Valley on 24th March 1975 and, remarkably, in a bramble bush at Nash on 9th October 1977: the latter bird flew strongly when released at Goldcliff later the same day. The most recent record concerns an individual seen flying across the M4 at Castleton on 10th February 1983; this occurrence seems likely to have been related to the very large wreck of Little Auks on the east coast at the time.

(Atlantic) **Puffin** *Fratercula arctica*
Pal

A very rare visitor

The Puffin is the smallest of the British breeding auks, and breeds in large numbers on the Pembrokeshire islands. It winters further out to sea than our other breeding auks and as a consequence is very rarely storm-blown, which is probably the main reason for there being just a single Gwent record, of an exhausted juvenile picked up at Cefntilla Court on 17th October 1965.

Auk sp.

There are approximately 24 records involving 60 birds, where observers have been unable to identify auks to species level. It is likely that all refer to Guillemot or Razorbill. Records are most common in May and June, but there are also a few in winter. Since 1971, records have occurred about once in every two years on average.

Jan	Feb	Mar	Apr	May	Jun	Jul	Aug	Sep	Oct	Nov	Dec
1	1	0	0	10	7	1	1	0	0	2	1

Monthly distribution of unidentified auk records

The majority of these records are of birds seen flying distantly offshore following a periods of south-westerly gales. Goldcliff Point is the best vantage for such sightings, and 16 of the 24 records originate from there. Records are generally of single birds, although 12 were seen flying past Goldcliff Point on 3rd June 1994, 7 on 3rd June 1988 and 6 on 6th June 1987.

Feral Pigeon *Columba livia*
Colomen Ddof

A common resident in built-up areas

The Feral Pigeon is descended from the domestic pigeon, which in turn is descended from the truly wild Rock Dove. The Rock Doves that formerly bred around the Welsh coasts have interbred with Feral Pigeons, and the 1994 *Birds in Wales* suggests that the last pure-bred Rock Doves in Wales were probably to be found on the remoter headlands of Pembrokeshire and on Ramsey Island in the 1930s and 1940s.

Where its wild ancestor used cliffs, the Feral Pigeon uses buildings and is very much at home in our towns and cities where it is so successful that it has become a pest in some public places. Its diet includes almost anything discarded by humans and is gleaned from parks, streets and rubbish tips, though flocks will also move into agricultural areas for grain and wild seeds. The 1988–91 National Atlas records a major extension of breeding range into the countryside during the 1970s, i.e. between the two national atlas projects, but cautions that this might be partly explained by observers in the second project being more aware of the validity of recording this species.

The 1st Gwent Atlas showed it to be present in most of the county's towns, especially Newport, Cwmbran and the western valley towns. A similar distribution is seen in the 2nd Gwent Atlas, with *probable* and *confirmed* breeding in an identical total of tetrads, though with considerably fewer *possible* records in the rural areas, resulting in a decline of 19% in the total occupied tetrads. Just as the national expansion, referred to above, may be partly artefactual, so the decline in Gwent may not be entirely real, as observers still vary greatly in their recording of the species, and distinguishing them from domestic pigeons may have been a problem for some observers. For these reasons we have not attempted to estimate a Gwent population size.

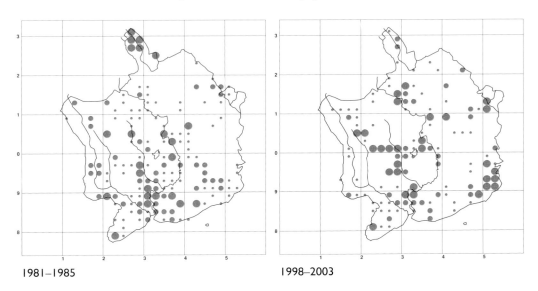

1981–1985   1998–2003

In recent years the largest counts in towns have been up to 300 in Newport, 68 in Cwmbran and 76 in Abergavenny, while the largest rural count is of 150 feeding in stubble at Marshfield in September. In the neighbouring city of Cardiff, Feral Pigeons have been visiting suburban gardens increasingly in recent years, with flocks of 30 or more taking food from bird tables and spilt seed from beneath feeders, and in some cases successfully taking seed directly from feeders by a combination of perching and hovering. This behaviour has not been reported from Gwent, though it may yet occur.

Gwent Breeding Atlas data and population size

Gwent Atlas	Confirmed tetrads	Probable tetrads	Possible tetrads	Total tetrads	Change in total	Gwent population
1981–1985	23	43	82	148	–	–
1998–2003	29	37	54	120	−19%	1,000–1,800

Stock Dove
Colomen Wyllt

Columba oenas

A common resident and irregular passage migrant

The Stock Dove is a widely distributed resident in Britain, absent only from northern Scotland, high moorland and built-up areas generally. In Wales it occurs up to around 300m and is most common in lowlands (2000 *Birds in Wales*).

The species was described in the 1937 *Birds of Monmouthshire* as breeding sparsely scattered in the central, northern and north eastern districts of the county, and numerous in autumn and winter in some years. During the 1950s the population in many parts of England suffered a severe decline as a direct result of the use of toxic

dressings on grain, though numbers in Wales had remained largely unaffected owing to the predominance of pastoral farming in the country (1994 *Birds in Wales*). However, it is possible that Gwent, being one of the less pastoral counties in Wales, may have been more comparable to England in this respect, so perhaps the 1963 *Birds of Monmouthshire* was reflecting such a decline when it described the Stock Dove's status as 'uncertain', though still known 'to breed in the Wye Valley cliffs and old quarries'.

It seems likely, though, that the species' status was somewhat understated in 1963, as the 1977 *Birds of Gwent* considered it to be a fairly common breeding resident and this was supported by the 1st Gwent Atlas, which showed it to be widely distributed in the county, with the western valleys as the only area where it was absent.

The 2nd Gwent Atlas map shows a largely unchanged distribution, with presence in 60% of tetrads covering all parts of the county apart from the west, and with *probable* or *confirmed* breeding in 47%: down slightly from 50% in the 1st Gwent Atlas. Breeding locations have included holes in trees, barns, where it sometimes nests between hay bales, outhouses and crevices in quarry cliffs. Analysis of BBS data gives a breeding population of 530–710 pairs, but this may be an underestimate owing to the exclusion of flying birds from all BBS analysis. By contrast, the estimate produced by the atlas-based method is considered too high (Appendix 1).

From August onwards, sometimes as early as July, and through the winter until March, Stock Doves collect in flocks at locations where farming activities provide good food sources. Such flocks are often reported from ploughed land and maize stubbles, and occasionally feeding on fresh young growth of foliage or root crops. The largest flocks recorded are of 300 at Llanover in March 1972, 250 near Uskmouth in January 1976, 160 at Castleton in March 1990, 120 at Peterstone in August 1989 and 120 at Llanvapley on 6th May 2003: where they fed on newly emerging pea plants. More usually flock sizes are in the range of around 10–50, less frequently up to 90 or 100. Since 1994 reports of medium-large flocks have been much less frequent, suggesting a possible decline in numbers.

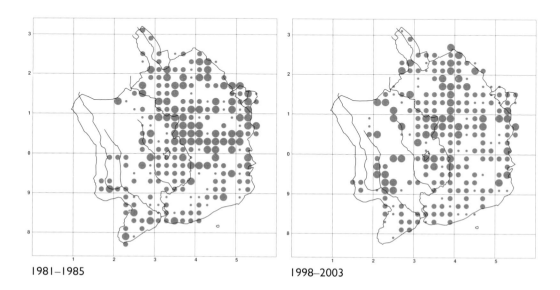

1981–1985

1998–2003

British-bred Stock Doves are generally very sedentary, and among a handful of ringing recoveries involving Gwent birds, the longest movement recorded is 27km. Despite this, some small-scale visible movements have been occasionally reported in Gwent in autumn. Totals of nine and eight flew south-west along the coast on 10th and 16th October respectively in 1976, while the coastal movement of Wood Pigeons on 9th November 1979 (see that species) contained 'some' Stock Doves. Also small flocks were observed on several occasions flying south over Llangybi in early October 1993, with a maximum of 71 birds on the 5th. Unprecedented coastal movements were recorded in the Uskmouth/Goldcliff area in autumn 2005, with westerly movements of 14 on 29th October, 42 in three hours on 5th November, and 42 again on 13th November, and a south-easterly movement of ten on 7th November. Drift migrants originating from northern Europe are known to occur on the east coast of England in autumn but the origins of birds seen moving over Gwent is unknown.

Gwent Breeding Atlas data and population size

Gwent Atlas	Confirmed tetrads	Probable tetrads	Possible tetrads	Total tetrads	Change in total	Gwent population
1981–1985	80	117	45	242	–	–
1998–2003	56	131	49	235	−3%	530–710 pairs

National breeding data and conservation status

Estimated Welsh population	Welsh CBC/BBS trend 1985–2003	UK CBC/BBS trend 1985–2003	Welsh & UK conservation status
10,000 pairs	+68%	+19%	Amber-listed

(Common) **Wood Pigeon**   *Columba palumbus*
Ysguthan

An abundant resident; large-scale movements are observed in autumn in some years

The Wood Pigeon was formerly a bird of deciduous woodland but in recent centuries it has expanded its range into a wide variety of habitats, including farmland, parkland, and suburban gardens, and it is absent only from the higher hills and mountains.

The 1st Gwent Atlas (1981–85) showed the Wood Pigeon to be a widespread breeding species in the county, present in 97% of tetrads and with *probable* or *confirmed* breeding in 91%. Most of the tetrads from which it was absent comprised high moorland and it had almost certainly been overlooked in the one or two cases where it was apparently absent from tetrads containing suitable habitat. The 2nd Gwent Atlas showed its status to have changed little, with presence in 98% of tetrads, though with an increase in *probable* or *confirmed* breeding records to 96%, which may reflect an increase in population density. In the UK as a whole, Wood Pigeon populations have increased greatly in the period between the two Gwent Atlases, but the increase in Wales has been small. Based on BBS data the current population for Gwent is estimated as 13,000–14,000 pairs,

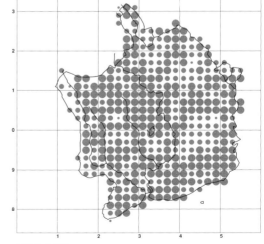

1998–2003

which corresponds to an average of about 33 pairs per tetrad. The 1st Gwent Atlas suggested a population of 16,000 pairs based on CBC analysis.

Outside the breeding season, Wood Pigeons congregate into large flocks at suitable food sources, and in Gwent these have included fields with stubble or kale, and woodlands where fallen acorns or beech mast are abundant. They may also gather into large roosts in woodland trees. During the 1960s maximum flock sizes were usually no larger than around 400, but they have increased steadily over the years, and in the decade 1994–2003 flocks of 750 or more have been recorded in no fewer than eight years. 3,000 birds on an unharvested barley field at Ysgyryd Fach in the winter of 1992/93 is the largest flock ever recorded feeding in the county. Table 88 shows that the very largest flocks always occur from November to February, and the persistence into April of gatherings of around 400 reflects the relatively late breeding season of this species. Movements of Wood Pigeons are often observed during the winter, sometimes in direct response to hard weather. They usually involve moderate numbers, so an estimated 3,500+ passing over Llandevaud on 5th January 1997 was quite exceptional.

Month	Jan	Feb	Mar	Apr	May	Jun	Jul	Aug	Sep	Oct	Nov	Dec
No.	1,100	1,000	400	400	180	150	150	200	200	400	1,600	3,000

Table 88. Maximum Wood Pigeon flock sizes (feeding or roosting) recorded since 1965

Although the occurrence of huge winter flocks may give the impression that immigration has occurred, ringing studies provide no evidence of any significant seasonal migration of Wood Pigeons into Britain, and the local influxes seem to derive solely from the congregation of birds in areas that provide a good food source at that time (*Migration Atlas*). Ringing data that relates to Gwent confirms the sedentary nature of local birds: among five birds ringed or recovered in the county, the greatest distance moved was 18km.

In many years large-scale movements of Wood Pigeons are seen along the Gwent coast during late October and early November, usually soon after dawn, and generally in a south or south-west direction. The largest such movements recorded are (number of birds, location, date): 2,000, Goldcliff, 7th November 1976; 2,200, Goldcliff, 9th November 1979; 4,000, Goldcliff, 29th October 1983; 17,000, Peterstone, 6th November 1999; 10,000, Newport Wetlands Reserve, 29th October 2001; 1,020 in 90 minutes, Goldcliff, 31st October 2005. On some of the dates the birds have been seen to approach from the north and turn southwest on reaching the coast, which may relate therefore to the large southerly movements occasionally observed inland in the county at this time of year. Similar large movements have been recorded along the east coast of England: for example over 31,000 moving south along the Suffolk coast on 2nd November 1994. These observations are not easy to reconcile with the lack of ringing evidence for migration. The *Migration Atlas* suggests that the east coast movements may comprise mainly birds that are *en route* from Fennoscandia to wintering areas in Iberia and which do not spend long enough in Britain to contribute to ringing data. It is possible the Gwent coastal movements have a similar origin.

Gwent Breeding Atlas data and population size

Gwent Atlas	Confirmed tetrads	Probable tetrads	Possible tetrads	Total tetrads	Change in total	Gwent population
1981–1985	259	99	25	383	–	–
1998–2003	242	138	6	386	+1%	13,000–14,000 pairs

National breeding data and conservation status

Estimated Welsh population	Welsh CBC/BBS trend 1985–2003	UK CBC/BBS trend 1985–2003	Welsh & UK conservation status
225,600 pairs	+4%	+56%	Green-listed

(Eurasian) **Collared Dove**
Turtur Dorchog

Streptopelia decaocto

A common and widespread resident

The Collared Dove is a relatively recent addition to the British avifauna. Having spread westwards across Europe during the first half of the 20th century, it reached southern England in 1955, and subsequently expanded northwards and westwards to colonise the whole of Britain. Wales was colonised widely during the early 1960s. It was first recorded in Gwent at Bassaleg in 1961, and then at Llanarth in the following two years. In 1964 four pairs were noted in the Newport area during the breeding season, one of which was proved to have bred, and at the end of the year a flock of 30 birds, by far the largest then recorded, was counted in an orchard. The remainder of the 1960s was a period of rapid expansion across the county and of growth of the breeding population. The increase of the Usk population from a single pair in 1967 to around 60 birds in 1969 typifies the growth of numbers during this period.

Collared Doves show a strong preference for habitats associated with human dwellings, particularly farms where spilt grain may be available, and also parks and suburban gardens where coniferous trees provide dense cover for nesting. Accordingly, colonisation of Gwent occurred initially in the more populated areas. In the 1st Gwent Atlas, 66% of tetrads in the county were occupied (55% *probable* or *confirmed*), but there were notable gaps in distribution on the higher ground in the north and north-west, in the more sparsely populated and rural areas of the east, and also in the western valleys. In the 2nd Gwent Atlas, the number of occupied tetrads has increased to 79% (72% *probable* or *confirmed*), and many of the previous gaps have been filled: for example in the 10-km square SO20 (western valleys) the number of occupied tetrads has doubled from 11 to 22, while in SO40 (a rural area in the east) it has increased from ten to 22. Based on BBS analysis, the county population is estimated at 1,900–2,400 pairs.

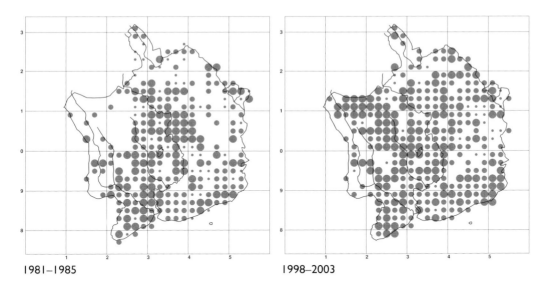

1981–1985

1998–2003

Collared Doves can be gregarious in winter and the occurrence of flocks is common at locations, such as farmyards, grain barns and stubble fields, where grain is available. During 1973–82 congregations of as 150–200 birds were not unusual but in more recent years reported flock sizes have been somewhat smaller, and apart from flocks of 110–120 at Peterstone in 1994 and 1996, the biggest groups have seldom exceeded 50.

Local ringing data confirm the generally sedentary nature of the species and one recovery demonstrates survival to the age of 13 years.

Gwent Breeding Atlas data and population size

Gwent Atlas	Confirmed tetrads	Probable tetrads	Possible tetrads	Total tetrads	Change in total	Gwent population
1981–1985	92	125	43	260	–	–
1998–2003	130	155	26	311	+20%	1,900–2,400 pairs

National breeding data and conservation status

Estimated Welsh population	Welsh CBC/BBS trend 1985–2003	UK CBC/BBS trend 1985–2003	Welsh & UK conservation status
16,250 pairs	+17%	+67%	Green-listed

(European) **Turtle Dove** **Turtur** *Streptopelia turtur*

A scarce summer visitor

The Turtle Dove is a summer visitor to Britain that winters in sub-Saharan Africa. It has the distinction of being the only member of the pigeon family to undertake long-distance migrations of over 4,000km (*Migration Atlas*). It was formerly widespread in most parts of England from Yorkshire southwards, though scarce in Wales apart from the lowland border counties.

The 1963 *Birds of Monmouthshire* described it as a regular summer visitor to the county, though with restricted breeding areas that were mainly in the central eastern districts. It also suggested that the species might be declining in the county, but in the succeeding years there was little evidence for this, as breeding records continued to be received from widespread locations to the east of the western valleys. For example, from 1966 to 1968, sites from which pairs were reported in the breeding season included Cwmyoy, Abergavenny, Llanover, Llanellen, Llanarth, Bettws Newydd, New Inn, Trelleck, Wentwood, Llanvaches, and Caldicot. In the last of these years, records (including passage birds) were received from a total of forty locations, with proven breeding at four.

In the 1960s and early 1970s there were also regular spring and autumn passage records from the coast, sometimes involving small flocks: as at Undy on 24th August 1968 when there were 11 on the seawall, and again on July 1972 when there were 10 at the same place. On 26th/27th April 1975, a steady passage of ones and twos was recorded throughout both days.

However, the Turtle Dove population began to decline nationally during the 1970s, and this accelerated during the 1980s, accompanied by a contraction of breeding range to the south and east. In parallel with the national decline, breeding in Gwent began to decline in the early 1970s and in 1974, for the first year on record, there were no proven instances of breeding in the county. Confirmed breeding subsequently became sporadic, and from the mid 1980s was restricted mainly to locations around the Wye Valley, particularly Trelleck and Cleddon Bog, though reports of singing males continued to be more widespread. There was a similar decline in coastal passage records, which despite a very good autumn passage at Peterstone in 1981, also became sporadic, with no records at all in many years.

The decline in the county has continued, and is illustrated by the period 1997–2000, when the total numbers of records received for the four years were six, five, seven, and four respectively. There have now been no proven breeding records since 1997, though singing males and pairs continue to be recorded at Trelleck. There was an encouraging increase in records during 2004, when eight singing males were recorded in the Trelleck and Cleddon area, but numbers were down again in 2005.

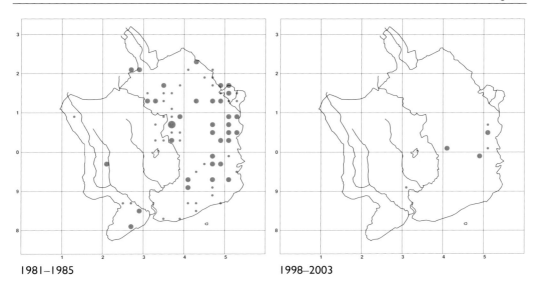

1981–1985   1998–2003

The two Gwent Atlases illustrate the local decline of the Turtle Dove very effectively. In the 1st Gwent Atlas it was recorded in 72 tetrads, mostly scattered over the eastern half of the county, and although breeding was *confirmed* in only one, the county population was estimated at no higher than 50 pairs. In the 2nd Gwent Atlas it was recorded in only six tetrads, a decline of 92% in distribution, and the current population is estimated as fewer than three pairs, possibly none.

First arrival dates are generally from mid-April to early May, and the earliest is 3rd April 1988. Last records of the year have usually been in September, but there are a few October records of which 10th and 11th October are the latest.

Gwent Breeding Atlas data and population size

Gwent Atlas	Confirmed tetrads	Probable tetrads	Possible tetrads	Total tetrads	Change in total	Gwent population
1981–1985	1	33	38	72	–	–
1998–2003	0	3	3	6	−92%	0–3 pairs

National breeding data and conservation status

Estimated Welsh population	UK BBS trend 1994–2004	UK CBC/BBS trend 1985–2003	Welsh & UK conservation status
Probably 0 pairs	−45%	−69%	Red-listed

Rose-ringed Parakeet (Ring-necked Parakeet)   *Psittacula krameri*
Paracit torchog

A very rare visitor

There are six Gwent records, which are presumed to relate to either escapees or wanderers from the feral breeding population in south-eastern England. Following a single bird at Sluice Farm on 6th December 1975, three were present at Peterstone during 30th–31st October 1976, and then single birds at Brockwells, Caldicot on 13th August 1981 and during 25th November–12th December 1985, at Pontnewydd on 14th December 1985 and at Llandegfedd Reservoir on 30th May 1994.

(Common) **Cuckoo**
Gog

Cuculus canorus

A fairly common but declining summer visitor

As elsewhere in the Britain, the Cuckoo is a fairly common summer visitor to Gwent, usually arriving in late April and disappearing in the late summer. The 1963 *Birds of Monmouthshire* described it as common, and most numerous among the hills and on the coastal flats, but it has undoubtedly declined since then.

In most years the first birds in the county are heard between 11th and 21st April, but the earliest spring arrivals have been noted on 27th 1975 and 31st March 1976, on 2nd April and twice on 3rd April. Most adults leave during late July or August but juveniles are thought to remain somewhat longer, although there is little evidence from ringing data to support this. The latest birds are seen up to 23rd September. In 1989 a Cuckoo was heard and seen at Bettws Newydd during 14th–15th January, and again during 22nd–26th January, a most unusual record.

Cuckoos are heard from some distance and their song is usually unmistakable, so their presence is easy to detect. Obtaining proof of breeding is much more difficult as the observer must either find a nest with a Cuckoo egg or see a host bird feeding a Cuckoo juvenile. In the 1st Gwent Atlas, *confirmed* breeding was obtained for 9% of occupied tetrads, whilst in the 2nd Gwent Atlas breeding was *confirmed* in only 3% of occupied tetrads. In Gwent, Cuckoos commonly parasitise Meadow Pipits on the hills and on the coastal levels, but the Dunnock is also a common host, noted especially around Raglan and at Magor. There are also four records of Pied Wagtails serving as hosts, and one record each for Skylark, Linnet and Yellow Wagtail hosts. Surprisingly, despite the coastal reedbeds in the county, there are no Gwent records of Reed Warblers as hosts. In 1989 a juvenile was found out of a nest and being fed by a Dunnock, as early as 7th May.

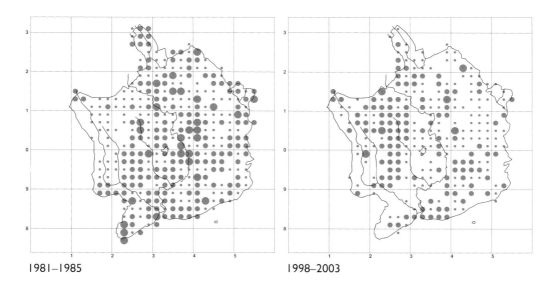

1981–1985   1998–2003

Cuckoos occur in a wide variety of habitats, from moorland and woodland, to farmland and reedbeds. In the 1st Gwent Atlas Cuckoos were widespread throughout the county, being found in 87% of tetrads. In the 2nd Gwent Atlas they were noted in only 67% of tetrads. This indicates a marked decline between the two atlas periods. Even in the late 1970s observers were noting declines in some areas such as the Llanthony Valley, and since then Cuckoos have continued to decline as elsewhere in Britain. The BTO has found a 19% reduction in populations between 1994 and 2004 (Raven & Noble, 2005).

Cuckoos occur at low densities, each pair covering a large area. In 1985 it was suggested that if on average just one pair occurred in each occupied tetrad, a county population of 300–350 pairs would be realistic. At present, there are some areas where there may be five or more pairs/tetrad, but in farmland, where a reduction has been most marked, there are many fewer. This disparity is illustrated by the following observation: in a 1-km square on the Blorenge up to five birds were noted between 1998 and 2003, whereas on a lowland 1-km square at Llansoy one bird was heard from 1995–2000, but subsequently none recorded (Andrew Baker, pers. comm.). An average of 2–3 pairs in tetrads where *confirmed* or *probable* breeding has been recorded would give a population of 240–360 pairs, and this is our recommended estimate for the county. Our standard methods give estimates varying from 9–730 pairs (Appendix 1), the upper end of which is clearly too high.

The rufous hepatic phase has occasionally been recorded in the county.

Gwent Breeding Atlas data and population size

Gwent Atlas	Confirmed tetrads	Probable tetrads	Possible tetrads	Total tetrads	Change in total	Gwent population
1981–1985	29	156	159	344	–	–
1998–2003	6	114	143	263	−21%	240–360 pairs

National breeding data and conservation status

Estimated Welsh population	Welsh CBC/BBS trend 1985–2003	UK CBC/BBS trend 1985–2003	Welsh & UK conservation status
1,200 pairs	−68%	−51%	Amber-listed

Barn Owl
Tylluan Wen

Tyto alba

An uncommon resident (some possibly the result of earlier re-introductions)

The Barn Owl is a species of open habitats, mainly farmland areas, especially if there is a proportion of rough grazing in which the preferred prey of small mammals can be found. It will nest in a variety of crevices, from those in buildings and rock faces to tree cavities. Its distribution in Britain is widespread but characterised by high densities in some areas with few birds between.

A national Barn Owl survey in 1932 suggested a population of 120 pairs for the county (Blaker, 1933). The 1963 *Birds of Monmouthshire* described it as fairly common but probably less common than Tawny Owl. However by the time of the 1977 *Birds of Gwent*, the descriptor 'fairly common' was no longer appropriate and, although it was frequently recorded in rural areas, it was much less so in the coalfield valleys in the west of the county. Numbers were considered fairly stable during the 1970s and during 1981–85 the 1st Gwent Atlas recorded presence in 70 tetrads, but with few *confirmed* breeding records and a high number of *possible* records. At the time of this fieldwork, it was known that captive bred birds were being released at a number of sites in Gwent and many of the sightings were undoubtedly attributable to these releases. Generally such release schemes were ill-conceived, as in most cases the released birds soon died. Legislation was subsequently introduced to ensure that any future releases had to be licenced.

Surprisingly, no county population estimate was given in the 1st Gwent Atlas. However, a survey by the Hawk and Owl Trust during 1982–85 (Shawyer, 1987) estimated just 25 pairs: a 79% decline since the earlier national survey in 1932. This reflected a major national decline during the 20th century, which was still on-going at the time of this survey. It should also be noted that the survey followed the severe winter of 1981/82 and this may have contributed to the low numbers found. The two National Atlases (1968–72; 1988–91) confirmed losses from western Gwent. Breeding estimates are complicated, owing to short-term fluctuations that are known to follow the three-year vole population cycle, and by the species' susceptibility to the adverse effects of cold wet winters. Breeding success and survival rates have increased since the mid 1970s, which could reflect a recovery from the pesticide era (1988–91 National Atlas), but these improvements have not yet reversed the overall decline.

In the period following the 1st Gwent Atlas, the number of confirmed breeding records received has varied from zero in 1986, 1987, 1988, 1995 and 1999, to five or six in 1993, 1998, 2000 and 2003, with no clear trend but a suggestion of an increase. Many of the breeding records during this period come from central Gwent and it is clear that the species can do well in habitats that are managed for shooting (Roberts, 1989). The 2nd Gwent Atlas suggests an improvement, with an estimated population of 25–50 pairs. Although the total number of records is reduced from the 1981–85 figure, the number of *confirmed* breeding records shows a modest increase. These increases have been mainly in the north-west and south-east, with a loss of *possible* records from central parts, where most of the earlier releases had taken place. The 2002 *Birds in Wales* estimated the Gwent population during 1992–2000 to be 23 pairs, with a recent stability in numbers, as in the majority of Welsh counties.

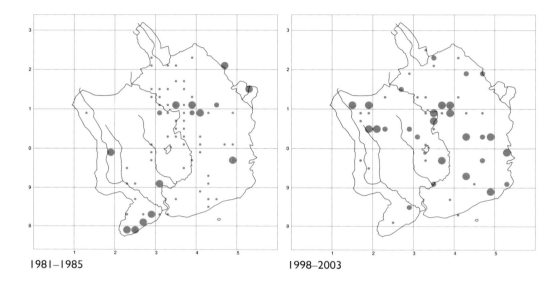

1981–1985   1998–2003

The Winter Atlas shows a distribution on farmland, generally below 300m where winter weather is not too severe. There are few Gwent records at this season but birds are easily overlooked. The species is largely sedentary (*Migration Atlas*). Young birds disperse soon after fledging, and any movements are more or less completed within 4–5 months. The median distance for ringing recoveries is just 12km, with females more likely to move further than males. Once established at a breeding site, birds remain faithful to the area throughout their lives: the median movement thereafter is only 3km.

There are a total of 39 ringing recoveries relevant to Gwent on the BTO database: 13 involved movements of less than 9km, 21 of 10–99km and five of over 100km. Of the five long distance movers, three were ringed as nestlings and two were ringed as fully grown females, probably during their first winter, and their recoveries show movements between Gwent and Yorkshire, Gwynedd, Powys, Wiltshire and Devon (full details are listed in Appendix 9).

There are occasional influxes to Britain of continental birds, following a good breeding season and a crash in prey abundance (as occurred in 1990); these involve the dark-breasted subspecies *T. a. guttata* of northern Europe. There is only one Welsh record of this subspecies, a bird that was shot at Blaenavon in 1908.

Gwent Atlas data

Gwent Atlas	Confirmed tetrads	Probable tetrads	Possible tetrads	Total tetrads	Change in total	Gwent population
1981–1985	12	3	55	70	–	(25)
1998–2003	15	12	25	52	−26%	25–50

National breeding data and conservation status

Estimated Welsh population	Welsh CBC/BBS trend 1985–2003	UK CBC/BBS trend 1985–2003	Welsh & UK conservation status
462 (1984)	Not available	Not available	Amber-listed

Snowy Owl
Tylluan yr Rira

Bubo scandiaca

A very rare vagrant

There are two Gwent records of this Arctic owl. The first was a single bird at Bishton on 23rd December 1952 (1963 *Birds of Monmouthshire*), and the second, one reported from several locations during late January 1976 from the Abergavenny/Raglan area.

Little Owl
Tylluan Fach

Athene noctua

A fairly common resident

The Little Owl is a species of agricultural areas where there are hedgerows, hollow trees or buildings that provide shelter and a location for a nest. It is more frequently seen during daylight hours than other owls, owing to its habit of perching in a prominent position near the nest site. It is not a native to the UK and became established only following several introduction attempts, mainly in southern England. It was first recorded in the county at Chepstow on 5th December 1901 and first bred there in 1914. Subsequently it spread further north and west into Wales and peak numbers were recorded in the 1930s; this expansion may have been aided by the decrease in the numbers of gamekeepers during and after the first World War. By the time of the 1937 *Birds of Monmouthshire*, it was described as a common resident breeding species. There was a decline during the next decade, probably as a result of a series of harsh winters, with local extinctions during the 1946/47 winter (1994 *Birds in Wales*).

By the early 1960s it had become a common resident, especially in the central parts of the county where it was associated with orchards (1963 *Birds of Monmouthshire*), and during the 1968–72 National Atlas the Welsh distribution showed it as being common only in Gwent and Glamorgan. Although it was more widespread in Wales by the time of the 1988–91 National Atlas, there had been declines in these former Welsh strongholds (1994 *Birds in Wales*). Increases in the late 1970s after a succession of mild winters, were followed by declines in the 1981/82 and 1984/85 winters (1988–92 National Atlas).

The 1st Gwent Atlas, which was carried out during a period of decline, showed the main distribution to be in central parts of the county, with an absence from the major urban areas and the more extensively wooded parts, and a patchy distribution in the western valleys. The population was estimated at 500–1,500 pairs (2–6 pairs per occupied tetrad), and it was noted that some nests were as close as 0.5km in central Gwent.

From 1985, the number of records received has declined, especially since the mid 1990s, when an annual maximum of four or five confirmed breeding records were the norm. Despite this, it was the most commonly reported owl from 1996–1999, possibly because it is active during daylight hours. The distribution in the 2nd Gwent Atlas shows an overall decline throughout the county but with the same general distribution in the core area of central Gwent. The current population is estimated at 250–390 pairs which, if correct (even at the lower end), would require the assessment of the current Welsh population as 300 pairs (2002 *Birds in Wales*) to be reconsidered. The UK CBC/BBS index for the period between the Gwent Atlases shows a 43% decline, which is consistent with that suggested by the two Gwent population estimates.

Little Owls are unable to tolerate prolonged periods of cold weather and the lack of suitable shelter accounts for their absence from many upland areas (Winter Atlas). Birds are largely sedentary, although they disperse on average slightly further than Tawny Owls. Most ringing recoveries are within 10km (median 7km) although occasional individuals can move up to 45km (*Migration Atlas*). In Britain, as in the rest of Europe, the species breeds at low densities and in declining numbers.

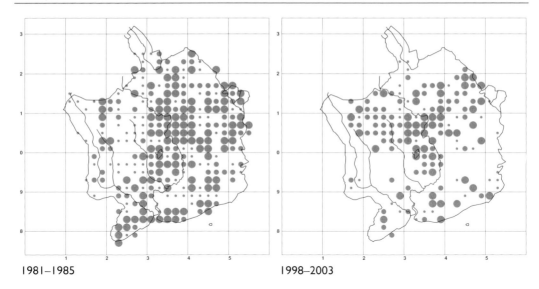

1981–1985   1998–2003

There are ten Gwent ringing recoveries. All had been ringed as nestlings and five were found dead close to the nest site, four within a month of fledging and the fifth a year later. Three others were found 2–4km from the nest site up to two years later. The remaining two had travelled further: one had moved within the county from Raglan to Brynmawr; the other had made an exceptional movement in the period when the species must have been colonising South Wales: after being ringed in July 1925 at Caerwent it was subsequently controlled in January 1926 at Wick, Glamorgan, some 57km to the west.

Gwent Breeding Atlas data and population size

Gwent Atlas	Confirmed tetrads	Probable tetrads	Possible tetrads	Total tetrads	Change in total	Gwent population
1981–1985	110	76	89	275	–	–
1998–2003	48	64	34	146	–47%	250–390 pairs

National breeding data and conservation status

Estimated Welsh population	Welsh CBC/BBS trend 1985–2003	UK CBC/BBS trend 1985–2003	Welsh & UK conservation status
380 pairs	Not available	–43%	Not listed

Tawny Owl   *Strix aluco*
Tylluan Frech

A common and widespread resident

The Tawny Owl is primarily a woodland bird, found in a variety of broadleaved and coniferous woods, and in more open country and urban areas wherever there are sufficient trees and copses to provide secure roosting and nesting areas. It was heavily persecuted along with other raptors during the 19th and the first half of the 20th centuries. However, it was able to survive and numbers increased considerably in most Welsh counties from the 1920s or 1930s onwards (1994 *Birds in Wales*). It has consistently been the most numerous and widespread owl in Gwent (1937 and 1963 *Birds of Monmouthshire*, 1977 *Birds of Gwent*, 1st Gwent Atlas) and, during the early 1980s, it was absent only where there was a local absence of nesting habitat.

The 1988–91 National Atlas indicates that this species differs from other common raptors (Sparrowhawk and Kestrel), in that its numbers have remained fairly stable over the previous 30 years. There was an increase in numbers from around 1900, probably due to an absence of intense persecution, but this could also be due to an adaptability in surviving severe winter weather and a very catholic diet (Winter Atlas). The amount of woodland in an area is the most important factor affecting numbers and density. It is found in all woodland types, and a well wooded county like Gwent supports high numbers.

In the years following the 1st Gwent Atlas (1981–85), there were noticeably fewer records submitted in the years 1992, 1995, 1999 and 2002. This was presumably a reflection of years with poor prey numbers, when some pairs do not attempt to breed and are less easily detected. However, the species is able to exploit other mammal and bird species when the preferred small rodents are not available.

The 2nd Gwent Atlas recorded Tawny Owls in 281 tetrads, compared with 301 in the 1st Gwent Atlas, and the number of tetrads with *confirmed* breeding fell markedly from 145 to 99. There have also been subtle changes in the overall distribution: several widely scattered 10-km squares show small losses while there have been small increases from a handful of others. The current population is estimated at 380–840 pairs, which overlaps the range suggested by the 1st Gwent Atlas of 600-1,200 pairs. The national CBC/BBS index shows a 39% decline between the two Gwent Atlas periods which is consistent with the decrease estimated for the Gwent population.

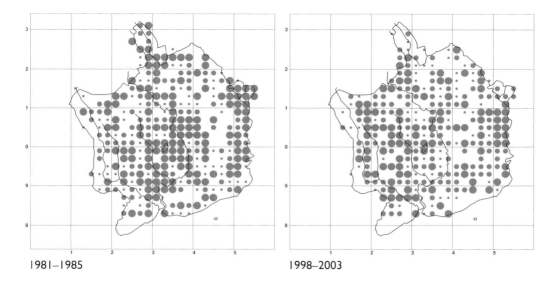

1981–1985   1998–2003

The Winter Atlas confirms that the winter range corresponds to that during the breeding season, which is not surprising as territories are established in the autumn and retained through to breeding. Few species show such site fidelity as the Tawny Owl (*Migration Atlas*) and the young generally establish territories close to their natal area; their median displacement distance is 4km, with few dispersing over 20km. Once established on a territory, movements are reduced to less than 1km.

There are 47 ringing recoveries relevant to Gwent: of these 43 had moved less than 9km, and four between 10km and 99km (mainly at the lower end of this range). One exceptional bird had moved 121km, from Shrewsbury, Shropshire, where it had been ringed as an adult in April 1983, to Llanwern, where it was found freshly dead in August. However, the possibility that this bird had been struck by a vehicle and then inadvertently carried cannot be ruled out.

Gwent Breeding Atlas data and population size

Gwent Atlas	Confirmed tetrads	Probable tetrads	Possible tetrads	Total tetrads	Change in total	Gwent population
1981–1985	145	79	77	301	–	–
1998–2003	99	120	62	281	−7%	380–840 pairs

National breeding data and conservation status

Estimated Welsh population	**Welsh trend 1985–2003**	**UK CBC/BBS trend 1985–2003**	**Welsh & UK conservation status**
2,100 pairs	Not available	−39%	Green-listed

Long-eared Owl
Tylluan Gorniog

Asio otus

A scarce breeder and winter visitor, being found in increasing numbers

The Long-eared Owl has distinctive orange-red eyes and long ear-tufts, although at rest its tufts are lowered and not visible. During the breeding season it is found in upland coniferous woods where these back onto hill grazing and moorland, and also in copses, thorn thickets and tall hedges; always where there is open country nearby.

The 1937 *Birds of Monmouthshire* records the Long-eared Owl as being a scarce and local breeding species and lists only three records: a nest and young collected at Chepstow (also referenced in the *Birds of Glamorgan 1900*), breeding near Abergavenny around 1900, and a bird shot near Usk in October 1926. The 1977 *Birds of Gwent* adds four additional spring records: Llandenny (1967), Llanellen (1969), Wentwood (1970) and Oakdale (1972), and two winter records: near Cwmcarn (1973) and a long dead bird found at Llantrisant (1975). There were no breeding records during the 1st Gwent Atlas (1981–85). However a bird wintered at Gobion in December 1985, but was subsequently killed on a nearby road.

Breeding Long-eared Owls are easily overlooked. Their basic requirements are for an area of rough grazing, moorland or restocked forest for hunting small mammal prey, with adjacent woodland where the old nests of other species are used for breeding. They are mainly restricted to the upland fringes as this is where their habitat requirements are met, although there is also speculation that they are restricted by competition with Tawny Owl. The 1988–91 National Atlas indicates that an unknown but significant number remain undetected. Apparent absence from some areas can be attributed to a shortage of the preferred habitat or competition with Tawny Owl, although both can coexist in well-structured woodlands. Afforestation is likely to have benefited Long-eared Owls, which can use artificial nesting platforms successfully.

There was a 25% decrease between the two National Atlases (1968–72 and 1988–91) but despite this, breeding records have increased in Gwent. At Mynydd Du Forest, three young were raised in 1992 and in the following year two pairs were present. Elsewhere in 1993, breeding was confirmed at two other sites: an adult and fledgling near Abergavenny and a pair with two young at a lowland site in the Usk Valley. Mynydd Du continued to be the main site, with one pair in 1994, two in 1995 and three in 1998. In 2001, breeding was also confirmed at another upland site in the Afon Lwyd valley, where three pairs were located. In that same spring a bird was also found at Llandegfedd Reservoir and pellets believed to be of this species were found near Monmouth. In 2002, three nests were found: one at Mynydd Du and two at Afon Lwyd, but only one was successful. In the following year, three young were raised at the Mynydd Du site. The number of confirmed breeding records is directly related to the time spent searching by a few enthusiasts, and between 1992 and 2000, Gwent accounted for approximately one-third of the 30 or so Welsh breeding records.

During the 2nd Gwent Atlas breeding was *confirmed* in four tetrads within the county and in one marginal tetrad where the nest site was over the border, and on this basis the population is estimated to be around ten pairs. In 2004–2005, two additional sites were found in the hills of the western valleys and, given the amount of potential hunting habitat on the upper fringes of Gwent's conifer plantations, the species is clearly being under-recorded.

Although this is one of our most elusive and least studied winter visitors its winter range is genuinely very patchy and the species is scarce in Wales. This patchy distribution developed in the 20th century and coincided with the successful expansion of the Tawny Owl (Winter Atlas).

Invasions of large numbers of continental birds occur in some winters, for example in 1975/76, and are attributable to crashes in numbers of prey species. Wintering birds have been recorded almost annually in Gwent since 1990, when single birds were found at Coldharbour Pill and Clytha in December. In 1991, a bird frequented Peterstone in March, which was probably from a roost of up to 12 birds reported in November/December 1990 from just over the county boundary in Glamorgan. This roost moved further into Glamorgan in subsequent winters, but two birds were still seen in Gwent during the 1992/93 winter, plus another at Rogiet in December. One was found dead at Caldicot in August 1994. During the winter 1995/96, and in March/April 1997, two birds were found roosting in a high hedgerow at Clytha. In January–March 1998, there were at least 12 birds using this roost, with additional birds found at St Arvans and Skirrid Fach in January.

The *Migration Atlas* confirms that this is one of the few British owl species to undertake long distance movements. In Britain it is a resident breeder and a regular, semi-irruptive winter visitor from the north and east. High numbers in Britain are correlated with the number of winter roosts reported in County Bird Reports, but these are mainly in undisturbed areas in the east of the country. High numbers were reported on the east coast at Spurn Bird Observatory in 1975, 1978, 1989 and 1990. Most winter visitors come from Fennoscandia (which may reflect ringing effort) and more females than males reach Britain (a 5:1 ratio). The main arrival peak is in November and departure takes place from February onwards. A bird found dead at Chepstow in February 1999 had been ringed in Finland in September 1997. The only other recovery was of a bird ringed at the Clytha roost in 1998, which was subsequently found dead at Usk two months later.

Gwent Atlas data

Gwent Atlas	Confirmed tetrads	Probable tetrads	Possible tetrads	Total tetrads	Change in total	Gwent population
1981–1985	0	0	0	0	–	–
1998–2003	5	0	6	11	+	10 pairs

National breeding data and conservation status

Estimated Welsh population	Welsh CBC/BBS trend 1985–2003	UK CBC/BBS trend 1985–2003	Welsh & UK conservation status
30	Not available	Not available	Green-listed

Short-eared Owl
Tylluan Glustiog

Asio flammeus

An uncommon winter visitor and passage migrant

The Short-eared Owl breeds on moorland in Britain, including in the uplands of Wales where a few dozen pairs nest, but to most British birdwatchers it is more familiar as winter visitor to coastal farmland and marshes, where it can provide an exciting diversion from wildfowl and wader counting. Large numbers of birds originating from northern and eastern Europe, and some from Iceland, arrive during late August–November but many remain close to east coast and relatively few find their way to Wales and the south-west.

Short-eared Owls have been recorded in Gwent every winter since 1972/73. They had previously been described as irregular visitors by the 1963 *Birds of Monmouthshire*, but had, no doubt, been under-recorded prior to the 1970s. They occur mainly on the coast where they hunt over the foreshore, saltmarshes and wet pastures of the Gwent Levels, though the extent of the latter habitat has become much reduced in recent years. Most records are in the November–February period, but it is not unusual for a few birds to arrive in October, or linger into March, or even April.

Numbers coming to Britain vary considerably from year to year. In years when populations of voles, their principal prey, are high on the northern breeding grounds, the owl populations increase correspondingly and many more make the long migration to Britain. Severe winter weather on the European mainland can also increase the numbers coming to Britain. These fluctuations can be seen in Gwent records, which show some winters with only a few reports of ones and twos, others with about 4–7 wintering birds, and occasional years when numbers get into double figures. Because they are very mobile, and records from different coastal locations may, therefore, refer to the same birds, it is always difficult to assess how many individuals are present in the years when they are most numerous. With this proviso in mind, the largest numbers recorded in the county are as follows: at least 14 in winter 1978/79, including ten at Peterstone; about ten widely scattered in the county in 1982/83; and at least 14, including 11 at Peterstone, in 1992/93. The 1963 *Birds of Monmouthshire* reported 1938/39 to have been another winter with unusually high numbers, but no figure was given.

The high numbers of winter of 1978/79 were part of a hard weather influx that occurred widely in Wales (1994 *Birds in Wales*), and Gwent records included three birds that spent the winter hunting over the grounds of Ebbw Vale Comprehensive School.

Inland records occur in most years but are much scarcer than coastal records. Nevertheless, there have been some notable numbers, including four at Bettws, Newport in 1982/83, six at Bryn Bach, near Tredegar in 1985/86 and six flushed from a young conifer plantation near Raglan during a pheasant drive in 1983/84. The latter record raises the suspicion that many inland birds may pass unrecorded.

A few birds occur on passage in many years and although, as with wintering birds, most are again recorded on the coast, there is a higher proportion from inland locations, which can be any open situations ranging from moorland to Llandegfedd Reservoir. Spring passage records occur typically in April but can also be in March and May. Autumn passage records occur from mid-August through to October.

Summer records are occasional on moorlands but breeding has never occurred in the county. However a pair did breed within one of the tetrads of the 2nd Gwent Atlas, but just outside the county border.

(European) Nightjar   *Caprimulgus europaeus*
Troellwr Mawr

An uncommon summer visitor, now at the highest level ever recorded

Nightjars are summer visitors, not arriving on our shores until May. The first indication that they have arrived is usually the males' churring song. They are nocturnal, hawking silently for insects especially at dusk and dawn.

The earliest record of the Nightjar in Gwent is of a male shot at Newport on 1st June 1926, the skin of which is now in the National Museum of Wales, Cardiff. The 1937 *Birds of Monmouthshire* described the species as being a fairly common visitor breeding rather locally on fern-covered hillsides, commons and heaths and in open woodlands or on sites of felled woods. By the time of the 1963 *Birds of Monmouthshire*, however, it was listed as a rather uncommon summer visitor, breeding very locally and thought possibly to be decreasing. The status had changed little by the 1977 *Birds of Gwent*, although there had been an increase in records since 1965. The main site was the forest restocks of Wentwood, with up to eight pairs in 1970, though there was a decline in numbers in following years. Regular reports, of not more than three birds were recorded from Bassaleg (Park Wood), Cwmcarn Forest, the Blorenge and the Sugar Loaf. The traditional habitat is lowland heathland, but its alternative folklore name of fern-owl alludes to its occurrence in bracken areas as well. By the time of the 1st Gwent Atlas, although Wentwood retained suitable areas, the species' stronghold had shifted to the east of the county. During the national survey of 1981, 25 males were found, and although one pair was found in Ebbw Forest in 1980, none were recorded there during the Gwent atlas fieldwork. A population of 30 pairs was thought likely. Although an easy species to detect, since the male's song is very distinctive, it does require special nocturnal efforts on the part of the observer.

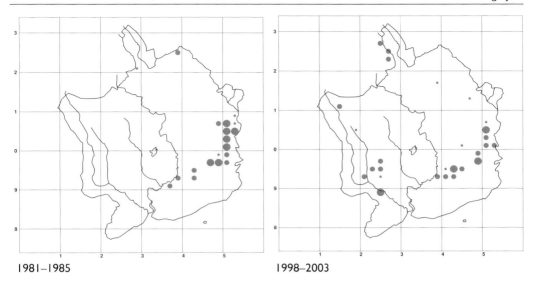

1981–1985   1998–2003

Year	Total males	Ebbw Forest	Wentwood	Wye Valley	Other
1981	26	0	2	23	1
1992	28	13	4	11	0
2003	33	no count	20	12	1
2004	48	7	28	10	3

The 2003 survey took place only in the eastern part of Gwent

Table 89. Counts of singing males in Gwent during Nightjar National Surveys

Between 1986 and 1998, the numbers of males recorded varied from ten (1996) to 28 (1992). The variation was chiefly a reflection of effort: 1992 was a national survey year with good coverage. During the late 1980s, the bulk of churring males were found in the Trelleck woodlands and in Chepstow Park, both in the Wye Valley and with a maximum of 17 in several years, with five in the Western Valleys (Ebbw Forest) in 1988. This period coincided with a low point in Wentwood where none were recorded in 1989. The 1992 survey showed a shift towards Ebbw Forest, which held 13 males, with 11 in the Wye Valley and four in Wentwood. The Ebbw Forest birds were retained until the mid 1990s when the population there and in the Wye Valley began to decline. By the time of the 2nd Gwent Atlas, Wentwood had once again risen to become the prime area.

The 1994 *Birds in Wales* records the Nightjar as common and widespread up to the 1920s/1930s in most counties. There were declines until the 1970s and increases from the 1980s as restocks were widely colonised. The 1981 National Survey found 57 males in the whole of Wales, including 26 in Gwent, and the 1992 survey found 193 males: 28 in Gwent. There had been major increases in most other Welsh counties where large areas of suitable restock were being created.

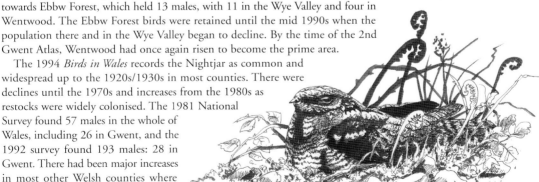

A survey of the eastern half of the county in 2003 recorded 33 males, of which 20 were in Wentwood and 11 in the Trelleck area (Lewis, 2003). The shifting centre of population undoubtedly reflected forest management and the extent of suitable habitat in the form of recently felled plantations. The National Survey, having been postponed to 2004, covered the whole county and gave a higher estimate of 48 males (Lewis, 2004), which represented the highest ever number recorded in Gwent.

The 1988–91 National Atlas indicated a decline in the number of squares occupied, but not in the species' range. As many of the restock sites were at higher altitudes than the traditional heathland sites, it suggests an altitudinal tolerance. It is therefore unlikely that climatic change was the cause of the decline, being more influenced by heathland management, which was not geared specifically for a species that requires small bare areas for nesting. The creation of bare ground areas improved numbers locally. Restocks are mainly occupied for up to five years after planting, with progressive declines thereafter. To maintain populations at their current levels therefore requires the creation of new restocks, an unlikely scenario with the move towards continuous cover forestry and limited clearfelling.

The *Migration Atlas* suggests that birds pass through France and Spain to and from wintering areas in West Africa. There are only two African recoveries, both in Morocco during the passage periods. Most birds arrive on the breeding grounds in late April/May. The average first date for Gwent is 15th May with early arrivals noted in 1987 (24th April), 1998 (4th May), 1971 (7th May) and an exceptionally early record of a pair seen at Pontymoile, near Pontypool on 26th March 1962. Most depart the breeding grounds in late August/September but there are a few October/early November records in Britain. The median last date for Gwent is 16th August with none later than 27th August: in 1989 and 1990.

There have been only two Gwent ringing recoveries, of adult males ringed and recaught in a subsequent year at the same site. This is consistent with studies in Dorset, which have shown high site fidelity of breeding birds (Alexander & Cresswell, 1990).

Gwent Breeding Atlas data and population size

Gwent Atlas	Confirmed tetrads	Probable tetrads	Possible tetrads	Total tetrads	Change in total	Gwent population
1981–1985	7	8	5	20	–	–
1998–2003	4	16	7	27	+35%	48 territories

National breeding data and conservation status

Estimated Welsh population	Welsh trend	UK trend	Welsh & (UK) conservation status
193 (in 1992)	Not available	Not available	Amber(Red)-listed

(Common) **Swift**   *Apus apus*
Gwennol Ddu

A common and widespread summer visitor

The Swift is a widespread summer visitor to Britain, most numerous in the south and east where the climate is warmer and aerial insects more abundant (1988–91 National Atlas). Although it breeds almost entirely in holes in buildings, nests occur in crevices in coastal cliffs in a few places in South Wales (1994 *Birds in Wales*).

The main influx of Swifts into Gwent occurs in the first two weeks of May although there are always a few early records. The earliest arrival on record was on 12th April 1982, and the most commonly reported first arrivals are from 19th–26th April. On 10th May 1993, migrating birds were seen in misty weather flying from the south at low altitude over Brynmawr, and the observer estimated many thousands moving north, west and east. Movements are also recorded along the coast in some years, such the 500+ birds that flew west past Uskmouth in a period of 20 minutes on 18th May 1996.

Usually Swifts feed too high to be seen, but large flocks, commonly of 100 to 300 birds, can be seen anywhere in the county during the summer months when they fly lower to feed on winged ants or on an emergence of moths. Thunderstorms will also bring Swifts down to levels where they can be seen. Flocks of up to 500 have regularly been reported from Llandegfedd Reservoir early in the summer. Flocks of 500–700 have been reported, for example over an uncut hay field at Pontypool on 1st August and at Peterstone in June.

In the 1st Gwent Atlas, Swifts were recorded in 84% of tetrads and *confirmed* breeding in 31%. In the 2nd Gwent Atlas they were found in 78% of the tetrads, but confirmed breeding in only 27%. This suggests some population decline. Although not easily overlooked when flying, obtaining proof of breeding by seeing birds entering nests under eaves is not always easy. The breeding population in Gwent, estimated from sample tetrads is 2,000–3,000 pairs, but this is a notoriously difficult species to census and the true figure could be very different. Although there appears to have been a slight decline in range between the two Gwent Atlases, this is small. Nonetheless, the BBS population trend shows reductions for both Wales and the UK between 1994 and 2004.

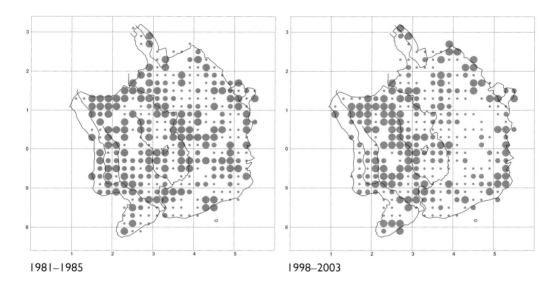

1981–1985   1998–2003

Traditional breeding sites that have been recorded include Monmouth's Monnow Bridge, the arched 13th road bridge, buildings in Monmouth market place, Nantyderry House, Llanfoist School, Panteg Hospital, Chepstow, DuPont plc at Pontypool, Park Crescent in Abergavenny and St John's Church in Newport. Elsewhere at Usk, Newport and New Inn, other tall buildings with suitable roof spaces and entrance holes are used. However, many old houses no longer afford nest sites because of blocking up of entrance holes, whilst modern houses afford few suitable nest sites. Nestboxes can provide an alternative and have been used for many years at Pilstone House near Whitebrook.

Young birds leave Britain soon after they fledge, adults following later. Although most birds leave during August for Africa, departure can be earlier in some years, for example in 1989 when few were seen in Gwent during August after large movements had been noted at the end of July. A small number remain beyond August, and late birds have been seen in Gwent up to the end of September, but there are also several October records, with two very late birds reported, on 20th October 1982 and 23rd October 1976.

There is only one ringing record of interest: an adult ringed in Hampshire on 10th June 1974 was recovered 171km north-west in Monmouth on 5th July the following year.

Gwent Breeding Atlas data and population size

Gwent Atlas	Confirmed tetrads	Probable tetrads	Possible tetrads	Total tetrads	Change in total	Gwent population
1981–1985	123	76	132	331	–	–
1998–2003	97	81	128	306	−7%	2,000–3,000 pairs

National breeding data and conservation status

Estimated Welsh population	Welsh BBS trend 1994–2004	UK CBC/BBS trend 1985–2003	Welsh & UK conservation status
13,000 pairs	−11%	−22%	Green-listed

Alpine Swift
Gwennol Ddu'r Alpau

Apus melba

A very rare vagrant

There are two Gwent records of this aerial visitor from southern Europe. Single birds were seen over the River Wye at Monmouth on 15th April 1988 and again on 11th April 1991.

(Common) **Kingfisher**
Glas y Dorlan

Alcedo atthis

An uncommon resident

Breeding Kingfishers are widespread on rivers and streams throughout most of lowland England and Wales, requiring shallow, slow-moving freshwater with vertical banks soft enough to allow excavation of nesting burrows (1988–91 National Atlas).

The 1937 *and* 1963 *Birds of Monmouthshire* reported the Kingfisher as a fairly common breeding resident that visited the coastal levels in 'fair numbers' in winter. The species is very susceptible to severe winters that produce prolonged freezing of inland waters. Consequently it was hard-hit in Gwent by the winters of 1961/62 and 1962/63, but the 1977 *Birds of Gwent* noted that its population recovered rapidly in the succeeding few years.

Kingfishers occur widely on Gwent's rivers, except on upland fast-flowing rocky stretches. Nests are to be found on the River Usk from the border with Breconshire to the tidal reaches near Newbridge-on-Usk, and on many tributaries such as on the Olway Brook and the Afon Llwyd up to Abersychan. They also occur throughout the Wye catchment, even on narrow streams such as the Mally Brook at Dixton near Monmouth. The Gwent population appears to be the largest in Wales.

In the 1st Gwent Atlas, Kingfishers were found in 100 tetrads (25 %) with *confirmed* or *probable* breeding in 44 (11%). Apart from on the River Rhymney, where there were several pairs, they were scarce in the western valleys, the uplands of the north-west and on the coastal levels. They were, however, frequent along the rivers Usk, Wye and Monnow, and also on the Trothy, Afon Llwyd and small streams. It was suggested that one pair per 2–3km on suitable rivers would give a population of 50 pairs.

In the 2nd Gwent Atlas, they were found in 118 tetrads (30%), slightly more than in 1981–85, and with *confirmed* or *probable* breeding in 57 (14%). The largest numbers were again found along the River Usk, and they were also frequent on the River Monnow, where there were at least 14 territories in 2002 and 2003. There were also at least seven pairs along the River Ebbw and at least one pair on the River Sirhowy, which represents a significant spread into the western valleys and may be a consequence of improvement in water quality. Birds were also seen on the Wye tributaries, such as the Trothy, Angidy and Mally Brook, as well as on the River Wye itself.

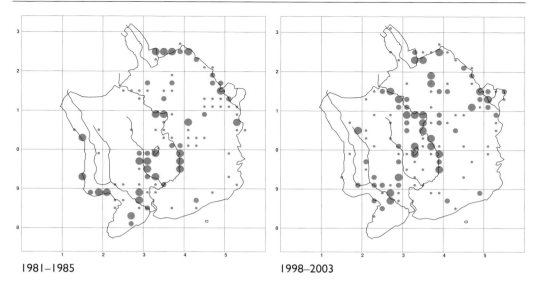

| 1981–1985 | 1998–2003 |

Using an average of 1.34 pairs per tetrad (from sample tetrads) for all tetrads with *confirmed* or *probable* breeding, a county population of up to 75 pairs is obtained. The Kingfisher is on the national Amber list because of a marked decline from 1970–1985, but since then there has been a good recovery, with the WBS showing an increase of over 80% in the period between the two Gwent Atlases. This appears to be reflected in the Gwent population, which seems to be increasing, partly owing to a spread into the western valleys.

In the autumn and winter, a wider range of aquatic habitats are frequented. These include garden ponds, lakes, canals, reedbeds and estuaries and even upland stretches of streams, as on the Afon Honddu. Records on the coastal levels are generally limited to the winter, when they can be found fishing at Peterstone Gout and in many of the reens (drainage channels).

Gwent Breeding Atlas data and population size

Gwent Atlas	Confirmed tetrads	Probable tetrads	Possible tetrads	Total tetrads	Change in total	Gwent population
1981–1985	24	20	56	100	–	–
1998–2003	25	32	61	118	+4%	34–75 pairs

National breeding data and conservation status

Estimated Welsh population	Welsh trend	UK WBS trend 1985–2003	Welsh & UK conservation status
c.400* pairs	Not available	+83%	Amber-listed

* From 1994 *Birds in Wales*.

(European) **Bee-eater** *Merops apiaster*
Gwybedog y Gwenyn

A very rare vagrant

There are two records of this exotically colourful Mediterranean species. Two birds were seen at close range perched on telephone wires at Caldicot on 6th June 1981, and a single bird, seen to fly east past Peterstone on the evening of 25th July, was (remarkably) found again at Black Rock several hours later.

(European) **Roller**
Rholydd

Coracias garrulus

A very rare vagrant

The Roller is summer visitor to southern and eastern Europe and no more than a vagrant to Britain. There is only one Gwent record. This involved a single bird at Michaelstone-y-Fedw on 30th September 1987, which was said by local people to have been in the area for the previous three weeks at least.

Hoopoe
Copog

Upupa epops

A very scarce passage migrant, mostly in spring

The striking and unmistakable Hoopoe is a summer visitor to much of southern Europe. A few northward-bound bound migrants regularly overshoot in spring, landing in Britain for a sojourn that is usually quite short, though on rare occasions pairs have stayed to breed.

There are a total of 30 Gwent records. There were seven records between 1934 and 1963, six more between 1965 and 1974, and from 1975 to 2005 it has occurred in 13 years with a total of 17 records.

Records have been well spread around the county, apart from the western valleys. Figure 22 shows that records are generally concentrated in the period April–June, although there is an exceptionally early one from the grounds of Maindiff Court Hospital, Abergavenny during the 1st week of March 1992. Records are scarcer during the summer/autumn period, and there is an exceptionally late record from Nantyderry on 6th December 1990. All records are of single birds except for two at Skenfrith on 20th August 1962 and two at Tredunnock-on-Usk during 18th–20th April 1990.

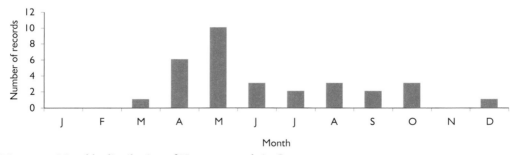

Figure 22. Monthly distribution of Hoopoe records in Gwent

Wryneck
Pengam

Jynx torquilla

Formerly a summer visitor that bred; now a rare autumn passage migrant

The Wryneck is Europe's only migratory woodpecker and a little over 100 years ago it was a common breeding summer visitor in Britain. In some parts of the country it was even the commonest of the woodpeckers (Mead, 2000), but it declined steadily during 20th century and may now be extinct as a breeding species in Britain (Ogilvie, 2004).

The 1937 *Birds of Monmouthshire* quoted four breeding records in the county from around 1900, and otherwise described it as an uncommon, but probably regular, spring passage migrant. However there were no documented records of such occurrences on passage and this was still the case when the 1963 *Birds of Monmouthshire* was published.

The first documented record was not until 1964 and concerned a bird at Llanellen in July. Since then it has occurred in 17 out of the 40 years to 2004, with a total of 21 records. The frequency of records has decreased since the 1970s, when there were 11 birds, to five in the 1980s and four in the 1990s, with no further records since 1997.

Its passage status in Gwent has clearly changed since the early part of the 20th century, as the monthly distribution of modern records (Figure 23) shows none in spring, and most within the autumn passage period, particularly September, which accounts for almost half of them. There are also several records from June–July, the earliest of which was at Wentwood on 14th June 1965, which raises the possibility of breeding. The three remaining summer records came from Llanellen in July 1964, Mamhilad on 11th July 1974 and Wentwood on 24th July 1977. There is a particularly late record of an individual at Triley Mill on 12th November 1993.

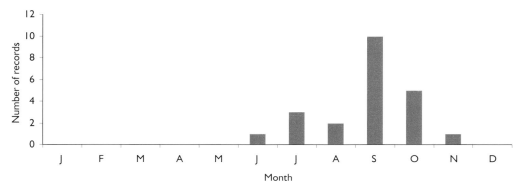

Figure 23. Monthly distribution of Wryneck records in Gwent

Green Woodpecker
Cnocell Werdd

Picus viridis

A fairly common resident

The Green Woodpecker is mainly a woodland bird, breeding in deciduous and mixed woodland, parkland and large gardens. Its distinctive laughing call, giving it the vernacular name of yaffle, makes this species unlikely to be overlooked. It is the woodpecker most likely to be seen on the ground, as it often feeds on anthills, be they in upland or lowland pastures or, in the case of Gwent, on reclaimed spoil heaps of former coal mines in the western valleys. Feeding birds can adopt a sky-pointing posture if disturbed but most are quick to fly, with a typical sighting comprising a flash of vivid lime green as the bird 'bounces' away.

The 1963 *Birds of Monmouthshire* described the Green Woodpecker as a common breeding species found in all suitable localities. In the 1977 *Birds of Gwent* it was described as a breeding resident which, by 1968, had recovered its former numbers following the hard winter of 1962/63. It was recorded as being well spread throughout the county including occasional sightings on the bare high ground of the north-west and the relatively open areas of the coastal levels.

In 1995 a breeding survey found birds in 170 tetrads of the county (Tyler, 1977). However, the more comprehensive 1st and 2nd Gwent Atlas surveys recorded Green Woodpeckers in 326 and 333 tetrads respectively. Although the increase in distribution was marginal, there were substantially more records in the *confirmed* and *probable* breeding categories in the later atlas.

According to the 1994 *Birds in Wales*, the distribution in Wales has not varied much over the past one hundred years, apart from losses due to severe winters as mentioned above. The 2002 *Birds in Wales* states that the Welsh stronghold for this species is in the east, particularly in Gwent. These accounts, combined with the historic information summarised above, indicate that Gwent has always been a stronghold for the species.

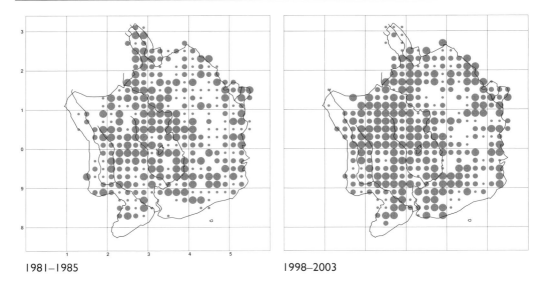

| 1981–1985 | 1998–2003 |

The 1st Gwent Atlas estimated the number of breeding pairs as 1,200–1,500 based upon density levels suggested by CBC figures. The latest estimate of 420–770, although significantly lower, reflects the different basis on which the two calculations have been made rather than an actual drop in numbers of pairs. This latest estimate is also consistent with an estimate of 550 pairs reported in the 2002 *Birds in Wales*.

The species is Amber-listed in both the UK and Wales owing to its unfavourable conservation status in Europe. In the period between the two Gwent Atlases there has been a substantial population increase at the UK level but a decrease in Wales. It is not clear from the Gwent Atlas data which of these conflicting national and regional trends have been reflected in Gwent, but the large increase in the number of tetrads with *probable* and *confirmed* breeding is strongly suggestive of a population increase in the county. The 1994–2004 BBS trend for Wales shows a 61% increase rather than the decrease seen over the longer (1985–2003) period.

The two Gwent ringing recoveries showed local movements of 3km and 4km. This provides strong local evidence to confirm the sedentary nature of this resident species, as summarised by the Winter Atlas.

Gwent Breeding Atlas data and population size

Gwent Atlas	Confirmed tetrads	Probable tetrads	Possible tetrads	Total tetrads	Change in total	Gwent population
1981–1985	123	106	97	326	–	–
1998–2003	150	126	57	333	+2%	420–770 pairs

National breeding data and conservation status

Estimated Welsh population	Welsh CBC/BBS trend 1985–2003	UK CBC/BBS trend 1985–2003	Welsh & UK conservation status
1,000+	−24%	+96%	Amber-listed

Great Spotted Woodpecker
Cnocell Fraith Fwyaf

Dendrocopos major

A common resident

The Great Spotted Woodpecker is a species of broad-leaved and coniferous woodland, parkland, gardens and hedgerows where there is a concentration of mature trees. It is the most widespread and numerous woodpecker in the UK. The 1988–91 National Atlas notes the Great Spotted Woodpecker as being most abundant in the well-wooded southern counties of England, with other concentrations in Gloucestershire, Gwent and through the Welsh Marches. The species has become a regular visitor to garden feeders, and its distinctive calls and noisy drumming in early spring make it relatively easy to detect.

The earliest record of this species in Gwent is of a bird being taken at Abergavenny on 2nd March 1926, the skin of which is now in the National Museum of Wales, Cardiff. The 1994 *Birds in Wales* notes that historically the species was far from common in South Wales, but that in Glamorgan it was considered to be increasing by the end of the 19th century and that increases were noted in many parts of Wales during the first half of the 20th century. Such increases were noted in the 1937 and the 1963 *Birds of Monmouthshire*, both describing the Great Spotted Woodpecker as a not uncommon

breeding species showing some increase. In the 1977 *Birds of Gwent* it is described as a breeding resident, only slightly less numerous than the Green Woodpecker, being well spread throughout the county and scarce only in the western valleys.

In the 1st Gwent Atlas, the species was found in 292 tetrads, with *confirmed* breeding in 152 of these, and a concentration in lowland regions. It was found more widely in the 2nd Gwent Atlas, with presence in 319 tetrads and *confirmed* breeding in 160, and a noticeable colonisation of tetrads at higher altitude in the west and north-west. This pattern of expansion is also seen in many other species and is probably attributable to improvement of habitat in formerly industrialised areas of the county (see 'Conclusions and Comparisons'), amelioration of winter climate and possibly pressure to expand due to a general increase in population in lowland areas.

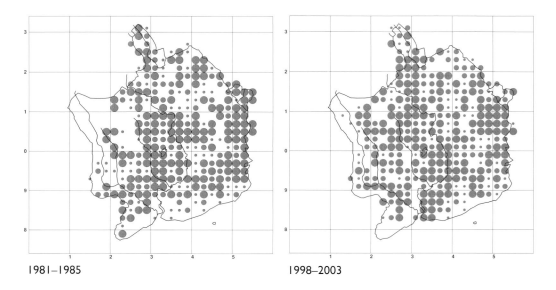

1981–1985   1998–2003

An increase in range is also apparent from the pattern of records published in *Gwent Bird Reports*, where it is now the most frequently reported woodpecker species. Sightings at bird tables at all times of year have now become commonplace. The provision of food in gardens is thought to have been a factor in the increase in the species range nationally (Gorman, 2004).

The range expansion between the two Gwent Atlases would be expected to reflect an increase in the county population, and such an increase would conform to the UK and Welsh population trends, which show marked increases for this species over the period in question. However, the current calculated population size of 670–1,000 pairs shows no change from the estimated figure at the time of the 1st Gwent Atlas (c.1,000 pairs). This is probably attributable to the different methods on which the two estimates are based and it is felt that the current estimate is the more reliable of the two.

The British breeding population is known to be very sedentary and there is no significant immigration of the species into the country. Two Gwent ringing recoveries reflect this sedentary nature, with the longer of the two recorded movements being only 6km.

Gwent Breeding Atlas data and population size

Gwent Atlas	Confirmed tetrads	Probable tetrads	Possible tetrads	Total tetrads	Change in total	Gwent population
1981–1985	152	68	72	292	–	–
1998–2003	160	101	58	319	+9%	670–1,100 pairs

National breeding data and conservation status

Estimated Welsh population	Welsh CBC/BBS trend 1985–2003	UK CBC/BBS trend 1985–2003	Welsh & UK conservation status
3,500 pairs	+22%	+55%	Green-listed

Lesser Spotted Woodpecker
Cnocell Fraith Leiaf

Dendrocopos minor

An uncommon resident

The Lesser Spotted Woodpecker is a bird of mature deciduous woodland, parks, orchards and alders alongside streams and canals. It can be a difficult bird to locate except when it calls noisily in the early spring. It is acknowledged to be the least common of the three resident woodpecker species to be found in Britain. Although locally common throughout Europe, Gwent is towards the north-west limit of its range. The 1994 *Birds in Wales* describes it as a mainly lowland bird, rarely occurring above an altitude of 180 metres.

The 1937 and 1963 *Birds of Monmouthshire* describe the Lesser Spotted Woodpecker as a resident breeding species less numerous than either of the other two woodpeckers, but nesting in scattered pairs throughout the county except in the higher valleys. The 1977 *Birds of Gwent* stated that there were only isolated sightings from about 15 localities each year and never more than one breeding record a year, but also that it is an elusive species and may be overlooked.

In both Gwent Atlases the Lesser Spotted Woodpecker's breeding range is confined to the central and eastern parts of the county. This reflects its preferred breeding habitat of lowland deciduous woodlands, parks and orchards as opposed to the upland conifer plantations, which are more prevalent in the west. Gorman (2004) drew attention to the species' requirement for plenty of old growth and much standing dead wood. It also favours alder trees along streams and canals, and has been observed nesting in alders alongside the Monmouthshire and Brecon Canal at Goetre, adjacent to the GOS woodland reserve at Goytre House Wood.

The 2nd Gwent Atlas recorded birds in 60 tetrads with *confirmed* breeding in 11. This represents a considerable (46%) reduction in range compared to the 1st Gwent Atlas, which located birds in 112 tetrads, with *confirmed* breeding in 20. The species has retreated noticeably from the southern half of the county and is now completely absent from the far south-east. Current strongholds are the Usk Valley running north of Usk town, and the valleys of Wye and Trothy rivers. The species has a secretive and essentially sedentary nature with a breeding territory of 50–100ha. Given these factors, it is likely that a record of *possible* breeding is more significant for this species than for many others.

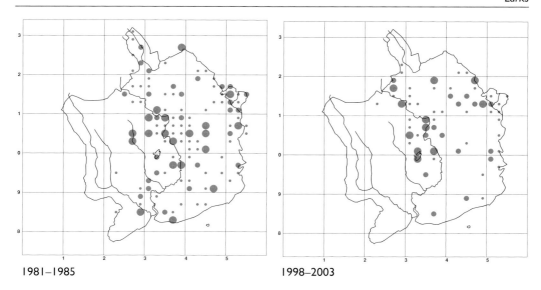

1981–1985   1998–2003

The reduction in the Gwent breeding range mirrors the decline noted nationally, which has seen a decrease of 74% in the years between the Gwent Atlases, putting the species in the Red-listed category. Longer-term trends in the UK show a low point in the early 1970s, then an increase up to the early 1980s followed by a further decline to a point where it is less numerous than in the 1970s. The 1st Gwent Atlas was therefore conducted at a period (1981–85) when the species was at its most prevalent in the UK. The national decline is probably due to the lack of suitable breeding habitat, caused by loss of hedgerow elms and the tendency for conifer plantations to replace broadleaved woodland. In addition, managed woodland has fewer of the standing dead trees preferred by the species. The 2002 *Birds in Wales* refers to the importance of riverine alders as an important nesting site for the species and notes that disease in these trees may be causing decline in this habitat.

Gwent Bird Reports continue to list up to 15 or so records in most years, often of single birds located in the eastern lowlands. Many such sightings occur year after year in the same location in suitable habitat, but confirmed breeding records are always much scarcer.

Gwent Breeding Atlas data and population size

Gwent Atlas	Confirmed tetrads	Probable tetrads	Possible tetrads	Total tetrads	Change in total	Gwent population
1981–1985	20	26	66	112	–	–
1998–2003	11	15	34	60	−46%	30–70 pairs

National breeding data and conservation status

Estimated Welsh population	Welsh CBC/BBS trend 1985–2003	UK CBC/BBS trend 1985–2003	Welsh & UK conservation status
c.300 pairs	−62%	−74%	Red-listed

Woodlark
Ehedydd y Coed

Lullula arborea

A very scarce visitor; has recently bred

Formerly a widespread breeding resident in Britain, the Woodlark underwent serious decline during most of the 20th century and is now restricted mainly to southern England. Between the two National Atlases (1968–72 and 1988–91) its distribution declined by 62%, leading to its Red-listing as a species of high conservation concern. Its numbers have recently begun to increase rapidly and a significant recovery looks distinctly possible (Mead, 2000).

The 1963 *Birds of Monmouthshire* described it as an uncommon and local breeding resident, with small flocks on the coast during the winter months, though the most recent breeding season records quoted were from the 1940s. In the 1977 *Birds of Gwent* it is described as a very scarce breeding resident, with breeding confirmed from an area close to Pen-y-fan Pond in 1967: a nest with five eggs found, suspected at the same site in 1971, and again confirmed there in 1974. There were further records of birds singing at this site on 1st July 1975 and seen there on both 31st May 1976 and 16th July 1977. Other notable sightings around this time included 25 flying east over Llanarth on 20th February 1964, eight at Abergavenny Sewage Works on 8th December 1967 and up to 12 at Wentwood during June–July 1968.

Since 1977 the Woodlark has declined in Gwent and can now only be described as a very scarce visitor, with just ten records in the 27 years 1978–2005. These records have usually been in the October–December period, and generally of only one or two birds, though at Dingestow there were six during 31st October–1st November 1993, up to ten during 25th–31st October 1994, and seven on 25th November 1995. The only records outside this period were in spring and involved single birds at Llanvihangel Crucorney on 20th April 1985 and at Trelleck on 7th and 14th May 1987.

Successful breeding by a pair in the east of the county was reported in 2006.

Skylark   *Alauda arvensis*
Ehedydd

A widespread and common resident; some occur on passage

The Skylark is one of the most ubiquitous of Britain's breeding birds, traditionally occurring on a wide variety of open habitats from wild moorlands to lowland farms, both arable and pastoral.

The 1963 *Birds of Monmouthshire* described the Skylark as a widespread breeding species up to 2,000 feet above sea-level, and very numerous on the coastal flats in winter. In the 1977 *Birds of Gwent* it was described as a common breeding resident, most numerous on the hills but occurring throughout the county. At the time of the 1st Gwent Atlas it was still widespread, breeding everywhere except in the more populated areas. Some 85% of tetrads held birds although, because of the difficulty of finding nests, breeding was *confirmed* in only 28% of occupied tetrads. An average of 30 pairs per tetrad, estimated from CBC data, put the county population at 10,000 pairs.

The Skylark population of the UK declined by 54% during 1970–2001 (Eaton & Gregory, 2003). This decline has been noted in Gwent, as in other parts of Wales. In the 2nd Gwent Atlas, Skylarks were found in only 71% of tetrads although breeding was *confirmed* in 30% of them. Although still widespread throughout, most of the tetrads with *confirmed* breeding records were in the west and north, where birds occur at much higher densities on moorland than on the intensively-managed farmland in the centre and east of the county. For example, 30–50 pairs bred on 300ha at Mynydd Garn Clochdy in 1988. On intensive farmland, cultivation and other mechanical operations destroy nests in crops and there is little undisturbed land at the field edges for birds to breed. A reduction in insect prey from the use of insecticides and herbicides may also have affected them. With the encouragement of environmentally sympathetic farming practices, such as creating conservation headlands and leaving land fallow, Skylarks should benefit.

During 1998–2003 the county population was estimated as 2,900–5,900 pairs using the BBS and atlas-based methods respectively. The lower (BBS) figure is likely to be an underestimate because the calculation includes a halving step, designed to convert total birds to total pairs, whereas in the case of this species, it will be almost entirely singing males that are detected by BBS transects.

By late October, birds have moved off the hills to lower land and then occur in flocks. Winter flocks are usually of 40–70 birds but 250 were seen at Sluice Farm in January 1985 and 500 at St Brides on 11th February 1985. Hard-weather movements have not been recorded in recent years but 4,000 were noted at Abergavenny in February 1969.

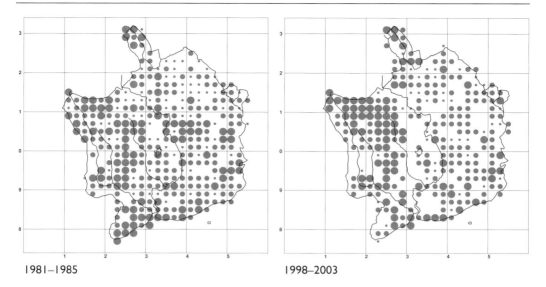

| 1981–1985 | 1998–2003 |

Passage movements regularly occur, generally involving small flocks, typically up to about 50 birds, flying along the coast in October and in February. Exceptionally large passage movements occurred at Goldcliff on 19th October 1968 (500 birds) and at Peterstone on 11th October 1975 (350). On 5th October 1985 over 500 were observed flying south-west over Goldcliff in a 90-minute period. Some inland movements have been recorded, as at Garn Clochdy in September 1992 and Llanwenarth in the same year.

Gwent Breeding Atlas data and population size

Gwent Atlas	Confirmed tetrads	Probable tetrads	Possible tetrads	Total tetrads	Change in total	Gwent population
1981–1985	96	169	71	336	–	–
1998–2003	85	151	43	279	0%	2,900–5,900 pairs

National breeding data and conservation status

Estimated Welsh population	Welsh CBC/BBS trend 1985–2003	UK CBC/BBS trend 1985–2003	Welsh & (UK) conservation status
120,000–142,000	−45%	−28%	Amber (Red)-listed

Sand Martin   *Riparia riparia*
Gwennol y Glennydd

A frequent breeding summer visitor and passage migrant

The Sand Martin is one the first summer visitors to arrive and it is a widespread breeding bird throughout the UK. Nest sites include newly eroded banks of rivers and lakes and sandy sea cliffs, and also freshly worked cliffs at sand and gravel quarries, vertical roadside banks, and drainage pipes in riverside walls. It is well distributed in Wales but scarce in some areas, including the rivers in the South Wales valleys, and on the coastal levels.

The population in Britain and Ireland has had mixed fortunes in recent decades with apparent increases in the 1950s and 1960s (possibly linked to the expansion of the gravel and sand extraction industry), followed by widespread, major declines after the 1968/69 winter when there was a severe drought in the Sahel region (1968–72 National Atlas). Numbers remained low in the early 1970s, increased thereafter, but dropped again in 1985. The population may have been as high as one million pairs before 1968/69 but the 1968–72 National Atlas gave a population estimate of 250,000–500,000 pairs and it may have dropped to as low as 40,000 pairs in the early 1970s. By the 1988–91 National Atlas there were an estimated 77,500–250,000 pairs in Britain.

Since then there has been a partial recovery linked to better rainfall in the Sahel zone, with an 84% increase in populations during 1994–2004. The Sand Martin was listed as a candidate Red Data bird species by Batten *et al.* (1990) and is now included in the Amber list of birds of conservation concern.

The 1937 and 1963 *Birds of Monmouthshire* described the Sand Martin as a summer visitor, breeding very locally and by no means numerous, though large numbers were recorded as passing on migration mainly along the valleys of the Usk and Wye, and also along the coast. In the 1977 *Birds of Gwent* Sand Martins were described as locally common along the Rivers Usk, Wye and Monnow with an estimated 1,500 pairs along the River Usk alone in 1965. Since then the species has declined in numbers. There is however, little difference in distribution between the 1st Gwent Atlas, when birds were recorded in 66 tetrads, and the 2nd Gwent Atlas when birds were found in 70 tetrads. The Rivers Usk and Monnow remain the strongholds in the county.

On the River Usk, Sand Martins are frequent along meandering sections down to Newbridge-on-Usk, wherever there is an extensive area of actively eroding cliff bank that provides nest sites. Colony sizes vary from year-to-year, and they frequently move to nearby banks including those on the opposite side of the river. For example, at Llanwenarth there were 100 holes in a bank on the south side of the Usk in 1975; in 1977 there were 90 in a bank some 200–300 m from the 1975 location, whilst in 1982–84 the colony transferred to the north bank between the two former sites. The largest colonies on the River Usk have been recorded at Llanfoist, between Llanfoist and Llanwenarth, and at Gobion, Clytha and Llanlowell, although the latter site has now been lost through bank protection works. Elsewhere, small colonies also occur on the Afon Llwyd near Ponthir, the River Rhymney at Machen, the Afon Honddu and at Penhow Quarry, where birds nest in quarry spoil. A small colony on the Ebbw at Rogerstone was lost in 2001, mostly due to bank improvements.

On the River Monnow there are scattered and generally small colonies. In 1994, 130 nest holes were recorded at six sites between Altyrynys and Monmouth Cap (personal observation). The most important colony, with 80+ nest holes, was near Llangua church but in 1995 much of the cliff bank was destroyed by the landowner with the consent of the former National River Authority. Small colonies of 12 or more holes occur above and below Kentchurch weir and at a few sites down to Skenfrith. A colony at Tregate Bridge has now gone as has a large colony of up to 100 pairs upstream of Rockfield.

In 2002, some 230 pairs nested along the Monnow. Colonies larger than 20 nest holes were found at only three sites. Smaller numbers occurred near Pandy, downstream of Rockfield and in Monmouth: where birds bred in drainpipes in walls below the old abbatoir and near the road arch at Overmonnow, some of which were lost when the wall was demolished in 2003/04. On the main River Wye small colonies are scattered between Dixton and Bigsweir.

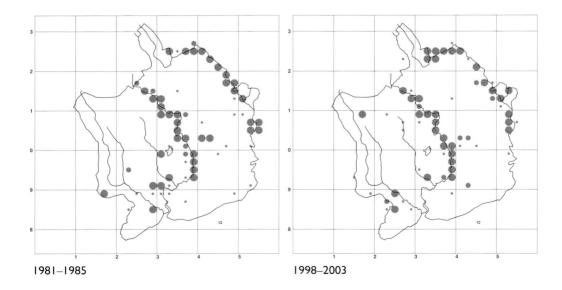

1981–1985

1998–2003

In the 1st Gwent Atlas the total county population on both the Usk and the Wye was estimated to be only 500 pairs. This is probably now an underestimate and the current figure may be closer to 700–800 or higher. One method of estimation suggested a population of 1,200 pairs (Appendix 1).

Sand Martins typically arrive in Gwent in early to mid-March, and the earliest date on record is 1st March 1966. Most leave the county during late summer and early autumn, and latest dates are 1st November 1969 and the exceptionally late date of 4th December 2005.

Many Sand Martins have been ringed at breeding colonies in the county and at colonies and roosts elsewhere. Consequently there have been many recoveries involving birds dispersing from their natal colony in Gwent to breed elsewhere, or of adults changing colonies. For example, a juvenile bird from Tregate Bridge on the River Monnow bred the following year at Sutton Sugwas near Hereford, one originating from Stretton Sugwas later bred near Abergavenny, and an adult from a Gobion colony was controlled three years later breeding at Talybont. Many other Gwent birds have been caught at summer roosts or on migration, including at Llangorse Lake, Chew Valley Lake, and Icklesham in Sussex: 270km away. Others first caught at Icklesham have been controlled on the River Usk at Gobion and Llanwenarth. There have been several recoveries of Gwent Sand Martins in Europe, and one in Africa, or of birds caught in Europe turning up in Gwent. For example, a bird ringed at Loir et Cher in France in July 1989 was found breeding at Abergavenny in July 1991 and a Rockfield bird caught in July 1989 was recovered at Somme in France in September 1990. A Sand Martin ringed at Llanvaches in July 1991 was controlled in Senegal, over 4,000km away, in March 1993.

Sand Martins migrating south through Britain in the late summer and early autumn will stop off to roost in unoccupied nest burrows at colonies. The protection of colonies is therefore important outside the main breeding season. Away from the breeding colonies, late summer and early autumn roosts are recorded at the Uskmouth reedbeds where 200–400 birds are recorded during late evenings most years. Diurnal coastal movements are also noted regularly during this time, especially at Goldcliff.

Gwent Breeding Atlas data and population size

Gwent Atlas	Confirmed tetrads	Probable tetrads	Possible tetrads	Total tetrads	Change in total	Gwent population
1981–1985	38	7	21	66	–	–
1998–2003	35	12	23	70	4%	c.900 pairs

National breeding data and conservation status

Estimated Welsh population	Welsh CBC/BBS trend 1985–2003	UK BBS trend 1994–2004	Welsh & UK conservation status
14,500 pairs	Not available	+84%	Amber-listed

(Barn) **Swallow**
Gwennol

Hirundo rustica

A widely distributed and common summer visitor and passage migrant

The Swallow is probably one of our most familiar summer visitors. In Wales, it is widely distributed, being one of the few species to breed in every 10-km square. The birds have a close association with man and breed wherever suitable farm buildings, sheds, porches and other sites are available. A pair may have up to three broods in a season, with young birds often still being in the nest in September. One very late brood in Gwent fledged from a nest at Chain Bridge on 10th October 1978.

The main influx of this summer visitor is during early April, but since 1976 the earliest records of arrivals in Gwent have ranged from 10th March to 11th April, with 28th March the median first arrival date. The earliest date on record for the county is 9th March, 1968. Large parties are not usually seen until late April or early May, when they can be encountered on the coast and especially at inland reservoirs. For example, 250 were at Llandegfedd Reservoir on 26th April 1968 and 1,000 were there on 5th May 1973; on the coast, approximately

100 birds per hour moved east past Undy on 29th April 1978 and 110 were with martins feeding over the reens at St Brides on 21st April 1985.

The Swallow was described in the 1937 and 1963 *Birds of Monmouthshire* as a summer visitor that was apparently decreasing in numbers but was widely distributed and breeding throughout the county except in the higher valleys amongst the hills. It was thought to be most numerous in the south amongst the farms on the coastal Gwent Levels.

In the 1st Gwent Atlas Swallows occurred in 94% of tetrads and there was *confirmed* breeding in 75%. In the 2nd Gwent Atlas birds were found in slightly more tetrads (98%) with breeding confirmed in 77%, showing that the species is still very widespread. Birds and nests are easily located. The latest estimated Gwent population is 4,300–5,300 pairs. Nationally there has been a small increase in population levels between 1994 and 2004.

Swallows are Amber-listed in both the UK and Wales because of a decline in numbers in many European countries. They depend on a good supply of insects, and intensive farming, with widespread use of pesticides, may have reduced prey availability. Another concern is the loss of nest sites in barns and other farm buildings when these are converted for human dwellings.

From August and September large flocks can be seen gathering on wires and there is a notable build-up of birds on the coast. Some of the larger gatherings recorded include 4,000 on telegraph wires at Goldcliff on 27th August 1968, 2,500 at Llandegfedd Reservoir on 25th August 1970 and 2,000 at Llanvaches on 30th August 1994.

Autumn roosts of Swallows, often mixed with smaller numbers of Sand Martins, have been recorded in late summer at the reedbeds on the Caldicot Level. For example, some 500 birds roosted at Greenmoor Pool in 1989 and, close by at Llanwern, a small roost of c.100–300 birds, has been recorded annually around the steelworks

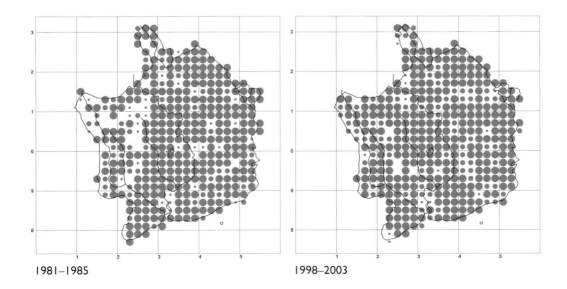

1981–1985

1998–2003

filter beds since 2003. The most significant roost however has been at Uskmouth, where 500 birds were present in September 1988, 1,500–3,000 in early September 1991 and 1,000 in 1997. More recently, the number of birds using the reedbeds at Uskmouth has diminished, which is perhaps surprising given the improvement of the habitat at the site, although c.100–250 are still found most years. Ringing at the Uskmouth roost suggests that it comprises birds that have bred locally and others from further afield. For example, one ringed in August 2002 was found two years later in a barn at St Brides Netherwent, and a juvenile ringed on the nest at Abercraf, Powys, in July 2004 was trapped at the roost in September of the same year.

During the autumn, large passage movements may occur at any time from late August through to early October, but mostly during September. Such movements are very evident at the county's reservoirs and on its southern coastline, where birds are seen predominantly flying east/southeast. Such movements can involve thousands of birds with anything from 200–550 passing during the course of an hour. For example, 235 passed Peterstone in 30 minutes on 24th September 1980 and 550 in an hour there on September 12th 1985. Very heavy passage has also been observed on occasions with 4,000 in an hour passing Black Rock on 17th September 1986, 6,500 per hour at Goldcliff on 24th September 1994, and 15,000 in three hours at West Pill on 24th September 2004. Passage continues into October: for example, 2,000 passed Goldcliff in 2.5 hours on 1st October 2000, 1,200 passed Peterstone on 2nd October 1973, and 1,000+ passed West Pill in one hour on 15th October 1988.

The latest dates that birds have been recorded range from 8th October to 28th November with a median late date of 4th November. A bird seen at the Olway Meadow, Usk on 23rd January 1990 and a freshly dead male found at Abergavenny on 20th January 1993 might have been overwintering birds, but they could possibly have been extremely early migrants.

Ringing of nestlings and of adults at roosts has generated a few recoveries, which give an insight into the migration movements of Gwent birds across the UK during the autumn. A young bird ringed at Fishguard in Pembrokeshire in August 1995 was found dead at Llandegfedd Reservoir a month later. One ringed in the nest in August 1984 at Newchurch West moved to Purbeck in Dorset a month later. Another Swallow, ringed as a nestling at Nantyglo in July 1978, was caught at Southampton two months later, and a Penallt nestling, ringed in June 1978 was caught three months later at Farlington Marshes near Portsmouth. Some have been controlled on migration through southern Europe and Africa, and there are two records of birds being found some 9,500km south in their winter quarters in South Africa having originally been ringed at the Uskmouth reedbed roost on the same evening in August 1997: one of these was found dead after electrical storms on 30th November 1997 at Mt Currie, Kokstad in KwaZulu Natal; and the second bird was trapped at Bloemfontein, Free State, Republic of South Africa on 27th February 1999.

Gwent Breeding Atlas data and population size

Gwent Atlas	Confirmed tetrads	Probable tetrads	Possible tetrads	Total tetrads	Change in total	Gwent population
1981–1985	296	44	30	370	–	–
1998–2003	304	67	13	384	+3.5%	4,300–5,300 pairs

National breeding data and conservation status

Estimated Welsh population	Welsh CBC/BBS trend 1985–2003	UK CBC/BBS trend 1985–2003	Welsh & UK conservation status
80,000 pairs	+41%	+36%	Amber-listed

House Martin
Gwennol y Bondo

Delichon urbicum

A common summer visitor and passage migrant

The House Martin is a common summer visitor that breeds throughout most of Britain wherever there are suitable nest sites, which usually means buildings, but nests can also be found on cliffs in some locations (1988–91 National Atlas). The long-term trend for the species is one of steady decline, leading to its

Amber-listing in the UK, but the BBS trend over the last decade has shown a strong increase (+31% in UK; +43% in Wales).

First arrival dates in Gwent over the last 27 years range from 15th March to 19th April with the median date being 3rd April. However, although there are always a few such early birds, the main arrival does not occur until late April or early May.

The 1963 *Birds of Monmouthshire* describes the House Martin as a well distributed species, but less common on the coastal levels than elsewhere in the county. In the 1st Gwent Atlas they were located in 86% of tetrads in the county, with *confirmed* breeding in 71%. There were notable gaps only in the western valleys and on the high moorland of the north-west. In the 2nd Gwent Atlas they were located in slightly more tetrads, 89%, and with *confirmed* breeding in almost 72%. Tetrads where the species was absent were scattered throughout the county but again with a concentration of empty tetrads in the western valleys, particularly in 10-km square SO29.

The county population is currently estimated at 3,600–4,700 pairs. In the period between the two Gwent Atlases, the UK and Wales population trends have been positive, which is consistent with the increase in distribution found in the county.

Often House Martins nest in small colonies of two or more pairs on houses, but there may be much larger concentrations of pairs at favoured sites. Good nesting locations over the last three decades have included Skenfrith Mill where a maximum of 58 nests, 34 of them occupied, were once noted; Tredegar House (31 nests), Monmouth School (40), Mamhilad Park factory (41), Goytre House (up to 56) and a house at Raglan (60). St Lawrence Hospital in Chepstow held a record 120 nests at one time but the site has now been demolished. Numbers fluctuate from year to year. For example the large count at Skenfrith Mill was in 1986, but in 2001 only 12 nests were seen there. Two or three broods may be reared, with the last young still in the nest in late September.

Flocks after the breeding season may be of 300 to 400 birds. Passage has been noted along the coast: such as 250 flying south-west from St Brides in two hours on 16th September 2001, and 700 south-east from Goldcliff on 1st October. There was an exceptional movement east from Black Rock of 14,000 birds per hour over three hours on 22nd September 1986. Last dates of the year vary from 4th October to 15th December with a median date of 26th October. There are only two records for late November: on the 17th and 30th, and two for December: one in Monmouth on the 16th in 1980 and one in Whitebrook on the 15th in 1979.

There are only three ringing records relevant to Gwent, all of which are consistent with movement through, or from, the county to the south coast of England, prior to the trans-Saharan journey undertaken by this species. A young bird ringed near Chepstow in July 1987 was recovered on the Dorset coast about eight weeks later; one ringed on the Sussex coast in mid-October 1988, was recovered in Usk in June of the following year and one ringed at Portland Bill, Dorset, in October 1986 was recovered in Cwmbran in August 1989.

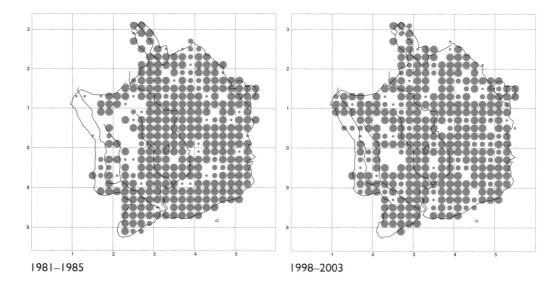

1981–1985   1998–2003

Gwent Breeding Atlas data and population size

Gwent Atlas	Confirmed tetrads	Probable tetrads	Possible tetrads	Total tetrads	Change in total	Gwent population
1981–1985	282	27	30	339	–	–
1998–2003	283	50	19	352	+3%	3,600–4,700 pairs

National breeding data and conservation status

Estimated Welsh population	Welsh BBS trend 1994–2004	UK CBC/BBS trend 1985–2003	Welsh & (UK) conservation status
76,000 pairs	+43%	+25%	Green (Amber)-listed

Richard's Pipit
Corhedydd Richard
Anthus richardi

A very rare vagrant

There are three records of this large pipit from Siberia. All involved single birds and were from Peterstone on 26th September 1951, Sluice Farm on 26th September 1977 and Newport Wetlands Reserve on 6th November 2004.

Tawny Pipit
Corhedydd Melyn
Anthus campestris

A very rare visitor

The Tawny Pipit is a widespread breeder on the European mainland and is a rare but regular passage migrant to the UK. There are two Gwent records, both of single birds: on the foreshore at Chepstow Wharf on 27th April 1989 and at Llandegfedd Reservoir on 6th October 1991.

Tree Pipit
Corhedydd y Coed
Anthus trivialis

A fairly common passage migrant and summer visitor

The Tree Pipit is a summer visitor to Britain and is widely distributed in the country apart from central and eastern England. It may occupy a wide variety of fairly open habitats so long as they contain tall song-posts, which can include man-made structures such as telegraph poles and pylons, as well as, more typically, trees and shrubs.

The 1937 and 1963 *Birds of Monmouthshire* described the species as fairly numerous and generally distributed, and occurring up to the tree limit in the hills, though scarce in the coastal districts.

In the 1st Gwent Atlas Tree Pipits occurred in 41% of tetrads, and with *probable* or *confirmed* breeding in 77% of these. Strongholds were in Wentwood, the woodlands on the Trellech plateau, Ebbw Forest and Carno Forest, as well as hill slopes in the western valleys and on the

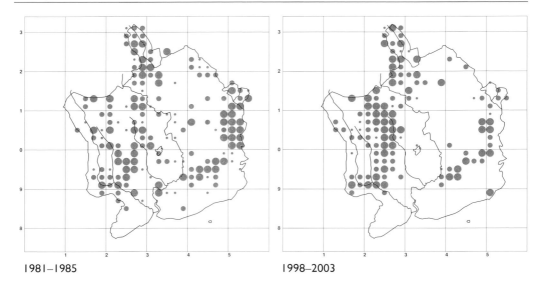

1981–1985   1998–2003

Blorenge and Black Mountains. In the 2nd Gwent Atlas fewer tetrads (31%) were occupied, but among these the proportion with *probable* or *confirmed* breeding had risen to 87%. The reduction in occupied tetrads between the two atlases suggests that there had been a decline over the intervening period. This is particularly evident in the east of the county where in Wentwood and the Wye Valley areas there were 23 tetrads with *confirmed* breeding records in the 1st Atlas but only ten in the 2nd Atlas. However, in the north and west of the county there had been some increase in distribution between the two atlases.

Habitats in Gwent typically used for breeding are clear-fell areas, or young restocks in conifer forests where there are some remaining scattered trees or clumps of trees as song-posts. Tree Pipits also favour bracken-covered grassy hillsides in the north and west of the county, especially where there are scattered hawthorns or other bushes or trees. New set-aside farmland and newly planted shelter belts between fields may also be used.

The BBS and atlas-based methods give county population estimates of 1,300 and 1,900 pairs but both figures are derived from small numbers of sample sites that may not be adequately representative. The lower end of the range is suggested as the more likely. The 1st Gwent Atlas suggested a population of about 1,500 pairs for the 1981–85 period.

The decrease in distribution in Gwent reflects the national situation. There has been a very marked long-term decline in the UK since 1970 (Eaton *et al.*, 2003), which has been very steep since 1985, the last recording year for the 1st Gwent Atlas, but has since levelled out. In the period between the Gwent Atlases, the UK index declined by 71%, and in Wales the 1994–2003 BBS index shows a decline of 45%.

The main arrival of Tree Pipits in the county is in mid-April but the earliest arrivals are in the first week of April with 2nd or 3rd April being typical dates, and 25th March 1989 the earliest on record. The main autumn passage is in August though late birds are recorded up to the first week of October.

After breeding, they soon leave the country, passing along the coast in small flocks from early August until mid-September. For example, at Uskmouth in 1998, passage was noted from 7th–29th August with a maximum of 20 or more birds on 27th. Other recent peak counts at Uskmouth, all during 21st –26th August have been 20 in 2001, 12 in 2003 and 15+ in 2004.

Gwent Breeding Atlas data and population size

Gwent Atlas	Confirmed tetrads	Probable tetrads	Possible tetrads	Total tetrads	Change in total	Gwent population
1981–1985	59	67	37	163	–	–
1998–2003	49	49	16	124	−9.5%	1,300–1,900 pairs

National breeding data and conservation status

Estimated Welsh population	Welsh BBS trend 1994–2003	UK CBC/BBS trend 1985–2003	Welsh & UK conservation status
14,500 pairs	−45%*	−71%	Amber-listed

*From *The State of Birds in Wales 2003*.

Meadow Pipit
Corhedydd y Waun

Anthus pratensis

A common resident/summer visitor in open hill country; also a common passage migrant

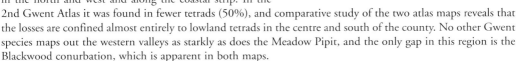

The Meadow Pipit is a widespread breeding species in the UK, occupying a variety of open habitats, but is most numerous in the uplands of Wales, Scotland and northern England. Passage birds and winter visitors occur widely in the lowlands and on coasts.

In Gwent it is common in the breeding season on the hills of the north and west, and breeds too along the sea wall on the Levels and occasionally elsewhere, as on Gray Hill near Wentwood. It is a noticeable passage migrant and substantial numbers occur during the winter months. In the 1st Gwent Atlas the Meadow Pipit occurred in some 57% of all tetrads, but with a marked concentration in the north and west and along the coastal strip. In the 2nd Gwent Atlas it was found in fewer tetrads (50%), and comparative study of the two atlas maps reveals that the losses are confined almost entirely to lowland tetrads in the centre and south of the county. No other Gwent species maps out the western valleys as starkly as does the Meadow Pipit, and the only gap in this region is the Blackwood conurbation, which is apparent in both maps.

It is a difficult species to census so an accurate estimate of the county population is not easily achieved. In the 1st Gwent Atlas, a population of 4,000 pairs was estimated, based on CBC data. In the 2nd Gwent Atlas the BBS and atlas-based methods give a much higher figure of 15,000–19,000 (Appendix 1). This corresponds to a mean of 80–100 pairs per occupied tetrad, which is well within the range of densities that can be expected in suitable habitat (1968–72 National Atlas). The plausibility of this estimate is also supported by the finding of about 25 pairs on a BBS 1-km square on the Blorenge (Andrew Baker, pers. comm.), which equates to 100 pairs per tetrad.

In the autumn, birds move down from the hills. Many are presumed to winter locally and can be found throughout the period, in flocks of usually fewer than 100 birds, in lowland areas of the county. In hard weather when snow covers the ground or when the ground is frozen, winter flocks may move to sewage works or farmyards where there is a supply of available invertebrates at the filter beds or dung-heaps respectively.

Some of our breeding birds cross the English Channel and migrate down the west coast of France to wintering grounds around the Mediterranean basin. In addition, many from more northern latitudes pass through Britain *en route* to the Mediterranean, with those from southern Greenland and Iceland probably passing down the west coast, and Scandinavian birds down the east coast (*Migration Atlas*).

Meadow Pipits are primarily daytime migrants, and their passage is very obvious on the Gwent coast during September and October, when large numbers can be seen moving in a southerly or south-westerly (occasionally easterly) direction in the hours after dawn. Numbers of birds passing are commonly a few hundred per hour, but can be over 2,000 per hour. Examples of larger recorded movements are: 1,000 west in two hours on 25th September 1978; 2,500 west in 2.5 hours on 25th September 1981; 3,500 south-west in 1.5 hours on

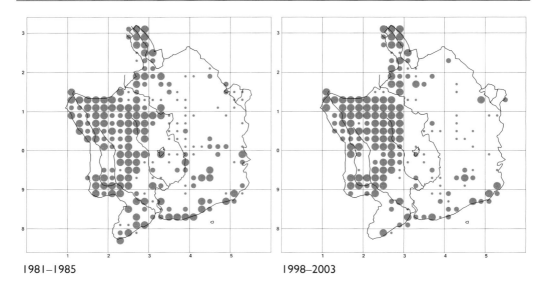

1981–1985   1998–2003

5th October 1985 and 2,000 west in three hours on 25th September 1987. Since the early 1990s, visible passage has continued to be reported annually, but there have been very few systematic counts so, whether the scale of these movements remains the same as in earlier years is unknown.

During the autumn passage months, large flocks are also seen feeding on the coast and elsewhere in the county. Examples of the larger flocks are: 100 at Llandegfedd Reservoir in September 1975, 200 at Raglan on 10th October 1981, 750 at Collister Pill on 26th September 1983, 300 at St Brides on 3rd October 1993, 200 at Garnlydan Reservoir on 21st September 1998 and 190 at Llanwenarth on 7th October 2001. Since the mid-1990s, sizes of the largest reported flocks have generally been smaller than in previous years.

Return passage in spring is less noticeable, with much smaller flocks and less visible passage. Notable movements include: 100 flying north at Peterstone 20th March 1979 and a similar record one day in March 1983; and 300 over Abergavenny on 17th March 2001. Notable flocks include: up to 100 at Nash on 11th April 1977, 185 at Llangybi on 8th April 1986 and 160 at Llanvihangel Gobion on 11th April 1986.

There is only one significant ringing recovery relevant to Gwent, which involves a bird ringed as a nestling and recovered locally during the following winter.

Gwent Breeding Atlas data and population size

Gwent Atlas	Confirmed tetrads	Probable tetrads	Possible tetrads	Total tetrads	Change in total	Gwent population
1981–1985	101	64	58	223	–	–
1998–2003	89	52	44	185	−7%	15,000–19,000 pairs

National breeding data and conservation status

Estimated Welsh population	Welsh CBC/BBS trend 1985–2003	UK CBC/BBS trend 1985–2003	Welsh & UK conservation status
200,000 pairs	+228%	+4%	Green-listed

Rock Pipit
Corhedydd y Graig

Anthus petrosus

An uncommon autumn/winter visitor; also a rare resident

The Rock Pipit is found predominantly within sight of the sea. It is widespread as a breeding bird around the coasts of Britain and Ireland and a notable winter visitor. It is larger and darker than the other pipits with greyish, not white, outer tail feathers. It breeds on rocky coasts but in winter it is also found feeding along the tideline.

In Gwent it is mostly recorded along the coastline from Chepstow in the east to Rumney Great Wharf in the west. This is particularly so during late September to the end of March. Usually small numbers, from 1–6 birds, are noted each year. However, larger groups have been recorded, especially at Peterstone saltmarsh where there were 48 during the winter of 1980/81, 20 in March 1984 and 25 in December 1984. Elsewhere, there were 20 at Mathern in December 1990, 20+ at Sluice Farm in October 1992 and, c.20 at Black Rock in November 1993. Inland records are rare and include single birds at Gobion in October 1985, November 1990 and 1995; Ynysyfro Reservoir in March 1987 and Llandegfedd Reservoir in November 1995.

Suitable breeding habitat is found at just a few locations in the county. The 1937 *Birds of Monmouthshire* described the Rock Pipit as possibly a scarce resident breeding species at one time, but despite having searched at the only possible nesting sites in the county they were unable to find it. This did not however take account of Denny Island and by the time of the 1963 *Birds of Monmouthshire* the species was described as breeding regularly there. However, only two records were used to qualify this statement, with birds being present on the island in June 1951 and then seen feeding young there in May 1961. There was then an absence of breeding records in the county until 1969, when breeding was confirmed at both Peterstone Pill and Denny Island, and it was subsequently suspected at Goldcliff in 1974 (1977 *Birds of Gwent*).

No evidence of breeding was found during survey work for the 1st Gwent Atlas (1980–81) and this remained the case until 1992 when birds were present at Goldcliff in July, whilst in the following year two birds were recorded at Denny Island on 17th August. Breeding was probable at Goldcliff during 1995–1997. During the 2nd Gwent Atlas, breeding was *confirmed* at Goldcliff in 1998 and *possible* there in 1999 and 2000. A single bird was noted in early July at Porton in 1998, possibly suggesting breeding, while at Denny Island, breeding was *confirmed* in 2002. Breeding has since occurred annually at Denny Island during 2003–06: four nestlings were ringed there in 2004 and two pairs were thought to be breeding in 2006.

The Rock Pipit has a Green-listed conservation status in Wales and the UK, and its population in Wales has been estimated at 3,300 pairs (2002 *Birds in Wales*).

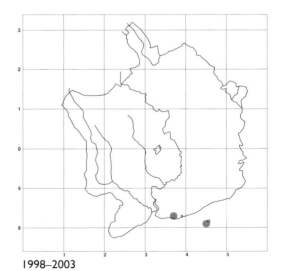

1998–2003

Gwent Breeding Atlas data and population size

Gwent Atlas	Confirmed tetrads	Probable tetrads	Possible tetrads	Total tetrads	Change in total	Gwent population
1981–1985	0	0	0	0	–	–
1998–2003	2	0	1	3	–	2–3 pairs

Rock Pipit   *Anthus petrosus littoralis*

The Scandinavian race of the Rock Pipit *A. p. littoralis* occurs commonly as a winter visitor and passage migrant in Britain, particularly on the east and south-east coasts (*Migration Atlas*). Birds showing characteristics of this race were seen at Sluice Farm on 1st March 1991, while 'some' of the Scandinavian race were there on 29th October 1992, and six 'probably all *A. p. littoralis*' on 22nd March 2003. Elsewhere, two were seen at Goldcliff on 22nd April 2002.

Water Pipit   *Anthus spinoletta*
Corhedydd y Dŵr

An uncommon winter visitor and passage migrant

The Water Pipit breeds in montane habitats of continental Europe and is an uncommon winter visitor and passage migrant to Britain, most numerous in the south.

The first fully documented Gwent record for this species, which at the time was still classified as a subspecies of Rock Pipit, was of a single bird in the grounds of the Abergavenny sewage works during 1st November 1967–29th February 1968, with a second bird seen there briefly on 27th November. Wintering birds were then noted annually at the site until 1972, with maxima of nine on 26th November 1969 and five on 20th November 1971. The only other record during this period was at Llandegfedd Reservoir, where a single bird was seen on 8th November 1969.

A further bird occurred at Llandegfedd Reservoir on 20th January 1974 and two at Abergavenny Castle Meadows on 25th April 1974. The first record on the coast was at St Brides on 24th April 1976 followed by two at Peterstone on 6th November 1977. A single bird was present at Sluice Farm during 9th–11th December 1977 and records have since occurred there in every year up to the present time, with occasionally as many as 12 being noted. Exceptionally, a flock of up to 25 was present during January–April 2005.

Birds may be present at Sluice Farm throughout the period October–April, by the end of which some individuals have often acquired their distinctive breeding plumage. Numbers often increase in late March to early April, indicating the arrival of passage migrants. An exceptionally late individual was noted in the Gout at Peterstone on 16th May 1980.

Records from elsewhere in the county have been mostly from the River Usk at Llanfihangel Gobion, where birds have been noted intermittently since 1990. Otherwise up to two were seen at Ynysyfro Reservoir during the 1978/79 winter and other sites where it has been recorded comprise (numbers of records in brackets): Uskmouth (3), Nash Pools (1), St Brides (1), Collister Pill (1) and the River Usk at Abergavenny Castle Meadows (2).

Yellow Wagtail   *Motacilla flava flavissima*
Siglen Felen

An uncommon summer visitor and passage migrant

The brilliant yellow plumage of a male Yellow Wagtail, freshly arrived from winter quarters in Africa, is a stunning sight but one that has become much less common over the past three decades. Widespread decline has put Gwent on the extreme western edge of the Yellow Wagtail's range, and the county population is now very small. By contrast, some forty years ago, the 1963 *Birds of Monmouthshire* described it as a not uncommon visitor that was most numerous on the coastal flats and river valleys, while the 1977 *Birds of Gwent* indicated that there had been little change from that position.

Yellow Wagtails arrive rather late in the spring, with the first birds usually seen around the first week of April and the main influx in the last two weeks of the month. Key areas for breeding birds have always been the low-lying fields on the Gwent Levels and floodplains along the Rivers Usk, Monnow and Trothy, as well as cereal and other crops on higher ground. They breed in loose and localised colonies, which may be present one year

but absent the next. During the 1970s about five pairs were reported each year, though in 1974 there were 11 breeding records, including five pairs at Llandegfedd Reservoir. However, these records would have represented only a fraction of the true breeding strength.

A population decline began around the late 1970s to early 1980s, and this resulted in a range contraction that affected Wales and southern and north-western England (1988–91 National Atlas). A long-term decline in the UK of 66% during 1978–2003 is indicated by the CBC/BBS index, and a short-term BBS index of –27% for 1994–2004 shows that the decline continues. The species has been placed on the Amber List of conservation concern and is a candidate for moving to the Red List.

The 1st Gwent Atlas was carried out in the early years of the national decline and the species was reported in 29% of tetrads, with *confirmed* breeding in 12%, mostly on flood meadows, pastures and some arable land. An RSPB survey conducted in this period (1984) detected 15 pairs on the Gwent Levels.

In the 2nd Gwent Atlas it was recorded in only 15% of tetrads, with *confirmed* breeding in just 4%. This indicates a substantial decline between the two atlases. The main strongholds in the period of the 2nd Gwent Atlas were in the Usk Valley, the Raglan/Dingestow/Hendre/Monmouth area and the extreme south-west part of the county in the Peterstone area.

Gwent Bird Reports record that in the 16 years from 1986 to 2001, there were breeding records in all but four years. Records ranged from two in one year, 7–10 in eight of the years and 13–15 in three years. The highest number of breeding records was reported in 2000. Habitats where birds were recorded were flood meadows, grassland on a disused golf course at Peterstone and arable fields. It seems that there has been a shift away from flood pastures to arable crops.

In the Usk Valley the favoured areas are Llanbadoc/Llanlowell/Llangybi, from Llanvihangel Gobion to The Bryn, and near Llanwenarth. In 1991 ten pairs were noted in just 2km at Llanvihangel Gobion. The Olway meadows near Gwernesney also formerly held small numbers. In 2002 only two pairs were found within the main Monnow Valley: one near Llancillo Monnow and the other in cereal and rape fields at Osbaston (Tyler, 2002). Three pairs were also found near Monmouth in an arable field at the end of Scud Brook, a tributary of the Monnow. Other records from between Raglan and Monmouth and near Trellech Grange were from a range of fields containing crops ranging from cereals, potatoes, onions and peas to turnips, strawberries and set-aside.

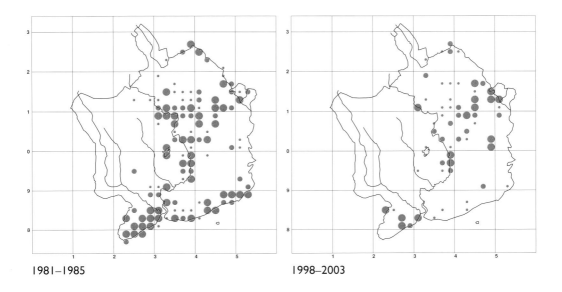

1981–1985   1998–2003

A county population of fewer than 200 pairs was estimated in the 1st Gwent Atlas, although it was subsequently believed that the total was no more than 100 pairs (S. J. Tyler, pers. comm.) The population during the 2nd Gwent Atlas based on extrapolation from sample tetrads, is estimated to be 37–75 pairs.

Passage birds occur in spring and autumn on the coast and also at suitable inland locations, such as damp river pastures and at reservoirs. The 1937 *Birds of Monmouthshire* referred to migratory flocks being seen along the coast at the end of April and beginning of May and again at the end of August up to the third week of September. Numbers these days are generally small in spring, and concentrations such as 14 at Llanvihangel Gobion on 25th April 1979 and 59 at Peterstone on 26th April 1982 are unusual. Much larger numbers occur in autumn, and during the 1970s and 1980s large roosts of passage birds occurred annually in the *Spartina* beds on the shore at Peterstone. These roosts commonly comprised around 75–150 birds in the last week of August and the largest count was c.250 at Sluice Farm on 23rd August 1990. Large numbers also occurred, though less regularly, at inland locations, examples being c.100 at Llandegfedd Reservoir on 25th August in both 1984 and 1989, 75 at Ynysyfro Reservoir in early September 1987 and up to 41 at Llangybi during mid-September 1985. In late August 1989, flocks at Llandegfedd Reservoir, Peterstone and Undy totalled 410 birds and, with moderate numbers reported at several other locations, the total present in the county then must have been well above 500. Also during the above period there were many records of visible passage at Peterstone, usually in a south-west direction in the 3–4 hours after dawn. A total of 962 birds was counted over 41 dawn watches in 1981 and 906 from 11 watches in 1989.

Since 1990, passage numbers have been much smaller and, apart from 150 at Peterstone in 1995, the largest annually reported flocks have been in the range 12–93. There have been no significant records of visible movements in recent years but this may to some extent reflect a paucity of observations. The last date is usually in late September but there have been a few early October records, the latest on 6th October.

Gwent Breeding Atlas data and population size

Gwent Atlas	Confirmed tetrads	Probable tetrads	Possible tetrads	Total tetrads	Change in total	Gwent population
1981–1985	49	30	34	113	–	–
1998–2003	16	17	27	60	−47%	37–75 pairs

National breeding data and conservation status

Estimated Welsh population	Welsh trend	UK CBC/BBS trend 1985–2003	Welsh & UK conservation status
c.100 pairs	Not available	−50%	Amber-listed

Blue-headed Wagtail   *Motacilla flava flava*

A scarce passage migrant

This continental subspecies is regularly recorded in Wales and occasional pairs breed (1994 *Birds in Wales*). There have been one or two records in Gwent in most years, the majority being in April or May, though with two June records, 1 July record and two September records. Birds are most often seen on the coast in the Peterstone or St Brides area, although there are two records from Llandegfedd Reservoir, one from the River Monnow and three from the River Usk. More recently records came in April 2000 from the Newport Wetlands Reserve. Birds are usually seen singly, and are mainly males, but females are hard to separate rom those of *flavissima*. In June 1978 a male *flava* was seen with a female *flavissima* at Peterstone and a pair of indeterminate race was then seen in July that year at Peterstone.

Grey-headed Wagtail   *Motacilla flava thunbergi*

A very rare migrant

There have been two accepted records, both in May: one at Goldcliff on 26th May 1994 and another at the Golf Course pools at Peterstone on 30th May 1996.

Grey Wagtail
Siglen Lwyd

Motacilla cinerea

A fairly common resident on fast-flowing streams and rivers throughout the county; also a passage migrant

The Grey Wagtail is widely distributed in Wales, and also in the rest of mainland Britain apart from the lowlands of central and eastern England (1988–91 National Atlas).

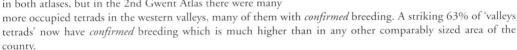

In the 1st Gwent Atlas Grey Wagtails were found in 55% of all tetrads with breeding *confirmed* in 27%. In the 2nd Gwent Atlas there were many more occupied tetrads (66%) and more with *confirmed* breeding records (38%), strongly suggesting an increase in population. The northern rivers in the Black Mountains and tributaries of the Usk and lower Wye were obvious strongholds in both atlases, but in the 2nd Gwent Atlas there were many more occupied tetrads in the western valleys, many of them with *confirmed* breeding. A striking 63% of 'valleys tetrads' now have *confirmed* breeding which is much higher than in any other comparably sized area of the county.

The Grey Wagtails of Gwent have been the subjects of several studies on the river catchments of the central, eastern and northern parts of the county. They have been found to be widespread and common throughout the Usk catchment, occurring from headwater streams to tidal sections, and on both minor and more major tributaries down to Newport. Up to 20 pairs have bred on the Afon Llwyd. A pair in 1994 and 1995 bred near the Usk estuary on buildings at Uskmouth Power Station. On wider, lower sections of the main River Usk, pairs are more widely dispersed, and then often associated with tributary confluences or bridges. In the Wye catchment they breed on all the tributaries, from the River Monnow to tiny wooded streams such as the Angidy Brook and White Brook. These are excellent streams for Grey Wagtails with seven or eight pairs regularly breeding on a 4km stretch of the Angidy down to the tidal reaches at Tintern, and eight or nine pairs on the White Brook. There are 24–30 pairs on the Monnow, six or seven pairs on the Olchon Brook (mostly in Herefordshire) and over 16 pairs on the Afon Honddu. At least three pairs bred on the Afon Trothy in 2002, and at least four pairs on the Mally Brook. On the main Wye, pairs breed at a range of sites especially where small side streams enter

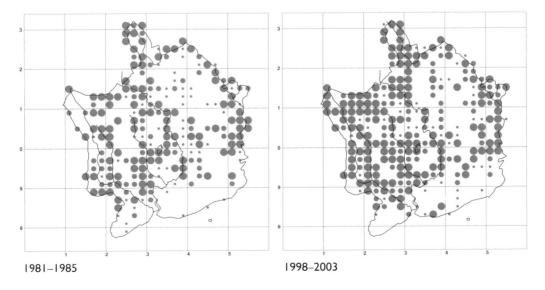

1981–1985

1998–2003

the main river, on riverside cliffs or in walls or associated with bridges. Some pairs nest in or on buildings at some distance from any stream or river, but often where there are nearby pools.

Tyler (2004) showed that there had been no decline in the population since the 1980s on lower Wye tributaries. A series of mild winters has enabled high survival of adults and first-year birds. The species is, moreover, little affected by pollution and as an opportunist feeder it can survive high water levels. On wooded tributaries, pairs commonly occur at 400–500m intervals, and on certain particularly good sections, territories may be as short as 200–300m.

It was suggested in the 1st Gwent Atlas that each occupied tetrad in the county might hold four pairs. Stott *et al.* (2004), however, suggest a density of four birds/km^2 (i.e. 16 birds or eight pairs per tetrad) in Cumbria, with one bird/km^2 on slower flowing rivers (i.e. four per tetrad). On this basis the current population in Gwent could be as high as 1,000 pairs. The estimate from BBS was, however, only 290 pairs, whilst the estimate from sample tetrads was 430–610 pairs. The upper end of the latter figure is the most likely. Although the Grey Wagtail was placed in the UK Amber List because of a long-term decline in the UK, populations have increased nationally in the last decade and the WBS trend for the period between the two Gwent Atlases is +44%. The Grey Wagtail is Green-listed in Wales.

Grey Wagtails are present throughout the year but some birds migrate south or south-west in the autumn. Many remain in southern or south-west England for the winter. From July to September small numbers can be observed moving along the Gwent coast. Counts have included 45 per hour at Black Rock for three hours on 17th September 1986, 20 per hour flying west at Collister Pill on 29th August 1988, and 154 east and 121 west on 19th August and 21st September 1989 at Peterstone. Some British birds reach France; others from Scotland and northern England may move south to overwinter in Gwent, and elsewhere in the south and west (Tyler, 1979). Our wintering populations also include some continental birds. For example, a Grey Wagtail ringed at Jylland in Denmark in August 1975 was found at Ponthir in Gwent in February 1977.

Most dispersive movements between natal and breeding sites are quite short. For example, a Llanthony breeding bird originated from a site near Builth Wells, 30km away, two years previously and one from Llanbedr moved to The Bryn near Abergavenny, 16km away. Another originating from a nest at Skenfrith was caught the following year as a breeding male at Llanbedr, 22km to the west, whilst a bird reared in 1992 at Brymnmawr was caught seven years later as a breeding male at Grwyne Fawr Reservoir 17km to the NNE. This was a very long-lived bird as most Grey Wagtails survive only one or two years.

In the winter some of our local breeding birds from upland areas move down onto low-lying and coastal areas such as the Gwent Levels, where other migrants may join them. Then they forage, often away from streams and rivers, wherever insects and other small invertebrates are numerous, for example at slurry pits and manure heaps at farms, and at sewage works as well as at garden pools. Unlike Pied Wagtails they do not gather in large winter roosts, and six or seven birds together is the maximum likely to be seen. On passage, however, roosts may be larger than this.

Gwent Breeding Atlas data and population size

Gwent Atlas	Confirmed tetrads	Probable tetrads	Possible tetrads	Total tetrads	Change in total	Gwent population
1981–1985	108	55	55	218	–	–
1998–2003	151	63	46	260	+11%	430–610 pairs

National breeding data and conservation status

Estimated Welsh population	Welsh WBS* trend	UK WBS* trend 1985–2004	Welsh & (UK) conservation status
6,000 pairs	Not available	+44%	Green (Amber)-listed

*WBS = Waterways Bird Survey

Pied Wagtail
Siglen Fraith

Motacilla alba yarrellii

A common resident, partial migrant, winter visitor and passage migrant

Pied Wagtails are very widely distributed in Britain, occurring by rivers and lakes, but also in towns and villages, at farms and in gardens. They favour feeding by water, on areas of short grass, or around manure and silage heaps. Because they are so widespread and conspicuous, finding birds and proving breeding is relatively easy. Adults are often seen carrying food or feeding recently fledged juveniles.

In the 1st Gwent Atlas Pied Wagtails were found in 90% of tetrads, with *confirmed* or *probable* breeding in 74%, but were rather scarce on the levels and hills in the west. In the 2nd Gwent Atlas they were again very widespread, being present in 94% of tetrads, with *confirmed* or *probable* breeding in 88%. In both atlases, tetrads where they were absent were scattered throughout the county rather than showing any particular pattern.

The increase in tetrads with *confirmed* or *probable* breeding is indicative of an increased population, and this would be consistent with the strongly positive UK and Welsh trends between the two Gwent Atlases. The current estimate for the county population, based on BBS analysis, is 2,200–2,600 pairs, which shows a small increase on the total of 2,100 pairs suggested in the 1st Gwent Atlas for the period 1981–85, but the very different methods used necessitates caution when making comparisons.

Post-breeding, Pied Wagtails congregate in flocks, perhaps joined by birds from further north. Although usually 100–200 strong, some of these post-breeding flocks can number up to 500 birds or more. Such large flocks were noted at Pencoed in October 1996, at Newhouse Industrial Estate at Chepstow in August 1999, and in a field at Llanwenarth in September 2001. Many birds are found in Gwent during the winter, feeding singly or in flocks of up to 200 birds throughout the county. Flocks usually occur on fields or other open spaces, such as the cricket ground at Abergavenny in December 1997. They occur frequently at sewage works, and at Monmouth sewage works small numbers occur in most winters on the clinker beds, with numbers building up to a peak in December or January. In cold weather numbers are higher with a maximum of 120 recorded on 1 January 1979, during a severe winter.

Pied Wagtails roost communally from the late summer through to the spring. Prior to entering the roost, there may be large pre-roost evening gatherings of wagtails, as have been observed at Magor Services off the M4 and at Raglan Services on the A40. Roosts may be occupied for several years and then suddenly abandoned. A regular large winter roost at Neville Hall Hospital, Abergavenny was first noted in 1974, and was still in use ten years later, with peak numbers of up to 500 in December and January. Woodstock Pond, which was in use mainly during the autumn in the late 1970s and early 1980s, held over 200 birds. Other roosts of up to 400 or 500 birds have been noted in buildings, trees or shrubs such as at Llanfoist, Llandegfedd Reservoir,

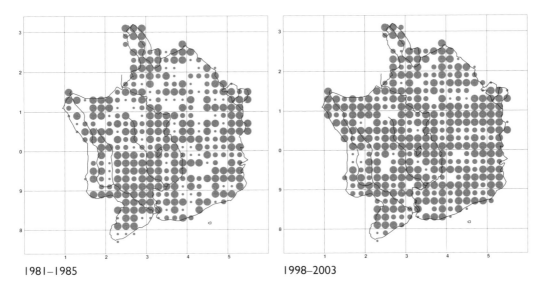

1981–1985

1998–2003

Newhouse, Safeways' supermarket at Abergavenny, Cwmbran town centre, Sainsbury's supermarket in Newport, Monmouth town centre and Usk.

From mid August to October, migrating Pied Wagtails show a steady passage on the coast, with birds generally flying south-east and south-west. Observers at Black Rock, Peterstone, St Brides, West Pill and Goldcliff have frequently recorded up to 40 per hour passing along the coast. Occasionally even more are noted, as at Goldcliff on 15th October 1988 when 90 flew south-east in 90 minutes, or on 6 October 1994 when 100 flew west in 75 minutes. Dawn watches in 1981 from 11th August to 30th September showed from 20–39 birds per hour flying west with maximum numbers passing in late September.

Despite their abundance, rather few Pied Wagtails are ringed each year and the number of recoveries is low. One ringed as a nestling at Long Hope in Gloucestershire was found in Gwent at Wernrheolydd, 30km away, in November of the same year. Two juveniles from Gwent were recovered in Dorset and Hampshire, respectively, the following winter, and a juvenile ringed in the county in July 1983 was caught again at Orense, in Spain, in early December 1984, 1,109km south-south-west. These records are consistent with fact that some British Pied Wagtails move south for the winter, reaching as far as the Iberian peninsula.

Gwent Breeding Atlas data and population size

Gwent Atlas	Confirmed tetrads	Probable tetrads	Possible tetrads	Total tetrads	Change in total	Gwent population
1981–1985	212	79	64	355	–	–
1998–2003	251	96	23	370	+4%	2,200–2,600 pairs

National breeding data and conservation status

Estimated Welsh population	Welsh CBC/BBS trend 1985–2003	UK CBC/BBS trend 1985–2003	Welsh & UK conservation status
30,600 pairs	+222%	+38%	Green-listed

White Wagtail   *Motacilla alba alba*

The nominate (continental) race, the White Wagtail, is a passage migrant in Gwent that has been recorded every year since 1975, with the exception of 1988. It occurs particularly on spring passage from mid-March to mid-May but also on autumn passage. Of 197 records involving many hundreds of birds up to 2002, almost 85% were of spring birds, the rest being seen in late August, September or early October. However, as they are not so easily identified in autumn, many may be overlooked at that time of year. Most records are of single birds or small numbers but larger flocks are recorded, such as 40 at Abergavenny sewage works in September 1970, 25 at Llandegfedd Reservoir in September 1971 and 27 on the Wentlooge Level on 16th April 1985. The most regularly recorded localities are Peterstone, Sluice Farm and Llandegfedd Reservoir, but White Wagtails are also recorded at other coastal locations and at many other inland sites, including Monmouth sewage works, and the River Usk at Llangybi, Llanwenarth, Llanllowell, Gobion and The Bryn.

(Bohemian) Waxwing   *Bombycilla garrulus*
Cynffon Sidan

A rare winter visitor, chiefly in years of large irruptions

The Waxwing breeds in the boreal forests of Fennoscandia and northern Russia. Although it regularly moves south and west into into eastern and central Europe for the winter, very few reach Britain. However, in years of population peaks or poor berry crops, it irrupts spectacularly into western Europe far beyond its usual wintering range, and may invade Britain in substantial numbers. Arrival dates during such irruptions are very variable and can range from early autumn to late winter. Most of the birds reaching Britain remain in the eastern parts of the country, so numbers reaching Gwent are usually very small.

The 1963 *Birds of Monmouthshire* listed only two records prior to 1965, of a single bird shot at Magor in January 1914 and six at Risca during 12th–28th February 1947, the latter record coinciding with the large invasion of winter 1946/47. There were no further Gwent records until the big invasion of 1965/66 when around 115 birds were recorded in the county: these were generally in small flocks of fewer than ten, although two groups of up to 20 birds were seen in Cwmbran in December, 19 in Newport during 24th January–21st February, and 15 in Beechwood Park, Newport, on 8th January.

Following winter 1965/66, records occurred in every winter to 1973/74. In 1967/68, another invasion year, over 40 individuals were recorded, including a flock of 20 at Treworgan Common in December. In 1969/70 a flock of 20 was recorded near Ysgyryd Fawr in November, and a 'small party' at Caldicot in December, while in 1970/71 a total of about 30 was recorded.

There were no further records until ten birds occurred at Mamhilad on the unusually early date of 13th October 1976, and then a further long gap to 1986/87 when two birds were seen in Newport during January/February. Subsequently there have been records in just seven winters, of which the first six of these are as follows (number of records/total birds in brackets): 1988/89 (2/12); 1990/91 (1/2); 1995/96 (3/6); 1996/97 (1;3); 2000/01 (1/4); and 2003/04 (1/1).

The winter of 2004/05 produced a spectacular widespread invasion of Britain, and many more Waxwings were recorded in Gwent than ever before. Records began in late December with eight birds at Wyesham on 20th and two at Magor on the 24th. The main influx came in January, with flocks of 50–100, often more, becoming widespread in the county, and numbers remaining at similar levels during February and March. As is usually the case with this species, many of the largest flocks occurred in parks and gardens where they fed on the berries of ornamental shrubs and trees.

The 2004/05 flocks were extremely mobile and appeared to feed in one area until the berry supply had become exhausted, and then move on to another. For this reason it is not possible to to estimate the total numbers of birds involved with any confidence. However, the largest single flock recorded was of 270 on 26th January at Chepstow, and analysis of the records shows that the greatest single day total, most of which were seen in the Cwmbran area, was approximately 720 birds on 29th January. Smaller numbers were recorded into April and the last birds were seen on April 24th.

(White-throated) **Dipper**
Bronwen y Dŵr

Cinclus cinclus

A fairly common resident on suitable watercourses throughout the county

The Dipper is a widespread breeding resident in the hills in the north and west of the UK. The 1937 *Birds of Monmouthshire* described it as most numerous in the north and north-west of the county, and also breeding on the Rivers Usk and Wye, and some of their tributaries. A further comment that it is 'frequently met in coastal districts in the winter', appears not to have been the case in the last fifty or so years, possibly because winters have been generally much milder.

In Gwent, the Dipper is frequent on rocky rivers and streams where it requires unpolluted, well-oxygenated water with abundant and accessible invertebrates including caddis larvae and mayfly nymphs. Such watercourses generally occur in upland areas. Suitable conditions may, however, also occur at lower altitudes as on some of the small tributaries in steep-sided valleys in the lower Wye. In the winter months, birds may also be seen on lowland rivers because, although most Dippers are resident, there may be some altitudinal movements, with birds moving down from the highest streams in severe weather.

Some 35% of tetrads were occupied in the period of the 1st Gwent Atlas with breeding *confirmed* in 19.5%. During the 2nd Gwent Atlas period birds were present again in 34.5% of tetrads, but with *confirmed* breeding in slightly fewer (17%). The current breeding distribution therefore shows rather little change from that between 1981 and 1985. The favoured areas are still the Black Mountain streams and lower Wye tributaries, but many more records for the 2nd Gwent Atlas came from the western valleys where numbers have undoubtedly increased as the river quality has improved. There is however, evidence of a recent decline in numbers on the Grwyne Fawr and on some Wye tributaries, with many former territories unoccupied in 2002 and 2003 (J. M. S. Lewis, pers.comm.; Tyler, 2004). For example, birds no longer occurred or were very scarce on the lower Mally Brook, the lower Trothy and lower Monnow. In 2005 there was evidence of some recovery.

Dippers may occur on rivers at the density of one pair per 500–1,000m. Breeding abundances are generally higher though on narrower rivers and streams (as narrow as 2-3m) where water depth is less than one metre and where there are abundant riffles. These are well-oxygenated areas where the water is shallow but rushes fast over rocks and stones. Typically territories are 400-500m in length on these streams, with territories abutting as on the Angiddy, which drops over 700m in about 5km to Tintern. Given a density of 1–5 pairs per occupied tetrad, a county population of 200–300 pairs was previously suggested in 1981–85. In view of the subsequent large increase in numbers in the western valleys, the current population is likely to be at the top end of this range or possibly higher.

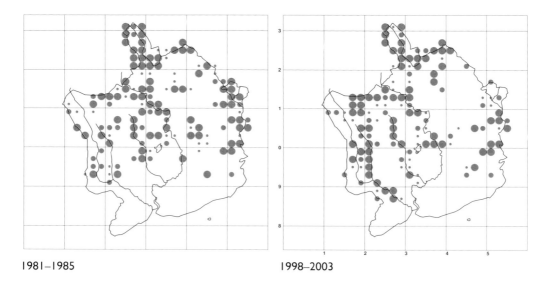

1981–1985   1998–2003

Male Dippers tend only to move a few kilometres from where they were hatched and where they subsequently breed (Tyler & Ormerod 1994). Females, however, may disperse some distance, up to 30–40km, from their natal site and may even move on to different rivers. For example, there have been short movements between the Angidy and Mounton Brooks; between the River Monnow, in Herefordshire, and Gwernesney on a tributary of the River Usk, and between Llantilio Crossenny on the Afon Trothy and Bigsweir on the River Wye. Other birds moved from Brynmawr to Forest Coal Pit, and another from Llanvihangel Crucorney to Cinderford in the Forest of Dean, a distance of 35km. Other movements of less than 20km were between Monmouth and Llanthony and between Pandy and Monmouth. Although Dippers do not usually live more than two to three years, one caught in July 1984 was still alive in April 1991, almost seven years later.

Reasons for declines in the Wye catchment may possibly be a succession of poor springs with flash floods or prolonged high flows and high turbidity, with less favourable Dipper territories on the lower sections being the first to be vacated. Run-off from surrounding ploughed land, or from overgrazing by stock or trampling of banks, all increase the sediment load that eventually is deposited on the river bed. The turbidity makes it difficult for Dippers to see prey whilst the sediment itself may smother invertebrates.

Re-pointing of bridges and associated walls has led to loss of some former nest sites, although if the territory is suitable, tree roots or drainpipes in nearby bridges would probably be used. Disturbance cannot be ruled out at a few sites such as close to the Mitchel Troy Caravan site. Other possible reasons for local declines may include local pollution incidents (e.g. the diesel spill on Mally Brook in 2002) or a higher loss from predation of juveniles or immature birds by introduced feral mink or other predators, notably Sparrowhawks and Peregrines. Rings from Dippers have been found at Sparrowhawk nests and Peregrine eyries.

Gwent Breeding Atlas data and population size

Gwent Atlas	Confirmed tetrads	Probable tetrads	Possible tetrads	Total tetrads	Change in total	Gwent population
1981–1985	76	29	33	138	–	–
1998–2003	68	32	36	136	−1%	200–300 pairs

National breeding data and conservation status

Estimated Welsh population	Welsh trend 1985–2003	UK trend 1985–2003	Welsh & UK conservation status
1,750 pairs	Not available	No significant trend*	Green-listed

*From Waterways Birds Survey

(Winter) **Wren**
Dryw

Troglodytes troglodytes

An abundant resident

The Wren occurs in most habitats and at all altitudes, and is a widely distributed breeding resident in the UK. It is one of Britain's most well-known birds and, although small and often nesting and foraging low down in dense foliage, its distinctive loud song and alarm call make it relatively easy to locate.

The Wren was described in the 1937 and 1963 *Birds of Monmouthshire* as a common resident breeding in all districts. The 1977 *Birds of Gwent* summarised its status in similar terms, and noted its recovery from being almost wiped out during the harsh winter of 1962/63, when the ground was frozen for 10–12 weeks.

The 1st Gwent Atlas confirmed its widespread distribution, showing it to be present in 98% of tetrads in the county including, a little surprisingly, in the company of the gulls on Denny Island. The run of relatively mild winters in the past two decades has precluded any recent population crashes and, in consequence, the 2nd Gwent Atlas again shows a very wide distribution. The number of occupied tetrads has increased by two, giving a rounded figure of 99%, but with no evidence of presence on Denny Island this time. *Probable* or *confirmed* breeding was recorded in 98% of tetrads, reflecting its abundance, the ease with which its loud song is detected and recognised, and its conspicuous alarm when it has fledged young nearby.

In the 1st Gwent Atlas the suggested county population was a wide-ranging 20,000–60,000 pairs, and the current estimate has produced the narrower range of 31,000–40,000 pairs. At a national level, both the UK and Welsh population indices show increases of 42% in the period between the two Gwent Atlases probably mainly as a consequence of milder winters.

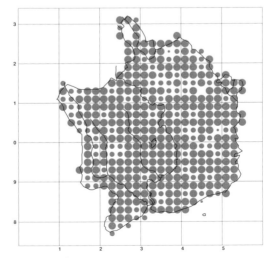

1998–2003

The British population of Wrens is boosted to a minor extent in winter by arrival of some continental birds of the nominate race *troglodytes*. The Winter Atlas considers this phenomenon of little or no importance in terms of overall numbers in southeast England, where the evidence for these movements is strongest. No evidence exists of the continental race occurring in Gwent. Although they are predominantly sedentary, the Winter Atlas indicates that some British Wrens do engage in southerly movements, or movements from moorland breeding territories to the lowlands. This, coupled with different habitats being favoured in winter: reedbeds as opposed to hedgerows or moorland for example, does mean that the fine-scale winter distribution of Wrens in Gwent could be different from that in the breeding season.

There are three ringing records relevant to Gwent: two show no movement, and are thus consistent with the species' mostly sedentary nature, but a third concerns a bird ringed in Hampshire in October 1974 being recovered in Monmouth the following June, 130km to the north-west, which possibly relates to the return of a bird that had moved south for the winter.

Gwent Breeding Atlas data and population size

Gwent Atlas	Confirmed tetrads	Probable tetrads	Possible tetrads	Total tetrads	Change in total	Gwent population
1981–1985	270	91	26	387	–	–
1998–2003	308	78	3	389	1%	31,000–40,000 pairs

National breeding data and conservation status

Estimated Welsh population	Welsh CBC/BBS trend 1985–2003	UK CBC/BBS trend 1985–2003	Welsh & UK conservation status
783,000 pairs	+42%	+42%	Green-listed

Dunnock (Hedge Accentor) Llwyd y Gwrych

Prunella modularis

An abundant resident

The Dunnock favours the edges of woods, hedgerows and gardens. Its ubiquity in Britain stems from its willingness to use virtually any low dense shrubs for breeding, although it is uncommon in more exposed stands of hillside gorse. It is an unassuming species, overlooked by most non-birdwatchers who, nevertheless, will have this delicately marked bird regularly gracing their garden. The scientific name *Prunella modularis* means 'small brown singing bird', which just about sums it up.

There are fascinating complexities to its sexual behaviour, which has been elegantly and euphemistically described as a variable mating system (Davies & Lundberg, 1984). The studies have shown whilst simple pairs do occur, a male can have two females, a female can have two or three males, and two or three males can share two to four females.

In both the 1937 and 1963 *Birds of Monmouthshire* the Dunnock is referred to as the British Hedge Sparrow, where it is described as a common resident breeding species in all districts except the barren hill country. This status was confirmed by the 1st Gwent Atlas, which recorded it in 96% of tetrads in the county, with gaps confined mainly to the bare moorland tops

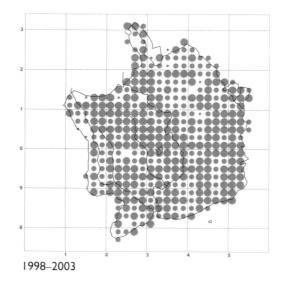

1998–2003

of the north-west. A similar distribution was found in the 2nd Gwent Atlas, but with an extra five occupied tetrads, raising percentage occupancy to 97%.

The UK population underwent a steep decline from the mid-1970s to the mid-1980s and the reasons for this are not known. It has recovered considerably over the most recent decade, but the conservation status of the species in the UK remains as amber-listed. As the 1st Gwent Atlas was carried out toward the end of the period of national decline, when the population size would have been near its lowest, the 2nd Gwent Atlas would be expected to show an increase in numbers that reflects the positive national trends apparent between the two atlases. An indication of such an increase is seen in the expansion in the numbers of tetrads with *confirmed* or *probable* breeding (85% to 94%), but not in the population estimate of 8,500–11,000 pairs, which is lower than the population of about 18,000 suggested by the 1st Gwent Atlas. As with some other species the differing methods of population estimation between the atlases means that caution should be used when comparing these figures.

The Dunnock is subject to parasitism by the Cuckoo, and there are references in *Gwent Bird Reports* to this being prevalent in Raglan and Magor. With the decline in the population of the Cuckoo, such parasitism is unlikely to be the reason for the decline in the numbers of Dunnocks. Another cause could be the frequency of hedge cutting, with many farmers now cutting their hedges annually whereas in past times they might have been left several years. This could be detrimental to the Dunnock, which is said to favour overgrown mature hedgerows

Birds of the race *occidentalis*, which is found in most of Britain, with the exception of western Scotland and Ireland, are known to be extremely sedentary (*Migration Atlas*). There have been 14 recoveries of birds ringed in Gwent, and all were close to the site of ringing. In contrast, those of the nominate race *modularis*, breeding in Fennoscandia, the former USSR and north-east Europe, migrate south-west. The Migration Atlas suggests that passage numbers in Britain are small and are restricted to the east coast.

Gwent Breeding Atlas data and population size

Gwent Atlas	Confirmed tetrads	Probable tetrads	Possible tetrads	Total tetrads	Change in total	Gwent population
1981–1985	218	119	40	377	–	–
1998–2003	240	132	9	381	1%	8,500–11,000 pairs

National breeding data and conservation status

Estimated Welsh population	Welsh BBS trend 1994–2003	UK CBC/BBS trend 1985–2003	Welsh & (UK) conservation status
213,000 pairs	+27%	+19%	Green (Amber) listed

(European) **Robin**
Robin Goch

Erithacus rubecula

An abundant resident

The Robin is a woodland species which has also adapted to sites, notably gardens, which provide a few trees or shrubs. It is widespread throughout the British Isles and is one of the most familiar and easily identified birds. It sings for much of the year, including at night, particularly where there is good artificial lighting.

The Robin is described in both the 1937 and 1963 *Birds of Monmouthshire* as a common resident found breeding everywhere. The 1977 *Birds of Gwent* also reported it as widespread and abundant, having recovered rapidly from the effects the harsh winter of 1962/63, which may have reduced its numbers by as much as 50%.

Its widespread distribution was demonstrated by the 1st Gwent Atlas, which showed it to be present in 99% of the county's tetrads, and absent only from Denny Island and those coastal tetrads that included only small fragments of land. Although the 2nd Gwent Atlas recorded it in one fewer tetrad than previously, its distribution was essentially unchanged with over 98% of tetrads occupied. The 1st Gwent Atlas suggested a population estimate of 38,000–47,500 pairs. The current estimate of 30,000–43,000 is somewhat lower, despite big increases in the national population indices during this period, but is based on different methods of estimation

(Appendix 1). A population of up to 43,000 pairs puts the Robin among the top three most numerous birds in the county, along with the Blackbird and the Wren.

Despite its sentimental image, the Robin can be very aggressive when establishing and defending territory, and there are several anecdotes in *Gwent Bird Reports* of rivals being killed in territorial battles.

British-breeding Robins are generally resident, and this appears to be true of those that breed in Gwent, as ringing data show that out of 29 recoveries of birds ringed in the county, 25 were local. The Winter Atlas records some altitudinal movements, with birds vacating higher altitude breeding sites. There is no evidence yet as to whether this occurs at the modest altitudes found in the Gwent hills.

A small proportion of British Robins have been known to migrate to south-west Europe for the winter. There is also a marked passage migration through Britain of birds of the nominate race *rubecula* from northern European breeding grounds to wintering areas in south-west Europe and north Africa, which is sometimes strikingly demonstrated by falls of migrant robins on the east coast. There is some evidence of passage in Gwent during the autumn from late August through into October, with ringing on the coast recording numbers of birds higher than would normally be expected. There are also occasional small 'falls' on the Gwent coast when Robins are noted at above average densities. Such passage has, however, not been noted in the spring. There are four ringing records relevant to Gwent that show movements of greater than 100km: two of these suggest autumn movements of birds into Gwent from northern and eastern England, and the other two involve movements between Gwent and Portland Bill that are suggestive of autumn migration of local birds, possibly to continental Europe.

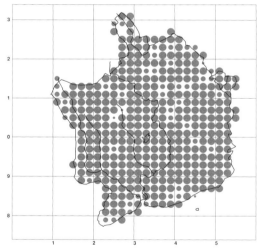

1998–2003

Gwent Breeding Atlas data and population size

Gwent Atlas	Confirmed tetrads	Probable tetrads	Possible tetrads	Total tetrads	Change in total	Gwent population
1981–1985	337	34	18	389	–	–
1998–2003	342	42	4	388	0%	30,000–43,000 pairs

National breeding data and conservation status

Estimated Welsh population	Welsh CBC/BBS trend 1985–2003	UK CBC/BBS trend 1985–2003	Welsh & UK conservation status
485,000 pairs	+46%	+61%	Green-listed

(Common) **Nightingale** *Luscinia megarhynchos*
Eos

A rare summer visitor and passage migrant; has bred

The 1963 *Birds of Monmouthshire* described it as formerly not uncommon in the Wye Valley and Raglan areas. In addition, the name Pant-yr-eos (given to a valley and brook near Newport), translates as valley of the Nightingale, thus hinting at a former abundance in this area. However, by the 1960s it had obviously become something of a rarity, as evidenced by the observation that a bird in song at Risca in May 1961 'attracted large audiences'.

There is a small breeding population in the neighbouring county of Gloucestershire, but Gwent is now on the extreme western fringe of this powerful songster's breeding range in Britain, and since 1960 there have been only 36 records. The yearly distribution of these records (Figure 24) shows a slight increase from 1960 up to the mid 1970s, but there was a subsequent decline and the Nightingale is now a very rare visitor with no records since 1998.

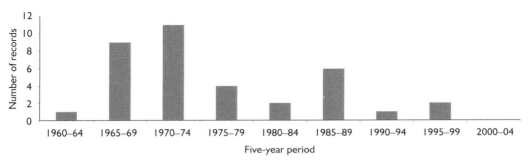

Figure 24. Numbers of Nightingale records in Gwent

All occurrences fall in the late April to early July period, with the earliest on 20th April 1971, and the latest at Llanwenarth on 10th July 1965. May is the best month to listen out for the species, with over 60% of birds recorded in this month. The only confirmed breeding record was at Lord's Grove, Monmouth in 1975, when a male was heard singing briefly on 7th June and a female with a fledged young was seen carrying food on 24th June. However, there have been several instances where birds have sung for extended periods, thus suggesting breeding activity: examples of this occurred near Raglan in 1980, at Nash in 1983, and Llanwern Steelworks in 1985. Neither of the latter two records found their way into the 1st Gwent Atlas, so they have been retrospectively included here in the atlas data table. During the 2nd Gwent Atlas there was one *possible* and one *probable* record, at Gwernesney and Wyesham respectively, both in 1998.

Gwent Atlas data

Gwent Atlas	Confirmed tetrads	Probable tetrads	Possible tetrads	Total tetrads	Change in total	Gwent population
1981–1985	0	2	0	2	–	–
1998–2003	0	1	1	2	0	0

Bluethroat *Luscinia svecica*
Bronlas

A very rare visitor

The Bluethroat is a regular though uncommon migrant to Britain. Although it occurs chiefly on the east coast, there have been 38 records in Wales since 1946, mostly in Caernarfon and Pembrokeshire (2002 *Birds in Wales*). The only Gwent record is of a single bird seen along the foreshore at Newport Wetlands Reserve on 1st October 1999.

Black Redstart
Tingoch Du

Phoenicurus ochruros

A scarce winter visitor and passage migrant

In Britain the Black Redstart has adapted to living in industrial and urban sites. Greater London, Birmingham and the Black Country are its main breeding areas, where it is often found nesting at power stations, disused factories, building sites, cliffs and old quarries. With fewer than 100 breeding pairs in the UK, the species is on the Amber List of Birds of Conservation Concern. The small UK wintering population tends to be found mostly at coastal sites, along cliffs and sheltered beaches, but also on ploughed fields and in gardens.

In Gwent it occurs predominantly on the coastal levels, where it is found amongst the boulders of the sea-defences and at industrial areas such as Uskmouth power station, Newport Docks and Llanwern steelworks, but it has also occurred rarely inland at Monmouth, Abergavenny, Cwmbran, Llanellen, Llandegfedd Reservoir and Llangovan. The majority of records relate to the period October–January, with November being the peak month.

The 1937 *Birds of Monmouthshire* described the species as being a rare winter visitor but considered it to be probably overlooked. Two specific records were referred to, both relating to the 1930s from the Newport area. The 1963 *Birds of Monmouthshire* gave no new records for the species and it was not recorded again until 1967 when a female was seen at Newport in January. The 1977 *Birds of Gwent* added 14 new records between 1967 and 1975, all of which concerned single birds. The authors thought that the increase in records during this time suggested that the species had been overlooked in the past. This view is further supported by the fact that the species has now been recorded annually in the county since 1974 with a mean of 4.75 birds a year.

Between 1976 and 2005 there were 110 records involving some 133 individual birds. Unlike previous years, fifteen of the records during this period involved more than one bird, the largest numbers being from Uskmouth, where four were recorded during November–December 1992, and then up to five during January–March 1995. Some spring passage has been noted, and examples include single birds on 5th May 1997 and 20th March 2005 at Goldcliff, 10th May 1998 at Sluice Farm, 19th–22nd April at the Newport Civic Centre, and inland at Llandewi Rhydderch on 3rd May 2000.

(Common) Redstart
Tingoch

Phoenicurus phoenicurus

A locally common summer visitor and a scarce passage migrant

One of our most attractive summer visitors, the Redstart is a typical species of deciduous woodlands in the uplands in the north and west of Britain. It can also be found in open parkland and farmland, where mature hedgerows and scattered trees provide insect food and holes for nesting. It is common and widespread in much of upland Wales, the Principality being one of its strongholds in Britain (1994 *Birds in Wales*).

The species' stronghold in Gwent is in the sessile oak woods of the northern uplands, the slopes of the western valleys, and also on upland farmland wherever there are mature hedgerows and trees, especially beech and hawthorn. The Wye Valley woodlands have traditionally supported a good population, though this has diminished of late, and central areas of the county have also held scattered pairs.

Nest sites recorded in the county have usually been in cavities in dry-stone walls, old or derelict farm buildings and natural tree holes, but other sites have included former Green Woodpecker nests, a log pile, old farm machinery and several ground nests among tree roots or forest floor debris. The woodland nest boxes provided in Gwent during the 1970s and 1980s often held a few successful pairs during their time, and since 1999 the groups of 71 boxes at Forest Coal Pit and nearby Mynyddisllwyn have held one or two pairs annually.

The 1937 *Birds of Monmouthshire* recorded the species as being a summer visitor that was apparently not so numerous as in the past, although a welcome increase was noted in 1937. It went on to say that the Redstart was very local and scarce in the south as a breeding species, but found in fair numbers in central districts and amongst the hills of the north up to heights of 1,000 feet.

The 1963 *Birds of Monmouthshire*, in a very brief coverage of the species, described it as fairly common but local, especially in the central districts of the county and the hilly districts of the north. The western valleys were thus not mentioned, perhaps because there were fewer birds there during the industrial era or, perhaps more likely, because they had been overlooked. Records for the western valleys first appeared in the mid 1970s, when two pairs were recorded annually at a CBC plot at Mynyddislwyn, and certainly by the 1980s the valleys had become recognised as one of the species strongholds in the county, as the 1st Gwent Atlas demonstrated very clearly. Comparison of the maps from the 1st and 2nd Gwent Atlases reveals a shift in distribution in recent years, with an even higher number of occupied tetrads in the western valleys, and a pronounced decline in the centre of the county and in the Wye Valley area to the east. The decline in the Wye Valley area has been supported by numerous reports from local observers and appears to have taken place during the early 1990s. The total number of occupied tetrads in Gwent has declined by 14% between the two Gwent Atlases, and this tallies with the Wales short-term population decline of 25% over the same period, rather than the UK trend of a 14% increase. The Redstart has a history of population fluctuations in Britain (Mead, 2000): there was a steep decline during the late 1960s and early 1970s, the local effects of which were recorded by the 1977 *Birds of Gwent*.

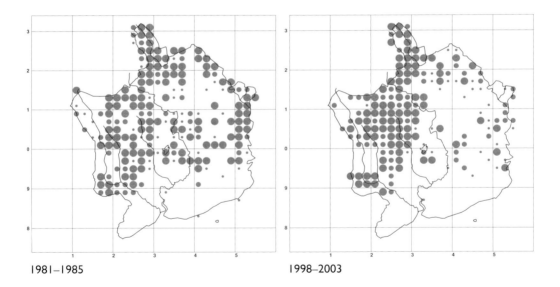

1981–1985   1998–2003

The 1st Gwent Atlas suggested a county population of about 1,500 pairs. Based on the BBS and atlas-based methods, the current Gwent population is estimated in the wide range of 600–2,600 pairs (see Appendix 1). This corresponds to an average of 3.5–15 pairs per occupied tetrad. A few observers who counted Redstart territories found as many as 20 in some tetrads and as few as one in some others, but with a mean of around 7–10, which would suggest a likely population near the middle of the above range (1,200–1,700 pairs). These densities are low in comparison to parts of mid-Wales where densities as high as 40–50 singing males/km^2 (=160–200 per tetrad) may occur (1994 *Birds in Wales*).

First arrivals in Gwent are typically during the second or third week of April, though sometimes earlier, and the earliest on record was on 30th March 1990. The main arrival is usually in late April. Autumn passage is sometimes noted as early as July, but is strongest during August and early September when ones and twos, occasionally up to six or seven are regularly recorded at well-watched sites such as Llandegfedd Reservoir and the coast at Peterstone. Very few birds are recorded after mid-September but in many years late stragglers have been recorded into October, and the latest was on 15th November 1992.

The only long-distance ringing recovery refers to a nestling ringed in the county in June 1976 that was recovered 1,164km to the south in Zaragoza, Spain in October of the same year. This fits the generally accepted migration route that follows the west coast of France and then across to the east coast of Spain.

Gwent Breeding Atlas data and population size

Gwent Atlas	Confirmed tetrads	Probable tetrads	Possible tetrads	Total tetrads	Change in total	Gwent population
1981–1985	118	41	41	200	–	–
1998–2003	90	52	31	173	−14%	600–2,600 pairs

National breeding data and conservation status

Estimated Welsh population	Welsh CBC/BBS trend 1985–2003	UK CBC/BBS trend 1985–2003	Welsh & UK conservation status
28,260 pairs	−25%	+14%	Amber-listed

Whinchat
Crec yr Eithin

Saxicola rubetra

A fairly common summer visitor to the uplands; occurs more widely as an uncommon passage migrant

The Whinchat is a summer visitor to Britain, occupying open habitats in the hills of the north and west. It was formerly more widespread but in the latter part of the 20th century it underwent a range contraction, mainly from lowland England. The causes of this contraction are not fully understood but loss of marginal farmland habitats is probably a significant factor (1988–91 National Atlas).

The 1937 and 1963 *Birds of Monmouthshire* describe the Whinchat as breeding regularly on the coastal levels, railway embankments and other lowland habitats as well as in the hills. Until the 1970s there were still some sporadic breeding records in lowland districts, but such records are rare today, and the Whinchat now resides predominantly in the hills of the north and west of the county. The moorland edges and hillsides where the land undulates and where there are deep gullies to give shelter and adequate nesting sites, are the favourite haunts of this species, especially where the vegetation includes heather, bilberry and bracken. The Whinchat also benefited in the short term from the planting of coniferous forests in the uplands of Gwent. These provided good habitat during their early stages of growth and were rapidly colonised but, as the trees grew larger, the habitat lost its attraction to chats and their populations declined.

Between the two Gwent Atlases there have been declines of 16% in the number of occupied tetrads, and also in the number with *probable* or *confirmed* breeding. This reflects the short-term UK population decline of 15% seen in the last decade, which, as with earlier losses, may be related to changes in land management and possibly also to climate change. Smith (2002) notes that recent wet summers have depressed breeding success in Gwent.

Before 1999 there were few estimates of Whinchat populations in Gwent, the only figures of real note being estimates of 77 pairs above the 220m contour of the Henllys to Penyrheol ridge in 1980, and 20 pairs on the slopes of Mynydd Llwyd at Cwm Lickey in 1985. However, detailed studies by Smith (2002) over the period

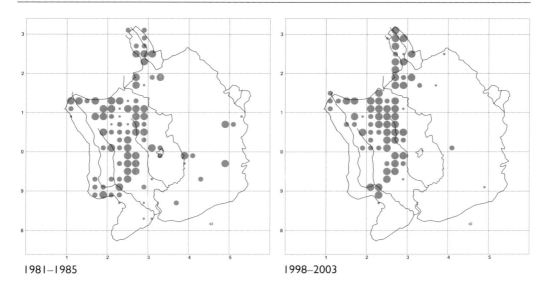

| 1981–1985 | 1998–2003 |

1999–2001 have produced average population densities (pairs in suitable habitat) of one pair per 3.3 hectares on the Blorenge, per 2.6 hectares on Mynydd-y-garn-fawr and per 5.5 hectares on Mynydd Garnclochdy, with a mean annual total of around 106 pairs on these three sites plus Coity Mountain. The current breeding population for Gwent is estimated at around 550 pairs (S. J. Smith, unpublished) but is subject to considerable annual variation.

Whinchats are one of the later summer migrants and generally do not begin to arrive on their breeding grounds until the third week of April, after which there is a steady influx that continues into the first week of May. Arrivals in early April have been recorded in some years, but March arrivals are exceptional and have been recorded on only two occasions, on 17th March 1974 and 24th March 1981.

There is a definite movement away from the breeding grounds as early as the end of June and early July, and individuals and family parties are then recorded at open lowland habitats throughout the county, such as Llandegfedd Reservoir. The movement off the uplands can continue through August and some birds may linger on their breeding grounds even into October, despite migration having long been underway. Migration is most obvious along the coast where groups of up eight, occasionally more, occur throughout August and early September at favoured sites such as Peterstone, St Brides, and Uskmouth. The last records of the year are normally on the coast, and usually in October, though there have been four records of migrating birds in November, the latest being on 15th November 1986. A rare overwintering bird frequented Peterstone from 14th November 1982 until 8th January 1983, and a bird observed there two months later on the exceptionally early date of 6th March could have been the same individual. Two birds at Goldcliff on 6th December 1970 and a single bird on 27th December 1993, at Peterstone, are the only other winter records.

British Whinchats spend their winter in sub-Saharan Africa, moving down the west coast of France, and onward to the southern coasts of Spain and Portugal where they refuel prior to their trans-Saharan flight (*Migration Atlas*). In accordance with this pattern, birds ringed as nestlings in Gwent have been recovered later in the same year in south-west France on 15th August, and in the Algarve, Portugal, on 15th September. Apart from providing information on migration routes and destinations, ringing studies can be used to study longevity, and in this respect it interesting to note that one male Whinchat from the Blorenge population has reached an age of at least six years (Smith, 1999).

Gwent Breeding Atlas data and population size

Gwent Atlas	Confirmed tetrads	Probable tetrads	Possible tetrads	Total tetrads	Change in total	Gwent population
1981–1985	41	35	14	90	–	–
1998–2003	45	22	9	76	−16%	c.550 pairs

National breeding data and conservation status

Estimated Welsh population	Welsh trend	UK BBS trend 1994–2004	Welsh & UK conservation status
2,400 pairs	Not available	−15%	Green-listed

Stonechat
Clochdar y Cerrig

Saxicola torquatus

An uncommon, but recently increasing resident, partial migrant and winter visitor

The Stonechat is a largely resident species, found mainly in the milder areas of Britain, chiefly in the west and south, and along the coasts. It shares its breeding requirements with its more migratory cousin, the Whinchat, being associated with gorse, bracken and heather in open situations. Stonechats, however, can be found nesting on the remotest of heather-clad hilltops where Whinchats are completely absent, and also on roadside verges and lowland gorse embankments somewhat reminiscent of past Whinchat haunts. They are very susceptible to prolonged cold winter weather, and were particularly hard hit by the winter of 1962/63, which resulted in their virtual extinction in several counties of South Wales (1994 *Birds in Wales*).

The earliest records for the county are of birds taken at Marshfield in November 1926 and at Wentwood Forest in July 1930. The 1937 *Birds of Monmouthshire* described the Stonechat as a resident breeding species that was more numerous and more widely distributed than the Whinchat. It was most numerous in the northern and north-western areas but local in the south. During winter it wandered widely, the hill breeding birds being thought to descend to lower ground. By the time of the 1963 *Birds of Monmouthshire* the Stonechat was a very local, resident breeding species, confined to the coast and one or two inland areas. In the years following the 1962/63 winter, breeding records were extremely scarce in Gwent, with no more than one or two annually and occasionally none.

This situation persisted until 1975 when a total of six pairs were proved to have bred in the western valleys, raising the suspicion that a significant increase in breeding strength might have occurred undetected. However, this was not supported by records received in subsequent years, and the *Gwent Bird Reports* for the late 1970s continued to refer to the Stonechat as mainly a winter visitor to the county.

The winters of 1978/79 and 1981/82 both included periods of severe weather that reduced the Stonechat populations of Wales. The first of these winters was only two years before the commencement of the 1st Gwent Atlas survey work and the second followed the initial summer of recording, so in retrospect it is perhaps not surprising that the atlas results showed a rather small county population. A mere 31 tetrads were found to be occupied, mainly scattered throughout the hills in the north and west. The county population was estimated at 20–30 pairs.

The years following the 1st Gwent Atlas have been a great success story for the Stonechat. A series of short, mild winters, coupled with its ability to raise three broods in a breeding season lasting from April to September,

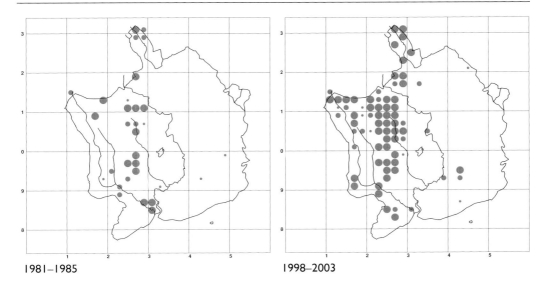

1981–1985   1998–2003

has produced a remarkable increase in numbers. The 2nd Gwent Atlas shows a striking expansion, with the total number of occupied tetrads increasing to 75, and the number with *probable* or *confirmed* breeding more than tripling from 15 to 50. The hills of the north and west are still the species' stronghold in the county but there is also a significant scattering of occupied tetrads in the central and southern regions.

The current Gwent population is estimated as 110–210 pairs, and probably at the top end of this range. This represents an enormous increase over the population of the early 1980s, and is an increase that reflects the recent national trends. The population in Wales in 2000 has been estimated at 3,000–3,500 pairs compared to a census figure in 1968 of 420 pairs (2002 *Birds in Wales*), while the UK trend for the last decade is +135%. Since the conclusion of the 2nd Gwent Atlas, the Stonechat has continued to expand its breeding range in the county, and new locations have included Llanwenarth, Pen-y-fan Pond, and Cwmfelinfach in the west of the county, Beacon Hill in the east, and several locations on the Gwent Levels in the south.

British Stonechats are generally regarded as resident breeders, often remaining, weather permitting, in their hillside breeding haunts throughout the winter. This is true of many of Gwent's Stonechats, which have been observed in habitat as high as 500m above sea level during the winter period. However, ringing studies have shown British Stonechats to be partial migrants, with an unknown proportion moving mainly to southern Iberia and the northern coast of Africa for the winter. This is well illustrated by the case of a bird ringed in July 1997 as a nestling at Trefil, Gwent, and recovered some 1,800km to the south in Algeria in November of the same year, and also by the case of a female ringed in Spain in November 1999 that was subsequently discovered breeding in Gwent, near Blaenavon, 1,090km to the north, in July 2000.

In September, Stonechats begin to appear on the Gwent Levels and they are present there throughout the winter until March. They are often seen in pairs, but single birds frequently 'team up' with a Robin. Summation of the counts received from various well-watched locations on the coast often gives a total of 20–30 birds, so assuming their presence at other less well watched sites, a population of 30–50 birds is likely in many winters. In some years, coastal numbers show a pronounced peak in October indicative of passage birds: notable examples include about 20 at Uskmouth on both 1st October 1995 and 8th October 2000. In some years there is a slight, but not very convincing, suggestion of return passage in March.

Gwent Breeding Atlas data and population size

Gwent Atlas	Confirmed tetrads	Probable tetrads	Possible tetrads	Total tetrads	Change in total	Gwent population
1981–1985	15	10	6	31	–	–
1998–2003	50	18	7	75	+142%	150–210 pairs

National breeding data and conservation status

Estimated Welsh population	Welsh CBC/BBS trend 1985–2003	UK BBS trend 1994–2004	Welsh & UK conservation status
3,000–3,500 pairs	Not available	+135%	Amber-listed

(Northern) Wheatear
Tinwen y Garn

Oenanthe oenanthe oenanthe

A fairly common summer visitor and passage migrant

The British distribution of the Wheatear is mainly in the uplands of the north and west, where it prefers close-grazed swards and nests in cavities provided by drystone walls, rocky screes or rabbit burrows (1968–72 National Atlas). Wales is well-endowed with appropriate habitat, particularly in the uplands and on parts of the coast, and is one of the species' strongholds in Britain.

The earliest record of the Wheatear being found in Gwent came in 1899 when a male bird was 'taken' at Newport. By the time of the 1937 *Birds of Monmouthshire* the species was known as a summer visitor 'breeding in the hill districts in fair numbers' and this continued to hold true by the time of the 1963 *Birds of Monmouthshire*.

The 2nd Gwent Atlas shows a breeding distribution almost entirely restricted to the uplands in the north and west of the county. In these areas it inhabits moorland, grassland, hillsides and quarries, and seems particularly attracted to sites where drystone walls and water are in close proximity. The distribution is almost identical to that found earlier in the 1st Gwent Atlas and, although the total number of tetrads has dropped by ten, the difference lies mostly in the number of *possible* breeding records outside the main range, many of which probably refer to passage birds.

Based on extrapolation from sample tetrads, the current Gwent population is estimated at 170–230 pairs. The mid-point of this range (200) is exactly the figure suggested by the 1st Gwent Atlas which, in the absence of other data, was based mainly on the authors' personal perceptions of population densities. Recent population trends for Wales and the UK for 1994–2004 are contradictory, the Welsh trend being –21% and UK trend +7%.

The Wheatear is one of the earliest summer migrants to arrive. In Gwent, the first arrivals are always in March and usually on the coast where, resplendent in their fresh breeding plumage, they provide a welcome diversion from wildfowl and wader counting. The earliest arrival date on record is 4th March 1980 at Manmoel. The median first arrival date has got steadily earlier over the past 39 years, moving from 27th March during 1965–73, to 10th March in 1994–2003 (see Table 90). The short-cropped and sea-washed turf of the Gwent foreshore, with scattered rocks to act as lookout posts, is ideal feeding habitat, and appears to be a favoured land-fall for passage birds. Their numbers build-up throughout April, with concentrations of 10–25 not unusual at the favoured haunts of Peterstone and St Brides. On 24th April 1986, counts at Sluice Farm, Peterstone, St Brides, Goldcliff and Undy produced a total of 100 birds, which gives a useful indication of the scale of passage that occurs in good years. Small numbers of passage birds are also recorded inland, and 130 in the vicinity of Garnlydan Reservoir on 5th April 1987 is by far the highest spring passage concentration recorded anywhere in

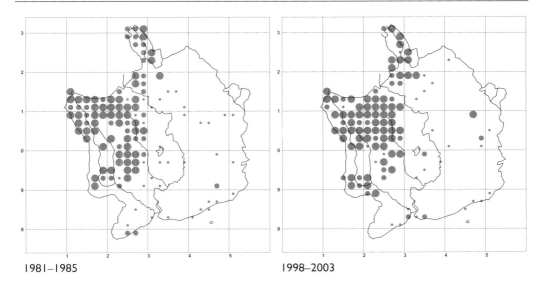

1981–1985   **1998–2003**

the county. On the coast, spring passage males sometimes engage in song and display flights but coastal breeding, as occurs in some other parts of South Wales, has never been recorded in Gwent. This may stem from a lack of suitable nest sites; although the cavities between the boulders of the sea defences would appear to be appropriate, they are subject to flooding on the higher tides.

Period	1965–73	1974–83	1984–93	1994–2003
Date	27 March	17 March	14 March	10 March

Table 90. Median first arrival dates for Wheatears in Gwent

Return passage is recorded widely throughout the county in suitable open habitat in both uplands and lowlands. It is most noticeable on the coast, where it usually commences with a trickle of juvenile birds, often as early as mid-June but with larger numbers in July. Passage records peak in late August and early September, when concentrations of around 15–35 are not unusual at the favoured locations. Few birds are recorded after mid-September but a few stragglers occur every year during October. There have been November records in 12 years, and one such bird stayed at Peterstone from 9th November to 9th December 1985.

British-bred Wheatears migrate through western France, Spain and west Africa to wintering grounds south of the Sahara (*Migration Atlas*). In this context there are two records of birds ringed as nestlings in Gwent that were recovered 2,200km and 2,600km to the south-south-west in western Morocco in late September and mid-October, respectively, the same year.

Gwent Breeding Atlas data and population size

Gwent Atlas	Confirmed tetrads	Probable tetrads	Possible tetrads	Total tetrads	Change in total	Gwent population
1981–1985	54	32	36	122	–	–
1998–2003	64	23	25	112	−8%	170–230 pairs

National breeding data and conservation status

Estimated Welsh population	Welsh BBS trend 1994–2003*	UK CBC/BBS trend 1994–2003*	Welsh & UK conservation status
5,000–10,000 pairs	−21%	+7%	Green-listed

*CBC/BBS trends for 1985–2003 not available owing to small sample sizes.

Greenland Wheatear   *Oenanthe oenanthe leucorhoa*

Wheatears of this subspecies make the somewhat astonishing flight across the North Atlantic to breed in Iceland, Greenland and eastern Canada. With experience they are recognisable in the field by their larger size and darker, more uniformly buff underparts. Typically they migrate later than the common subspecies, passing northward through Britain in late April and early May, and returning in late September and early October.

The 1963 *Birds of Monmouthshire* describes the Greenland Wheatear as occurring regularly as a passage migrant, in both spring and autumn, but with rarely more than a dozen seen together. However, this description did not correspond to the situation of the succeeding 20 years, which produced only five county records, with fewer than five birds on each occasion. Since then, however, occurrences have become more regular, and from 1990 it has been recorded in twelve out of fourteen years, with numbers ranging from 1–7 birds. Spring records have occurred between 17th April and 23rd May with a median date of 5th May. Autumn records have been much more widely spread, from 24th August to 13th October, but with a concentration in late August which accounts for around half of them.

Desert Wheatear   *Oenanthe deserti*
Tinwen y Diffaethwch

A very rare vagrant

This species is a rare vagrant to Britain from Africa, with records generally during late November and December. The only record for Gwent, which was only the second for Wales, was of a single bird that frequented the seawall at Peterstone during 16–20th December 1996.

Ring Ouzel   *Turdus torquatus*
Mwyalchen y Mynydd

A scarce and declining summer visitor; also a passage migrant

The Ring Ouzel is known in some areas as the mountain blackbird and indeed it is found breeding only in the uplands of Britain, generally above 250m. It is a summer visitor and one of the earliest to arrive.

Ring Ouzels usually arrive in Gwent in late March or April: the mean first date up to the end of the 1990s was 29th March but birds have been reported as early as 18th March. More recently though, they have not been seen until into April. Formerly they bred on cliffs, in quarries and on the ground in moorland in the north and west of the country, notably in the Black Mountains, the hills between Abergavenny, Ebbw Vale and Pontypool, and at Trefil Quarries near Tredegar, but their range now is very restricted.

In the 1st Gwent Atlas Ring Ouzels were found in 31 tetrads (8%) with *confirmed* breeding in six (1.5%), all in the northwest of the county. In the 2nd Gwent Atlas birds were found in only six tetrads and were not *confirmed* breeding in any. No birds were found in the Black Mountains, a former local stronghold. The only two *probable* breeding records came from the extreme north-west of the county, and there were four *possible* records in the western hills. A marked decline has therefore occurred over the last 20 years. Trefil Quarries remained a reliable site with 3–4 pairs present from 1990 up to 1997 but, although birds have been seen there in all years to 2005, there was no evidence of breeding during the 2nd Gwent Atlas period other than a report of birds nest-building in 2003. None were seen in 2006.

Other sites where birds have been seen since 1990 include Mynydd Garnclochdy, Mynydd Maen, Mynydd-y-garn-fawr, Ysgyryd Fawr, Talywain, Blaenavon, Varteg, Coity Mountain, Garnlydan, Gilwern Hill and the Blorenge.

Nationally, a decline occurred between the 1968–72 National Atlas and the 1988–91 National Atlas, and since then a 58% percent decline in the UK between 1988–91 and 1999 has prompted the inclusion of the species on the Red List of birds of conservation concern (Gregory *et al.*, 2002). In Wales, Tyler & Green (1994)

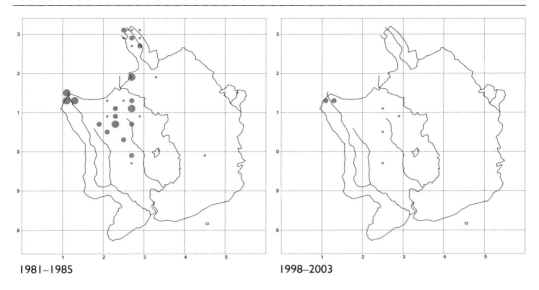

1981–1985   1998–2003

drew attention to a worrying decrease in breeding birds and suggested possible reasons. These range from loss of habitat in their winter quarters in Morocco to deterioration of habitat in the uplands due to excessive sheep numbers and increasing soil acidification. Competition with Blackbirds and Mistle Thrushes has also been suggested as a reason for the species' decline. At many of the Ring Ouzel's former haunts, such as Trefil and Gilwern Hill, there is also now heavy disturbance from motor cyclists.

In the 2002 *Birds in Wales* a continuing decline was noted throughout the Principality, with the only Gwent breeding record between 1994 and 2002 being in 1997 at Trefil Quarries. Ring Ouzels now appear to be lost as a breeding bird in the county.

In the autumn, passage birds can turn up anywhere: there was one in Wentwood on 25 October 1994. They are occasionally reported as coastal migrants: as at Uskmouth in October 1991. The average last date for Ring Ouzel in Gwent is 13th October but birds have been reported up to late October. The latest record is of an immature male at Collister Pill on 2nd November 1985.

There have been only two recoveries of Gwent-ringed birds, both of them ringed as nestlings at Trefil in May 1980. One ringed on 21st May was recovered on 20th September near Lewes in Suffolk, 249km east-south-east. Presumably this bird was heading for the south coast on the way to its winter quarters. The other recovery is from the winter quarters: a bird ringed on 23rd May and found around 14th February 1982 in Morocco, 2216km from its natal site.

Gwent Breeding Atlas data and population size

Gwent Atlas	Confirmed tetrads	Probable tetrads	Possible tetrads	Total tetrads	Change in total	Gwent population
1981–1985	6	11	13	30	–	–
1998–2003	0	2	4	6	−80%	0–1 pairs

National breeding data and conservation status

Estimated Welsh population	Welsh trend	UK trend 1991–99*	Welsh & UK conservation status
293–392 pairs	Not available	−58%	Red-listed

*See Gregory *et al.* (2002)

(Common) **Blackbird** *Turdus merula*
Mwyalchen

An abundant resident and winter visitor

The Blackbird is a ubiquitous bird of both rural and urban habitats. Although sometimes referred to as a bird of the woodland edge it is equally at home in town gardens, moorland, farmland hedgerows and scrub. The Blackbird is described in both the 1937 and 1963 *Birds of Monmouthshire* as a very common resident breeding species, penetrating farther and higher into the hills than the Song Thrush. It is also described in the 1977 *Birds of Gwent* as abundant and widespread. As this noisy thrush can thrive in nearly all habitats that occur in Gwent it is not surprising that both the 1st and 2nd Gwent Atlases show it breeding in 99% of tetrads. The 1st Gwent Atlas estimated the size of the county population in the very wide range of 40,000–100,000 pairs. Estimates for the 2nd Gwent Atlas are toward the lower end of this range, and coupled with the level trend in Wales suggest that numbers have been fairly stable over the intervening period.

The species is easy to detect and the nests are often found in obvious places, particularly in urban areas where it is more confiding than in farmland and woodland. With 2–4 broods and clutches of 3–5 young it is a productive breeder, but suffers predation of eggs and nestlings often by the Magpie (Groom, 1993). Recently fledged young are fed by parents on the ground adjacent to the nest and are vulnerable to cat predation in urban areas.

There are few records of winter flocks though 300 were noted roosting with Redwings at Panteg in January 1981.

It is well established that Blackbirds move westwards in autumn from Scandinavia and Eastern Europe, many spending the winter months in Britain (*Migration Atlas*). Recent ringing returns show that these immigrants reach Gwent, with birds ringed during winter months in Gwent being reported in Norway, Sweden, Denmark and Germany from March to June. One ringed in Heligoland, Germany, in March 1983 was controlled in Newport the following December. Further evidence of the winter influx is provided by an older record of a recovery in January 1932 of a bird which had been ringed in Denmark in June 1929 (1977 *Birds of Gwent*).

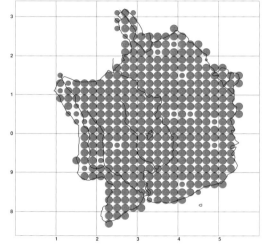

1998–2003

Gwent Breeding Atlas data and population size

Gwent Atlas	Confirmed tetrads	Probable tetrads	Possible tetrads	Total tetrads	Change in total	Gwent population
1981–1985	364	23	5	392	–	–
1998–2003	365	26	1	392	0%	41,000–46,000 pairs

National breeding data and conservation status

Estimated Welsh population	Welsh CBC/BBS trend 1985–2003	UK CBC/BBS trend 1985–2003	Welsh & UK conservation status
480,000 pairs	stable	+6.6%	Green-listed

Fieldfare
Socan Eira

Turdus pilaris

A common winter visitor, typically arriving in mid October

Fieldfares are winter immigrants, feeding on lowland fields and in berry-bearing hedges. Like Redwings, with which they regularly associate, they leave their Scandinavian breeding grounds when the weather makes feeding difficult for them, and move to western Europe where they spend the winter. Fieldfares are also known to frequent orchards and gardens when the weather makes other feeding ground difficult, particularly when there is a covering of snow.

The Fieldfare is described in both the 1937 and 1963 *Birds of Monmouthshire* as a regular winter visitor, and in the 1977 *Birds of Gwent* as a regular winter visitor sometimes in very large numbers. Although there are records of arrivals from the first week in September, and an extremely early record on 20th August 1974, the main influx is usually in mid-October with the latest recorded arrival in mid November. It then occurs throughout Gwent with flocks of over 500 birds reported most years. They normally leave between early March and mid-April, but a couple of records show them still present in the first week of May; the latest record for Gwent being 9th May 1989.

Fieldfares can occur in very large flocks during passage. This is particularly the case prior to the onset of severe winter weather, and was noted in Gwent during the winters of the 1960s, for example, before the heavy snow falls of 1962/63. Very severe weather in mid February 1969 resulted in large concentrations of Fieldfares in low-lying areas of the county, while on 18th February thousands were seen in the frozen riverside fields between Caerleon and Usk. On the coastal levels, large flocks have been recorded regularly over recent decades. Exceptional concentrations of several thousand were noted along the levels during the winter of 1973. In 1978, some 2,000 were at Peterstone in mid-December and several thousand on the Caldicot Level during November and December. During mid-December 1985, flocks of up to 4,000 birds were evident from different parts of the levels suggesting a total population of at least 15,000 birds, but with most having moved on by Christmas. Good numbers were again apparent in mid-December 1990 with 3,000 at Redwick, 1,500 at Caldicot, 2,000 at Goldcliff and 3,000 at both Undy and Peterstone.

Inland, larger flocks reported include: several thousand with Redwings at Llanarth at the beginning of the year in 1976; 6,000, again with Redwings at Llandenny in January 1977; and 1,500–2,000 at Penhow in January 1985. Maximum flock sizes for each winter during the last decade are shown in Table 91. During the 2nd Gwent Atlas period, winter records of Fieldfare flocks were mostly in the 100–200 range, though with a flock of 1,500 seen at Uskmouth in November 2000.

Year	Date	Number	Location
1994	5 March	500	Olway Meadows
1995	1 November	200	Trellech
1996	24 Feb	4,200	Llanarth
1997	21 October	200	St Brides
1998	20 November	1,000+	Goldcliff
1999	4 November	1,000	Goldcliff
2000	19 November	2,000	Uskmouth
2001	28 October	700	Newport (overflying)
2002	11 November	354	Newport Wetlands Reserve
2003	7 November	1,000+	Undy

Table 91. Maximum winter Fieldfare flock sizes during 1994–2003

Several winter roost sites have been noted in Gwent, generally in association with Redwings and occasionally other species of thrush. In the winter of 1976/77, 400 were at a roost at Monmouth. A mixed roost of Fieldfares and Redwings was at Ysgyryd Fach, where 5,000–10,000 birds were present in early February 1977. Elsewhere, there were 2,000 at Llantilio Pertholey in February 1981, 1,250 at Cwmavon in November 1985, 1,200 at Chepstow Park Wood in February 1989 and 4,200 at Llanarth in February 1996.

There are no records of the species having bred in Gwent, or indeed anywhere in Wales, although they have bred in more northerly English counties. There is, however, an interesting Gwent record of a bird observed clearly on 31 July 1979 over woodland adjacent to County Hall, Cwmbran that did raise some intriguing possibilities at the time. Sadly, there were no subsequent sightings. The species is Amber-listed as a breeding species at the UK level owing to a moderate decline in population.

There are no relevant ringing records for this species.

Song Thrush
Bronfraith

Turdus philomelos

A widely distributed and fairly common resident, formerly abundant; also a winter visitor and passage migrant

The Song Thrush is widespread in Britain and breeds in a wide range of habitats, but is more commonly to be seen in woodland and farmland than the ubiquitous Blackbird. It has a distinctive song regularly repeating phrases three or four times, often from a prominent perch.

The 1937 and 1963 *Birds of Monmouthshire* both described the Song Thrush as a common resident breeding species throughout the county, but the 1963 edition stated that it was probably not as common as formerly, and that the decline appeared to coincide with an increase in the number of Blackbirds, which had come to out-number it greatly in all areas. Results of a study on Gwent farmland in 1946–47 were quoted, which showed a ratio of Blackbirds to Song Thrushes of 4:1. Based on local CBC data, the 1977 *Birds of Gwent* indicated that this ratio was still the case. The latest population estimates for the county based on analysis of BBS data (Appendix 1) suggest a ratio more in the order of 7:1.

In the 1st Gwent Atlas the Song Thrush was present in 97% of tetrads, and this remained the case in the 2nd Gwent Atlas, though the proportion of tetrads in the county with *confirmed* or *probable* breeding rose from 87% to 94%.

There has been concern for this species owing to a decline of 59% between 1970 and 1998 in the UK, and it has been designated a Biodiversity Action Plan species. It is an Amber-listed bird in Wales, but recent population data for the Principality shows an increase of 30 per cent for the period 1994–2003, and an increase of 117% between the two Gwent Atlas periods. It appears therefore that it is recovering from a low point, for reasons that are not apparent at present.

The 1977 *Birds of Gwent* noted that small flocks of about 25 birds had been recorded in autumn and winter and that these presumably comprised winter immigrants. Reports of such influxes are, however, rare. One was noted in the Dingestow area on 27th December 1995 and this included c.50 probably continental birds. A further recorded influx was of some 80 birds at Llandegfedd Village on 16th November 2002. Influxes of Song Thrushes from continental Europe, from Belgium and the Netherlands, are well documented (Goodacre, 1960).

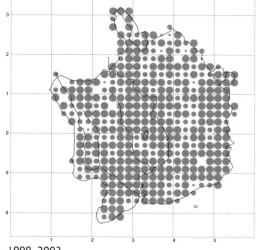

1998–2003

Local ringing data indicate that most of Gwent's Song Thrushes are sedentary, but there are three records of birds ringed in Gwent in the autumn and winter being recovered in the east Midlands in the spring, and of another ringed in Warwick in August 1965 and recovered in Monmouth in December 1967. These records suggest that Gwent is winter host to a substantial number of birds originating from further to the north-east in Britain. The autumn movement of some British Song Thrushes to south-west Europe is well documented (*Migration Atlas*) and the case of a bird, ringed in October 1978 at Monmouth, and recovered on the Cherbourg Peninsula, Northern France (254km SSE), the following January, shows that some of these originate in, or pass through, Gwent.

Gwent Breeding Atlas data and population size

Gwent Atlas	Confirmed tetrads	Probable tetrads	Possible tetrads	Total tetrads	Change in total	Gwent population
1981–1985	294	50	37	381	–	–
1998–2003	283	88	9	380	0%	5,500–6,100 pairs

National breeding data and conservation status

Estimated Welsh population	Welsh CBC/BBS trend 1985–2003	UK CBC/BBS trend 1985–2003	Welsh & (UK) conservation status
93,000 pairs	+117%	+15%	Amber (Green)-listed

Redwing
Coch Dan-aden

Turdus iliacus

A common winter visitor and passage migrant, typically arriving in early October

The soft '*seep*' of the Redwings' flight call on their night migration, typically on an October evening, is often the first indication of their arrival from colder climes. They leave their Scandinavian breeding grounds when the weather is too harsh for them to feed, and move to western Europe, including Britain, France and Spain. Redwings have bred in the Highlands of Scotland in varying but generally small numbers since the 1930s. The species is Amber-listed at the UK level because of the small size of the breeding population.

The 1963 *Birds of Monmouthshire* describes Redwings as a regular and numerous winter visitors near the coast and on lower ground. In the 1977 *Birds of Gwent* they are described as regular winter visitors, which is as true today as it was 30 years ago. Redwings occur in most habitats in Gwent and are noticeably more numerous in cold winters. They can be found feeding in open pasture, on berry-bearing trees and hedges, and also foraging on the woodland floor. The Gwent Levels are a particular stronghold for the species, where flocks of 1,000–2,000 are not unusual. Their numbers depend on the availability of berries in early winter, but they rely on invertebrates when the supply of berries is exhausted. Many of the birds arriving in Britain from September to November move on to south-west France and western Spain later in winter. Flock sizes are often smaller than for Fieldfares with which they often associate.

Redwings arrive in Gwent during early October, with the median first date falling in the first week of the month, though first arrivals in either the previous or following week are also common. The earliest for the county is 10th September, a date when birds were first noted in both 1996 and 2005. In the spring, latest departure dates occur from mid March to the end of April; the latest record for Gwent being the exceptionally late date of 8th June 1969.

In common with Fieldfares, Redwings can be seen in large flocks on passage, especially prior to the onset of very severe winter weather. Such passage was noted during the winters of the 1960s. In particular, immediately before the heavy snow falls of the 1962/63 winter when a 'great migration' of Fieldfares and Redwings was seen flying west at Pontypool on 26th December. Similar exceptional movements were noted in 1968 during anticyclonic weather, when on 19th February around 12,000 birds landed in the fields between St Brides and Peterstone. In February the following year, very heavy concentrations of both species were again apparent with flocks of up to 5,000 flying SSW at Newport, Abergavenny and Pontypool.

No exceptional movements were noted during the 1970s, but in the following decade, some 3,300 birds flew past Sluice Farm in under three hours on 22nd February 1981 and 3,000+ flew over Monmouth in early November 1983. There were no further recorded large movements during the remainder of the 20th century, but subsequently a very heavy passage of thousands was noted at Chepstow on 30th October 2003 and 7,500 were seen flying east-north-east up the Usk Valley during the morning of 16th October 2004.

Several large winter roosts have been recorded in Gwent, usually in association with Fieldfares, but other thrushes also congregate at such sites. At Whitehill, Monmouth in 1976 a roost reached 1,000 birds in January, and towards the end of the year held 2,800 in November. In the Panteg area several large flocks were seen going to roost: 4,300 on 16th November 1980 rising to 5,250 by 23rd November and then 8,750 on 10th December, and remaining at 8,000–9,000 birds until the first week March 1981, after which numbers declined rapidly. At Lasgarn, 1,000 birds roosted in October 1979 and a maximum of 1,800 birds were present in November 1983. Elsewhere, 5,000 birds roosted at Cwm-Ysgubor-tier, Pontypool, in December 1982, and 2,000 roosted near Llandegfedd in February 1984. Other roosts of some 1,000 birds have been recorded in November at Ysgyryd Fawr (1976), Ysgyryd Fach (1979) and Blaina (1992).

Maximum flock sizes for the decade 1994–2003 are shown in Table 92; during 1997–2002 flocks were noticably smaller than past years, mostly in the 50–200 range with the exception of 2,000 at Trellech in December 2000.

Year	Month	Number	Location
1994	Late December	800+	Llandegfed Reservoir
1995	22 October	2,750	Monmouth
1996	3 Feb	1,000	Llangybi
1997	21 February	300	Wyesham
1998	2 February	400	Llandevaud
1999	11 February	350	Llandegfed Reservoir
2000	23 December	2,000	Trellech
2001	18 October	700	Llanwenarth
2002	13 November	300	Goldcliff
2003	30 October	1,000+	Chepstow

Table 92. Maximum winter Redwing flock sizes during 1994–2003

Redwings have a flexible migration pattern, in which individuals may go to the same or widely different wintering areas in successive winters, and they may also make further movements during the winter, according to weather conditions and food availability. Although there are only five ringing records relevant to Gwent, they illustrate all these behaviours. Two birds ringed at Clytha in 1992 and 1994, each returned to the same location in a subsequent winter (1994 and 1995 respectively), whereas another, ringed in Monmouth in January 1977, was controlled in France the following November at a distance of 1,000km south of its previous known wintering site. A bird ringed in Chepstow in November 1985 was controlled in Avon three months later. Finally, one ringed at Clytha in 1998 was controlled in Norway in early October 2001, presumably just prior to its main migratory flight to the south.

Mistle Thrush
Brych y Coed

Turdus viscivorus

A common resident; small passage movements have been recorded in autumn

The preferred habitat of the Mistle Thrush is open woodland, large gardens, farmland and parks. It is sometimes referred to as the 'Storm Cock' from its habit of singing loudly from a prominent treetop on windy days in early spring. It can sometimes be seen guarding a well-berried holly tree, which it vigorously defends from all comers during winter. It is a species that has spread north from its original stronghold in south-east England only in the last two hundred years, but has become a widely distributed breeding resident in the UK.

The 1937 and 1963 *Birds of Monmouthshire*, and the 1977 *Birds of Gwent*, all describe the Mistle Thrush as a common breeding resident and a widely distributed species, locally more common than the Song Thrush. In the 1st Gwent Atlas it was found to be widely distributed in the county, recorded in 90% tetrads, and conspicuously absent only from the treeless moorlands of the far north-west, and several coastal tetrads. In some upland areas it was considered more common than Song Thrush. In the 2nd Gwent Atlas it was found in slightly more tetrads (92%), with gaps in the north-west largely filled, though those on the coast remain.

The long term UK trend shows a 36% fall in population, whilst between the two Gwent Atlases there were declines of 14% in the UK and 5% in Wales. The greatest reductions seem to have occurred in farmland habitats. The slightly increased distribution in Gwent coupled with a significant increase (307 to 340) in tetrads with *confirmed* or *probable* breeding, are suggestive of an increased population, but the figure of 1,200–1,500 pairs derived from BBS data for the 2nd Gwent Atlas (see Appendix 1) represents a considerable reduction from the 3,500 estimated in the 1st Gwent Atlas, equating to a drop from about ten to about four pairs per tetrad. However, owing to the completely different methods of estimation used in the two atlases, the figures should be compared with caution.

In the post breeding period it is often seen in flocks of 30 or so, but slightly larger flocks have been recorded, including 50 at Mynydd Garn Clochdy, Wentwood and Sor Brook on 15th June 1968, 30th July 1970 and 4th August 1999 respectively. There are two March records of flocks, which might suggest a possible spring movement: 75 at Llangeview on 26th March 1976 and 50 at Glascoed on 13th March 1976. Winter records include 60–75 at Penallt on 28th December 1979 and an exceptionally large flock of 400 in Penpergwm on 3rd February 1973. Numbers are known to decline following hard winters. There is only one ringing record relevant to Gwent, which shows a bird to have been present in the same area in November and the following April and is thus consistent with the view that this is a mainly sedentary species.

Despite the sedentary nature of British Mistle Thrushes, modest autumn movements were recorded along the Gwent coast during dedicated migration watches in 1974 and 1975. Most records related to October; the largest however was of 27 birds at Goldcliff on 13th November 1974.

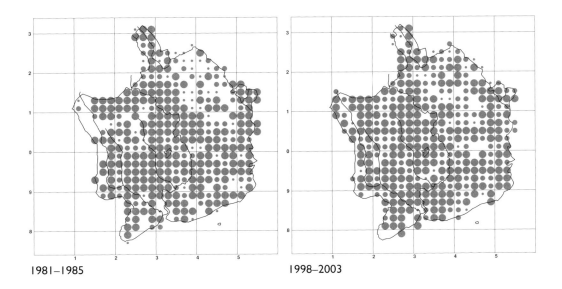

1981–1985   1998–2003

Gwent Breeding Atlas data and population size

Gwent Atlas	Confirmed tetrads	Probable tetrads	Possible tetrads	Total tetrads	Change in total	Gwent population
1981–1985	239	68	42	349	–	–
1998–2003	232	108	23	363	+4%	1,200–1,500 pairs

National breeding data and conservation status

Estimated Welsh population	Welsh CBC/BBS trend 1985–2003	UK CBC/BBS trend 1985–2003	Welsh & (UK) conservation status
22,000 pairs	−5%	−14%	Green (Amber)-listed

Cetti's Warbler
Telor Cetti

Cettia cetti

An uncommon resident; breeding since 2001

Cetti's Warbler is found in dense, damp cover such as brambles and willow scrub, and where reeds are present. Most of its population breeds by sizeable reedbeds. Its skulking nature makes it very difficult to see but it usually makes its presence known with loud bursts of song.

A fairly recent colonist to Great Britain, it arrived in the early 1960s and has extended its status and range since then. Distribution has mostly been to the south of a line from south Wales to the Wash, but with a more recent bias to the south-west where there are milder winters. Probable breeding was first recorded near Canterbury in 1972 and the expanding UK population was approaching 1,000 pairs by the end of the century (Mead 2000).

Since first arriving in Gwent, it has gone from strength to strength and, after a gradual increase in the size of the population during the mid 1990s, some 50 singing males are now apparent, making the county one of Wales' strongholds for the species.

It was first recorded in Gwent in 1988 when a male was heard calling regularly between 16th March and 22nd June at Greenmoor Pool, near Llanwern, and there were further records at this site over the next two years. In 1989 a male was also heard at the grounds of the Monsanto (Solutia) plant adjacent to the Nash Pools, Newport between 5th–7th June and again at this site in 1993.

From 1994 onwards there was a noticeable increase in the number of birds being recorded. In that year up to five were singing at the Nash Pools and a further two were at the Uskmouth reedbeds from 29th August. Since then birds have been recorded annually at Uskmouth, which has become the stronghold for the species.

Ringing at Uskmouth has contributed greatly to our knowledge of Cetti's Warbler in the county. The trapping of a female on 28th August 1998 constituted the first proof of the presence of female Cetti's Warbler in the county. This same individual successfully fledged at least three young in 2001, the first time that there had been conclusive proof of breeding in the county. As an indication of site fidelity and longevity of the species, this bird continued to be caught in subsequent years, showing a brood patch each time and was present at Uskmouth for at least seven years. Since breeding was first confirmed, there has been a significant increase in the number of birds being recorded annually. The number of singing males in the breeding season has gone from 11 in 2001 to 51 in 2005 (Figure 25).

Further evidence of the continued growth of the population is found by looking at the number of birds trapped in the Newport area, with five in 2001, 31 in 2002, 34 in 2003 and 62 in 2004. Perhaps significantly,

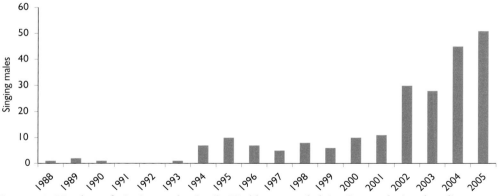

Figure 25. Number of singing male Cetti's Warblers recorded in Gwent during breeding seasons 1988–2005

this increase coincides with the new and managed habitat of the Newport Wetlands Reserve, where the majority of birds are recorded (Clarke 2001–2004).

Following the increase in population there has been a modest expansion in range. The majority of birds are found in the area around Nash near Newport, including the Newport Wetlands Reserve, Nash Pools and various locations at the steelworks complex at Llanwern. Within this area is a matrix of reedbeds and drainage ditches that provide suitable habitat. Drainage ditches, known locally as reens, are a key feature of the Gwent Levels and therefore it is not surprising that where these are overgrown or form part of larger water bodies, they provide further suitable sites for the species' expansion in range. On the Caldicot Level small numbers of singing males have been recorded at various locations as far east as Chepstow since 2002 and, to the west of Newport, at Peterstone since October 2002 and during the breeding season at Coedkernew in 2003 and Marshfield and Peterstone in 2004. The only inland records relate to Llandegfedd Reservoir in September 2004 and February 2005.

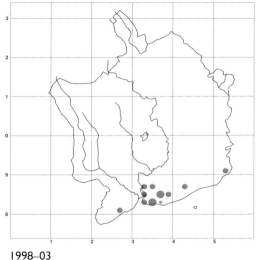

1998–03

There have been two ringing controls in the county, both at Uskmouth. The first, in May 1996, was of an adult male ringed in June 1994 at Littleton Warth, Avon. The second was a female in October 2001 that had been ringed at Thatcham Marsh, Berkshire in August 2000.

Gwent Breeding Atlas data and population size

Gwent Atlas	Confirmed tetrads	Probable tetrads	Possible tetrads	Total tetrads	Change in total	Gwent population
1981–1985	0	0	0	0	–	–
1998–2003	2	8	1	11	–	50–60 pairs

National breeding data and conservation status

Estimated Welsh population	Welsh trend	UK trend	Welsh & UK conservation status
60–80 pairs*	Increasing	Increasing	Green-listed

*The estimate in 2002; true figure must now be much higher.

(Common) **Grasshopper Warbler** *Locustella naevia*
Troellwr Bach

An uncommon summer visitor and passage migrant

The Grasshopper Warbler is a summer visitor arriving in late April–May and departing for wintering grounds in sub-Saharan Africa during August–October. It is an inconspicuous species that is difficult to observe due to its skulking behaviour and liking for low tangled ground cover. It can occupy a wide spectrum of nesting habitats in both wet and dry situations that include marshy areas, rank ground flora habitats on which some scrub is present (especially that associated with clear-felled woodland and new plantations), water meadows, low-grade farmland (where it is ill-drained or in an unkempt state), arable crops, post industrial ground and wet, heathy, 'rhos' pasture. It can be easily overlooked and generally the only clue to its presence is its distinctive 'reeling' song, delivered from a low perch. It is best listened for between late April/May and July when the birds sing from song-posts, mostly at dawn and dusk, but often through the night.

The *Birds of Monmouthshire* (both 1937 and 1963) described the species as a summer visitor that was very local in breeding habitats and not numerous; possibly overlooked in many suitable districts. The 1937 account records breeding near Pant-yr-eos, Cwmbran, Usk, Abergavenny, Raglan, Tintern and Llandogo. In the 1960s singing birds in suitable breeding habitat were noted at Pen-y-fan Pond, Upper Cwmbran, Ysgyryd Fawr and Magor Marsh. A breeding bird survey of the reedbeds at Newport docks in May 1966 recorded six singing males.

The 1977 *Birds of Gwent* noted that since 1963 there had been an apparent increase in numbers during 1967–1971 and a steady decline thereafter. The species' dependence on young forestry plantations was noted, and the decline was attributed to the growth of trees to too great a height and density. The forest at Wentwood was a stronghold for the species from the late 1960s until the mid 1970s. Breeding was first recorded there in 1968, with six pairs in 1969 and 18 heard in the Little Oak area in 1972, but declining thereafter with seven at Little Oak in 1973, four there in 1974, and three at Five Paths in 1974. By the late 1970s there were just two or three records a year and then a seven-year absence of records until three were heard there during the breeding season in 1988. Apart from two, possibly spring passage, records in 1989 there have been no records for the species at the forest since then.

The species was first recorded at Park Wood, Bassaleg in 1969 when there were three singing males, and it was then recorded annually until 1972 when nine were noted, but declining shortly after this until none were recorded after 1975. Elsewhere, during this period breeding was confirmed at Glascoed Common in 1969, Minnetts Wood and Crick in 1971, whilst singing birds were noted regularly at Reddings Inclosure.

From 1976, new strongholds were being reported for the species in the south and east of the county with two confirmed nests in the south during 1976 and six singing males in the east in 1977.

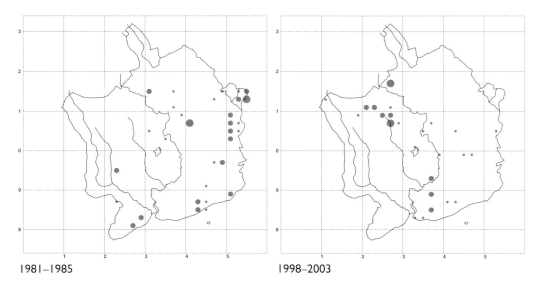

1981–1985   1998–2003

During the 1st Gwent Atlas (1981–1985) the species was recorded in 31 tetrads mainly in the east, especially in the young conifer plantations along the Trellech ridge, where six singing males were recorded in 1982, and in the Wye Valley. There was also a small pocket of birds in and around Magor Reserve, where two singing males were recorded in 1984, and on the Wentlooge Level where breeding was probable in two tetrads. Breeding was also confirmed near Raglan in 1982. Some 50 pairs were thought to be breeding in Gwent at this time.

Between 1986 and 1997 there were no confirmed breeding records although breeding was probable at a number of sites including Chepstow Park Wood and Lady Park Wood in 1986, near Penhow in 1990, Uskmouth reedbeds in 1994 and Llanfair Kilgeddin in 1995.

Distribution in the 2nd Gwent Atlas shows a remarkable change when compared to the earlier atlas, with just two tetrads recording birds during both surveys. It was recorded mainly in the north-west in the area around Blaenavon, along the Usk Valley and on the Caldicot Level; the easterly bias to distribution shown in the previous atlas no longer being apparent. The species was recorded in 25 tetrads, six fewer than in the previous atlas and representing a 19% reduction in range. Both atlases recorded *confirmed* breeding in only two tetrads and the number of tetrads where breeding was *possible* is also comparable. There is a however a 50% decrease from 14 to seven tetrads between the two atlases where breeding was *probable*. No comprehensive survey has been undertaken to enable an accurate assessment to be made of the number of breeding pairs in Gwent. However, based upon atlas data and casual records in *Gwent Bird Reports*, a population size of no more than 35 breeding pairs is suggested.

Spring passage is generally first noted on the coast from the third week of April and into May. The earliest records are 13th April 1997 at Uskmouth and 14th April near Newport in 1996, Uskmouth in 1993, Wentwood in 1980 and Minnetts Wood in 1971. There was an unusually large passage concentration of 22 singing males at Magor Reserve on 4th May 1969.

Unlike spring, the species is unobtrusive during autumn passage and is rarely seen. In Gwent, passage is first noted in late July after cessation of song and runs through into September. Records during this period are few, and those that there are relate predominantly to the county's coastal belt, particularly the reedbeds at Uskmouth where trapping during the autumn now accounts for the majority. Exceptional catches were 12 in 1996, 13 in 2003 and nine in 2005. Late records for the county include 15th September 1991 at Porton, 16th September 2001 at Uskmouth, 24th September 1989 at Lydart (an unusual inland record), and 29th September 1999 at Uskmouth.

The species is Red-listed as available data indicate a rapid population decline between the mid 1960s and mid 1980s (Marchant *et al.*, 1990). The BBS shows wide fluctuations in abundance since 1994, and recently an overall moderate increase. Given suitable habitat and conditions, the species has high reproductive potential, as demonstrated by analysis of nest record data (Glue, 1990).

Gwent Breeding Atlas data and population size

Gwent Atlas	Confirmed tetrads	Probable tetrads	Possible tetrads	Total tetrads	Change in total	Gwent population
1981–1985	2	14	15	31	–	–
1998–2003	2	7	16	25	−19%	<35 pairs

National breeding data and conservation status

Estimated Welsh population	Welsh trend	UK BBS trend 1994–2004	Welsh & UK conservation status
1,700 pairs	Not available	+59%	Red-listed

Aquatic Warbler
Telor y Dŵr

Acrocephalus paludicola

A very rare passage migrant

The Aquatic Warbler is the rarest passerine found in mainland Europe and the only globally threatened one. It has undergone a considerable decline in the last century. It is a summer visitor to eastern Europe, its major breeding strongholds being in Belarus, Ukraine, Poland and Hungary. A global population of around

13,000–19,000 singing males was estimated in 2005 (*AWCT, 2005*). Although not breeding in the UK, it is recorded whilst on passage during the autumn when birds move west through the Netherlands, Belgium, northern France and the southern part of Britain. Sites where it is found on migration are of considerable importance as they provide suitable habitats for feeding and resting. The species is Red-listed in both the UK and Wales.

The 2002 *Birds in Wales* gives a total of 65 individuals as having been recorded in Wales up to 2000. In Gwent, the species has been recorded on 11 separate occasions. All records relate to juvenile birds and occurred during the month of August. The first county record was on 20th August 1989 at Sluice Farm on the Gwent Levels. The following year a bird was found at the same site on 10th August. All subsequent records involve birds that were trapped in the reedbeds of the lagoons at Uskmouth (Table 93) during a dedicated programme of ringing. This confirmed that the species was a regular but rare migrant to the area, and identified Uskmouth as probably the second most significant known site for the species in Wales, after Kenfig National Nature Reserve (Clarke 2006).

Year	Date
1996	11 August
1997	20 August
2001	16 & 22 August
2002	14 &19 August
2003	6 & 18 August
2006	15 August

Table 93. Dates of Aquatic Warblers trapped and ringed at the Uskmouth reedbeds

Sedge Warbler
Telor yr Hesg

Acrocephalus scoenobaenus

A fairly common summer visitor and passage migrant

The Sedge Warbler is found in rank vegetation, usually reeds or sedge swamp with bushes, and along overgrown ditches and ponds. It is often conspicuous as it delivers its song from a branch or a reed stem, making short flights during its singing.

It was described in both the 1937 and 1963 *Birds of Monmouthshire* as a not uncommon summer visitor breeding regularly in suitable localities, most numerous amongst the reens (drainage channels) of the coastal levels and locally distributed along river valleys. Its presence on the coastal levels is further confirmed by a skin at the National Museum, Cardiff, which records that the bird was collected at Peterstone on 21st April 1940. The 1977 *Birds of Gwent* reaffirmed earlier assessments of status and distribution up to 1972, after which there was thought to be a reduction in numbers up until at least the mid-1970s, reflecting an overall national decline that was evident from CBC data. The CBC shows that the population nationally reached a peak in 1968 but thereafter fell progressively to a low point in 1974 and lower again in 1985. The impact of serious rainfall deficits in wintering grounds in the Sahel region of Africa has been identified as the cause of these population declines.

A partial survey of the Wentlooge Levels during 1977 found at least 38 singing males, including at least 17 confirmed or probable breeding pairs. This survey demonstrated that there were fewer Sedge Warblers than Reed Warblers, which was contrary to the indications of previous records. That Sedge Warblers were more widespread than Reed Warblers might have inflated the general impression of Sedge Warbler numbers previously. A complete survey of the Gwent Levels during 1978–79 (Table 94) revealed a maximum of 168 breeding pairs (Mortimer *et al.*, 1978, 1979; Venables & Titcombe 1980).

	Confirmed	Probable	Possible	Total
Wentlooge Level (Glam.)	2	5	23	30
Wentlooge Level (Gwent)	21	13	51	85
Newport docks	0	3	10	13
Caldicot Level	18	19	3	40

Table 94. Number of breeding pairs of Sedge Warblers recorded during surveys of Gwent Levels 1978–1979

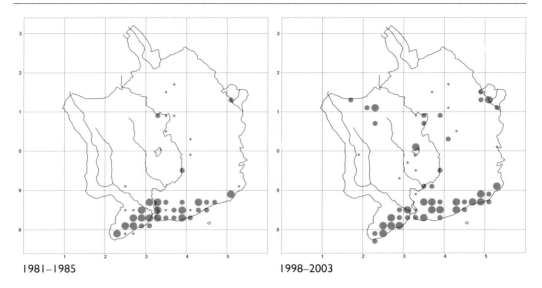

1981–1985   1998–2003

The 1st Gwent Atlas described the Sedge Warbler as being 'surprisingly scarce'. *Confirmed* breeding was recorded only on the Caldicot and Wentlooge Levels, where suitable vegetation was found fringing reens, and at the Magor Marsh and Llanwern. Elsewhere, birds were recorded singing or holding territory in the Usk Valley, and an isolated bird was noted near Monmouth. The Gwent population during the atlas period was estimated to be as high as 100–200 pairs.

Data from the 2nd Gwent Atlas confirms that the stronghold for the species continues to be the Gwent Levels. Elsewhere, breeding was *confirmed* at Llandegfedd Reservoir, in the Monmouth area and in the north of the county, and *probable* in the Usk valley. A comparison of atlas data shows a 29% expansion of range and a 50% increase of *probable* and *confirmed* breeding records between survey periods. The expansion in range relates largely to new sites along the Usk Valley, Llandegfedd Reservoir, Monmouth area and, perhaps more surprisingly, at higher altitude in the north of the county in the Heads of the Valleys area, where birds were present at ponds, the legacy of industrial activity. This expansion in range is consistent with a national increase of +29% in the period between the two Gwent Atlases.

Although difficult to calculate, the current estimated breeding population based upon previous survey work and the noted increase in range is likely to be some 150–250 breeding pairs, though extrapolation from sample tetrads during the atlas period suggests a lower range of 60–140 pairs.

There have been two exceptionally early records of single birds: on 25th March 1965 and 31st March 2003, but more typically birds start arriving from the second week of April with the main passage occurring in the last week of April.

Autumn passage starts in late July and peaks in the second or third week of August before trailing off in September. Good numbers of migrants pass through the reedbeds on the coastal levels during this time. Systematic ringing at the Uskmouth reedbeds provides an insight into the true strength of this passage with 153, 361, 205 and 499 being trapped during August during 2002–2005 respectively. Last migrants are usually recorded in late September, the latest being at Uskmouth on 10th October 1993.

The pattern from ringing recoveries in Gwent demonstrates that birds from the west and north of Britain move south-east or south through South Wales during the autumn. Birds controlled at Uskmouth, Newport include individuals ringed originally in Eire, Northern Ireland, Scotland and Anglesey and Powys in Wales. Subsequent movements are of birds travelling in the same direction through the English West Country counties, and the south coast, before crossing to mainland Europe. Such movement is well illustrated by a bird ringed originally at Uskmouth on 25th July 2004 that was subsequently controlled initially ten days later at Walberswick in Suffolk, and then in Loire-Atlantique, France after a further 14 days. The reedbeds of South Wales, southern England and northwest France are known locations where Sedge Warblers lay down fat reserves before undertaking rapid long-haul flights across Iberia, North Africa and the Sahara to wintering grounds. There are seven records of birds ringed at Uskmouth being trapped subsequently in mainland Europe. A single bird at Brabant, Belgium and in France, two at Finistère (418km south-south-west) and four in Loire-Atlantique (480km south). A further bird trapped at Magor Marsh in July 2002 had originally been ringed in Charente-Maritime, France, the previous August.

Gwent Breeding Atlas data and population size

Gwent Atlas	Confirmed tetrads	Probable tetrads	Possible tetrads	Total tetrads	Change in total	Gwent population
1981–1985	15	15	15	45	–	–
1998–2003	20	25	13	58	+29%	150–250 pairs

National breeding data and conservation status

Estimated Welsh population	Welsh trend	UK CBC/BBS trend 1985–2003	Welsh & UK conservation status
17,700	Not available	+52%	Green-listed

Marsh Warbler
Telor y Gwerni

Acrocephalus palustris

A rare summer visitor; has bred

The Marsh Warbler is a scarce breeding bird in Britain and has a Red-listed conservation status. During the 1970s and 1980s it was a regular breeder in the Severn Valley in Worcestershire but in recent years it has been confined mainly to south-east England. It is a rare bird in Wales.

There have been five records in Gwent. The first was of a pair that successfully bred, raising five young, at the steelworks complex at Llanwern in 1972 (1994 *Birds in Wales*). This is the only proven breeding record for Wales. The remaining four records were of single birds, generally in song, at St Brides during 4th–5th June 1981, alongside the River Usk at Llanhennock during 1st–2nd June 1983, at Magor Reserve on 9th July 1991 and at Peterstone during 22nd June–10th July 1996; the latter bird was obviously holding a territory.

(Eurasian) **Reed Warbler**
Telor y Cyrs

Acrocephalus scirpaceus

A fairly common summer visitor and passage migrant

The Reed Warbler, as its name suggests, is closely associated with *Phragmites* reeds. It is found predominantly in extensive reedbeds and in the reed fringes of suitable water bodies. It is not always the easiest bird to see as it spends a great deal of its time low down in deep vegetation, even when singing. Its song does however give away its presence, its chattering being a conspicuous feature of reedbeds during the summer.

The species is at the north-western limits of its range in southern Britain and, until it expanded its range into Wales, Lancashire and south-west England from the 1960s onwards, it was a rare breeding bird in Wales and a very scarce passage migrant (1994 *Birds in Wales*). Its range in Gwent is limited by the distribution of suitable habitat, which is confined largely to the southern part of the county on the Gwent Levels, where reed-fringed reens and reedbeds are found. The 1937 and 1963 *Birds of Monmouthshire* both referred to this species as a scarce and very local summer visitor noted as breeding in the Marshfield district, near Abergavenny and near Llanrothal on the Herefordshire border. Several records of breeding were noted near Rumney in 1951, 1952 and 1960.

In the 1960s over 50 and 41 birds were reported at Newport Docks in 1964 and 1967 respectively, and 20 were heard there in May 1966. Nevertheless during this and the first half of the following decade, the species was still regarded as an uncommon summer visitor to Gwent. During the 1970s the species was recorded more widely with a greater number of records from the Wentlooge Level, but rarely of more than three birds at any one site. The 1977 *Birds of Gwent* referred to the species as being an uncommon but fairly regular visitor, mainly to areas on the coastal levels, notably Newport Docks, which at the time had extensive reedbeds that supported a sizeable colony of birds, and also Magor Marsh and the Wentlooge Level.

In the 1970s it was suspected that the species might be under-recorded in the county and consequently a partial survey of the Wentlooge Level was undertaken in 1977. From this, an estimate of some 70–100 pairs was derived (Mortimer *et al.*, 1978). A complete survey of the Gwent Levels was undertaken during 1978–79 and this revealed a maximum of 196 breeding pairs (Mortimer *et al.*, 1979; Venables & Titcombe 1980). Over half of the birds (57%) were found on the reens of the Wentlooge Level whereas only 10% were found in the equivalent habitat of the Caldicot Level (Table 95). The survey hypothesised that

this was as a consequence of the relative amounts of reedbed on the two levels. The importance of reedbeds found at industrial sites was particularly noteworthy, with about 1/3 of the total breeding pairs on the levels being recorded around Newport at sites on the east bank of the River Usk, Newport Docks and Llanwern Steelworks.

	Confirmed	Probable	Possible	Total
Wentlooge Level (Glam.)	4	9	8	21
Wentlooge Level (Gwent)	14	36	41	91
Newport docks	0	11	16	27
Caldicot Level	3	45	9	57

Table 95. Number of breeding pairs of Reed Warblers recorded during surveys of Gwent Levels 1978–1979

The 1st Gwent Atlas noted that breeding was confined largely to the low-lying southern part of the county at edges of reens, and in more extensive reedbeds as at Magor Marsh, Llanwern Steelworks and areas adjacent to the River Usk near Newport. Elsewhere, *probable* breeding was recorded only at Llanarth, and *possible* breeding records in the Usk Valley, which at the time were considered almost certainly to refer to passage birds.

The 2nd Gwent Atlas data confirm that the stronghold for the species continues to be the Gwent Levels. Elsewhere, breeding was *confirmed* at Llandegfedd reservoir and *probable* breeding in the Usk valley. A comparison of data from the two atlases shows a 29% expansion of range and a 48% increase of *probable* and *confirmed* breeding records between survey periods. The expansion relates largely to the levels, especially to the east of Newport on the Caldicot Level.

The species has expanded its range in the UK since the 1960s but its long-term trend is uncertain. CBC/BBS and WBS surveys show progressive moderate increases, but CES census data shows a decline from 1983 until the early 1990s, followed by a partial recovery and another much more recent decline.

The Gwent population was estimated to be as high as 200–300 pairs at the time of the 1st Gwent Atlas. The current estimate, based on sample tetrads, is 310–570 pairs.

The establishment of the Newport Wetlands Reserve and the consequent provision of new reedbeds at Uskmouth, together with the management of pre-existing reedbeds there, have been noticeably beneficial for the species, especially since the maturing of the new beds and the raising of water levels in existing beds from 2002.

Typically birds first arrive in Gwent from the third week of April. The 1977 *Birds of Gwent* noted an exceptionally early record of a single bird at Magor Marsh on 7th March 1965, but more recently the earliest record has been two birds at Uskmouth on 11th April 1997.

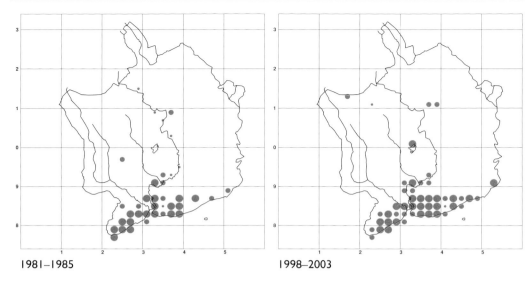

1981–1985   1998–2003

Adult Reed Warblers start to leave their breeding grounds in Britain and Ireland in late July, with peak passage across the south coast of England in the last third of August. The passage of juveniles extends into October (*BWP*). Systematic ringing during the autumn at the Uskmouth reedbeds provides an insight into the strength of this passage through Gwent, with 177, 311, 269 and 342 being trapped during August over the years 2002–2005 respectively. Ringing at the coastal reedbeds has also provided some evidence that there is a passage of birds moving through from further west in Wales and Ireland. Subsequent movement of these, and locally-bred birds, is then south through England before reaching western France, the Iberian Peninsula, then crossing into Africa via Morocco. Such movements can be swift: for example a bird ringed at the Uskmouth reedbeds on 15th August 2003 was re-trapped six days later in the Vendée region of France some 585km to the south. Other examples of autumn migration include a bird ringed at Uskmouth on 24th August 2003 reaching Lot-et-Garonne, France some 834km and 24 days later, and one ringed at Magor Marsh on 23rd August 1993 reaching Guipuzcoa, Spain some 918km and also 24 days later.

There is just one record relating to wintering grounds: a bird retrapped at Uskmouth on 3rd August 1997 had been ringed originally in Senegal five years earlier on 29th March 1992. Latest departure dates from Gwent are 8th October 1995 at Uskmouth and 9th October 2001 at Goldcliff.

Gwent Breeding Atlas data and population size

Gwent Atlas	Confirmed tetrads	Probable tetrads	Possible tetrads	Total tetrads	Change in total	Gwent population
1981–1985	20	11	7	38	–	–
1998–2003	25	21	3	49	+29%	310–570 pairs

National breeding data and conservation status

Estimated Welsh population	Welsh trend	UK CBC/BBS trend 1985–2003	Welsh & UK conservation status
3,600	Not available	+46%	Green-listed

Melodious Warbler
Telor Pêr

Hippolais polyglotta

A very rare visitor

The Melodious Warbler is a south-western European species which occurs regularly during passage periods, mostly in autumn, on the south-west coasts of England and west coast of Wales, although it winters in West Africa. There is only one accepted Gwent record: a single bird at Goldcliff on 2nd August 1969.

Dartford Warbler
Telor Dartford

Sylvia undata

A very rare visitor, but seen with increasing frequency in recent years; has bred

This is one of only two resident warbler species to be found in Britain. It favours heathland habitats, breeding principally in gorse and heather, and its stronghold is in the southern counties of England.

Gwent has little suitable habitat for the species, and there are just six records for the county, one of which represents the first breeding record for Wales. A female, present at Peterstone during 3rd December 1984–1st January 1985, constituted the first county record and was followed by another female at the Uskmouth ashponds during 28th November 1992–13th March 1993. The first breeding record for Wales occurred in 1998 at a site in the north-west of the county, where two broods of four and three young successfully fledged. A third brood failed owing to predation. Birds then remained in the area until at least 9th December, with a further sighting of an adult male on 15th March 1999. Disappointingly, following a very cold spell of weather with heavy snow during April 1999 there were no further records from this site. There are three other records: a male in song at Cefn Bach, Abertillery on 28th May 2000, up to two females/immatures at the Uskmouth reedbeds during November 2003–January 2004, and up to two at Bryn Arw, Abergavenny, during November–December 2003.

Barred Warbler
Telor Rhesog

Sylvia nisoria

A very rare visitor

The Barred Warbler is an eastern European species that occurs in Wales only as a rare passage migrant, chiefly on the coast. An immature bird at Uskmouth during 29th August–1st September 1994 is the only Gwent record.

Blackcap
Telor Penddu

Sylvia atricapilla

A common summer visitor and passage migrant; also an uncommon winter visitor

The Blackcap is a common and widespread summer visitor to all parts of Britain south of the Scottish Highlands (1988–91 National Atlas). It is found in most habitats that provide a combination of trees and shrubs, including deciduous woods and copses that have a good understorey of brambles or shrubs, overgrown hedgerows with trees, and large mature gardens.

The 1937 and 1963 *Birds of Monmouthshire* both indicated it was a numerous summer visitor to the county, with a distribution similar to Garden Warbler, which was in turn described as 'well distributed and breeding in suitable wooded localities'.

In the 1st Gwent Atlas it was found in 85% of tetrads, being completely absent only from the relatively treeless regions of the north-west. Additionally, large areas in the eastern half of the county, where deciduous woodland is scarce, had only *possible* breeding records, suggesting a relative scarcity in these parts.

The 2nd Gwent Atlas shows presence of Blackcap in 93% of tetrads, and an increase from 71% to 86% in the number of tetrads with *probable* or *confirmed* breeding, indicating an expansion of range in the county, and an increase in population density. Most of the newly occupied tetrads are in the north-west, while many of those with enhanced evidence of breeding are in the east. This undoubted expansion reflects the national situation where numbers of breeding Blackcaps have shown a steady increase since the 1950s (1988–91 National Atlas). In the period between the two Gwent Atlases the UK population

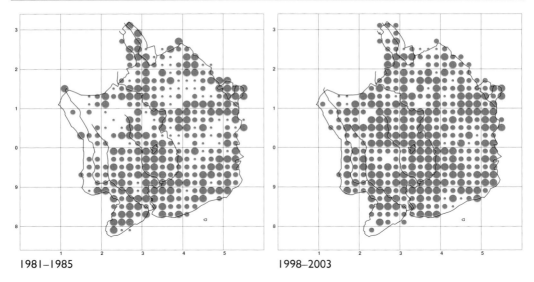

| 1981–1985 | 1998–2003 |

trend has been +46%, while the recent trend in Wales (1994–2004) has been +62%. Using the BBS and atlas-based methods (see Appendix 1), the current breeding population for Gwent is estimated at 8,500–13,000 pairs, compared with a figure of 9,000 pairs estimated from CBC data during the 1st Gwent Atlas.

The first singing birds are generally recorded in the last few days of March or the first two weeks of April, and these are generally considered to be the newly arrived breeders, freshly returned from winter quarters. At the end of the breeding season, numbers decline rapidly during late August to mid-September and records in the second half of September are greatly reduced. Ringing at Uskmouth gives an insight into autumn passage, with peak movements of birds being noted during September, and smaller numbers still being trapped into early October. During the mornings of the first three weeks of September, catches of 20–30 birds are usual: for example 28 birds on 22nd September 2002, 34 on 3rd September 2004 and 24 on 13th September 2005 (Goldcliff Ringing Group). Most of the British breeding population is thought to spend the winter in southern Iberia and north-west Africa, but there have been a few ringing recoveries south of the Sahara (*Migration Atlas*), including a young bird ringed in Gwent that was recovered in Ivory Coast, 5,160km to the south.

The 1963 *Birds of Monmouthshire* refers to 'several instances of Blackcaps wintering in the county in recent years', and during the early 1970s these occurrences became annual, with at least nine birds in some winters. The winter of 1976/77 was remarkable for a total of at least 30 birds and, since then, numbers have been in double figures in most winters, with a maximum of 38 in 1995/96. When wintering Blackcaps first started to be recorded in Britain, it was assumed that they were British breeders that had not left for their usual wintering grounds. However, ringing studies have conclusively demonstrated that they are birds from west-central and central Europe that have migrated to Britain in a north-westerly direction (*Migration Atlas*). They are recorded in Gwent from October to mid-March, with largest numbers usually in January and February, and most reports are from gardens, where they visit feeders and take a wide variety of foods. In 1994, one bird that had become a regular garden visitor during the winter stayed until 14th April, showing that not all April birds are new arrivals.

There are two ringing records that show wintering individuals returning to Gwent in subsequent winters, one returning to the same Monmouth garden the following winter, and the other turning up four winters later, less than 2km from the ringing site. Other interesting ringing records of winter birds concern one ringed on the Suffolk coast, due east of Gwent, on 14th September that was recovered at Uskmouth 25 days later, and a young bird ringed in Slovenia on 16th September that was recovered at Tintern on 26th March the next year.

Gwent Breeding Atlas data and population size

Gwent Atlas	Confirmed tetrads	Probable tetrads	Possible tetrads	Total tetrads	Change in total	Gwent population
1981–1985	151	127	56	334	–	–
1998–2003	186	163	19	368	+10%	8,500–13,000 pairs

National breeding data and conservation status

Estimated Welsh population	Welsh BBS trend 1994–2003*	UK CBC/BBS trend 1985–2003	Welsh & UK conservation status
106,000 pairs	+64%	+46%	Green-listed

*Welsh CBC/BBS trend 1985–2003 not available

Garden Warbler
Telor yr Ardd

Sylvia borin

A fairly common summer visitor and passage migrant

The Garden Warbler has similar habitat requirements to Blackcap, favouring woodland and woodland edge with a dense understorey of shrubs or bramble thicket, or overgrown hedgerows, and areas of dense scrub with small trees. It is a widely distributed summer visitor in Britain apart from northern Scotland. In Wales, it is generally much less abundant than the Blackcap but, according to the 1994 *Birds in Wales*, it often becomes the more numerous of the two in sessile oak woodlands at higher altitudes owing to its greater tolerance of less dense undergrowth. The 1937 and 1963 *Birds of Monmouthshire* both described it as fairly numerous and breeding widely in suitable wooded localities.

Although the Garden Warbler's song is distinctive to the experienced ear, it can be confused with that of the Blackcap, and it is not as far carrying as that of many other woodland songsters. In addition, the bird itself is not visually conspicuous, and all these factors may have led to its presence in some tetrads being overlooked in both Gwent Atlases. The 1st Gwent Atlas showed it to occur mainly in the lowland agricultural areas of the Usk Valley and the relatively well-wooded areas of the east and north-east, while it was largely absent from the coastal levels and substantial parts of the central plateau and western valleys.

The 2nd Gwent Atlas shows an 11% increase in the number of occupied tetrads, and 95% of this increase has occurred to the west of gridline East 30, the line that runs through western Newport, Pontypool and eastern Abergavenny, and for much of its length forms a border between the western valleys and the rest of the county. Many of the gaps seen in the western valleys have thus been filled in the period between the two atlases. The number of tetrads with *probable* or *confirmed* breeding has also risen by 24%, suggesting a general increase in population density during this period. However, these observations are not reflected in corresponding national trends: in the period between the Gwent Atlases both UK and Welsh trends were negative, in the latter case very strongly negative at −38%.

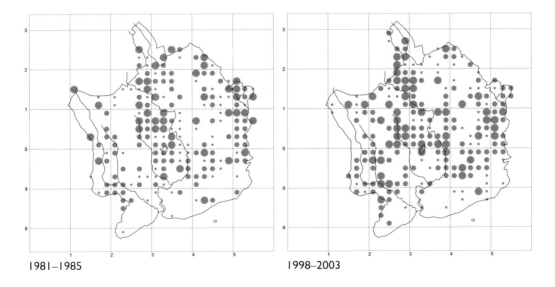

1981–1985

1998–2003

Estimates of the Gwent population for this species have been particularly problematic, with the BBS and atlas-based methods producing widely differing estimates (see Appendix 1) of 540 and 2,270 pairs. The lower estimate implies a mean of only 2–3 pairs per occupied tetrad, whereas local observers' experience suggests perhaps twice this value. The middle of the range is proposed as a realistic approximation.

There have been two March records in Gwent, both prior to 1977, the earliest being on 19th March. However, first arrivals are usually in April with a wide spread of dates across the month, and a median date of 20th April. Passage records in habitats adjoining the coast are regular during late August and September but involve very small numbers, usually ones and twos. There have been two October occurrences: on 2nd October 2002 and 8th October 1995.

British Garden Warblers winter in sub-Saharan Africa and both ringing and direct observation indicate that many of them, including those from Wales and the West, converge on southeast England in autumn, before making the relatively short crossing of the English Channel (*Migration Atlas*). Of three ringing records relevant to Gwent, two are consistent with this pattern: one involving a Glamorgan-hatched bird passing through Gwent in its in first autumn and another, an adult ringed in Gwent, being recovered near Calais. The third record is of an adult ringed in Gwent in early August, which was recaptured a week later 115km to the south-south-west on the coast of southern Devon.

Gwent Breeding Atlas data and population size

Gwent Atlas	Confirmed tetrads	Probable tetrads	Possible tetrads	Total tetrads	Change in total	Gwent population
1981–1985	43	88	64	195	–	–
1998–2003	55	107	54	216	+11%	540–2,300 pairs

National breeding data and conservation status

Estimated Welsh population	Welsh CBC/BBS trend 1985–2003	UK CBC/BBS trend 1985–2003	Welsh & UK conservation status
31,000 pairs	−38%	−16%	Green-listed

Lesser Whitethroat
Llwydfron Fach

Sylvia curruca

An uncommon summer visitor and passage migrant, which has recently declined

The favoured habitats of the Lesser Whitethroat are dense scrub, or farmland with thick overgrown hedgerows and scattered trees. It was formerly a bird of southern and central England, and of limited occurrence in Wales beyond the lowlands and river valleys of the border counties.

The 1937 *Birds of Monmouthshire* described it as being an uncommon and very local summer visitor, although having possibly increased 'in recent years', that was absent from the hill districts of the north and north-west. Breeding was noted in the south-west of the county, but was also considered probable near Llanrothel and possible where singing birds had been recorded: near Abergavenny, Usk, Monmouth, Chepstow Newport and Peterstone. The 1963 *Birds of Monmouthshire* described it as breeding rather locally, and commented that it was easily overlooked and might therefore be commoner than suspected.

Between the National Atlases of 1968–72 and 1988–91, its range expanded to the north and west, and it became more common and widespread in Wales. This development was very apparent in Gwent, where *Gwent Bird Reports* documented a very obvious increase in numbers during the early 1970s, while in the late 1970s and early 1980s local CBC plots at Nash and Llanhennock recorded doublings in the numbers of Lesser Whitethroat territories. At the time of the 1st Gwent Atlas (1981–85) the county population was probably higher than it had ever been before. The main stronghold was the south of the county, particularly the coastal levels, where the old hawthorn hedgerows provided ideal habitat, but there was also a good scatter of occupied tetrads in the central farmland areas, and a few on the eastern border.

Starting in the late 1980s, there has been a national decrease in Lesser Whitethroat numbers, with the UK BBS showing a decline of 44% since the time of the 1st Gwent Atlas. Reasons for this are not understood but are thought to stem from problems on migration and/or in the winter range. The national decline is reflected in the 2nd Gwent Atlas, which shows a decrease of 15% in the number of occupied tetrads. However, the distribution of this decrease is very uneven: the 10-km squares prefixed ST (roughly the southern 40% of the county) show a decrease of 38% in the number of occupied tetrads, whereas the squares prefixed SO (the northern part of the county) show an increase of 27%. The severe loss of old hawthorn hedges, which has occurred on much of the coastal levels in recent years, has probably contributed to the loss of Lesser Whitethroats from several tetrads in this particular area.

On the basis of sample tetrads, the county population is currently estimated to be in the range 70–180 pairs, which corresponds closely to the estimate produced by analysis of BBS data (see Appendix 1). Even allowing for the difficulties involved in comparison of numbers obtained by different methods, this represents a dramatic decline from the population of 3,000 pairs estimated from CBC data at the time of the 1st Gwent Atlas.

Since 1971, first arrivals in the county have fallen between 12th April and 5th May, but with a very obvious cluster in the period 22nd–26th April, and a median date of 24th April. The main influx usually occurs during either the last week in April or the first in May. Return passage is sometimes noted in late July, but most passage records occur during August and the first half of September. Although passage birds may turn up at Llandegfedd Reservoir and many other inland locations, they are most frequently recorded on the coast. Late September records are very scarce, and single sightings on 5th October 1998 and 7th November 1999, at Pandy and Gobion respectively, are exceptional.

Unlike most of our other warblers, the Lesser Whitethroat takes a south-easterly migration route in the autumn, and passes around the eastern end of the Mediterranean to reach east Africa. This is nicely illustrated by the case of a bird that was ringed during the 1973 breeding season in Gwent, and recovered some months later (date uncertain) in the Lebanon. The only other ringing record relevant to Gwent concerns a young bird

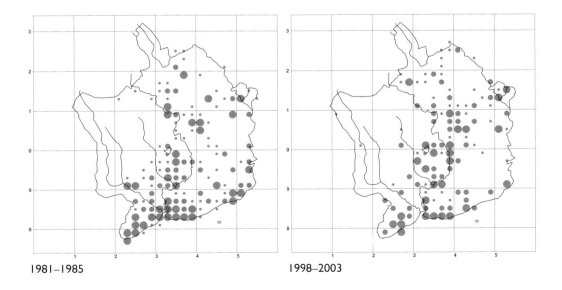

1981–1985   1998–2003

ringed in June at Aberthaw in Glamorgan, and recovered in August at Llandegfedd Reservoir, presumably heading for a sea-crossing from the coast of south-east England.

Gwent Breeding Atlas data and population size

Gwent Atlas	Confirmed tetrads	Probable tetrads	Possible tetrads	Total tetrads	Change in total	Gwent population
1981–1985	36	34	61	131	–	–
1998–2003	27	42	42	111	−15%	70–180 pairs

National breeding data and conservation status

Estimated Welsh population	Welsh CBC/BBS trend 1985–2003	UK CBC/BBS trend 1985–2003	Welsh & UK conservation status
3,800 pairs	−35%	−44%	Green-listed

(Common) **Whitethroat**   *Sylvia communis*
Llwydfron

A common summer visitor and passage migrant

The Whitethroat is a widespread summer visitor to the UK, absent only from the higher mountains and the far north. It is a bird of scrub, bramble patches and hedgerows, and seemingly at home even in the severely-cut hedgerows that are so often a feature of our modern farmland.

The first records for the county both relate to 1934, when two birds were 'taken' at Peterstone in April and July. Later in the same decade, the 1937 *Birds of Monmouthshire* described it as a common warbler, 'second in numbers to the Willow Warbler, and nesting everywhere, except far into the hill districts'. In the early 1960s it was again noted as common, and particularly so in the hedgerows of the coastal areas (1963 *Birds of Monmouthshire*). This situation changed in 1969, when around two-thirds of the British breeding population failed to return from their winter quarters in the Sahel region of Africa. This population crash was a consequence of poor winter survival, related to the prolonged drought in the Sahel (1988–91 National Atlas). In succeeding years there was a slow recovery, though not to its former strength, and with fluctuating numbers from year to year.

Work for the 1st Gwent Atlas (1981–85) began at a time when the population had recovered fairly well, so despite another national decline in 1984, Whitethroats were nevertheless recorded in 70% of the county's tetrads. Their distribution showed a bias toward the south and east of the county and there were notable gaps in the western valleys and some northerly areas. In 1991, several observers reported large drops in numbers of Whitethroats in Gwent, and it transpired that this was the result of yet another crash on a national scale (1988–91 National Atlas). Since then, populations have again shown some recovery and the UK short-term index shows a 39% increase during 1994–2004.

The 2nd Gwent Atlas took place at a time of relatively high numbers, and shows a slight increase in occupied tetrads to 73%. The bias to the south of the county appears to have become more pronounced compared to 1981–85, but there is increased penetration into the western valleys, while numerous gaps have appeared at the northern end of the Gwent section of the Wye Valley. The proportion of *probable* and *confirmed* breeding records has increased by 15%, which suggests an increase in population density in occupied areas, and this contention is supported by an increase in the Welsh population index of 13% in the period between the two Gwent Atlases. The county population is estimated at 3,600–4,400 pairs, compared with an estimate of 3,000 pairs during the 1st Gwent Atlas.

Since 1965, first arrivals have generally been noted from 11th April to the end of the month, though there are two earlier dates: – 4th April 1980 and 6th April 1965. There are no March records, and in 1966, 1970 and 1978, first reports were as late as early May. The median date for first arrival is 18th April. In most years the main influx of local breeders appears to occur in the last week of April or the first in May. Return passage can

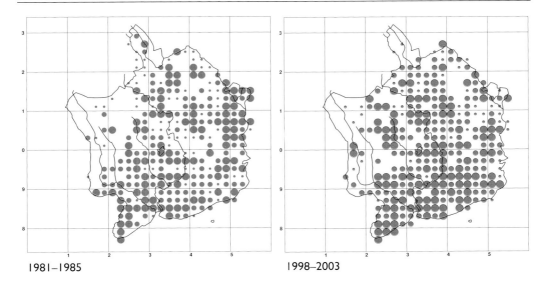

1981–1985   1998–2003

be noted on the coast as early as late July, but in most years is not noticeable until late August and early September. Stragglers frequently occur in the last week of September and there have been three October records: 1st October 1996, 2nd October 1988 and on the extremely late date of 30th October 1986. There are no ringing recovery records relevant to Gwent, but as the total number of Whitethroats ringed in the county is only about 270 (by comparison, the number for Willow Warblers is about 3,400), this is not altogether surprising.

Gwent Breeding Atlas data and population size

Gwent Atlas	Confirmed tetrads	Probable tetrads	Possible tetrads	Total tetrads	Change in total	Gwent population
1981–1985	105	105	67	277	–	–
1998–2003	113	129	44	286	+3%	3,600–4,400 pairs

National breeding data and conservation status

Estimated Welsh population	Welsh CBC/BBS trend 1985–2003	UK CBC/BBS trend 1985–2003	Welsh & UK conservation status
69,000 pairs	+13%	+136%	Green-listed

Yellow-browed Warbler
Telor Aelfelyn

Phylloscopus inornatus

A very rare autumn passage migrant

The Yellow-browed Warbler breeds in Siberia but occurs in Britain as a regular autumn passage migrant in very small numbers. There are three Gwent records, all of single birds: at West Pill on 14th October 1988, St Brides on 3rd October 1993 and in a copse near the Uskmouth reedbeds at Newport Wetlands Reserve on 26th October 2003.

Wood Warbler
Telor y Coed

Phylloscopus sibilitrix

A fairly common if declining summer visitor

The Wood Warbler is one of the characteristic species of the Welsh woodlands and the Principality is its major stronghold in Britain. Its basic requirement is closed canopy woodland with little or no understorey, and this can be provided in both broadleaved and conifer woodlands: in the former generally through grazing and in the latter through shading. In Gwent, mature Larch woods are now regularly occupied, some of them with a denser ground flora than is normally associated with this species, but evergreen woods are usually occupied only if some broadleaved trees remain.

The 1963 *Birds of Monmouthshire* recorded the Wood Warbler as a regular summer visitor, not numerous and breeding very locally, while the 1977 *Birds of Gwent* described it as locally fairly numerous in areas of sessile oak and mixed deciduous woodland on hillsides.

The unmistakeable accelerating trill that announces the arrival of the Wood Warbler in the county is first heard during April. The mean first date is 18th April, though arrivals have been as early as 4th April 1999 and 5th April in both 1987 and 1996. The mean last date of the year is 23rd August, and the latest records are 2nd September 2000 and 10th October 1969. Concentations of birds on autumn passage are unusual and ten at Llandegfedd Reservoir on 7th August 1969 is the most notable example in the county.

During 1981–85, the 1st Gwent Atlas recorded the species in 156 tetrads with strongholds in the upland sheep-grazed woods of the north and west of the county, and in some woods in the Wye Valley, and occasionally in conifer plantations, especially larch. Using an estimated figure of ten pairs/occupied tetrad the suggested county population was 1,000–1,500 pairs.

During the late 1980s, and 1990s, few systematic counts were made but breeding was regularly reported from woodlands in the Wye Valley, Wentwood and the western valleys. A decline was suggested in Wentwood and at Trelleck in 1996, but subsequent records indicate a recovery. Conifer plantation nesting was first reported in the western valleys in 1995, and this habitat is being increasingly used in Wentwood: all eight nests found there in 2000 were under larch.

The 2nd Gwent Atlas recorded the Wood Warbler in only 121 tetrads, representing a 22% decline in distribution since the 1st Gwent Atlas. The strongholds are still in the uplands of the north and west, and and a decline has occurred in some central and north-central regions of the county. Interestingly, the number of tetrads with *confirmed* breeding has not shown any decline. The county population is now estimated at 720–1,600

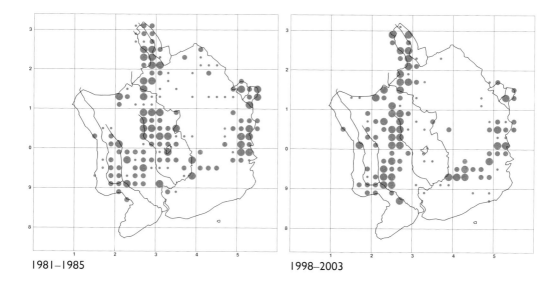

1981–1985

1998–2003

pairs, although this is likely to be high, given the estimated size of the Welsh population and the difficulty of making estimations based on singing males. The UK CBC/BBS data indicate a 68% decline during the same period, considerably greater than has been found for Gwent, presumably because much of the national decline would have been from non- optimum habitat, particularly in south-east England.

Since 2001, regular counts have been made in 1.5km² plots in part of Wentwood and in Chepstow Park Wood (J Lewis, pers. obs.). Wentwood is predominantly larch and Chepstow Park has mixed broadleaves and conifers. The numbers of locations where singing males were recorded is compared with the number of pairs/nests found in Table 96. Despite the difficulties of finding females or nests (which may mean that some were missed), the data show that the number of singing locations is not a good indication of breeding numbers. Discrepancies arise because all males may not be mated, and others can be polygynous and move to new areas in attempt to find additional mates.

Year	Wentwood		Chepstow Park Wood	
	Singing males	Pairs/nests	Singing males	Pairs/nests
2001	28	14	18	7
2002	20	11	10	3
2003	no count	no count	16	7
2004	25	15	6	1

Table 96. Number of singing locations and pairs/nests of Wood Warblers found in study plots in Wentwood and Chepstow Park Wood 2001–2004

The *Migration Atlas* indicates that the Wood Warbler is the most common trans-Saharan migrant for which there are no recoveries of British birds on the wintering grounds, and consequently, many of its movements remain unknown. The species winters in Africa, and migrates via the central and eastern Mediterranean route, returning via a more westerly route. Some records suggest a lack of fidelity to the natal area among young birds, with recoveries in a subsequent season up to 350km away, although some of these birds could still have been on passage, while others have been recovered close to the natal site. Most adults are faithful to their breeding areas year on year, but two males have been recorded 19km and 66km away in subsequent breeding seasons.

There is only one ringing recovery on the BTO database for Gwent: a chick ringed near Tintern in 1983, was caught at St Albans Head, Dorset on its autumn migration. However, between 2003 and 2005, the Wentwood/Chepstow Park study has yielded eight local recoveries of birds ringed during the study. Of six recoveries of birds ringed as nestlings, four females were subsquently found breeding between 200m and 800m away from their natal site, whereas two males were found 400m and 9km away. Among birds ringed as adults, one adult male retained the same territory between years, and an adult female moved 200m. Because of the local nature of this study there would be a bias against detecting more distant movements, but the ringing data do suggest that a substantial proportion of the breeding population returns to the same area.

The future does not look particularly good for the Wood Warbler. Those nesting in larch plantations can have their nests destroyed during felling operations, while in the more traditional upland oak woods, changing agricultural practices and grant incentives to reduce winter grazing to encourage regeneration could also have a negative impact.

Gwent Breeding Atlas data and population size

Gwent Atlas	Confirmed tetrads	Probable tetrads	Possible tetrads	Total tetrads	Change in total	Gwent population
1981–1985	39	70	46	155	–	–
1998–2003	40	49	32	121	−22%	720–1,600 pairs

National breeding data and conservation status

Estimated Welsh population	Welsh trend	UK CBC/BBS trend 1985–2003	Welsh & (UK) conservation status
2,800	Not available	−68%	Green (Amber)-listed

(Common) **Chiffchaff** **Siff-saff**

Phylloscopus collibita

A common summer visitor and passage migrant, and a scarce winter visitor

In Britain the Chiffchaff is a widespread summer visitor, though more numerous in the south, breeding in mature deciduous woodlands that include good ground cover for nesting. The 1994 *Birds in Wales* notes that in many Welsh woodlands, sheep grazing results in a lack of ground cover and a corresponding absence of Chiffchaffs.

In Gwent, the proportion of woodland that is sheep-grazed is lower than in most parts of Wales, and perhaps as a consequence, the species is common and widely distributed in the county. In former times, however, it seems to have been rather local on the coastal levels, and absent from the 'wilder country in the north' (1963 *Birds of Monmouthshire*). In the 1st Gwent Atlas Chiffchaffs were found in 87% of tetrads, being completely absent only from the relatively treeless regions of the northwest. In large areas in the eastern half of the county, where deciduous woodland is scarce, there were many occupied tetrads with only *possible* breeding records, suggesting a relatively low population density in these parts.

The 2nd Gwent Atlas shows the presence of Chiffchaffs in 95% of tetrads, and an increase from 65% to 89% in the number of tetrads with *probable* or *confirmed* breeding. This indicates an expansion of range in the county and probably an increase in population density. Most of the newly occupied tetrads are in the north-west, while many of those with enhanced evidence of breeding are in the east. Chiffchaff populations in Britain underwent a short-term decline in the early 1980s but recovered later in the decade (1988–91 National Atlas), and in subsequent years they have continued to increase, with indices of +76% in the UK and +46% in Wales during 1994–2004. The 1st Gwent Atlas was, therefore, conducted at a time when national populations were low, and the data from the 2nd Gwent Atlas reflects the species' subsequent recovery and expansion. Using the BBS and atlas-based methods (see Appendix 1) the current breeding population for Gwent is estimated to be in the range of 5,600–21,000 pairs. Based on CBC data, the population in the 1st Gwent Atlas was estimated at 7–8,000 pairs.

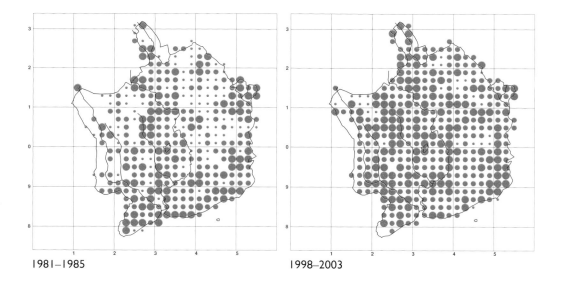

1981–1985   1998–2003

The Chiffchaff is one of the earliest of our summer visitors to arrive and with its distinctive but monotonous song it is a characteristic herald of spring. In the 1960s and 1970s new arrivals were seldom heard in Gwent until the second half of March, but they have got steadily earlier and in the decade 1994–2003 the average first date was 6th March. In recent years, the first major influx of birds has followed the first record by one to two weeks, and has ranged from 11th–24th March. Return passage begins in late August and sometimes produces large 'falls' such as the mixed concentration of 150 Chiffchaffs and Willow Warblers at Llandegfedd Reservoir on 21st August 1994. Passage continues during September with sizeable numbers, often 20–30 birds, being seen at coastal locations throughout the month, and smaller numbers well into October.

British Chiffchaffs are known to migrate initially in a south-easterly direction to take advantage of the shorter crossing over the English Channel, and from there to follow the Atlantic coasts of France, Spain and Portugal to the Mediterranean basin, with many progressing down the west coast of Africa to winter as far south as Guinea Bissau (*Migration Atlas*). Ringing data suggests that the migration of Gwent's Chiffchaffs conforms to this pattern. Of the five Gwent-ringed birds recovered more than 100km from the ringing site, two have been recovered during passage periods at Dungeness, Kent, a third from the west coast of France, and a fourth from Agadir, Morocco. However, although all the above birds were juveniles, they were ringed during the migration season in August or September, and may have been passing through the county from natal sites elsewhere in Britain. This possibility is emphasised by the fourth recovery at over 100km, which concerned a juvenile ringed in August at Llandegfedd Reservoir and recovered the next spring in Derbyshire. The recovery, at Usk, in April 1993 of an individual ringed two winters previously in Senegal suggests that this country is the ultimate destination of at least some of Gwent's birds. Chiffchaffs that breed in Britain belong to the race *P. c. collybita*, but passage migrants include Fennoscandian and Siberian birds of the races *P. c. abietinus* and *P. c. tristis*. Single birds showing the characteristics of *abietinus* were recorded in Gwent at Peterstone on 19th October 1992, and near Usk during 7th–22nd November of the same year. Despite the last-mentioned record, Chiffchaffs are not recorded regularly in Gwent during November, having been noted in only eleven of the last twenty years, but with increased frequency in the last decade.

The 1963 *Birds of Monmouthshire* makes no mention of wintering Chiffchaffs, but since regular recording began in the county, about 40 years ago, records in the mid-winter period of December–February have been almost annual. The number of birds reported each winter has varied from two to eight, but these must represent only a small fraction of the true winter population. Records are scattered widely across the county, often coming from gardens and the coastal levels where Magor Marsh appears to be a favoured locality.

As with passage Chiffchaffs, the British winter population is diverse and includes, in addition to birds of the British race, representatives of both *abietinus* and *tristis*. Among Chiffchaffs wintering in Gwent, a possible example of the race *tristis* was recorded at Magor during 21st December–1st January in winter 1996/97.

Gwent Breeding Atlas data and population size

Gwent Atlas	Confirmed tetrads	Probable tetrads	Possible tetrads	Total tetrads	Change in total	Gwent population
1981–1985	93	164	87	334	–	–
1998–2003	144	207	27	378	+13%	5,600–21,000 pairs

National breeding data and conservation status

Estimated Welsh population	Welsh CBC/BBS trend 1985–2003	UK CBC/BBS trend 1985–2003	Welsh & UK conservation status
75,000 pairs	+127%	+154%	Green-listed

Willow Warbler
Telor yr Helyg

Phylloscopus trochilus

A common summer visitor and passage migrant; much declined in recent years

The Willow Warbler is abundant and widespread throughout Britain, breeding in most areas where there are trees or scrub in combination with ground cover for nesting. Closed-canopy woodland is avoided, but woodland rides and edges are often occupied and young plantations are particularly favoured.

The 1963 *Birds of Monmouthshire* implies that the Willow Warbler was the most widespread and abundant summer visitor to the county at that time. This status was certainly the case by the early 1980s when the 1st

Gwent Atlas showed it to occur in 95% of the tetrads in the county, with *confirmed* breeding in 57%. Densities were low on the coastal levels, but CBC plots elsewhere in the county had high densities, with approximately 150 pairs per tetrad at Penallt and even higher in some other areas. On the basis of these data the county population was estimated at 55,000 pairs.

Subsequently, in the early 1990s, there was a population crash on a national scale that appeared to be the result of low adult survival, probably caused by conditions in their winter quarters south of the Sahara. Since then, numbers in the UK overall have recovered to some extent and stabilised, so although the long-term index shows a decline of 45%, the ten-year trend shows no overall change in recent years. In Wales, by contrast, the short-term trend shows a decline of 34%. It is interesting to note that despite the national decline, which was beginning at the time, the newly developed Bryn Bach country park was impressively colonised by Willow Warblers in the early 1990s, as new plantations of birch, oak and other tree species began to reach heights of 3–5 metres. A survey of the park by Gwent County Council in 1995 found 45–47 territories at a density of 0.78/ha, which compares with an average for Wales at the time of 0.19/ha (1994 *Birds in Wales*).

The national decline is reflected in the results from the 2nd Gwent Atlas, which show that the number of tetrads with Willow Warblers has dropped to 91% and, perhaps more tellingly, the number with *confirmed* breeding has dropped to only 42%. In consequence, the Willow Warbler has been replaced by the Chiffchaff as the county's most widespread warbler, and in 2002 it was reported to be less numerous than the Chiffchaff in both the Wye and Monnow valleys. The BBS and Atlas-based methods indicate a county population in the range 5,000–11,000 pairs. Even if it is allowed that these estimation methods are very different from that used in the 1st Gwent Atlas, this represents a calamitous drop in the population.

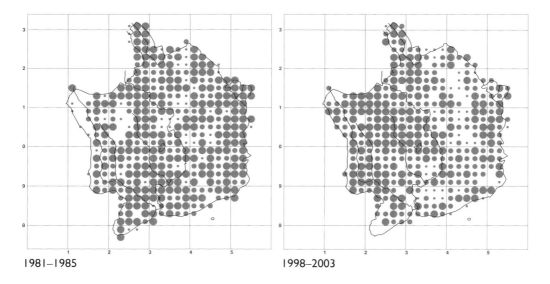

1981–1985   1998–2003

The Willow Warbler typically arrives some three weeks later than the Chiffchaff, and in the last decade the average first date for Gwent has been 27th March. The main influx has followed some ten days behind, usually between 5th and 10th April.

After the breeding season, return passage is noted throughout August, occasionally as early as late July, and examples of larger passage concentrations have included 40+ at Peterstone on 12th August 1977, 50+ at Llandegfedd Reservoir on 9th August 1997, 30 at Newport Wetlands Reserve on 19th August 2001 and about 30 at the same location on 8th August 2002. Small numbers continue to be recorded during September, becoming scarcer as the month progresses, while there are just three October records: in 1983, 1990 and 1994, and two very late records on 18th November 1970 and 11th November 1983. There have been only two winter records, both in January 1983, when there was bird at Magor Reserve on the 9th and another at Osbaston on the 10th and 17th. Such records are very scarce in Britain generally, and occurred in only ten 10-km squares during the three winters of the Winter Atlas.

Of Willow Warblers ringed in Gwent, there have been no recoveries of adults ringed on territories, and only three of birds ringed as nestlings, two of which were very local and within a few days of the ringing date. Ringing data, therefore, give little direct information on the migratory movements of the Gwent breeding population. On the other hand, data from other categories, mostly young birds ringed in their first autumn, provide an excellent illustration of the direction of passage movements through the county. Of the ten relevant recoveries, five that had been ringed in Gwent were recovered, variously, in the Isle of Man the following spring, Dorset, Hampshire, Somerset and Sussex, whereas four that were recovered in Gwent had been ringed in the Isle of Man, Merseyside, Portland the previous year and Guernsey the previous year (see Appendix 9 for details). These locations lie on a north/north-north-west to south/south-east axis though Gwent, suggesting this is a major migratory direction through the county, and concurring with the conclusion of the *Migration Atlas* that the initial migration of young birds is oriented in a south/south-easterly direction. The only foreign recovery of a Gwent-ringed bird was in southwest France, and illustrates the route of onward passage to wintering grounds to the south of the Sahara.

Gwent Breeding Atlas data and population size

Gwent Atlas	Confirmed tetrads	Probable tetrads	Possible tetrads	Total tetrads	Change in total	Gwent population
1981–1985	225	103	47	375	–	–
1998–2003	165	162	34	361	−4%	5,000–11,000 pairs

National breeding data and conservation status

Estimated Welsh population	Welsh CBC/BBS trend 1985–2003	UK CBC/BBS trend 1985–2003	Welsh & UK conservation status
160,000–200,000 pairs	−64%	−52%	Amber-listed

Goldcrest
Dryw Eurben

Regulus regulus

Resident; abundant in favoured habitats. Also a passage migrant in small numbers

The Goldcrest is a diminutive bird, with a thin high-pitched song to match, and a preference for feeding in conifer foliage. These factors conspire to make it easily over-looked, though it is often tame and confiding when it is seen. It is common and widespread in the UK wherever there are coniferous woodlands but will also breed in deciduous woodland, particularly where there is a good covering of ivy on the trees. Its status in Wales has benefited greatly from the afforestation programmes of the mid 20th century (1994 *Birds in Wales*). Although the 1988–91 National Atlas states that Goldcrests are less likely to be found in woods smaller than 10ha, gardens in Gwent with just a few mature conifers are commonly occupied, as are churchyards with mature yew trees.

The 1937 *Birds of Monmouthshire* indicated that the Goldcrest was widespread in the county at that time. Systematic records, however, date only from 1963, when its population was in the first stages of recovery from the disastrous effects of the previous very severe winter. It was evidently quite rare at this time, and from 1963 to 1966 the *Gwent Bird Report* published all records received, which were few and far between. However, the species can raise two large broods per year and has a great capacity for rapid recovery, so by the late 1960s it was being described as widespread and common again. Its recovery was doubtless aided by the maturation of the commercial forestry plantations that now form its most important habitat.

The 1st Gwent Atlas showed Goldcrests to be present in 77% of tetrads, with *confirmed* or *probable* breeding in 57%. Their breeding strongholds were in the large forestry blocks, and they were absent only from the largely treeless hills of the northwest, and from the coastal levels. The 2nd Gwent Atlas shows an expansion of breeding range, with 84% of tetrads now occupied. The general distribution has remained unchanged, with gaps again concentrated in the northwest and on the coastal levels. The proportion of tetrads with *confirmed* or *probable* breeding has risen substantially to 75%, suggesting an increase in population density, but this contrasts with negative trends over the same period for both the UK and Wales. Using the BBS and atlas-based methods (see Appendix 1) the county population is estimated to be in the range 7,000–11,000 pairs, which is more than double the total of 3,600 suggested in the 1st Gwent Atlas.

Despite its diminutive size, the Goldcrest is an accomplished migrant. Significant numbers migrate to Britain from northern Europe during autumn, many of them crossing the North Sea directly rather than taking the much shorter route across the English Channel. By contrast, the movements of British Goldcrests are not well known because so few are ringed in breeding habitat owing to the practical difficulties presented by birds that nest high in coniferous trees. What ringing data there are, suggest a general southerly or south-easterly movement in autumn, with a north to north-westerly return in spring (*Migration Atlas*). However, despite a statement in the 1963 *Birds of Monmouthshire* that numbers of Goldcrests in the county are considerably increased in winter by immigration, there are no Gwent records of large flocks in the mid-winter months that might support this assertion. The only good evidence for Goldcrests being winter visitors to the county is provided by two December recoveries of juveniles that were ringed earlier in the year in Merseyside and the Isle of Man, respectively. The latter of these was ringed in mid-November, showing that passage movements are still occurring late in the year.

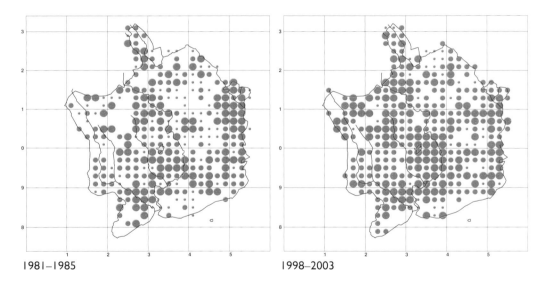

1981–1985   1998–2003

Although evidence for winter immigration may be sparse, there are many observations to suggest that Goldcrests are regular passage migrants through the county. Light autumn passage is recorded annually from September to November (occasionally in August), and peaks during late September–early October. It is most often manifested as the occurrence of birds in habitats where they are not usually seen, including gardens, Llandegfedd Reservoir and, particularly, along the coast, and its scale is probably under-recorded. The more notable passage records on the coast include ten at Collister Pill on 2nd October 1989, 20 at Goldcliff Pill on 10th October 1992, c.22 at West Pill on 27th September 1998 and 10+ at Newport Wetlands Reserve during October 2002, and again there on 25th September and 3rd October 2004.

Flocks of 20–50 are sometimes recorded in woodland habitats from September to November, and gatherings of up to 100 have been recorded in late November at Cilfeigan Park in 1980 and Manor Wood in 1983. However, although these woodland flocks may refer to passage birds, they could also be gatherings of local birds.

Spring passage is not well marked in the county but is sometimes detected in the form of ones and twos at coastal sites in March.

Gwent Breeding Atlas data and population size

Gwent Atlas	Confirmed tetrads	Probable tetrads	Possible tetrads	Total tetrads	Change in total	Gwent population
1981–1985	106	118	78	302	–	–
1998–2003	138	158	35	331	+10%	7,000–11,000 pairs

National breeding data and conservation status

Estimated Welsh population	Welsh CBC/BBS trend 1985–2003	UK CBC/BBS trend 1985–2003	Welsh & UK conservation status
85,000 pairs	−28%	−6%	Green-listed

Firecrest
Dryw Penfflamgoch

Regulus ignicapilla

A scarce passage migrant and winter visitor; has bred

The Firecrest and Goldcrest share the accolade of being Europe's smallest species of bird. The Firecrest is a rare breeder in southern Britain and has bred in only a handful of Welsh counties, the first being Gwent, most probably during the late 1970s. It is Amber-listed throughout the UK.

The 1937 *Birds of Monmouthshire* noted that the species had been recorded only twice: a skin in the collection at Newport museum was labelled Pontypool Park, 1926; and a male had been picked up dead near Peterstone on 1st February 1937. The 1963 *Birds of Monmouthshire* added only one further record of one seen at Llandegfedd Churchyard on 11th January 1942. Thirty years elapsed before the next record, a single bird at Henllys on 11th January 1972, and a second bird in the same year on 30th October and 1st November at Mamhilad. Birds have been recorded almost annually since this time, the exceptions being 1981, 1985, 1992–93 and 1998–99.

The 1977 *Birds of Gwent* noted that the species was an irregular winter visitor, but had become a recent resident and probable breeder in one area. The first suggestion of breeding in the county came in March 1974 when a bird was heard in song at Llandegfedd Reservoir. The following year began a series of records from the Wentwood Forest with at least three birds heard in song on a number of occasions between May and June. Singing was also heard in June 1976, and between May and July 1977 when up to three birds were present, two at least being in song. Nest building was subsequently reported, but was abandoned following the theft of nesting material by a Chaffinch. There was just one record of song in May 1978 and then up to five birds in song throughout the breeding season in 1979, when a nest was seen to be robbed of its material by a Chiffchaff. Singing was heard again in the forest during survey work for the 1st Gwent Atlas: in 1980, when two birds were present and in 1983, when one was heard on a single date. Successful breeding was eventually confirmed in 1987 when a party of two adults and at least four juveniles were seen on several dates in August. Then in 1988, at least four pairs were present and possibly as many as five additional singing males. One pair probably had two broods and a total of possibly 15 juveniles was estimated. Breeding reached a peak at the Wentwood in 1989 when 21 singing males were noted, and subsequently 11 pairs were recorded breeding with at least five raising two broods. A minimum total of 75 fledged young resulted. The breeding population declined thereafter, possibly due to cold weather, though 12 males were singing in 1990 and newly fledged young were seen in three areas. There have been no further confirmed breeding records, although singing was recorded during the survey work for the 2nd Gwent Atlas, when a bird was heard in May 2000 for two days and again in 2002, when possibly two birds were present.

Breeding has possibly occurred elsewhere in Gwent with a number of singing birds recorded from other sites with suitable habitat. At least three were noted in the Trelleck area during May and June 1987 and up to two birds were singing at Fedw Wood in 1988, 1989 and again in 1990. Tintern, Highmeadow Woods, Whitebrook and Cwmyoy all had singing birds in April and May during 1990. During the 2nd Gwent Atlas period there were up to three at Coed-y-Prior Common in 2002 and one at Llanfair Kilgeddin.

Most records in March and April relate to the arrival of birds at breeding grounds and very few suggest an obvious spring passage.

There are two September records at Mynydd Garn Wern on the 12th in 1983 and at Llandegfedd Reservoir on the 7th in 1994. Although early, these records probably relate to migrant birds but it is possible they may have originated locally. Autumn migrants are noted chiefly during October, with a total of 12 birds recorded, the majority being in the second half of the month. Most records relate to single birds, but two were at Goytre on 19th October 1973 and at Peterstone on 17th October 1979. Passage birds continue into November with four records between 1995 and 2001, the latest being 18th November 2001 at Allt-yr-yn, Newport.

There are two clear cases of overwintering in the county, involving three birds: two were seen frequenting a hedgerow at Henllys between 30th October 1988 and 6th March 1989 and one was at Abergavenny between 25th October and 31st December 1990. A further four December records, between 1986 and 2000, and eight January records are also likely to relate to wintering birds.

Gwent Breeding Atlas data and population size

Gwent Atlas	Confirmed tetrads	Probable tetrads	Possible tetrads	Total tetrads	Change in total	Gwent population
1981–1985	0	0	0	0	–	–
1998–2003	0	2	1	3	+3 tetrads	0

Spotted Flycatcher
Gwybedog Mannog

Muscicapa striata

A passage migrant and fairly common summer visitor, now declining

The Spotted Flycatcher is widely distributed throughout the British Isles. It is a bird of open woodland or woodland edge and is often found in parks and gardens during the summer. From an exposed perch it stands sentinel waiting for flying insect prey, launching itself into flight after its quarry and frequently returning to the favoured perch.

The 1937 and 1963 *Birds of Monmouthshire* both described the Spotted Flycatcher as a well distributed and fairly numerous summer visitor and breeding species, although it was noted as being absent from the higher and wilder country in the north of the county. The 1977 *Birds of Gwent* also referred to it being fairly common and breeding widely, but added that records from the coastal strip referred to mostly passage birds in August or September. During 1970s, there were some noticeable records where the species was breeding at high density. For example, 11 pairs were reported in an area 200m in diameter at Llanfihangel Crucorney in 1976, while at Lasgarn Wood, 15 pairs bred in 1977, 12 in 1978 and 14 in 1979. Good numbers of breeding pairs continued to be reported during the 1980s, especially from the central districts, and by the time of the 1st Gwent Atlas the species was still described as being widespread. Its distribution was, however, noted as being patchy and it was considered to be generally scarcer on the Gwent Levels and in the west of the county by comparison to the central and eastern areas.

Since the 1960s the species has shown a national decline, especially in southern Britain. The position is less clear in Wales, due to the limited availability of data, although there is some evidence of a decline since the 1980s. In Gwent, there was a very noticeable decline in casual records from 1990 onwards. The national decline has been linked to a noted decrease in the annual survival rates of birds in their first year of life (Freeman & Crick, 2003), and possibly as a result of a deterioration in woodland habitats. However, conditions on the wintering grounds or along migration routes are most likely to be significant factors (Fuller *et al.*, 2005).

A comparison between the 1st and 2nd Gwent Atlases shows that the species' range in the county has declined by 22%. Although still widespread, it is patchily distributed and the number of tetrads occupied has fallen, especially on the Gwent Levels and in the mid-county area of the Usk Valley. There has been a significant 37% decline in the number of tetrads where breeding was *confirmed* and a further decline of 14% where breeding was thought *probable*. In the 1st Gwent Atlas, a county population of about 1,250 pairs was calculated based on there being five pairs per occupied tetrad. At the time, this was considered likely to be an underestimate.

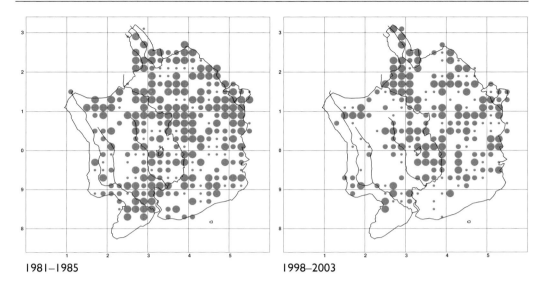

1981–1985   1998–2003

From data collected from sample tetrads during the 2nd Gwent Atlas, albeit a small sample, the current popu-lation is thought to be some 490–830 pairs. Although the approach to calculating populations between Gwent Atlases is different, there can nevertheless be no doubt that the species has undergone a significant decline in both range and population density between the atlas periods.

The Spotted Flycatcher is one of our latest summer migrants to arrive with first sightings in the county generally being in late April/early May. The earliest records are 14th April 1984 and 16th April 1981. Autumn passage begins in August and is generally over by mid-September. There have, however, been a few records from the early days of October and one exceptionally late bird at Kilgwrrwg on 11th November 1973. Flocks are very seldom seen and, when encountered, relate to post breeding, possibly migratory parties. The largest groups on record are of 30 birds at St Woolas' cemetery in August 1980, 20 at Llandewi Skirrid in late July 1986 and 14 at Black Rock on 17th September 1986.

There is just one notable ringing record: a bird ringed at Twyn-Y-Sheriff, Raglan in July 1986 was subsequently controlled at Cádiz, Spain some 1,675km to the south in November of the same year.

Gwent Breeding Atlas data and population size

Gwent Atlas	Confirmed tetrads	Probable tetrads	Possible tetrads	Total tetrads	Change in total	Gwent population
1981–1985	145	73	59	277	–	–
1998–2003	92	63	60	215	−22%	490–830 pairs

National breeding data and conservation status

Estimated Welsh population	Welsh CBC/BBS trend 1985–2003	UK CBC/BBS trend 1985–2003	Welsh & (UK) conservation status
9,400 pairs	−39%	−72%	Amber (Red)-listed

Pied Flycatcher
Gwybedog Brith

Ficedula hypoleuca

A fairly common passage migrant and summer visitor

This attractively marked summer visitor is a characteristic bird of upland deciduous woodland, and Wales is its stronghold in Britain. Pied Flycatchers arrive in Gwent in early April: the median first date is 15th April and ranges from 9th April to 5th May. They are conspicuous whether breeding in natural holes, such as in Alder trees along the River Honddu, or in nest boxes in woodland. Until the mid 1960s they were regarded as rare in the county with only 19 records between 1899 and 1962 (1963 *Birds of Monmouthshire*). The provision of nest boxes in the 1960s undoubtedly helped the initial increase in numbers of breeding Pied Flycatchers and it is now a numerous breeding bird, mainly in the north-west of the county but also in some other woodlands.

In the 1st Gwent Atlas Pied Flycatchers were found in 97 tetrads (almost 25%) with breeding *confirmed* or *probable* in 16%. Birds were concentrated in the Black Mountains, on the Blorenge and in woods in the northern part of the Afon Llwyd and Usk valleys. In the Wye Valley breeding was confirmed in nine tetrads but birds were more thinly scattered than in the north-west. In the 2nd Gwent Atlas the species was found in 96 tetrads (24%), but with *confirmed* or *probable* breeding in 19%. This indicates very little change in distribution between the two atlas surveys. Birds were again mainly concentrated in the north-west although they bred in ten tetrads in the Wye Valley and Trellech plateau, with others in Wentwood and in the Usk Valley and an isolated occurrence west of Newport. There has been a marked decline in the east of the county (see below).

Using a sample-based average of 4–5 pairs/tetrad in those tetrads with *probable* or *confirmed* breeding, the county population is estimated as 400–450. Numbers vary greatly between tetrads, with some having 30 or more pairs and some only one. This estimate compares with the 500 pairs suggested in the 1st Gwent Atlas. More widely in the UK, the Pied Flycatcher appears to be declining with a 35% decline detected by BBS between 1994 and 2004. A decline has also been noted in the Netherlands, where it is thought that climate change has advanced the peak period of food availability in deciduous forests, and the birds have not so far compensated for this change by breeding earlier (Both, 2002).

Nest box colonies have been monitored at a range of sites including Whitebrook, Penallt, Bettws Newydd, Lasgarn Wood, Llanellen, Penperlleni, Cwmyoy and the Grwyne Fawr. In the 1970s and 1980s numerous boxes had been erected and regular nest box reports appeared in *Gwent Bird Reports*. However, colonies were monitored for a few years and then for various reasons, such as the death of key recorders such as Percy Playford, reduced interest of observers, vandalism, or old nest boxes falling into disrepair, the colonies were abandoned. However, new ones have since been started. In the nest box colony heyday, as in 1981, as many as 120 boxes contained Pied Flycatchers. One of the largest and regularly monitored colonies was at Cwmyoy along the Afon Honddu, with 26 boxes occupied in 1977, but that colony no longer exists, although a few birds nest in riverside Alders. Another large nest box colony was in the Grwyne Fawr Valley: where 30 boxes were in use in 1984, 33 in 1985 and 36 in 1986. In 2003, 52 occupied boxes were checked at a new colony in the Grwyne Fawr. Elsewhere colonies at Llanellen, Lasgarn Wood and Cwmavon varied in size from year to year but until the early 1990s often exceeded 10 pairs: for example 20 at Cwmavon in 1991. At Penallt Old Church wooden boxes were put up in 1979 and three were occupied by 1986. Six boxes were occupied there in 1989, 1991 and 1992, after which a decline set in: to four pairs in 1993, two pairs 1997 and 2002 and none in 2003 or 2004. It was noted at this wood, and at another wood at Penallt, that males were singing in April but there was an apparent absence of females.

The highest numbers of nestlings were ringed in the 1980s with a maximum of 780 (and also 110 adults) ringed in 1984. Numbers ringed have been very much lower in the last decade. In all, almost 9,000 nestlings and over 1,300 adults were ringed between 1980 and 2003. Young birds ringed in Gwent have returned in their second year to other colonies either nearby or further afield, including elsewhere in Gwent and locations in Breconshire, Herefordshire, Gloucestershire, Shropshire, Lancashire and Devon. Birds originating from other colonies in neighbouring counties, such as at the Nagshead Reserve in Gloucestershire, also turn up as breeding birds in Gwent. Movements from a greater distance have included one at Fforest Coal Pit that originated from Breconshire, one at Llanvair Kilgeddin from Shropshire, and two at nest boxes in a Penallt wood: one from

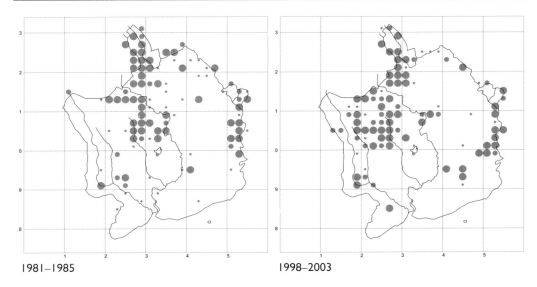

| 1981–1985 | 1998–2003 |

Clwyd,139km to the north and the other from Shropshire, 73km away. A Pied Flycatcher whose ring was found in a Sparrowhawk nest in Lasgarn Wood was hatched in Rifton in Devon.

Adults however, are generally quite faithful to their breeding location from season to season. This is exemplified by an observation of Percy Playford's that one female returned to the same colony for six successive seasons in the 1970s, having migrated each year to its wintering quarters in West Africa and back again. There have been no recoveries of Gwent Pied Flycatchers in West Africa. However, some have been recovered on migration at intermediate locations, mostly on the return passage in April. These have included two in north-west France, two in south-west France, one in south-west Spain, one in Algeria and one in Switzerland.

Once the young have fledged they are rarely seen and so it is difficult to give departure dates. In some years birds are seen up to the end of August but occasionally there are October records. The median last date seen is 23rd August but if two June and July records are excluded then it is 28th August. The latest date recorded is 6th October.

Gwent Breeding Atlas data and population size

Gwent Atlas	Confirmed tetrads	Probable tetrads	Possible tetrads	Total tetrads	Change in total	Gwent population
1981–1985	48	15	34	97	–	–
1998–2003	52	23	21	96	–1%	400–450 pairs

National breeding data and conservation status

Estimated Welsh population	Welsh trend	UK BBS trend 1994–2004	Welsh & UK conservation status
18,000 pairs	Not available	–35%	Green-listed

Bearded Tit
Titw Barfog

Panurus biarmicus

A rare passage migrant and winter visitor, but bred for the first time in 2005

The Bearded Tit has a very local distribution in Britain owing to its requirement for extensive areas of common reed, and eastern England has been its traditional stronghold. In the last half century it has spread westwards and from the mid 1960s to late 1990s it bred erratically at several locations in Wales, the nearest to Gwent being the Kenfig National Nature Reserve (1994 *Birds in Wales*).

Until recently, extensive reedbeds have been a scarce habitat in Gwent, and this is reflected in the meagre total of just twelve records of Bearded Tits to 2003. The first of these was at Newport Docks in 1966, where up to three birds, including at least one male, were present from 29th January to at least 6th March. The remaining records up till 2002 (listed in Table 97) came exclusively from reedbeds at Uskmouth and Magor Marsh, and occurred mostly from November through to April. The species can be very difficult to see, and some records have been based entirely on recognition of its distinctive and characteristic 'pinging' call.

1974	15 December	Uskmouth	3	a male and two females
1979	2 December	Uskmouth	3	
1981	5 November	Magor Marsh	2	
1986	4 November	Uskmouth	1	
1988	1 April	Uskmouth	1	
1992	28 November	Uskmouth	1	heard only
1993	14 March	Uskmouth	2	
1993	27–30 November	Uskmouth	4	at least 2 males
1997	30 March	Magor Marsh	1	heard only
2002	22 July	Uskmouth	1	heard

Table 97. Bearded Tit records in Gwent 1974–2002

The expansion of the Uskmouth reedbeds, following their incorporation into the Newport Wetlands Reserve, has resulted in more frequent records at this site (increased observation may also be a factor in the apparent increase), with up to two birds seen in late November and December 2003, and presumably the same individuals noted intermittently until at least 30th March 2004. At least three were recorded during November and December 2004, and after further records in spring 2005, a group of 6–9 juveniles was seen on 10th July, confirming the first ever breeding record in Gwent, and the first in Wales since 1988. Breeding was again confirmed at this site in 2006.

Long-tailed Tit
Titw Gynffon-hir

Aegithalos caudatus

A common and widespread resident

The Long-tailed Tit is a bird of woodland and woodland edge but also frequents hedgerows and scrub, particularly where gorse or thorn bushes are present. Its familiar domed nest, made of cobwebs and lichen and lined with feathers, is normally placed in dense bushes. It is common and widespread in Wales and most other parts of Britain.

The 1st Gwent Atlas found Long-tailed Tits to be widespread in the county, present in 79% of tetrads, and with *probable* or *confirmed* breeding in 71%. Notable gaps were identified in parts of the western valleys, particularly at the northern end, and also in the urban areas around Newport. This distribution appears similar to that described in earlier years by both the 1937 and 1963 *Birds of Monmouthshire*, which indicated a widespread presence apart from in the 'remote hill country'.

The 2nd Gwent Atlas shows that there has been a significant increase in range in recent years, with presence in 88% of tetrads, and *probable* or *confirmed* breeding in 82%. Many of the formerly vacant tetrads in the western valleys, and the urban tetrads in Newport, have been colonised and the only substantial gap in distribution remains in the treeless moorland of the extreme north-west.

Use of the BBS and atlas-based methods gives a current county population in the range 6,700–12,000 pairs, as compared with 3,000+ pairs suggested by the 1st Gwent Atlas on the basis of CBC data. The population has, however, not always been in such a healthy state. Long-tailed Tits are very sensitive to severe weather in winter, particularly when ice forms on trees and prevents foraging among the twiggy growth. The winter of 1962/63 was extremely bad in this respect and the Gwent population took several years to recover the losses sustained at that time. More recently, a very cold spell in February 1991 reduced breeding numbers on two local CBC plots by 50%, and no flocks exceeding ten birds were seen in the county during the following autumn/winter periods.

However, in the absence of really severe winters in recent years, the British Long-tailed Tit population has flourished, and the long-term UK trend (1973–2004) shows an increase of 57%. This is reflected in the 11% increase in distribution recorded in Gwent between the two county atlases. In view of this, it is surprising that the trend in Wales has been strongly negative (-24%) during the same period, but this figure is based on a much smaller sample size than the UK trend and needs to be treated with caution.

Long-tailed Tits have unusual social behaviour in which birds that are unmated, or whose current breeding attempt has failed, will often assist in tending the young of their close relations. In this context it is interesting to note that a nest at Penallt was attended by four adults in 1981.

In late summer, family parties gather into large flocks that forage together. These are often seen in Gwent at any time from July to early October and though flock sizes are generally in the 10–50 range, groups of up to 100 have occasionally been reported. Later in the autumn these groups split into family units that can include the 'helpers' from the previous summer, and each group defends a territory vigorously (Winter Atlas). Winter flock sizes are therefore rather smaller, and in Gwent have typically contained about 10–20 birds. Long-tailed Tits are essentially sedentary, with national ringing data showing that 95% of birds move less than 60km from their natal territory. A record of 12 birds that flew out over the estuary from St Brides on 23rd October 1990 was therefore most unusual.

In late winter, young females tend to move to adjacent territories, whereas males are likely to remain on the home range. An interesting ringing record concerns 16 birds that were caught in a garden at Ysgyryd Fach in October 1980. Seven of these birds had been ringed in a single catch at the same location in December the previous year. This is an impressive demonstration of the way in which flocks that split into pairs for breeding will reform again at the end of the breeding season.

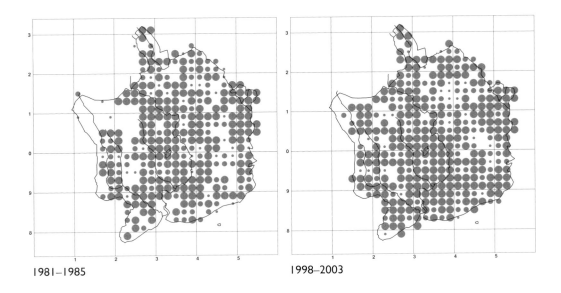

1981–1985

1998–2003

The use of garden feeding stations by this species was recorded in Gwent as early as 1967, but was unusual at that time and tended to occur only in hard weather. However it increased markedly during the 1980s and has now become a common winter occurrence. The food taken commonly includes peanuts, which is unexpected for this very insectivorous species.

Gwent Breeding Atlas data and population size

Gwent Atlas	Confirmed tetrads	Probable tetrads	Possible tetrads	Total tetrads	Change in total	Gwent population
1981–1985	206	74	34	314	–	–
1998–2003	247	76	25	348	+11%	6,700–12,000 pairs

National breeding data and conservation status

Estimated Welsh population	Welsh CBC/BBS trend 1985–2003	UK CBC/BBS trend 1985–2003	Welsh & UK conservation status
33,000 pairs	−24%	+56%	Green-listed

Willow Tit
Titw'r Helig

Poecile montanus

A scarce and declining resident

The Willow Tit is a patchily distributed breeding resident in England, Wales and south-west Scotland. Its preferred habitat is damp mixed woodland with willow, birch or alder trees, where nest holes are excavated in suitably rotten wood. Conifer woodland is extensively occupied in continental Europe but only to a very small extent in Britain (1988–91 National Atlas).

Separation of Willow and Marsh Tits in the field can be difficult unless the distinctive calls are heard. The 1988–91 National Atlas and the Winter Atlas both refer to this problem, and concede that some records for these species may, consequently, be based on misidentification. The same is no doubt true for some records in the two Gwent Atlases.

Despite its similarity to the Marsh Tit, it is still surprising that the occurrence of the Willow Tit went unrecognised in Britain until 1900. The 1963 *Birds of Monmouthshire* listed the first county record as a pair seen at Llandegfedd in 1942, and reported only six further records to 1953. By 1963 it had been reported from several central and northern parts of the county.

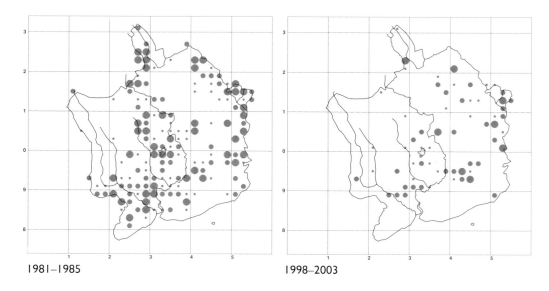

1981–1985   1998–2003

In the 1st Gwent Atlas the Willow Tit was found to have a scattered distribution in the county. It was present in 156 tetrads concentrated mainly in the central and southern lowlands, Wentwood and the Wye Valley Woodlands, but also with notable clusters in the uplands to the north of the county. It was absent or rare in the western valleys, and surprisingly scarce on the coastal levels, where pollarded willows have traditionally lined the damp fields and might have been expected to have provided good nesting habitat, as in other parts of Britain. Since the 1st Gwent Atlas, the species has undergone serious decline within the county. The 2nd Gwent Atlas records its presence in only 63 tetrads, representing a decline of 60% in its distribution, while the number of tetrads with *confirmed* breeding has dropped from 48 to eight. Losses have occurred throughout the county but are most severe in the western half.

Local ringing totals over the three decades from 1974 to 2003 also suggest a decline, with the proportion of fledged Willow Tits to fledged Blue Tits falling by 51% between the first and second decades, and by a further 25% between the second and third decades. The average number of breeding pairs per occupied tetrad is unlikely to exceed two, so based on its current distribution, a county population of 70–125 pairs is likely. This compares with an estimate of 300–450 pairs, based on 2–3 pairs per occupied tetrad, in the 1st Gwent Atlas.

The fortunes of the Willow Tit in Gwent mirror the national situation, which has been one of steady decline since the early 1970s, with a long-term trend (1973–2004) of –85%. Causes of the decline are uncertain but Siriwardena (2004) cites the drying out of woodlands caused by climate change and reduction of woodland flora caused by deer grazing as probable factors. However, as Gwent's deer population is currently limited to woodlands in the east of the county, notably Wentwood and the Wye Valley woodlands, whereas the Willow Tit's decline has been most severe in the west of the county, it seems unlikely that deer browsing is a major cause of decline in this instance.

This species is generally sedentary, so numbers reported in the county vary little between seasons. Winter flocks are rare, and reported winter counts in woodland have only twice reached double figures, on both occasions at Wentwood, with ten there in October 1992 and 15 in January 1995. Most records outside the breeding season are from woodlands and old hedgerows, but there are numerous records of feeding in mature gardens as well. The use of garden feeders has also been recorded, though much less frequently than in the case of Marsh Tit, with only five such reports in the last 25 years. Three birds foraging in jetsam at the edge of the River Wye in Monmouth in July 1980 is an unusual record.

Gwent Breeding Atlas data and population size

Gwent Atlas	Confirmed tetrads	Probable tetrads	Possible tetrads	Total tetrads	Change in total	Gwent population
1981–1985	48	52	56	156	–	–
1998–2003	8	28	27	63	–60%	70–125 pairs

National breeding data and conservation status

Estimated Welsh population	Welsh trend	UK CBC/BBS trend 1985–2003	Welsh & UK conservation status
2,300 pairs	Uncertain	–71%	Red-listed

Marsh Tit
Titw'r Wern

Poecile palustris

A scarce resident

The Marsh Tit is a bird of deciduous woodland and is a widely but patchily distributed breeding resident, mostly in the southern half of Britain. As discussed under Willow Tit, the similarity of these two tit species may have resulted in a few misidentifications in the Gwent Atlases.

The 1937 and 1963 *Birds of Monmouthshire* reported Marsh Tit as a local but not uncommon breeding resident that appeared to be distributed over the greater part of the county except on the hills. This status was broadly confirmed by the 1st Gwent Atlas, which showed a scattered distribution that excluded most of the coastal levels, the treeless hills of the north and north-west and also, perhaps surprisingly, the woodlands of the western valleys. In total, 45% of tetrads in the county were occupied and breeding was *probable* or *confirmed* in 28%.

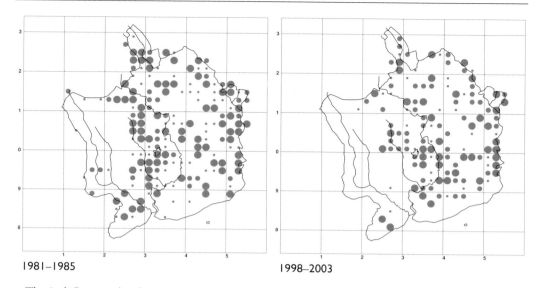

1981–1985   1998–2003

The 2nd Gwent Atlas shows a marked decline, with the number of occupied tetrads decreasing to 33%, though the number of tetrads in the county with *probable* or *confirmed* breeding has held up fairly well and remains at 25% of the total. Losses appear well spread, with no particular areas of the county being more noticeably affected than others.

Gwent ringing totals over the three decades from 1974 to 2003 also suggest a decline, with the proportion of fledged Marsh Tits to fledged Blue Tits declining by 30% between the first and second decades, and by a further 35% between the second and third decades. With a scarce woodland species such as this, population size is difficult to estimate, as data are few. Use of the atlas-based method (see Appendix 1) gives a county population of around 510–1,200 breeding pairs, but this figure is based on a small sample and should be treated with caution. Experienced local opinion considers the lower end of the range to be most likely. The 1st Gwent Atlas was equally circumspect when estimating the county population, suggesting that a total of 500 pairs, based on a single CBC plot plus extrapolation from the densities quoted in the 1968–72 National Atlas, was possibly a considerable underestimate.

The situation of Marsh Tit across the UK has been one of serious long-term decline, though this has levelled off in the last decade and recent trends show some possible signs of recovery. Causes of the national decline are not fully understood, though degradation of woodland understorey as a result of grazing by deer is a likely factor (Fuller *et al.*, 2005), This factor seems unlikely to be of importance in Gwent, as the county's deer population is currently confined to eastern areas whereas there is no evidence for Marsh Tit decline being more severe in these areas than elsewhere in the county.

The generally sedentary nature of the Marsh Tit means that numbers of birds reported in Gwent vary little between seasons. Winter flocks are rare, but counts in suitable woodland have occasionally reached double figures: notably about 18 in Coed-y-Prior Wood in November 1980, ten in Piercefield Woods in December 1986 and 12 in woodland near Tintern in November 1997.

Visits to garden feeding stations are not common but have been regularly reported, and in several years during the early 1990s there were almost daily occurrences during the October–May period in a garden at Goytre. Use of nest boxes for breeding has been occasionally reported.

There is just one ringing recovery relevant to Gwent. An adult ringed at Brynmawr in February 1998 was recovered near Crickhowell (7km north) in November 2000.

Gwent Breeding Atlas data and population size

Gwent Atlas	Confirmed tetrads	Probable tetrads	Possible tetrads	Total tetrads	Change in total	Gwent population
1981–1985	77	35	65	177	–	–
1998–2003	43	55	32	130	−27%	510–1,200 pairs

National breeding data and conservation status

Estimated Welsh population	Welsh CBC/BBS trend 1985–2003	UK CBC/BBS trend 1985–2003	Welsh & UK conservation status
9,400 pairs	−16%	−28%	Red-listed

Coal Tit
Titw Penddu

Periparus ater

A common resident. There is evidence of small autumn passage movements

The Coal Tit is a widespread resident in Britain and is most common in coniferous woodland, where its small size and fine bill enable it to forage effectively among pine needles. It is usually much less common in deciduous woodland, where it tends to be out-competed by the larger Great and Blue Tits, although it can survive in single large conifers in predominantly broadleaved woods (1988–91 National Atlas).

The 1937 and 1963 *Birds of Monmouthshire* both reported the species to be considerably scarcer in the county than the Blue or Great Tits, and to breed in cultivated and wooded districts together with hillside larch plantations. The 1st Gwent Atlas showed it to widely distributed as a breeding bird in the county, with records from 75% of tetrads. It was notably absent from the coastal levels and the treeless moorlands of the extreme north-east, and was patchily distributed in the more open farmland of north/central areas.

The Coal Tit's range in Britain increased greatly during the middle of the last century in association with the extensive planting of coniferous forests (1988–91 National Atlas), and the population has continued to expand in recent years, with the UK trend showing an increase of 46% between 1970 and 2003. Between the two Gwent Atlases, the UK population has increased by 23% and the Welsh population by 18%. These national trends have been reflected in the 2nd Gwent Atlas, which shows that the percentage of occupied tetrads has increased from 75% to 82%.

The proportion of tetrads in the county in which *probable* and *confirmed* breeding was recorded has increased from 59% to 73%, suggesting an increase in population as well as range. It is interesting that local ringing totals for the last 30 years show the ratio of fledged Coal Tits to Blue Tits increasing from 1:25 in the first 15-year period to 1:9 in the second 15-year period, again suggestive of an increase in numbers. Based on the BBS and atlas-based methods (Appendix 1), the Gwent population is now estimated to be in the range 4,300–6,400 pairs. This compares with a suggested population of 3,000 pairs in the 1st Gwent Atlas but, owing to the very different methods used, comparisons should be made only with caution.

Nests are generally located in natural holes in trees or sometimes walls. Cavities at ground level between tree roots are often used, and one such nest at Trellech in 1979 was reported to have been predated by an adder. Nest boxes are used only occasionally: the Gwent Nest Box Schemes (see Pied Flycatcher) recorded only 12 instances of breeding Coal Tits in eighteen years, though all of these were very successful in producing fledged young. Very unusually, a pair at Glascoed built a nest on top of a Blue Tit nest after the latter's young had fledged.

Flocks of up to 20 birds are frequently encountered in woodland during the autumn and winter months, and several flocks of 30–50 birds have been recorded in Wentwood. A flock of about 47 at this location on 24th July 1977 was remarkably large for the time of the year. Small gatherings are often reported from garden feeding stations in winter: up to ten is not unusual and the record is 14 in a Monmouth garden in 1984.

Coastal records are scarce. They are limited to the months of September and October and involve small numbers, often engaged in visible passage to the southwest. The most notable of such movements comprise ten at Black Rock on 21st September 1997 and 25 in a period of 90 minutes at Goldcliff on 5th October 1985, while smaller numbers have been recorded in five other years. The *Migration Atlas* states that although British Coal Tits *P. a. britannicus* are largely sedentary, ringing returns provide evidence for autumn movements of young birds, and possibly their subsequent return to their natal area. Also, irruptions from continental Europe occur in some years, with immigrants reaching as far as the southwest extremes of Britain. It is interesting to note that an influx of around 170 Coal Tits onto Ramsey Island occurred in late September 1997, following the above-mentioned movement at Black Rock, and some of those captured for ringing showed characteristics of the continental race *P. a. ater* (2002 *Birds in Wales*).

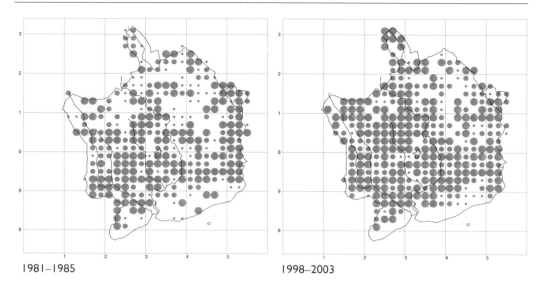

1981–1985   1998–2003

Gwent Breeding Atlas data and population size

Gwent Atlas	Confirmed tetrads	Probable tetrads	Possible tetrads	Total tetrads	Change in total	Gwent population
1981–1985	150	80	66	296	–	–
1998–2003	195	94	33	322	+9%	4,300–6,400 pairs

National breeding data and conservation status

Estimated Welsh population	Welsh CBC/BBS trend 1985–2003	UK CBC/BBS trend 1985–2003	Welsh & UK conservation status
63,000 pairs	+18	+23%	Green-listed

Blue Tit
Titw Tomos Las

Cyanistes caeruleus

An abundant resident. There is evidence of south-westerly movements in autumn

The Blue Tit is the commonest and most familiar of its family and occurs throughout Britain. It is most abundant in mature oak woodland but will breed in almost any habitat that provides suitable nest holes.

It has a wide breeding distribution in Gwent, recorded in over 98% of tetrads in both Gwent Atlases, and absent only from bare moorlands and tetrads comprising small fragments of coast. Parents carrying food to young are very obvious and young birds are very noisy, both in the nest and when recently fledged, so coupled with its habit of using nest boxes in gardens, these features make it a conspicuous breeder and account for the fact that over 90% of atlas records refer to *confirmed* breeding.

In recent years, unusual nesting sites have included natural House Martin nests, while both natural and artificial versions have been used as winter roosting places. There have been two records of mixed broods of Blue and Great Tits being successfully raised in nest boxes: in one case this was known to have arisen from a Blue Tit laying five eggs in a Great Tit nest. Blue Tits are normally single-brooded, so a record in 1987 of two broods being reared consecutively in the same nest box was extremely unusual. Fledging dates for the young were 14th June and 18th August. The adults were not ringed, and could not therefore be individually identified, but as tits often show fidelity to nest boxes, it seems likely to have been the same pair that reared both broods.

The Gwent breeding population of Blue Tit is estimated at 33,000–39,000 pairs, making it at least twice as abundant as Great Tit. In the period 1972–2003 totals of about 17,000 fledged Blue Tits and 6,000 fledged Great Tits were ringed in Gwent, suggesting that Blue Tits may outnumber Great Tits by almost three to one, but as most of these birds were ringed in gardens, the comparison may suffer from site-related bias. It is interesting to note, however, that the ratio remains constant for both the sub-periods 1972–87 and 1988–2003, indicating that the relative

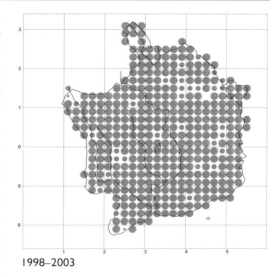

1998–2003

proportions of the two species visiting gardens has remained constant for over 30 years.

Blue Tits are widespread and plentiful in winter, and flocks of up to 50 are not unusual, often in company with smaller numbers of Goldcrests and other tit species. Although the largest winter flocks are normally encountered in deciduous woodland, smaller numbers occur in a diverse variety of habitats ranging from hedgerows, scrub and gardens, to reedbeds, and even the strand line on the estuary. The large numbers that visit garden feeders in winter are best demonstrated by ringing studies: the 166 individuals ringed in a Monmouth garden during a ten-day period in 1979 are a good example of this in Gwent.

In Britain, the Blue Tit is a mainly sedentary species but some young birds make modest movements in autumn (*Migration Atlas*). In Wales there is evidence for most such movements being westerly, with a return movement in the late winter or early spring (1994 *Birds in Wales*). This pattern is clearly seen in Gwent, where in many years there are observations of moderate numbers moving in a southerly or south-westerly direction at the coast, particularly during October, though occasionally in September or November. A selection of some of the notable movements, mostly seen at Goldcliff, is shown in Table 98.

Date	14 Sep 74	2–5 Oct 85	12 Oct 85	3 Oct 88	8 Oct 88	3 Oct 93	9 Oct 93
No./Direction	30 S	120 SW	80 SW	120 SW	80 SW	50 W	100 SW
Period (hours)	?	1.5	2.75	?	2.0	?	?

Table 98. Examples of coastal Blue Tit movements in Gwent

Analysis of local ringing recoveries from the last 40 years supports the view that these movements comprise mainly first-year birds, migrating west or south-west in the autumn, and possibly returning in the late winter or early spring. Thus, among medium distance movements of birds ringed as nestlings in Gwent, most have been recovered during the following winter to the south or south-west, while in the case of winter recoveries in Gwent of birds ringed as nestlings outside the county, all have involved immature birds from locations up to 109km east or north-east of the recovery site. Also, recoveries in Gwent of birds ringed in winter outside the county, have involved mostly first-winter birds making journeys from the south-west compass quarter, including one that flew 70km northwards from Bridgwater, Somerset between the 8th and 27th March 1975, and another that moved 131km eastwards from Pembroke to Monmouth between February and June 1976.

The longest movement recorded is 358km south-south-west and involved a bird ringed as a nestling in North Yorkshire in June 2000, which was recovered at Uskmouth in June 2003. This bird, like those above, may have migrated in a south-westerly direction in its first autumn but, in this case, never returned to its natal area. (full details of ringing recoveries are listed in Appendix 9).

Gwent Breeding Atlas data and population size

Gwent Atlas	Confirmed tetrads	Probable tetrads	Possible tetrads	Total tetrads	Change in total	Gwent population
1981–1985	341	35	11	387	–	–
1998–2003	355	31	2	388	<1%	33,000–39,000 pairs

National breeding data and conservation status

Estimated Welsh population	Welsh CBC/BBS trend 1985–2003	UK CBC/BBS trend 1985–2003	Welsh & UK conservation status
377,000 pairs	3%	+8%	Green-listed

Great Tit
Titw Mawr

Parus major

An abundant resident

The Great Tit breeds throughout Britain, the only gaps in distribution occurring where there is a shortage of tree cover or in mountainous areas. In Gwent it is a widespread and abundant bird, breeding in all habitats with trees, including deciduous woodland and copses, hedgerows with trees, and both urban and suburban gardens. Coniferous woodland is also occupied, though at a lower density than deciduous woodland.

It has a wide breeding distribution in Gwent, recorded in over 98% of tetrads in both Gwent Atlases, (1981–85 and 1998–2003) and absent only from bare moorlands of the north-west, and tetrads comprising small fragments of coast. As with the Blue Tit, proof of breeding is relatively easy to obtain, as adults feeding young are conspicuous, as also are the noisy fledglings. As a consequence, around 85% of breeding records referred to *confirmed* breeding.

On the basis of the BBS and atlas-based methods (see Appendix 1) the Gwent population is estimated to be in the region of 16,000–18,000 pairs. This figure is considered more realistic than the much larger figure given in the 1st Gwent Atlas, which was based largely on limited CBC data.

In common with other tits, the Great Tit is usually single brooded, but there have been two records of second broods in the county: one at Skenfrith in 1979 and the other at Ysgyryd Fach in 2000.

Adult males are known to be very sedentary, often remaining on their territories throughout the year, but females and young birds form roaming flocks in autumn and winter, often in company with Nuthatches, Goldcrests and other tits (Winter Atlas). Numbers of Great Tits in winter flocks in Gwent are smaller than those of Blue Tits, and have not usually exceeded 20 birds.

Ringing data confirm the largely sedentary nature of local Great Tits. Of birds ringed in Gwent, most recoveries have been within 10km of the ringing site. The majority of the remainder have been within 50km and show no apparent directional pattern. The most notable ringing record concerns an adult ringed in February that was recorded 15 months later, 180km north-north-east in Cheshire. There are only two records of visible passage movements: of 30 birds moving west at Goldcliff on 9th October 1993 and of a small but steady passage down the Llanthony Valley on 10th September 1978.

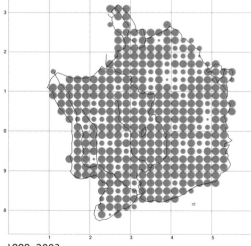

1998–2003

Gwent Breeding Atlas data and population size

Gwent Atlas	Confirmed tetrads	Probable tetrads	Possible tetrads	Total tetrads	Change in total	Gwent population
1981–1985	329	42	17	388	–	–
1998–2003	328	53	6	387	<1%	16,000–18,000 pairs

National breeding data and conservation status

Estimated Welsh population	Welsh CBC/BBS trend 1985–2003	UK CBC/BBS trend 1985–2003	Welsh & UK conservation status
200,000 pairs	stable	+11%	Green-listed

Nuthatch
Delor Y Cnau

Sitta europaea

Resident, increasing in both numbers and range

The Nuthatch is well-known for two characteristics unique among British woodland species. Unlike other tree-climbers, it is equally adept at climbing both down and up a trunk or branch. Also, instead of excavating its nest hole, it reduces the entrance of an existing hole to its preferred size by plastering it with mud. Both characteristics can assist the field worker: a small bird, seen creeping head first down a tree trunk or a hole of almost artificial circularity in a tree often suggest 'Nuthatch'. As it also has a loud and distinctive voice, and is especially noisy early in the breeding season, it is probable that few pairs will have been entirely overlooked.

Comparison of the maps for the two Gwent Atlases show a considerable extension of range within the county, with the number of occupied tetrads increasing by 19%. It is also notable that evidence of *confirmed* or *probable* breeding has been obtained in the vast majority of the tetrads where Nuthatches have appeared since the 1st Gwent Atlas. Thus it is fair to expect that the 2nd Gwent Atlas map reflects the current situation reasonably accurately.

Many of the tetrads without Nuthatch records are those in which trees of sufficient maturity to provide nest sites are either absent or very sparsely present. Thus the gaps on the coastal levels and the high ground of the north and west are easily explained. More surprising is the distribution of the newly-occupied tetrads, being most numerous in those 10-km squares containing the upper parts of the western valleys. Even allowing for increased observation in this area, there seems little doubt that this reflects a real extension of range; this is all the more remarkable for a bird known to be extremely sedentary. The Winter Atlas noted that, in the history of the BTO ringing scheme up to 1979, there had been only two recoveries of Nuthatches more than 5km from the ringing site. Thus a bird ringed at Forest Coal Pit in May 1987 and recovered two years later 5km away was an unusually well-travelled member of its species. The 1977 *Birds of Gwent* indicates the Nuthatch to be 'apparently most numerous in the east (of Gwent)': this is clearly no longer the case.

The 1st Gwent Atlas estimate of a county population of 750–1,250 pairs was based on the assumption of an average of 3–5 pairs per occupied tetrad. The current estimate, which incorporates BBS data is considerably higher at 1,300–4,100 pairs. A significant increase in population would be expected as a result of the 19% increase of occupied tetrads in the county, and the 17% increase in the number with *confirmed* or *probable*

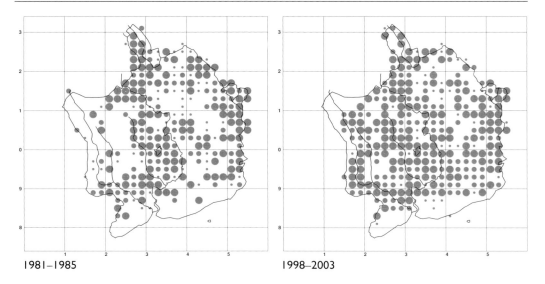

1981–1985   1998–2003

breeding, and would also be predicted from the strongly increasing national trends in the period between the two Gwent Atlases.

Gwent Breeding Atlas data and population size

Gwent Atlas	Confirmed tetrads	Probable tetrads	Possible tetrads	Total tetrads	Change in total	Gwent population
1981–1985	120	75	56	251	–	–
1998–2003	154	106	38	298	+19%	1,300–4,100 pairs

National breeding data and conservation status

Estimated Welsh population	Welsh CBC/BBS trend 1985–2003	UK CBC/BBS trend 1985–2003	Welsh & UK conservation status
c.38,000 pairs	+42%	+53%	Green-listed

(Eurasian) **Treecreeper**   *Certhia familiaris*
Dringwr Bach

A widespread resident in moderate numbers

The Treecreper is a widely distributed resident throughout most parts of the UK. Bird watchers familiar with the species will readily recognise descriptions like 'inconspicuous' and 'unobtrusive'. Its jerky climbing up and around a tree trunk and its subsequent flight to the bottom of a neighbouring tree are easily overlooked. Its high-pitched song is not easy to detect from any great distance, and its call-notes and those of its young can easily be confused with those of Goldcrests or Coal Tits, often present in the same habitat. Its nest is equally inconspicuous, usually hidden in a crevice in a mature tree trunk, often behind a piece of loose bark. It is therefore not surprising that examination of the distribution maps from the 1st and 2nd Gwent Atlases reveals a change of breeding status has occurred in about three-quarters of the tetrads with Treecreeper records; nor (as shown below) that consistent estimates of the county population are hard to obtain. Noisy juveniles or family parties, however, readily draw attention to themselves, and their detection is often the easiest way to obtain proof of breeding.

The broad swathe of tetrads showing *confirmed* and *probable* records coincides roughly with the Usk Valley, with other concentrations along the Wye Valley and parts of the western valleys. Some of the gaps on this map are readily accounted for by lack of trees: for instance, those on the north-western edge, where treeless high

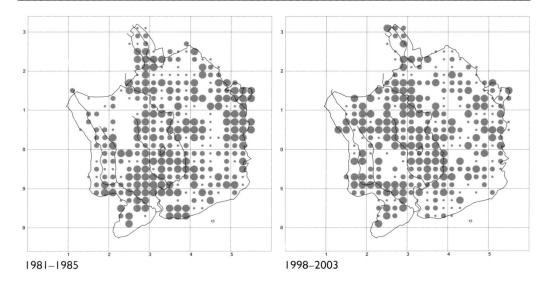

1981–1985   1998–2003

ground predominates, and along the coast, where trees are often thinly scattered. Treecreepers are, however, less particular about species or maturity of trees than Nuthatches or woodpeckers, and pollarded willows may afford suitable breeding sites on the coastal levels. It may be that the relative scarcity shown on the coastal levels indicates a thinly scattered population, for which evidence of presence or breeding would be hard to obtain.

Comparison of the data from the two atlases shows that in the western valleys the numbers of tetrads showing upgrading and downgrading of breeding status are almost equal; this may be due in some measure to the readiness of Treecreepers to colonise conifer plantations, many of which have appeared at and around reclaimed mining and industrial sites. The net decreases in numbers of tetrads with *probable* and *confirmed* records indicated in the Table have occurred in other parts of the county.

The 1st Gwent Atlas, using an estimate of five pairs per occupied tetrad, gave a county population estimate of about 1,500 pairs. The 1988–91 National Atlas, while giving figures implying a nationwide average of just under 100 pairs per occupied 10-km Square, and thus about four pairs per tetrad, also remarked that South Wales contains many high abundance areas, so that the higher average of five pairs per tetrad may be reasonable for Gwent. On this assumption, the present county population, based on the 2nd Gwent Atlas data, would be about 1,450 pairs, a slight decrease from the earlier *Atlas*. This compares with an estimate of 2,300–2,900 pairs obtained from current population analyses (Appendix 1). Such an increase in population is, however, not supported by changes in distribution between the two Gwent Atlases or by the strongly negative national trends over the same period, implying that the current estimate is too high or the former too low (or a combination of both).

Several *Gwent Bird Reports,* however, note substantial local fluctuations in numbers, attributable in at least some cases to the effects of hard winter weather. Small birds like Treecreepers are especially vulnerable to both hard winters and, according to recent BTO indications, to wet winters. However, the 1977 *Birds of Gwent* indicated that, after the large decreases following the severe winter of 1962/63, numbers had recovered by the summer of 1965. The impression left by the entries in more recent *Gwent Bird Reports* is of similar rapid recoveries in numbers after other hard, though less extreme, winters. The widespread distribution of Treecreepers, both in Gwent and in Wales as a whole, gives grounds for optimism that they will remain as an established part of our avifauna even after future hard or wet winters.

Gwent Atlas	Confirmed tetrads	Probable tetrads	Possible tetrads	Total tetrads	Change in total	Gwent population
		Gwent Breeding Atlas data and population size				
1981–1985	132	107	73	312	–	–
1998–2003	120	102	75	297	−5%	2,300–2,900 pairs

	National breeding data and conservation status		
Estimated Welsh population	**Welsh CBC/BBS trend 1985–2003**	**UK CBC/BBS trend 1985–2003**	**Welsh & UK conservation status**
c.41,300 pairs	−38%	−19%	Green-listed

(Eurasian) **Golden Oriole** *Oriolus oriolus*
Euryn

A formerly rare summer migrant; a little more frequent in recent years

The Golden Oriole is a summer visitor that breeds very locally in eastern England but occurs elsewhere in Britain as a scarce spring migrant. The male is an unmistakeable bird with a golden yellow body contrasting with black wings and red bill, but it is generally a secretive species and its beautiful fluty whistle or its screaming, almost Jay-like, call are usually the first indicators of its presence.

The 1963 *Birds of Monmouthshire* lists three records of single birds: at Abergavenny on 8th September 1939, Caerleon on 21st June 1942 and Abercarn on 23rd April 1944. The next record in the county was not until 1967 when a male and a female were seen separately on several occasions in the Wentwood/Llanvaches area from late April to late June. This began a series of sightings around the southern fringes of Wentwood that continued until 1982, and involved records of up to two birds in seven of the sixteen years during this period.

From 1983 to 1995 it occurred in only one year, when two were heard singing at different locations in 1988. Since then there has been an increase in frequency with records in 1996, 1997 and 2000, and more recently in 2004 when a well-watched immature bird was present at Castle Meadows, Abergavenny on the very late dates of 13th–16th October.

Figure 26 shows that most county records have occurred in the May–June period, which is typical for Britain generally. The earliest spring record was on 21st April 1971 and the latest of the summer records was on 26th July 1970, when two females/immatures were seen in Wentwood.

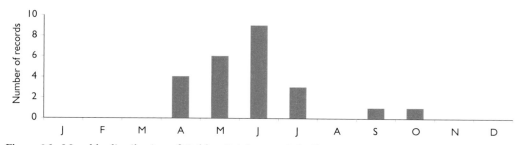

Figure 26. Monthly distribution of Golden Oriole records in Gwent

Red-backed Shrike *Lanius collurio*
Cigydd Cefngoch

Formerly more common but now a very rare visitor; has recently bred

As elsewhere in Britain, the Red-backed Shrike was formerly much more common in Gwent than it has been in recent years. This is evidenced by the presence in the Baker-Gabb collection of eggs and nests taken from Abergavenny: five in 1889 and two in 1890, both from the same field. Also the 1963 *Birds of Monmouthshire* noted that breeding had previously been recorded at Marshfield, Newport, Portskewett, Llantarnum, Monmouth, Abergavenny and the Llanthony Valley. In 1944 a pair attempted unsuccessfully to breed near Maesglas, Newport, whilst another pair bred successfully at Llanfoist in three successive years, 1944–1946. Single birds were also recorded at Trelleck in July 1952 and near Caldicot on 21st June 1958.

The species' range in Britain has contracted throughout the 20th century, and it ceased to be a regular breeder in the country some 25 years ago. Consequently it has also become far rarer in Gwent, and since 1958 there have been only ten records. Four of these have involved autumn passage birds, with individuals at both Peterstone and Wentwood in September 1969, Shirenewton for two days in August 1970 and Caerleon in August 1979. The remainder are from the breeding season and all but one comprise single birds all seen in June: at Fforest Coalpit in 1973, Magor in 1973, Wentwood in 1976, Llangovan in 2004 and Llanwenarth in 2006. The remaining record involved, somewhat remarkably, successful breeding at the Kymin, Monmouth, during 1981.

At the time of going to press reports of breeding have been received. Two recently fledged young were found at a site in the north of the county in 2005. It subsequently transpired that they probably also bred in 2004. Four chicks were fledged at the same site in 2006.

Great Grey Shrike
Cigydd Mawr

Lanius excubitor

A very scarce winter visitor and passage migrant

The Great Grey Shrike is a widespread breeding bird in northern regions of continental Europe. The more northerly populations are migratory and some Scandinavian birds occur in Britain as both passage migrants and scarce, but widespread, winter visitors. The winter population in Britain is small; the Winter Atlas put the figure at above 150 birds, but numbers have since decreased (*Migration Atlas*). Based on the data from the Winter Atlas, the 1994 *Birds in Wales* proposed an average of only 5–10 per winter in Wales, and data presented in the 2002 *Birds in Wales* suggests no increase on this figure.

There are approximately twenty-two records of Great Grey Shrike in Gwent. The 1963 *Birds of Monmouthshire* includes just one documented record (a second is no longer considered acceptable – see Appendix 2): of a single bird at Peterstone on 9th April 1933. Since 1966 it has been recorded on a further twenty occasions, and in seventeen out of forty-one winters ('winter' is used in this context to mean the entire October–April period). There has usually been only one record per winter and all records have been of single birds, with the exception of a brief period at the end of March in 1995 when two were present in Wentwood.

The monthly distribution of records is shown in Figure 27 and demonstrates the occurrence of passage migrants, particularly in spring, in addition to winter visitors. Earliest and latest dates are 4th October 1997 near Trellech, and 18th April 1989 at Wentwood.

Most individuals have been present on only a single day or occasionally for a few days, but there are four recorded stays of 20 days or more, including two of four and five months respectively. The long-stayers were one in Park Wood Chepstow from 17th March 1984–6th April 1985; one in the Little Oak/Nine Wells area in Wentwood Forest from 4th November 1990–1st April 1991, with one in the same area from 15th November 1992–19th March 1993; and one in Maypole from 12th February 1993–29th March 1994. The species is known to establish winter territories and to show site-fidelity from year to year, so the records in 1990/91 and 1992/3 in Wentwood may well have involved the same individual. Winters 2003/04 and 2004/05 have also had records of single birds in Wentwood which may again involve a single individual. Fraser and Ryan (1995), classify records of Great Grey Shrikes as passage migrants, winter residents, or winter wanderers (which are seen only for a few days at any one location); on this basis, records for Gwent can be divided into autumn passage migrants (five), winter wanderers (nine), winter residents (three) and spring passage migrants (five).

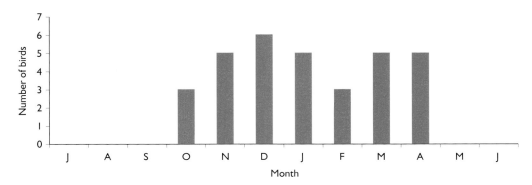

Figure 27. Monthly distribution of Great Grey Shrike records in Gwent

Records have occurred widely around the county but four of the six records prior to 1976 were on the Wentlooge Level at Peterstone, where the small damp pastures with mature hedgerows for observation posts provided good habitat. However, the Wentlooge Level has since lost many of its hedgerows, and the pattern of land usage in much of the area has changed, with the result that it is now less attractive to this species. In recent years seven out of ten records have been at Wentwood, where young restocked forestry plantations have been the favoured habitat.

Woodchat Shrike   *Lanius senator*
Cigydd Pengoch

A rare vagrant

There are four records of this southern European species, all of single birds. Immature birds were present at Peterstone during 1st October–8th November 1983 and St Brides during 29th August–6th September 1988, while in 1993 a female was at Magor Reserve during 14th–18th May, with what was presumably the same individual at nearby Magor Pill on 8th June and Caldicot Moor during 8th–16th August. The remaining record concerns a spring passage bird, a female at Newport Wetlands Reserve on 24th April 2004.

(Eurasian) Jay   *Garrulus glandarius*
Ysgrech y Coed

A common resident and an irregular autumn passage migrant

The Jay is a relatively secretive woodland breeder but has recently been venturing much more often into gardens, where it makes a striking sight. Although it is particularly associated with oak woodland, where acorns are its staple diet, it also breeds very successfully in both mixed broadleaved woodland and conifer plantations, and is widespread in England and Wales except from areas where tree cover is lacking.

The Jay was formerly much persecuted by gamekeepers, and in the 19th century its population in Gwent, as elsewhere in Wales, would have been much lower than it is today (1994 *Birds in Wales*). Evidence of this persecution in Gwent comes from estate game books, a good example being from Talycoed that recorded the shooting of small numbers of birds around the turn of the 20th century, including two in October 1899 at Penrhos Grange and five in November 1911 at Pontysychan Grange. As with other birds persecuted by game interests, expansion of its numbers is generally considered to date from the time of the First World War, and some 45 years after this the 1963 *Birds of Monmouthshire* was able to describe its local status as fairly numerous in wooded districts.

It remains a common species today and maps from the two Gwent Atlases are more or less identical, showing a presence in 83% and 84% of tetrads, respectively, and a widespread distribution in all wooded parts of the county. Only those areas with sparse tree cover are unoccupied: notably the moorlands of the northwest, open farmland of the north and east and the coastal levels in the south. The 1st Gwent Atlas commented that the Jay's secretive nature when breeding can cause it to be overlooked and speculated that this might account for some of the apparent gaps in the east of the county where suitable habitat exists. However, the existence of a similar pattern of gaps in the 2nd Gwent Atlas makes this explanation less likely to be valid. When the numbers of tetrads with either *probable* or *confirmed* breeding are added together, the totals are almost identical between the two atlases (262 and 261), but the number with *confirmed* breeding is down by a striking 42% in the 2nd Gwent Atlas. This suggests a generally lower visibility of breeding pairs, and may reflect a reduction of population size between the two atlas periods. Over the same period the UK population index shows a small decline. The Welsh index shows no change between the Gwent atlas periods, but an 8% decline in the last decade (1994–2004).

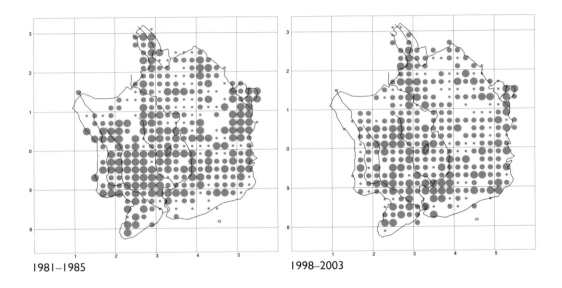

1981–1985   1998–2003

The BBS and atlas-based methods give the disparate figures of 530 and 3,000 pairs, respectively, for the county population (see Appendix 1). As discussed in Appendix 1, BBS counts exclude birds seen in flight, and as this is how Jays are most often seen, the data generated is likely to underestimate population size. The true population is likely, therefore, to be in the upper half of the above range, corresponding to 5–9 pairs per occupied tetrad.

Jays are well known for their irruptive behaviour in years when the acorn crop is poor or fails completely. In such years large numbers move westward into Wales during late September and October, occurring in unusually large flocks and in places where they are not normally recorded, such as coastal habitats. The 1994 *Birds in Wales* lists the following years when irruptive movements were also observed in Wales (years in which notable flocks and movements were also observed in Gwent are italicised): *1923*, 1935, 1947, *1975*, *1977*, *1981*, *1983*, *1993* and 1996. The irruption of 1983, which included birds from continental Europe, was the largest in recent times (*Migration Atlas*) and observers in Gwent reported several associated records, including 45 passing south over Monmouth in late September, 21 moving west-south-west over Caldicot on 4th October, and 22 moving north over Mamhilad the following day. A flock of 25 at Newport on 25th September 1975 was another exceptionally large flock. A small influx into the Newport and Wentwood areas of Gwent, involving groups of up to ten birds was also noted in autumn 1994, not a year when irruptions were reported more widely in Wales. More recently, small late-autumn flocks of 5–8 birds have been recorded in each of the years 2002 to 2004, while in 2005, up to 20 were recorded at Newport Wetlands Reserve during 29th September–2nd October.

Over the last 30–40 years, Jays have been venturing increasingly into gardens and making use of bird tables and other food supplies. There have been several reports from Gwent of Jays using their intelligence and ingenuity to hang and feed successfully from nut-feeders.

Gwent Breeding Atlas data and population size

Gwent Atlas	Confirmed tetrads	Probable tetrads	Possible tetrads	Total tetrads	Change in total	Gwent population
1981–1985	149	113	67	329	–	–
1998–2003	87	174	65	326	−1%	530–3,000 pairs

National breeding data and conservation status

Estimated Welsh population	Welsh CBC/BBS trend 1985–2003	UK CBC/BBS trend 1985–2003	Welsh & UK conservation status
21,600 pairs	stable	−7.6%	Green-listed

(Black-billed) **Magpie** **Pioden**   *Pica pica*

An abundant resident

With its distinctive plumage, strikingly long tail and harsh cackling calls, the Magpie is recognised by all, but those who appreciate it for its good looks and engaging behaviour are probably outnumbered by those who detest it as a nest predator.

It is a versatile species that occupies a very wide variety of habitats throughout most parts of Britain, and it increased greatly during the 20th century, mainly as a result of reduced persecution from gamekeepers and others. In parts of Wales, another beneficial factor has been the great increase of sheep numbers that has provided food in the form of carrion and stock-feed stations (1994 *Birds in Wales*). However, despite this increase and spread, it was evident even as late as 1963, that the Magpie was still basically a bird of the countryside, with the 1963 *Birds of Monmouthshire* describing it as widespread and common, nesting everywhere in the county, including 'just outside all the towns'.

By 1981–85, the period of the 1st Gwent Atlas, the towns had also been colonised, and the Magpie was identified as the most widespread breeding bird in the county, occurring in all mainland tetrads, and absent only from 48K, the tetrad in the middle of the Severn Estuary that contains Denny Island as its only piece of dry land. More recently, however, the Magpie's fortunes appear to have reversed, and the 2nd Gwent Atlas shows evidence of a significant decline in which the Magpie has ceded its position as Gwent's most widespread bird to the Blackbird, and now ranks

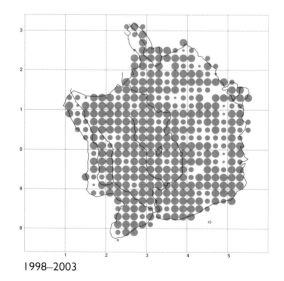

1998–2003

only 10th on this criterion. It is absent from 12 mainland tetrads, and the number of tetrads with *confirmed* breeding has dropped dramatically from 336 to 282. The Magpie is a conspicuous and noisy breeder with a large and unmistakeable nest, so this change in status is most unlikely to have resulted from its being overlooked. On the contrary, it is noteworthy that several atlas recorders mentioned having difficulty in finding Magpies in some farmland tetrads, and also encountered anecdotal evidence of increased control of the species in certain farmland areas. In addition, *Gwent Bird Reports* from the 1990s note a number of local declines, and its occurrence in Gwent BBS squares has also decreased. In conclusion there appears to be a convincing case for a significant decline of the Magpie in Gwent during the last 20 years. The population trend for Wales is also negative, indicating that this decline may not be confined to Gwent.

Woodland and suburban habitats in Britain can hold over 40 pairs per tetrad (1968–72 National Atlas), and upland farmland near Brynmawr and Trefil was shown to hold around 30–40 pairs per tetrad (*1994 Gwent Bird Report*), whereas many Gwent farmland tetrads at lower altitudes may hold fewer than five pairs. An average of 20–25 pairs per tetrad would give a county population of around 8,500 pairs, which lies between the figures of 5,300 and 18,000 produced by our BBS and atlas-based methods, both of which have some disadvantages when applied to this species (see Appendix 1). A population of about 15,000 pairs was suggested at the time of the 1st Gwent Atlas.

Decline has also been noted in the size of non-breeding flocks. In the 1970s, flocks of 30–40 birds were reported regularly, and 50–80 more occasionally, with a record of 29 in the same tree at Llanwenarth in March 1978. By contrast, during the decade 1994–2003 the largest flock-size recorded has been 33, and in most years has ranged from 20 to 30. A roost at Ynysyfro Reservoir that contained up to 131 birds in winter 1987/88 declined steadily over subsequent years and held a maximum of only 55 in winter 1991/92.

Magpies have had a bad press in recent years, being blamed for the decline in passerine populations in urban and suburban areas, but this is generally unsubstantiated in recent research literature (1988–91 National Atlas). Predation of Magpie nests by squirrels and Carrion Crows has been reported in Gwent, showing that they can be victims as well as aggressors. The fact that they have long been considered vermin by the human population is shown by the following extract from *Shooting in Monmouthshire, 1923*: 'The County abounds with vermain – 30 crow, 80 magpies together with a number of sparrowhawks killed at Llangibby Estate during past year'.

Gwent Breeding Atlas data and population size

Gwent Atlas	Confirmed tetrads	Probable tetrads	Possible tetrads	Total tetrads	Change in total	Gwent population
1981–1985	336	40	17	393	–	–
1998–2003	282	86	13	381	−3%	5,300–18,000 pairs

National breeding data and conservation status

Estimated Welsh population	Welsh CBC/BBS trend 1985–2003	UK CBC/BBS trend 1985–2003	Welsh & UK conservation status
100,000 pairs	−7.2%	stable	Green-listed

(Spotted) Nutcracker
Malwr Cnau

Nucifraga caryocatactes

A very rare vagrant

The Nutcracker is an irruptive vagrant from central and eastern Europe. There are two Gwent records, both of single birds, the first at St Julian's Wood on either the 19th or 20th October 1954, and the second at Llanhilleth on 12th November 1968. The latter was one of three birds that reached Wales in an unprecedented irruption that brought more than 300 Nutcrackers to Britain, chiefly to the east coast (1994 *Birds in Wales*).

(Red-billed) **Chough**
Brân Goesgoch

Pyrrhocorax pyrrhocorax

A very rare vagrant

The 1963 *Birds of Monmouthshire* mentions three records from between about 1880 and 1905, and states that it was said to have nested on Ysgyryd Fawr in about 1880. It also gives two unconfirmed reports for 1959, but classes all these as doubtful occurrences.

In more modern times there are two records: a single bird was present at Abergavenny sewage works during 30th September–1st October 1972 and two birds flew over Mynydd-Garnclochdy on 16th May 1985.

(Eurasian) **Jackdaw**
Jac-y-do

Corvus monedula

An abundant resident

The Jackdaw, our smallest crow, is a conspicuous and noisy bird that breeds in a wide variety of habitats, including urban areas, parkland, farmland and woodland. It often nests colonially and nest sites include holes in trees and old buildings, crevices in cliff and quarry faces, and chimneys of both old and new buildings. Pairs of Jackdaws are an endearing feature of the rooftops in many of our towns, and their large, chattering flocks make a striking spectacle as they fly to roost late on winter afternoons.

The 1937 and 1963 *Birds of Monmouthshire* and the 1977 *Birds of Gwent* all describe the Jackdaw as a common and widespread breeding species, the first of these sources mentioning 'big colonies among the cliffs of the Wye Valley, and in the mining towns of the coalfield'. This status had probably obtained for some decades previous to 1937, as the 1994 *Birds in Wales* states that numbers are likely to have been stable and high in most parts of Wales throughout the 20th century.

The 1st Gwent Atlas showed the Jackdaw to be a widely distributed breeding species, found in 92% of tetrads in the county, and with gaps in distribution confined almost entirely to open farmland areas of the north, the east and the coastal levels. The 2nd Gwent Atlas paints a very similar picture, with 90% of tetrads occupied, and with absence from five moorland tetrads in the extreme northwest as the only significant change in distribution. However, the proportion of tetrads in the county with *confirmed* or *probable* breeding has risen from 80% to 85%, suggesting an increase in population. This interpretation is supported by national population trends in the period between the Gwent Atlases, which show significant increases in both the UK and Wales indices.

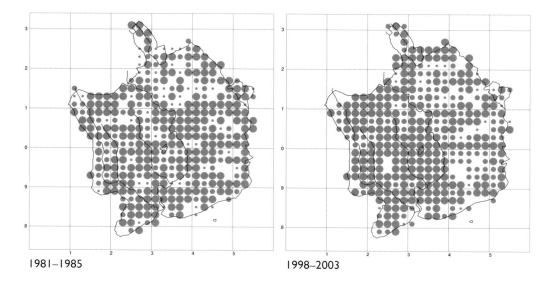

1981–1985   1998–2003

The colonial breeding habit of the Jackdaw and its preference for urban areas make it difficult to estimate a Gwent population size (see Appendix 1). The BBS-based method gives a figure of 5,300–6,400 pairs but this is clearly too low. The highest densities occur in the urban parts of the western valleys where, in many places, almost every terraced house seems to have a pair of Jackdaws in its chimney. In such areas, densities must greatly exceed 100 pairs per tetrad. In contrast, many occupied farmland tetrads in the north and east of the county have only a handful of pairs. An average of 30–40 pairs per tetrad would give a county population of around 10,000–15,000 pairs and is considered a reasonable estimate.

In winter, Jackdaws congregate into large flocks for feeding and roosting. In recent years several large roosts have been reported in Gwent, the largest of which have been 500 near Aberbeeg in September 2000, around 1,000 flying down Clydach Gorge in December 2001; and 1,000+ at Llanfoist and 800 flying over Newport, both in 2003. This last record probably relates to birds flying to roost at Tredegar Park, Newport which is possibly the largest roost in the county and can hold several thousand birds. Jackdaws from the Ebbw and lower Rhymney valleys, as well as Newport and the surrounding area, fly to Tredegar Park to roost, in flocks varying from tens to hundreds (R. M. Clarke, pers. comm).

Partial albinos are occasionally seen in the county often with varying numbers of white secondary feathers. Complete albinos were reported in 2001 and 2002.

Gwent Breeding Atlas data and population size

Gwent Atlas	Confirmed tetrads	Probable tetrads	Possible tetrads	Total tetrads	Change in total	Gwent population
1981–1985	237	80	47	364	–	–
1998–2003	242	94	20	356	–2%	10,000–15,000 pairs

National breeding data and conservation status

Estimated Welsh population	Welsh CBC/BBS trend 1985–2003	UK CBC/BBS trend 1985–2003	Welsh & UK conservation status
59,000 pairs	+33%	+24%	Green-listed

Rook
Ydfran

Corvus frugilegus

A common and widespread resident

In Britain the Rook is a widespread and common breeding resident, absent only from the highest hills. In Gwent, it is widely distributed in all parts of the county except for the the hills and the valleys in the west, where it is scarce.

The 1963 *Birds of Monmouthshire* described the Rook as common throughout the county, even on the higher ground in the north, and with 'many of the small towns in the mining valleys' having small rookeries of up to about six pairs.

In the 1st Gwent Atlas the species was found breeding in 139 well spread tetrads (35%), but only three of these occupied tetrads were in the western valleys, suggesting a decline had occurred in this region of the county since 1963. In the 2nd Gwent Atlas it was found in slightly fewer tetrads (131), but the number in the western valleys had increased to seven. In particular, in the first atlas there were no breeding records from the 10-km squares ST19 and SO10, whereas in the second atlas birds were found breeding in five tetrads in these squares. Elsewhere in the county, seven tetrads were occupied in ST28 in the first atlas compared with only three in the second, SO40 dropped from 19 to 14 occupied tetrads, and SO32 increased from five to eight. Other 10-km squares in the county also showed small losses and gains.

As Rooks are colonial breeders, and birds may forage well away from their colony, all *possible* breeding records for Rooks in both Gwent Atlases were discarded and presence of nests was required for inclusion in the *probable* or *confirmed* breeding categories. They are noisy and conspicuous when breeding, so proof of breeding is easily obtained.

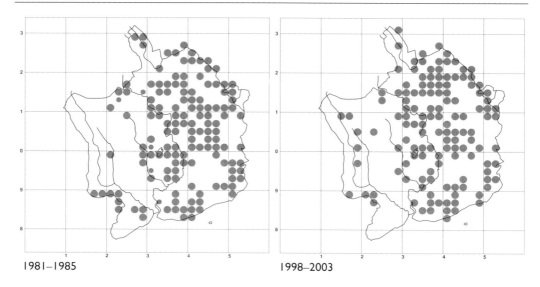

1981–1985   1998–2003

The Rook is one of the few species that has been the subject of national censuses on a regular basis. The Gwent results for all full surveys are shown in Table 99. In 1996, a sample survey was carried out and there was no evidence for any decline in numbers since the census of 1986. The 1996 survey estimated the Welsh population as 53,140 pairs but with a possible range of 35,900–73,600 pairs (Marchant & Gregory, 1996).

Year of survey	No. of nests	No. of rookeries
1945	5,625	96
1975	3,124	178
1980	3,233	155
1985	4,588	214

Table 99. Numbers of nests and rookeries found in Gwent during national surveys

Rookeries can range in size from two to three nests in the smallest colony to over 100 nests, with most having 20–60 nests. The largest rookeries in Gwent have been recorded at Whitson: 98 nests in 1999 and 110 in 2004, at Llansoy: 100+ nests 1982–89, with 167 in 1987; and at Machen church: where over 100 nests were counted in 2002. Although most rookeries are in trees in woods or copses, along hedgerows and streams or even in single trees, a pylon may sometimes be used, as at Black Rock in 1993 where there were seven nests.

Powell (1990) reported a study of rookeries in 10-km square SO40 during 1975–89. He found the average number of nests per colony was 18.7 in 1985 (when the Gwent average was 16.8), 33.3 in 1980 and 25.7 in 1989. Rookeries were found at 64 sites during the study period but only 11 were in continuous occupation in this period. The actual number of rookeries varied from 30 in 1975 to only 23 in 1980 and 36 in 1989.

In 10-km squares ST38 and ST39 ten colonies were found in 2001, containing 469 nests in that year and 483 the following year. Some observers have monitored the increase in Rook nests along the A449 between Usk and Monmouth. On this stretch they nest in relatively low trees, mostly Alders lining streams alongside the dual carriageway. There were 190 nests in ten rookeries in 1998 and 223 nests in eight rookeries in 2001.

A decline in Rook numbers occurred nationally from the 1950s to 1975 but this was followed by an increase that saw numbers in Gwent rise by 30% between 1980 and 1985 in the BTO surveys (Table 99).

Rooks are still shot in some parts of the county and this, or other types of distrubace, can sometimes be a factor in a well-established rookery suddenly becoming inactive. However, although they have long been considered a pest species, Rooks mainly eat insect pests such as wireworms and leatherjackets and so should be valued by farmers. Nevertheless, in some instances Rooks do cause damage to young maize crops.

Outside the breeding season Rooks may gather in very large flocks and roost communally. Flocks of 100–200 birds are not uncommon whilst a roost of 250 birds was noted at Pontllanfraith in September 2003.

Gwent Atlas	Confirmed tetrads	Probable tetrads	Possible tetrads	Total tetrads	Change in total	Gwent population
Gwent Breeding Atlas data and population size						
1981–1985	134	5		139	–	–
1998–2003	131	0		131	−2%	4,600–7,100 pairs

Estimated Welsh population	Welsh BBS trend 1994–2004	UK CBC/BBS trend 1985–2003	Welsh & UK conservation status
National breeding data and conservation status			
34,000–76,000 pairs*	−11%	13%	Green-listed

*1996 BTO survey

Carrion Crow
Brân Dyddyn

Corvus corone

An abundant resident

The Carrion Crow is a very adaptable species, which occupies an extremely wide range of habitats, including towns, suburbs, woodland, farmland at all altitudes and moorland. In coastal areas it will forage extensively in the intertidal zone of the shore. It is widely distributed thoughout Britain, except for north-west Scotland where it is replaced by its close relative the Hooded Crow. The 1994 *Birds in Wales* states that 'all historical accounts agree the ubiquity and abundance of the species throughout Wales, and there seems no reason to assume it has ever been anything other than numerous'.

The 1937 and 1963 *Birds of Monmouthshire* both attested to the ubiquity of the Carrion Crow in the county, and listed the coastal levels, the western valleys and the vicinity of towns as areas where it was most numerous.

In the early 1980s the 1st Gwent Atlas found the species to be present in 99% of tetrads, and a virtually identical distribution was found in the 2nd Gwent Atlas. Numbers of tetrads with *probable* or *confirmed* breeding were also essentially unchanged between the two atlases. In the 2nd Gwent Atlas it was absent from only three mainland tetrads, two of which comprise mainly high moorland, and the third a fragment of coastal land. Breeding was confirmed in 82% of tetrads, reflecting the ease with which incubating adults or large young can been seen in nests, and also the conspicuous nature of recently fledged young. The similarity of the figures from the two Gwent Atlases suggest no change of distribution or density in the intervening years.

Our two standard methods for estimation of the current breeding population of the county give very different figures, both of which we have discarded as likely to be very inaccurate (see Appendix 1). At the time of the 1st Gwent Atlas the population estimate was based on data from the following three CBC plots (territories/tetrad in brackets): lowland farmland at Llanhennock (31); upland farmland and woodland at Penallt (27); and the Gwent Levels at Nash (51). Of these, the figure from Nash, based on an area of only 60ha, was perhaps the least statistically reliable, and has been replaced by two very significant counts carried out over 12km² of the Wentlooge Level in 1979 and 1992 that yielded figures of 28 and 20 occupied nests per tetrad respectively. Use of these figures, together with the Llanhennock and Penallt CBC data, suggests an average occupancy of perhaps 25–30 pairs per tetrad, corresponding to a county breeding population of around 10,000–12,000 pairs during the

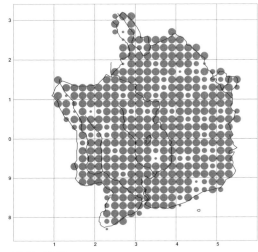

1998–2003

1980s. The 1994 *Birds in Wales* concluded that Carrion Crow populations in Wales had been static for some years owing to saturation of habitats, and the BBS trend in Wales for the last decade has also shown little change, so the above figures, though rather dated, are almost certainly still relevant.

Carrion Crow populations in Britain comprise territorial breeding pairs and also substantial numbers of non-breeding birds that will often feed and roost communally. Thus flocks of up to 150 birds feeding or roosting in Gwent during the height of the breeding season from March to May, are not unusual, and groups of as many as 300 have been occasionally reported in this period. In autumn and winter, the communal gatherings are swollen by the young of the year, and the largest roosts recorded in Gwent have been 800 near Llandegfedd Reservoir during September–November 1992, up to 1,000 at the same roost in winter 1994–95, 1,500–2,000 at Goytre in December 1994 and over 1,000 at Llanwern in February 1997. These roosts are frequently mixed, commonly including Jackdaws and also Rooks.

As implied by its name, the Carrion Crow is most likely to feed on meat from carcasses, but it will also kill for food when the opportunity arises. In Gwent it has been recorded killing young Starlings on two occasions and a young Wood Pigeon on another.

Gwent Breeding Atlas data and population size

Gwent Atlas	Confirmed tetrads	Probable tetrads	Possible tetrads	Total tetrads	Change in total	Gwent population
1981–1985	323	53	15	391	–	–
1998–2003	325	53	12	390	<1%	10,000–12,000 pairs

National breeding data and conservation status

Estimated Welsh population	Welsh BBS trend 1994–2004	UK CBC/BBS trend 1985–2003	Welsh & UK conservation status
126,000 pairs	−4%	+32%	Green-listed

Hooded Crow   *Corvus cornix*
Brân Lwyd

A rare winter visitor; no records since 1992

The Hooded Crow is a handsome grey-bodied crow that breeds in Ireland, northern Scotland and in northern and central regions of continental Europe. In September 2002 it was elevated by the British Ornithologists Union Records Committee (BOURC) to the status of full species, having previously been classed as a subspecies of the Carrion Crow.

There are twelve Gwent records (Table 100), all of single birds during the period October–April. Except perhaps for the 1953 bird, which was apparently paired with a Carrion Crow and reputed to have bred in the area for the two previous years, all records are likely to represent birds from the Scandinavian breeding population, which are much more migratory than those from the British and Irish breeding populations.

1925	12 October	Undy foreshore	1	shot near Severn Tunnel Junction
1926	6 February	Newport	1	
1931	27 October	Maesycwmmer	1	shot along the Glamorgan border
1953	25–26 March	Bettws Newydd	1	apparently paired with a Carrion Crow.
1966	9–10 November	Llanwernarth	1	
1967	date unknown	Abergavenny	1	
1969	14 November	Wentwood Forest	1	
1969	18 November	Twmbarlwm	1	
1972	1 October	Magor Pill	1	
1979	6–27 February	Gwernesney	1	
1989	9 April	Peterstone	1	
1992	22–23 February	Llandegfedd Reservoir	1	with Carrion Crows

Table 100. Hooded Crow records in Gwent

(Common) **Raven**
Cigfran

Corvus corax

A fairly common resident

The Raven is often thought of as a bird of the mountains, nesting on high crags, but in the absence of persecution it will also nest in trees and on buildings and can take advantage of a wide range of habitats. However, it has always been high on gamekeepers' and farmers' lists of vermin, and its eggs were formerly much sought after by collectors (1994 *Birds in Wales*). Such persecution severely limited its numbers and range, and in the early years of the 20th century the Raven populations of Wales were confined to the least accessible mountain areas. Since the First World War, when keepering activities began to decline, it has slowly recovered, spreading back into the lowlands and even nesting in some town centres.

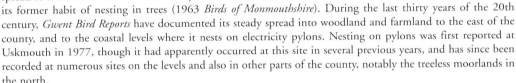

The recovery of the Raven in Gwent, however, was a slow process, and in 1937 it was still thought to nest only on crags in the extreme northwest of the county and at not more than two or three regular sites (1937 *Birds of Monmouthshire*). By the early 1960s it had spread to sites in the centre of the county, where it resumed its former habit of nesting in trees (1963 *Birds of Monmouthshire*). During the last thirty years of the 20th century, *Gwent Bird Reports* have documented its steady spread into woodland and farmland to the east of the county, and to the coastal levels where it nests on electricity pylons. Nesting on pylons was first reported at Uskmouth in 1977, though it had apparently occurred at this site in several previous years, and has since been recorded at numerous sites on the levels and also in other parts of the county, notably the treeless moorlands in the north.

The 1st Gwent Atlas showed that in the early 1980s the Raven was a widespread breeder, but still sparsely distributed in the east of the county, and with only two occupied sites on the coastal levels. In subsequent years there has been a considerable expansion in the east and on the levels. This spread is well illustrated by the 2nd Gwent Atlas, which also shows a much higher density of occupied tetrads in the traditional breeding haunts in the north and west. Between the two atlases the number of occupied tetrads has increased by 40%, and the number with *confirmed* or *probable* breeding by 76%. This increase is reflected in the 1994–2004 BBS population indices of +91% for the UK and +22% for Wales.

With its large size, loud calls, dramatic displays and early breeding season, the Raven is a most obvious and striking bird and it is most unlikely to have been overlooked anywhere in the county. However, these same features, coupled with the large territories of breeding pairs, may sometimes have led to the same pair or family party being recorded in more than one tetrad. This factor, and also the possibility of some pairs nesting in different tetrads in different years of the atlas period, may have resulted in a small degree of over-recording. Based on extrapolation from sample tetrads, a county population of 170–340 breeding pairs is estimated.

Ravens in Wales are strongly associated with the farming of livestock, particularly sheep, and the availability in late winter and early spring of carrion, in the form of afterbirths and still-born lambs, is an important factor in their the breeding success. Numerous local reports have illustrated this association, notable examples being of 60 birds feeding around lambing flocks at Cross Ash in early April, 35 feeding on a sheep carcase at Penhow in January, and large numbers 'patrolling' sheep flocks near Raglan throughout January–March. Other livestock may be taken advantage of, and in 2000–2001, gatherings of up to 40 fed at a pig farm near Manmoel in autumn and winter. They also make use of rubbish tips, and dozens are usually to be seen around the Silent Valley landfill site and the adjoining hill, just south of Ebbw Vale.

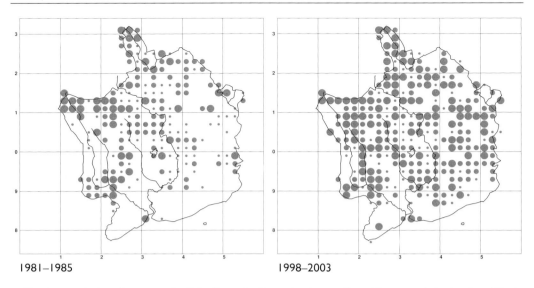

1981–1985   1998–2003

The increase in breeding strength of the Raven in Gwent has been reflected in a growth in the size of flocks recorded in the county. During the 1970s and 1980s flocks of up to 20 were common, up to 30 occasional, and anything larger, such as 57 at Coity Mountain in July 1975 and 60 at Cross Ash in 1988, was quite exceptional. During the 1990s and into the present century, the largest flocks of the year have almost always exceeded 30 birds, and 40–60 has not been unusual. A winter roost at Llandegfedd Reservoir in the mid 1990s commonly held up to 60 birds but, surprisingly, by far the largest flock recorded in Gwent was on 5th May 1931, when 120 birds were present at a site in the north-west of the county where slaughterhouse offal had been dumped.

Gwent Breeding Atlas data and population size

Gwent Atlas	Confirmed tetrads	Probable tetrads	Possible tetrads	Total tetrads	Change in total	Gwent population
1981–1985	45	78	76	199	–	–
1998–2003	109	107	63	279	+40%	170–340 pairs

National breeding data and conservation status

Estimated Welsh population	Welsh BBS trend 1994–2004	UK BBS trend 1994–2004	Welsh & UK conservation status
2,100 pairs	+22%	+91%	Green-listed

(Common) **Starling**   *Sturnus vulgaris*
Drudwen

A widespread and common resident, passage migrant and winter visitor

The Starling is widespread in Britain and Ireland in urban, suburban and rural habitats, being absent only from the highest moors and mountains, but less numerous than two to three decades ago. It was Amber-listed in the 1990s, and was moved in 2004 to the Red List owing to a long-term decline in excess of 50%. Although no real contraction in range was noted at the time of 1988–91 National Atlas, marked declines in numbers in lowland habitats had been first noted in the early 1980s, and have continued since, resulting in a 78% fall in UK numbers during 1978–2003. The decline has been especially severe in woodland.

The 1963 *Birds of Monmouthshire* noted that the Starling was a very common and widespread bird in the county, and this was still the situation in the early 1980s when it was found in 96% of tetrads during the 1st

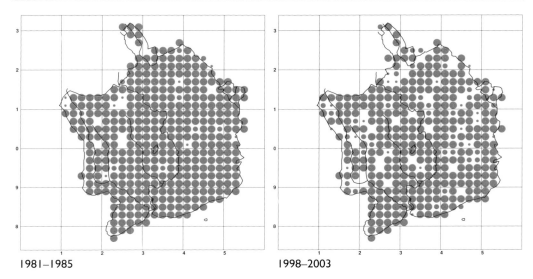

1981–1985   1998–2003

Gwent Atlas, and with *confirmed* breeding in 91%. It is still widespread as a breeding bird in the county, but in the 2nd Gwent Atlas was found in only 90% of tetrads, and with *confirmed* breeding in only 76%. The vacant tetrads were widespread, but with a bias towards the west, and particularly the Black Mountains in the north.

The current Gwent population is estimated as 7,200–9,100 pairs by use of the BBS-based method (Appendix 1). This compares with an estimate during the 1st Gwent Atlas of at least 18,000 pairs, which was based on local CBC data. This decline in local numbers reflects the decline in the national indices that has occurred in the period between the two Gwent Atlases.

The decline had been noted in Gwent, as elsewhere in Britain, as early as 1986 and further concerns about a continuing drop in numbers were expressed during the 1990s in *Gwent Bird Reports*. In 1994 there were few breeding records and winter flocks were only of 100–200 birds. On the Penallt CBC there were 16 pairs in 1981 but by the early 2000s only 4–5 pairs bred.

Starlings breed in cavities in houses and in holes in trees. Possibly some nest sites have been lost due to felling of old dying trees and through renovation work on houses and conversion of barns, but agricultural changes are thought to be mainly responsible for the losses. As breeding birds, Starlings are still common in towns such as Newport.

Starlings prefer to feed in short grass swards, where they probe for leatherjackets and earthworms, and permanent pasture with short swards, as created by stock-grazing, is a favoured feeding area. Whilst there are still abundant pastures in the Gwent, many of them have been ploughed and re-seeded with rye-grass, and treated with artificial fertiliser so that the grass grows quickly and can then be cut two or three times in the season as a silage crop. Whilst the tall grass is unsuitable for Starlings, recently-cut silage fields and sheep-grazed swards provide ideal feeding conditions so this development is not wholly negative for the birds. In the winter birds tend to forage in intensively managed fields (Atkinson *et al.*, 2005). The national decline may be due to decreased survival rates of first year birds, but it is still unclear why these rates have decreased.

Adults and juveniles join up to form large summer and autumn post-breeding flocks from June onwards, sometimes earlier. At Llandegfedd Reservoir 2000 were noted on a silage field in May 1990 and again in 1991. Apple crops have also attracted flocks, as at Goytre where 500 were noted in an orchard from August to November 1990. Wet pastures are commonly used, for example in Llangybi Bottom, where 500-1,000 birds were seen in June 1993. Other large summer or autumn flocks have included 1,000 at Llanvair Discoed in October 1989. Post-breeding flocks appear to be smaller than 20–30 years ago with flocks of only 100–200 birds seen since 1999.

Starlings in summer and autumn roost communally, typically in gatherings of 500–5,000 birds. One well-documented roost used from 1981 to at least 1987 was in spruce trees by Carno Reservoir. Other notable roosts have been in Cwmbran town centre in 1988, on a pylon in the Wye estuary near Chepstow in the late 1980s and early 1990s, and at Uskmouth from June to August 1997 and in August 1998.

Winter numbers are augmented by the arrival of thousands of migrants from Europe. Flocks of several hundreds to up to 1,000 birds are still commonly reported from many locations, although perhaps larger flocks are less common now than in the 1970s and 1980s. A selection of the largest winter feeding flocks recorded in the county is shown in Table 101.

Large roosts of Starlings are also a feature of winter, and the largest of these are also shown in Table 100. All previous roosts have recently been eclipsed by the enormous gathering at Uskmouth in the last three years, which was estimated to hold 50,000 birds in January 2005. Pre-roost gatherings are also often observed, such as 450 at Monmouth School in July 1991 and several thousand in February 1997 at Neville Hall, Abergavenny.

Winter roosts			Winter feeding flocks		
Goytre	1965	20,000	Peterstone	1983	2,000–3,000
Ebbw Vale	1965	15,000	Glascoed	1973/4	10,000
Netherwent	1976	3,000	Newport Docks	1979	5,000–10,000
Cwmcarn	1981	4,400	Llandegfedd Res	1991	2,000
Llanarth	1996	3,000	Goldcliff	1995	2,000–3,000
Monmouth	1995	4,500	Monmouth	1996	20,000
Uskmouth	2003–4	30,000–40,000	Wilcrick Wood	1997	20,000
Uskmouth	2005	50,000	Llandevaud	2003	3,500

Table 101. Largest winter roosts and feeding flocks of Starlings in Gwent

Passage birds have been recorded on the coast, such as at Collister Pill, where flocks of 200–10,000 birds passed by between August and December 1978, and a movement of 500 birds/hour was recorded in May 1973. In mid March 1976 about 10,000 flew north-east over Magor with 4,000 more a few minutes later, and at Peterstone 5,000 flew east at dusk in mid-August 1987. Some flocks flying over are more likely be going to or from a roost than on passage. For example, 9,000 flew east over Monmouth on the evening of 23 March 1976, 3,000 flew east over Garnlydan in 30 minutes on 22 June and 5,000 flew north over Aberbeeg in mid January 1981.

Ringers in Gwent have caught rather few Starlings, with the exception of Dave Proll who ringed many hundreds at Nantyglo in the late 1970s and early 1980s. From these he had a number of interesting recoveries. Several young Starlings from Nantyglo were recovered locally as at Oakdale, at Builth Wells (47km away) and at Gloucester (65km) whilst others moved further. Young females were recovered in the spring in Broughton Astley, Leicestershire (157km) and in Kenilworth, Warwickshire (126km) whilst another ringed in October 1978, was found dead at Blackwell Quay, London, 221km away, in February 1980. An adult ringed in Monmouth in February 1986 was a road casualty at Hillingdon, Middlesex in May 1990. These recoveries suggest that many birds at Nantyglo during the winter came from east and north-east England but some came from breeding areas further afield. For example, one young female ringed in January 1977 was found in Jylland, Denmark in April 1978, and an adult male ringed in November 1980 was shot in Friesland in the Netherlands in April 1982 (623km east-north-east). The longest-distance recovery of a Starling in Gwent was of a bird ringed in July 1982 in Kalingrad, Russia, and found at New Inn, Pontypool, on 10 January 1983, 1,615km west-south-west.

Gwent Breeding Atlas data and population size

Gwent Atlas	Confirmed tetrads	Probable tetrads	Possible tetrads	Total tetrads	Change in total	Gwent population
1981–1985	360	9	9	378	–	–
1998–2003	302	33	20	355	−6%	7,200–9,100 pairs

National breeding data and conservation status

Estimated Welsh population	Welsh CBC/BBS trend 1985–2003	UK CBC/BBS trend 1985–2003	Welsh & UK conservation status
80,300 pairs	−74%	−64%	Red-listed

Rose-coloured Starling (Rosy Starling)
Drudwen Wridog

Sturnus roseus

A very rare vagrant

Despite a recent increase in the number of Rosy Starlings recorded nationally, two very old records, of birds shot at Magor in 1836 and at Monmouth on 11th September 1937, remain the only Gwent records (1963 *Birds of Monmouthshire*).

House Sparrow
Aderyn y Tô

Passer domesticus

A fairly common resident

The House Sparrow is probably one of the most familiar species to us all, living as it does in close proximity to man. It is one of the most widely distributed and numerous land species in the world.

The 1937 and 1963 *Birds of Monmouthshire* both recorded it as being a common breeding resident, especially in and around towns and villages. It was, however, practically absent from the wilder hill-districts, but could be found near human habitations up to the heads of the mining valleys. The 1977 *Birds of Gwent* recorded much the same as the previous publications, but noted the species as being very common although also slow to colonise newly developed rural areas.

The 2002 *Birds in Wales* states that significant declines were noted in most areas during 1970–1990, but that the position might have been reversed by the end of the century. There is no clear evidence of any significant decline occurring in Gwent. Both National Atlases (1968–72; 1988–91) recorded the species in all 10-km squares in the county and the 1st Gwent Atlas recorded the species in 94% of all tetrads with 81% of tetrads having *confirmed* breeding. The position remains largely unchanged in the 2nd Gwent Atlas, with a small decrease (1%) in the number of tetrads occupied. This is perhaps not surprising given the close association of the species with human habitation and the presence of such habitat in almost all tetrads in Gwent. The maintenance of breeding numbers in Gwent is consistent with the strongly positive trend in Wales during the period between the the two Gwent Atlases. The 1st Gwent Atlas assumed a Gwent population in the range of about 15,000–30,000 pairs calculated on the basis of there being 40–80 pairs per tetrad. The latest county estimate is 23,000–33,000 pairs based on analysis of BBS and atlas data (Appendix 1).

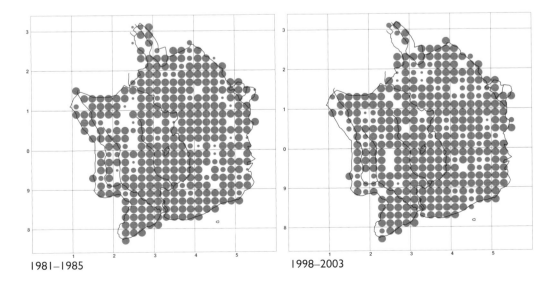

1981–1985 1998–2003

The 1963 *Birds of Monmouthshire* noted that the House Sparrow was known to invade the rural cornlands in numbers in summer, although it did not usually stray far from the local nesting areas. These days there is little evidence of such invasions, most probably due to changing agricultural practice resulting in there being fewer cornfields in the summer. This change in behaviour was noted in the 1988–91 National Atlas which recorded a noticeable decrease in the sizes of post-breeding flocks at the ripening grain fields. In Gwent, flocks of up to 100 birds are recorded during most years, but larger flocks are seldom seen and this has been especially so in the new millennium. Larger flocks noted include: 500 at Ynysfro Reservoir in July 1987, 1,500–2,000 roosting in fir trees near Cwmbran Boating Lake in 1985, 350+ at St Brides in August 1983 and 300 at Ynysyfro Reservoir in August 1990.

Gwent Breeding Atlas data and population size

Gwent Atlas	Confirmed tetrads	Probable tetrads	Possible tetrads	Total tetrads	Change in total	Gwent population
1981–1985	317	33	18	368	–	–
1998–2003	308	50	7	365	−1%	23,000–33,000 pairs

National breeding data and conservation status

Estimated Welsh population	Welsh CBC/BBS trend 1985–2003	UK CBC/BBS trend 1985–2003	Welsh & UK conservation status
484,000 pairs	+291%	−36%	Green-listed

(Eurasian) **Tree Sparrow**   *Passer montanus*
Golfan y Mynydd

An uncommon resident and passage migrant

The Tree Sparrow's breeding habitat includes pollarded willows and other trees with nest-holes along lowland watercourses, together with free-standing trees along roadsides or in groups on farmland. Woodlands are also frequented, especially where they are small, isolated and in open countryside, with well-spaced mature broadleaved trees.

The earliest record of the species in the county is of a bird found at Newport in 1896, the skin of which is now in the National Museum of Wales, Cardiff. The 1937 *Birds of Monmouthshire* reported the species as being a very local resident breeding species with small colonies of 3–10 pairs recorded from the Abergavenny and Usk districts, and two local-ities on the coastal levels. In the latter area, birds had been recorded for at least 40–50 years, but numbers varied greatly with just one or two pairs in some years. It was noted as breeding in considerable numbers in 1935–36, but having declined afterwards. Although not generally noted in breeding areas during the autumn, it was found in small flocks along the coast in winter.

It was found breeding in the Llandegfedd and Llangybi areas in 1945, principally associated with old orchards. A small colony was nesting in elms near the River Usk at Llabadoc in 1948, 1949 and 1950, while two pairs were recorded at Peterstone in 1949 and at least three pairs near Severn Tunnel Junction in 1960. However, the 1977 *Birds of Gwent* described the species as fairly common in all areas apart from the industrial valleys, and noted that it was often seen in flocks of up to 30 and occasionally up to 80.

A traditional nesting site for the species in Gwent has been the pollarded willows on the coastal levels and along the Usk Valley, but the custom of pollarding trees has greatly diminished over the years, depriving the species of potential nesting sites. Increased use of nest boxes was noted locally in the 1970s, possibly owing to a reduction in natural holes caused by the clearance of old orchards and trees at that time. Several nest box colonies have emerged in Gwent over the years. At the Llandegfedd Reservoir colony 6–10 pairs were present from 1968 into the early 1970s, and small numbers intermittently up to 1992. At New Inn, the colony produced 43 clutches at its peak, resulting in 189 fledged young in 1981, and still had 40 nests in 1984. At Raglan, up to seven pairs used boxes in 1985–1987. At Porton, a small colony was established in the early 1990s and up to five boxes were occupied regularly up to 1997, at which time breeding ceased for several years until it started again in 2002. Successful breeding has continued at Porton since 2002, with the provision of new nest boxes aiding the recovery, so that by 2006 at least ten pairs were nesting successfully in the area.

The 1st Gwent Atlas recorded the species as being patchily distributed with records from 52% of total tetrads. However, because the species could easily be overlooked, it was suggested that it might be under-recorded. Strongholds were noted as being the farmlands of the coastal levels and the Usk Valley, while smaller numbers occurred in woodlands, and scattered pairs in the uplands, usually associated with farms, where grain was an important food source. The lowland CBC plots were noted as having the most favourable habitat for the species with more than 20 pairs per tetrad. Nevertheless, an estimated Gwent population of 4,000 pairs based on these CBC densities was conceded as being a little high even at the time.

The Tree Sparrow has been declining nationally in both numbers and range for a large part of the last century. There was an 85% decline in numbers in Britain between the two National Atlases (1968–72 and 1988–91), the largest decline of any common species during this period. Its range also decreased by 20% during the same period, with the largest losses being in Wales and Scotland. The dramatic national decline of the species was mirrored at the Goldcliff CBC plot. Although based on a small sample, successive five-yearly averages from 1975 to 1989 were 5.2, 4.4 and 2.0 territories, and then none after 1989 (Bailey, 1995). The 2nd Gwent Atlas recorded the species in just 34 tetrads, a reduction in range of 88% compared to the 1st Gwent Atlas. Populations recorded previously in the western valleys and at Peterstone have all but completely disappeared. Furthermore, the obvious stronghold of the species in the centre of the county in the Usk Valley has also disappeared, along with the populations that once existed in the Wye Valley. Breeding was *confirmed* in only 12 tetrads including at Trelleck (5–6 pairs in 1999), Dingestow, Llanllowell, Porton, Llandenny and near Cwmbran and Pontypool. Perhaps surprisingly, nine of the tetrads (26%) that held birds during the 2nd Gwent Atlas did not do so during the previous atlas period.

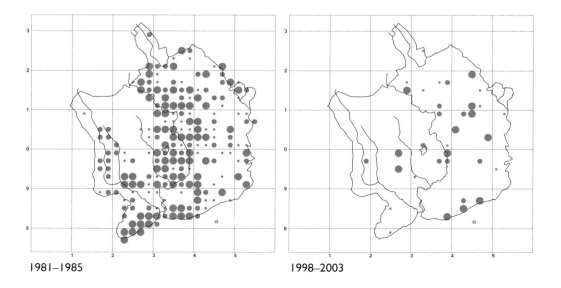

1981–1985   1998–2003

The size of the current population is difficult to determine, in part due to limited information. However, assuming ten pairs per tetrad (the estimated population density in occupied tetrads), and applying this to the number of tetrads where breeding was either *confirmed* or *probable*, an estimated total of about 240 pairs is produced. It is strongly recommended that further work be done on establishing the true strength of the residual Gwent population of this threatened species.

There has sometimes been evidence of passage along the coast during the autumn, especially when the national population was higher. By far the largest flock recorded during passage was over 130 birds at Goldcliff on 6th October 1968, but smaller flocks of 10–60, mostly moving south-south-west, were recorded on the coast in October during the 1970s. Light passage was also noted at St Brides in September/October 1990, with a maximum of 26 on 16th October. There is an interesting movement of a bird ringed as a nestling in Warwickshire in May 1980 and then re-trapped 100km away at Abergavenny in December of the same year.

The 1977 *Birds of Gwent* noted that flocks of up to 30 and occasionally up to 80 were often seen. Flock sizes give an insight into population densities. The largest were recorded in the 1970s: with 200 at Newport rubbish tip in December 1975, 200 at Magor in August 1976, 150 at Coldharbour Pill in November 1976 and 300 at Monmouth from November 1976 to mid June 1977. Good-sized flocks continued into the 1980s: with 150 near Tredegar Park House during February 1980, 75 at Llancayo in November 1983, 70 at Llangybi in December 1983 and 100+ in the Peterstone area during August–September 1989. Also in 1989 there were 90 at Goldcliff in late August and 220 at Llandewi Skirrid during January/February. Flock sizes since the 1990s have been considerably smaller, rarely exceeding 30 birds, and this decline has continued since 2000, with flocks of 10 or more birds now being very unusual.

Little is known about the factors affecting the species' decline but it has occurred at the same time as decreases in the numbers and/or ranges of other farmland birds that share its diet of grass, wildflower and cereal seeds, and also feed their young on insects. It is likely therefore that the reasons associated with the decrease in breeding numbers include changing agricultural practices and the reduced availability of suitable nest sites.

Gwent Breeding Atlas data and population size

Gwent Atlas	Confirmed tetrads	Probable tetrads	Possible tetrads	Total tetrads	Change in total	Gwent population
1981–1985	79	64	60	203	–	–
1998–2003	12	10	12	34	−84%	c.240 pairs

National breeding data and conservation status

Estimated Welsh population	Welsh trend	UK CBC/BBS trend 1985–2003	Welsh & UK conservation status
4,600 pairs	Not available	−39%	Red-listed

Chaffinch
Ji-binc

Fringilla coelebs

A common resident and winter visitor

The Chaffinch is one of Britain's most widespread, abundant and familiar birds. It was described in the 1963 *Birds of Monmouthshire* as a common resident breeding species, whose numbers were increased by immigration in winter. The 1977 *Birds of Gwent* describes it as one of the commonest birds in the county, breeding from the coast to the limit of bushy vegetation in the hills. In the 1st Gwent Atlas it was found in 99% of tetrads and it was similarly abundant at the time of the 2nd Gwent Atlas, being widespread and very common throughout the county, and again found in 99% of tetrads, with confirmed breeding in as many as 64%.

It still occurs in the highest numbers in broadleaved woodland but is also common in parks, gardens and conifer plantations. Based on estimates of 165 pairs per tetrad in the lowlands and 90 pairs in the uplands, the 1st Gwent Atlas put the county population at about 55,000 pairs, but current estimates based on BBS and other data give a figure of 32,000–36,000 pairs. National trends in the period between the two Gwent Atlases have been fairly stable.

In the winter, large flocks of up to 200 birds, occasionally to 400, occur on arable land where weed seeds are plentiful. Some of the largest flocks recorded over the last decade include over 300 at Castleton on 6th January 1993 and 400 at Penpergwm on 7th November 1993. In 1988 a flock of 450 birds was feeding on buds of *Corydalis claviculata*. Flocks may also feed in woodland especially under beech trees in years of good mast, but also in conifers where they favour larches. Feeding on larch cones often occurs in mixed flocks with Redpolls, Goldfinches and Siskins.

About 50% of Chaffinches present in Britain in winter have migrated from continental Europe, mainly Fennoscandia, and most of these immigrants comprise young of the year and females (Winter Atlas). The occurrence of such birds in Gwent is demonstrated by ringing data: two Chaffinches ringed in winter in Gwent have been recovered during spring in the Netherlands and Germany respectively, while another two have been recovered in south-east England, possibly *en route* to the continent. In the reverse direction, birds ringed in autumn in the Netherlands, Sweden and south-east England have been recovered in Gwent during the winter months. Significantly, six of these seven records involved young birds.

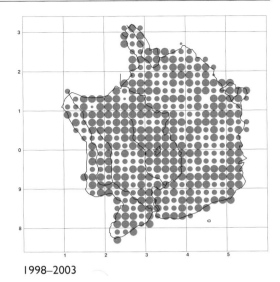

1998–2003

Passage birds occur along the coast in the autumn. Records are generally of 60–150 passing east or west per hour during October or early November, but 720 were observed flying west in two hours at Goldcliff on 8th October 1988 and several thousand east in three hours at West Pill on 15th October 1988. A number of large movements occurred in 1992, including 473 flying east in 105 minutes on 7th October at Peterstone, 180 east in an hour at Black Rock on 10th October, and 1,000+ north-east in two hours at Peterstone on 8th November.

Gwent Breeding Atlas data and population size

Gwent Atlas	Confirmed tetrads	Probable tetrads	Possible tetrads	Total tetrads	Change in total	Gwent population
1981–1985	284	90	15	389	–	–
1998–2003	251	135	4	390	0	32,000–36,000 pairs

National breeding data and conservation status

Estimated Welsh population	Welsh CBC/BBS trend 1985–2003	UK CBC/BBS trend 1985–2003	Welsh & UK conservation status
464,000	−3.7%	+7.6%	Green-listed

Brambling
Pinc y Mynydd

Fringilla montifringilla

A fairly common but local winter visitor and passage migrant

Bramblings migrate south-west to southern Scandinavia in autumn, only moving further south-west to Britain if they find a scarcity of beechmast. Accordingly, irregular influxes into Britain can occur, causing wintering numbers to vary between 50,000 and two million birds (*BWP*). This fluctuation occurs in microcosm in Gwent, with maximum annual flock sizes ranging from three individual birds to five hundred.

The 1963 *Birds of Monmouthshire* stated that the Brambling occured somewhat infrequently in winter in hard weather, and that numbers rarely exceeded three or four. It does however record a flock of about 100 in a field near Chepstow from 26th February until mid-March 1956, feeding on weed seeds. Subsequent to 1963 it has been recorded annually in the county, in varying numbers, and feeding on beechmast, stubbles and weed seeds.

Bramblings in Gwent are most commonly observed in the company of Chaffinches, usually in small numbers but occasionally in flocks of 100 or more. Flocks of c.200 have been recorded eight times between 1971 and 2003, at sites dispersed throughout the county: at Manmoel, Llantrisant, Lydart Hill, Sudbrook, Caldicot Castle, Abergavenny, Pen-y-fan Pond and Whitestone in the Wye Valley. The two largest flocks recorded are 350 feeding on beechmast at Wentwood on 11th February 1993 and c.500 under Beeches at Llanover in December 1993.

The species was first observed feeding at bird tables in Gwent at Wentwood on 11th January 1968. This has gradually become more widespread, with peanuts and sunflower seeds becoming important food sources, especially in years with a poor availability of beechmast (*Migration Atlas*).

Bramblings usually arrive in Gwent from mid-October and leave for their breeding grounds in Scandinavia in mid-April. They migrate principally at night but light diurnal passage movements have been observed in October and November on six occasions between 1968 and 2000. These were all at coastal sites, with four records of between one and four birds, ten birds at Blackrock on 2nd November 1991, and 17 at Peterstone on 26th November 1975. Return passage movements have been recorded only in 2000 with two birds on 6th April and three on 15th April at Skirrid Fach, and two on 16th April at Beacon Hill. The earliest and latest county records are one at Peterstone on 4th October 1972, and a male singing at Cadira Beeches, Wentwood on 14th May 1978.

There have been two recoveries of Gwent-ringed birds, both ringed at Nantyglo in 1994: the first was ringed in February and recovered in October of the same year in the Netherlands; the second, ringed on 21st March was recovered some four weeks later in Lincolnshire (217km east-north-east), a direction that, if continued, would have taken it back to Scandinavia.

With a milder climate due to global warming occurring in northern Europe, good beechmast crops may be produced more regularly in Scandinavia, causing British numbers to decrease as birds are able to find food further north. The very low numbers occurring in Gwent in the years 1999 until 2002 may be due to this phenomenon, and it will be interesting to see if the trend continues.

(European) **Greenfinch**   *Carduelis chloris*
Llinos Werdd

A common and widespread resident; increasing. Also a partial post-breeding migrant and winter visitor

Greenfinches breed in most areas that contain trees and bushes, particularly favouring gardens, parks and churchyards in towns and villages, and are widespread in Britain. They nest either alone or in loose colonies. Outside the breeding season they are gregarious, forming feeding flocks and roosting communally in hedges, particularly evergreens.

The1963 *Birds of Monmouthshire* describes the Greenfinch as a common, resident breeding species except in the hill districts, and this was confirmed during 1981–85 by the results of the 1st Gwent Atlas, which showed it to be present in 80% of tetrads in the county, with gaps limited mostly to the high ground in the north-west.

The 2nd Gwent Atlas revealed it to be present in 92% of tetrads, which represents an increase in range of 43 tetrads over the 1st Gwent Atlas. The increase in range is most noticeable in the northern and western hill areas and has probably resulted from improving habitat, with birds now occupying the matured conifer plantations on hill flanks. Colonisation of gardens in towns and villages of the western valleys has also occurred, where conifers have provided nest sites and bird tables and seed-bearing shrubs and trees a food source. This increase in range is also evident in the urban areas generally throughout the county. By contrast, the species has become scarcer on farmland, owing to changes in agricultural practice, such as increased herbicide use, increased autumnal planting of cereals and more efficient harvesting, all of which have reduced food availability.

In Gwent, the overall result of the above changes of habitat use has been an increase in population. The number of tetrads in the county with *confirmed* breeding has increased from 31% to 54% between the two Gwent Atlases and, in combination with the extension in range, a large population increase is indicated. This is borne out by the estimated population size of 11,000–12,000 pairs, which represents a substantial increase on the 7,000 pairs suggested in the 1st Gwent Atlas. At a UK level there has been a 43% increase in the population index over the same time period, while in Wales the increase has been 63%.

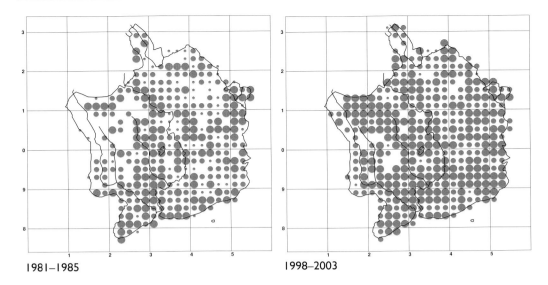

1981–1985

1998–2003

The increase in the UK index disguises the fact that the CBC index showed a relatively stable Greenfich population level from 1966 until the mid 1990s, and most of the growth has occurred in the years since then. On a very local scale, it interesting to record that changes in the number of Greenfinch territories on the Penallt CBC site have followed the rising trend in the mid-1990s with eight territories during 1991–1994, 10–11 in 1995 and 16 in 1996.

The species has always been considered largely sedentary but ringing data provides evidence that this is not always the case. Movements in the post breeding period often occur, particularly in juveniles (Newton, 1972), and the majority of birds return to their natal or previous breeding location in the spring (*Migration Atlas*). There have been 87 recoveries of birds originally ringed in Gwent. Of these 60 were recovered in Gwent, eight in the rest of Wales, 17 in southern England and single birds reached as far as northern England and Scotland.

There have also been 23 recoveries in the county of birds ringed elsewhere in the UK. Of these, one was from the north of England, 19 from the south of England and three from other parts of Wales. There is also one exceptional record of a bird ringed on Guernsey being recovered in Llangybi on 14th April 1990. Full details of all such long-distance movements are given in Appendix 9. Interpretation of these data suggests that birds breeding in Gwent are largely sedentary, but with some exchanges with neighbouring counties. However, it also suggests that a significant proportion of the Gwent wintering population are migrants from southern England and in particular from the south-east.

There is some evidence of a small movement of birds at coastal sites during the autumn, mostly in October and early November. Such passage was first reported in the 1977 *Birds of Gwent*, which noted small parties moving along the coast at Goldcliff and Sudbrook during the autumn months of 1974 and 1975. Subsequent records, although not plentiful and probably a reflection of under-recording rather than anything else, include two of 20 and 22 birds respectively, and 60 flying south-west in 90 minutes at Goldcliff on 5th November 1985.

The 1963 *Birds of Monmouthshire* stated that flocks are usually to be seen on the coastal flats during winter but, while this remains a favoured area, the majority of very large flocks in the past forty years have been further inland. A notable early record was of 100+ at Undy in 1966, but since then such flocks have become more common, and there have been nine of 200–300 birds since 1970, with all but one (which was in August), occurring between October and April. There have been two record-sized flocks of 400 recorded: one near Raglan in December 1981 and the other at a roost at Black Rock in November 1997.

Otherwise, gatherings of up to twenty are common in the post-breeding and winter periods, and are regularly seen at garden feeding stations. The taking of food from bird feeders is thought to have originated during the harsh winter of 1962/63, and its increase was noted in the *1967 Gwent Bird Report*. The trend has continued to the extent that peanuts and sunflower seeds can form the main food source of many birds during the winter.

Gwent Breeding Atlas data and population size

Gwent Atlas	Confirmed tetrads	Probable tetrads	Possible tetrads	Total tetrads	Change in total	Gwent population
1981–1985	123	138	58	319	–	–
1998–2003	213	140	10	363	+14%	11,000–12,000 pairs

National breeding data and conservation status

Estimated Welsh population	Welsh CBC/BBS trend 1985–2003	UK CBC/BBS trend 1985–2003	Welsh & UK conservation status
44,000	+63%	+43%	Green-listed

(European) Goldfinch   *Carduelis carduelis*
Nico

A resident and summer visitor. Also a passage migrant and possibly a winter visitor in small numbers

The Goldfinch is a small attractive finch that is easily identified by its red face, broad yellow wing-bars and rapid twittering song. It is widespread in Britain and breeds in trees, located in parks, gardens, woodland edges and farmland, particularly where weedy areas are also present. Goldfinches are usually observed in pairs during spring and summer, but form flocks in the post-breeding period and are most conspicuous during the autumn or winter when feeding on thistles.

The species was a popular British cage bird and large numbers were caught in Wales in the 19th century. The cagebird trade inevitably had a negative impact on the wild population, and it was not until legal protection was introduced in the early part of the 20th century that the population started to increase again. This is reflected in the 1937 *Birds of Monmouthshire,* which described the Goldfinch as breeding in fair numbers and as having recently increased considerably throughout the county, with the exception of the mining districts. By the time of the 1963 *Birds of Monmouthshire* it was described as a common resident, breeding in fair numbers and having penetrated into the more sheltered valleys amongst the hills of the northern area. Since then it has had mixed fortunes: the CBC index has shown large fluctuations with an initial rapid increase from 1972–1975, followed by a 50% decline from 1975–1987 and Amber-list status. Since 1987, it has made a gradually accelerating recovery, especially in Wales, resulting in its transfer to Green-list status.

The 1st Gwent Atlas revealed a widespread distribution in the county, with presence in 85% of tetrads and *confirmed* or *probable* breeding in 75%, but with absence from large areas of the higher ground in the north-west. The 2nd Gwent Atlas shows presence in 93% of tetrads, an increase of 33 tetrads (10%), and *confirmed* or *probable* breeding in 88% of tetrads. The expansion has been achieved primarily by colonisation of the previously vacant areas in the north-western valleys, and has probably been driven by a burgeoning population moving into more marginal areas, but also by the environmental improvement that has occurred in these areas and possibly by the amelioration of climate.

The methodologies employed in the 2nd Gwent Atlas give a population range of 6,400–14,000 pairs, which is a very substantial increase on the 5,500 pairs suggested in the 1st Gwent Atlas. The upward trend in numbers evident in Gwent mirrors the 72% UK increase in population between the Gwent Atlases and also the BBS trend in Wales from 1994-2003, which was even more positive at +110%.

Severe winters such as 1962/63, those of the mid 1970s and 1980/81 contributed to a sharp decline in the population of Welsh-wintering Goldfinches. However, the recent mild winters have contributed to a continu-

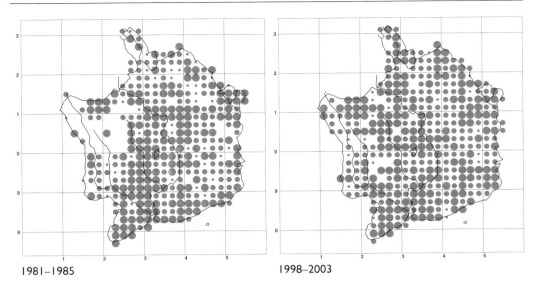

1981–1985   1998–2003

ing recovery. Another factor implicated in the recovery is the increased use of garden bird tables as a source of food, particularly Nyger seed. Feeding in gardens was first recorded in Gwent on 1st April 1992, at Abergavenny, and has gradually become a widespread behaviour. In conjunction with several mild winters this is likely to have resulted in a higher survival rate than formerly among Gwent's wintering birds. Certainly the number of Goldfinches wintering in Gwent has visibly increased and a large majority of these are male birds, which then have first choice of territories in spring. This could be a major factor in the surge of numbers, and in the medium term, resident birds could become the majority.

The largest flocks or 'charms', are generally observed during the post-breeding period. Groups of greater than 50 birds are seen regularly, whereas flocks of over 200 birds are uncommon. From the late 1970s on, reported charms were smaller, reflecting the species' decline. However, since 1988 charms of over 150 have been recorded almost annually.

The majority of British-breeding Goldfinches migrate to the continental mainland, mostly to Belgium, western France and Spain to winter, although a small number also migrate to Ireland. The *Migration Atlas* states that Irish, Scottish and Welsh Goldfinches are believed to follow a predominantly south-westerly migratory path, similar to those from southern England. It has been suggested that as much as 80% of the breeding population in southern Britain is made up of birds that are summer visitors (Newton, 1972). Although it is not clear if such a high percentage of Welsh birds migrate, the 1994 *Birds in Wales* does note that many of the Welsh-breeding Goldfinches migrate at the end of the summer.

Visible movement of Goldfinches at coastal sites in Gwent is often observed during September and October. The first record of this kind was on 6th August 1968 when 'several' flew south-west at Undy, but large flocks had previously been noted on the levels during the autumn which might have involved passage birds. Such flocks are still evident: for example, 500 at Peterstone on 11th October 1964, 330 at Sluice Farm in early October 1977, 350 at St Brides in September 1991 and 300+ at West Pill in October 1991. Away from the coast there were 200 at Henllys in September 1988 and 500 were at Penhow in October 1991. Since 1972, movements have been recorded almost annually, usually in an easterly

direction. The largest single movement involved 650 birds moving east in two hours on 21st October 1990, at Collister Pill. A light passage observed during May 1996 at Peterstone is the only recorded instance of spring movement in the county.

The migration of Goldfinches to Spain is illustrated by two records of birds ringed in Gwent. One ringed at Gwehelog, Usk on 2nd August 1992 was recovered almost 1,000km south in Navarra, northern Spain on 20th October of the same year, while another ringed in Monmouth on 13th August 1975 was recovered later that year over 1,100km to the south in Valladolid, northern Spain on 17th November.

With a majority of the local breeding Goldfinch population migrating, the sizes of winter flocks are much reduced compared with those seen in autumn, although the 1937 *and* 1963 *Birds of Monmouthshire* both noted that large flocks could be found on the coastal districts during the winter. Winter flocks are commonly observed feeding on weed seeds on the coastal levels, and elsewhere in Alder trees, sometimes in the company of Siskins. It is possible that our resident birds may be joined by migrants from the north, but there is no ringing evidence to support this. An exceptional winter flock was at Wentwood during the first half of 1977 when thousands of birds were present.

Gwent Breeding Atlas data and population size

Gwent Atlas	Confirmed tetrads	Probable tetrads	Possible tetrads	Total tetrads	Change in total	Gwent population
1981–1985	172	125	38	335	–	–
1998–2003	184	164	19	367	+10%	6,400–14,000 pairs

National breeding data and conservation status

Estimated Welsh population	Welsh CBC/BBS trend 1985–2003	UK CBC/BBS trend 1985–2003	Welsh & UK conservation status
39,000	+203%	+72%	Green-listed

(Eurasian) Siskin   *Carduelis spinus*
Pila Gwyrdd

An increasing breeding species, numerous winter visitor and passage migrant

The Siskin breeds in mature conifers, preferably with alder and birch nearby. In Britain, it has historically been restricted in breeding range to the Caledonian pinewoods (Newton, 1972). The maturing of spruce, larch and pine planta-tions to the stage where they could produce cones, provided a food source and nesting site ideal for Siskin, allowing an expansion in its breeding range.

The colonisation of conifer plantations in Gwent may have begun in the early 1970s, although breed-ing was not confirmed until much later. The first record of singing males was at Wentwood on 12th April 1971, and a pair observed there on 1st July 1974 was the first breeding season record for Gwent. Other contemporary records were of a pair at Whitebrook in April 1974 and at Abergavenny in June 1975. There were no further breeding season records until May 1978 when pairs were seen, twice in Wentwood and once at Buckholt, in spruce and larch. Subsequently, summer records became more frequent, though still irregular. Breeding was first proven in 1984, when family parties were observed both at Wentwood and at a wood near the River Wye, and occurred again in 1985 when two nests were found at Trelleck in Douglas Firs.

It follows from the above, that at the time of the 1st Gwent Atlas (1981–85) the colonisation of the county by Siskins was still at an early stage, and this is reflected in the atlas map, which shows presence in only 40 tetrads, and *confirmed* or *probable* breeding in only 21 of these. By contrast, the 2nd Gwent Atlas shows the Siskin to be present in 112 tetrads (28%), which corresponds to an approximately three-fold increase in breeding range between atlases. This has been achieved by the colonisation of large tracts of suitable, unoccupied breeding habitat, namely mature conifer forest. The majority of conifer forests in the county are now occupied, and in consequence the species' strongholds are in the areas of greatest afforestation. These are the western valleys, which have 45% of all occupied tetrads and 62% of tetrads with *confirmed* breeding, together with the Llanthony area, the Wye Valley woods, and Wentwood. Young Siskins are reared on a mixture of insects, and the seeds of spruce, larch or pine. As the availability of these seeds is dependent on the size of the cone crop, which is very variable from year to year, it follows that large annual fluctuations in breeding numbers can occur. However, the broad local trend seems to be upward, even though overall BBS trend for the UK (1994–2004) is one of decline. The Gwent population of 1,380 pairs was derived using an average density of one pair per five hectares, as suggested in the 1988–91 National Atlas as a conservative estimate, and a conifer expanse in Gwent of 69km². This is a massive increase on the 100 pairs suggested in the 1st Gwent Atlas for the period 1981–85.

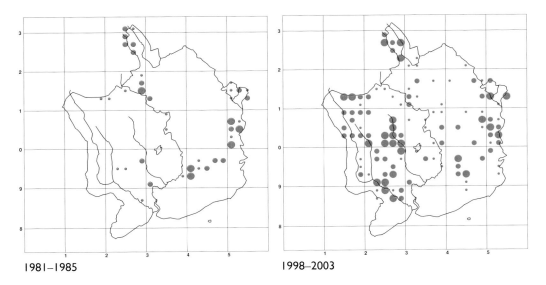

1981–1985 | 1998–2003

Historically the Siskin was merely a winter visitor to the county in small numbers (1963 *Birds of Monmouthshire*), migrating from northern Britain and areas of northern and eastern Europe. This migration still occurs and the county population is swollen by the arrival of migrants arriving mainly from September onwards. The size of winter flocks, though variable, has increased steadily since the 1960s, mirroring the growth of the UK population. The Siskin is sometimes subject to irruptive behaviour which can be triggered by severe winter weather, or a poor birch or alder seed crop, resulting in the irregular appearance of very large and numerous flocks.

Table 102 shows maximum flock sizes recorded at Llanwenarth over the last 40 years, and illustrates the variable but increasing trend in the pattern of winter numbers.

Year	1966	1967	1970	1975	1986	1995	1997	2003
Number	16	40	60	95	140	50	300	30

Table 102. Annual maximum Siskin counts at Llanwenarth

The years 1980 and 1981 were possibly irruptive years with large flocks observed at numerous locations. For example, in 1980: 170 at Cadira Beeches, 100 at Whitebrook, 150 at Gobion and 200 at Cwmbrwrch; and in

1981: 120 at Monmouth, 200 at Wentwood and 250 at Llantarnam. Wentwood has been the most productive area for large flocks with four of 200: in 1991, 1993, 1994 and 1997.

The use of bird tables for feeding was first observed in Gwent during January and February of 1971, with 30 to 40 Siskins present at a Mardy garden. This practice remained at a low level for a number of years but has since increased to the stage where Siskins are now present at most birdfeeders during the late winter period, when natural seed crops are becoming exhausted. Such behaviour is likely to have increased their winter survival rates.

Ringing data suggest that this species is extremely mobile, particularly in winter. There are thirteen recoveries of birds that were ringed in Gwent, and of these only three recoveries were at Gwent sites. There have been nine records of birds ringed elsewhere in the United Kingdom and Ireland, but recovered in Gwent, and of these, eight were movements of over 100km. There is also one record of a bird ringed at La Fougeraie, Sark on 28th October 1985 that was recovered at Cross Keys, Gwent on 2nd March 1986, a movement of 247km north-north-west.

Details of all movements over 100km are given in Appendix 9. Their analysis suggests that the most commonly recorded movement is of birds recorded in spring and summer in Scotland, and wintering in Gwent. There are five such records: three from Highland, one from Oban and one from Dumfries and Galloway. Two records of birds that were recovered shortly after ringing (in Gwent), showed a due north orientation of movement and were presumably returning to breeding sites further north. A bird recovered in Belgium is likely to have been returning to breeding grounds in Fennoscandia or the Baltic States, and three records from south-east England may also have been *en route* to these areas. There is a single record of a bird summering in Clwyd, North Wales and wintering in Gwent. Ringing data therefore suggest that most of Gwent's wintering population comes from the north, probably migrating from Scotland, with smaller numbers arriving from northern Europe and possibly a few from North Wales. The relative abundance of these different population groups is likely to vary between winters.

Visible passage is often recorded in autumn, and movements of between three and 50 birds have been observed almost annually along the coast since 1986, usually moving south-westwards. During September–October 1997, migrants were observed in unprecedented numbers, totalling at least 1,420 birds. Of these c.500 were flying west at Uskmouth in three hours on 6th September, 130+ at Peterstone on 20th September, c.200 at Black Rock on 21st September and c.200 at Uskmouth on 21st September.

Gwent Breeding Atlas data and population size

Gwent Atlas	Confirmed tetrads	Probable tetrads	Possible tetrads	Total tetrads	Change in total	Gwent population
1981–1985	6	15	19	40	–	–
1998–2003	26	44	42	112	+173%	c.1,380 pairs

National breeding data and conservation status

Estimated Welsh population	Welsh trend	UK BBS trend 1994–2004	Welsh & UK conservation status
27,000	Not available	−40%*	Green-listed

*Wide fluctuations are concealed in this figure.

(Common) **Linnet**   *Carduelis cannabina*
Llinos

A common resident, summer visitor and passage migrant

Cock Linnets are easily identified during the breeding season, having bright red feathering on the head and breast. In all other plumages the Linnets' pale wing flashes and white outer tail feathers are probably the most useful distinguishing features. These are birds of open country, particularly uplands and farmland, often nesting in loose colonies in gorse, heather and young forestry plantations in the former, and in hedgerows and scrubby thickets in the latter.

The 1937 *Birds of Monmouthshire* described the Linnet as a common breeding species throughout the county, up to the limit of bushy vegetation in the hills, and very numerous in flocks in autumn and winter. However, the 1963 *Birds of Monmouthshire* was less confident about its status, and expressed the view that it might be declining. It transpired that this was an accurate observation, as during the subsequent forty years, there was a major population decline nationally, with a particularly rapid decline between the mid-1970's and mid-1980's, followed by a stable period. This resulted in a 51% reduction in the UK population between 1970 and 2001 and Red list status. The main factor responsible for this decline is considered to have been a reduction in weed seeds, due to an increased use of herbicides, scrub clearance in the lowlands and intensive sheep grazing in the uplands. In Wales however, the BBS results show a recovery between 1994 and 2003 of 26%.

The 1st Gwent Atlas was carried out towards the end of the period of steep decline, but despite this showed presence of Linnets in 78% of tetrads, and with *confirmed* or *probable* breeding in 63%. The 2nd Gwent Atlas shows a small expansion in distribution, with 83% of tetrads now occupied, and *confirmed* or *probable* breeding in 76%, reflecting the upward trend seen in Wales as a whole in the period between the two atlases. The current calculated population range of 4,900–5,800 pairs is little different from the upper limit of 6,000 pairs suggested in 1st Gwent Atlas. The main gains between the two atlases are in the far north of the county, which has fifteen additional tetrads occupied. Factors contributing to this change of fortunes are an increase in the area of set-aside land, and the widespread planting of oilseed rape, which Linnets now use as a food source.

Illustrative breeding records include a series from Mynydd Garnclochdy from 1987 to 1991 showing a constant population of 12–15 pairs, including 14 nests which contained 61 eggs and produced 48 young in 1989. The Newport Wetlands Reserve recorded 39 pairs in 2002 and 37 pairs in 2004.

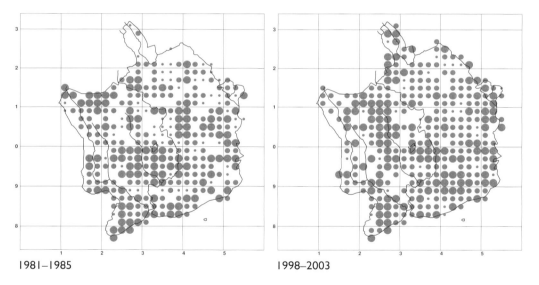

1981–1985   1998–2003

Large flocks occur in the post-breeding period, with the largest from late July until October. They are most concentrated along the coast where they probably include birds on passage. Flocks of 500 or more recorded in this period are: 700 at Uskmouth on 8th October 1995, 500 at Sluice Farm on 2nd September 1996, 500 at St. Brides on 14th September 2003 and 500+ at Llanllowell on 3rd October 2003.

There are no ringing data directly relevant to Gwent, but national data show that a proportion of the UK breeding population migrates between September and November to France and Iberia, returning between mid-March and early May (*Migration Atlas*). Gwent birds are presumably no exception this, and the reduction in size and frequency of flocks recorded during the winter supports the conclusion that only a minority of birds remain in the county through the winter.

Visible passage is often observed on the coast, usually from Goldcliff or Peterstone, and the 1977 *Birds of Gwent* stated that Linnet was the most numerous finch observed on autumn migration, with several hundreds regularly being seen. The direction of movement is generally south-west along the coast, and Ferns (1977) presented evidence for such birds continuing in this direction to Lavernock Point (Glamorgan) and then crossing the Bristol Channel in the vicinity of the islands of Steepholm and Flatholm. However, north-easterly movements are occasionally recorded, tending to occur into easterly winds. The largest single movement was of 2000+ south-west in two hours at Goldcliff on 6th October 1968.

Those that remain in the county in winter, group together into flocks at food sources, such as stubbles or saltmarsh, whilst the hills become deserted. The most productive site for winter records of over 100 birds, with eight occurrences in the last forty years, has been Llandegfedd Reservoir. Flocks of 200 have also occurred at Llandegfedd Reservoir, at Llanfihangel Gobion and at a fruit farm near Abergavenny, while a flock of 300 was at Llanfihangel Crucorney on 13th February 2000.

An observation of four Linnets feeding at a bird table at Goytre on 11th February 1978 is the only recorded example of this behaviour in Gwent.

Gwent Breeding Atlas data and population size

Gwent Atlas	Confirmed tetrads	Probable tetrads	Possible tetrads	Total tetrads	Change in total	Gwent population
1981–1985	108	142	58	308	–	–
1998–2003	120	178	29	327	+14%	4,900–5,800 pairs

National breeding data and conservation status

Estimated Welsh population	Welsh CBC/BBS trend 1985–2003	UK CBC/BBS trend 1985–2003	Welsh & (UK) conservation status
62,000	+10%	+6%	Amber (Red)-listed

Twite
Llinos y Mynydd

Carduelis flavirostris

A scarce winter visitor, rare in recent years

The Twite breeds in upland areas of northern and western Britain and generally moves to the milder coastal districts, particularly the English east coast, during the winter period. It is a rare visitor to Gwent, principally recorded during the October–February. Prior to 1939 it was considered to be very rare, with records only from Abergavenny and Llantarnum (1937 *Birds on Monmouthshire*).

In modern times there have been fifteen records in the county, the first involving six birds seen in Tredegar Park, Newport on 1st and 2nd February 1972. This and other inland records are listed in Table 103a. However, birds occur more typically on the coast (Table 103b). Temporal distribution of records is strongly biased toward the 1970s (four records) and 1980s (nine records), with only one record in the 1990s and one since.

a) Inland records

1972	1–2 February	Tredegar Park, Newport	6	
1975	24–25 October	Mardy, Abergavenny	2	
1979	23 February	Chain Bridge, Usk Valley	4	
1986	24 January	Llangybi Bottom	1	with Redpolls
1991	4 May	Trefil Quarries	2	presumed pair

b) Coastal records

1977	26 December	Peterstone	1	
1982	7 January	Magor Reserve	1	
1983	22 November–2 April 1984	Sluice Farm	25	4 birds noted till 2nd April
1983	29 December	Undy Foreshore	2	
1984	1 April	Collister Pill	2	
1985	11 January–11 March	Peterstone	9	
1986	2 January	Sluice Farm	5	also noted on 1st February

1987	8 January	Sluice Farm	3	one on 15th January
1987	4 October	West Pill	5	
2001	30 December–1 January	Chepstow Wharf	5	on the foreshore

Table 103. Records of Twites in Gwent

(Lesser) **Redpoll**   *Carduelis cabaret*
Llinos Bengoch

A partial migrant, breeding locally but declining; also a passage migrant and winter visitor in fluctuating numbers

The harsh metallic rattling call is often the first indication of the presence of Redpolls in the area. Redpolls are fairly well distributed breeding birds in Britain, with gaps in their distribution limited mainly to the west midlands and south-west England (1968–72 National Atlas), but a national decline in numbers over the last 30 years has led to its being Amber-listed in the UK. In Gwent, Redpolls can be found in young conifer plantations and gorse scrub during the breeding season, and feeding on alder and birch seed in the winter.

The 1937 *Birds of Monmouthshire* mentioned breeding records from Newport, Llantarnam and some western valleys, and the next record of confirmed breeding was at Cwmyoy in 1969. At about this time Redpolls began to nest in Gwent's young conifer plantations, resulting in big increases in the Gwent breeding population: in 1971, 12 and 20 pairs were recorded in this habitat in Ebbw Vale and Tredegar respectively, while from 1974 there were numerous summer records from widespread locations in the county.

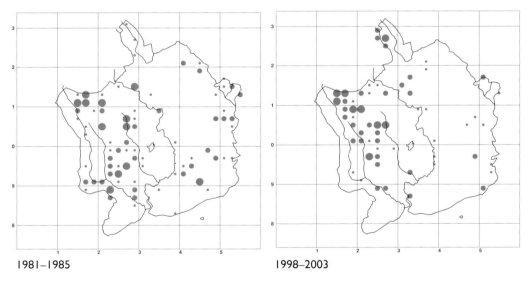

1981–1985   1998–2003

The 1st Gwent Atlas then showed that a rapid expansion had occurred, with 80 tetrads occupied and an estimated population of 400 pairs. The growth in numbers at that time can to some extent be explained by changes in the Forestry Commission's management of young plantations: historically, plantations were weeded of the birch trees, which otherwise self-seed and grow throughout them, but in the early 1980s this practice was discontinued owing to shortages of manpower. This allowed ideal nesting habitat for Redpolls to develop, comprising young conifer plantations intermixed with large numbers of birches, their favoured source of food.

The 2nd Gwent Atlas illustrates a decline in the county, with a decrease of occupied tetrads from 80 to 59 (a 25% range reduction), and of tetrads with *confirmed* breeding from 12 to nine. This reduction includes the loss of the Redpoll as a breeding species from the woods of Wentwood, the Sirhowy Valley, Ynysyfro Reservoir, Twmbarlwm and much of the Wye Valley. The western valleys and the Llanthony area are now the strongholds for this species in Gwent and contain 75% of tetrads with *probable* and *confirmed* breeding, and all *confirmed* records. Half of the *confirmed* records were in young conifer plantations, with the rest in scrubby areas.

Further analysis on a tetrad by tetrad basis of distribution maps for both Redpoll and woodland, uncovers some interesting trends. In the 1st Gwent Atlas, 70% of all occupied tetrads also contained conifer plantations, whereas this had reduced to 44% in the 2nd Gwent Atlas. This amounts to a 37% decline of breeding in tetrads containing this habitat. It appears that if coniferous woodland becomes unsuitable for occupation, Redpolls are lost from the area unless alternative suitable habitat is available, and this has happened in most areas of the county. Only in the north-west quarter of the county have Redpolls maintained their overall occupancy levels, by breeding more widely in birch woodland and in scrub. The move in the north-west from conifer woodland to other habitats is shown by the fact that in this area only one-third of the occupied tetrads contained conifers in the 2nd Gwent Atlas compared to two-thirds in the 1st Gwent Atlas.

The decline of Redpolls in Gwent's coniferous woods may be explained by a decrease in the area of young plantations, with trees maturing and producing a closed canopy unsuitable for occupation. Since the mid-1990s the decline of suitable conifer habitat has been exacerbated by a resumption of the removal of birch from some Gwent plantations, this time by a company specialising in constructing horse jumps. The affected plantations include Wentwood, Trelleck and the Wye Valley, all of which are areas in which Redpolls are either much reduced or have become extinct. The Forestry Commission's policies of replanting clear-felled areas with broadleaved or mixed woodland, and of having continuous cover does not bode well for the future breeding success of this species in coniferous woodland.

The estimate for the county population of this species is 45–180 pairs, and is based on a mean density of five pairs per tetrad in those tetrads that have either *probable* or *confirmed* breeding. Nationally, the Redpoll has undergone an 87% decline between the two Gwent Atlases (1985–2003), which identifies it as the species with the most rapid national population reduction in this period.

In winter, varying numbers of resident Redpolls are joined by migrants from more northerly areas of Britain. Evidence for this is provided by a record of a bird ringed in Cumbria in July 1981 and recovered 316km to the south in Gwent during the following December. There are two other ringing records relevant to Gwent: a bird ringed in November 1983 in Herefordshire was recovered in Gwent in February 1988 and another ringed in Monmouth in the winter of 1979/80 was recovered in Nottingham during winter 1981/82. Some of the UK breeding birds migrate to the continent via south-east England (*Migration Atlas*), and this may include Gwent birds, but there is no ringing evidence to support this as yet. A light autumn passage, mainly along the coast, has been observed during October/November almost annually, the highest count being 58 in three hours at Blackrock on 26th October 1991.

During winter, Redpolls are most frequently observed feeding on alder, often in the company of Siskins. They have been commonly noted in the county in small parties and occasionally in large flocks. The highest concentrations recorded were at Wentwood (Table 104). Other notable counts include: 170 in St Dials Wood, Monmouth in 1977, 200 at Mescoed Mawr in 1981, 230 at Penallt in 1993 and 150 at Forest Coal Pit in 2001.

Year	1970	1971	1978	1979	1983	1985	1991
Number of birds	200	200	300	150	100	150	170

Table 104. Redpoll flocks recorded at Wentwood

Prior to 1981, records of large flocks occurred regularly, but have since decreased in both size and frequency. Since 1995 there has been only one report of a flock with more than 50 birds. This decrease is likely to be a reflection of the steep UK decline in breeding numbers from around the early 1980s.

			Gwent Breeding Atlas data and population size			
Gwent Atlas	Confirmed tetrads	Probable tetrads	Possible tetrads	Total tetrads	Change in total	Gwent population
1981–1985	12	27	40	79	–	–
1998–2003	9	27	23	59	−25%	45–180 pairs

National breeding data and conservation status

Estimated Welsh population	Welsh CBC/BBS trend 1985–2003	UK CBC/BBS trend 1985–2003	Welsh & (UK) conservation status
13,000	Not available	−87%	Green (Amber)-listed

(Common) **Crossbill** *Loxia curvirostra*
Gylfin Groes

An uncommon winter visitor and breeder, in very variable numbers; also an occasional irruptive immigrant

The Crossbill is a large hefty finch that is found in coniferous forest. Its large head and mandibles crossed at the tip enable it to extract seeds from cones. In flight, the male's red rump and female's greenish-yellow rump are striking, and the metallic 'kip-kip' call is very distinctive, and often the first indication of Crossbills being present. It is not currently a species of conservation concern and is Green-listed.

The 1937 *and* 1963 *Birds of Monmouthshire* both mention the Crossbill as being observed frequently in the county, especially in north-eastern districts. However, the 1963 edition reported it as chiefly a winter visitor. Up to 1930, there were only ten records, but it has been recorded every year from 1966, with increasing frequency from 1970. The species had become widespread in Wales from the late 1950s/early 1960s, as the new plantations developed. By the time of the 1977 *Birds of Gwent,* it was known as an uncommon visitor and a probable resident in small numbers.

Breeding was first suggested by the shooting of a female with a bare breast indicative of recent nesting at Michaelson y Fedw on 28th June 1898 (*Birds of Glamorgan* 1900). The 1937 *Birds of Monmouthshire* noted that the species occasionally bred, as in Newport in 1901 and near Abergavenny in 1909. Subsequently the 1963 *Birds of Monmouthshire* recorded family groups on the canal between Pontypool and Abergavenny in July 1956 and at Llanover in August and September 1958.

In Gwent, most breeding records are from Wentwood, although the 1st Gwent Atlas reported a stronghold in the Monmouth/Trelleck area. Between the two Gwent atlases there have been breeding records in every year except 1987 and 1995: mainly from Wentwood (eight years), Trelleck (four), Ebbw Forest (three), Mynydd Du (two) and the Wye Valley (three records in 1992). These same areas of the county are represented in the distribution seen in the 2nd Gwent Atlas. The abundance of records along the Trelleck ridge and Wentwood, and the sparsity of records from the western valleys, is probably a reflection of the availability of seed crops during the period, itself a reflection of the relatively fewer conifer species that are grown in the western valleys.

At the time of the 1st Gwent Atlas the county population was estimated at 30–50 pairs and this estimate holds true today, with probably fewer than 50 pairs nesting in most years. The difficulty in estimating numbers of breeding pairs of this highly irruptive species cannot be overemphasised, which underlies the fact that no population figure for Wales is given in the 2002 *Birds in Wales*. Crossbills often nest during the winter months, when the seed crop is at its most abundant, and many birds may have completed nesting before most observers consider the 'breeding season' to have started. The Gwent Atlas maps show a 48% increase in occupied tetrads in the period between the two atlases, but as numbers and distribution fluctuate greatly from year to year, depending on whether there has been a recent invasion, this should not be interpreted as a range expansion during the period. For the same reasons, no figures for national population trends are produced.

The Crossbill eats conifer seeds and little else. It is a Norway Spruce specialist and can breed prolifically during good seed years, often synchronised over large areas. During poor seed years however, birds can erupt in their thousands to find a new food source to exploit, such as Sitka Spruce, Douglas Fir and the various larches. In

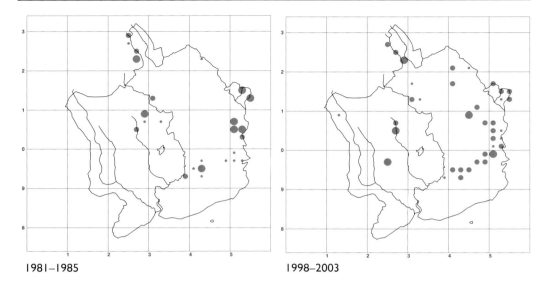

1981–1985   1998–2003

such years, numbers in Britain can vary dramatically, with birds vacating their breeding grounds in northern Europe earlier than most other species. They often reach Britain in the summer and generally remain for just one season, during which they may breed. If conditions are suitable they may remain longer and form new breeding populations. Both National Atlases (1968–72 and 1988–91) gave untypically wide distributions owing to annual variation in numbers, and because there was a major irruption in summer 1990. The Winter Atlas also exaggerated the distribution for the same reasons, eruptions having occurred in 1982 and 1983.

The 1994 *Birds in Wales* lists the main irruption years as 1953, 1956, 1958, 1959, 1962, 1963, 1972, 1983, 1985 and 1990. High numbers were recorded in Gwent in the winters of 1985/86, 1990/91 (following a build up in summer), 1993/94 (following an autumn influx and followed by a dramatic drop in numbers in the 1994/95 winter), and 1997/98 (following a June influx), with 80–100 in Wentwood in August, 150 there in October-December, and c.200 in three flocks in Ebbw Forest in October. Although lower numbers were reported in the intervening years, the species was recorded annually, with moderate influxes in 1992/93, 1997/98 and 2002/03.

There are no ringing recoveries relevant to Gwent.

Gwent Breeding Atlas data and population size

Gwent Atlas	Confirmed tetrads	Probable tetrads	Possible tetrads	Total tetrads	Change in total	Gwent population
1981–1985	8	6	11	25	–	–
1998–2003	5	23	9	37	+48%	c.50

(Common) **Bullfinch**   *Pyrrhula pyrrhula*
Coch y Berllan

A fairly numerous, but declining resident

Bullfinches are widespread within the UK, and also in Gwent, but can be locally scarce. They frequent woodland, copses, large hedgerows and scrub. For such an attractive bird, they are surprisingly inconspicuous, but are often given away by their soft piping call or the flash of a white rump in flight. In comparison to other finches they eat many more tree-flowers, buds and berries, a habit that can damage orchards. They are usually found in pairs during spring and summer, and in flocks of up to ten during autumn and winter.

The earliest record for the county is (perhaps disappointingly) that of over 30 birds being shot in a garden near Caerleon during February 1930. The 1937 *Birds of Monmouthshire* described the Bullfinch as a fairly common resident that was numerous in winter. Subsequently, the 1963 *Birds of Monmouthshire* described it as a common resident that appeared to have increased and which bred in practically all districts, except the more barren hill country of the north-west.

From 1966, the UK CBC index showed a slight increase which peaked in 1974, followed by a steady decline that continued to the early 1990s. Within Wales, the BBS shows that a population collapse occurred between 1994 and 1999, resulting in a 50% decline during this period, followed by a small but fluctuating recovery, resulting in a 28% overall decline in Wales between 1994 and 2003 and Red-list status.

The above changes are reflected in the Gwent Atlases. In the 1st Gwent Atlas the Bullfinch was found in 85% of tetrads with notable gaps limited to the treeless moorland tops of the north and west. In the 2nd Gwent Atlas it was found in only 73% of tetrads indicating a total range contraction of 48 tetrads between the two atlases. There has also been a 19% reduction in the number of tetrads in which breeding was confirmed between the two atlases, which strongly suggests a population reduction resulting in thinly scattered nests that are more difficult to find. The 2nd Gwent Atlas gives an estimated population of 1,390–3,110 pairs which represents a substantial reduction from the 5,000 pairs suggested in the 1st Gwent Atlas. This is consistent with a UK population decline of 33% over the same time period (1985–2003). Interestingly, these declines have not been in evidence on the Penallt CBC site, which has had a relatively stable population of 4–6 pairs from 1978 until 2004.

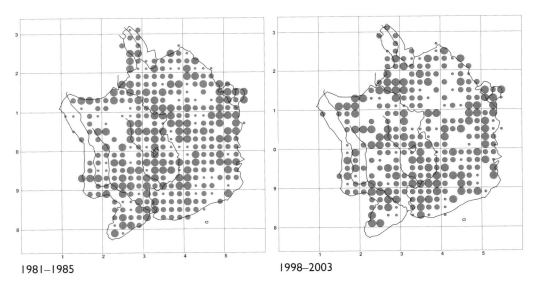

1981–1985

1998–2003

There are two main areas where the range contraction in Gwent is most evident. The north-eastern quarter of the county, bounded by a line from Cwmyoy south to Little Mill and then due east to the border at Tintern via Llansoy, has seen a significant increase in the number of unoccupied tetrads, to 33 compared with six. Similarly the coastal strip has 13 unoccupied tetrads compared to four previously. As these are principally farming areas, this is consistent with national survey results showing greater losses on farmland compared with woodland (CBC 1972–96, -62% in farmland versus -36% in woodland), and may be caused by agricultural intensification. A factor in the decline, observable in Gwent, is the loss of large straggling hedgerows, which are a preferred nesting site.

Bullfinches that breed in Britain belong to the race *P. p. pileata*, and are almost entirely sedentary. Consistent with this, all six recoveries of Gwent-ringed birds have been local, and there have been no recoveries in Gwent of birds ringed outside the county. There are a few records of visible passage being noted; all relate to Goldcliff and involve very small numbers of birds. In 1974 two flew south on 12th October, and again in 1986, two and three birds flew south-west on the 2nd and 11th of November respectively. It is difficult to determine the nature of these records, but it is worth considering comments in the 1994 *Birds in Wales* that continental birds *P. p. pyrrhula* are more prone to winter movements, and have occasionally been reported in Wales and, furthermore, that such continental birds might be responsible for the occasional visible passage which occurs in autumn and spring. A male bird thought to be of the continental race was observed feeding on honeysuckle buds at Pontypool on 2nd February 1970.

During winter the Bullfinch is found generally in small numbers, with records of more than ten together being quite uncommon. Two exceptionally large flocks, both containing a record 30 birds have been observed: at Whitehill Wood, Monmouth on 4th January 1976 and at Chepstow on 11th January 1987. Also during the winter of 1986–87 a 'notable influx' into the county was recorded during December, with numerous small flocks of up to 25 birds, mainly males. Since then the largest recorded flocks have been of ten birds, mirroring the population decline of this sedentary bird.

A pair seen feeding on a nut-feeder at Croesyceiliog on 1st December 1974 constituted the first record of this behaviour in the county, but although it has been reported irregularly since, the habit does not appear to have become widespread, as it has with Goldfinches, Greenfinches and Siskins.

Gwent Breeding Atlas data and population size

Gwent Atlas	Confirmed tetrads	Probable tetrads	Possible tetrads	Total tetrads	Change in total	Gwent population
1981–1985	122	153	60	335	–	–
1998–2003	99	140	48	287	−14%	1,390–3,110 pairs

National breeding data and conservation status

Estimated Welsh population	Welsh BBS trend 1994–2003	UK CBC/BBS trend 1985–2003	Welsh & UK conservation status
9,500 pairs	−28%	−33%	Red-listed

Hawfinch
Gylfinbraff

Coccothraustes coccothraustes

An uncommon and local resident

The Hawfinch, despite being the largest finch found in Gwent, is surprisingly secretive and can be easily overlooked. It is found in deciduous woodland, feeding on the seeds of trees such as Wild Cherry, beech, maple and hornbeam. The availability of such trees determines its distribution in the county.

The earliest detailed record of a Hawfinch in Gwent came in 1937 when a male bird was collected at Peterstone on 10th May; the skin is now in the National Museum of Wales, Cardiff. The 1937 and 1963 *Birds of Monmouthshire* recorded it as a somewhat local resident breeding species found in the central and southern portions of the county. It was apparently most numerous in the districts around Chepstow, Monmouth and Abergavenny, but it had also been recorded in the coastal districts. The 1977 *Birds of Gwent* shows that the Hawfinch had a similar status throughout the 1960s and 1970s as a local resident breeder in small numbers. It listed three pairs in a garden near Chepstow in April 1953, a female at Wyndcliff in May 1961 and regular sightings in the Abergavenny area since

1970, with breeding reported in three years, giving an estimated population of four pairs. Breeding was also reported from Abercarn in 1975 and probably from Monmouth in 1974 and 1975. There were also sporadic sightings at Cwmcarvan, Grwyne Fawr and the countryside from Pontypool and Chepstow.

The 1st Gwent Atlas suggests the status of the Hawfinch had remained unchanged for the previous 40/50 years. It was widely distributed in the Wye Valley, with a small colony of six pairs in the 5.5ha Priory Wood near Usk (fewer in 1985), and the county population was estimated at 50–100 pairs. Gwent is a well-wooded county with a high proportion of mixed hardwood stands, and the availability of large tree seeds such as hornbeam, cherry, wych elm, yew, hawthorn and beech, ensures a suitable food source for Hawfinches. Because of the mixture of seeding trees in many woods, there is generally an alternative food source if the preferred one fails, and this ensures the species continued presence.

Sightings in Gwent have been annual since the mid-1980s. Noteworthy, were the results of RSPB surveys of the Wye Valley in 1986, which found Hawfinches in 17 separate woods. During the five-year period 1986–1990 there was an average of 12 locations/35 birds in each year, with peak years in 1988 and 1989. The maximum flock sizes during the period were 15 at Priory Wood in 1986, and 12 at both Piercefield (1988) and The Cott (1990). Breeding evidence, for 5–10 pairs per year, was also widespread, with records from Priory Wood and several locations in the Wye Valley annually, as well as occasional records from Chepstow Park Wood, The Hendre and St Pierre Great Wood. Records began falling from 1991, reaching a low point in the years 1992 to 1994, when only approximately ten birds were reported, at four or fewer sites. There was a count of 15 birds at Wyesham in 1995. Numbers picked up again to 10 locations/25–45 birds in 1996 and 1997, with flocks of about ten at both Tintern and Monmouth in 1996.

No birds have been recorded from the former stronghold of Priory Wood since 1994, and it can be no coincidence that the majority of the cherry trees were removed during felling operations in 1990. The exact habitat requirements of the species are not entirely understood, but routine woodland management can have a detrimental effect at the local level. Most records since 1992 have been from the Wye Valley woodlands, and six nests were found in a newly discovered 'colony' in 1996. During the 2nd Gwent Atlas years, the species was generally reported from only three locations in any one year, with a maximum of five in 2000. Breeding was *confirmed* at only two sites, one of which has been omitted on the distribution map at the request of the observers. The largest flocks were six at Tintern in April 2001 and 10 there in February 2003.

Although the number of occupied tetrads has only shown a modest decline, the two distribution maps show a loss of the central Gwent (Priory Wood/Clytha) population. Given the greater interest in the species in recent years, the decline is likely to be more extensive than the comparison between atlas maps suggests. National data show a long-term decline, and the county population is now probably within the range of 30–100 pairs, but perhaps closer to the lower end of the range.

The Hawfinch is one of the least-known, and possibly most under-recorded of Welsh birds, and Gwent was previously regarded as being the Welsh stronghold (1994 *Birds in Wales*). This position changed however in the

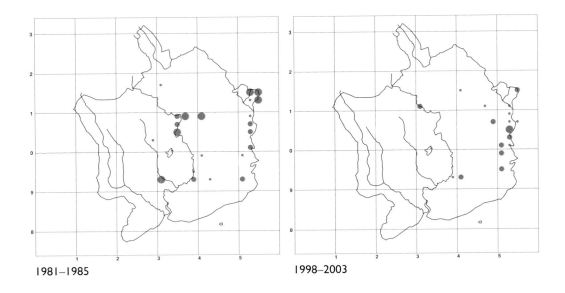

1981–1985   1998–2003

1990s, when large roosts were discovered in Merionydd and Caernarfon in North Wales (2002 *Birds in Wales*). Most Welsh breeding records nevertheless continue to come from Gwent.

Passage is only exceptionally recorded in Wales, with some movements noted in October/November on the offshore islands including Bardsey, Skokholm and Ramsey. Two passage records have however come from Lavernock Point in Glamorgan in the 1960s, and in Gwent, there was a notable passage report of five birds at Goldcliff Point on 5th November 2005.

Although there is some evidence of northern European birds moving into Britain during autumn, there is little ringing data to support long distance movements of British birds. The only ringing recovery relevant to Gwent is of a bird colour-ringed near Chepstow (as a nestling or as a breeding adult) in May 2004 that was sighted at Nagshead Reserve in the Forest of Dean in March 2005.

Gwent Breeding Atlas data and population size

Gwent Atlas	Confirmed tetrads	Probable tetrads	Possible tetrads	Total tetrads	Change in total	Gwent population
1981–1985	7	7	8	22	–	–
1998–2003	2	8	8	18	−18%	30–100 pairs

National breeding data and conservation status

Estimated Welsh population	Welsh trend	UK trend	Welsh & UK conservation status
300 pairs	Not available	Not available	Amber-listed

Lapland Bunting (Lapland Longspur) Bras y Gogledd

Calcarius lapponicus

A rare winter visitor

There are eight Gwent records of this rare winter visitor from arctic regions and all have occurred on the coast, usually on the foreshore, during October–January. The first record for the county was a single bird on the Undy foreshore on 13th December 1970. Apart from a group of up to three birds at West Pill during 25th November–1st December 1990, all other records have been of single birds, which have occurred as follows: at West Pill on 11th October 1986, Peterstone on 7th December 1986, Black Rock on 30th December 1990 and 26th October 1991, Newport Wetlands Reserve (Saltmarsh Grasslands) on 10th November 2000 and Collister Pill on 24th January 2004.

Snow Bunting Bras yr Eira

Plectrophenax nivalis

A scarce winter visitor

Although it breeds in the Scottish Highlands, the Snow Bunting is more familiar to most British bird watchers as a winter visitor, frequenting the seashores and salt-marshes in the east and north. Most of these birds appear to derive from the Iceland and Greenland breeding populations (*Migration Atlas*). The species is regular in Wales but only in small numbers.

The 1937 *Birds of Monmouthshire* described it as a rare winter visitor to the county, listing only five records and the 1963 *Birds of Monmouthshire* added no further occurrences.

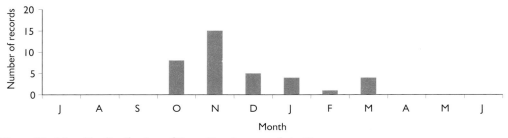

Figure 28. Monthly distribution of Snow Bunting records in Gwent

Since 1963 there have been over 30 further records for the county. These have been fairly evenly spread over the years, but with a gap of five years between 1989 and 1995.

Snow Buntings in Gwent occur mostly along the coast, mainly in October and November and less often during the remainder of the winter period (Figure 28). The earliest record was at St Brides on 9th October 1983 and the latest at Undy on 28th March 1964. Most records are either of single birds or of parties of up to four, but there are three records of larger parties from the Undy foreshore, where there were seven on 2nd February 1964, ten on 1st March 1964 and eight on 8th November 1967.

There are also several inland records which comprise: one at Abergavenny on 29th December 1890, which is the first documented record for the county, three at Abergavenny Sewage Works on 9th January 1968, one at Twmbarlwm during 30th October–1st November 1997, one flying over Ynysyfro Reservoir on 4th December 1997 and one at Bryn Arw, Abergavenny, during 27–30th November 2003.

Yellowhammer   *Emberiza citrinella*
Melyn yr Eithin

Resident but declining

The Yellowhammer's favoured habitat is arable farmland, although it also occurs in young conifer plantations, mountain pastures, overgrown coal tips, gorse commons and uncultivated areas. Males are extremely conspicuous in spring, with their brilliant yellow plumage and 'little-bit-of-bread-and-no-cheese' refrain, delivered from the tops of trees and hedgerows.

The 1937 *Birds of Monmouthshire* described the Yellowhammer as a widespread breeding species, fairly common on the gorse-covered foothills and in the agricultural areas, and twenty-six years later the 1963 *Birds of Monmouthshire* confirmed this status as still being the case. In the 1977 *Birds of Gwent*, however, some concern was expressed over marked declines in certain areas of the county.

These concerns proved to be prescient, as at a national level the CBC index for the Yellowhammer, which had been fairly stable from 1966 until 1987, began a steady and continuing decline. Consequently, the conservation status of the species moved from being Green-listed in 1996, to Red-listed. The decline was, and still is more marked in Wales, than in other UK areas. It is interesting that during the decline, breeding performance actually improved, but survival rates worsened, mainly owing to a reduction in winter food availability. This resulted largely from a loss of winter stubbles caused by the autumn planting of cereals, and a reduction in weed density caused by greater herbicide use. Other reasons for the decline include an increase in livestock grazing (and therefore fewer cereal crops), hedgerow removal, intensive sheep grazing and ploughing of marginal land which caused the loss of rough uncultivated patches.

The Gwent Atlases illustrate the Yellowhammer's decline very effectively. The 1st Gwent Atlas just preceded the start of the decline, and showed a widespread distribution in the county with a total of 305 tetrads (78%) occupied, whereas the 2nd Gwent Atlas records the Yellowhammer in a mere 194 tetrads (49%). This equates to a 111-tetrad reduction (36%) in range between the two atlases. The reduction in range has not occurred evenly throughout the county and a line of demarcation can be identified, from the Sugar Loaf Mountain in the

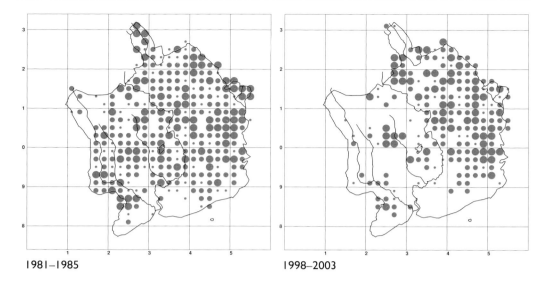

1981–1985   1998–2003

north, through Usk to a point south-west of Caerwent, and then due east to the border. To the west and south of this line the Yellowhammer has become scarce, with only 14% of tetrads having *probable* or *confirmed* breeding. Given the conspicuous nature of this bird, these tetrads probably represent all areas in which it actually bred. Of these, two-thirds are clustered in four areas, centred on Michaelstone-y-Fedw, Llandegfedd, Abersychan (where old coal workings provide important habitat) and Risca. This represents a dramatic 70% range decline between the two Gwent Atlases in this part of the county.

To the east of the line, 73% of tetrads have *probable* or *confirmed* breeding, which represents a comparatively small reduction in range of 9% over the same time period. This area has a higher proportion of arable farming, and therefore has more chance of providing optimum habitat. It is likely, however, that this comparatively small reduction in range masks a more significant population decline, as only one pair needs to be present in each tetrad to indicate breeding, whereas the 1st Gwent Atlas estimated a population of 30–40 pairs per occupied tetrad.

Counts of breeding pairs within the county are fairly few but notable examples include: nine and ten pairs on the Sugar Loaf slopes and St. Mary's Vale in 1974 and 1975 respectively, seven pairs at Dingestow in 2001 and 26 territories in the Monnow Valley in 2002. As an illustration of the decline in the county, there were ten pairs in the Lasgarn area in 1978 and six on Mynydd Garnclochdy in 1979, whereas a total absence was recorded in both of these areas in 1995. Annual totals on the CBC site at Penallt from 1980 to 2003 are shown in Figure 29, and demonstrate a decline from 18 territories in 1980 to zero pairs in 2003 and a slight recovery to three pairs in 2005.

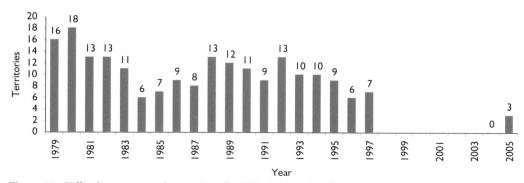

Figure 29. Yellowhammer numbers at Penallt CBC site (no data from 1998–2003)

The county population is currently estimated to be in the range of 2,400–3,100 pairs, which represents a small fraction of the 9,000–12,000 pairs suggested in the 1st Gwent Atlas. The UK has seen a population decline of 48% between 1985 and 2003, but the reduction in range and population shown in the 2nd Gwent Atlas is far more severe and equates to a crisis that should be urgently addressed. The best hope for recovery in the short term is provided by agri-environmental schemes such as set-aside, providing weedy stubbles in winter, and hedges with grass buffer strips to encourage invertebrates, which are an essential food source for breeding.

The Yellowhammer winters mainly in its breeding range, especially in milder winters. Flock formation and local movements to new feeding areas are typical, and small movements can occur in autumn, when birds vacate higher ground. The only Gwent ringing recovery is consistent with this sedentary behaviour, being of a bird ringed in February 1986 at Llanfair Kilgeddin, and recovered locally in April of the same year. Also in keeping with its sedentary nature, is the scarcity of visible movements on the coast, of which there are only two, both in 1976: 45 flew east on 16th October and 10 flew east on the 28th of November. These movements were preceded by an exceptionally dry summer, though whether the two events have any connection is unknown.

Given that Yellowhammers rely on seed as a winter food source, it is important that good winter foraging habitat, particularly stubbles, is available close to breeding areas (*Migration Atlas*). Winter flocks of 10–20 have been recorded regularly in Gwent and flocks over 100 were sometimes recorded in past years, but are now very rare. Flocks of over 150 comprise c.400 at Pontllanfraith in December 1973, c.200 at New Inn in January 1978 and 200+ at Penallt in December 1982. In more recent years, the only flocks of this magnitude have been 150 at Dingestow in November 1995 and again in January 1998, as a result of winter stubble provision and the planting of 'game crops'.

The first Gwent records of feeding under a birdtable for scraps were in January 1985 at Garnlydan and in February 1985 at Abergavenny. Subsequently there have been only three further records of this behaviour: a single bird at Trelleck in autumn 1989, six at Pontypool in 2000 and one at Aberbeeg in January/February 2003.

Gwent Breeding Atlas data and population size

Gwent Atlas	Confirmed tetrads	Probable tetrads	Possible tetrads	Total tetrads	Change in total	Gwent population
1981–1985	87	151	67	305	–	–
1998–2003	59	97	38	194	−36%	2,400–3,100 pairs

National breeding data and conservation status

Estimated Welsh population	Welsh CBC/BBS trend 1985–2003	UK CBC/BBS trend 1985–2003	Welsh & UK conservation status
38,850	−59%	−48%	Red-listed

Cirl Bunting
Bras Ffrainc

Emberiza cirlus

Formerly resident but now a very rare visitor

During the early 20th century the Cirl Bunting was considered to be a very local resident in the county, with breeding recorded from Abergavenny, Usk, Rogerstone and Newport, and with occasional reports from other districts up to 1925 (1937 *Birds of Monmouthshire*).

The species declined nationally during the second half of the 20th century, and its British breeding population is now limited to Devon and Cornwall (Ogilvie, 2004). There are only four recent records for Gwent, which are confined to the years 1968–1970. A single bird was seen at Glascoed on 31st May and 25th June 1968, while at Llanarth a male was in song during July–September 1968, and breeding was confirmed when two young were seen. In 1969 a male was again in song at Llanarth throughout most of the breeding season, and in 1970, a male was seen along the motorway verge at Magor on 27th June.

Reed Bunting
Bras y Cyrs

Emberiza schoeniclus

A fairly common resident

The Reed Bunting is widely distributed throughout Britain. During the breeding season it is found in all kinds of marsh habitats where rushes, reeds and osiers are present but it has also occupied some drier sites, such as agricultural land and young conifer plantations, especially when population levels have been high. In winter, birds generally leave the higher ground and move to freshwater, coastal marshes and farmland, often associating with finch flocks, but can also be found visiting bird tables in small numbers.

The 1937 and 1963 *Birds of Monmouthshire* and the 1977 *Birds of Gwent* recorded the species as being a local, but not uncommon breeding resident that was present at all altitudes in suitable habitat, but most numerous among the reens of the coastal levels and, to a lesser extent, along the river valleys. The 1st Gwent Atlas recorded much the same, with the species' strongholds being firmly based on the levels, the valleys of the Usk and its tributaries, and the marshes and ponds of the uplands at the heads of the western valleys. Fewer than 20% of records came from outside these areas. Results from the 2nd Gwent Atlas show that the position remains largely unchanged today. The Gwent Levels continue to be the stronghold for the species as does the lower Usk Valley and its tributaries, while there has been an increase in the uplands in the north-west of the county. However, there has been an 11% decline in range between the Gwent Atlas periods, with the number of occupied tetrads decreasing from 111 to 99, though the proportion of tetrads with *probable* or *confirmed* breeding records has increased from 77% in the 1st Gwent Atlas to 84% in the 2nd Gwent Atlas. The Welsh population trend was strongly positive (+112%) during this period.

The 1968–72 National Atlas noted that there was an absence of Reed Buntings from eastern Gwent, affecting 10-km squares ST49, SO40, SO41 and SO50; the inclusion of the latter square was thought surprising as it contains part of the Wye Valley. Both the 1st and 2nd Gwent Atlases show a similar situation with a scarcity or absence in all these squares, and also in ST59, another Wye Valley square.

Only a limited amount of work has been done on establishing the size of the Gwent Reed Bunting population. A survey of the Gwent Levels during 1978–79 revealed a maximum of 67 confirmed/probable breeding pairs (Mortimer *et al.*, 1978, 1979; Venables & Titcombe 1980) (Table 105). In 1984, an RSPB survey of the Gwent Levels indicated one confirmed, four probable and 45 possible breeding records: the greatest concentration being at Bowleaze Common, an area now threatened by the proposed M4 relief road. An incomplete survey of the Llanwern Steelworks site in 1995 found at least 25 pairs and a further 12 pairs were at the nearby Uskmouth BBS area during the same year. The 1st Gwent Atlas estimated a population of 1,000 pairs based upon local CBC data. The latest estimate using BBS data suggests a range of between 970–1,800 pairs. The lower end of the range, and therefore a population somewhere close to that suggested by the 1st Gwent Atlas estimate, is considered most likely.

Area	Confirmed	Probable	Total
Wentlooge Level	4	19	23
Caldicot Level	2	42	44

Table 105. Number of breeding pairs of Reed Buntings recorded during surveys of Gwent Levels 1978–1979

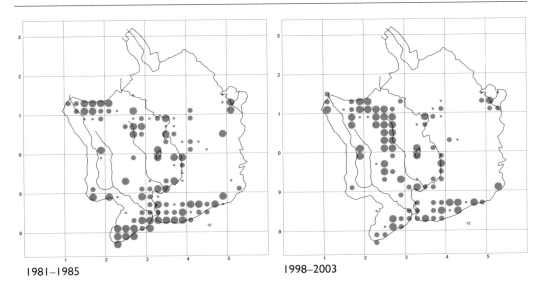

1981–1985   1998–2003

The species is Red-listed nationally and Amber-listed in Wales, as a consequence of a significant decline being noted on CBC plots between 1974 and 1999. Both CBC/BBS and WBS indices declined rapidly during the 1970s, but abundance has since remained remarkably stable. CES data indicate that the decline has continued and that it is associated with falling productivity and driven by decreasing survival rates (Peach *et al.*, 1999).

The Reed Bunting is predominantly sedentary, but some directional autumn dispersal to milder areas by a minority of birds has been noted (*Migration Atlas*). There is some evidence in Gwent of such movements with two ringing controls showing movement between Uskmouth and Lewell in Dorset, 100km to the south, and a third bird ringed at Uskmouth subsequently being retrapped in the winter at Newton Abbot, Devon. Two individuals trapped in Gwent during the winter were recovered to the north in Droitwich, Worcestershire, and in Shropshire.

There is also some indication of a light passage movement on the Gwent coast during the autumn with small parties of up to 20 birds seen occasionally flying west from late September through October and sometimes into November. Examples include c.50 birds recorded over three hours on 17th November 1999 and 74 during 90 minutes on 21st October 1980.

Large flocks are often recorded during the winter months through to February, with groups of up to 50 birds being recorded most years, especially from the coast. More significant flocks have included 200 in the Peterstone area during October in 1967 and 1984, and 150 at Uskmouth in 1993. An exceptionally large flock of 250–300 was at Peterstone from mid-February to early March 1984.

Gwent Breeding Atlas data and population size

Gwent Atlas	Confirmed tetrads	Probable tetrads	Possible tetrads	Total tetrads	Change in total	Gwent population
1981–1985	47	38	26	111	–	–
1998–2003	41	42	16	99	−11%	970–1,800 pairs

National breeding data and conservation status

Estimated Welsh population	Welsh CBC/BBS trend 1985–2003	UK CBC/BBS trend 1985–2003	Welsh & UK conservation status
16,000 pairs	+112%	+3%	Amber (Red)-listed

Corn Bunting
Bras yr Ŷd

Emberiza calandra

A rare visitor

The Corn Bunting formerly bred in all counties of Wales and was numerous in some coastal areas, but declined in the early 20th century and now has no more than a toehold in the Principality (1994 *Birds in Wales*). It has also declined elsewhere in the UK, though not so drastically as in Wales, and changes in agricultural practice are probably the major causative factors.

Other than two breeding records at Pant-yr-eos Reservoir in 1903 and at Llanvapley in 1970, there are just thirteen records of Corn Buntings in Gwent. The 1937 *Birds of Monmouthshire* described the species as a rare visitor to the coastal districts of the county, a comment that seems to stand the test of time, as ten of the 13 modern records (Table 106) have been from the coastal regions. Occurrences were fairly regular during 1966–73 but have since become very rare.

1962	8 January	Chepstow	1
1966	27 June	Peterstone	4
1968	19 January	Undy Foreshore	2
1968	9 July	Caldicot Moor	1
1970	18 August	Undy Foreshore	4
1971	20 May	Carno Reservoir	2
1972	July	Llandegfedd Reservoir	1
1972	29 August	Risca	1
1973	17 March	Collister Pill	1
1980	15 February	Sluice Farm	1
1985	15–19 April	Black Rock	1
1990	1 July	Peterstone	1
1990	29 July	Llandevaud	2

Table 106. Corn Bunting records in Gwent

CONCLUSIONS AND COMPARISONS

This chapter briefly reviews the changes that have occurred in the county's avifauna since the 1977 *Birds of Gwent*. No attempt has been made to mention every species, and the intention is simply to highlight some of the more interesting and important changes. The 1977 *Birds of Gwent* included records only up to the end of 1976. For this reason developments such as new additions to the county list, or new breeding birds, are subsequent to 1976, not 1977.

The number of species recorded in Gwent

Since 1976 another 53 species have been added to the list of wild birds recorded in Gwent, bringing the county list to 288 as of 31st December 2005. While many of these have been vagrants or rare passage migrants, spending only limited periods within the county, a small number, including the Little Egret and Dartford Warbler, have bred and seem likely to become established as regular breeders in future years.

The full list of all species added to the county list is in Appendix 5.

Increases in records of formerly rare or very scarce seabirds

Regular coastal bird-watching has revealed that many seabirds are much more frequent visitors to the county than previously thought. The discovery that westerly or south-westerly gales almost invariably bring seabirds into the Severn Estuary has encouraged observation during and immediately after such weather, with the result that birds such as Kittiwake, Manx Shearwater, Gannet and Fulmar are now known to occur more or less annually in the county. In the case of Kittiwakes, the numbers can be very large on occasion. Other examples include Arctic Skua and Great Skua for which, in 1976, there were only seven and two records, respectively, compared with 83 and 39 today.

Trends in arrival dates of summer visitors

For several decades there has been a climate-related trend for summer visitors to arrive at increasingly early dates in the UK. This has been reflected in the arrival dates of many of Gwent's summer migrants, and data for the most obvious examples are shown in Figure 30. The Wheatear and the Sand Martin are particularly striking examples in which the median date for first arrivals has moved forward by 16 and 12 days respectively.

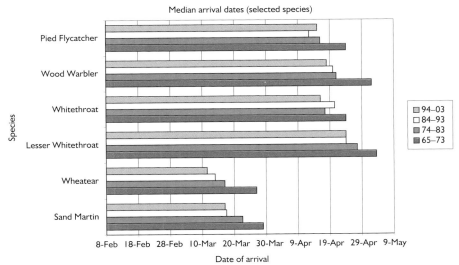

Figure 30. Arrival dates for selected summer visitors to Gwent since 1965

Number of breeding species

The range of species breeding in the county has increased considerably between the two atlas periods of 1981–85 and 1998–2003; the *probable* plus *confirmed* total has risen from 118 to 132, and the total for all categories from 120 to 136. However, analysis at the tetrad level tells a different story, with the mean number for all breeding categories dropping by 2.3 species (54.7 to 52.5), reflecting the fact that the recently arrived species have often colonised limited specialised habitats, such as the Newport Wetlands Reserve, whereas the commoner, more widely distributed species have, on average, declined in distribution. By contrast, the mean number of *probable* plus *confirmed* species per tetrad has risen from 42.8 to 44.5, which suggests that the decline in diversity is not due to any lower level of effort on the part of the atlas recorders.

Changes in general distribution of breeding birds

Two obvious trends have occurred in the county: a large increase in the diversity of breeding species in the formerly industrialised area of the north-west, contrasting with a significant decrease almost everywhere else.

The increase in the north-west derives from a number of very positive ecological developments in this area that have undoubtedly produced real benefits for breeding birds. Most such developments come under the heading of the 'greening' of the valleys, which started before the 1st Gwent Atlas and has continued ever since. This has involved improvement of water quality in rivers, growth and maturation of trees that were planted on the cleared mining spoil tips, and the advent of parks such as Bryn Bach: which have been formed by landscaping and planting on extensive former industrial wastelands, sometimes surrounding open waters that also were formerly industrial in purpose.

Indeed, Bryn Bach Park provides an excellent illustration of such a development. In 1989, soon after its completion, a census of breeding birds produced only six species. Six years later, in 1995, when planted trees had put on growth and other vegetation, including emergent vegetation around the lake, had become more established, a repeat census found 20 breeding species. The incomers included many common species such as the Wren, Dunnock, Robin and Goldfinch, and waterbirds such as the Mallard and the Great Crested Grebe (Venables, 1989 & 1995). By the end of the 2nd Gwent Atlas (2003) many other species had been added, including the Coot, Moorhen, Pied Wagtail and Grey Wagtail.

It is also possible that the effects of global climate change will have had an ameliorating effect on the winter temperatures on the higher ground of north-west Gwent, thus allowing better winter survival of resident species.

In most of the remainder of the county, particularly in those areas that are predominantly farmland, there have been statistically significant decreases in species diversity at the tetrad level, with an average of around 4–5 fewer species per tetrad. This result reflects national trends for farmland species, which have declined seriously owing to the the loss of habitat diversity arising from agricultural intensification. In Gwent, the loss of bird species has been particularly marked on the coastal levels, where the mean reduction in species per tetrad has been 5.9 (Wentlooge Level) and 7.5 (Caldicot Level). The Gwent Levels have suffered in recent years from enhanced drainage, loss of reens and associated mature hedgerows, conversion from pastoral to arable farming, construction of golf courses and industrial premises, and the opening of at least one land-fill site.

The most widely distributed species

Table 107 shows the 20 most widely distributed birds in Gwent during the period 1998–2003 as found by the 2nd Gwent Atlas, and compares them with the equivalent list for 1981–85. The Blackbird now tops the table as the county's most widespread breeding bird, very closely followed by the Carrion Crow and the Chaffinch. In the 1st Gwent Atlas, the Magpie had topped the table, but since then it has shown some decline and has slipped to joint 10th place. Reflecting their national declines, the Starling (12th to 23rd), the Willow Warbler (13th to 21st), and the Cuckoo (19th to 44th) have all dropped precipitously out of the top 20. The Jackdaw has also dropped out of the top 20 (17th to 22nd), but not so much as a result of a change in its own range (which has declined only slightly), but as a consequence of the increases in range shown by the Blackcap, Goldfinch and Greenfinch. These are three of the species that have spread significantly into the western hills and valleys, and have joined the top 20 by increasing their ranking position by some 7–10 places. The most dramatic entry to the top 20 is the Buzzard, which has risen from 30th to become our 10th most widely distributed bird though, owing to its large territory size and conspicuousness, it is possible that this position overstates its true rank a little.

Rank	2nd Gwent Atlas (1998–2003)	Tetrads	1st Gwent Atlas (1981–85)	Tetrads
1	Blackbird	392	Magpie	393
2	Carrion Crow	390	Blackbird	392
3	Chaffinch	390	Carrion Crow	391
4	Wren	389	Chaffinch	389
5	Robin	388	Robin	389
6	Blue Tit	388	Great Tit	388
7	Great Tit	387	Wren	387
8	Woodpigeon	386	Blue Tit	387
9	Swallow	384	Woodpigeon	383
10	Buzzard	381	Song Thrush	381
11	Dunnock	381	Dunnock	378
12	Magpie	381	Starling	378
13	Song Thrush	380	Willow Warbler	375
14	Chiffchaff	378	Swallow	370
15	Pied Wagtail	370	House Sparrow	368
16	Blackcap	368	Jackdaw	364
17	Goldfinch	367	Pied Wagtail	355
18	House Sparrow	365	Mistle Thrush	349
19	Mistle Thrush	363	Cuckoo	345
20	Greenfinch	363	Chiffchaff	344

Table 107. The 20 most widely distributed breeding species in the two Gwent Atlases

Species showing greatest percentage increases in range

Table 108 shows species for which there was a 10% or greater increase in the number of tetrads in which they were recorded. They comprise 34 very diverse species, which have increased for a variety of different reasons. With the exception of Garden Warbler, for which the national trend has been slightly negative in recent years, all these increases in the Gwent distribution reflect population trends for the UK as whole.

Several waterbirds have significantly expanded their ranges. Goosanders have been expanding southwards since the late 1800s and their increase in Gwent is a continuation of this long-term trend. Canada Goose, Tufted Duck, the two grebes, and Coot have been increasing in numbers and expanding their British range in recent years, while Mute Swan populations have been recovering from the lead poisoning problems of the 1970s-1980s. Although not increasing their British range, which has always been extensive, Mallard have shown substantial population increases, which probably underlie the observed extension of their range in Gwent. Most of the species in this group have benefited to varying degrees from the creation of new recreational and ornamental water bodies, and their increased colonisation of urban water habitats.

Several of the notable increases concern resident species that can be badly affected by hard winters. Herons and Kingfishers both require ice-free water to feed, while Long-tailed Tits and Goldcrests are diminutive birds with very low body mass, and which therefore have difficulty surviving the night during very cold weather. Many Stonechats, and most Grey Wagtails and Nuthatches remain on their territories throughout the winter, and can suffer severely in hard winters. All species in this group have probably benefited from the absence of any severe and prolonged cold winters since the years of the 1st Gwent Atlas

Lesser Black-backed and Herring Gulls have continued to expand their colonisation of inland rooftops, an increase that has been fuelled by the availability of abundant food, especially at open refuse tips, and there is some indication that even Great Black-backed Gulls (not shown in Table 108), the most marine of our resident gull species, might begin to follow the same pattern.

Ravens, together with birds of prey, feature prominently in Table 108. In this group, enlightened attitudes have resulted in reduced levels of persecution, and have thus been a major factor in their recent increases and spread. The current ubiquity of Buzzards in the county is the most strikingly visible example of this development. In the case of the Hobby, its westward and northward expansion in Britain may also be related to the advent of warmer, drier summers leading to a greater availability of large insect prey, particularly certain dragonfly species (Prince & Clarke, 1993). Some of the expansion of the Peregrine's range can be attributed, particularly in the earlier years of the period, to their continued recovery from the pesticide-induced crash of the 1960s, while the escape and/or release of falconers' birds, and maturation of coniferous forests have contributed to the spread of the Goshawk.

Among the warblers, the increases seen for Reed Warbler, Sedge Warbler, Blackcap and Chiffchaff all reflect the national trends for these species, and may be to some extent be climate-related, though Sedge Warbler and Chiffchaff populations in Britain are known to fluctuate according to rates of winter survival in northern and sub-Saharan Africa.

Siskin, Crossbill and Nightjar are associated with coniferous forestry plantations. Siskin and Crossbill have expanded into maturing forests, and are still spreading, though in the case of Crossbill, periodic irruptions are also a source of variation in breeding numbers. Although Nightjars are associated with heathland in many parts of Britain, in Gwent they are found almost exclusively in forestry restocks (plantations that have been recently felled and replanted), so numbers and distribution tend to be controlled by local forestry activity.

The increase in Collared Doves appears to be a continuation of their expansion following their colonisation of Britain some 50 years ago. Greenfinch and Goldfinch have shown strong increases nationally in the years since the 1st Gwent Atlas, and they may be benefiting from milder winters, but their increased use of garden food sources is probably a major factor in assisting winter survival.

Species	% Change in total tetrads occupied	Species	% Change in total tetrads occupied
Canada Goose	6,100	Sedge Warbler	29
Goshawk*	875	Collared Dove	20
Lesser Black-backed Gull	540	Grey Wagtail	19
Hobby	295	Nuthatch	19
Herring Gull	220	Kingfisher	18
Goosander	188	Buzzard	18
Siskin	180	Mallard	17
Tufted Duck	157	Peregrine	16
Little Grebe	142	Mute Swan	14
Stonechat	142	Greenfinch	14
Coot	110	Long-tailed Tit	11
Great Crested Grebe	89	Garden Warbler	11
Grey Heron	60	Blackcap	10
Crossbill	48	Chiffchaff	10
Nightjar	42	Goldcrest	10
Raven	40	Goldfinch	10
Reed Warbler	29		

Table 108. Breeding species for which the number of tetrads occupied has increased by 10% or more.
Species that were not found in at least ten tetrads in either of the Gwent Atlases are considered in the rare and sporadic breeders section. * From the 1st Gwent Atlas, only tetrads with *confirmed* breeding records of Goshawks have been recorded, so the figure shown represents increase in tetrads with *confirmed* breeding rather than total tetrads in which recorded.

Widespread species showing greatest percentage decreases in range

Table 109 lists those species that have shown a 10% or greater reduction in the number of tetrads in which they were recorded in Gwent. In the cases of the Water Rail, Barn Owl and Common Sandpiper the data may be misleading, as although all three were recorded in fewer total tetrads, they showed significant increases in the number of tetrads with *probable* or *confirmed* breeding, and it is likely that their populations in the county have actually increased. This is particularly true of Water Rail, which now has a large breeding population at Newport Wetlands Reserve. The apparent declines of Feral Pigeon and Hawfinch may also be false, as (for very different reasons) they are both frequently overlooked, and certainly under-recorded.

The decline in Redstart distribution has occurred despite an increase in the UK population index, but the decreases noted for other species in Table 109 all reflect recent UK trends.

The species referenced as (A) in Table 109 are predominantly farmland species, or those for which farmland has been one of the significant habitats occupied. Changes in agricultural practice have been identified as an important causative factor in their decline, although not necessarily the only one. The more intensive regimes introduced during the second half of the 20th century have included drainage of wet meadows, loss of marginal habitats, mechanised hedge cutting, hedge loss, lack of winter stubble, sowing of cereals in autumn instead of spring and increased use of herbicides and insecticides. Different factors have affected different species, the Whinchat, for example, being affected by the loss of marginal habitat; the Yellow Wagtail and Lapwing by the loss of wet meadows and the Yellowhammer by the loss of winter stubbles, but the combined effects have resulted in a serious overall decline of our traditional farmland bird populations. It is noticeable that the decline of Skylark and Meadow Pipit in Gwent has been almost entirely on farmland, whereas no decline has been detected on moorlands. Reed Buntings, although mainly inhabiting wetlands, have also lost habitat for some of the above reasons.

The species referenced as (B) in Table 109 are woodland birds that have undergone declines in the UK, probably for a number reasons. Loss of ground flora as a result of deer grazing has been suggested as an important factor in the declines of Marsh Tit, Willow Tit, Woodcock and Bullfinch in parts of the UK, and this may be significant in woodlands in the east of Gwent where deer are known to be well-established. Competition with, and predation by, Great Spotted Woodpeckers may be a factor in the cases of Willow Tit and Lesser Spotted Woodpecker. The maturation of conifer plantations, although beneficial to species such as Siskin, is probably a cause of recent declines in Tree Pipit, which tend to colonise plantations only in the early years prior to canopy closure.

For some of our migratory species referenced as (C) Table 109, factors outside the UK may have contributed to their decline. Hunting pressures during migration may be significant for Turtle Dove and Ring Ouzel, and environmental changes, either at passage stopovers or in winter quarters may be important in some cases. The Willow Warbler does not feature in Table 109 as the number of tetrads occupied has dropped by only 4% but, as elsewhere in southern Britain, a severe decline has occurred in Gwent, which is shown up by a drop of 27% in the number of tetrads with *confirmed* breeding.

Species (text reference)	% Change in total tetrads occupied	Species (text reference)	% Change in total tetrads occupied
Turtle Dove (A,C)	−90	Redpoll (B)	−25
Tree Sparrow (A)	−84	Tree Pipit (C)	−24
Grey Partridge (A)	−83	Cuckoo (A)	−24
Ring Ouzel (C)	−80	Hawfinch	−23
Woodcock (B)	−61	Wood Warbler (B,C)	−22
Willow Tit (B)	−60	Spotted Flycatcher (C)	−22
Redshank (A)	−59	Kestrel (A)	−21
Snipe (A)	−50	Feral Pigeon	−20
Little Owl (B)	−47	Grasshopper Warbler (C)	−19
Yellow Wagtail (A)	−47	Common Sandpiper	−18
Lesser Spotted Woodpecker (B)	−46	Meadow Pipit (A)	−17
Red-Legged Partridge (A)	−46	Skylark (A)	−17
Lapwing (A)	−43	Whinchat (A)	−16
Yellowhammer (A)	−36	Water Rail	−15
Curlew (A)	−30	Lesser Whitethroat (C)	−15
Red Grouse	−27	Bullfinch (B)	−14
Marsh Tit (B)	−26	Redstart	−14
Barn Owl	−26	Reed Bunting	−11

Table 109. Species for which the number of tetrads occupied has decreased by more than 10%

New breeding species

New breeding species that have begun to breed in the county since 1976 are shown in Table 110. A total of ten new species have been proved to breed, while another two have probably bred and it seems likely that proven breeding will occur for these in the near future.

The new acquisitions to our breeding list have all been species that, for various reasons, are extending their range in Britain, and their arrival was not altogether unexpected.

The appearance of southern species such as the Little Egret, Dartford Warbler, Cetti's Warbler and Bearded Tit forms part of a long-term pattern of expansion that appears to be related to climatic warming. The construction of the extensive reedbeds at the Newport Wetlands Reserve was thus a timely development for Cetti's Warbler and Bearded Tit, while the saline lagoons there provided a suitable habitat for the Avocet, another species that has been extending its range in Britain. The Gadwall has been expanding west from England, as also have the feral populations of Greylag Goose and Mandarin, while the colonisation of Denny Island by Cormorants was not wholly unexpected, given the species' recent population expansion. The striking success of the introduction of Red Kite to several sites in England, together with the continued expansion of the Welsh population, has resulted in its appearance in many new counties, and breeding in Gwent was a more or less inevitable development. Honey Buzzards appear to be taking advantage of the current state of our conifer forests where felling of the most mature trees, and replanting, is creating a more varied structure that favours this species. The probable breeding of Pochard at Newport Wetlands Reserve may reflect a current readiness of this species to take rapid advantage whenever an appropriate new habitat is created, as happened in the 1990s after the creation of the Penclacwydd WWT in Carmarthenshire.

The Short-eared Owl appears in the 2nd Gwent Atlas as a confirmed breeding species, but this is not a Gwent breeding record as it occurred in a border tetrad just outside the county boundary.

Species	Status	1st Year of breeding
Greylag Goose	Confirmed	1994
Dartford Warbler	Confirmed	1998
Great Cormorant	Confirmed	1999
Gadwall	Confirmed	2006
Honey Buzzard	Probable	2000
Little Egret	Confirmed	2001
Cetti's Warbler	Confirmed	2001
Pochard	Probable	2003
Avocet	Confirmed	2003
Mandarin	Confirmed	2003
Bearded Tit	Confirmed	2005
Red Kite	Confirmed	2006

Table 110. Species that have begun to breed in Gwent since 1976

Rare and irregular breeding species

Teal, Shoveler and Garganey have all bred irregularly in the county in the past, and although they have not been proved to breed for some years now, all three have recently summered at Newport Wetlands Reserve and the situation looks promising for the near future. At the time of the 1st Gwent Atlas, the Goosander would also have featured in this section, but its breeding status can no longer be considered as rare and irregular.

The Goshawk, like the Goosander, is a formerly rare species that is now well established, but another of our raptors, the Merlin, has remained very scarce, and although it was recorded at similar numbers of sites in both Gwent Atlases, the number with *probable* or *confirmed* breeding declined by two-thirds.

Among the waders, the Ringed Plover and the Little Ringed Plover have both improved their breeding strength since the 1st Gwent Atlas, the former being another species that has taken advantage of the Newport Wetlands Reserve, and the latter expanding its total of breeding sites from three to seven. In contrast, the position of Golden Plover and Dunlin remains weak, though behaviour suggestive of breeding was observed at single locations during the 2nd Gwent Atlas, and it is possible that both retain a tenuous foothold on the northern moorlands. In the same area of the county, a similar comment can be made about a rather different bird, the Ring Ouzel, which appears to hanging on precariously at Trefil quarries.

The Long-eared Owl has been a recent success story. It was not known to have bred in the county since the start of the 20th century until 1992, since when it has become established in Gwent's mature conifer plantations, with possibly in excess of ten pairs breeding. The Firecrest, another forest breeder, has remained characteristically erratic, with good numbers in the mid 1970s and late 1980s, and a sprinkle of suggestive records since 2000, but nothing in between.

The Rock Pipit was not recorded during the 1st Gwent Atlas, although it had been known to breed in previous years, but has since become regular at two or more coastal sites, while the Red-backed Shrike, which last bred in 1981, was a surprise breeder in the north of the county in 2005.

Wintering Wildfowl

Most wintering wildfowl species have maintained their numbers in the county, but there have been some significant redistributions between sites. Perhaps most obviously, there has been a decline in numbers using Llandegfedd Reservoir, coupled with corresponding increases at other sites, with the result that the estuary has now become the most important site for Wigeon, Teal and Mallard, while Ynysyfro Reservoir has become the most important site for Tufted Duck. The saltmarsh grasslands at the Newport Wetlands Reserve have been very successful at attracting Wigeon and numbers are still increasing there. From the late 1980s the estuary held very large numbers of Pochards and Tufted Ducks, but there have been very few there since sewage discharge ceased during 2000.

Pintails have increased greatly on the estuary, and the Gwent shore now holds internationally important numbers, while Shoveler numbers have increased to the level of national importance.

On the debit side, Bewick's Swan has declined from being a regular winter resident numbering 40–80 birds, to a scarce visitor. This appears to be caused by recent milder winters, which have resulted in birds wintering further east.

Wintering and passage waders

As with Bewick's Swan (above) the trend to milder winters in Europe has led also to several wader species travelling less far from their breeding grounds than previously. Thus, numbers of Ringed Plovers and Grey Plovers reaching Gwent and other parts of western Britain have dropped very significantly. Although never very high, the numbers of wintering Turnstones in the county have also fallen, and this reflects a general decline in UK winter populations. Sanderlings on spring passage have also decreased drastically, but this appears not to be typical among Welsh sites for this species, and may have more local causes.

The Severn Estuary remains a site of international importance for Dunlin, and a substantial proportion of the Severn population still feeds on the Gwent shore. In very recent years there has been a remarkable increase in wintering Black-tailed Godwits on the Gwent coast, with nationally important numbers now commonly recorded.

Concluding remarks

At the time when the 2nd Gwent Atlas was proposed, and linking it to the production of a new *Birds of Gwent* was planned, there was an anticipation that we would have a rather depressing tale to tell. In the event, we have been very pleasantly surprised. It was, of course, inevitable that many of the negative national trends would be reflected in the state of Gwent's birds, and we have confirmed that this is the case. However, we have also been able to describe many positive developments, in terms of individual species and also the regional species diversity, several of which were not expected. The future is not all bleak.

ESTIMATES OF BREEDING POPULATIONS

The estimation of numbers of breeding birds, particularly for the more common species, is often a difficult task. For the last two decades, the methodology used for tracking the population trends of bird species in the wider countryside has been the Breeding Bird Survey (BBS) of the BTO/JNCC/RSPB. The survey is undertaken in randomly selected 1-km squares, and involves walking a 2km route on two occasions during the breeding season. All birds are counted (though as the survey is intended to track breeding birds, juvenile birds are excluded wherever possible) and assigned to various distance categories (see Raven & Noble, 2006, for full details). Although not originally intended to produce population estimates, BBS survey data have been employed in both of the methods used for assessing the numbers of widespread and common species in Gwent.

Widespread and Common Species. Method 1 (termed the BBS analysis method in the species accounts)

This has involved analysis by the BTO of Gwent BBS returns for the year 2000 (n = 38). The BTO have been undertaking experimental analysis of BBS data to establish population numbers (Newson *et al.*, 2005), and the methodology is therefore likely to be further refined in the future. Their analysis of the Gwent BBS data has been used to give a population estimate for many species in the county. The locations of the individual BBS squares are plotted on the map in Figure A1. Data from the early season visit has been used for resident species, and data from the latter visit for migrants. The number of individual observations (excluding flying birds) are multiplied up to give 1-km square populations and then county populations. The habitat for each section of each 2-km route is recorded, and species populations are adjusted for the proportion of their preferred habitat in the county. Also, as detectability generally decreases with distance, an additional factor allows for undetected individuals. The final figures are divided by two to give the number of pairs. This analysis was carried out by Stuart Newson of the BTO, and his detailed description of the method is given in the addendum at the end of this appendix.

Widespread and Common Species. Method 2 (termed the atlas-based method in the species accounts)

This has involved GOS analysis of BBS returns and additional 2-km walks (n = 101). This analysis included the same data for the year 2000 used in method 1, together with data from three further 'official' BBS squares from a different year. Also included is data from an extra eight 'unofficial' BBS surveys and from a further 52 surveys where BBS-type 2-km walks were undertaken in a tetrad (all plotted in Figure A1). As habitat was not recorded on the 2-km walks, this variable could not be factored in the analysis. The higher count from the two visits to each square was used for each species, and as with method 1 the observations are multiplied up to give a population per 1-km square. This figure is multiplied by four to give a population per tetrad. The number per tetrad is then multiplied by the number of tetrads in which *confirmed* breeding was recorded in the 2nd Gwent Atlas: to give a minimum county population figure, or by the number of tetrads in which *confirmed* plus *probable* breeding was recorded: to give a maximum county population figure. No detectability factors are included and the final range is taken to represent the number of pairs.

Discussion of the merits of the different methods.

In many cases, e.g. Wren, Dunnock, Blackbird, all of the tits, House Sparrow, Chaffinch, Greenfinch, Linnet and Yellowhammer, the two methods came up with remarkably similar numbers, whereas other species differed by a factor of two and some by a greater amount. Each method has some advantages and disadvantages:-

a) greater sample size – an advantage of Method 2
b) species detectability taken account of – an advantage of Method 1
c) habitat type/extent taken account of – a general advantage of Method 1 (the random selection of the BBS squares has however resulted in two squares being chosen on the Newport Wetlands, which could give an over-representation of wetland species in the county using Method 1)

d) the inclusion of flight records – an advantage for Method 2 for those species that are more commonly seen in flight (e.g. raptors, corvids, pigeons, woodpeckers) but could also give an overestimate of numbers for conspicuous and wide-ranging species (e.g. Buzzard, Raven)

e) the assumption that the final figure represents individuals (Method 1) or pairs (Method 2) – for some species, detectability of the sexes is near equal, but for others the male is much more easily recorded, so both methods could have advantages for different species. During the breeding season however, it is probably unlikely that both members of a pair will be detected, as one may be tending the nest.

Less Common Species. Method 3 (sample tetrads method; n = 151 cards, covering 128 tetrads)

Similar cards to the standard recording card were used, with scarce and colonial species highlighted. Observers were asked to give their best estimate for each of the required species in each of their tetrads, and the method by which they arrived at the number was also recorded (e.g. survey, count, estimate). The location of the tetrads for which cards were returned are plotted on the map in Figure A2. In most cases records for only a few species were entered on each card. A population density was calculated for those cards (tetrads) that held the species, and, as in Method 2, the population range was estimated by multiplying by the number of tetrads in which *confirmed* breeding was recorded in the 2nd Gwent Atlas: to give a minimum county population figure, or by the number of tetrads in which *confirmed* plus *probable* breeding was recorded: to give a maximum county population figure.

Rare Species. Method 4 (expert opinion)

For a limited number of species that breed in small numbers, and whose range is intensively watched, e.g. some waders and wildfowl and Cetti's Warbler, all pairs are probably detected. Others, e.g. Cormorant and rare raptors, have been intensively studied, while Grey Heron and Nightjar have been systematically surveyed.

The figures derived from each of the above methods for all breeding species are shown in Table A1. In the cases of species where there are two or more estimates, we have carefully considered the ways in which the advantages/disadvantages listed above might have impacted on them, before choosing a figure that we consider to be the best estimate. The figure(s) on which we have based this estimate are in **bold type** in the table, and the final estimate is shown in the last column of the table. Where available, Sample Tetrad data has generally been preferred above other sources, as it represents actual counts or estimates within tetrads, rather than extrapolations from transects. In some instances where two methods have produced very different figures, the relative merits of the figures are discussed in the individual species accounts.

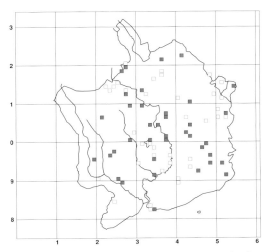

Figure A1. Locations of counts used in Methods 1 and 2. Filled squares show official BBS squares used in Method 1. Open squares show sites where additional BBS-style censuses were conducted, or counts were made along 2-km transects. Data from all sites (filled and open symbols) were combined for use in Method 2.

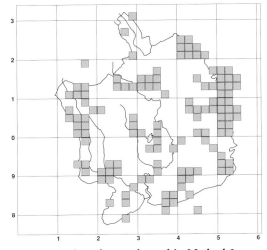

Figure A2. Sample tetrads used in Method 3

Table A1. Population estimates for breeding birds in Gwent

Species	Method 1		n	Method 2		n	Method 3	Method 4	Chosen figure
	Mean	Range		Mid-point	Range				
Mute Swan	350	240–460						**30–50**	30–50
Greylag Goose								**4**	4
Canada Goose						5	65	**c.50**	c.5.0
Shelduck							45	**100–200**	100–200
Mallard	3,110	**2,680–3,510**	34	12,300	11,470–13,140				2,700–3,500
Tufted Duck	–	–		–	–	4	30	**20–30**	20–30
Goosander								**c.10**	c.10
Red Grouse						2	**38–65**	**c.60**	60
Red-legged Partridge						6	**40–65**		40–65
Grey Partridge								**50–100**	50–100
Pheasant	1,600	1,460–1,750	39	7,100	5,970–8,230			**c.3,000**	1,500–1,800
Little Grebe						3	35–46	**30–45**	30–45
Great Crested Grebe								**6–14**	6–14
Cormorant								**50–90**	50–90
Little Egret								**5**	5
Heron								**140–160**	140–160
Goshawk	–	–				21	40–65	**c.50**	c.50
Sparrowhawk	520	**430–610**				61	130–290		430–610
Buzzard	870	780–980				91	**500–800**		500–800
Kestrel	80	50–100				57	**90–200**		90–200
Merlin								**3**	3
Hobby						2	**20–28**	**20–30**	20–28
Peregrine								**15**	15
Water Rail								**c.30**	c.30
Moorhen	230	190–280				42	**325–380**		330–380
Coot	420	330–510				8	**130–160**		130–160
Oystercatcher								**c.10**	c.10
Avocet								**5**	5
Little Ringed Plover								**8–12**	8–12
Ringed Plover								**4–8**	4–8
Lapwing						23	**220–500**		220–500
Snipe								**20–30**	20–30
Woodcock						10	**c.100**		c.100
Curlew	330	280–390				12	**21–130**		21–130
Redshank								**15–30**	15–30
Common Sandpiper						3	**22–38**	**30–40**	25–40
Lesser Black-backed Gull								**c.375**	c.180
Herring Gull								**170+**	170+
Great Black-backed Gull								**20–30**	20–30
Feral Pigeon			5	1,420	**1,044–1,800**				1,000–1,800
Stock Dove	630	**530–710**	21	2,840	1,850–3,830				530–710
Wood Pigeon	12,970	**12,300–13,670**	93	35,230	27,400–43,050				13–14,000
Collared Dove	2,130	**1,900–2,390**	35	8,620	8,240–9,000				1,900–2,400
Cuckoo	600	460–730				25	9–180	**240–360**	240–360
Barn Owl						2	15–27	**25–50**	25–50
Little Owl	310	**250–390**				42	174–410		250–390
Tawny Owl	470	390–570				64	**380–840**		380–840
Long-eared Owl								**10**	10
Nightjar						3	9–45	**c.48**	c.48
Swift						34	**2–3,000**		2–3,000
Kingfisher						21	**34–75**		34–75
Green Woodpecker	400	330–460	34	2,940	2,070–3,810	77	**420–770**		420–770
Great Spotted Woodpecker	480	430–530	39	3,370	2,580–4,150	67	**670–1090**		670–1,100
Lesser Spotted Woodpecker						33	**28–67**		30–70

Species	Method 1		Method 2			Method 3		Method 4	Chosen figure
	Mean	Range	n	Mid-point	Range	n			
Skylark	2,910	2,650–3,120	34	5,910	3,140–8,680				2,900–5,900
Sand Martin						12	c.900		c.900
Swallow	4,880	4,330–5,300							4,300–5,300
House Martin	4,130	3,570–4,720							3.600–4,700
Tree Pipit	1,320	1,040–1,630	9	1,920	1,200–2,640				1,300–1,900
Meadow Pipit	15,400	12,700–17,580	22	18,600	14,400–22,810				15–19,000
Rock Pipit								2–3	2–3
Yellow wagtail						7	37–75		37–75
Grey Wagtail	290	200–380				46	430–610		430–610
Pied Wagtail	2,420	2,180–2,640	40	8,100	6,800–9,370				2,200–2,600
Dipper						27	100–140	200–300	200–300
Wren	38,380	36,710–40,250	97	34,750	30,900–38,600				31–40,000
Dunnock	8,460	7,970–8,910	77	11,000	8,500–13,500				8,500–11,000
Robin	42,610	40,850–44,620	89	30,240	28,490–31,990				30–43,000
Redstart	600	510–720	22	2,590	2,010–3,170				600–2,600
Whinchat	1,550	1,190–1,940						c.550	c.550
Stonechat	210	150–280				11	91–120	c.150	150–210
Wheatear	110	70–140				17	170–230		170–230
Ring Ouzel								0–1	0–1
Blackbird	41,490	40,130–42,870	97	46,230	44,640–47,820				41–46,000
Song Thrush	5,760	5,440–6,090	77	16,550	14,320–18,770				5,500–6,100
Mistle Thrush	1,340	1,200–1,500	53	6,860	5,550–8,140				1,200–1,500
Cetti's Warbler								50–60	50–60
Grasshopper Warbler								<35	<35
Sedge Warbler	630	440–820				7	63–140	150–250	150–250
Reed Warbler	3,050	2,270–4,070				8	310–570		310–570
Blackcap	8,430	7,840–8,990	69	13,140	9,160–17,110				8,500–13,000
Garden Warbler	540	470–610	35	2,270	1,150–3,390				540–2,300
Lesser Whitethroat	130	90–170				13	71–180		70–180
Whitethroat	4,050	3,620–4,420	31	3,500	2,230–4,770				3,600–4,400
Wood Warbler			15	1,160	720–1,600				720–1,600
Chiffchaff	5,610	5,270–5,960	45	21,100	12,280–29,940				5,600–21,000
Willow Warbler	5,020	4,560–5,520	70	10,800	7,200–14,390				5–11,000
Goldcrest	11,270	10,025–12,310	45	7,040	4,470–9,600				7–11,000
Spotted Flycatcher	1,580	1,390–1,770	12	2,150	1,590–2,700	52	491–830		490–830
Pied Flycatcher						16	400–450		400–450
Long-tailed Tit	6,740	6,080–7,440	34	11,850	10.250–13,410				6,700–12,000
Blue Tit	39,030	37,450–40,570	11	33,350	31,950–34,740				33–39,000
Great Tit	15,910	15,150–16,580	81	17,870	16,530–19,200				16–18,000
Coal Tit	4,300	3,770–4,730	39	6,400	5,110–7,690				4,300–6,400
Willow Tit								70–125	70–125
Marsh Tit			11	830	507–1,160				510–1,200
Nuthatch	1,250	1,110–1,390	36	4,080	3,030–5,120				1,300–4,100
Treecreeper	2,630	2,320–2,930	29	2,850	1,990–3,690				2,300–2,900
Jay	530	450–600	41	3,010	1,505–4,520				530–3,000
Magpie	5,300	4,970–5,670	80	17,810	15,450–20,170				5,300–18,000
Jackdaw	5,780	5,310–6,360						10–15,000	10–15,000
Rook	7,090	5,560–8,920				26	3350	4,600	4,600–7,100
Carrion Crow	6,380	6,100–6,700	93	32,580	30,130–35,040			10–12,000	10–12,000
Raven	140	100–180	19	3,670	2,460–4,880	58	171–340		170–340
Starling	8,080	7,210–9,100	58	44,590	42,280–46,900				7,200–9,100
House Sparrow	23,300	21,510–25,190	60	32,870	30,400–35,340				23–33,000
Tree Sparrow								c.240	200–240
Chaffinch	33,440	32,430–34,510	93	31,530	24,850–38,214				32–36,000
Greenfinch	11,380	10,690–12,150	64	13,520	10,180–16,870				11–12,000
Goldfinch	6,350	5,700–6,930	62	13,730	9,500–17,960				6,400–14,000
Siskin								c.1,400	c.1,400

Species	Method 1			Method 2		Method 3	Method 4	Chosen figure
	Mean	Range	n	Mid-point	Range			
Linnet	5,330	**4,900–5,810**	44	7,300	4,200–10,400			4,900–5,800
Lesser Redpoll							**45–180**	45–180
Crossbill							**c.50**	c.50
Bullfinch	**1,390**	1,190–1,580	31	**3,110**	1,820–4,400			1,390–3,100
Hawfinch							**30–100**	30–100
Yellowhammer	2,730	**2,390–3,050**	21	2,920	1,600–4,230			2,400–3,100
Reed Bunting	1,400	**970–1,810**	6	2,580	1,710–3,460			970–1,800

Addendum to Appendix 1.

Method for the production of population size estimates for Gwent, based on BBS data

Based on data for 2000 from the BTO/JNCC/RSPB Breeding Bird Survey. The method is based on that of Newson *et al.* (2005) with further refinements.

Estimating population size from BBS data

Distance sampling software developed by Buckland *et al.*, 2001 (DISTANCE, version 4.1 Release 2; Thomas *et al.*, 2004) was used to model the decline in detectability with distance from the transect line to allow an estimate of undetected individuals to be incorporated into the real estimate of density. Birds recorded in the final distance band (100 m or more) were excluded from the analyses, because counts within an unbounded category are difficult to interpret. Birds in flight were also excluded. Because the BBS is designed to monitor breeding birds, which tend not to flock during the breeding season, we assume that counts are a collection of individual birds rather than modelling the detectability of flocks.

Heterogeneity in detectability is commonly minimised using stratification, but this may be precluded by small sample sizes or result in biased estimates. In this study we take advantage of recent developments in the program DISTANCE that allow the effect of multiple covariates to be incorporated into the estimation procedure using a conditional likelihood approach (Marques & Buckland 2003). We consider fitting half-normal and hazard-rate key functions only because other key functions available in the software Distance (Thomas *et al.*, 2004) either do not allow the inclusion of covariates (uniform key) or have an implausible shape (exponential key). To take potential differences in detectability between specified habitats (see Table A2) and regions (11 regions: 9 English Government Office Regions, Scotland and Northern Ireland) into account, we adopt the following stepwise approach. For each species in turn we start by estimating $f(0)$ (the value of the probability density function of perpendicular distances, at zero distance) without including habitat or region covariates to both half-normal and hazard rate models. We then add a single covariate habitat or region and establish whether the model fit was improved by identifying the model with the smallest AIC (i.e. best relative fit). We then fitted a model with both habitat and region as covariates and used AIC to see whether the relative fit of the model was improved further. If there was no improvement to the relative fit of the model, a model with the single covariate was chosen as the model that best explained the observed heterogeneity in detectability. Once the 'best' model had been chosen for a particular species, it was applied to the encounters from surveyed squares to produce an estimate of the number of individuals of that species for each 1-km square surveyed.

To obtain estimates of population size and confidence intervals, we used a bootstrap resampling procedure of 400 iterations (Crowley 1992). For each iteration, 1-km squares were randomly resampled within Gwent (38 1-km squares surveyed), the sample drawn being equal to the total number of 1-km squares in the county. The values for each sampling region were then added to derive an estimate of each species in that region. The 200th, 10th and 390th ordered bootstrap values across iterations were taken to given the median and lower and upper 95% confidence limits of the Gwent estimates.

Table A2. Breeding Bird Survey habitat classes recorded by volunteers and used in the distance-sampling analyses. Habitat classes are based on Crick (1992).

Covariate	Name	Description
Habitat	Broadleaved woodland	Broadleaved woodland
Habitat	Coniferous woodland	Coniferous woodland
Habitat	Mixed woodland	Broadleaved and coniferous (min. 10% of each)
Habitat	Scrub	Young regenerated woodland, downland scrub, heath scrub, young coppice, young plantation and clear-felled woodland (< 5m in height)
Habitat	Semi-natural grassland	Chalk downland, grass moor (unenclosed), grass moor mixed with heather and other dry grassland, Machair, water meadow, grazing marsh, reed swamp, saltmarsh and other open marsh
Habitat	Heath and bog	Dry heath, wet heath, mixed heath and breckland, bog, drained bog and bare peat
Habitat	Farmland	Improved and unimproved grass farmland, mixture of grassland and tilled farmland, arable farmland including standing crop, plough and bare earth awaiting cultivation, orchard and other farmland not specified above
Habitat	Human sites	Land relating to human habitation in a city or town, on the outskirts of a city or town or in the countryside, e.g. village or hamlet
Habitat	Water bodies and coastal	Freshwater pond, lake, reservoir, stream, river, canal and ditch

RECORDS EXCLUDED FROM THE SYSTEMATIC LIST

The following records, some of which have been published previously, are excluded from the species accounts for one or more of the following reasons:

(a) Bird(s) considered to be escapes from captivity;
(b) Locality is not believed to be in Gwent;
(c) Records reconsidered or reviewed, and identification considered not fully established;
(d) Records previously published but now considered unacceptable.

Black-necked Grebe   *Podiceps nigricollis*
Birds offshore at Peterstone on 31st July and two birds in the Gout on 18th September 1983 **(d)**.

Cattle Egret   *Bubulcus ibis*
A single bird of the 'eastern race' in Llangibby village on 19th May 1993 **(a)**.

White Stork   *Ciconia ciconia*
An immature at St Brides on 8th November and then at Peterstone on 9th November 1996 **(a)**.

Pink-footed Goose   *Anser brachyrhynchus*
A single bird at the Rhymney Estuary on 3rd February 1963 **(b)**.

Barnacle Goose   *Branta leucopsis*
One in the gout at Peterstone on 7th May 1985 **(a)**, one in the Peterstone area with a large free-flying flock of Canada Geese during 13th March–3rd May 1997 **(a)**, one present throughout 1998–2001 at the Warrage / Dingestow Court / the Hendre area **(a)**, two birds associating with a large flock of Canada Geese at Marshfield on 15th December 1998 **(a)**, one at YR on 9th October 2001 **(a)**, one at the NWR in February 2002 and up to five, again with Canada Geese during January–May 2003 at the NWR **(a)**.

Ruddy Shelduck   *Tadorna ferruginea*
Single birds at Undy Foreshore on 23rd May 1965 and at Peterstone on 3rd May 1978 **(a)**. Up to two at Collister Pill from 21st May–late Jun 1978, one at Tredegar House Country Park throughout 1995 and three flying past Sluice Farm on 26th July 1998 **(a)**.

Shoveler   *Anas clypeata*
A flock of 28 females at Ynysyfro Reservoir on 12th November 1970 **(d)**.

Ferruginous Duck   *Aythya nyroca*
A record included in the 1977 *Birds of Gwent* at Llandegfedd Reservoir on 30th October 1965 **(d)**.

Eider   *Somateria mollisima*
A male shot at Pant-yr-eos Reservoir during the winter of 1894/95 **(c)**.

Smew   *Mergellus albellus*
A single female shot at the Rhymney estuary on 24th Dec 1938 **(b)**.

Golden Pheasant   *Chrysolophus pictus*

Six records (**a**): a very tame male seen in a Goytre garden during 29th November 1978–29th January 1979, with further males being seen at Cwmfelinfach during 14th–17th November 1980 and in a Newport garden on 8th November 1981. A female at Peterstone on 23rd January 1985 and 26th October 1986, and a female mated to a male Common Pheasant at Magor Reserve in 1990.

Wood Sandpiper   *Tringa glareola*

One 'was considered almost certainly to be this species' published in the 1963 *Birds of Monmouthshire* as seen on 27th August 1939, although no location was given (**d**).

Grey Phalarope   *Phalaropus fulicarius*

One probably of this species at Peterstone on 5th December 1950 (**d**).

Long-tailed Skua   *Stercorarius longicaudus*

One was apparently shot in January 1892 at Rhymney (**b**). This record was given in *The Birds of Pembrokeshire* as coming from the collection of the late W. S. M. D'Urban of Exmouth.

Kittiwake   *Rissa tridactyla*

One at the mouth of the Rhymney estuary on 1st June 1960 (**b**).

Snowy Owl   *Bubo scandiacus*

Details included within the 1977 *Birds of Gwent* of a bird reported in the Abergavenny Chronicle and said to have been in the vicinity during the 1915/16 winter (**c**).

Shore Lark   *Eremophila alpestris*

Two on the foreshore near the Rhymney estuary on 2nd November 1972 (**b**).

Red-breasted Flycatcher   *Ficedula parva*

Three records only (**c**), one in a garden at Llanvaches on the edge of Wentwood forest on 20th–21st August 1969, a party of six or seven at Cleddon Wood on 14th July 1973, and a male in Wentwood forest on 21st May 1975.

Red-backed Shrike   *Lanis collurio*

One in a garden at Croesyceiliog on 10th September 1974 (**c**).

Great Grey Shrike   *Lanus excubitor*

Records within the 1963 *Birds of Monmouthshire* include a specimen at the National Museum of Wales which is labelled Monmouthshire but with no other details, and two at Trelleck in April 1954 (**c**).

Rose-coloured Starling   *Sturnus roseus*

A record in the 1977 *Birds of Gwent* of one at Llandenny on 16th April 1959 (**c**).

Ortolan Bunting   *Emberiza hortulana*

A record in the 1974 *Gwent Bird Report* of a pair on the Blorenge on 24th June 1971 (**c**).

Snow Bunting   *Plectrophenax nivalis*

A male was apparently shot during the winter of 1897/98 near the Rumney Pottery (**b**). Seven reported in reedbeds at Goldcliff Pill on 21st January 1967 are considered unlikely to have been of this species (**c**).

Cirl Bunting   *Emberiza cirlus*

A pair at Abernant Farm, Bulmore on 14th March 1984 (**c**).

Corn Bunting   *Emberiza calandra*

Two at Goldcliff on 23rd August 1969 (**d**).

APPENDIX 3

SUMMARY OF ALL TETRAD DATA
AND OBSERVERS FOR THE
2ND GWENT BREEDING ATLAS

The table lists all tetrads in the atlas survey together with the numbers of species recorded in each breeding category (possible, probable and confirmed). It also identifies the observers who took responsibility for carrying out atlas recording each tetrad. Observers who submitted casual records are listed separately in Appendix 6.

Tetrad	Tetrad Name	Observer(s)	Number of Species			
			Possible	Probable	Confirmed	Total
10E	Llechryd	J Avon	2	5	24	31
10H	Abertysswg	A Venables	4	24	9	37
10I	Cwm Tysswg	A Venables	2	9	15	26
10J	Bryn Bach S	C Cheeseman, R Morris, E Powell	6	27	18	51
10L	New Tredegar	A Venables	1	19	10	30
10M	Mount Pleasant	A Venables	3	25	11	39
10N	Bedwellty Pits	J Avon, G Waite	9	20	13	42
10P	Mountain Air	J Avon, G Waite	3	18	22	43
10Q	Markham	L Taswell, A Venables	9	19	26	54
10R	Hollybush	R Clarke	4	28	7	39
10S	Cruglwyn	J Avon	11	14	25	50
10T	Garden City	J Avon, G Waite	9	17	41	67
10U	Ebbw Vale	J Avon, G Herbert	4	13	50	67
10V	Pen-y-fan Pond	J Walton	4	24	14	42
10W	Mynydd Pen-y-fan	J Walton	6	26	17	49
10X	Cwm	K Richards	6	15	54	75
10Y	Cwm Merddog	G Herbert	14	12	25	51
10Z	Mynydd Carn-y-cefn	G Herbert	14	7	49	70
11A	Blaen Rhymney	J Avon, M Preece	6	18	13	37
11B	Trefil Ddu	J Avon, J Bennett	4	15	15	34
11C	Ffos-y-wern	J Avon	2	19	9	30
11F	Brynbach N	C Cheeseman, J Avon	10	10	12	32
11G	Trefil	J Avon, J Bennett	3	13	11	27
11K	Waun y Pound	A Moon, G Herbert	10	8	40	58
11L	Rassau	A Moon, M Preece	7	11	25	43
11Q	Beaufort	G Herbert	11	7	36	54
11R	Garnlydan	A Moon, M Preece	15	8	50	73
11V	Brynmawr	G Herbert	12	5	52	69
11W	Clydach Terrace	R Morris, E Powell	1	7	32	40
18U	Bedwas	P Bristow	2	27	14	43
18Z	Trethomas	P Bristow	6	27	5	38
19L	Twyn Shon-Ifan	C Hodgson	9	27	22	58
19Q	Mynydd Y Grug	A Venables, C Hodgson	11	19	21	51
19R	Ynysddu	A Venables	2	18	29	49
19S	Gelligroes	A Venables, R Clarke	13	9	19	41
19T	Blackwood	A Venables, R Clarke	4	16	24	44
19U	Penycoed	L Taswell	15	11	20	46
19V	Graig-goch	A Venables	1	18	31	50

Tetrad	Tetrad Name	Observer(s)	Number of Species			
			Possible	Probable	Confirmed	Total
19W	Pant-glas	R Clarke	7	20	26	53
19X	Mynyddislwyn	A Venables, R Clarke	11	18	16	45
19Y	Pentwyn mawr	R Clarke	5	17	23	45
19Z	Oakdale	A Venables, R Clarke	3	14	29	46
20A	Brynithel	J Walton	6	24	25	55
20B	Aberbeeg	J Walton	5	29	21	55
20C	Cwmtyleri	K Richards	5	13	49	67
20D	Mynydd James S	J Walton	6	31	4	41
20E	Cwmcelyn	G Herbert	9	16	34	59
20F	Llanhilleth	J Walton, K Richards	7	14	41	62
20G	Abertyleri	J Walton	4	26	7	37
20H	Gwastad	K Richards	6	11	40	57
20I	Twyn Gwryd	C Hatch, T Griffiths	5	12	52	69
20J	Coity Pond	C Hatch, T Griffiths	9	10	39	58
20K	Graig Ddu	C Hatch, T Griffiths	6	9	53	68
20L	British	C Hatch, T Griffiths	5	6	55	66
20M	Cwm Ffrwd	C Hatch, T Griffiths	5	6	54	65
20N	Mynydd Farteg Fawr	C Hatch, T Griffiths	4	12	36	52
20P	Blaenavon	C Hatch, T Griffiths	4	13	46	63
20Q	Wainfelin	C Hatch, T Griffiths	0	10	50	60
20R	Snatchwood	C Hatch, B King, G Saunders	2	10	52	64
20S	Garndiffaith	P Boddington	5	8	59	72
20T	Gallowsgreen	P Boddington	5	11	59	75
20U	Coedcae	C Hatch, T Griffiths	7	10	46	63
20V	Pontypool (N)	E Hankey	3	10	41	54
20W	Little Mountain	E Hankey	5	16	36	57
20X	Garn-wen	E Hankey	4	25	28	57
20Y	Craig-yr-Allt	A Williams, E Hankey	5	19	21	45
20Z	Upper Llanover	K Bradley, E Hankey	8	12	32	52
21A	Twyn Carncanddo	R Howells, C Hatch	5	12	39	56
21B	Cwm Clydach	C Hatch, T Griffiths, M Preece	6	11	58	75
21F	Llanelly Hill	C Hatch, T Griffiths	11	9	45	65
21G	Clydach	S Williams, C Cheeseman	18	21	21	60
21H	Llanelly	S Williams, G Herbert, J Avon	14	19	38	71
21K	Keepers Pond	C Hatch, T Griffiths, D Smith	3	15	51	69
21L	Twyn Allws	A Baker, J Avon	12	22	17	51
21M	Gilwern	A Balshaw, A Baker	14	17	28	59
21N	Cwn Gwenffrwdd	A Balshaw, A Venables	4	15	25	44
21Q	Blorenge (S)	B King, S Williams, G Saunders	15	25	9	49
21R	Blorenge (N)	A Baker, G Herbert	6	19	34	59
21S	Llanwenarth	R Brown	12	12	35	59
21T	Mynydd Llanwenarth	S Butler, J Davies	13	6	45	64
21U	Sugar Loaf	S Butler, J Davies	17	15	31	63
21V	Blorenge (E)	R Moeller, A Venables	15	12	38	65
21W	Llanfoist	F Branagan	5	12	41	58
21X	Abergavenny (W)	F Branagan, E Meredith, G Herbert	7	4	44	55
21Y	Twyn-yr-Allt	A Rowlands, S Butler, J Plumb	9	8	43	60
21Z	Bettws	R Beck, A Venables, A Rowlands	8	23	24	55
22N	Mynydd Du Forest	S Butler, J Lewis	6	18	15	39
22P	Mynydd Du Forest (N)	S Butler	9	17	11	37
22Q	Trewysgoed	J Harper	2	10	39	51

Tetrad	Tetrad Name	Observer(s)	Number of Species			
			Possible	Probable	Confirmed	Total
22R	Partrishow	J Harper	6	13	38	57
22S	Cadwgan	R Beck, G Ashwell	12	28	13	53
22T	Bal Mawr	R Beck	5	9	6	20
22U	Dol Alice	S Butler	3	15	16	34
22V	Forest Coal Pit	W Keen, Mr & Mrs Judd, A Venables, R Clevely, J Swift	7	22	33	62
22W	Cwmyoy	F Kenward, G Ashwell, J Evans	13	2	54	69
22X	Henllan	G Ashwell, J Evans	15	13	20	48
22Y	Llanthony	S Butler, J Davies	7	10	46	63
22Z	Loxidge Tump	S Butler, J Davies	1	15	44	60
23K	The Monastery	C James, J Lewis	14	13	15	42
23Q	The Vision Farm	C James, S Butler, J Davies	17	7	36	60
23V	Charity Farm	C James, A Baker	3	24	12	39
27I	Lamby	H P Jones	11	10	7	28
27J	Rumney	H P Jones	6	26	9	41
27P	Sluice Farm	H P Jones, A Venables	6	11	21	38
27U	Peterstone Gt Wharf	M Love, R Price	5	4	28	37
28E	Machen	P Bristow	5	25	19	49
28F	Llanrumney	M Love	3	2	30	35
28G	Began	H Mortimer, B Dowrick	10	21	15	46
28H	Cefn llwyd	H P Jones, D Spittle	14	22	15	51
28I	Coed Craig Ruperra	R Clarke, D Spittle	10	19	28	57
28J	Lower Machen	A Venables, R Clarke	4	17	30	51
28K	Wern Gethin	M Love	6	7	39	52
28L	Castleton	J Rosser	4	10	31	45
28M	Michaelston-y-Fedw	A Venables, P Bristow, B Dowrick	7	9	38	54
28N	Parkwood	R Clarke	10	20	21	51
28P	Coed y Squire	R Clarke, K Binmore	3	16	38	57
28Q	Peterstone	M Love	6	11	40	57
28R	Coedkernew	J Rosser	4	10	44	58
28S	Cefn Llogel	I Walker	6	18	27	51
28T	Bassaleg	I Walker	12	6	46	64
28U	Rogerstone	I Banner, G Savery	6	19	26	51
28V	St Brides (S)	C Jones, A Venables	6	18	20	44
28W	St Brides (N)	R Price	5	26	11	42
28X	Duffryn	M Love	6	7	39	52
28Y	Glasllwch	I Walker	4	4	41	49
28Z	Ynys-y-fro Res.	I Banner	5	14	37	56
29A	Wattsville	A Venables	4	16	31	51
29B	Mynydd-y-Lan	R Clarke	4	29	16	49
29C	Abercarn	G Thorne	6	6	35	47
29D	Newbridge	G Thorne	0	4	32	36
29E	Crumlin	R Clarke	2	19	21	42
29F	Crosskeys	G Thorne, G Savery	1	5	50	56
29G	Pontywaun	G Thorne	2	9	39	50
29H	Cefn Rhyswg	G Thorne	2	6	35	43
29I	Cil-lonydd	P O'Duffy	5	26	20	51
29J	Hafodyrynys	R Clarke	4	21	13	38
29K	Pant-yr-eos Res.	G Thorne, G Savery	4	7	50	61
29L	Mynydd Henllys (S)	P O'Duffy, G Thorne	3	11	38	52
29M	Mynydd Henllys (N)	P O'Duffy	0	20	19	39

Tetrad	Tetrad Name	Observer(s)	Number of Species			
			Possible	Probable	Confirmed	Total
29N	Mynydd Maen	P O'Duffy	9	24	14	47
29P	Mynydd Llwyd	P O'Duffy	8	21	19	48
29Q	Golynos	P O'Duffy	6	27	14	47
29R	Henllys	P O'Duffy, S Busson	2	14	27	43
29S	Cwmbran (W)	P O'Duffy, M Bailey	4	11	44	59
29T	Blaen Bran Res.	P O'Duffy	2	16	24	42
29U	Cwm Lickey	P O'Duffy	5	22	25	52
29V	Bettws	M Bailey	5	13	30	48
29W	Pant-glas	M Bailey	7	17	33	57
29X	Cwmbran (C)	J Woolway	4	15	26	45
29Y	Cwmbran (N)	J Woolway	6	12	32	50
29Z	Sebastopol	J Woolway	9	17	29	55
30A	Pontymoel	E Hankey	2	12	35	49
30B	Mamhilad	J Davies	5	12	43	60
30C	Goytre House	A Williams, B Morgan	6	12	36	54
30D	Pencroesoped	A Williams	12	14	34	60
30E	Llanover Estate	A Williams	6	13	39	58
30F	Llandegfedd Res. (N)	R Poole	22	7	56	85
30G	Little Mill	G Herbert	10	14	27	51
30H	Goetre	R Brown, A Williams	9	10	37	56
30I	Nant-y-derry	A Williams	5	21	19	45
30J	The Bryn	G Herbert, S Roberts	10	4	30	44
30K	ROF Glascoed	A & S Cruttenden, J Davies	9	14	35	58
30L	Monkswood	A & S Cruttenden, S Butler	7	17	26	50
30M	Chain Bridge	N Nethercott, A Williams	15	11	47	73
30N	Llanfair Kilgeddin	S Roberts	4	25	50	79
30P	Pant-y-Goitre	S Roberts, A Williams	6	19	50	75
30Q	Usk (W)	J Bennett	6	10	49	65
30R	Llancayo	J Bennett, B Burgess	4	13	41	58
30S	Trostrey Court	J Branscombe	9	24	22	55
30T	Clytha Hill	A Williams, A Venables	7	20	30	57
30U	Clytha	G Herbert	12	11	42	65
30V	Usk (E)	J Bennett, S Haslett	13	12	37	62
30W	Park Wood	J Bennett	7	16	31	54
30X	Gwehelog	A Venables, H Horrex	5	38	9	52
30Y	Rhiwlas Farm	A Venables, R Horrex	5	45	7	57
30Z	Bryngwyn	S Roberts	3	26	41	70
31A	Llanellen	M Hamar, A Venables, A Baker, S Butler, P Bengelaar	11	25	30	66
31B	Ysgyryd fach	J Lewis	6	24	41	71
31C	Abergavenny (E)	G Noakes, P Bengelaar	6	9	43	58
31D	Llantilio Pertholey	G Noakes, G Smith	12	6	46	64
31E	Bryn Arw	S Kelly	9	17	30	56
31F	Parc Llettis	G Noakes, A Venables	3	16	35	54
31G	Ty Hir	J Lewis	15	22	29	66
31H	Ty Draw Farm	J Lewis	8	21	18	47
31I	Ysgyryd Fawr (S)	G McQuade	14	27	15	56
31J	Ysgyryd Fawr (N)	G McQuade	9	18	15	42
31K	Coed Morgan	E Humphreys, A Venables, B Hood	5	33	8	46
31L	Llandewi Rhydderch	J Lewis	8	21	21	50
31M	Parc-gwyn	J Lewis	8	20	17	45

Tetrad	Tetrad Name	Observer(s)	Possible	Probable	Confirmed	Total
31N	The Court	A Baker	2	38	9	49
31P	Tump	F Lester, G Bromwell	4	26	14	44
31Q	Llanarth	G J Lewis, A Venables	9	26	21	56
31R	Llanvapley	A Venables	8	21	11	40
31S	Llanvapley (N)	G Marchant	13	22	14	49
31T	Llanvetherine	R Brown, F Lester	10	10	47	67
31U	Great Pool Hall	F Lester, G Bromwell	8	16	39	63
31V	Millbrook	A Rowlands, S Roberts	10	20	36	66
31W	Wernrheolydd	A Rowlands	21	13	23	57
31X	Llantilio Crossenny	A Rowlands, J Clement	7	33	21	61
31Y	Brynderi	A Rowlands, Mrs Bluett	20	22	20	62
31Z	Llanfair Grange	R Brown	9	10	21	40
32A	Stanton	W Keen, J Lewis	15	18	22	55
32B	Pont-Rhys-Powell	R Brown	6	10	31	47
32C	Hatterall Hill	I & D Hart	5	10	27	42
32F	Llanvihangel Crucorney	G Motley, J Evans	14	18	23	55
32G	Tre-Wyn	R Brown, S Tyler	7	12	38	57
32H	Oldcastle	I & D Hart	12	14	19	45
32K	Cefn Campstone	J Lewis, Mr & Mrs Price	11	18	7	36
32L	Wern Gounsel	D & M Marples, S Tyler	7	16	27	50
32M	Grove Farm	S Tyler	13	10	19	42
32Q	Kathlea	G McQuade	12	17	15	44
32R	Camston Hill	W Evans, J Lewis	13	13	17	43
32S	Llancillo Court	S Tyler	16	9	19	44
32V	Dan-y-Graig	R Brown	4	11	23	38
32W	Birches	I Rabjohns, J Pullen	14	21	19	54
32X	Llangua	J Pullen, S Tyler	29	15	21	65
32Y	Monmouth Cap	S Tyler	14	11	26	51
38A	Coast fragment	A Venables	0	18	13	31
38B	Uskmouth (W)	D Wood, C Jones	1	18	32	51
38C	Newport Docks (W)	D Wood, M Plunkett	8	21	30	59
38D	Newport (SW)	I Walker	3	10	22	35
38E	Newport (Civic Centre)	D Wood, I Walker	4	11	30	45
38G	Uskmouth (E)	R Clarke	12	31	22	65
38H	Newport Docks (E)	A Hickman, I Walker, M Plunkett	7	20	31	58
38I	Somerton	I Walker	7	11	29	47
38J	St Julians	I Walker	8	15	29	52
38L	Nash	R Clarke, H P Jones	11	20	44	75
38M	Pye corner	J Marsh	9	19	24	52
38N	Liswerry	P O'Duffy	5	16	35	56
38P	Christchurch	J Marsh, I Walker	7	9	31	47
38R	Goldcliff	I Walker	7	11	42	60
38S	Whitson Court	I Walker, P O'Duffy	8	21	34	63
38T	Llanwern Works (C)	P O'Duffy, I Walker	10	11	38	59
38U	Llanwern	I Walker	7	12	32	51
38W	Great Porton	I Walker	6	13	34	53
38X	Green Moor	I Walker, P O'Duffy	4	27	28	59
38Y	Bishton	P O'Duffy, I Walker	12	15	30	57
38Z	Llanmartin	I Sandeman, I Walker	8	15	29	52
39A	Malpas	M Beard	5	24	20	49
39B	Llantarnam	P O'Duffy	5	16	32	53

Tetrad	Tetrad Name	Observer(s)	Possible	Probable	Confirmed	Total
			Number of Species			
39C	Llanyrafon	J Lewis, S Roberts	7	24	20	51
39D	Croesyceiliog	M Bailey	6	13	33	52
39E	New Inn	M Bailey	7	25	21	53
39F	Caerleon (W)	C Jones, K Jones	14	12	40	66
39G	Ponthir	G Waite	12	17	27	56
39H	Cefn Tila	M Bailey	7	15	28	50
39I	Walnut Tree Farm	M Bailey, J Walker	10	23	22	55
39J	Llandegfedd Res. (S)	R Poole, M Stevens	22	11	49	82
39K	Caereon (E)	C Jones, K Jones, R Evans	9	19	36	64
39L	Llanhennock	S Busson, V Picken	9	12	34	55
39M	Llwncelyn	H P Jones	18	19	17	54
39N	Graigwith House	I Walker, M Stevens	5	18	32	55
39P	T'yn-y-Caeau Hill	A Venables, M Stevens	5	14	39	58
39Q	Catsash	I Walker, C Pennant	7	18	35	60
39R	Kemeys Inferior	I Walker	4	23	34	61
39S	Tredunnock	M Evans, V Picken	10	13	36	59
39T	Llangybi	M Evans, A Venables, V Picken	8	15	32	55
39U	Cwm Dowlais	A Venables, J Bennett	10	17	27	54
39V	Llnabeder	I Walker, J Kennett	5	13	33	51
39W	Wentwood (W)	I Walker	8	21	33	62
39X	Newbridge	I Walker	8	21	34	63
39Y	Llantrisant	I Walker, K Jones	5	15	46	66
39Z	Llanllowel	I Walker, J Bennett	8	10	50	68
40A	Gwernesney	K Haslett	21	20	18	59
40B	Llandenny	K Haslett, A Venables	7	22	24	53
40C	Twyn-y-Sherriff	D Lewis	0	7	45	52
40D	Raglan	M Langley, A Venables, S Tyler	5	21	24	50
40E	Raglan Castle	M Langley, A Venables, S Tyler	2	22	20	44
40F	Llangwm (N)	B Gregory	6	21	24	51
40G	Llandenny Court	R Davies, S Haslett	18	22	12	52
40H	Kingcoed	A Baker	15	26	18	59
40I	Twyn-yr-argoed	A Baker, S Tyler	3	22	19	44
40J	The Warrage	M Langley	20	16	24	60
40K	Lan-Pill Woods	R Medland	14	20	18	52
40L	Llansoy	R Davies	13	18	14	45
40M	Llangovan	P Blake, R Medland	6	21	18	45
40N	Pen-y-clawdd	R Medland, S Tyler	7	20	23	50
40P	Dingestow Court	S Bosanquet	11	12	40	63
40Q	Cobbler's Plain	M Plunkett, R Medland	16	24	8	48
40R	Llanishen	M Plunkett, R Medland	4	18	28	50
40S	Cwmcarfan Hill	J Harper	14	25	19	58
40T	Cwmcarfan	J Howells, S Tyler	11	7	36	54
40U	Bailey Glace	H Colls	13	4	42	59
40V	Trellech grange	R Armstrong	6	24	16	46
40W	Parkhouse	R Armstrong	22	14	21	57
40X	Woolpitch Wood	R Armstrong	9	18	21	48
40Y	Fedw Fawr	R Armstrong	16	18	22	56
40Z	Craig-y-dorth	J Howells, S Tyler	13	2	33	48
41A	Wern-y-Melyn	J Lewis	7	23	17	47
41B	Pen-twyn	J Lewis	14	26	11	51
41C	Talycoed	J Clement	9	25	6	40

Tetrad	Tetrad Name	Observer(s)	Number of Species			
			Possible	Probable	Confirmed	Total
41D	Pantygoida	K & G Adams	20	13	28	61
41E	Cross Ash	R Brown, J Lewis	6	7	30	43
41F	Pen-yr-Heol	S Bosanquet, M Yule, T Russell	8	9	32	49
41G	Cefn Garw Farm	J Lewis, M Yule	3	27	20	50
41H	Onen	J Lewis	7	31	9	47
41I	Llanvaenor	A Rowlands, J Lewis, M & S Eggleton	13	9	20	42
41J	Lettravane Farm	J Lewis	9	25	19	53
41K	Dingestow	S Bosanquet	10	17	20	47
41L	Parc-Grace Dieu	I Banner	12	10	13	35
41M	The Duffryn	I Banner, J Lewis	10	19	28	57
41N	Newcastle	P Waghorn, W & T Tyler-Ritt	6	15	34	55
41P	Crossway	P Waghorn, W & T Tyler-Ritt	7	21	18	46
41Q	Jingle Street	H Colls	11	8	34	53
41R	Kings Wood	P Johns, W Keen	13	21	28	62
41S	Rockfield Farm	J Lewis, B Gregory	9	31	5	45
41T	St Maughans Green	P Waghorn	10	18	39	67
41U	Llanrothal	P Waghorn	21	11	21	53
41V	Mitchel Troy	S Tyler	11	6	32	49
41W	Monmouth (W)	P Johns	6	23	42	71
41X	Rockfield	B Gregory	9	20	14	43
41Y	The Cwm	M Woods, B Gregory	14	25	20	59
42A	Duke's Farm	B Gregory	6	21	15	42
42B	Cross	J Pullen, B Gregory	6	22	33	61
42C	Grosmont	B Gregory, S Tyler	8	20	33	61
42F	Blackbrook House	B Gregory	12	8	18	38
42G	Lower Dyffryn	B Gregory	9	24	9	42
42K	Skenfrith	B Gregory, J Pullen	11	28	34	73
42L	Tennersfield	B Gregory	7	17	13	37
42Q	Woodside Farm	B Gregory	10	20	15	45
48B	Redwick coast	K Thomas	16	11	17	44
48C	Redwick	K Thomas, M Bailey	14	17	16	47
48D	Llandevenny	I Sandeman	8	30	14	52
48E	Pencoed Castle	I Sandeman	5	35	17	57
48H	Magor Pill	K A Jones, C Rutter	18	6	30	54
48I	Magor Reserve	K A Jones, C Rutter	14	11	42	67
48J	St Brides Netherwent	C Hodgson, M Bailey, K Roylance	11	17	23	51
48K	Denny Island	C Jones	1	0	4	5
48M	Collister Pill	B Maskery, P Willis, K A Jones	10	25	7	42
48N	Caldicot Moor	B Maskery, K A Jones	9	20	13	42
48P	The Minnetts	N Bird	8	14	26	48
48T	Rogiet	N Bird, P Willis	5	12	27	44
48U	Brockwells	B Maskery, M Bailey, K Roylance	10	21	21	52
48Y	Caldicot (S)	N Bird, P Willis	10	13	21	44
48Z	Nedern wetlands	N Bird, K A Jones	7	18	40	65
49A	Parc Seymour	C Hodgson	7	13	27	47
49B	Wentwood Gate	D Davies, A Venables	3	15	27	45
49C	Darren Wood	D V Thomas, L Mainwaring	2	31	17	50
49D	Gwern ddu Hill	A Venables	1	34	8	43
49E	Coed Cwnwr	A Venables	2	20	19	41
49F	Penhow	C Hodgson	7	19	24	50
49G	Wentwood Res.	J Bennett, D V Thomas	3	25	34	62

Tetrad	Tetrad Name	Observer(s)	Number of Species			
			Possible	Probable	Confirmed	Total
49H	Cadira Beeches	J Bennett	4	23	23	50
49I	Golden Hill	A Venables	1	19	28	48
49J	Llangwm (S)	A Venables	3	24	16	43
49K	Five-lanes	R Jones	13	8	33	54
49L	Llanvair Discoed	R Belle, P Willis	8	15	41	64
49M	Earlswood	R Belle	8	25	27	60
49N	Gaerllwyd	A Venables	2	17	23	42
49P	Wolvesnewton	A Venables	3	23	15	41
49Q	Caerwent	A Venables, M Plunkett	0	22	19	41
49R	Shirenewton (W)	R Belle	2	24	21	47
49S	Gilbrook Wood	R Belle	6	26	21	53
49T	Hale Wood	K & J Futcher, A Venables	7	33	13	53
49U	Cwm-fagor	M Plunkett, B Gregory	4	19	30	53
49V	Kilcrow Hill	M Plunkett	10	21	18	49
49W	Shirenewton (E)	R Belle	7	17	22	46
49X	Itton	G Jones, R Belle	10	21	20	51
49Y	Chepstow Park Wood	J Vernon, M Jenkins, M Plunkett	9	32	11	52
49Z	Devauden	N Saunders	6	25	26	57
50A	Whitelye	B Gregory, R Medland	10	16	37	63
50B	Catbrook	R Armstrong, B Gregory	10	23	25	58
50C	Trellech	R Armstrong, B Gregory, D Adams	9	9	45	63
50D	Trellech Common	R Armstrong, B Gregory, D Adams	9	15	39	63
50E	The Craig	B Gregory, S Tyler	7	15	29	51
50F	Tintern	M Plunkett, B Gregory	10	17	42	69
50G	Bargain Wood	B Gregory	5	24	19	48
50H	Cuckoo Wood	B Gregory, S Tyler	14	12	38	64
50I	Whitebrook	B Gregory, S Tyler	16	15	26	57
50J	Pen-Twyn	B Gregory, J Harper	8	13	50	71
50M	Lower Meend	B Gregory	10	21	19	50
50N	Wyegate Green	B Gregory	13	20	12	45
51A	Troy House	B Gregory	12	28	18	58
51B	Monmouth (C)	B Gregory	9	9	44	62
51C	Monmouth (N)	B Gregory	9	19	21	49
51D	Buckholt	B Gregory	9	28	15	52
51F	Penallt	B Gregory,	12	18	34	64
51G	Kymin	B Gregory	7	16	32	55
51H	Hadnock Court	B Gregory	12	19	28	59
51L	Staunton	B Gregory	6	23	28	57
51M	Seven Sisters	B Gregory	5	22	20	47
58D	Sudbrook	P Willis	7	11	15	33
58E	Black Rock	P Willis	7	17	28	52
58J	Mathern Oaze	G Jones	0	4	1	5
59A	St Pierre	B Catlin, A Gabriel	3	8	38	49
59B	Mounton	B Catlin, A Gabriel	4	7	34	45
59C	Fryth Wood	B Gregory	4	17	24	45
59D	St Arvans	A Gabriel	4	16	28	48
59E	The Cot	N Saunders, R Medland	9	24	38	71
59F	Mathern	B Catlin, G Jones, A Gabriel	10	10	38	58
59G	Chepstow	A Gabriel, B Catlin	16	2	33	51
59H	Chepstow Racecourse	G Newman, A Gabriel	13	3	45	61
59I	Wyndcliff	G Newman, M Plunkett	13	20	24	57
59J	Black Cliff	M Plunkett	4	17	40	61

PREVIOUSLY UNPUBLISHED DATA FROM THE MID- AND SOUTH GLAMORGAN BREEDING ATLAS SURVEY (1984–1989)

The table shows data from the five tetrads not published in either the 1995 *Birds of Glamorgan* or the 1st Gwent Atlas. These data have been included in revised maps for the 1st Gwent Atlas as presented in the the species accounts.

A = Confirmed breeding; B = Probable breeding; C = Possible breeding

Species	Tetrad					Species	Tetrad				
	10I	18Z	27I	27J	28E		10I	18Z	27I	27J	28E
Shelduck			A	A		Whinchat		A			B
Mallard			A	A		Wheatear	A				
Red-legged Partridge				A		Blackbird	C	A	A	A	A
Grey Partridge			B	A		Song Thrush		A	A	A	A
Sparrowhawk		B		A	B	Mistle Thrush		A	C	A	B
Buzzard		B			B	Sedge Warbler				A	
Kestrel		B	C	A	A	Reed Warbler			A	A	
Moorhen			A	A		Lesser Whitethroat			A	A	
Oystercatcher			A	B		Whitethroat		B	A	A	A
Ringed Plover			C			Garden Warbler		B		C	B
Lapwing	B		A	A		Blackcap		A		A	A
Snipe	C					Wood Warbler					A
Curlew	C					Chiffchaff		B		A	A
Redshank			A	A		Willow Warbler		B	A	A	A
Lesser Black-backed Gull				B		Goldcrest		B			
Herring Gull				C		Spotted Flycatcher		B			B
Feral Pigeon		B		A	A	Long-tailed Tit		A		A	A
Stock Dove			B	A		Willow Tit		B			A
Woodpigeon		A	A	A	A	Coal Tit		B			A
Collared Dove		B	B	A	A	Blue Tit	C	A	A	A	A
Cuckoo		B	A	A	B	Great Tit	C	A	A	A	A
Barn Owl			A			Nuthatch		B			A
Little Owl			A	A		Treecreeper		A			A
Tawny Owl		B			B	Jay		A		A	A
Swift		B		A	A	Magpie	B	A	A	A	A
Kingfisher		A			A	Jackdaw	A	A			A
Green Woodpecker		A			B	Rook		A			A
Great Spotted Woodpecker		B		A	A	Carrion Crow	C	A	A	A	A
Skylark	A		A	A		Raven	C	B			B
Swallow	B	A	A	A	A	Starling	A	A	A	A	A
House Martin		A		A	A	House Sparrow	A	A	A	A	A
Tree Pipit		B				Tree Sparrow		B	A	A	B
Meadow Pipit	A	B	A	B	A	Chaffinch	C	A	A	A	A
Yellow Wagtail			B	A		Greenfinch		B	A	A	A
Grey Wagtail		A			A	Goldfinch		B	A	A	A
Pied Wagtail	C	A	C	C	A	Linnet		A	A	A	A
Wren		A	A	A	A	Bullfinch		B		A	A
Dunnock		A	A	A	A	Yellowhammer		B			A
Robin		A	A	A	A	Reed Bunting			A	A	A
Redstart		A			B						

SPECIES ADDED TO THE GWENT LIST SINCE 1976*

Species	Year of first record	Species	Year of first record
Ruddy Duck	1977	Roller	1987
Crane	1978	Mandarin	1987
Kentish Plover	1978	Cetti's Warbler	1988
Buff-breasted Sandpiper	1978	Alpine Swift	1988
Red-necked Grebe	1978	Tawny Pipit	1988
Broad-billed Sandpiper	1979	Greater Sand Plover	1988
Gull-billed Tern	1979	Yellow-browed Warbler	1988
Spotted Sandpiper	1980	Little Egret	1989
Cattle Egret	1981	Aquatic Warbler	1989
Ring-billed Gull	1981	White-winged Black Tern	1991
Bee-eater	1981	Purple Heron	1993
Lesser Yellowlegs	1981	Little Bittern	1994
American Bittern	1981	Whiskered Tern	1994
Roseate Tern	1982	Barred Warbler	1994
Egyptian Goose	1983	Great White Egret	1995
Pomarine Skua	1983	White-rumped Sandpiper	1995
Night Heron	1983	American Wigeon	1995
Sabine's Gull	1983	Bean Goose	1996
Cory's Shearwater	1983	Desert Wheatear	1996
Woodchat Shrike	1983	Baird's Sandpiper	1997
Iceland Gull	1984	Bluethroat	1999
Dartford Warbler	1984	Ring-necked Duck	2000
Yellow-legged Gull	1984	Black-winged Pratincole	2001
Golden Eagle	1985	Squacco heron	2003
Black Kite	1985	Little Swift	2004
Long-billed Dowitcher	1985		
White Stork	1986	Hooded Crow	**1925
Temminck's Stint	1987	Water Pipit	**1967

*Records for the 1977 Birds of Gwent included records up to 1976. **Although recorded in the county prior to 1977, these species were not accorded full species status until recently.

CONTRIBUTORS OF CASUAL RECORDS

The following people also submitted breeding records that were used in the 2nd Gwent Atlas of Breeding Birds.

H J Allen, Jane Beazley, Diana Bevan, P Bowles, Sheila Chapman, Mrs Y Chivers, D Clarke, E Collard, Grahame Cox, B M Davies, Anne C. Dunton, Vera Easton, S & K Gittins, B A Gulliford, Gwent Wildlife Trust, Bob Harding, E V Haxworth-Williams, Katherine M. Henderson, F Hoet, Steve Howell, Lyn Jackson, Roger James, H Jones, Jenny Jones, C A E Kenry, M Kilner, Andrew Long, Michael J Marshall, D Mayo, David Morgan, Ken Morgan, Sally Neale, Will O'Keefe, Mr & Mrs J H Paling, B M Pearce, Suzanne Peebles, Marion Poole, Dave Powell, Oscar Puls, Mrs M Randall, Rob Roome, B Sheppard, E G Smith, WA Smith, R & C Spillards, H Stephenson, Bill Symondson, Colin Titcombe, Upper Red House farm SO428131, D. Walker, P Warwick, Carolyne Watkins, Diana Westmoreland, L Williams-Davies, Mary Williams, Peter Williams, N Williamson, Adrian Wood.

APPENDIX 7

AUTHORSHIP OF SECTIONS AND SPECIES ACCOUNTS

The authors take collective responsibility for the text, but the lead authors for each section are as follows:

Introduction – Al Venables

The County of Gwent – Stephanie Tyler and Alan Williams

Geology of Gwent – Stephen Howe

Bird habitats in Gwent
Woodland – Jerry Lewis
Moorland – Andrew Baker
Wetlands – Stephanie Tyler
Urban and Industrial – Ian Walker
Farmland – Stephanie Tyler

Where to watch birds in Gwent
Introduction – Andrew Baker
Newport Wetlands Reserve – Helen Jones
Llandegfedd Reservoir – Chris Hatch
Wentlooge Coast – Al Venables
The River Usk – Andrew Baker, Robert Moeller, Jerry Lewis
Wentwood Forest – John Bennett
Ynysyfro Reservoirs – Ian Walker
Graig Goch Woodlands – Al Venables
The Blorenge – Andrew Baker
Wye Valley Woodlands – Stephanie Tyler

The Gwent breeding bird atlases – Al Venables

Systematic List
Introduction
Al Venables

Species accounts

Al Venables:
Mute Swan, Bewick's Swan, White-fronted Goose, Greylag Goose, Canada Goose, Brent Goose, Shelduck, Wigeon, Gadwall, Teal, Mallard, Pintail, Garganey, Shoveler, Pochard, Tufted Duck, Scaup, Common Scoter, Goldeneye, Goosander, Ruddy Duck, Red-legged Partridge, Pheasant, Little Ringed Plover, Feral Pigeon, Stock Dove, Wood Pigeon, Collared Dove, Turtle Dove, Short-eared Owl, Common Redstart, Northern Wheatear, Blackcap, Garden Warbler, Lesser Whitethroat, Whitethroat, Chiffchaff, Willow Warbler, Goldcrest, Long-tailed, Blue, Great, Coal, Willow and Marsh Tits.

Al Venables and Mary Plunkett:
Jay, Magpie, Jackdaw, Carrion Crow, Raven.

Al Venables and Chris Jones:
Eider, Long-tailed Duck, Smew, Slavonian Grebe, Black-necked Grebe, Wryneck, Waxwing, Nightingale, Great Grey Shrike, Snow Bunting.

Steve Smith and Al Venables:
Whinchat, Stonechat.

Andrew Baker:
Brambling, Greenfinch, Goldfinch, Siskin, Linnet, Redpoll, Bullfinch, Yellowhammer.

Richard Clarke:
Little Grebe, Great Crested Grebe, Cormorant, Little Egret (with Chris Jones), Grey Heron, Red Grouse, Grey Partridge, Water Rail, Rock Pipit, Black Redstart, Cetti's, Grasshopper, Aquatic, Sedge and Reed Warblers, Firecrest, Spotted Flycatcher, House Sparrow, Tree Sparrow, Reed Bunting.

Chris Jones:
Rare species, comprising: Whooper Swan, Bean, Pink-footed, Barnacle Goose, Egyptian Goose, Mandarin, American Wigeon, Red-crested Pochard, Ring-necked Duck, Ferruginous Duck, Velvet Scoter, Red-breasted Merganser, Black Grouse, Quail, all divers, Red-necked Grebe, Fulmar, Cory's and Manx Shearwaters, European and Leach's Storm-petrels, Gannet, Shag , Bittern, American and Little Bitterns, Night Heron, Cattle and Great Egrets, Purple Heron, White Stork, Glossy Ibis, Spoonbill, Black and Red Kites, Marsh, Hen and Montagu's Harriers, Rough-legged Buzzard, Golden Eagle and Osprey, Spotted Crake, Corn Crake, Crane, Black-winged Stilt, Avocet, Stone Curlew, Black-winged Pratincole, Kentish and Greater Sand Plovers, Dotterel, Temminck's Stint, White-rumped, Baird's, Pectoral, Purple, Broad-billed and Buff-breasted Sandpipers, Long-billed Dowitcher, Lesser Yellowlegs, Wood and Spotted Sandpipers, Red-necked and Grey Phalaropes, all skuas, Mediterranean, Little, Sabine's, Ring-billed, Yellow-legged, Iceland and Glaucous Gulls, Kittiwake, Gull-billed, Sandwich, Roseate, Little, Whiskered, Black and White-winged Terns, Guillemot, Razorbill, Little Auk, Puffin, Rose-ringed Parakeet, Snowy Owl, Alpine Swift, Bee-eater, Roller, Hoopoe, Wood Lark, Richard's, Tawny and Water Pipits, Bluethroat, Desert Wheatear, Marsh, Melodious, Dartford, Barred and Yellow-browed Warblers, Bearded Tit, Golden Oriole, Red-backed and Woodchat Shrikes, Nutcracker, Chough, Hooded Crow, Rosy Starling, Twite, Lapland, Cirl and Corn Buntings.

Jerry Lewis:
Honey Buzzard, Goshawk, Sparrowhawk, Buzzard, Kestrel, Merlin, Hobby, Peregrine, Woodcock, Barn, Little, Tawny and Long-eared Owls, Nightjar, Wood Warbler, Crossbill, Hawfinch.

Stephanie Tyler:
Goosander, Moorhen Coot, Green and Common Sandpipers, Cuckoo, Swift, Kingfisher, Skylark, Sand Martin, Swallow, House Martin, Tree and Meadow Pipits, Yellow, Grey and Pied Wagtails, Dipper, Ring Ouzel, Pied Flycatcher, Rook, Starling, Chaffinch.

Ian Walker:
Oystercatcher, Ringed, Golden and Grey Plovers, Lapwing, Knot, Sanderling, Little Stint, Curlew Sandpiper, Dunlin, Ruff, Jack and Common Snipes, Black-tailed and Bar-tailed Godwits, Whimbrel, Curlew, Spotted Redshank, Redshank, Greenshank, Turnstone, Black-headed, Common, Lesser Black-backed, Herring and Great Black-backed Gulls, Common and Arctic Terns, Nuthatch, Treecreeper.

Alan Williams:
Green, Great Spotted and Lesser Spotted Woodpeckers, Wren, Dunnock, Robin, Blackbird, Fieldfare, Song Thrush, Redwing, Mistle Thrush.

Conclusions and Comparisons
Al Venables

Appendix 1. Populations
Jerry Lewis

LIST OF VIGNETTES AND ARTISTS

Artist	Vignette
Chris Hodgson	Bewick's Swan, Canada Goose, Barnacle Goose, Gadwall, Tufted Duck, Goosander, Red-legged Partridge, Grey Partridge, Great Northern Diver, Great Crested Grebe, Black-necked Grebe, Slavonian Grebe, Manx Shearwater, Cormorant, Little Egret, Coot, Sanderling, Great Skua, Black Tern, Kingfisher, Meadow Pipit, Grey Wagtail (one of two), Redstart, Whinchat, Stonechat (one of two), Wheatear, Cetti's Warbler, Reed Warbler, Pied Flycatcher, Nuthatch, Tree Sparrow, Goldfinch (one of two), Siskin.
Steve Roberts	Long-tailed Duck, Grey Heron, Honey Buzzard, Marsh Harrier, Sparrowhawk, Kestrel, Hobby, Avocet, Ringed Plover, Golden Plover, Dunlin, Woodcock, Curlew, Greenshank, Common Sandpiper, Stock Dove, Turtle Dove, Barn Owl, Long-eared Owl, Nightjar, Great Spotted Woodpecker, Swallow, Tree Pipit, Yellow Wagtail, Grey Wagtail (one of two), Dipper, Stonechat (one of two), Fieldfare, Lesser Whitethroat, Blackcap, Long-tailed Tit, Red-backed Shrike, Raven, Goldfinch (one of two), Crossbill, Hawfinch, Snow Bunting, Reed Bunting.
Helen Scourse	White-fronted Goose, Shelduck, Teal, Pintail, Shoveler, Herring Gull, Great Black-backed Gull, Robin, Mistle Thrush, Goldcrest, Blue Tit, Jay.

SELECTED RINGING DATA

In cases where species accounts have included analyses of ringing data, details of individual recoveries are listed here.

KESTREL: Recoveries of birds ringed in Gwent with movements >100km

Ringed Gwent	Recovered	Distance/direction
Monmouth	Aug 77 Denbigh, Denbighshire	152km NNW
Pandy	Mar 79 La Garnache, France	557km S
Penallt	Jan 79 Barnstaple, Devon	124km SW
Llangeview, Usk	Nov 84 Helston, Cornwall	246km SW
Trefil Quarry	Nov 88 Tidworth, Hampshire	128km ESE
Llanfair Kilgeddin	Nov 89 Gyllyngiase, Cornwall	235km SW
Llanarth	Dec 91 Plougonven, France	367km S
Llanfair Kilgeddin	Nov 92 Ockley, Surrey	189km ESE
Nantyglo	Jan 97 Weymouth, Dorset	139km SSE
Abergavenny	Jul 02 Birmingham	110km NE

KESTREL: Recoveries in Gwent with movements >100km

Ringed	Recovered in Gwent	Distance/direction
Skipton, North Yorkshire	Oct 06 Newbridge on Usk	260km S
East Grinstead, Sussex	Sep 79 Caerleon	206km WNW
Roundwood, Co Wicklow, Ireland	Nov 81 Caldicot	292km SE
Nr Winslow, Buckinghamshire	Nov 89 Usk	135km W
Nr Bygate Hill, Northumberland	Dec 89 Llandenny	408km S
Nr Angle, Pembrokeshire	Aug 96 Abergavenny	130km E
Nr Warwick, Warwickshire	Dec 97 Ebbw Vale	127km WSW

Just two birds that had moved more than 100km survived beyond their first winter.

BARN OWL: Recoveries with movements >100km

Ringed	Found dead	
Feb 47 Wiltshire	Sep 48 Llangeview, Usk	110km NW
May 90 Sidmouth, Devon	Oct 90 Llandenny, Usk	100km N
Jul 92 Gwynedd	Jan 93 Abergavenny	135km SSE
Jul 93 Machynlleth, Powys	Feb 94 Magor, Gwent	133km SSE
Dec 97 Monmouth	Jan 98 Whitby, N Yorks	329km NNE

WILLOW WARBLER: Recoveries of young birds ringed in Gwent with movements >100km

Ringed Gwent	Recovered	Distance/direction
5 Jun 73 Monmouth	20 Apr 75 Hampshire	183km SE
14 Aug 77 Monmouth	23 Aug 77 Dorset	154km SSE
8 Jul 79 Blaina	26 Aug 79 Beachy Head, Sussex	264km ESE
1 Jul 84 Chepstow	17 Aug 84 Gironde, France	783km SSE
28 Jul 93 Pontypool	23 Apr 94 Isle of Man	289km NNW
30 Jul 97 Pontypool	2 Jul 98 South Yorkshire	225km NNE

WILLOW WARBLER: Recoveries in Gwent with movements >100km

Ringed	Recovered in Gwent	Distance/direction
12 Jul 97 Isle of Man	30 Jul 97 Pontypool	309km SSE
15 Jun 84 Merseyside	6 Aug 85 Chepstow	214km S
22 Apr 97 Portland Bill	25 Apr 99 Newport	125km NNW
3 Aug 89 Guernsey	2 Aug 90 Llansoy	252km N

CHAFFINCH: Recoveries of birds ringed in Gwent with movements >100km

Ringed Gwent	recovered	Distance/direction
2 Feb 86 Clytha, Raglan	16 May 86 Brewood, Staffs.	112km NNE
4 Feb 84 Nr Raglan	5 May 84 Thursley, Surrey	164km ESE
5 Nov 83 Clytha, Raglan	26 Mar 92 Stavenisse, Netherlands	477km E
12 Dec 81 Monmouth	18 Mar 82 High Wycombe	135km E
16 Feb 72 Monmouth	15 Apr 72 West Germany	769km E

CHAFFINCH: Recoveries in Gwent with movements >100km

Ringed	Recovered in Gwent	Distance/direction
15 Nov 61 Surrey	25 Feb 62 Abergavenny	182km WNW
24.Nov 79 Netherlands	27 Feb 81 Abergavenny	504km W
18 Sep 88 Sweden	12 Mar 90 Cwmbran	1180km SW

GREENFINCH: Recoveries of birds ringed in Gwent with movements >100km

Ringed in Gwent	Recovered	Distance\Direction
23 Feb 76 Monmouth	24 Apr 77 Essex	207km E
22 Feb 76 Monmouth	16 Apr 76 Buckinghamshire	128km ENE
13 Dec 82 Brynmawr	03 Apr 83 Harlow, Essex	221km E
03 Feb 83 Brynmawr	10 Apr 84 Potters Bar, Hertfordshire	206km E
28 Dec 84 Monmouth	24 Feb 86 Corby, Northants	155km ENE
04 Mar 84 Monmouth	26 Apr 86 Black Notley, Essex	223km E
20 Mar 85 Clytha	13 May 86 Withernsea, Humberside	297km NE
05 Nov 90 Nantyglo	22 Apr 91 Minster-in-Thanet, Kent	313km E
25 Feb 92 Abergavenny	28 Mar 93 Glen Caple, Dumf & Gall	355km N

GREENFINCH: Recoveries in Gwent with movements >100km

Ringed in UK	Recovered in Gwent	Distance\Direction
22 Nov 70 Shropshire	07 Aug 72 Monmouth	138km SSW
04 Sep 71 Warwickshire	17 Jan 78 Monmouth	123km WSW
21 Dec 74 Leicester	06 Mar 76 Monmouth	151km SW
14 Feb 79 Exeter, Devon	22 Jan 80 Monmouth	133km NNE
21 Jan 82 Hertfordshire	06 Apr 83 Cwmbran	198km W
03 Apr 82 Merseyside	15 Dec 83 Brynmawr	187km S
25 Sep 82 Northants	03 Mar 85 Chepstow	171km WSW
25 Jun 00 Shropshire	06 Jul 03 Newport 139km SSW	
08 Feb 04 Buckinghamshire	26 Apr 04 Monmouth 133km W	

SISKIN: Recoveries of birds ringed in Gwent with movements >100km

Ringed in Gwent	Recovered	Distance/Direction
25 Jan 87 Llanvaches	03 Apr 87 Bidston, Wirral	199km N
18 Mar 92 Nantyglo	27 Mar 93 Dingwall, Highland	651km N
08 Apr 92 Abergavenny	11 Mar 95 Halstead, Essex	254km E
09 Feb 94 Nantyglo	10 Apr 95 Limburg, Belgium	577km E
18 Feb 94 Llanvaches	25 Sep 94 Llangadfan, Powys	127km NNW
20 Feb 00 Nantyglo	09 Aug 02 Golspie, Highland	689km N
05 Mar 03 Nantyglo	11 Feb 04 Crampmoor, Romsey	147km SE
11 Mar 03 Nantyglo	28 Jan 04 Fermanagh, Ireland	416km NW

SISKIN: Recoveries in Gwent with movements >100km

Ringed in UK and Ireland	Recovered in Gwent	Distance/Direction
28 Feb 92 Retford, Notts	18 Jan 95 Abersychan	227km SE
05 Mar 93 Crewkerne, Somerset	10 Mar 93 Abergavenny	105km N
13 May 96 Oban, Scotland	27 Mar 98 Langstone	548km SSE
31 Mar 00 Marley Com., Sussex	15 Feb 02 Pen y cae-mawr	159km WNW
27 Apr 00 Glencaple, Scotland	22 Feb 02 Sebastopol	372km S
26 Mar 02 Runcorn, Cheshire	03 Mar 03 Nantyglo	173km S
13 Apr 02 Blairgorm, Scotland	25 Mar 03 Penallt	612km S
07 Jun 03 Llwynmawr, Clwyd	29 Mar 04 Oakdale	139km S

LOCATIONS OF PLACES

Four-figure grid references are given for all places mentioned in the text.

Aberbeeg	SO2102	Coed Morgan	SO3511
Abercarn	ST2194	Coed Parciau	SO2500
Abergavenny	SO2914	Coed Pen-y-wern	SO2214
Abersychan	SO2603	Collister Pill	ST4585
Abertillery	SO2104	Craig Llwyfas	ST2194
Angidy Valley	SO5100	Crosskeys	ST2291
Bargoed	ST1499	Crumlin	ST2198
Bassaleg	ST2787	Cwm	SO1804
Beacon Hill	SO5105	Cwm Gofapi	ST2394
Beaufort Ponds	SO1712	Cwm Lickey	ST2698
Bedwas	ST1788	Cwmbran	ST2895
Bedwellty	SO1600	Cwmcarn	ST2293
Biblins	SO5514	Cwmcarn Forest Drive	ST2393
Bigsweir	SO5304	Cwmfelinfach	ST1891
Black Rock	ST5188	Cwmtillery	SO2105
Blackrock	SO2112	Cwmyoy	SO3023
Blackwood	ST1797	Denny Island	ST4581
Blaenafon	SO2508	Devauden	ST4899
Blaen Bran	ST2697	Dingestow	SO4510
The Blorenge	SO2611	Dingestow Court	SO4509
Boat Lane	ST3683	Dunlop Semtex Pond	SO1811
Branches Fork Meadow	SO2701	Ebbw Vale	SO1609
Broad Meend	SO5004	Fisherman's Lane	ST4686
The Bryn	SO3309	Forest Coal Pit	SO2820
Bryn Bach Park	SO1210	Fourteen Locks	ST2888
Brynmawr	SO1911	Garn Lakes	SO2309
Bulmore	ST3591	Garnlydan Reservoir	SO1713
Caerleon	ST3390	Garn-yr-erw	SO2310
Caldicot Castle	ST4888	Gelligroes	ST1794
Caldicot Moor	ST4586	Gilwern	SO2414
Caldicot Pill	ST4987	Gilwern, Lower Common	SO2515
Campston Hill	SO3622	Glascoed	SO3301
Carno Reservoir	SO1613	Gobion	SO3409
Castrogi Brook	ST4593	Goldcliff	ST3683
Celtic Manor Golf Club	ST3690	Goldcliff lagoons	ST3682
Chwarel y Fan	SO2529	Goldcliff Pill	ST3682
Chepstow	ST5393	Goldcliff Point	ST3781
Chepstow Park Wood	ST4897	Goetre	SO3205
Cleddon Bog	SO5103	Goytre House Wood	SO3104
Clydach	SO2312	Greenmoor Pool	ST3885
Clytha	SO3608	Gwyddon Valley	ST2295
Coedkernew	ST2783	Hafod Farm, Brynmawr	SO2012

Hatterrall Hill	SO3025	Nant Gwyddon	ST2395
Henllys, Cwmbran	ST2693	Nant-y-derry	SO3306
Highmeadow Woods	SO5513	Nash	ST3483
The Hoop Ponds	SO5107	Nedern Wetlands	ST4889
Hunger Pill	ST5490	Newbridge-on-Usk	ST3894
Ifton Great Wood	ST4589	Newhouse Ind. Est.	ST5392
Kentchurch	SO4125	New Inn	ST3099
The Kymin	SO5212	Newport	ST3088
Lady Hill Wood	SO5414	Newport Wetlands (central)	ST3482
Lady Park Wood	SO3702	Oakdale	ST1898
Llanarth	SO3710	Ochrwyth	ST2489
Llanbadoc	ST3799	Oldcastle	SO3224
Llancillo	SO3625	Osbaston	SO5014
Llandegfedd Reservoir	SO3300	Pandy	SO3321
Llandenny	SO4103	Pant-yr-eos Reservoir	ST2591
Llandevaud	ST4090	Pant-y-Goitre	SO3408
Llanddewi Skirrid	SO3417	Pantygasseg	SO2509
Llandogo	SO5204	Parkhouse	SO4902
Llanellen	SO3010	Penallt	SO5209
Llanfair Kilgeddin	SO3407	Pencoed	ST4089
Llanfoist	SO2813	Pen-y-clawdd	SO4507
Llangattock Lingoed	SO3620	Pen-y-fan Pond	SO1900
Llangovan	SO4505	Pen-yr-heol	SO4311
Llangybi	ST3796	Peterstone Gout	ST2780
Llanllowell	ST3998	Peterstone Wentlooge	ST2680
Llanover	SO3108	Piercefield Park	ST5295
Llansoy	SO4402	Pontllanfraith	ST1795
Llantilio Crossenny	SO3914	Pontymister	ST2390
Llanthony	SO2827	Pontnewydd	ST2996
Llanwenarth	SO2714	Pontypool	SO2901
Llanwern	ST3688	Porton	ST3882
Llanwern steelworks	ST3586	Prisk Wood	SO5309
Lodge Wood	ST3291	Redbrook	SO5310
Lower Machen	ST2288	Risca	ST2391
Loysey Wood	SO4906	Rockfield	SO4814
Machine Pond	SO1811	Rogerstone	ST2788
Magor	ST4287	Rogiet	ST4587
Magor Pill	ST4384	Sirhowy Country Park	ST1891
Magor Marsh	ST4286	Skenfrith	SO4520
Mally Brook	SO5115	Skirrid Fach	SO3113
Malpas	ST3090	Skirrid Fawr	SO3217
Manmoel	SO1703	Sluice Farm	ST2579
Marshfield	ST2682	Solutia Reserve	ST3483
Mathern foreshore	ST5289	Springdale Farm	ST4199
Michaelston-y-Fedw	ST2484	Stanton	SO3121
Minnetts Wood	ST4589	St Brides Wentlooge	ST2982
Mitchel Troy	SO4910	Sugar Loaf	SO2718
The Moorings, Newport	ST3389	Talywain	SO2604
Monmouth	SO5012	Tintern	SO5200
Mynydd Carn-y-cefn	SO1808	Tredegar Park	ST2885
Mynydd Henllys	ST2593	Tredunnock	ST3794
Mynyddislwyn	ST1994	Trefil Quarries	SO1213
Mynydd Maen	ST2696	Tregate Bridge	SO4717

Trellech	SO5005	Waun Lwyd	SO1806
Trostrey	SO3604	Waun Rydd	SO1712
Treowen	ST2098	Waun Wen	SO2111
Twmbarlwm	ST2492	Wentwood Forest	ST4094
Undy	ST4387	Wentwood Reservoir	ST4393
Undy foreshore	ST4485	Wernrheolydd	SO3912
Usk	SO3700	West Pill	ST4686
Uskmouth	ST3282	Whitebrook	SO5306
Uskmouth reedbed pools	ST3383	Woodstock/ Morgan Pool	ST3090
Varteg	SO2606	Wye Valley Woods	SO5415
Wattsville	ST2091	Wyndcliff	ST5197
Waunafon	SO2210	Whitson	ST3883
Waunfawr	ST2291	Ynysyfro Reservoir	ST2889

BIBLIOGRAPHY

General References

The following ornithological works have frequently been referred to in the species accounts and we have used short and descriptive forms of reference in an attempt to make the text more readable and accessible for the general reader. The list below gives the reference form used in the text, followed by the full reference for the work in question.

1968–72 National Atlas: Sharrock, J. T. R. 1976. *The Atlas of Breeding Birds in Britain and Ireland*. T & AD Poyser, Calton.

1988–91 National Atlas: Gibbons, D. W., Reid, J. B. & Chapman, R. A. 1993. *The New Atlas of Breeding Birds in Britain and Ireland:1988–1991*. T & AD Poyser, London.

Winter Atlas: Lack, P. 1986. *The Atlas of Wintering Birds in Britain and Ireland*. T & AD Poyser, Calton.

Migration Atlas: Wernham, C., Toms, M., Marchant, J., Clark, J., Siriwardena, G. & Baillie, S. 2002. *The Migration Atlas*. T & AD Poyser, London.

1994 *Birds in Wales*: Lovegrove, R., Williams, G. & Williams, I. 1994. *Birds in Wales*. T & AD Poyser, London.

2002 *Birds in Wales*: Green, J. 2002. *Birds in Wales 1992–2000*. Welsh Ornithological Society.

1937 *Birds of Monmouthshire*: Ingram, G. C. S. & Salmon, H. M. 1937. *The Birds of Monmouthshire*. Cardiff Naturalists' Society.

1963 *Birds of Monmouthshire*: Humphreys, P. N. 1963. *The Birds of Monmouthshire*. Newport Museum.

1977 *Birds of Gwent*: Ferns, P. N., Hamar, H. W., Humphreys, P. N., Kelsey, F. D., Sarson, E. T., Venables, W. A. & Walker, I. R. 1977. *The Birds of Gwent*. Gwent Ornithological Society.

1st Gwent Atlas: Tyler, S., Lewis, J., Venables, W. A. & Walton, J. 1987. *The Gwent Atlas of Breeding Birds*. Gwent Ornithological Society.

2nd Gwent Atlas: Survey carried out 1998–2003 and published for the first time in this book.

Gwent Bird Report. 1963–2005. Published annually. Gwent Ornithologial Society.

BWP: Cramp, S. *et al.* (Eds) 1977–1994. *The Birds of the Western Palearctic*. Oxford University Press.

Popular Handbook: Hollom, P. A. D. 1968. *The Popular Handbook of British Birds*. H. F. & G. Witherby Ltd, London.

WeBS: Waterbirds in the UK: The Wetland Bird Survey. BTO/WWT/RSPB/JNCC, Thetford.

Other References

Aebischer, N. J. & Ewald, J. A. 2004. Managing the UK Grey Partridge *Perdix perdix* recovery: population change, reproduction, habitat and shooting. *Ibis* 146:181–191.

Alexander, I. H. & Cresswell, B. 1990. Foraging by Nightjar *Caprimulgus europaeus* away from their nesting areas. *Ibis* 132: 568–574.

Alexander, W. B. 1945. The Woodcock in the British Isles. *Ibis* 87: 512–550.

Alexander, W. B. 1946. The Woodcock in the British Isles. *Ibis* 88: 1–24, 159–179, 271–286, 427–444.

Alexander, W. B. 1947. The Woodcock in the British Isles. *Ibis* 89:1–28.

Atkinson, P. W., Fuller, R. J., Vickery, J. A., Conway, C. J., Tallowin, J. R. B., Smith, R. E. N., Hayson, K. A., Ings, T. C., Asterak, E. J. & Brown, V. K. 2005. Influence of agricultural management, sward structure and food resources on grassland field use by birds in lowland England. *Journal of Applied Ecology* 42: 932–942.

Bailey, M. 1995. Twenty-one years of the Common Birds Census at Goldcliff. *Gwent Bird Report* 31: 11–13.

Bibby, C. J. 1989. A survey of breeding Wood Warblers, *Phylloscopus sibilatrix,* in Britain 1984 –1985. *Bird Study* 36: 56–72.

Blaker, G. B. 1934. *The Barn Owl in England and Wales*. RSPB, London.

Both, C. 2002. Nemen Bonte Vliegenvangers *Ficedula hypoleuca* af door klimaatsverandering? [Decrease of European Pied Flycatchers due to climate change?] *Limosa* 75: 73–78.

Boyd, H J. 1963. The Denny. In *Steep Holm Gull Research Station Report* 28. Mimeograph.

Buckland, S. T., Anderson, D. R., Burnham, K. P., Laake, J. L., Borchers, D. L. & Thomas, L. 2001. *Distance sampling: estimating abundance of biological populations.* Oxford University Press, Oxford.

Burton, N. H. K., Musgrove, A. J., Rehfisch, M. M., Sutcliffe, A. & Waters, R. J. 2003. Numbers of wintering gulls in the UK, Channel Islands and Isle of Man: a review of the 1993 and previous gull roost surveys. *British Birds* 96: 376–401.

Batten, L. A., Bibby, C. J., Clement, P., Elliot, G. D. & Porter, R. F. 1990. *Red Data Birds in Britain.* T & AD Poyser, London.

BirdLife International Aquatic Warbler Conservation Team AWCT 2005. http://www.aquaticwarbler.net/sar/

Burton, N. 2006. Impacts of the Cardiff Bay barrage. *BTO News:* 265: 6–7.

Clarke, R. M. 2001–2006. *Goldcliff Ringing Group Annual Reports.*

Clarke, R. M. 2004. Great Cormorants in Gwent. *Gwent Bird Report* 38: 14–24.

Clarke, R. M. 2006. An investigation into the importance of the Uskmouth reedbeds in relation to the autumn passage of Aquatic Warbler. *Gwent Bird Report* 41: 68–69.

Clarke, R. M. 2006. Survey to determine the population of breeding pairs of Water Rail at the Uskmouth lagoons. *Gwent Bird Report* 41: 62–65.

Crick, H. 1992. A bird-habitat coding system for use in Britain and Ireland incorporating aspects of land management and human activity. *Bird Study* 39: 1–12.

Crowley, P. H. 1992. Resampling methods for computation-intensive data analysis in ecology and evolution. *Ann. Rev. Ecol. Systematics* 23: 405–447.

Davies, N. B. & Lundberg, A. 1984. Food distribution and a variable mating system in the Dunnock, *Prunella modularis. Journal of Animal Ecology* 53: 895–912.

Dixon, A. & Lawrence, A. M. 1999. The historical status of the Peregrine Falcon in Gwent. *Gwent Bird Report* 34: 68–69.

Dobson, A. P. & Hudson, P. J. 1992. Regulation and stability of a free-living host-parasite system: *Trichostrongylus tenuis* in Red Grouse. II: Population models. *Journal of Animal Ecology* 61: 487–498.

Dudley, S. P., Gee, M., Kehoe, C., Melling, T. M. and the British Ornithologists' Union Records Committee (BOURC). 2006. The British List: A Checklist of the Birds of Britain (7th edition). *Ibis* 148: 526–563.

Eaton, M. A. & Gregory, R. D. 2003. 'Red-listing' birds in the UK: a provisional comparison of 'the population status of birds in the UK' with IUCN regional guidelines. In: de Iongh H. H., Banki, O. S., Bergmans, W. & van der Werff ten Bosch, M. J. (Eds). *The Harmonization of Red Lists for threatened species in Europe.* The Netherlands Commission for International Nature Conservation, Leiden: 137–148.

Ferns, P. N., Green, G. H. & Round, P. D. 1979. The significance of the Somerset and Gwent Levels in Britain as feeding areas for migrant Whimbrel *Numenius phaeopus. Biological Conservation* 16: 7–22.

Ferns, P. N., & Mudge, G. P. 1979. Breeding and wintering populations of gulls in Gwent. *Gwent Bird Report* 14: 8–13.

Ferns, P. N. 1977. Migration. In Ferns, P. N., Hamar, H. W., Humphreys, P. N., Kelsey, F. D., Sarson, E. T., Venables, W. A. & Walker, I. R. *The Birds of Gwent* 48–64. Gwent Ornithological Society.

Fraser, P. A. S. & Ryan, J. F. 1995. Status of the Great Grey Shrike in Britain and Ireland. *British Birds* 88: 478–484.

Freeman, S. N. & Crick, H. Q. P. 2003. The decline of the Spotted Flycatcher *Muscicapa striata* in the UK: an integrated population model. *Ibis* 145: 400–412.

Fuller, R. J., Baker, J. K., Morgan, R. A., Scroggs, R. & Wright, M. 1985. Breeding populations of the Hobby *Falco subbuteo* on farmland in the southern Midlands of England. *Ibis* 127: 510–516.

Fuller, R. J., Noble, D. G., Smith, K. W. & Vanhinsbergh, D. 2005. Recent declines in populations of woodland birds in Britain: a review of possible causes. *British Birds* 98: 116–143.

Glue, D. E. 1990. Breeding biology of the Grasshopper Warbler in Britain. *British Birds* 83: 131–145.

Goodacre, M. J. 1960. The origin of winter visitors to the British Isles. 6. Song Thrush (*Turdus philomelos*). *Bird Study* 7: 108–110.

Gorman, G. 2004. *The Woodpeckers of Europe.* B. Coleman, Chalfont St Peter, England.

Gregory, R. D., Wilkinson, N. I., Noble, D. G., Robinson, J. A., Brown, A. F., Hughes, J., Procter, D., Gibbons, D. W. & Galbraith, C. A. 2002. The population status of birds in the United Kingdom, Channel Islands and Isle of Man: an analysis of conservation concern 2002–2007. *British Birds* 95: 410–448.

Groom, D. W. 1993. Magpie, *Pica pica,* predation on Blackbird, *Turdus merula,* nests in urban areas. *Bird Study* 40: 55–62.

Hudson, P. J. 1992. *Grouse in space and time : the population biology of a managed gamebird : the report of the Game Conservancy's Scottish Grouse Research Project & North of England Grouse Research Project.* Game Conservancy Ltd: Fordingbridge, Hampshire, UK.

Humphreys, P. N. 1975. House Martins as a hobby. *Gwent Bird Report*, 1(10): 505–507.

Hurford, C. & Lansdown, P. G. 1995. *Birds of Glamorgan.* Published by the authors.

Hurford, C. 1996. The decline of the Ring Ouzel *Turdus torquatus* breeding population in Glamorgan (v.c.41). *Welsh Birds* 1(3): 45–51.

Kershaw, M. & Cranswick, P. A. 2003. Numbers of wintering waterbirds in Great Britain, 1994/1995–1998/1999: I. Wildfowl and selected waterbirds. *Biological Conservation* 111: 91–104.

Lewis, J. 1991. Red Grouse in Gwent. *Gwent Bird Report* 26: 16–17

Lewis, J. 1992. The Peregrine survey 1991. *Gwent Bird Report* 27: 6.

Lewis, J. 2003. A Survey of Nightjar in East Gwent in 2003. *Gwent Bird Report* 39: 4–5.

Lewis, J. 2004. The National Nightjar Survey 2004. *Gwent Bird Report* 40: 5–6.

Locke, G. M. L. 1987. Census of woodlands and trees 1979–82. *Forestry Commission Bulletin* 63, HMSO, London.

Lovegrove, R. R., Hume, R. A. & McLean, I. 1980. The status of breeding wildfowl in Wales. *Nature in Wales* 17: 4–10.

Marchant, J. H., Freeman, S. N., Crick, H. Q. P. & Beaven, L. P. 2004. The BTO Heronries Census of England and Wales 1928–2000: new indices and a comparison of analytical methods. *Ibis* 146: 323–334.

Marchant, J. H., Hudson, R., Carter, S. P. & Whittington, P. 1990. *Population trends in British breeding birds.* British Trust for Ornithology, Tring.

Marques, F. F.C. & Buckland, S.T. 2003. Incorporating covariates into standard line transect analyses. *Biometrics* 59: 924–935.

Martin, P. N. & Venables, W. A. 1982. A visit to Denny Island (1981). *Gwent Bird Report* 17: 16–20.

Matthew, M. A. 1894. *The birds of Pembrokeshire and its islands.* R.H. Porter, London.

Mead, C. 2000. *The State of the Nation's Birds.* Whittet Books.

Mitchell, P. I., Newton, S. F., Ratcliffe, N. & Dunn, T. E. 2004. *Seabird Populations in Britain and Ireland. Results of Seabird 2000.* T & AD Poyser, London.

http://www.jncc.gov.uk/page–2888

Mortimer, H. M., Venables, W. A. & Walker, I. R. 1978. Reed Warblers on the Wentlooge Level. *Gwent Bird Report* 13: 19–20.

Mortimer, H. M., Venables, W. A. & Walker, I. R. 1979. A complete survey of Reed and Sedge Warbler populations on the Wentlooge Level. *Gwent Bird Report* 14: 24–27.

Newson S. E., Woodburn, R. J. W., Noble, D. G., Baillie, S. R. & Gregory, R. D. 2005. Evaluating the Breeding Bird Survey for producing national population size and density estimates. *Bird Study* 52: 42–54

Newton, I. 1972. *The Finches.* Collins, London.

Newton, I. 2004. The recent declines of farmland bird populations in Britain: an appraisal of causal factors and conservation actions. *Ibis* 146: 579–600.

Nicholson, E. M. 1929. Report on the 'British Birds' census of heronries, 1928. *British Birds* 22: 270–323, 334–372.

Ogilvie, M. 2004. Rare breeding birds in the UK in 2002. *British Birds* 97: 492–536.

Peach, W. J., Siriwardena, G. M. & Gregory, R. D. 1999. Long-term changes in over-winter survival rates explain the decline of reed buntings *Emberiza schoeniclus* in Britain. *Journal of Applied Ecology* 36: 798–811.

Pollit, M. S., Hall, C., Holloway, S. J., Hearn, R. D., Marshall, P. E., Musgrove, A. J., Robinson, J. A. & Cranswick, P. A. 2003. *The Wetland Bird Survey 2000–2001: Wildfowl and Wader Counts*. Slimbridge: BTO/WWT/RSPB/JNCC.

Prater, A. J. 1981. *Estuary birds of Britain and Ireland*. T & AD Poyser, Calton.

Prince, P. & Clark, R. 1993. The Hobby's breeding range in Britain. What

factors have allowed it to expand? *British Wildlife* 4: 341–346.

Potts, G. R. 1986. *The partridge: pesticides, predation and conservation.* Collins, London.

Powell, M. N. 1993. Rooks in Gwent, SO40 1975–89. *Gwent Bird Report* 28: 8–11

Ratcliffe, D. A. 1980. *The Peregrine Falcon*. T & AD Poyser, Calton.

Raven, M. & Noble, D. 2005. Recent changes in common bird populations. *BTO News* 260: 12–15.

Raven, M. J. & Noble, D. G. 2006. The Breeding Bird Survey 2005. *BTO Research Report 439*. BTO, Thetford.

Roberts, S. & Lewis, J. 1985. The Hobby in Gwent. *Gwent Bird Report* 21: 7–14.

Roberts, S. & Lewis, J. 1986. Nest observations of Gwent Hobbies. *Gwent Bird Report* 22: 6–10.

Roberts, S. & Lewis, J. 1988. Hobby – a nest history. *Gwent Bird Report* 24: 16–17.

Roberts, S. & Lewis, J. 1989. The Peregrine in Gwent. *Gwent Bird Report* 25: 7–9.

Roberts, S. & Lewis, J. 1990. Breeding Hobbies in Gwent – a status review. *Gwent Bird Report* 26: 7–11.

Roberts, S. J. 1989. Gwent Barn Owls score a first for Britain. *Gwent Bird Report* 25: 14–16.

Robinson, R. A., Siriwardena, G. M. & Crick, H. Q. P. 2005. Size and trends of the House Sparrow *Passer domesticus* population in Great Britain. *Ibis* 147: 552–562.

Rowell, H. E., Ward, R. M., Hall, C. & Cranswick, P. A. 2004. *The Naturalised Goose Survey 2000*. WWT, Slimbridge.

RSPB, 1978. *A survey of birds of the River Wye, 1977. A report to the Nature Conservancy Council*. Unpublished report.

SAS Institute. 2001. *SAS/STAT user's guide, version 8.02*. North Carolina: Cary.

Seabird 2000 project: JNCC website: http://www.jncc.gov.uk/page–2888

Shawyer, C. 1987. The Barn Owl in the British Isles; its past, present and future. Hawk Trust. London.

Siriwardena, G. M. 2004. Possible roles of habitat, competition and avian nest predation in the decline of the Willow Tit *Parus montanus* in Britain. Bird Study 51: 193–202.

Forestry Commission. 2002. *National Inventory of Woodland and Trees: Wales*. Forestry Commission, Edinburgh.

Smith, S. J. 1999. The chats of the moorland edge. *Gwent Bird Report* 35: 63–66.

Smith, S. J. 2002. A study of Whinchats *Saxicola rubetra* on the moorland edge. *Welsh Birds* 3: 183–190.

Stott, M., Callion, J., Kinley, I., Raven, C. & Roberts, J. (eds). 2004. *The breeding birds of Cumbria – a tetrad atlas 1997–2001*. Cumbria Bird Club.

Thomas, L., Laake, J. L., Derry, J. F., Buckland, S. T., Borchers, D. L., Anderson, D. R., Burnham, K. P., Strindberg, S., Hedley, S. L., Burt, M. L., Marques, F., Pollard, J. H. & Fewster, R. M. 2004. Distance 4.1. Research Unit for Wildlife Population Assessment, University of St. Andrews, UK.

Titcombe, C. 1998. *Gwent – its landscape and natural history*. Published by the author

Tyler, J. O. 1923. Shooting in Monmouthshire 1789–1923. Pontypool

Tyler, S. J. 1979. Movements and mortality of the Grey Wagtail. *Ringing and Migration* 2: 122–131.

Tyler, S. J. 1993. Status of the Lapwing in Gwent. *Gwent Bird Report* 29: 7–9.

Tyler, S. J. 1995. Green Woodpeckers in Gwent. *Gwent Bird Report* 31: 16–18.

Tyler, S. J. 2002. Birds of the River Monnow. *Gwent Bird Report* 38: 6–13.

Tyler, S. J. 2004. The status of Dippers and Grey Wagtails in south and mid Wales. *Welsh Birds* 4: 4–10.

Tyler, S. J. & Green, M. 1994. The status and breeding ecology of Ring Ouzels *Turdus torquatus* in Wales with reference to soil acidity. *Welsh Bird Report* 7: 78–79.

Tyler, S. J. & Ormerod, S. J. 1991. The influence of stream acidification and riparian land-use on the breeding biology of Grey Wagtails *Motacilla cinerea* in Wales. *Ibis* 133: 286–292

Tyler, S. J. & Ormerod, S. J. 1994. *The Dippers*. T & AD Poyser, London.

Venables, W. A. 1989. *Census of breeding birds at Bryn Bach Park*. Report to Gwent County Council Planning Department. Unpublished Report.

Venables, W. A. 1995. *Breeding Birds at Bryn Bach Park 1995.* Report to Gwent County Council Planning Department. Unpublished Report.

Venables, W. A. & Titcombe, C. 1980. A survey of the breeding birds on the Caldicot Level. *Gwent Bird Report* 15: 31–33.

Index of scientific names

Index of Welsh common names

Index of English common names